Expert Oracle SQL

Optimization, Deployment, and Statistics

Tony Hasler

Apress

Expert Oracle SQL

ISBN-13 (pbk): 978-1-4302-5977-0

ISBN-13 (electronic): 978-1-4302-5978-7

Trademarked names, logos, and images may appear in this book. Rather than use a trademark symbol with every occurrence of a trademarked name, logo, or image we use the names, logos, and images only in an editorial fashion and to the benefit of the trademark owner, with no intention of infringement of the trademark.

The use in this publication of trade names, trademarks, service marks, and similar terms, even if they are not identified as such, is not to be taken as an expression of opinion as to whether or not they are subject to proprietary rights.

While the advice and information in this book are believed to be true and accurate at the date of publication, neither the authors nor the editors nor the publisher can accept any legal responsibility for any errors or omissions that may be made. The publisher makes no warranty, express or implied, with respect to the material contained herein.

Publisher: Heinz Weinheimer
Lead Editor: Jonathan Gennick
Development Editor: Matthew Moodie
Technical Reviewers: Frits Hoogland, Randolf Geist, Dominic Delmolino, Carol Dacko
Editorial Board: Steve Anglin, Mark Beckner, Ewan Buckingham, Gary Cornell, Louise Corrigan, Jim DeWolf, Jonathan Gennick, Jonathan Hassell, Robert Hutchinson, Michelle Lowman, James Markham, Matthew Moodie, Jeff Olson, Jeffrey Pepper, Douglas Pundick, Ben Renow-Clarke, Dominic Shakeshaft, Gwenan Spearing, Matt Wade, Steve Weiss
Coordinating Editor: Jill Balzano
Copy Editor: April Rondeau
Compositor: SPi Global
Indexer: SPi Global
Artist: SPi Global
Cover Designer: Anna Ishchenko

Distributed to the book trade worldwide by Springer Science+Business Media New York, 233 Spring Street, 6th Floor, New York, NY 10013. Phone 1-800-SPRINGER, fax (201) 348-4505, e-mail orders-ny@springer-sbm.com, or visit www.springeronline.com. Apress Media, LLC is a California LLC and the sole member (owner) is Springer Science + Business Media Finance Inc (SSBM Finance Inc). SSBM Finance Inc is a Delaware corporation.

For information on translations, please e-mail rights@apress.com, or visit www.apress.com.

Apress and friends of ED books may be purchased in bulk for academic, corporate, or promotional use. eBook versions and licenses are also available for most titles. For more information, reference our Special Bulk Sales–eBook Licensing web page at www.apress.com/bulk-sales.

Any source code or other supplementary material referenced by the author in this text is available to readers at www.apress.com. For detailed information about how to locate your book's source code, go to www.apress.com/source-code/.

To Marianne.

About IOUG Press

*IOUG Press is a joint effort by the **Independent Oracle Users Group (the IOUG)** and **Apress** to deliver some of the highest-quality content possible on Oracle Database and related topics. The IOUG is the world's leading, independent organization for professional users of Oracle products. Apress is a leading, independent technical publisher known for developing high-quality, no-fluff content for serious technology professionals. The IOUG and Apress have joined forces in IOUG Press to provide the best content and publishing opportunities to working professionals who use Oracle products.*

Our shared goals include:

- Developing content with excellence
- Helping working professionals to succeed
- Providing authoring and reviewing opportunities
- Networking and raising the profiles of authors and readers

To learn more about Apress, visit our website at **www.apress.com**. Follow the link for IOUG Press to see the great content that is now available on a wide range of topics that matter to those in Oracle's technology sphere.

Visit **www.ioug.org** to learn more about the Independent Oracle Users Group and its mission. Consider joining if you haven't already. Review the many benefits at www.ioug.org/join. Become a member. Get involved with peers. Boost your career.

www.ioug.org/join

apress®

Contents at a Glance

Contents

About the Author

Tony Hasler is an independent software consultant specializing in SQL tuning for Oracle databases. He graduated with an honor's degree in computer studies from Lancaster University in the United Kingdom in 1978 and spent the next 15 years working as a software developer.

Tony worked in the United Kingdom and the Netherlands for the first couple of years of his career and then moved to New Jersey, where he met his wife-to-be, Marianne. Tony returned to the United Kingdom in 1988 to join Digital Equipment Corporation (DEC) as a team leader on the OpenVMS operating system development team. During his five years at DEC Tony filed a patent on optimizations for logging protocols, and as a representative of the British Standards Institute (BSI) he participated in the creation of a number of publications from the International Standards Organization (ISO).

Soon after leaving DEC in 1993, Tony began his second career in support work, specializing mainly in performance tuning of an application by Wall Street Systems (http://www.wallstreetsystems.com/). In 2004 Tony moved away from applications and operating systems and began specializing in Oracle database technology. At the time of writing, Tony is working as a full-time SQL performance specialist.

Tony is a well-known speaker in the United Kingdom and has published several articles for the UK Oracle User Group. Tony also occasionally makes an entry in his blog, http://tonyhasler.wordpress.com/, when he finds something interesting to talk about.

Although Tony lives in Scotland with his wife, Marianne, none of his current clients have operations in Scotland; they are global financial institutions with UK headquarters in London. The world of telecommuting has arrived.

Tony has two grown-up children, both of whom have followed in their father's footsteps. Timothy has a degree in computer gaming from Abertay University in Dundee and is working as a software developer in Edinburgh, while Thomas is working as a software developer in London after obtaining a software engineering degree from Edinburgh.

About the Technical Reviewers

Frits Hoogland is an IT professional specializing in Oracle database performance and internals. Frits frequently presents on Oracle technical topics at conferences around the world. In 2009 he received an Oracle ACE award from the Oracle Technology Network, and a year later he became an Oracle ACE Director. In 2010 he joined the OakTable Network. In addition to developing his Oracle expertise, Frits works with MySQL, PostgreSQL, and modern operating systems. Frits currently works at Enkitec LP.

Randolf Geist has been working with Oracle software for 19 years now, and as a freelance database consultant since 2000. He focuses primarily on performance-related issues, in particular helping people to understand and unleash the power of the Oracle cost-based optimizer (CBO)—being available for short-term, short-notice assignments regarding Oracle performance troubleshooting and in-house seminars and consulting.

He blogs about CBO-related issues at oracle-randolf.blogspot.com, regularly contributes to the official OTN database-related forums, and is also co-author of *Expert Oracle Practices*, a book published in 2010 by the OakTable Press in which he contributed the performance-related chapters.

Randolf is a regular speaker at all major user conferences around the world and also acts as an instructor for the Oracle University as part of their "Celebrity Seminar" program, where he gives seminars on "Advanced Oracle Performance Troubleshooting." Randolf is a proud member of the OakTable Network and the Oracle ACE Director program.

Dominic Delmolino is the lead database technologist for Agilex. He specializes in Oracle and Agile database deployment methods and is a member of the OakTable Network. He enjoys researching and presenting on advanced database topics.

Acknowledgments

It may seem like an act of political correctness for an author to begin a list of acknowledgments by thanking their spouse. That is unless you are an author—or an author's spouse—in which case, you would understand. It has taken me somewhere between 1,000 and 1,500 hours to write this book. When you consider that I have kept a full-time job at the same time you may begin to see the impact that such a project has had on the lives of family and friends. On top of the usual stresses of life, we moved between houses a few months ago and Marianne had to do the vast majority of the work involved! Writing this book would have been utterly impossible without Marianne's support, and my thanks are heartfelt.

Although I would in no way wish to liken myself to Isaac Newton or the other great minds that have used this metaphor, I am but a dwarf standing in the shoulders of giants. My two main sources of both information and inspiration are books entitled *Cost Based Oracle* by Jonathan Lewis and *Troubleshooting Oracle Performance* by Christian Antognini. Jonathan's book was published by Apress in 2008 and the second edition of Christian's book was published in 2014, also by Apress. I am fortunate to know both authors personally. Jonathan has engaged in e-mail correspondence to help clear up my own misunderstandings on a couple of topics in this book, and Christian has provided me with a draft of his own chapter on optimizer transformations, thus saving me countless hours of work.

However, the idea for writing this book did not come from either Jonathan or Christian. It did, in fact, come from Dan Tow, author of *SQL Tuning*, a book published by O'Reilly in 2003, but a book that I only discovered in 2011. I'll come back to Dan's book in the introduction.

I have to admit that I am not inclined to spend a lot of my spare time trawling through large numbers of blog entries, but it would be wrong of me to suggest that my education and inspiration have come solely from words written on real paper. The Internet is a wonderful resource for filling holes in your knowledge, and one website in particular, www.hellodba.com, a Chinese website from Wei Huang, has provided me with a lot of details about many of the undocumented hints in the Oracle database.

Gordon Mitchell works for one of my clients and was the first to coin the term TSTATS for "Tony's statistics," but in fact I was not the first or only person to invent the sort of scheme that is discussed in Chapter 6 and Chapter 20 of this book. I must mention Adrian Billington in particular (http://www.oracle-developer.net/) for coming up with a key idea of deleting the maximum and minimum values from column statistics (but see the instructions for running the examples in the introduction for an issue in 12.1.0.1.)

I must, of course, acknowledge my technical reviewers as well as Chris Dunscombe, who provided one reader's perspective on some of my more controversial chapters, and my editors at Apress. It is impossible to produce a work of this magnitude that is completely free of technical or grammatical error, but the quality of the book is vastly improved as a result of their efforts. Thank you, all.

And finally, of course, I must thank you, my readers, for buying this book and giving it some life. I take full responsibility for any errors that remain, but I sincerely hope that you find reading *Expert Oracle SQL* an educational and enjoyable experience.

Foreword

When Jonathan Gennick from Apress approached me with a request to write the foreword for this book, I said yes without thinking for too long, as I already knew the quality of Tony's work. He has a good, practical approach to understanding and fixing Oracle problems and for optimizing inefficient code.

Optimizing SQL performance is not always about providing more-detailed optimizer statistics for faster execution plans. Sometimes you want to provide less-detailed information to the cost-based optimizer and freeze the statistics to achieve better stability in SQL performance. Such an approach may initially sound counterintuitive and off the mainstream, but it can avoid headaches and midnight phone calls later if SQL plan stability is important to you. As always, you will need to apply such techniques correctly and in the right situations. Tony explains the thought process behind SQL optimization and statistics management for both performance and stability, and also provides tools and examples to put his approach into use.

Another great value of this book lies in the numerous practical examples of how to optimize SQL by rewriting or adjusting your queries and statements. You absolutely need the mindset and skill for real-life SQL optimization, as desperately regathering the optimizer statistics, or creating yet another index, may not provide any noticeable performance gains for your problem SQL. Hence the need to rewrite or adjust, and multiple chapters in the second half of the book help by dealing with various ways you (or the Oracle optimizer) can optimize the form of your SQL.

In addition to Chapter 16 ("Rewriting Queries") and Chapter 17 ("Optimizing Sorts"), you have over 70 pages' worth of optimizer transformations explained in Chapter 13! The content in these three chapters helps you to understand why the final execution plan for a query may often look quite different from what the original SQL was supposed to do, while still delivering correct results, but faster. And this all, in turn, helps you to write more efficient SQL in the first place.

When reading this book, remember that roughly the first half of this book consists of a number of shorter chapters, each introducing you to different parts of the Oracle Database's SQL optimization and runtime features. These first chapters serve as building blocks ready to be put into use in the later parts of the book, where all the pieces fall together.

You will gain plenty of new knowledge and will also have fun reading this book!

—Tanel Põder

Tanel Põder is one of the leading Oracle Database performance specialists in the world, having helped solve complex problems for customers in 25 countries on five continents. He works for Enkitec as a technology evangelist, focusing on advanced Oracle, Linux, and Hadoop performance topics, including Exadata and the brand-new In-Memory Database Option. Tanel has received the "Oracle ACE Director" recognition for his community contribution, is a proud member of the OakTable Network, and he is a co-author of *Expert Oracle Exadata*, also published by Apress

Introduction

What is this book about?

How many of us have been woken at some antisocial hour because a SQL statement that was performing well suddenly started behaving badly because of a changed execution plan? In most circumstances, Oracle would probably recommend that customers suffering repeatedly from such issues investigate the use of SQL Plan Baselines, Oracle's strategic feature for stabilizing execution plans in a production environment. This book introduces TSTATS, the name given by one of my clients to a controversial technology that bypasses altogether the need to gather object statistics on a production system and can be thought of as an alternative to SQL Plan Baselines.

Although Chapter 6 and Chapter 20 are dedicated to the issue of deploying and managing statistics in a production environment, the main theme of the book is tuning SQL for Oracle databases. There are other excellent books covering Oracle database performance in general, but this book is focused specifically on SQL tuning.

In my opinion, the key to finding the best solution to a SQL tuning problem usually lies in fully understanding the problem that you are addressing as well as in understanding the technologies at your disposal. A large portion of this book is dedicated to a study of how the cost-based optimizer (CBO) and the runtime engine work and how to obtain and interpret diagnostic data, such as the execution plans displayed by functions from the DBMS_XPLAN package.

Some readers may find it surprising is that I make very little reference to the famous 10046 and 10053 traces that form the foundation of many books on SQL performance. In practice, I use a 10046 trace about once a year and a 10053 trace about once every three years. In my opinion, there are easier ways to diagnose the vast majority of SQL tuning problems, and I will explain the techniques that I use in detail.

You will notice that I have used the term "in my opinion" twice in the last few paragraphs, and I will use it many more times throughout this book. The fear of alienating audiences dissuades many authors from expressing controversial opinions, particularly if they are not perfectly aligned with Oracle-recommended practice. But there is often more than one way to look at a topic, and I hope this book provides you with something new to think about.

But don't be too worried that this book is all about philosophy and grandstanding. There is a lot of technical content in this book that you won't find in other books or in blogs and plenty of examples to help you through.

Why did I write this book?

The process that led me to write this book began with a talk by Kyle Hailey (http://www.oraclerealworld.com/) at the 2010 UK Oracle User Group (UKOUG) national conference. The topic of Kyle's talk is immaterial, but he mentioned en passant a book called SQL Tuning written in 2003 by Dan Tow and published by O'Reilly. I was sitting next to Jonathan Lewis (http://jonathanlewis.wordpress.com/) in the audience, and Jonathan agreed with Kyle that this was an excellent book, one of only a handful that he recommends on his blog. I felt obliged to buy the book and can confirm that it is an outstanding publication.

The small difficulty I have in 2014 with Dan's book is that it focuses almost entirely on a scientific and foolproof way to determine the correct join order for a set of tables. Although join order is still a performance concern, it is less so in 2014 than it was in 2003 for several reasons:

- Since the CBO was introduced into the Oracle database product in version 7, it has become increasingly more capable of identifying the correct join order.

- New options, such as right-deep join trees and star transformations, which I will cover in chapters 11 and 13 respectively, mean that there is even less possibility that the CBO will pick a disastrous join order.

- We now have at our disposal Wolfgang Breitling's *Tuning by Cardinality Feedback* (http://www.centrexcc.com/Tuning%20by%20Cardinality%20Feedback.pdf) tuning technique, which I will discuss briefly in Chapter 6 and which provides a simpler approach to solving simple problems like join order. Wolfgang's approach is nowhere near as formal and foolproof as Dan's, but it works 90% of the time and is easier to master.

Although join order is less of a problem in 2014 than it was in 2003, there are new challenges. The base database product (the part that requires no extra licensing) now includes analytic functions, parallel processing, and the MODEL clause, all of which open up ever more sophisticated options for business logic in the database layer and in SQL statements in particular. Licensed options, such as partitioning, can also help solve some performance problems that otherwise might be very cumbersome, at the very least, to solve. All these nice new features generate complexity, and with that complexity comes the need to understand more aspects of how a SQL statement behaves. Chapter 17, for example, is dedicated entirely to the topic of sorting.

And so the idea of this book was born. In December 2011, at the next UKOUG conference, I was still mulling over the idea of writing this book and looked for some encouragement from other authors that I knew. I received a mixed response. Yes, a new book on SQL tuning would be nice. But given the amount of work involved, I would be crazy to undertake it.

But I was already emotionally committed and a short while later I asked Christian Antognini, author of *Troubleshooting Oracle Performance*, to introduce me to his publisher at Apress.

Running the examples

Scripts to run the SQL statements in the listings in this book can be downloaded from http://www.apress.com/9781430259770. If you want to run the scripts yourself, I would recommend using version 12cR1 of the database product, although most of the scripts do run on 11gR2. The following are additional requirements:

- The database should have an 8k block size and you should set the initialization parameter db_file_multiblock_read to 128.

- The sample schemas (SCOTT, OE, HR, PM and SH) need to be installed. See the Sample Schemas manual and the $ORACLE_HOME/rdbms/admin/scott.sql script for more details.

As the book has been reviewed it has become clear that the different ways of installing the example schemas can lead to inconsistencies in execution plans. The downloadable materials include a set of object statistics for the example schemas that can be installed with datapump import. These statistics should help you reproduce the results shown in this book. Full instructions are included in the README file included in the materials.

At the time of publication, the only point release of Oracle database 12cR1 available is 12.1.0.1, and unfortunately there is a bug related to join cardinality estimates that renders one of the key elements of the TSTATS technology described in chapters 6 and 20 unworkable as described. Hopefully this bug will be fixed in a later point release, but in the meantime the downloadable code includes a workaround: rather than removing the high- and low-value column statistics altogether, the high value of the column statistic is set very high and the low value set very low.

The structure of this book

This book is composed of five parts:

Part 1 introduces some basic concepts. I cover the SQL language itself and the basics of execution plans. I introduce the cost-based optimizer (CBO) and the runtime engine and give an overview of my approaches to optimization and managing object statistics in a production environment. Even if you are very experienced with SQL I would recommend that you at least skim this first part as a command of the concepts covered is crucial to following the rest of the book.

Part 2 covers more advanced aspects of SQL and execution plans and explains how object statistics are used by the CBO to help it select an execution plan.

Part 3 provides a study of the CBO. I don't get bogged down with lots of formulas for costing; I cover the essential details of access method, join order, and join method that you will need during your SQL tuning life. I also take a detailed look at the all of the optimizer transformations that you are likely to encounter.

Part 4 covers optimizing SQL. Now that we have a firm grounding in the tools of the trade, it is finally time to look at how we can apply all this knowledge to solving real SQL performance issues. I cover physical database design and rewriting SQL, and then take a detailed look at that most controversial of topics: hints. There is also a chapter dedicated to sorts and another that covers a range of advanced techniques for solving unusual problems.

Part 5 is a single chapter dedicated to TSTATS, a technique for managing object statistics in a production environment. TSTATS virtually eliminates unwanted execution changes without the need to manage repositories of SQL Plan Baselines. A controversial chapter to be sure, but the techniques described in this chapter have proven themselves in a number of mission-critical applications over a number of years.

The key messages of the book

As with most problems in life, solving a SQL tuning problem or a production instability problem can be made much easier, and sometimes trivial, by fully understanding it. An obvious statement, perhaps, but I have lost count of the number of times I have seen people trying to solve a SQL performance problem *without* understanding it. For example, it may be that the best solution to a performance problem is to gather statistics. Perhaps you just need to stop and restart the SQL. Perhaps you need to run the SQL Tuning Advisor and create a SQL profile. But don't just pick one of these options at random and work through the list when it doesn't work. For example, if your SQL statement includes a temporary table then the SQL Tuning Advisor is unlikely to be of much use because the temporary table will be empty when the SQL Tuning Advisor runs. You need to begin by reviewing the SQL statement!

Why are so many problems with poorly performing SQL approached in a haphazard way? One reason is the pressure that technicians are put under, often at antisocial hours, to do *something* quickly. The other reason is that very few people have enough knowledge to approach a performance problem in a systematic way. I can't help you with the first of these two problems, but hopefully after reading this book you will at least have the knowledge and the skill, if not always the time, to approach your performance problems in a systematic way, starting with the problem and working towards a solution, rather than the other way around.

I want to end this introduction with a second message. Enjoy yourself! Enjoy reading this book and take pride and pleasure in your work. It will take time to master all the principles in this book, but the journey will hopefully be a rewarding one for your clients, your employers, and, above all, yourself

Basic Concepts

CHAPTER 1

■ ■ ■

SQL Features

This chapter discusses a selection of fairly independent SQL features that are of importance for the tuning process, many of which are somewhat poorly advertised. I'll begin with a quick review of just what SQL statements are and the identifiers used to refer to them. My second topic is the array interface that is used to move data from client processes to the database server in large batches. I will then discuss factored subqueries that make reading SQL statements much easier. My fourth and final topic in this first chapter is a review of the different types of inner and outer joins; I will explain how to write them, what they are used for, and why it isn't quite as easy to reorder outer joins as it is to reorder inner joins.

SQL and Declarative Programming Languages

Programs written in a *declarative programming language* describe what computation should be performed but not how to compute it. SQL is considered a declarative programming language. Compare SQL with *imperative programming languages* like C, Visual Basic, or even PL/SQL that specify each step of the computation.

This sounds like great news. You write the SQL any way you want and, providing it is semantically correct, somebody or something else will find the optimal way to run it. That something else in our case is the *cost-based optimizer* (CBO) and in most cases it does a pretty good job. However, despite the theory, there is a strong implication of an algorithm in many SQL statements. Listing 1-1 using the HR example schema is one such example.

Listing 1-1. Subqueries in the SELECT list

```
SELECT first_name
       ,last_name
       , (SELECT first_name
            FROM hr.employees m
           WHERE m.employee_id = e.manager_id)
           AS manager_first_name
       , (SELECT last_name
            FROM hr.employees m
           WHERE m.employee_id = e.manager_id)
           AS manager_last_name
    FROM hr.employees e
   WHERE manager_id IS NOT NULL
ORDER BY last_name, first_name;
```

What this statement says is: *Obtain the first and last names of each employee with a manager and in each case look up the manager's first and last names. Order the resulting rows by employees' last and first names.* Listing 1-2 appears to be a completely different statement.

3

Listing 1-2. Use of a join instead of a SELECT list

```
  SELECT e.first_name
        ,e.last_name
        ,m.first_name AS manager_first_name
        ,m.last_name AS manager_last_name
    FROM hr.employees e, hr.employees m
   WHERE m.employee_id = e.manager_id
ORDER BY last_name, first_name;
```

This statement says: *Perform a self-join on* HR.EMPLOYEES *keeping only rows where the* EMPLOYEE_ID *from the first copy matches the* MANAGER_ID *from the second copy. Pick the names of the employee and the manager and order the results.* Despite the apparent difference between Listing 1-1 and Listing 1-2, they both produce identical results. In fact, because EMPLOYEE_ID is the primary key of EMPLOYEES and there is a referential integrity constraint from MANAGER_ID to EMPLOYEE_ID, they are semantically equivalent.

In an ideal world, the CBO would work all this out and execute both statements the same way. In fact, as of Oracle Database 12c, these statements are executed in entirely different ways. Although the CBO is improving from release to release, there will always be some onus on the author of SQL statements to write them in a way that helps the CBO find a well-performing execution plan, or at the very least avoid a completely awful one.

Statements and SQL_IDs

Oracle Database identifies each SQL statement by something referred to as an SQL_ID. Many of the views you use when analyzing SQL performance, such as V$ACTIVE_SESSION_HISTORY, pertain to a specific SQL statement identified by an SQL_ID. It is important that you understand what these SQL_IDs are and how to cross-reference an SQL_ID with the actual text of the SQL statement.

An SQL_ID is a base 32 number represented as a string of 13 characters, each of which may be a digit or one of 22 lowercase letters. An example might be 'ddzxfryd0uq9t'. The letters e, i, l, and o are not used presumably to limit the risk of transcription errors. The SQL_ID is actually a hash generated from the characters in the SQL statement. So assuming that case and whitespace are preserved, the same SQL statement will have the same SQL_ID on any database on which it is used.

Normally the two statements in Listing 1-3 will be considered different.

Listing 1-3. Statements involving literals

```
SELECT 'LITERAL 1' FROM DUAL;
SELECT 'LITERAL 2' FROM DUAL;
```

The first statement has an SQL_ID of '3uzuap6svwz7u' and the second an SQL_ID of '7ya3fww7bfn89'.

Any SQL statement issued inside a PL/SQL block also has an SQL_ID. Such statements may use PL/SQL variables or parameters, but changing the values of variables does not change the SQL_ID. Listing 1-4 shows a similar query to those in Listing 1-3 except it is issued from within a PL/SQL block.

Listing 1-4. A SELECT statement issued from PL/SQL

```
SET SERVEROUT ON

DECLARE
   PROCEDURE check_sql_id (p_literal VARCHAR2)
   IS
      dummy_variable   VARCHAR2 (100);
      sql_id           v$session.sql_id%TYPE;
```

```
  BEGIN
    SELECT p_literal INTO dummy_variable FROM DUAL;

    SELECT prev_sql_id
      INTO sql_id
      FROM v$session
     WHERE sid = SYS_CONTEXT ('USERENV', 'SID');

    DBMS_OUTPUT.put_line (sql_id);
  END check_sql_id;

BEGIN
   check_sql_id ('LITERAL 1');
   check_sql_id ('LITERAL 2');
END;
/
```

d8jhv8fcm27kd
d8jhv8fcm27kd
```
PL/SQL procedure successfully completed.
```

This anonymous block includes two calls to a nested procedure that takes a VARCHAR2 string as a parameter. The procedure calls a SELECT statement and then obtains the SQL_ID of that statement from the PREV_SQL_ID column of V$SESSION and outputs it. The procedure is called with the same two literals as were used in Listing 1-3. However, the output shows that the same SQL_ID, 'd8jhv8fcm27kd', was used in both cases. In fact, PL/SQL modifies the SELECT statement slightly before submitting it to the SQL engine. Listing 1-5 shows the underlying SQL statement after the PL/SQL specific INTO clause has been removed.

Listing 1-5. An SQL statement with a bind variable

```
SELECT :B1 FROM DUAL
```

The :B1 bit is what is known as a *bind variable*, and it is used in PL/SQL whenever a variable or parameter is used. Bind variables are also used when SQL is invoked from other programming languages. This bind variable is just a placeholder for an actual value, and it indicates that the same statement can be reused with different values supplied for the placeholder. I will explain the importance of this as I go on.

Cross-Referencing Statement and SQL_ID

If you have access to the SYS account of a database running 11.2 or later, you can use the approach in Listing 1-6 to identify the SQL_ID of a statement.

Listing 1-6. Using DBMS_SQLTUNE_UTIL0 to determine the SQL_ID of a statement

```
SELECT sys.dbms_sqltune_util0.sqltext_to_sqlid (
       q'[SELECT 'LITERAL 1' FROM DUAL]' || CHR (0))
  FROM DUAL;
```

The result of the query in Listing 1-6 is '3uzuap6svwz7u', the SQL_ID of the first statement in Listing 1-3. There are a few observations that can be made about Listing 1-6:

- Notice how the string containing single quotes is itself quoted. This syntax, fully documented in the SQL Language Reference manual, is very useful but is often missed by many experienced Oracle specialists.

- It is necessary to append a NUL character to the end of the text before calling the function.

- You don't need access to a SYS account on the database you are working on to use this function. I often work remotely and can pop a statement into the 11.2 database on my laptop to get an SQL_ID; remember that SQL_IDs are the same on all databases irrespective of database version!

This isn't the usual way to cross-reference the text of an SQL statement and an SQL_ID. I have already explained how to use the PREV_SQL_ID column of V$SESSION to identify the SQL_ID of the previous SQL statement executed by a session. The SQL_ID column, as you might imagine, pertains to the currently executing statement. However, the most common approaches to identifying an SQL_ID for a statement is to query either V$SQL or DBA_HIST_SQLTEXT.

V$SQL contains information about statements that are currently running or have recently completed. V$SQL contains the following three columns, among others:

- SQL_ID is the SQL_ID of the statement.

- SQL_FULLTEXT is a CLOB column containing the text of the SQL statement.

- SQL_TEXT is a VARCHAR2 column that contains a potentially truncated variant of SQL_FULLTEXT.

If you are using data from the Automatic Workload Repository (AWR) for your analysis, then your SQL statement will likely have disappeared from the cursor cache, and a lookup using V$SQL will not work. In this case, you need to use DBA_HIST_SQLTEXT, itself an AWR view, to perform the lookup. This view differs slightly from V$SQL in that the column SQL_TEXT is a CLOB column and there is no VARCHAR2 variant.

Using either V$SQL or DBA_HIST_SQLTEXT, you can supply an SQL_ID and obtain the corresponding SQL_TEXT or vice versa. Listing 1-7 shows two queries that search for statements containing 'LITERAL1'.

Listing 1-7. Identifying SQL_IDs from V$SQL or DBA_HIST_SQLTEXT

```
SELECT *
  FROM v$sql
 WHERE sql_fulltext LIKE '%''LITERAL1''%';

SELECT *
  FROM dba_hist_sqltext
 WHERE sql_text LIKE '%''LITERAL1''%';
```

■ **Caution**   The use of the views V$ACTIVE_SESSION_HISTORY and views beginning with the characters DBA_HIST_ require enterprise edition with the diagnostic pack.

The two queries in Listing 1-7 will return a row for each statement containing the characters 'LITERAL1'. The query you are looking for will be in V$SQL if it is still in the shared pool and it will be in DBA_HIST_SQLTEXT if captured in the AWR.

Array Interface

The *array interface* allows an array of values to be supplied for a bind variable. This is extremely important from a performance point of view because without it, code running on a client machine might need to make a large number of network round trips to send an array of data to the database server. Despite being a very important part of the SQL, many programmers and database administrators (DBAs) are unaware of it. One reason for its obscurity is that it is not directly available from SQL*Plus. Listing 1-8 sets up a couple of tables to help explain the concept.

Listing 1-8. Setting up tables T1 and T2 for testing

```
CREATE TABLE t1
(
   n1    NUMBER
  ,n2    NUMBER
);

CREATE TABLE t2
(
   n1    NUMBER
  ,n2    NUMBER
);

INSERT INTO t1
   SELECT object_id, data_object_id
     FROM all_objects
    WHERE ROWNUM <= 30;
```

Listing 1-8 creates tables T1 and T2 that each contains two numeric columns: N1 and N2. Table T1 has been populated with 30 rows and T2 is empty. You need to use a language like PL/SQL to demonstrate the array interface, and Listing 1-9 includes two examples.

Listing 1-9. Using the array interface with DELETE and MERGE

```
DECLARE
   TYPE char_table_type IS TABLE OF t1.n1%TYPE;

   n1_array    char_table_type;
   n2_array    char_table_type;
BEGIN
   DELETE FROM t1
     RETURNING n1, n2
          BULK COLLECT INTO n1_array, n2_array;

   FORALL i IN 1 .. n1_array.COUNT
      MERGE INTO t2
          USING DUAL
            ON (t2.n1 = n1_array (i))
      WHEN MATCHED
      THEN
         UPDATE SET t2.n2 = n2_array (i)
      WHEN NOT MATCHED
      THEN
         INSERT     (n1, n2)
             VALUES (n1_array (i), n2_array (i));
END;
/
```

The first SQL statement in the PL/SQL block of Listing 1-9 is a DELETE statement that returns the 30 rows deleted from T1 into two numeric arrays. The SQL_ID of this statement is 'd6qp89kta7b8y' and the underlying text can be retrieved using the query in Listing 1-10.

Listing 1-10. Display underlying text of a PL/SQL statement

```
SELECT 'Output: ' || sql_text
  FROM v$sql
 WHERE sql_id = 'd6qp89kta7b8y';

Output: DELETE FROM T1 RETURNING N1, C2 INTO :O0 ,:O1
```

You can see that this time the bind variables :O0 and :O1 have been used for output. The PL/SQL BULK COLLECT syntax that signaled the use of the array interface has been removed from the statement submitted by PL/SQL to the SQL engine.

The MERGE statement in Listing 1-9 also uses the array interface, this time for input. Because T2 is empty, the end result is that T2 is inserted into all 30 rows deleted from T1. The SQL_ID is '2c8z1d90u77t4', and if you retrieve the text from V$SQL you will see that all whitespace has been collapsed and all identifiers are displayed in uppercase. This is normal for SQL issued from PL/SQL.

```
┌─────────────────────────────────────────────────────────────────────┐
│                      PL/SQL FORALL SYNTAX                            │
└─────────────────────────────────────────────────────────────────────┘
```

It is easy to think that the PL/SQL FORALL syntax represents a loop. It does not. It is just a way to invoke the array interface when passing array data into a Data Manipulation Language (DML) statement, just as BULK COLLECT is used to invoke the array interface when retrieving data.

The array interface is particularly important for code issued from an application server because it avoids multiple round trips between the client and the server, so the impact can be dramatic.

Subquery Factoring

Subquery factoring is the second theme of this chapter and probably the single most underused feature of SQL. Whenever I write articles or make presentations, I almost always find an excuse to include an example or two of this feature, and factored subqueries feature heavily in this book. I will begin by briefly explaining what factored subqueries are and then go on to give four good reasons why you should use them.

The Concept of Subquery Factoring

We all know that views in the data dictionary are specifically designed so that syntactically our SQL statements can treat them just like tables. We also know that we can replace a data dictionary view with an *inline view* if the data dictionary view doesn't exist or needs to be modified in some way. Listing 1-11 shows the traditional way of using inline views.

Listing 1-11. Traditional inline views without subquery factoring

```
  SELECT channel_id, ROUND (AVG (total_cost),2) avg_cost
    FROM sh.profits
GROUP BY channel_id;

  SELECT channel_id, ROUND (AVG (total_cost), 2) avg_cost
    FROM (SELECT s.channel_id
                ,GREATEST (c.unit_cost, 0) * s.quantity_sold total_cost
           FROM sh.costs c, sh.sales s
          WHERE     c.prod_id = s.prod_id
                AND c.time_id = s.time_id
                AND c.channel_id = s.channel_id
                AND c.promo_id = s.promo_id)
GROUP BY channel_id;
```

You write the first query in Listing 1-11 using the view PROFITS in the SH schema in a straightforward way. You then realize that some of the values of UNIT_COST are negative and you decide you want to treat such costs as zero. One way to do so it to replace the data dictionary view with a customized inline view, as shown in the second query in Listing 1-11.

There is another, and in my opinion, superior way to accomplish this same customization. Listing 1-12 shows the alternative construct.

Listing 1-12. A simple factored subquery

```
WITH myprofits
    AS (SELECT s.channel_id
               ,GREATEST (c.unit_cost, 0) * s.quantity_sold total_cost
          FROM sh.costs c, sh.sales s
         WHERE     c.prod_id = s.prod_id
               AND c.time_id = s.time_id
               AND c.channel_id = s.channel_id
               AND c.promo_id = s.promo_id)
  SELECT channel_id, ROUND (AVG (total_cost), 2) avg_cost
    FROM myprofits
GROUP BY channel_id;
```

What these statements do is move the inline view out of line. It is now named and specified at the beginning of the statement prior to the main query. I have named the factored subquery MYPROFITS and I can refer to it just like a data dictionary view in the main query. To clear up any doubt, a factored subquery, like an inline view, is private to a single SQL statement, and there are no permission issues with the factored subquery itself. You just need to have permission to access the underlying objects that the factored subquery references.

Improving Readability

The first reason to use factored subqueries is to make queries that include inline views easier to read. Although inline views are sometime unavoidable with DML statements, when it comes to SELECT or INSERT statements, my general advice is to avoid the use of inline views altogether. Suppose you come across Listing 1-13, once again based on the HR example schema, and want to understand what it is doing.

Listing 1-13. A SELECT having inline views

```
SELECT e.employee_id
       ,e.first_name
       ,e.last_name
       ,e.manager_id
       ,sub.mgr_cnt subordinates
       ,peers.mgr_cnt - 1 peers
       ,peers.job_id_cnt peer_job_id_cnt
       ,sub.job_id_cnt sub_job_id_cnt
   FROM hr.employees e
       ,(  SELECT e.manager_id, COUNT (*) mgr_cnt, job_id_cnt
             FROM hr.employees e
             ,(  SELECT manager_id, COUNT (DISTINCT job_id) job_id_cnt
                    FROM hr.employees
                 GROUP BY manager_id) jid
          WHERE jid.manager_id = e.manager_id
        GROUP BY e.manager_id, jid.job_id_cnt) sub
       ,(  SELECT e.manager_id, COUNT (*) mgr_cnt, job_id_cnt
             FROM hr.employees e
```

```
            ,(  SELECT manager_id, COUNT (DISTINCT job_id) job_id_cnt
                    FROM hr.employees
                 GROUP BY manager_id) jid
             WHERE jid.manager_id = e.manager_id
         GROUP BY e.manager_id, jid.job_id_cnt) peers
   WHERE sub.manager_id = e.employee_id AND peers.manager_id = e.manager_id
ORDER BY last_name, first_name;
```

This is all very daunting, and you take a deep breath. The first thing I would do is paste this code into a private editor window and move the outermost inline views into factored subqueries so as to make the whole thing easier to read. Listing 1-14 shows what the result looks like.

Listing 1-14. A revised Listing 1-13, this time with one level of inline views replaced by factored subqueries

```
WITH sub
     AS (  SELECT e.manager_id, COUNT (*) mgr_cnt, job_id_cnt
             FROM hr.employees e
                 ,(  SELECT manager_id, COUNT (DISTINCT job_id) job_id_cnt
                        FROM hr.employees
                     GROUP BY manager_id) jid
             WHERE jid.manager_id = e.manager_id
         GROUP BY e.manager_id, jid.job_id_cnt)
    ,peers
     AS (  SELECT e.manager_id, COUNT (*) mgr_cnt, job_id_cnt
             FROM hr.employees e
                 ,(  SELECT manager_id, COUNT (DISTINCT job_id) job_id_cnt
                        FROM hr.employees
                     GROUP BY manager_id) jid
             WHERE jid.manager_id = e.manager_id
         GROUP BY e.manager_id, jid.job_id_cnt)
   SELECT e.employee_id
         ,e.first_name
         ,e.last_name
         ,e.manager_id
         ,sub.mgr_cnt subordinates
         ,peers.mgr_cnt - 1 peers
         ,peers.job_id_cnt peer_job_id_cnt
         ,sub.job_id_cnt sub_job_id_cnt
     FROM hr.employees e, sub, peers
    WHERE sub.manager_id = e.employee_id AND peers.manager_id = e.manager_id
ORDER BY last_name, first_name;
```

The two inline views have been replaced by two factored subqueries at the beginning of the query. The factored subqueries are introduced by the keyword WITH and precede the SELECT of the main query. On this occasion, I have been able to name each factored subquery using the table alias of the original inline view. The factored subqueries are then referenced just like tables or data dictionary views in the main query.

Listing 1-14 still contains inline views nested within our factored subqueries, so we need to repeat the process. Listing 1-15 shows all inline views removed.

Listing 1-15. All inline views eliminated

```
WITH q1
    AS (  SELECT manager_id, COUNT (DISTINCT job_id) job_id_cnt
             FROM hr.employees
          GROUP BY manager_id)
    ,q2
    AS (  SELECT manager_id, COUNT (DISTINCT job_id) job_id_cnt
             FROM hr.employees
          GROUP BY manager_id)
    ,sub
    AS (  SELECT e.manager_id, COUNT (*) mgr_cnt, job_id_cnt
             FROM hr.employees e, q1 jid
            WHERE jid.manager_id = e.manager_id
          GROUP BY e.manager_id, jid.job_id_cnt)
    ,peers
    AS (  SELECT e.manager_id, COUNT (*) mgr_cnt, job_id_cnt
             FROM hr.employees e, q2 jid
            WHERE jid.manager_id = e.manager_id
          GROUP BY e.manager_id, jid.job_id_cnt)
  SELECT e.employee_id
        ,e.first_name
        ,e.last_name
        ,e.manager_id
        ,sub.mgr_cnt subordinates
        ,peers.mgr_cnt - 1 peers
        ,peers.job_id_cnt peer_job_id_cnt
        ,sub.job_id_cnt sub_job_id_cnt
    FROM hr.employees e, sub, peers
   WHERE sub.manager_id = e.employee_id AND peers.manager_id = e.manager_id
ORDER BY last_name, first_name;
```

Listing 1-15 moves the nested inline views in SUB and PEERS to factored subqueries Q1 and Q2. We can't use the original table aliases on this occasion as the names of factored subqueries must be unique and the table aliases for both nested inline views are called JID. I then referenced Q1 from SUB and Q2 from PEERS. One factored subquery can reference another as long as the referenced subquery is defined before the referencing one. In this case, that means the definition of Q1 must precede SUB and Q2 must precede PEERS.

■ **Tip**　Like any other identifier, it is usually a good idea to pick names for factored subqueries that are meaningful. However, sometimes, as here, you are "reverse engineering" the SQL and don't yet know what the factored subquery does. In these cases, try to avoid using the identifiers X and Y. These identifiers are actually in use by Oracle Spatial, and this can result in confusing error messages. My preference is to use the identifiers Q1, Q2, and so on.

This exercise has only served to make the query easier to read. Barring CBO anomalies, you shouldn't have done anything yet to affect performance.

Before proceeding, I have to say that in earlier releases of the Oracle database product there have been a number of anomalies that cause refactoring, such as shown in Listings 1-14 and 1-15, to have an effect on performance. But these seem to have been solved in 11gR2 and later. In any event, for most of us being able to read a query is an important step toward optimizing it. So just do the refactoring and the query will be much easier to read.

Using Factored Subqueries Multiple Times

When you look a little more closely at Listing 1-15, you can see that subqueries Q1 and Q2 are identical. This brings me to the second key reason to use factored subqueries: you can use them more than once, as shown in Listing 1-16.

Listing 1-16. Using a factored subquery multiple times

```
WITH jid
    AS (  SELECT manager_id, COUNT (DISTINCT job_id) job_id_cnt
            FROM hr.employees
        GROUP BY manager_id)
    ,sub
    AS (  SELECT e.manager_id, COUNT (*) mgr_cnt, job_id_cnt
            FROM hr.employees e, jid
           WHERE jid.manager_id = e.manager_id
        GROUP BY e.manager_id, jid.job_id_cnt)
    ,peers
    AS (  SELECT e.manager_id, COUNT (*) mgr_cnt, job_id_cnt
            FROM hr.employees e, jid
           WHERE jid.manager_id = e.manager_id
        GROUP BY e.manager_id, jid.job_id_cnt)
  SELECT e.employee_id
        ,e.first_name
        ,e.last_name
        ,e.manager_id
        ,sub.mgr_cnt subordinates
        ,peers.mgr_cnt - 1 peers
        ,peers.job_id_cnt peer_job_id_cnt
        ,sub.job_id_cnt sub_job_id_cnt
    FROM hr.employees e, sub, peers
   WHERE sub.manager_id = e.employee_id AND peers.manager_id = e.manager_id
ORDER BY last_name, first_name;
```

The change to use a single factored subquery multiple times *is* something that is likely to affect the execution plan for the statement and may change its performance characteristics, usually for the better. However, at this stage we are just trying to make our statement easier to read.

Now that you have made these changes, you can see that the subqueries SUB and PEERS are now identical and the JID subquery is superfluous. Listing 1-17 completes this readability exercise.

Listing 1-17. Listing 1-16 rewritten with just one factored subquery

```
WITH mgr_counts
     AS (  SELECT e.manager_id, COUNT (*) mgr_cnt, COUNT (DISTINCT job_id) job_id_cnt
             FROM hr.employees e
         GROUP BY e.manager_id)
  SELECT e.employee_id
        ,e.first_name
        ,e.last_name
        ,e.manager_id
        ,sub.mgr_cnt subordinates
        ,peers.mgr_cnt - 1 peers
        ,peers.job_id_cnt peer_job_id_cnt
        ,sub.job_id_cnt sub_job_id_cnt
    FROM hr.employees e, mgr_counts sub, mgr_counts peers
   WHERE sub.manager_id = e.employee_id AND peers.manager_id = e.manager_id
ORDER BY last_name, first_name;
```

UNDERSTANDING WHAT A QUERY DOES

After a few minutes of rearranging Listing 1-13 so its constituent parts stand out clearly, you have a much better chance of understanding what it actually does:

- The query returns one row for each middle manager. The boss of the company and employees who are not managers are excluded.

- The EMPLOYEE_ID, LAST_NAME and FIRST_NAME, and MANAGER_ID are from the selected middle manager.

- SUBORDINATES is the number of employees reporting directly to the selected middle manager.

- PEERS is the number of other people with the same manager as the selected middle manager.

- PEER_JOB_ID_CNT is the number of different jobs held by those peers.

- SUB_JOB_ID_CNT is the number of different jobs held by the direct reports of the selected middle manager.

Once you understand a query you are much better positioned to tune it if necessary.

Avoiding the Use of Temporary Tables

The third reason to use factored subqueries is to avoid the use of temporary tables. There are those who recommend taking complex queries and breaking them up into separate statements and storing the intermediate results into one or more temporary tables. The rationale for this is that these simpler statements are easier to read and test. Now that factored subqueries are available, I personally no longer use temporary tables purely to simplify SQL.

If you want to test individual factored subqueries, either to debug them or to look at performance, rather than use temporary tables, you can use a subset of your factored subqueries. Listing 1-18 shows how to test the MGR_COUNTS factored subquery in Listing 1-17 on its own.

Listing 1-18. Testing factored subqueries independently

```
WITH mgr_counts
    AS ( SELECT e.manager_id, COUNT (*) mgr_cnt, COUNT (DISTINCT job_id) job_id_cnt
           FROM hr.employees e
       GROUP BY e.manager_id)
    ,q_main
    AS ( SELECT e.employee_id
               ,e.first_name
               ,e.last_name
               ,e.manager_id
               ,sub.mgr_cnt subordinates
               ,peers.mgr_cnt - 1 peers
               ,peers.job_id_cnt peer_job_id_cnt
               ,sub.job_id_cnt sub_job_id_cnt
           FROM hr.employees e, mgr_counts sub, mgr_counts peers
          WHERE sub.manager_id = e.employee_id AND peers.manager_id = e.manager_id
       ORDER BY last_name, first_name)
SELECT *
  FROM mgr_counts;
```

What I have done in Listing 1-18 is take what was previously the main query clause and made it into another factored subquery that I have chosen to name Q_MAIN. The new main query clause now just selects rows from MGR_COUNTS for testing purposes.

In Oracle Database 10g, Listing 1-18 would have been an invalid SQL syntax because not all of the factored subqueries are being used. Thank goodness in Oracle Database 11g onward this requirement has been lifted, and we can now test complex SQL statements in stages without resorting to temporary tables.

The reason I generally prefer a single complex SQL statement with multiple simple factored subqueries to separate SQL statements integrated with temporary tables is that the CBO can see the whole problem at once and has more choices in determining the order in which things are done.

■ **Note**   I have stated that I don't use temporary tables just for testing. However, there are other reasons to use temporary tables, which I discuss in chapter 16.

Recursive Factored Subqueries

We now come to the fourth and final reason to use factored subqueries. That reason is to enable recursion.

Oracle Database 11gr2 introduced *recursive factored subqueries,* which are really a different sort of animal to the factored subqueries that we have dealt with up to now. This feature is explained with examples in the SQL Language Reference manual, and there is plenty of discussion of their use on the Web.

Suppose your table contains tree-structured data. One way to access those data would be to use hierarchical queries, but recursion is a more powerful and elegant tool. A fun way to learn about recursive factored subqueries is to look at Martin Amis's blog.

■ **Note**   You can visit Martin Amis's blog at: http://technology.amis.nl/. His article on solving Sudoku with recursive factored subqueries is at: http://technology.amis.nl/2009/10/13/oracle-rdbms-11gr2-solving-a-sudoku-using-recursive-subquery-factoring/.

Incidentally, a query can contain a mixture of recursive and non-recursive factored subqueries. Although recursive subquery factoring seems like a useful feature, I haven't yet seen it used in a commercial application, so I won't discuss it further in this book.

Joins

Let's move on to the final topic in this chapter: joins. I will begin with a review of inner joins and traditional join syntax. I will then explain the related topics of outer joins and American National Standards Institute (ANSI) join syntax before looking at how partitioned outer joins provide a solution to data densification problems with analytic queries.

Inner Joins and Traditional Join Syntax

The original version of the SQL included only inner joins, and a simple "comma-separated" syntax was devised to represent it. I will refer to this syntax as the *traditional syntax* in the rest of this book.

A Simple Two Table Join

Let's start with Listing 1-19, a simple example using the tables in the HR example schema.

Listing 1-19. A two table join

```
SELECT *
  FROM hr.employees e, hr.jobs j
 WHERE e.job_id = j.job_id AND e.manager_id = 100 AND j.min_salary > 8000;
```

This query just has one join. Theoretically this statement says:

- Combine all rows from EMPLOYEES with all rows in JOBS. So if there are M rows in EMPLOYEES and N rows in JOBS, there should be M x N rows in our *intermediate result set*.

- From this intermediate result set select just the rows where EMPLOYEES.JOB_ID = JOBS.JOB_ID, EMPLOYEES.MANAGER_ID=1, and JOBS.MIN_SALARY > 8000.

Notice that there is no distinction between the predicates used in the joins, called *join predicates*, and other predicates called *selection predicates*. The query logically returns the result of joining the tables together without any predicates (a *Cartesian join*) and then applies all the predicates as selection predicates at the end.

Now, as I mentioned at the beginning of this chapter, SQL is a declarative programming language and the CBO is allowed to generate the final result set in any legitimate way. There are actually several different approaches the CBO could take to deal with this simple query. Here is one way:

- Find all the rows in EMPLOYEES where EMPLOYEES.MANAGER_ID=1.

- For each matching row from EMPLOYEES, find all rows in JOBS where EMPLOYEES.JOB_ID = JOBS.JOB_ID.

- Select rows from the intermediate result where JOBS.MIN_SALARY > 8000.

The CBO might also take the following approach:

- Find all the rows in JOBS where JOBS.MIN_SALARY > 8000.

- For each matching row from JOBS, find all the rows in EMPLOYEES where EMPLOYEES.JOB_ID = JOBS.JOB_ID.

- Select rows from the intermediate result where EMPLOYEES.MANAGER_ID=1.

These examples introduce the concept of *join order*. The CBO processes each table in the FROM clause in some order, and I will use my own notation to describe that order. For example, the preceding two examples can be shown using the table aliases as E ➜ J and J ➜ E, respectively.

I will call the table on the left of the arrow the *driving* table and the table on the right the *probe* table. Don't attach too much meaning to these terms because they don't always make sense and in some cases will be in contradiction to accepted use. I just need a way to name the join operands. Let's move on to a slightly more complex inner join.

A Four Table Inner Join

Listing 1-20 adds more tables to the query in Listing 1-19.

Listing 1-20. Joining four tables

```
SELECT *
  FROM hr.employees e
      ,hr.jobs j
      ,hr.departments d
      ,hr.job_history h
 WHERE e.job_id = j.job_id AND e.employee_id = h.employee_id
       AND e.department_id = d.department_id;
```

Because the query in Listing 1-20 has four tables, there are three join operations required. There is always one fewer join than tables. One possible join order is ((E ➜ J) ➜ D) ➜ H. You can see that I have used parentheses to highlight the intermediate results.

When there are only inner joins in a query, the CBO is free to choose any join order it wishes, and although performance may vary, the result will always be the same. That is why this syntax is so appropriate for inner joins because it avoids any unnecessary specification of join order or predicate classification and leaves it all up to the CBO.

Outer Joins and ANSI Join Syntax

Although inner joins are very useful and represent the majority in this world, something extra is needed. Enter the outer join. *Left outer joins*, *right outer joins*, and *full outer joins* are three variants, and I will cover them each in turn. But first we need some test data.

I won't use the tables in the HR schema to demonstrate outer joins because something simpler is needed. Listing 1-21 sets up the four tables you will need.

Listing 1-21. Setting up tables T1 through T4

```
DROP TABLE t1;                  -- Created in Listing 1-8
DROP TABLE t2;                  -- Created in Listing 1-8

CREATE TABLE t1
AS
   SELECT ROWNUM c1
     FROM all_objects
    WHERE ROWNUM <= 5;

CREATE TABLE t2
AS
   SELECT c1 + 1 c2 FROM t1;

CREATE TABLE t3
AS
   SELECT c2 + 1 c3 FROM t2;

CREATE TABLE t4
AS
   SELECT c3 + 1 c4 FROM t3;
```

Each table has five rows but the contents differ slightly. Figure 1-1 shows the contents.

T1

C1
1
2
3
4
5

T2

C2
2
3
4
5
6

T3

C3
3
4
5
6
7

T4

C4
4
5
6
7
8

Figure 1-1. The data in our test tables

Left Outer Joins

Listing 1-22 provides the first outer join example. It shows a left outer join. Such a join makes rows from the second table, the table on the right-hand side, optional. You'll get all relevant rows from the table on the left-hand side regardless of corresponding rows in the right-hand side of the table.

Listing 1-22. A two table left outer join

```
SELECT *
    FROM t1 LEFT OUTER JOIN t2 ON t1.c1 = t2.c2 AND t1.c1 > 4
   WHERE t1.c1 > 3
ORDER BY t1.c1;

        C1         C2
---------- ----------
         4
         5          5
```

As you can see, the format of the FROM clause is now quite different, and I'll come back to this. The left operand of the join is called the *preserved row source* and the right operand the *optional row source*.

What this query (logically) says is:

- Identify combinations of rows in T1 and T2 that match the criteria T1.C1 = T2.C2 AND T1.C1 > 4.

- For all rows in T1 that do not match any rows in T2, output them with NULL for the columns in T2.

- Eliminate all rows from the result set that do not match the criteria T1.C1 > 3.

- Order the result by T1.C1.

Notice that there is a big difference between a selection predicate and a join predicate. The selection predicate T1.C1 > 3 resulted in the elimination of rows from the result set, but the join predicate T1.C1 > 4 just resulted in the loss of column values from T2.

Not only is there now a big difference between a join predicate and a selection predicate, but the CBO doesn't have complete freedom to reorder joins. Consider Listing 1-23 that joins all four tables.

Listing 1-23. Four table outer join

```
SELECT c1
      ,c2
      ,c3
      ,c4
  FROM (t3 LEFT JOIN t4 ON t3.c3 = t4.c4)
       LEFT JOIN (t2 LEFT JOIN t1 ON t1.c1 = t2.c2) ON t2.c2 = t3.c3
ORDER BY c3;
```

C1	C2	C3	C4
3	3	3	
4	4	4	4
5	5	5	5
	6	6	6
		7	7

To make things a little clearer, I have added optional parentheses so you can see the intention. Notice also that the keyword OUTER is optional and I have omitted it here.

With one special exception, which I'll come to when I discuss *hash input swapping* later, the CBO always uses the left operand of the left outer join (the preserved row source) as the driving row source in the join. Therefore, the CBO has limited choice in which join order to use here. The join order that was specified was ((T3 ➔ T4) ➔ (T2 ➔ T1)).

The CBO did, in fact, have a choice of five join orders. All the predicates mandate that:

- T3 precedes T4 in the join order

- T2 precedes T1 in the join order

- T3 precedes T2 in the join order

As an example, Listing 1-24 rewrites Listing 1-23 using the order (((T3 ➔ T2) ➔ T1) ➔ T4) to get the same results.

Listing 1-24. An alternative construction of Listing 1-23

```
SELECT c1
      ,c2
      ,c3
      ,c4
   FROM t3
        LEFT JOIN t2 ON t3.c3 = t2.c2
        LEFT JOIN t1 ON t2.c2 = t1.c1
        LEFT JOIN t4 ON t3.c3 = t4.c4
ORDER BY c3;
```

Because outer joins had not yet been conceived when SQL was first invented, the traditional syntax has no provision for separating join conditions from selection conditions or for differentiating preserved from optional row sources.

Oracle was an early implementer of outer joins and it devised a proprietary extension to the traditional syntax to denote outer join conditions. The syntax involves modifying the WHERE clause by appending columns from the optional row source with (+) in join conditions. Listing 1-25 rewrites Listing 1-24 using the proprietary syntax.

Listing 1-25. Rewrite of Listing 1-24 using proprietary syntax

```
SELECT c1
      ,c2
      ,c3
      ,c4
   FROM t1
      ,t2
      ,t3
      ,t4
  WHERE t3.c3 = t2.c2(+) AND t2.c2 = t1.c1(+) AND t3.c3 = t4.c4(+)
ORDER BY c3;
```

This notation is severely limited in its ability:

- Prior to Oracle Database 12cR1, a table can be the optional row source in at most one join.

- Full and partitioned outer joins, which I'll discuss shortly, are not supported.

Because of these restrictions, the queries in Listings 1-28, 1-29 and 1-30 can't be expressed in proprietary syntax. To implement these queries with proprietary syntax, you would need to use factored subqueries, inline views or set operators.

Personally I find this proprietary syntax difficult to read, and this is another reason why I generally advise against its use. You could, however, see this notation in execution plans in the predicate section, which will be discussed in Chapter 8.

The new syntax has been endorsed by the ANSI and is usually referred to as *ANSI join syntax*. This syntax is supported by all major database vendors and supports inner joins as well. Listing 1-26 shows how to specify an inner join with ANSI syntax.

Listing 1-26. ANSI join syntax with inner joins

```
SELECT *
 FROM t1
     LEFT JOIN t2
        ON t1.c1 = t2.c2
     JOIN t3
        ON t2.c2 = t3.c3
     CROSS JOIN t4;
```

C1	C2	C3	C4
3	3	3	4
3	3	3	5
3	3	3	6
3	3	3	7
3	3	3	8
4	4	4	4
4	4	4	5
4	4	4	6
4	4	4	7
4	4	4	8
5	5	5	4
5	5	5	5
5	5	5	6
5	5	5	7
5	5	5	8

The join with T3 is an inner join (you can explicitly add the keyword INNER if you want), and the join with T4 is a Cartesian join; ANSI uses the keywords CROSS JOIN to denote a Cartesian join.

Right Outer Joins

A right outer join is just syntactic sugar. A right outer join preserves rows on the right instead of the left. Listing 1-27 shows how difficult queries can be to read without the right outer join syntax.

Listing 1-27. Complex query without right outer join

```
  SELECT c1, c2, c3
    FROM    t1
        LEFT JOIN
             t2
           LEFT JOIN
             t3
          ON t2.c2 = t3.c3
        ON t1.c1 = t3.c3
ORDER BY c1;
```

Listing 1-27 specifies the join order (T1 ➜ (T2 ➜ T3)). Listing 1-28 shows how to specify the same join order using a right outer join.

Listing 1-28. Right outer join

```
SELECT c1, c2, c3
  FROM t2
       LEFT JOIN t3
          ON t2.c2 = t3.c3
       RIGHT JOIN t1
          ON t1.c1 = t3.c3
ORDER BY c1;
```

Personally, I find the latter syntax easier to read, but it makes no difference to either the execution plan or the results.

Full Outer Joins

As you might guess, a full outer join preserves rows on both sides of the keywords. Listing 1-29 is an example.

Listing 1-29. Full outer join

```
SELECT *
  FROM t1 FULL JOIN t2 ON t1.c1 = t2.c2
ORDER BY t1.c1;
```

C1	C2
1	
2	2
3	3
4	4
5	5
	6

Partitioned Outer Joins

Both left and right outer joins can be *partitioned*. This term is somewhat overused. To be clear, its use here has nothing to do with the *partitioning option*, which relates to a physical database design feature.

To explain partitioned outer joins, I will use the SALES table from the SH example schema. To keep the result set small, I am just looking at sales made to countries in Europe between 1998 and 1999. For each year, I want to know the total sold per country vs. the average number of sales per country made to customers born in 1976. Listing 1-30 is my first attempt.

Listing 1-30. First attempt at average sales query

```
WITH sales_q
     AS (SELECT s.*, EXTRACT (YEAR FROM time_id) sale_year
           FROM sh.sales s)
  SELECT sale_year
        ,country_name
        ,NVL (SUM (amount_sold), 0) amount_sold
        ,AVG (NVL (SUM (amount_sold), 0)) OVER (PARTITION BY sale_year)
           avg_sold
    FROM sales_q s
         JOIN sh.customers c USING (cust_id) -- PARTITION BY (sale_year)
         RIGHT JOIN sh.countries co
           ON c.country_id = co.country_id AND cust_year_of_birth = 1976
   WHERE     (sale_year IN (1998, 1999) OR sale_year IS NULL)
         AND country_region = 'Europe'
GROUP BY sale_year, country_name
ORDER BY 1, 2;
```

I begin with a factored subquery to obtain the year of the sale once for convenience. I know that some countries might not have any sales to customers born in 1976, so I have used an outer join on countries and added the CUST_YEAR_OF_BIRTH = 1976 to the join condition rather than the WHERE clause. Notice also the use of the USING clause. This is just shorthand for ON C.CUST_ID = S.CUST_ID. Here are the results:

SALE_YEAR	COUNTRY_NAME	AMOUNT_SOLD	AVG_SOLD
1998	Denmark	2359.6	11492.5683
1998	France	28430.27	11492.5683
1998	Germany	6019.98	11492.5683
1998	Italy	5736.7	11492.5683
1998	Spain	15864.76	11492.5683
1998	United Kingdom	10544.1	11492.5683
1999	Denmark	13250.2	21676.8267
1999	France	46967.8	21676.8267
1999	Italy	28545.46	21676.8267
1999	Poland	4251.68	21676.8267
1999	Spain	21503.07	21676.8267
1999	United Kingdom	15542.75	21676.8267
	Ireland	0	0
	The Netherlands	0	0
	Turkey	0	0

The AVG_SOLD column is supposed to contain the average sales for countries in that year and thus is the same for all countries in any year. It is calculated using what is known as an *analytic function,* which I'll explain in detail in Chapter 7. You can see that three countries made no qualifying sales and the outer join has added rows for these at the end. But notice that the SALE_YEAR is NULL. That is why I added the OR SALE_YEAR IS NULL clause. It is a debugging aid. Also, Poland made no sales in 1998 and Germany made no sales in 1999. The averages reported are thus incorrect, dividing the total by the six countries that made sales in that year rather than the ten countries in Europe. What you want is to preserve not just every country but every combination of country and year. You can do this by uncommenting the highlighted PARTITION BY clause, as shown in Listing 1-30. This gives the following, more meaningful, results:

SALE_YEAR	COUNTRY_NAME	AMOUNT_SOLD	AVG_SOLD
1998	Denmark	2359.6	6895.541
1998	France	28430.27	6895.541
1998	Germany	6019.98	6895.541
1998	Ireland	0	6895.541
1998	Italy	5736.7	6895.541
1998	Poland	0	6895.541
1998	Spain	15864.76	6895.541
1998	The Netherlands	0	6895.541
1998	Turkey	0	6895.541
1998	United Kingdom	10544.1	6895.541
1999	Denmark	13250.2	13006.096
1999	France	46967.8	13006.096
1999	Germany	0	13006.096
1999	Ireland	0	13006.096
1999	Italy	28545.46	13006.096
1999	Poland	4251.68	13006.096
1999	Spain	21503.07	13006.096
1999	The Netherlands	0	13006.096
1999	Turkey	0	13006.096
1999	United Kingdom	15542.75	13006.096

That's more like it! There are ten rows per year now, one for each country regardless of the sales in that year.

The problem that partitioned outer joins solves is known as *data densification*. This isn't always a sensible thing to do, and I'll return to this issue in Chapter 19.

■ **Note** Although partitioned full outer joins are not supported, it is possible to partition the preserved row source instead of the optional row source, as in the example. I can't think of why you might want to do this, and I can't find any examples on the Internet of its use.

Summary

This chapter has discussed a few features of SQL that, despite being crucial to optimization, are often overlooked. The main messages I want to leave you with at the end of this chapter are:

- The array interface is crucial for shipping large volumes of data in and out of the database.

- Outer joins limit the opportunity for the CBO to reorder joins.

- Understanding SQL is crucial and making it readable with factored subqueries is an easy way to do this.

I have briefly mentioned the role of the CBO in this chapter and in chapter 2 I give a more detailed overview of what it does and how it does it.

CHAPTER 2

■ ■ ■

The Cost-Based Optimizer

Chapter 1 introduced the CBO. It is the job of the CBO to determine how to set about running your SQL statement. An approach to executing an SQL statement is known as an *execution plan*, and for very simple statements, there may only be one way to set about doing the task. Therefore, there will only be one possible execution plan. However, for the vast majority of SQL statements, there are different possible execution plans from which the CBO must choose. In English language, *optimization* means picking the best from a number of options, and in this case the CBO is trying to pick the optimal execution plan from all of the possible plans it identifies.

THE RULE-BASED OPTIMIZER

When the database is mounted but not open, queries cannot use the CBO and the rule-based optimizer (RBO) is used. It is possible to use the RBO in other situations, but since the release of Oracle database 10gR1, the RBO is no longer supported for general purpose use. Therefore, I won't be discussing the RBO further in this book.

The vast majority of the CBO's work revolves around optimizing queries or the subqueries embedded in DML or Data Definition Language (DDL) statements. For DML and DDL statements, there are one or two other things to consider, such as whether to perform direct-path or conventional inserts, but these are normally determined by relatively fixed rules. For the sake of simplicity, I will ignore these and continue on the assumption that the CBO is there purely to optimize queries.

I begin this chapter with a discussion of the criteria that the CBO uses to determine the optimal execution plan. After that, I'll introduce the concept of cost, which is how the CBO quantifies the benefits of one plan over another. Finally, I'll give a brief overview of the process that the CBO uses to identify and cost the set of plans from which it must choose. I'll return to the topics introduced in this chapter later in the book and go into far more detail.

The Optimal Execution Plan

So if optimization is about picking the optimal execution plan, it is important to understand what an optimal execution plan is. Fortunately, or unfortunately, the CBO has a very simple view of what constitutes optimal: the optimal execution plan is the one that runs the quickest. That's it. Well that's *almost* it. If the optimizer is running using one of the FIRST_ROWS optimizer modes, then the optimal plan is the one that returns the first few rows the quickest rather than the one that returns all the rows the quickest. Be that as it may, the point is that the CBO does not encumber itself with concerns about resource consumption and the like. So, for example, if a serial execution plan is estimated to take 4.98 seconds and a plan involving 128 parallel query slaves is estimated to complete in 4.97 seconds, then the CBO will pick the latter! That is, it will do that if you let it. I'll discuss the optimization process a little later in this chapter, and as part of that discussion I'll return to the topic of parallel operations.

The Definition of Cost

So if the optimal execution plan is the one that would finish first, then the CBO needs to estimate how long each plan would take to run and then pick the one with the lowest predicted execution time. That estimated execution time is known as the *cost* of the plan. Now you might assume that the unit of execution time might be nanoseconds, milliseconds, seconds, or some such standard measurement. Unfortunately, for historical reasons, the unit of cost is defined as the length of time that a single block read takes to complete! So, if the CBO thinks that a query will take 5 seconds to run and that a single block read takes 10 milliseconds, then the assigned cost will be 500 as this is 5,000 milliseconds divided by 10 milliseconds.

CBO COST VS. REAL COST

The term *cost* in this book is used exclusively to refer to the estimate that the CBO makes of how long an SQL statement will take to execute. That estimate, of course, may be inaccurate. It is important to realize that when it comes to tuning, the human optimization process that attempts to better the CBO, the goal is to reduce the actual elapsed time a statement takes to run. It isn't important how high the CBO cost estimate is as long as the statement runs fast, and similarly you won't be impressed by a low cost estimate if the statement takes ages to run.

To arrive at the cost of an execution plan, the CBO doesn't just estimate the number of single block reads. It also tries to work out how long any multiblock read operations in the plan will take and how long central processing unit (CPU)-related operations, such as in-memory sorts, take to run, and it incorporates these times in the overall cost. Oddly enough, though, it translates all these times into equivalent single block reads. Here's an example. Suppose that a particular plan is estimated to involve:

- 400 single block reads
- 300 multiblock reads
- 5 seconds of CPU processing

Let's further assume that the CBO estimates that:

- A single block read takes 10 milliseconds

- A multiblock read takes 30 milliseconds

The cost of this plan is calculated as:

```
((400 x 10) + (300 x 30) + 5,000)/10 = 1800
```

These days, execution plans are typically printed with both a cost and an estimated elapsed time in hours, minutes, and seconds, so you don't have to do quite as much math as you used to!

The CBO's Cost-Estimating Algorithm

There are two big questions to answer at this point: How is the cost of an execution plan determined? How accurate is that guess? Let's take a look at these questions now.

Calculating Cost

The main inputs to the CBO's estimating process are the *object statistics* that are held in the data dictionary. These statistics will indicate, for example, how many blocks are in a table and, therefore, how many multiblock reads would be required to read it in its entirety. Statistics are also held for indexes, so the CBO has some basis for estimating how many single block reads will be required to read data from a table using an index.

Object statistics are the most important inputs to the CBO's costing algorithm but by no means the only ones. *Initialization parameter settings, system statistics, dynamic sampling, SQL profiles*, and *SQL baselines* are all examples of other things the CBO considers when making its cost estimates.

The Quality of the CBO's Plan Selection

Let's look at the accuracy of the CBO's cost-estimation process and why it sometimes matters but sometimes doesn't.

The Accuracy of the CBO's Cost Estimates

You may be surprised to learn that the CBO's cost calculations are frequently wildly inaccurate! Fortunately, these errors often turn out to be irrelevant. Suppose that the CBO is choosing between two possible execution plans for a query. It thinks that plan A will take 5 seconds to run and plan B 10 seconds, so it chooses plan A. Now it may be that when the query is run using plan A, it actually takes 50 seconds to run and the CBO was off by a factor of 10. Well that error won't be of any consequence if the estimate for plan B is a big underestimate as well. As long as when the query runs with plan B it isn't noticeably faster than when it runs with plan A, then no harm is done: the CBO made an acceptable selection of plan despite making wildly inaccurate cost estimates.

In many cases, particularly with interactive online transaction processing (OLTP)-style queries, the choice of plan is obvious and the CBO couldn't get it wrong even if the object statistics were very inaccurate or nonexistent. For example, if you are reading a single row from a huge table using equality predicates on all primary key columns, it is very difficult to see how the CBO could do anything but use the primary key index. The alternative approach of a full table scan would take hundreds or even thousands of times longer to run, so the correct plan would still be selected even if the CBO's cost estimates were way off.

Suboptimal Execution Plans

Although the CBO will often pick an acceptable execution plan, it is also quite common for it to pick a severely suboptimal plan, even when statistics are gathered correctly and are up to date. In other words, the CBO picks a plan that takes much longer to run than an alternative plan would have. I'll explain the reasons why this happens so often later in this book.

There are two main reasons these bad plan selections often go unnoticed:

- The first is that the performance of many SQL statements is of no concern. Suppose you have a five-hour batch that runs overnight and executes several thousand SQL statements. If one SQL statement takes 30 seconds to run instead of one second, it won't matter much, particularly if other statements in the batch are running concurrently and this statement isn't on the critical path.

- The second reason that these bad plan selections go unnoticed is that there is no easy way to know how long an SQL statement should take to run; people's expectations are often very low. The exception, of course, is when a plan changes for the worse; you would know that the new plan is bad because you experienced the previous good plan! I would hazard a conservative guess that the elapsed time of most overnight batch runs that have not been professionally tuned could be at least halved without any code changes (other than adding optimizer hints) given enough time for analysis. In real life, of course, tuning exercises usually involves physical database changes, such as adding indexes and rewriting some code. In these cases, it isn't uncommon to see batch times reduce by a factor of 10 or more!

The assertion that the CBO often gets it wrong may come as a surprise. But remember that the CBO is just making a *guess* as to what the right plan is. It can't be certain. Common sense tells us that when you guess over and over again you will guess wrong some of the time and some of the times you guess wrong you will be very, very wrong.

Now that you understand the concepts of optimization and cost, let's look at the three main tasks involved in both identifying and costing the various executions plan for a query.

The Optimization Process

The three main tasks for identifying and costing the various execution plans for a query are:

- Determine the degree of parallelism to be used.

- Determine what transformations are to be applied.

- Determine what I will refer to as the *final state optimization.* I have invented this term because the term optimization is ambiguous. On the one hand, optimization can be used to refer to the entire process including identifying the degree of parallelism and the necessary transformations. On the other hand, it can refer to the process of identifying and costing the various execution plans once transformations and the degree of parallelism have been settled on. To avoid confusion, I will use the term final state optimization to refer to the latter, narrower, concept.

These three tasks are not independent of one another. You can't really work out what degree of parallelism to use until you know what the serial execution plan looks like. After all, a table and its various indexes may have different degrees of parallelism specified in the data dictionary. But you often can't work out whether an index or a full table scan is better unless you know the extent to which a full table scan will be parallelized. Fortunately, you and I don't need to understand how the CBO sorts all this out. We just need to understand the basics, so let's get started.

Parallelism

If the CBO is entirely unconcerned about resource consumption, you may be wondering why it doesn't use parallel query most, if not all, of the time. The short answer is that by default the CBO is precluded from considering parallel query, parallel DML, and parallel DDL. To allow the CBO to consider parallel query, you need to do one of the following:

- Add the PARALLEL optimizer hint to the query.

- Alter one or more tables or indexes involved in the query to specify a nondefault degree of parallelism.

- Use an ALTER SESSION statement to specify a degree of parallelism for the session.

- Set up *automatic degree of parallelism* (auto DOP) on your system.

If you do any of these things, the CBO will be allowed to consider parallel operations, but in all cases the maximum degree of parallelism will be limited to ensure that resource consumption doesn't get too much out of control. Listing 2-1 provides examples of enabling parallel query operations.

Listing 2-1. Different ways to enable parallel query

```
CREATE TABLE t
AS
    SELECT ROWNUM c1 FROM all_objects;

CREATE INDEX i
    ON t (c1);

--
-- Use optimizer hints to allow the CBO to consider parallel operations
--
EXPLAIN PLAN
    FOR
        SELECT /*+ parallel(10) */
            * FROM t;

SELECT * FROM TABLE (DBMS_XPLAN.display);

--
-- Enable parallel operations on operations involving table T
--
ALTER TABLE t PARALLEL (DEGREE 10);
--
-- Enable parallel operations on index I
--

ALTER INDEX i
    PARALLEL (DEGREE 10);

--
-- Attempt to force parallel queries of degree 10 on all SQL statements.
-- Be aware that FORCE doesn't mean parallelism is guaranteed!
--
ALTER SESSION FORCE PARALLEL QUERY PARALLEL 10;
--
-- Setup Auto DOP for the system (logged in as SYS user, RESTART REQUIRED)
--

DELETE FROM resource_io_calibrate$;

INSERT INTO resource_io_calibrate$
    VALUES (CURRENT_TIMESTAMP
            ,CURRENT_TIMESTAMP
            ,0
            ,0
            ,200
            ,0
            ,0);

COMMIT;

ALTER SYSTEM SET parallel_degree_policy=auto;
```

Let's go through these examples one by one. After creating a table and an associated index, the next statement uses the variant of the PARALLEL optimizer hint introduced in Oracle database 11gR2 to enable parallel query with degree 10 for the statement. Be aware that contrary to the SQL Language Reference manual, this hint does not force a parallel query; it just allows the CBO to consider it. The point is that some operations, such as index range scans on non-partitioned indexes, can't be parallelized, and a serial index range scan might be more efficient than a parallel full table scan at the specified degree.

If you really want to force a parallel query, you might try the ALTER SESSION statement given in Listing 2-1. Here too I have specified the degree of parallelism to be used and here too parallelism isn't guaranteed for the same reasons! All the ALTER SESSION statement does is to implicitly add a PARALLEL hint to all statements in the session.

FORCING PARALLEL OPERATIONS

If the CBO picks a serial index range scan and you want to force a parallel full table scan, then using the ALTER SESSION statement as in Listing 2-1 may be insufficient despite the misleading FORCE keyword in the statement. You might also have to hint the code to force the full table scan as well.

I didn't have to specify the degree of parallelism in any of the examples in Listing 2-1. If I hadn't, then the CBO would pick the *ideal degree of parallelism* (ideal DOP), which is the degree of parallelism that allows the query to complete the fastest providing that degree is no more than the value specified by the initialization parameter PARALLEL_DEGREE_LIMIT.

DEGREE OF PARALLELISM AND COST

At some point, increasing the degree of parallelism becomes counterproductive for various reasons. Although the ideal DOP reflects this reality, the reported cost of plans with a degree of parallelism higher than the ideal DOP will be lower than the plan that uses the ideal DOP.

The final way to enable parallel query for a statement is to use the auto DOP feature introduced in Oracle database 11gR2. This feature basically means that the ideal DOP is used on all statements that are estimated to run for more than 10 seconds. Officially you are supposed to set up auto DOP using the DBMS_RESOURCE_MANAGER.CALIBRATE_IO routine so that the CBO can more accurately calculate the ideal DOP. Unofficially, the CBO team has suggested using the code in Listing 2-1 instead that specifies 200 MB per second throughput for the input/output (I/O) subsystem. All other metrics, like the number of disks, meaningless with enterprise storage, are left unspecified. Either way, you have to restart the database instance.

I have tried auto DOP using the unofficial approach on a large system with 64 processors and a 64GB System Global Area (SGA) and it worked really well. I have heard mixed reports from those who have used the documented approach. Some are happy and others have reported problems.

Query Transformation

The second of the CBO's main tasks in optimizing a query is to consider the potential transformations that might be applied to the statement. In other words, the CBO looks at rewriting the statement in a simpler or more efficient way. These days there are a lot of possible transformations that the CBO can consider, and I'll go through most of them in Chapter 13.

There are two types of query transformation:

- *Cost-based transformation*: The CBO should only apply the transformation when the optimal plan obtainable from the transformed query has a lower cost than the optimal plan available from the untransformed query.

- *Heuristic transformation*: This type of transformation is applied either unconditionally or based on some simple rules.

These days the vast majority of transformations are cost based, but there are one or two that are not. Regardless of the type of the transformation, you can always force it or suppress it with the aid of an optimizer hint. Listing 2-2 shows an example query where the CBO applies a heuristic query transformation inappropriately.

Listing 2-2. Simple view merging query transformation

```
CREATE TABLE t1
AS
        SELECT 1 c1
          FROM DUAL
   CONNECT BY LEVEL <= 100;

CREATE TABLE t2
AS
        SELECT 1 c2
          FROM DUAL
   CONNECT BY LEVEL <= 100;

CREATE TABLE t3
AS
        SELECT 1 c3
          FROM DUAL
   CONNECT BY LEVEL <= 100;

CREATE TABLE t4
AS
        SELECT 1 c4
          FROM DUAL
   CONNECT BY LEVEL <= 100;

EXPLAIN PLAN
   FOR
      WITH t1t2
           AS (SELECT t1.c1, t2.c2
                 FROM t1, t2
                WHERE t1.c1 = t2.c2)
          ,t3t4
```

```
            AS (SELECT t3.c3, t4.c4
                  FROM t3, t4
                 WHERE t3.c3 = t4.c4)
       SELECT COUNT (*)
         FROM t1t2 j1, t3t4 j2
        WHERE j1.c1 + j1.c2 = j2.c3 + j2.c4;

SELECT * FROM TABLE (DBMS_XPLAN.display (format => 'BASIC +COST'));

PAUSE

-- The above query is transformed into the query below

EXPLAIN PLAN
   FOR
      SELECT COUNT (*)
        FROM t1
            ,t2
            ,t3
            ,t4
       WHERE     t1.c1 = t2.c2
             AND t3.c3 = t4.c4
             AND t1.c1 + t2.c2 = t3.c3 + t4.c4;

SELECT * FROM TABLE (DBMS_XPLAN.display (format => 'BASIC +COST'));
-- The resulting execution plan is this:

Plan hash value: 2241143226
```

```
----------------------------------------------------
| Id  | Operation             | Name | Cost (%CPU)|
----------------------------------------------------
|   0 | SELECT STATEMENT      |      |  293  (89)|
|   1 |  SORT AGGREGATE       |      |           |
|   2 |   HASH JOIN           |      |  293  (89)|
|   3 |    TABLE ACCESS FULL  | T4   |    2   (0)|
|   4 |    HASH JOIN          |      |   36   (9)|
|   5 |     TABLE ACCESS FULL | T2   |    2   (0)|
|   6 |     MERGE JOIN CARTESIAN|    |   31   (0)|
|   7 |      TABLE ACCESS FULL| T1   |    2   (0)|
|   8 |      BUFFER SORT      |      |   29   (0)|
|   9 |       TABLE ACCESS FULL| T3  |    0   (0)|
----------------------------------------------------
```

Listing 2-2 creates four tables and then queries them. The query has been explicitly written to suggest that T1 and T2 are joined first; T3 and T4 are joined next; and then the two intermediate results joined. However, the CBO has applied *simple view merging* and replaced the original query with the simple join of four tables highlighted in bold. I'll explain this in detail and how to generate and analyze execution plans in Chapter 3, but now you just need to focus on the estimated cost for the query as a whole, which is reported on line 0 of the plan–293. Listing 2-3 adds some hints.

Listing 2-3. Simple view merging suppressed

```
WITH t1t2
    AS (SELECT /*+ NO_MERGE */
              t1.c1, t2.c2
          FROM t1, t2
         WHERE t1.c1 = t2.c2)
    ,t3t4
    AS (SELECT /*+ NO_MERGE */
              t3.c3, t4.c4
          FROM t3, t4
         WHERE t3.c3 = t4.c4)
SELECT COUNT (*)
  FROM t1t2 j1, t3t4 j2
 WHERE j1.c1 + j1.c2 = j2.c3 + j2.c4;
```

```
--------------------------------------------------------
| Id  | Operation               | Name | Cost (%CPU)|
--------------------------------------------------------
|  0  | SELECT STATEMENT        |      |   11   (28)|
|  1  |  SORT AGGREGATE         |      |            |
|  2  |   HASH JOIN             |      |   11   (28)|
|  3  |    VIEW                 |      |    4    (0)|
|  4  |     HASH JOIN           |      |    4    (0)|
|  5  |      TABLE ACCESS FULL| T1  |      |    2    (0)|
|  6  |      TABLE ACCESS FULL| T2  |      |    2    (0)|
|  7  |    VIEW                 |      |    4    (0)|
|  8  |     HASH JOIN           |      |    4    (0)|
|  9  |      TABLE ACCESS FULL| T3  |      |    2    (0)|
| 10  |      TABLE ACCESS FULL| T4  |      |    2    (0)|
--------------------------------------------------------
```

The two NO_MERGE hints have suppressed the simple view merging transformation and now the selected execution plan has a cost of 11! This is interesting, isn't it? Most people assume that the only reason to apply optimizer hints is to get the CBO to select a plan that it considers suboptimal but they know is optimal. However, on this occasion the CBO believes the hinted plan is better than the one it chose. It didn't pick the hinted plan itself because the unconditional nature of the simple view merging transformation meant that the optimal plan wasn't even considered! How does the query perform in real life? All of this discussion about CBO costing is all very interesting but at the end of the day you are most interested in actual elapsed times, not cost estimates. In fact, on this occasion there is nothing much wrong with the costing algorithm. If you try running these statements, you are likely to find that the hinted query runs much faster than the unhinted one, but perhaps not 26 times faster as the cost estimates might suggest.

Final State Query Optimization

Let's turn our attention briefly to the basic job of the CBO. Final state optimization involves determining:

- The join order for the various rows sources
- The join mechanisms
- The access method for each of the tables in a query
- Whether to use *in-list iteration*

I'll discuss all of these items in some detail in Chapter 12.

Summary

This chapter briefly introduced some basic CBO concepts such as cost and described at a very high level the sort of decisions the CBO has to make and how it makes them. Part 3 of this book is entirely dedicated to the CBO, and I'll explain query transformation and final state optimization in far more detail there. For now, let's wrap up this introduction with three key messages:

- The CBO is trying to do a very complex job in a short amount of time.

- The CBO is just a (very) fancy guessing machine, and although its guesses are usually acceptable, often they aren't and significant performance problems can arise.

- When the CBO costs an execution plan wrongly, it should not be of concern. But if it picks a slow running plan when a significantly faster one is available, this is of concern.

Now that I have introduced the CBO, it is time to start looking at what it produces. Chapter 3 takes a first look at execution plans.

CHAPTER 3

Basic Execution Plan Concepts

Now that you know what the CBO is and what it does, you need to begin understanding how to interpret its output: the execution plan. You will often hear an execution plan referred to as an *explain plan* because the SQL explain plan statement is a key part of one the most important ways to view an execution plan. This chapter looks in detail at the explain plan statement and other ways of viewing execution plans.

But there is little point in displaying execution plans if you can't understand what is displayed, and I will explain the process of interpreting execution plans in this chapter. Unfortunately, some execution plans are extremely complex, so I will look at the more advanced topics of execution plan interpretation in Chapter 8 after covering a little more groundwork.

Returning to this chapter, let us get started with a look at the various views that hold information about execution plans.

Displaying Execution Plans

Execution plans are to be found in several places in an Oracle database, but the following three places are the most important for the purposes of this book.

- `SYS.PLAN_TABLE$`: This system-owned global temporary table is usually referred to via the public synonym `PLAN_TABLE` and contains the results of `EXPLAIN PLAN` statements.

- `V$SQL_PLAN`: This view shows the execution plans of statements that are currently running or have recently completed running. The data that the view displays is held in the *cursor cache* that is part of the shared pool.

- `DBA_HIST_SQL_PLAN`: This view shows a useful subset of execution plans that were executed in the past. The data that the view displays is held in the AWR and is collected from the shared pool by the MMON background process.

Although it is possible to look at the table and the two views directly, it is inconvenient to do so. This is particularly true for the `OTHER_XML` column that, as you might guess, contains unformatted XML. It is far easier to use functions from the `DBMS_XPLAN` package that present the execution plans in a more human readable format. In the following sections I will discuss how to interpret the default output of three of the package's functions; I will look at non-default output formats in Chapters 4 and 8.

Displaying the Results of EXPLAIN PLAN

The raison d'être for the `EXPLAIN PLAN` SQL statement is to generate an execution plan for a statement without actually executing the statement. The `EXPLAIN PLAN` statement only writes a representation of the execution plan to a table. It doesn't display anything itself. For that, you have to use the `DBMS_XPLAN.DISPLAY` function. This function takes several arguments, all of which are optional; I will use the defaults for now. The intention is to pass the results of the function to the TABLE operator. Listing 3-1 shows an example that performs an EXPLAIN PLAN for a query using tables from the SCOTT example schema and then displays the results using DBMS_XPLAN.DISPLAY.

Listing 3-1. Join of EMP and DEPT tables

```
SET LINES 200 PAGESIZE O FEEDBACK OFF

EXPLAIN PLAN
    FOR
        SELECT e.*
                ,d.dname
                ,d.loc
                , (SELECT COUNT (*)
                    FROM scott.emp i
                    WHERE i.deptno = e.deptno)
                    dept_count
            FROM scott.emp e, scott.dept d
        WHERE e.deptno = d.deptno;

SELECT * FROM TABLE (DBMS_XPLAN.display);


Plan hash value: 4153889731
```

```
-------------------------------------------------------------------
| Id | Operation          | Name | Rows | Bytes | Cost (%CPU)| Time     |
-------------------------------------------------------------------
|  0 | SELECT STATEMENT   |      |   14 | 1638  |    7  (15)| 00:00:01 |
|  1 |  SORT AGGREGATE    |      |    1 |   13  |           |          |
|* 2 |   TABLE ACCESS FULL| EMP  |    1 |   13  |    3   (0)| 00:00:01 |
|* 3 |  HASH JOIN         |      |   14 | 1638  |    7  (15)| 00:00:01 |
|  4 |   TABLE ACCESS FULL| DEPT |    4 |  120  |    3   (0)| 00:00:01 |
|  5 |   TABLE ACCESS FULL| EMP  |   14 | 1218  |    3   (0)| 00:00:01 |
-------------------------------------------------------------------
```

```
Predicate Information (identified by operation id):
---------------------------------------------------

   2 - filter("I"."DEPTNO"=:B1)
   3 - access("E"."DEPTNO"="D"."DEPTNO")

Note
-----
   - dynamic sampling used for this statement (level=2)
```

The statement being explained shows the details of each employee together with details of the department, including the estimated count of employees in the department obtained from a correlated subquery in the select list. The output of DBMS_XPLAN.DISPLAY begins with a plan hash value. If two plans have the same hash value they will be the same plan. In fact, the same execution plan will have the same hash value on different databases, provided that the operations, object names, and predicates are all identical.

After the plan hash value you can see the operation table, which provides details of how the runtime engine is expected to set about executing the SQL statement.

- The first column is the ID. This is just a number to uniquely identify the operations in the statement for use by other parts of the plan. You will notice that there is an asterisk in front of operations with IDs 2 and 3. This is because they are referred to later in the output. For the sake of brevity I will say "operation 2" rather than "The operation with ID 2" from now on.

- The second column is the operation. There are some 200 operation codes, very few of which are officially documented, and the list grows longer with each release. Fortunately, the vast majority of operations in the vast majority of execution plans come from a small subset of a couple of dozen that will become familiar to you as you read this book, if they aren't already.

- The third column in the operation table is called name. This rather non-descript column heading refers to the name of the database object that is being operated on, so to speak. This column isn't applicable to all operations and so is often blank, but in the case of a TABLE ACCESS FULL operation it is the name of the table being scanned.

- The next column is rows. This column provides the estimated number of rows that the operation is finally going to produce, a figure often referred to as a *cardinality estimate*. So, for example, you can see that operation 2 uses the TABLE ACCESS FULL operation on EMP and will read the same number of rows as ID 5 that performs the same operation on the same object. However, ID 5 returns all 14 rows in the table while operation 2 is expected to return one row. You will see the reason for this discrepancy shortly. Sometimes individual operations are executed more than once in the course of a single execution of a SQL statement. It is important to understand that the estimated row count usually applies to a single invocation of that operation and not the total number of rows returned by all invocations. In this case, operations 1 and 2 correspond to the subquery in the select list and are expected to return an average of about one row each time they are invoked.

- The bytes column shows an estimate of the number of bytes returned by one invocation of the operation. In other words, it is the average number of rows multiplied by the average size of a row.

- The cost column and the time column both display the estimated elapsed time for the statement. The cost column expresses this elapsed time in terms of single-block read units, and the time column expresses it in more familiar terms. When larger values are displayed it is possible to work out from these figures how long the CBO believes a single-block read will take by dividing time by cost. Here the small numbers and rounding make that difficult. You can also see that the cost column shows an estimate of the percentage of time that the operation will spend on the CPU as opposed to reading data from disk.

ROUNDING ISSUES

The numbers displayed in this table are always integers or seconds, but in fact the CBO keeps estimates in fractions. The rows column is rounded up and is almost always at least one, even if the CBO believes that the chances of a row being returned by the operation are slim to none. The cost column is rounded up to the nearest whole number, and the time column is rounded up the nearest second. So as a rule of thumb, always read a cardinality estimate of 1 as meaning "0 or 1."

There are other columns that you might see in the operation table. These include columns relating to temporary space utilization, partition elimination, parallel query operations, and so on. However, these are not shown here because they aren't relevant to this query.

Following the operation table you can see a section on predicates. In this query there are two predicates.

- The first one listed relates to operation 2. This is a *filter predicate*, which means that the predicate is applied to rows after the operation has generated them but before they are output. In this case the rows are rejected from the TABLE ACCESS FULL operation unless the column DEPTNO matches a particular value. But what value? The value :B1 looks for all the world to be a bind variable, but there aren't any bind variables in this query! In fact, if you try and match up the operation to the original SQL text you will see that the table with an alias of I is, in fact, from a correlated subquery and the "variable" is actually just the corresponding DEPTNO appropriate to that invocation of the correlated subquery; in other words, it is the value from the table with alias E.

- The second predicate listed is an *access predicate*. This means that it is actually used as part of the execution of the operation, not just applied at the end like a filter predicate. In this case the HASH JOIN of operation 3 uses the predicate to actually perform the join.

The final section listed is a human readable note. This lists information that might be useful and that doesn't have a place elsewhere in the plan. In this case, there are no statistics for the tables in the data dictionary, and so dynamic sampling was used to generate some statistics on the fly.

EXPLAIN PLAN May Be Misleading

When you use EXPLAIN PLAN you might expect that when you actually run the statement the execution plan that the runtime engine uses will match that from the immediately preceding EXPLAIN PLAN call. This is a dangerous assumption! Let me provide one scenario where this may not be the case.

- You run a statement. The CBO generates a plan based on the statistics available at the time and saves it in the cursor cache for the runtime engine to use.

- You gather (or set) statistics without specifying NO_INVALIDATE=FALSE. As a consequence, the execution plan saved in the cursor cache is not invalidated.

- You issue EXPLAIN PLAN. The CBO generates a plan based on the new statistics.

- You run your statement. The CBO doesn't generate a new plan, as there is a valid execution plan already in the cursor cache. The runtime engine uses the saved plan based on the older statistics.

This isn't the only scenario where EXPLAIN PLAN may be misleading. I will look at a feature known as *bind variable peeking* in Chapter 8. It is also worth bearing in mind that, for some reason, possibly security related, the SQL*Plus AUTOTRACE feature uses EXPLAIN PLAN rather than attempting to retrieve the actual execution plan from the cursor cache. So AUTOTRACE can be misleading as well.

Let us move away from EXPLAIN PLAN now and look at other ways to display execution plans.

Displaying Output from the Cursor Cache

Since the call to EXPLAIN PLAN is potentially misleading, it is very fortunate indeed that actual execution plans from the cursor cache can usually be retrieved either while a statement is running or shortly thereafter. The code in Listing 3-2 actually runs a SQL statement and then retrieves the plan from the cursor cache. By default, DBMS_XPLAN.DISPLAY_CURSOR retrieves the plan from the most recently executed SQL statement of the calling session.

Listing 3-2. Looking at execution plans in the cursor cache

```
SELECT 'Count of sales: ' || COUNT (*) cnt
  FROM sh.sales s JOIN sh.customers c USING (cust_id)
 WHERE cust_last_name = 'Ruddy';
SELECT * FROM TABLE (DBMS_XPLAN.display_cursor);


Count of sales: 1385
```

SELECT * FROM TABLE (DBMS_XPLAN.display_cursor);

```
SQL_ID  d4sba28503nxy, child number 0
-------------------------------------
SELECT 'Count of sales: ' || COUNT (*) cnt   FROM sh.sales s JOIN
sh.customers c USING (cust_id)  WHERE cust_last_name = 'Ruddy'

Plan hash value: 1818178872
```

```
---------------------------------------------------------------------------------
| Id  | Operation              | Name      |X| Cost (%CPU)| Time     | Pstart| Pstop |
---------------------------------------------------------------------------------
|   0 | SELECT STATEMENT       |           |X|  832 (100)|          |       |       |
|   1 |  SORT AGGREGATE        |           |X|           |          |       |       |
|*  2 |   HASH JOIN            |           |X|  832    (1)| 00:00:08 |       |       |
|*  3 |    TABLE ACCESS FULL   | CUSTOMERS |X|  423    (1)| 00:00:04 |       |       |
|   4 |    PARTITION RANGE ALL |           |X|  407    (0)| 00:00:05 |    1  |    28 |
|   5 |     TABLE ACCESS FULL  | SALES     |X|  407    (0)| 00:00:05 |    1  |    28 |
---------------------------------------------------------------------------------
```

```
Predicate Information (identified by operation id):
---------------------------------------------------

   2 - access("S"."CUST_ID"="C"."CUST_ID")
   3 - filter("CUST_LAST_NAME"='Ruddy')

Note
-----
   - this is an adaptive plan
```

You will note that the output from this call looks a little different. The column in the operation table labeled "X" doesn't appear in reality. I have suppressed the rows and bytes columns so that the output fits on the page.

USE OF THE SH EXAMPLE SCHEMA AND THE CURSOR CACHE

- You will need SELECT privileges on V$SESSION, V$SQL, and V$SQL_PLAN to use the DBMS_XPLAN.DISPLAY_CURSOR function. Generally, I would recommend that any user doing diagnostic work is granted the SELECT_CATALOG_ROLE.

- Be aware that the SQL*Plus command SET SERVEROUTPUT ON interferes with DBMS_XPLAN.DISPLAY_CURSOR when called with no arguments.

- Use of the SH schema requires Oracle Enterprise Edition with the partitioning option.

- Although not required I will be using ANSI join syntax when accessing the SH schema (and for most examples from now on). In this case ANSI syntax is more concise than traditional syntax because the CUST_ID join column is named identically in both the SH.SALES and SH.CUSTOMERS tables.

The output begins with a line that identifies the SQL_ID of the statement. This is a useful piece of information unfortunately not provided by DBMS_XPLAN.DISPLAY. The child number indicates the specific child cursor that is being displayed.

THE TERM "CURSOR"

The word "cursor" is one of a few terms that Oracle uses in too many different contexts. My use of the term here has nothing to do with the PL/SQL data type or any related client-side concepts. When discussing the CBO and the runtime engine, the term "parent cursor" refers to information about the text of a SQL statement. The term "child cursor" refers to saved execution plan and security contexts. Child cursors are numbered and start at zero when a SQL statement is first parsed.

The next section displayed is a snippet of the SQL statement with whitespace compressed. For longer statements, the snippet is a truncated version of the code. After that there is the plan hash value and the operation table as with DBMS_XPLAN.DISPLAY.

You can see that in this case the operation table has two extra columns: pstart and pstop. These columns were not present in Listing 3-1 because no partitioned tables were involved. In Listing 3-2 the range of partitions accessed is listed for the SH.SALES table. In this case all 28 partitions are accessed because there is no predicate involving the partitioning column.

The predicate section should look familiar, as it's very similar to that in Listing 3-1.

The note section indicates that the plan is *adaptive*. I will discuss adaptive plans, a new feature of Oracle 12cR1, in Chapter 6.

Displaying Execution Plans from the AWR

The limitation of using the cursor cache as a source of execution plan information lies in the term "cache." This word suggests that the plan may disappear, and so it will if space in the shared pools starts to run short. Fortunately, the MMON process saves most long-running plans in the AWR. Listing 3-3 shows how you can retrieve an execution plan that may have long gone from the cursor cache.

Listing 3-3. Execution plan of an MMON statement

```
SELECT * FROM TABLE (DBMS_XPLAN.display_awr ('6xvp6nxs4a9n4'));

SQL_ID 6xvp6nxs4a9n4
--------------------
select nvl(sum(space),0) from recyclebin$ where ts# = :1

Plan hash value: 1168251937

-----------------------------------------------------------------------------------------
| Id  | Operation                    | Name           | Rows  | Bytes | Cost (%CPU)| Time     |
-----------------------------------------------------------------------------------------
|   0 | SELECT STATEMENT             |                |       |       |     1 (100)|          |
|   1 |  SORT AGGREGATE              |                |     1 |    26 |            |          |
|   2 |   TABLE ACCESS BY INDEX ROWID| RECYCLEBIN$    |     1 |    26 |     1   (0)| 00:00:01 |
|   3 |    INDEX RANGE SCAN          | RECYCLEBIN$_TS |     1 |       |     1   (0)| 00:00:01 |
-----------------------------------------------------------------------------------------
```

What I have done here is retrieve a SQL statement that is used by the MMON process itself to monitor space. It is executed on all 11gR2 and 12cR1 databases, and since the SQL_ID of a statement is invariant across databases the above query should work for you if you have an 11gR2 or 12cR1 database.

You can see that although there is clearly a predicate in the statement, there is no predicate section in this output. If you check the definition of the view DBA_HIST_SQL_PLAN you will see columns ACCESS_PREDICATES and FILTER_PREDICATES, but as of 12cR1 these are always NULL. This is a nuisance that I have heard multiple people complain about, but there are apparently insurmountable technical issues preventing the population of these columns.

Understanding Operations

Operations are parts of an execution plan that the CBO generates for the runtime engine to execute. To investigate performance issues you need to understand what they do, how they interact, and how long they take. Let me address these issues one by one.

What an Operation Does

Unfortunately, Oracle doesn't document all the operations in an execution plan (although from 12cR1 the SQL Tuning Guide introduces quite a few), and we are left to our own devices to work out what they actually do. I will cover the most important operations involving table access and joins in Part 3, but even if I could claim that I knew and understood them all (which I can't), I wouldn't have the space here to document them. Quite often you can work out what an operation does by referring back to your original statement, but be careful with this. For example, what do you think the SORT AGGREGATE operation in Listing 3-1 does? There is an aggregate function, COUNT, in the statement, and it would be a correct assumption that the SORT AGGREGATE function counts rows on input and produces that count on output. However, you may be put off by the word SORT. Where does sorting come into the picture? The answer is that it doesn't! I have done a fair amount of testing, and I have come to the conclusion that a SORT AGGREGATE operation never sorts; just run a query like the one in Listing 3-3 a few times from SQL*Plus with AUTOTRACE and you will see that after the initial parse there is no sort!

How Operations Interact

In common with many people, the first question I asked when I was shown my first execution plan was "Where do I start?" A second question was implied: "Where would the runtime engine start?" Many people answer these questions by saying, "the topmost operation amongst the furthest indented," or something like that. In Oracle 8i this was an oversimplification. After release 9i came out with the hash-join-input-swapping feature that I have already mentioned en passant, that sort of explanation became positively misleading. A correct, if somewhat glib, answer is that you start with the operation that has an ID of 0, i.e., you start at the top! To help explain where to go from there, you actually do need to understand all this indenting stuff. The operations are organized into a tree structure, and operation 0 is the root of the tree. The indentation indicates the parent-child relationships in an intuitive way. Figure 3-1 shows how you might draw the execution plan shown in Listing 3-1 to emphasize the parent-child relationships.

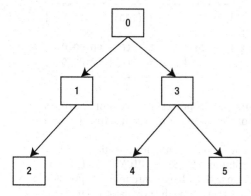

Figure 3-1. *Parent-child relationships in an execution plan*

Operation 0 makes one or more coroutine calls to operations 1 and 3 to generate rows, operation 1 makes coroutine calls to operation 2, and operation 3 makes coroutine calls to operations 4 and 5. The idea is that a child operation collects a small number of rows and then passes them back to its parent. If the child operation isn't complete it waits to be called again to continue.

THE CONCEPT OF COROUTINES

You may be comfortable with the concept of subroutine calls but be less comfortable with the concept of coroutines. If this is the case then it may help to do some background reading on coroutines, as this may help you understand execution plans better.

Let me go through the specific operations in Listing 3-1 the way the runtime engine would.

Operation 0: SELECT STATEMENT

The runtime engine begins with the SELECT STATEMENT itself. This particular operation always has at least one child and calls the *last* child first. That is, it calls the child with the highest ID—in this case operation 3. It waits for the HASH JOIN to return rows, and, for each row returned, it calls operation 1 to evaluate the correlated subquery in the select list. Operation 1 adds the extra column, and the now complete row is output. If the HASH JOIN isn't finished it is called again to retrieve more rows.

Operation 1: SORT AGGREGATE

Operations 1 and 2 relate to the correlated subquery in the select list. I have highlighted the correlated subquery and the associated operations in Listing 3-1. Operation 1 is called multiple times during the course of the SQL statement execution and on each occasion is passed as input the DEPTNO from the main query. It calls its child, operation 2, passing the DEPTNO parameter, to perform a TABLE ACCESS FULL and pass rows back. All SORT AGGREGATE does is to count these rows and discard them. When the count has been returned it passes its single-row, single-column output to its parent: operation 0. You can see that the estimated cardinality for this operation is 1, which confirms the understanding of this operation's function.

Operation 2: TABLE ACCESS FULL

Because operation 1 is called multiple times during the course of the SQL statement and operation 1 always calls operation 2 once, operation 2 is called multiple times throughout the course of the statement as well. It performs a TABLE ACCESS FULL on each occasion. As rows are returned from the operation, but before being returned to operation 1, the filter predicate is applied; the DEPTNO from the row is matched with the DEPTNO input parameter, and the row is discarded if it does not match.

Operation 3: HASH JOIN

This operation performs a join of the EMP and DEPT columns. The operation starts off by calling its *first* child, operation 4, and as rows are returned they are placed into an in-memory hash cluster. Once all rows from DEPT have been returned and operation 4 is complete, operation 5 begins. As rows from operation 5 are returned they are matched with rows returned from operation 4, and, assuming one or more rows match, they are returned to operation 0 for further processing. In the case of a HASH JOIN (or any join for that matter) there are always exactly two child operations, and they are each invoked once per invocation of the join.

Operations 4 and 5: TABLE FULL SCANs

These operations perform full table scans on the EMP and DEPT tables and just pass their results back to their parent, operation 3. There are no predicates on these operations and, in this case, no child operations.

How Operations Interact Wrap Up

You can see that in reality there are multiple operations in progress at any one time. As rows are returned from operation 5 they are joined by operation 3 and passed back to operation 0 that then invokes operation 1, and indirectly operation 2 as well. The "topmost innermost" operation is operation 2, which was the last to start and almost the last to finish, so that blows that theory.

How Long Do Operations Take?

I have to balance being emphatic with nagging, but let me remind you again that at this stage I am just talking about how long the CBO *thinks* that operations will take to run, not how long they actually take to run in practice. Even the figures presented from DBMS_XPLAN.DISPLAY_CURSOR and DBMS_XPLAN.DISPLAY_AWR are still the initial estimates (in the default display) rather than the actual elapsed times. Much of the job of analyzing SQL statement performance lies in identifying the difference between the initial estimates and the reality in practice. I'll come onto identifying the actual cardinalities and runtimes in Chapter 4.

I have already stated that the cardinality estimate (the column with heading "rows") is based upon a single invocation. The cost and time columns are also based on single invocations. If you look at Listing 3-1 again you will see that the cost for operation 2 and operation 5 are the same despite the fact that operation 2 is invoked multiple times and operation 5 just once. I am not sure why the figures are presented in this way, but there it is.

INLIST ITERATOR AND PARTITION RANGE OPERATIONS

One of the reasons it is so difficult to explain how to read an execution plan is that there are so many exceptions. In the case of the INLIST ITERATOR and the PARTITION RANGE operators, the rows, bytes, cost, and time columns reported by the child operation (in fact all descendants) reflect the accumulated cost of all invocations rather than those of individual calls.

The cost/time for a parent operation includes the cost of its child operations. So in Listing 3-1 you can see that the cost of operation 3 is 7, while the cost of its two child operations, 4 and 5, are 3 each. This means that the HASH JOIN itself is expected to have an overhead of 1 (all CPU it seems…that makes sense).

But hold on. The SELECT STATEMENT itself has a cost of 7. Where has the cost of the subqueries disappeared to? These have a cost of 3 each, and the runtime engine does several of them. This is simply a bug. If you want to see another bug take a look at the CPU percentages reported for the costs of operation 0 in Listings 3-2 and 3-3. These are 100%, and for operation 0 they are always 100% in the case of DBMS_XPLAN.DISPLAY_CURSOR and DBMS_XPLAN.DISPLAY_AWR. These sorts of anomalies abound, and I only point these issues out because when you first try to understand execution plans you are likely to assume that these anomalies reflect a fundamental lack of understanding on your part. Not in these cases.

Summary

In this chapter I have introduced, with examples, the techniques for displaying and interpreting some simple SQL statements with basic formatting. Even with these simple examples there is a lot still left unexplained, but some of these questions will be answered when I have covered a few more concepts.

The good news is that much of the anomalous behavior that we see when looking at the CBO's initial estimates disappears when we look at actual statistics produced by the runtime engine. So let us get on with that in Chapter 4.

■ ■ ■

The Runtime Engine

Chapter 3 focused on the plans that the CBO made. It is now time to look at how those plans work out in practice. I will explain the traditional ways of gathering and analyzing runtime data as well as a newer complementary approach called the SQL performance monitor. To fully understand SQL performance, it is very important to understand the role of workareas and the shortcuts the runtime engine uses to minimize overhead, and both of these topics are covered in this chapter.

Collecting Operation Level Runtime Data

As you'll learn in Chapter 5, we almost always need to get a breakdown of the behavior of an SQL statement at the operation level to determine how best to optimize that SQL statement. Some of the operation-level statistics that can be gathered are:

- How many times the operation ran in the course of the statement

- How long it took

- How many disk operations it performed

- How many logical reads it made

- Whether or not the operation executed entirely in memory

These statistics are not gathered by default. There are three ways to trigger the collection:

- *Add the GATHER_PLAN_STATISTICS optimizer hint to your SQL statement*: The collection will be done for that one statement only.

- *Change the initialization parameter STATISTICS_LEVEL to ALL*: If set at the session level, all SQL statements for the session will be affected. If STATISTICS_LEVEL is set to ALL at the system level, collection will be enabled for all SQL statements in all sessions in the instance.

- *Enable SQL tracing*: As with the STATISTICS_LEVEL parameter, SQL tracing can be enabled either at the session or system level.

Let's look at each of these options in turn.

The GATHER_PLAN_STATISTICS Hint

This optimizer hint has been around for a long time but is documented for the first time in Oracle Database 12cR1. Listing 4-1 updates Listing 3-2 by adding the GATHER_PLAN_STATISTICS hint.

Listing 4-1. Gathering operation data at the statement level

```
SELECT /*+ gather_plan_statistics */
       'Count of sales: ' || COUNT (*) cnt
  FROM sh.sales s JOIN sh.customers c USING (cust_id)
 WHERE cust_last_name = 'Ruddy';
```

Notice that, as with all optimizer hints, you can use uppercase or lowercase.

Setting STATISTICS_LEVEL=ALL

If you can't, or would prefer not to, change the code you are analyzing, you can set the STATISTICS_LEVEL parameter using one of the two statements in Listing 4-2.

Listing 4-2. Enabling runtime data collection at the session or system level

```
ALTER SESSION SET STATISTICS_LEVEL=ALL;
ALTER SYSTEM  SET STATISTICS_LEVEL=ALL;
```

Any Oracle performance specialist would be remiss not to advise you of the potential for serious performance problems when you set STATISTICS_LEVEL to ALL at the system level. The main concern is that the performance of your application could seriously degrade as a result of the additional overhead. However, many experts would go further and suggest that you should only set STATISTICS_LEVEL to ALL at the system level for short periods of troubleshooting, and that it is never appropriate to leave it set to ALL at the system level permanently. I wouldn't go that far.

The main contributor to the overhead of gathering runtime statistics is the numerous calls to the Unix operating system routine GETTIMEOFDAY or its equivalent on other platforms. Although this operating system call can be very inefficient on some operating systems, on others it can be very efficient. In addition, the sampling frequency (controlled by the hidden parameter _rowsource_statistics_sampfreq) has been reduced in later releases of Oracle Database. I have recently set STATISTICS_LEVEL to ALL at the system level on a heavily loaded Solaris/SPARC-64 production system and found no measurable impact on the elapsed time of a two-hour batch run.

Even if you leave STATISTICS_LEVEL permanently set to ALL at a systemwide level, the runtime engine statistics are not saved in the AWR. To work around this, I run my own scheduled job to capture these data. The code for doing all of this is quite lengthy, so I haven't included it here, but it is available in the downloaded materials.

The reason you might want to consider permanently setting STATISTICS_LEVEL to ALL at the system level is to deal with unexpected production performance problems after the event; if an SQL statement runs fine sometimes but not always, it may be that you can't reproduce the problem at will and having the data available from the actual incident can be invaluable.

As a final note of caution, you should be aware that between versions 10.1.0.2 and 11.1.0.7 you may run into bug 8289729, which results in a dramatic increase in the size of the SYSAUX tablespace. Have a look at the Oracle support note 874518.1 or this blog from Martin Widlake (http://mwidlake.wordpress.com/2011/06/02/why-is-my-sysaux-tablespace-so-big-statistics_levelall/), but don't be too disheartened as this extra data collection didn't harm performance in my case.

Enabling SQL Tracing

There are several ways to enable SQL tracing. The oldest and therefore most well-known way to enable SQL tracing is to set the 10046 event. So you will often hear people refer to SQL trace as the "10046 trace." However, the preferred way to enable SQL trace these days is to use the routine DBMS_MONITOR.SESSION_TRACE_ENABLE, and examples of how to call it are provided in the PL/SQL packages and types reference manual. Additional information can be found in the performance tuning guide (pre-12cr1) or the SQL tuning guide (12cR1 onward).

Apart from enabling statistics gathering from the runtime engine, SQL trace generates a text file with a lot of additional information about what is happening in the session. Among other things, this trace file can help you see:

- What SQL statements have run and how often they run.

- What recursive SQL statements (SQL statements in triggers or functions) have run.

- How much time was spent opening the cursor (executing the SQL statement), how much time was spent fetching the data from the cursor, and how much time was spent in so-called idle wait events, implying that the session is executing application logic outside of the database.

- Detailed information about individual wait events, such as the precise number of blocks read by individual database file multiblock read waits.

Although for many performance specialists the SQL trace is the primary diagnostic tool, I almost never use it for tuning individual SQL statements! For the vast majority of SQL tuning tasks, the runtime engine statistics are more than sufficient for the task, and as you'll see shortly, data dictionary views are available that present those data in a very convenient way.

Displaying Operational Level Data

Once you have gathered your runtime engine statistics by one of the ways described above, the next task is to display them. Let's look at the two ways to do this:

- With DBMS_XPLAN.DISPLAY_CURSOR

- With V$SQL_PLAN_STATISTICS_ALL

Displaying Runtime Engine Statistics with DBMS_XPLAN.DISPLAY_CURSOR

Using the nondefault parameters to DBMS_XPLAN.DISPLAY_CURSOR, you can see runtime engine statistics in the operation table. Listing 4-3 shows how to do this immediately after running the statement in Listing 4-1.

Listing 4-3. Displaying runtime engine statistics

```
SELECT * FROM TABLE (DBMS_XPLAN.display_cursor (format => 'ALLSTATS LAST'));
```

```
---------------------------------------------------------------------------------
| Id  | Operation                    | Name         | Starts | E-Rows | A-Rows |
---------------------------------------------------------------------------------
|   0 | SELECT STATEMENT             |              |      1 |        |      1 |
|   1 |  SORT AGGREGATE              |              |      1 |      1 |      1 |
|*  2 |   HASH JOIN                  |              |      1 |   7956 |   1385 |
|*  3 |    TABLE ACCESS FULL         | CUSTOMERS    |      1 |     61 |     80 |
|   4 |    PARTITION RANGE ALL       |              |      1 |   918K |   918K |
|   5 |     BITMAP CONVERSION TO ROWIDS |           |     28 |   918K |   918K |
|   6 |      BITMAP INDEX FAST FULL SCAN| SALES_CUST_BIX |  28 |        |  35808 |
---------------------------------------------------------------------------------
```

Listing 4-3 has been edited somewhat to remove various headings and some of the columns from the operation table. Once again, this is just so the output is readable on the page.

The DBMS_XPLAN.DISPLAY_CURSOR has a FORMAT parameter, and the way to get all the runtime execution statistics from the last execution of the statement is to specify the value of 'ALLSTATS LAST'; you can check the documentation for more variants. The resulting output is quite illuminating:

- First, look at the Starts column. This tells you that operations 0 through 4 ran once, but that operation 5 ran 28 times. This is because there are 28 partitions in the SALES table and it needs to run the TABLE ACCESS FULL operation for each one.

- The E-Rows and A-Rows columns are the estimated and actual row counts, respectively, and you can see that the biggest discrepancy lies with operation 2 where the estimate is over five times greater than reality.

- The actual elapsed time in column A-Time is reported with a greater degree of accuracy than the estimate displayed by DBMS_XPLAN.DISPLAY.

It is important to realize that all runtime engine statistics reflect the accumulated results of all executions of the operation. So operation 5 returned 918K rows after scanning all 28 partitions and the 0.46-second elapsed time also reflects the accumulated time to scan the entire SALES table.

ALL EXECUTIONS OF A STATEMENT VS. ALL EXECUTIONS OF AN OPERATION

I mentioned that the ALLSTATS LAST format displayed statistics for the LAST run of the SQL statement. However, I also stated that the A-Time column reflects the accumulated time from all executions of operation 5. Both statements are true because the 28 executions of operation 5 were all performed as part of the LAST execution of the SQL statement. If I had specified the ALLSTATS ALL format, then the value of Starts for operation 5 would have been a multiple of 28 if the statement had been run multiple times.

The A-Time column reflects the time taken to execute the operation and all its descendants. For example, look at the HASH join at operation 2 and its two children:

- The first child of operation 2 is the full table scan of the CUSTOMERS table at operation 3. Operation 2 is reported to have taken 0.2 second.

- The PARTITION RANGE ALL operation with ID 4 is the second child of operation 2 and apparently took 0.66 second.

- If we add 0.2 and 0.66, it totals to 0.86 second for the children of operation 2.

- Subtracting the value of 0.86 from the reported value of 1.22 in operation 2, you can see that the HASH JOIN itself took 0.36 second.

Displaying Runtime Engine Statistics with V$SQL_PLAN_STATISTICS_ALL

Although I find the output of DBMS_XPLAN functions superb when it comes to analyzing an execution plan and working out what it does, I find the format of the DBMS_XPLAN output very difficult to work with when doing detailed analysis of runtime statistics. The main problem is that there are a large number of columns, and even assuming you have an electronic page capable of displaying them all, it is difficult for the eye to navigate left and right.

The view V$SQL_PLAN_STATISTICS_ALL returns all the runtime engine statistics shown by DBMS_XPLAN. DISPLAY_CURSOR, and when I am doing any kind of detailed analysis of runtime engine data, I almost always use a tool to display the output of that view in a grid. Even if you do not have a graphical tool, such as SQL Developer, you can always get the data from the view in Comma Separated Variable (CSV) format and pop it into a spreadsheet; that works just as well.

The reason that displaying the statistics in a grid is useful is that you can order the columns as you wish and you can temporarily hide the columns you aren't currently focused on. There are a few extra tricks you can use that can make reading these data even easier:

- V$SQL_PLAN_STATISTICS_ALL contains all of the statistics for both the last execution of a statement and all executions of the statement. The columns containing information from the last execution are prefixed with "LAST_". Because these are probably all you need, most of the time you do not want to select the columns STARTS, OUTPUT_ROWS, CR_BUFFER_GETS, CU_BUFFER_GETS, DISK_READS, DISK_WRITES, and ELAPSED_TIME because these columns reflect all executions of the statement and will cause confusion.

- You can indent the OPERATION column using the DEPTH column.

- You can label potentially ambiguous columns to avoid confusion.

- Dividing LAST_ELAPSED_TIME by 1000000 changes microseconds to seconds, more readable for most of us.

Listing 4-4 shows a simple query against V$SQL_PLAN_STATISTICS_ALL that illustrates these points.

Listing 4-4. Selecting a subset of columns from V$SQL_PLAN_STATISTICS_ALL

```
   SELECT DEPTH
         ,LPAD (' ', DEPTH) || operation operation
         ,options
         ,object_name
         ,time "EST TIME (Secs)"
         ,last_elapsed_time / 1000000 "ACTUAL TIME (Secs)"
         ,CARDINALITY "EST ROWS"
         ,last_output_rows "Actual Rows"
     FROM v$sql_plan_statistics_all
    WHERE sql_id = '4d133k9p6xbny' AND child_number = 0
ORDER BY id;
```

This query just selects a few columns, but in practice you would select a lot more. The SQL_ID and child number for the statement you are interested in can be obtained using the techniques described in Chapter 1.

Displaying Session Level Statistics with Snapper

Although the most important statistics for analysis of runtime performance are those in V$SQL_PLAN_STATISTICS_ALL, there are a plethora of statistics that are gathered constantly by default. For some unfathomable reason, Oracle has left their customers with only a bunch of impenetrable views to see these statistics, and most of us are left too disheartened to try using them. Fortunately "most" does not equal "all," and there a number of people who have found ways to make this information easier to digest. One of the earliest examples of a script to display session statistics in a readable way came from Tom Kyte and can be found at http://asktom.oracle.com/runstats.html. In my opinion, the best tool for looking at this information comes from Oracle scientist Tanel Poder, who has published a general purpose script to extract and display numerous runtime statistics in an easily readable format. The latest version of his invaluable Snapper script is available at http://blog.tanelpoder.com/ and I encourage you to download this free and simple-to-use tool.

Snapper is particularly useful when a session is "stuck" on the CPU. On each occasion that I have used Snapper in these circumstances, I been able to see immediately what the problem was. Listing 4-5 shows a real-life extract from a Snapper run on a long-running query that was constantly on the CPU.

Listing 4-5. Contention issue highlighted by snapper

```
---------------------------------------------------------------------------
TYPE, STATISTIC                                    ,    HDELTA,
---------------------------------------------------------------------------
STAT, session logical reads                        ,     1.06M,
STAT, concurrency wait time                        ,         1,
STAT, consistent gets                              ,     1.06M,
STAT, consistent gets from cache                   ,     1.06M,
STAT, consistent gets - examination                ,     1.06M,
STAT, consistent changes                           ,     1.06M,
STAT, free buffer requested                        ,        17,
STAT, hot buffers moved to head of LRU             ,        27,
STAT, free buffer inspected                        ,        56,
STAT, CR blocks created                            ,        17,
STAT, calls to kcmgas                              ,        17,
STAT, data blocks consistent reads - undo records applied  ,     1.06M,
STAT, rollbacks only - consistent read gets        ,        17,
TIME, DB CPU                                        ,     5.82s,
TIME, sql execute elapsed time                     ,     5.71s,
TIME, DB time                                      ,     5.82s,
WAIT, latch: cache buffers chains                  ,   11.36ms,
--  End of Stats snap 1, end=2013-01-31 02:29:11, seconds=10
```

What stood out to me when I first saw the output in Listing 4-5 was that in the 10-second snapshot it applied 1.06 million undo records! The query was in conflict with a bunch of insertion sessions that had started shortly after the query did, and the query was busy making consistent read copies by backing out the insertions. I was immediately able to see that killing and restarting the query would allow it to finish quickly. I was asked if it was necessary to gather statistics before restarting. I am able to confidently state that that wasn't necessary. All the guesswork had been eliminated!

The SQL Performance Monitor

The statistics in V$SQL_PLAN_STATISICS_ALL have three major drawbacks:

- They are only available if you have set STATISTICS_LEVEL to ALL, which, as discussed previously, will not be problematic on some hardware platforms but may be problematic on others.

- They are only available after the statement finishes.

- The LAST statistics are missing or incorrect when parallel query operations are used.

These drawbacks make diagnosis of some problems difficult. Fortunately, SQL performance monitor was introduced in Oracle Database 11gR1 and that helps get around all of these deficiencies.

SQL performance monitor reports can be accessed either via Enterprise Manager or via a call to DBMS_SQLTUNE.REPORT_SQL_MONITOR from SQL*Plus. I'll focus on the latter mechanism here. Listing 4-6 shows two small scripts that can be used to generate an HTML report. Personally I am not a great fan of multicolored charts when it comes to detailed analysis. Give me text output and a spreadsheet any day. However, in this case even I always generate the HTML output. Let me show you why.

You should take the first two snippets of code in Listing 4-6 and place them into two separate scripts on your PC. The third snippet shows how the scripts are called. When you call the scripts, an HTML file is produced in C:\Temp, a location that is obviously changeable if you wish.

Listing 4-6. Scripts to generate an HTML report with SQL performance monitor

```
-- Place this code in GET_MONITOR_SID.SQL

SET ECHO OFF TERMOUT OFF LINES 32767 PAGES 0 TRIMSPOOL ON VERIFY OFF LONG 1000000 LONGC 1000000
SPOOL c:\temp\monitor.html REPLACE

SELECT DBMS_SQLTUNE.report_sql_monitor (session_id => &sid, TYPE => 'ACTIVE')
  FROM DUAL;

SPOOL OFF
SET TERMOUT ON

-- Place this code in GET_MONITOR_SQLID.SQL

SET ECHO OFF TERMOUT OFF LINES 32767 PAGES 0 TRIMSPOOL ON VERIFY OFF LONG 1000000 LONGC 1000000
SPOOL c:\temp\monitor.html REPLACE

SELECT DBMS_SQLTUNE.report_sql_monitor (sql_id   => '&sql_id'
                                       ,TYPE     => 'ACTIVE')
  FROM DUAL;

SPOOL OFF
SET TERMOUT ON PAGES 900 LINES 200

-- Example call to GET_MONITOR_SID.SQL from SQL*Plus

DEFINE SID=123
@GET_MONITOR_SID
```

Note the SQL*Plus formatting lines before the SPOOL statement. These are important to ensure the output is usable.

The next step is to place a bookmark in your browser to point to file:///c:/temp/monitor.html. You can just click this bookmark and your latest monitor report will appear!

The output contains almost all of the information that is available in V$SQL_PLAN_STATISTICS_ALL and much more besides. Figure 4-1 shows part of an SQL performance monitor report.

Operation	Name	Estimate...	Cost	Timeline(47s)	Exec...	Actual ...	Memory
⊟ SELECT STATEMENT					1	0	
⊟ SORT AGGREGATE		1			1	0	
⊟ HASH JOIN		120M	2,948		1	132M	61MB
⊟ PARTITION RANGE ALL		919K	343		1	919K	
└ TABLE ACCESS FULL	SALES	919K	343		28	919K	
⊟ PARTITION RANGE ALL		919K	343		1	708K	
└ TABLE ACCESS FULL	SALES	919K	343		17	708K	

Plan Hash Value 3515001197

Figure 4-1. *Fragment of an SQL performance monitor report*

The screenshot in Figure 4-1 is from an actively running query. You see the arrows on the left? These show the operations that are currently in progress. Data are being read from the SALES table and as the rows are produced they are being matched by the HASH JOIN and then aggregated by the SORT AGGREGATE operation. Remember, the SORT AGGREGATE doesn't sort!

The 47-second timeline in the fifth column shows that the first of the full table scans was fast but the second is running slower. You have to be careful here. The timeline figures shown by this report show when the operations first become active as well as the point when (or if) they ceased to be active; the time spent processing rows by both parent and child operations is included. Contrast this with V$SQL_PLAN_STATISTICS_ALL where the reported times include child operations but not parent ones. There is a lot of information in the SQL performance report, so play around with it.

Unfortunately, SQL performance monitor isn't a complete replacement for V$SQL_PLAN_STATISTICS_ALL. For example, it is impossible to tell from Figure 4-1 which of the four operations currently running is taking up the time. This will only be visible once the query finishes in V$SQL_PLAN_STATISTICS_ALL. Here are a few final notes on SQL performance monitor:

- Statements are normally only monitored after they have run for more than five seconds. You can override this rule by the MONITOR and NO_MONITOR hints.

- Data from monitored SQL statements are kept in a circular buffer, so it might age out quite quickly on a busy system.

Workareas

Lots of operations in an SQL statement need some memory to function, and these allocations of memory are called workareas.

Operations Needing a Workarea

Here are some of the operations that require a workarea:

- All types of joins, with the exception of nested loops that require no workarea.

- Sorts are required, amongst other things, to implement ORDER BY clauses and by some aggregate and analytic functions.

- Although some aggregate and analytic functions require sorts, some do not. The SORT AGGREGATE operation that has come up several times in this book so far still requires a workarea, even though no sorting is involved!

- The MODEL clause requires a workarea for the cells being manipulated. This will be discussed with the MODEL clause later in this book.

Allocating Memory to a Workarea

It is the runtime engine's job to determine how much memory to allocate to each workarea and to allocate disk space from a temporary tablespace when that allocation is insufficient. When costing operations, the CBO will hazard a guess as to how much memory the runtime engine will allocate, but the execution plan does not include any directive as to how much to allocate.

One common misconception is that memory for workareas is allocated in one big chunk. That is not the case. Workarea memory is allocated a bit at a time as it is needed, but there may come a point when the runtime engine has to declare that enough is enough and that the operation has to complete using space in a temporary tablespace.

The calculation of how much memory can be allocated to a workarea depends on whether the initialization parameter WORKAREA_SIZE_POLICY is set to MANUAL or AUTO.

Calculating Memory Allocation When WORKAREA_SIZE_POLICY Is Set to AUTO

We almost always explicitly set the initialization parameter PGA_AGGREGATE_TARGET to a nonzero value these days so automatic workarea sizing takes place. In this case, the runtime engine will try to keep the total amount of memory under the PGA_AGGREGATE_TARGET, but there are no guarantees. PGA_AGGREGATE_TARGET is used to derive values for the following hidden initialization parameters:

- _smm_max_size: The maximum size of a workarea in a statement executing serially. The value is specified in kilobytes.

- _smm_px_max_size: The maximum size of all matching workareas in a query executing in parallel. The value is specified in kilobytes.

- _pga_max_size: The maximum amount of memory that can be allocated to all workareas within a process. The value is specified in bytes.

The internal rules for calculating these hidden values seem quite complicated and vary from release to release, so I won't try documenting them here. Just bear in mind that:

- The maximum size of any workarea is at most 1GB with automatic WORKAREA_SIZE_POLICY set to AUTO.

- The total memory for all workareas allocated to a process is at most 2GB with automatic WORKAREA_SIZE_POLICY set to MANUAL.

- Increasing the degree of parallelization for a statement will cease to have an impact on the memory available for your operation after a certain point.

Calculating Memory Allocation When WORKAREA_SIZE_POLICY Is Set to MANUAL

The only way to get individual workareas larger than 1GB or to have an SQL statement operating serially to use more than 2GB for multiple workareas is to set WORKAREA_SIZE_POLICY to MANUAL. This can be done at the session level. You can then set the following parameters at the session level:

- HASH_AREA_SIZE: The maximum size of a workarea used for HASH JOINs. This is specified in bytes and must be less than 2GB.

- SORT_AREA_SIZE: The maximum size of a workarea used for all other purposes. This includes operations such as HASH GROUP BY, so don't get confused! The value of SORT_AREA_SIZE is specified in bytes and can be set to any value less than 2GB.

The HASH_AREA_SIZE and SORT_AREA_SIZE parameters are only used when WORKAREA_SIZE_POLICY is set to MANUAL. They are ignored otherwise.

Optimal, One-Pass, and Multipass Operations

If your sort, join, or other operation completes entirely within the memory allocated to the workarea, it is referred to as an optimal operation. If disk space is required, then it may be that the data have been written to disk once and then read back in once. In that case, it is referred to as a one-pass operation. Sometimes, if a workarea is severely undersized, data need to be read and written out more than once. This is referred to as a multipass operation. Generally, although there are some obscure anomalies, an optimal operation will complete faster than a one-pass operation and a multipass operation will take very much longer than a one-pass operation. As you might imagine, identifying multipass operations is very useful, and fortunately there are several columns in V$SQL_PLAN_STATISTICS_ALL that come to the rescue:

- LAST_EXECUTION: The value is either OPTIMAL or it specifies the precise number of passes taken by the last execution of the statement.

- ESTIMATED_OPTIMAL_SIZE: Estimated size (in kilobytes) required by this workarea to execute the operation completely in memory (optimal execution). This is either derived from optimizer statistics or from previous executions.

- ESTIMATED_ONEPASS_SIZE: This is the estimated size (in kilobytes) required by this workarea to execute the operation in a single pass. This is either derived from optimizer statistics or from previous executions.

- LAST_TEMPSEG_SIZE: Temporary segment size (in bytes) created in the last instantiation of this workarea. This column is null when LAST_EXECUTION is OPTIMAL.

Shortcuts

The runtime engine usually follows the instructions laid out by the CBO slavishly, but there are times when it uses its initiative and departs from the prescribed path in the interests of performance. Let's look at a few examples.

Scalar Subquery Caching

Take another look at the query in Listing 3-1. Listing 4-7 executes the query and checks the runtime behavior.

Listing 4-7. An example of scalar subquery caching

```
SET LINES 200 PAGES 900 SERVEROUT OFF
COLUMN PLAN_TABLE_OUTPUT FORMAT a200

SELECT e.*
      ,d.dname
      ,d.loc
      , (SELECT COUNT (*)
           FROM scott.emp i
          WHERE i.deptno = e.deptno)
          dept_count  FROM scott.emp e, scott.dept d
 WHERE e.deptno = d.deptno;

SELECT * FROM TABLE (DBMS_XPLAN.display_cursor (format => 'ALLSTATS LAST'));
```

```
-------------------------------------------------------------------
| Id  | Operation           | Name | Starts | E-Rows | A-Rows |
-------------------------------------------------------------------
|   0 | SELECT STATEMENT    |      |      1 |        |     14 |
|   1 |  SORT AGGREGATE     |      |      3 |      1 |      3 |
|*  2 |   TABLE ACCESS FULL | EMP  |      3 |      1 |     14 |
|*  3 |  HASH JOIN          |      |      1 |     14 |     14 |
|   4 |   TABLE ACCESS FULL | DEPT |      1 |      4 |      4 |
|   5 |   TABLE ACCESS FULL | EMP  |      1 |     14 |     14 |
-------------------------------------------------------------------
```

The output of DBMS_XPLAN.DISPLAY has been edited once again, but the important columns are listed. You can see that operation 5 was executed once and returned 14 rows. Fair enough. There are 14 rows in SCOTT.EMP. However, you might have expected that operations 1 and 2 from the correlated subquery would have been executed 14 times. You can see from the Starts column that they were only executed three times! This is because the runtime engine cached the results of the subqueries for each value of DEPTNO so the subquery was only executed once for each value of the three values of DEPTNO that appear in EMP. Just to remind you, E-Rows is the estimated number of rows returned by a single execution of the operation and A-Rows is the actual number of rows returned by all three executions of the operation.

Scalar subquery caching is only enabled when the results of the subquery are known not to vary from one call to the next. So if the subquery had a call to a routine in the DBMS_RANDOM package, for example, then subquery caching would be turned off. If the subquery included a call to a user written function, then scalar subquery caching would also have been disabled unless the keyword DETERMINISTIC had been added to the function declaration. I'll explain that a little bit more when we discuss the function result cache.

Join Shortcuts

Sometimes the runtime engine will cut short a join operation if there is no point in continuing. Listing 4-8 creates and joins two tables.

Listing 4-8. Shortcutting a join

```
SET LINES 200 PAGES 0 SERVEROUTPUT OFF

CREATE TABLE t1
AS
        SELECT ROWNUM c1
          FROM DUAL
   CONNECT BY LEVEL <= 100;

CREATE TABLE t2
AS
        SELECT ROWNUM c1
          FROM DUAL
   CONNECT BY LEVEL <= 100;

SELECT *
  FROM t1 JOIN t2 USING (c1)
 WHERE c1 = 200;

SELECT *

  FROM TABLE (DBMS_XPLAN.display_cursor (format => 'BASIC IOSTATS LAST'));
```

```
--------------------------------------------------------------
| Id | Operation            | Name | Starts | E-Rows | A-Rows |
--------------------------------------------------------------
|  0 | SELECT STATEMENT     |      |    1   |        |    0   |
|* 1 |  HASH JOIN           |      |    1   |    1   |    0   |
|* 2 |   TABLE ACCESS FULL| T1   |    1   |    1   |    0   |
|* 3 |   TABLE ACCESS FULL| T2   |    0   |    1   |    0   |
--------------------------------------------------------------
```

The execution plan for the join of tables T1 and T2 shows a hash join but operation 2, the full table scan of table T1 returned no rows. The runtime engine then realized that if there were no rows from T1, the join couldn't possible produce any rows. You'll see from the Starts column that operation 3, the full table scan of T2, was never run. A reasonable decision to override the CBO's instructions, I am sure you will agree!

Result and OCI Caches

The result cache was introduced in Oracle Database 11gR1 with the intention of avoiding repeated executions of the same query. The use of the result cache is controlled primarily by means of the RESULT_CACHE_MODE initialization parameter and two hints:

- If RESULT_CACHE_MODE is set to FORCE, then the result cache is used in all valid cases unless the NO_RESULT_CACHE hint is supplied in the code.

- If RESULT_CACHE_MODE is set to MANUAL, which it is by default, then the result cache is never used unless the RESULT_CACHE hint is supplied in the code and it is valid to use the result cache.

Listing 4-9 shows how you might use the result cache feature.

Listing 4-9. The result cache feature forced by an initialization parameter

```
BEGIN
   DBMS_RESULT_CACHE.flush;
END;
/

ALTER SESSION SET result_cache_mode=force;

SELECT COUNT (*) FROM scott.emp;

SELECT * FROM TABLE (DBMS_XPLAN.display_cursor (format => 'ALLSTATS LAST'));

SELECT COUNT (*) FROM scott.emp;

SELECT * FROM TABLE (DBMS_XPLAN.display_cursor (format => 'ALLSTATS LAST'));

ALTER SESSION SET result_cache_mode=manual;
```

Id	Operation	Name	Starts	E-Rows	A-Rows
0	SELECT STATEMENT		1		1
1	RESULT CACHE	2jv3dwym1r7n6fjj959uz360b2	1		1
2	SORT AGGREGATE		1	1	1
3	INDEX FAST FULL SCAN	PK_EMP	1	14	14

Id	Operation	Name	Starts	E-Rows	A-Rows
0	SELECT STATEMENT		1		1
1	RESULT CACHE	2jv3dwym1r7n6fjj959uz360b2	1		1
2	SORT AGGREGATE		0	1	0
3	INDEX FAST FULL SCAN	PK_EMP	0	14	0

For the purposes of running a repeatable example, I began by flushing the result cache with the DBMS_RESULT_CACHE package. I then ran a simple query twice. You can see that the execution plan now has a new RESULT CACHE operation that causes the results from the first execution to be saved. The second invocation after the flush call was made executed neither operation 2 nor 3, the results having been retrieved from the result cache.

I must say I have yet to take advantage of result caching. The usual way to deal with queries being executed multiple times is to execute them once! On the one occasion where I was unable to prevent multiple executions of a statement because they were automatically generated, the use of the result cache was not valid because the expression TRUNC (SYSDATE) appeared in the query and the nondeterministic nature of this query rendered the use of the result cache invalid. Nevertheless, I am sure there are some occasions where the result cache will be a lifesaver of last resort!

The OCI cache goes one step further than the server-side result cache and stores data with the client. On the one hand, this might give excellent performance because it avoids invoking any communication with the server at all. On the other hand, the consistency of results is not guaranteed and so its usefulness is even more limited than the server side result cache!

Function Result Cache

Assuming that a function call always returns the same result for the same set of parameters, then you can supply the RESULT_CACHE keyword in the function declaration. This will result in the returned value being saved in a systemwide cache together with the associated parameter values. Even if the function's result is only deterministic if the contents of some underlying tables remain unaltered, you can still use the function result cache. When the function result cache was first introduced in Oracle Database 11gR1, you had to specify a RELIES ON clause to specify the objects on which the function's deterministic nature depended. In Oracle Database 11gR2 onward, this is done for you, and the RELIES ON clause is ignored if specified.

The concept of a function result cache bears strong resemblance to the concept of deterministic functions that I briefly mentioned in the context of scalar subquery caching:

- Neither the DETERMINISTIC nor the RESULT_CACHE keyword will prevent multiple calls to a function if different parameters are supplied.

- A function declared as DETERMINISTIC will only avoid multiple calls to a function with the same parameter values within a single invocation of an SQL statement. The RESULT_CACHE keyword saves on calls across statements and across sessions.

- When a function is declared as DETERMINISTIC, no check is made on underlying data changes in midstatement. In this sense, DETERMINISTIC is less reliable than RESULT_CACHE. On the other hand, you probably don't want underlying data changes to be visible midstatement!

- DETERMINISTIC functions don't consume system cache and in theory at least should be a little more efficient than the function result cache.

You can specify both the DETERMINISTIC and the RESULT_CACHE keywords in a function declaration, but do bear in mind that DETERMINISTIC doesn't absolutely guarantee that the same result will be returned from multiple calls within the same SQL statement. The scalar subquery cache is finite, and in some cases the results of earlier calls can be removed from the cache.

TRANSACTION CONSISTENCY AND FUNCTION CALLS

One of the interesting things about preparing examples for a book like this is that sometimes, as an author, you learn something new yourself! I was previously of the opinion that the READ COMMITTED isolation level would guarantee that the results of a single SQL statement would be consistent even if the transaction level guarantees of SERIALIZABLE were not provided. However, it turns out that repeated recursive SQL calls (such as in function calls) are *not* guaranteed to generate consistent results unless the transaction isolation level is SERIALIZABLE!

Listing 4-10 shows the declaration and call of a function that has been declared with both the DETERMINISTIC and the RESULT_CACHE keywords.

Listing 4-10. Performance improvements by caching function results

```
CREATE TABLE business_dates
(
   location          VARCHAR2 (20)
  ,business_date     DATE
);

INSERT INTO business_dates (location, business_date)
     VALUES ('Americas', DATE '2013-06-03');

INSERT INTO business_dates (location, business_date)
     VALUES ('Europe', DATE '2013-06-04');

INSERT INTO business_dates (location, business_date)
     VALUES ('Asia', DATE '2013-06-04');

CREATE OR REPLACE FUNCTION get_business_date (p_location VARCHAR2)
   RETURN DATE
   DETERMINISTIC
   RESULT_CACHE
IS
   v_date    DATE;
   dummy     PLS_INTEGER;
BEGIN
   DBMS_LOCK.sleep (5);

   SELECT business_date
     INTO v_date
     FROM business_dates
    WHERE location = p_location;

   RETURN v_date;
END get_business_date;
/

CREATE TABLE transactions
AS
        SELECT ROWNUM rn
              ,DECODE (MOD (ROWNUM - 1, 3),  0, 'Americas',  1, 'Europe',  'Asia')
                  location
              ,DECODE (MOD (ROWNUM - 1, 2)
                      ,0, DATE '2013-06-03'
                      ,DATE '2013-06-04')
                  transaction_date
          FROM DUAL
    CONNECT BY LEVEL <= 20;

  SELECT *
    FROM transactions
   WHERE transaction_date = get_business_date (location);
```

This code creates a BUSINESS_DATE table that, quite realistically, has the BUSINESS_DATE for Americas one day behind that of Europe and Asia. A selection is then made from a TRANSACTIONS table that picks rows matching the BUSINESS_DATE for that LOCATION. Of course, in real life this simple example would probably be best done by a table join, but also in real life the logic in the function may well be more complex than provided here.

If you run this script, which has a deliberate 5-second pause inside the function, you will see that it returns after only 15 seconds (i.e., after only three function calls). This shows that the function has been called only once for each region.

Summary

The CBO creates an execution plan that it believes to be optimal given the information it has at the time. A key part of optimization is understanding the discrepancy between what the CBO thinks will happen and what transpires in practice. This chapter has explained how the runtime engine interprets the execution plan it is given by the CBO, how to track the runtime engine's performance, and how various forms of caching can influence its behavior.

You now have enough basic concepts under your belt so I can give you an overview of my approach to SQL statement optimization, and that is what I will cover in Chapter 5.

CHAPTER 5

■ ■ ■

Introduction to Tuning

This chapter introduces the first of the two major themes of this book: tuning a SQL statement. The systematic process described in this chapter is designed to identify an approach to the execution of a SQL statement that ensures that the SQL statement runs in a reasonable amount of time without undue consumption of resources. At this stage I am just going to give you an overview of the process. I will go into a lot more detail in part 4 of this book.

It is important to understand that the techniques used to identify the approach to getting a SQL statement to run fast may be different from the techniques used to implement or enforce that approach in a production system. We will start to look at deployment in the next chapter.

Understanding the Problem

In so many aspects of life, properly understanding the problem you are trying to solve is most of the work needed in finding a solution to that problem. Tuning a SQL statement is a prime example. The more you understand about the tuning problem the easier it will be to make tuning decisions with confidence.

Understanding the Business Problem

This is a technical book, not a training manual on management technique, but gaining clarity on the business problem is so important that I have to spend a short while discussing it. When you are first asked to look at a performance issue with one or more SQL statements it is very tempting to dive in straight away. But you should take a breath first.

Suppose you are called out of bed because a query in an overnight batch is overrunning. The first question you need to have answered is "So what?" You probably want to express the question a little more politely, but that is the actual question you need answered. What are the business implications of the query running late? Is there a Service Level Agreement (SLA) that needs to be met, and what happens if it is breached? When will the SLA be breached, or has it already been breached?

Understanding the business context is critical to your whole approach to the tuning exercise for several reasons. For one thing, you need to balance the need to get the query done with the need to collect diagnostic information for Root Cause Analysis (RCA), itself important in preventing recurrences of this issue.

A second reason that understanding the business problem is important is so that you can prioritize the allocation of resources. You might observe that the system is extremely busy running other processes. How important are these other processes? Can they be killed? The more severe your problem the more palatable drastic measures will be to the business community and vice versa. On the one hand, sometimes billions of dollars may be on the line, sometimes even human life might be at stake. In critical situations like these you might want to get one or two other people involved. On the other hand, I have been woken at night to discover that there were absolutely no consequences to the query running for a long time; I was just advised "in case I wanted to know." It is best to get a handle on this sort of thing before you get started.

Remedial performance tuning of production queries is not the only case when understanding the business problem is important. If a developer asks you for advice about a query that runs for 10 minutes you should also start with politely phrased variants of the "so what" question. Is the query intended for interactive use or part of a batch? What is the expectation of the business community? If the query runs once a year as part of a year-end overnight batch then maybe it isn't important—unless last year's year-end batch was a disaster of course!

The development scenario leads me to a third reason why it is important to understand the business problem. And that is to know when to stop! Suppose you have an SLA of 75 minutes and you have tuned your query so that it consistently runs in 15 minutes. You can see that with a little more work you might be able to bring the elapsed time down to 12 minutes. Is it worth it? Almost certainly your time would be best spent elsewhere, as the consumers of your service will see little benefit from the extra work.

Getting a complete and authoritative understanding of the business context can be quite difficult and in many cases hopelessly impractical. You can't spend 30 minutes getting a clear understanding of a problem that might take you 10 minutes to fix; your "professionalism" may itself precipitate an SLA Service Level Agreement (SLA) breach! However, the more urgent the issue appears and the more panic appears to abound, the more need there is to get a clear understanding of what the real issue is so that resources are correctly focused.

A considerable amount of judgment is required here, and we all get better with experience. I will close this topic with a little tip on status reports: you may want to write a short email about what you have been asked to do and why. Sending a copy of such an email to various key people is a good way to give those key people visibility of the assumptions you are being asked to make and provides a useful audit trail.

Understanding the Technical Problem

The technical problem may seem obvious: make the SQL statement run fast. Right? Once again, you need to take a breath.

I once spent two days tuning a query that never finished only to discover that the query was incorrect! The developer was new to the ANSI syntax that was a coding standard in her team and had specified LEFT JOIN each time she meant RIGHT JOIN and vice versa! I could have kicked myself for not checking, and I would like to say that I never made that mistake again, but I can't! Quite recently a developer deliberately altered a SQL statement before giving it to me to tune. The change was made with the best of intentions. The data on the test system I was given to work on was not representative of production, and the actual production query ran fine on that test system. The query was altered in good faith to reflect the test data, but the change completely changed the options for tuning.

Making sure that the statement you have been asked to look at (or have yourself written) is correct is not the only technical thing you need to get straight. You also need to understand whether the SQL statement is static or dynamic. In other words, you need to know if the statement will change every time it is run or not. You need to understand if this is the only statement that needs tuning or if there are hundreds of similar statements. You need to understand what else is going to be running at the same time so that you can avoid contention and allocate resources appropriately. There are probably other things that might trip you up so don't take this as an exhaustive list.

Understanding the SQL Statement

In Chapter 1 I introduced factored subqueries because I feel that being able to read a SQL statement and understand what it does is critical to tuning. It may be possible to rewrite a query completely to give precisely the same results. You remember the change from Listing 1-1 to Listing 1-2? Such transformations are very difficult to see if you don't have the faintest idea what the SQL statement is trying to do. Perhaps there is an ORDER BY clause in the query. Do you know why it is there? Does it fulfill a genuine requirement, or was it put there just because the developer could more easily verify that the output was correct? The ubiquitous "SELECT COUNT (*) FROM" queries are often used just to determine the existence of matching rows, and the exact count is irrelevant. If you wrote the query yourself then hopefully you know the answers to these questions, but if not then spending some time trying to understand what the query does and why will usually speed up the whole tuning process.

Understanding the Data

It is all very well getting your query to run fast on a test system, but is the test data representative of what you will find on the production system? Are the data volumes on your production system likely to grow and, if so, at what rate? I will admit that the specific questions about data may be difficult to frame at the very start of a tuning exercise. Until you have some understanding of what the performance issues are and what the possible execution plans are, it may be difficult to know which particular aspects of your query are sensitive to data volume or data distribution. However, once you discover some aspect of your query that is particularly sensitive to data volume or data distribution it may be best to pause and ask some questions.

Let me give you a real-life example of what can go wrong when you don't check your assumptions about the data. A regulatory requirement resulted in a table that I shall call AUDIT_TRAIL being added to a database. The rows in in the AUDIT_TRAIL table were populated with columns like USER_ID, PRODUCT_ID, and so on. The software that added rows to the table was tested, and half a dozen rows appeared in the AUDIT_TRAIL table. A report was then written. It took rows from the AUDIT_TRAIL table and joined it with USERS and PRODUCTS tables so that the meaningless USER_ID and PRODUCT_ID columns were replaced by more readable USER_NAME and PRODUCT_NAME columns. The report worked fine!

The very first day that the application was deployed in production some concerns were raised about the report, which seemed to be running a little longer than expected. The second day the concerns were voiced somewhat more strongly, as the report was now taking an unacceptably long time. The reason why the report was taking so long was that something like 100,000 rows were being added to the AUDIT_TRAIL each day! Who knew? Apparently not the tester of the report, who had signed off on the testing after reporting on about six rows!

Understanding the Problem Wrap Up

This discussion of the various aspects of a tuning problem should not be treated either as a mandatory checklist or as a comprehensive list of questions. The reason I have spent this long discussing the issue is to highlight the fact that no SQL tuning assignment is ever as simple as it first appears. If you make a premature start to technical analysis you are likely to end up making false assumptions and delivering a solution that is inapplicable or unsuitable for other reasons. If you do end up delivering a solution that your consumer is happy with you will do so more quickly and efficiently if you ask the right questions first. Finally, I would like to emphasize that once you have started your analysis you should always be wary of making deductions from your observations that are based on unverified assumptions. Don't be afraid to pause and check your facts.

Analysis

After getting a thorough understanding of the problem statement, the next stage in the tuning process is to analyze the behavior of the SQL statement. This is part of an iterative process; you analyze, make some changes, and reanalyze.

Running the Statement to Completion

Although you can get some understanding of how a SQL statement is working as it is running by using the SQL performance monitor, you can't really claim to have the full picture until you get the SQL statement to finish. And if you want to be able to try out a few things, you need to get the statement to finish in 5 to 10 minutes at most. Otherwise you will either be twiddling your thumbs for far too long or you will end up having to work on something else at the same time and end up losing track of where you are.

Suppose that a query has been running for two minutes and you look at a SQL performance monitor report and see that a full table scan of table T1 is in progress and that it is only 1% complete. My oh my. You didn't expect a full table scan to take so long. At this rate it will be 200 minutes before the full table scan completes, and who knows how much longer before the statement as a whole finishes. As a temporary measure you need to reduce the amount of data you are selecting from the table. Listing 5-1 shows one of the numerous methods that can be employed to reduce the data set on which you are operating.

Listing 5-1. Use of the SAMPLE keyword to reduce the size of a dataset

```
CREATE TABLE t1
AS
        SELECT 1 c1
          FROM DUAL
   CONNECT BY LEVEL <= 100;

CREATE TABLE t2
AS
        SELECT 1 c2
          FROM DUAL
   CONNECT BY LEVEL <= 100;

SELECT *
  FROM t1, t2
 WHERE t1.c1 = t2.c2;

WITH q1
     AS (SELECT *
           FROM t1 SAMPLE (5) SEED(0))
SELECT *
  FROM q1 t1, t2
 WHERE t1.c1 = t2.c2;

DROP TABLE t1;
DROP TABLE t2;
```

The first query in Listing 5-1 shows a typical query that joins two tables. The second query uses the SAMPLE keyword to select, in this case, 5% of the data in T1 in an attempt to get some kind of result in a reasonable amount of time. The SEED keyword is used to generate reproducible results. Of course, at some point you will have to remove this SAMPLE keyword, but only once you have figured out why the query is taking so long.

Analyzing Elapsed Time

Once the statement has finished, you need to get a breakdown of that elapsed time. In Chapter 4 I explained how to ensure that the view V$SQL_PLAN_STATISTICS_ALL was populated with information from the runtime engine about individual operations in an SQL statement. This is the main source of information for analysis.

When the Elapsed Times Doesn't Add Up

Sometimes you will look at the data from V$SQL_PLAN_STATISTICS_ALL and find that the total amount of elapsed time is nowhere near the length of time you spent waiting for the query to finish. Here are several reasons why this might be the case:

- **Recursive SQL.** If an SQL statement under test includes calls to functions that in turn include calls to other SQL statements, then the time spent executing these recursive SQL statements will not be included in the reported time for the statement under test. If a DML statement ends up invoking one or more triggers, then the time spent executing these triggers will be similarly excluded.

- **Sending and receiving data to the client process.** Once rows have been returned from a query they need to be sent to the client process. If the client process is not able to keep up, then that can hold up proceedings at the server. A slow network or a slow client will show up as numerous "SQL*Net message to client" wait events seen in V$ACTIVE_SESSION_HISTORY.

- **Parsing.** This is rarely an issue for SQL statements that run for multiple seconds, but I once worked with an application where the CBO took over 4 seconds to devise a query plan! The query plan was quite good and ran in under one second, but that was little consolation!

Most of the time the source of the lost time will soon become quite clear. It is on those rare occasions when you can't see where the lost time has gone that the 10046 SQL trace that I mentioned in Chapter 4 becomes invaluable.

When the Time Does Add Up

Once the figures in V$SQL_PLAN_STATISTICS_ALL make sense, you need to focus in on the most expensive operation first. Look at what the test script in Listing 5-2 does.

Listing 5-2. Analyzing the performance of a simple two-table join

```
CREATE TABLE t1 (c1 PRIMARY KEY)
ORGANIZATION INDEX
AS
   SELECT ROWNUM c1 FROM DUAL;

CREATE TABLE t2
PCTFREE 99
PCTUSED 1
AS
   WITH q1
       AS (    SELECT ROWNUM c2
                 FROM DUAL
            CONNECT BY LEVEL <= 100)
   SELECT a.c2, RPAD ('X', 2000) vpad
     FROM q1 a, q1;

BEGIN
   DBMS_STATS.gather_table_stats (SYS_CONTEXT ('USERENV', 'CURRENT_SCHEMA')
                               ,'T1'
                               ,no_invalidate   => FALSE);
   DBMS_STATS.gather_table_stats (SYS_CONTEXT ('USERENV', 'CURRENT_SCHEMA')
                               ,'T2'
                               ,no_invalidate   => FALSE);
END;
/

INSERT INTO t2 (c2, vpad)
   WITH q1
       AS (    SELECT ROWNUM c2
                 FROM DUAL
            CONNECT BY LEVEL <= 300)
   SELECT a.c2, RPAD ('X', 2000) vpad
     FROM q1 a, q1;

SET LINES 200 PAGES 900 TIMING ON

ALTER SESSION SET statistics_level=all;

BEGIN
   FOR r IN (SELECT *
               FROM t1, t2
              WHERE t1.c1 = t2.c2)
   LOOP
     NULL;
   END LOOP;
END;
/
```

```
COLUMN id FORMAT 99
COLUMN operation FORMAT a18
COLUMN options FORMAT a11
COLUMN actual_time FORMAT 99.999 HEADING "Actual|Time"
COLUMN object_name FORMAT a17 HEADING "Object|Name"
COLUMN last_starts FORMAT 9999999 HEADING "Last|Starts"
COLUMN actual_rows FORMAT 9999999 HEADING "Actual|Rows"

  SELECT id
        ,LPAD (' ', DEPTH) || operation operation
        ,options
        ,last_elapsed_time / 1000000 actual_time
        ,object_name
        ,last_starts
        ,last_output_rows actual_rows
    FROM v$sql_plan_statistics_all
   WHERE sql_id = 'cwktrs03rd8c7'
ORDER BY id;
```

Listing 5-2 includes some SQL*Plus-specific syntax and begins by creating two tables. T1 is an index-organized table, and T2 is a regular heap table. After the statistics are gathered on the two tables (superfluous in 12cR1 onwards as I shall explain later in the book) some more rows are added to table T2. The statistics for T2 are now slightly out of date. This is perhaps a little unusual; you can't always gather statistics on a table every time you insert data into it, but you don't normally increase the number of rows several fold before re-gathering statistics! The tables are then joined inside a PL/SQL block and, for the purposes of this test, the output is discarded. On my laptop the query took about 25 seconds. The final statement in Listing 5-2 examines some key columns from V$SQL_PLAN_STATISTICS_ALL using the SQL_ID that I determined separately using the techniques described in chapter 1.

The output from the final query in Listing 5-2 is shown in Listing 5-3.

Listing 5-3. Runtime statistics from a two-table join

ID	OPERATION	OPTIONS	Actual Time	Object Name	Last Starts	Actual Rows
0	SELECT STATEMENT		25.157		1	400
1	NESTED LOOPS		25.157		1	400
2	TABLE ACCESS	FULL	24.806	T2	1	100000
3	INDEX	UNIQUE SCAN	.258	SYS_IOT_TOP_97615	100000	400

We can see that operation 1 ostensibly took about 25.16 seconds, but do you remember what I said about the time allocated to children being included in the time for the parent? Operations 2 and 3 took about 24.81 seconds between them, so the NESTED LOOP itself was responsible for just 0.35 seconds. This is to be expected because a NESTED LOOPS join just gets rows from the driving row source and invokes the probe row source for matches. What is perhaps a little more surprising is that even though we can see that operation 3 was invoked 100,000 times, which we know form the LAST_STARTS column, the total elapsed time was still just 0.26 seconds!

■ **Tip** With the exception of semi-joins and anti-joins that I will cover in Chapter 11, the number of times the probe row source (the child with the higher ID) of a NESTED LOOPS join is executed (LAST_STARTS) is always precisely the same as the number of rows returned by the driving row source (the LAST_OUTPUT_ROWS column from the child with the lower ID). This is because the second child is probed once for every row returned by the first child. In this case the full table scan of T2 returned 100,000 rows, so the index of T1 was probed 100,000 times.

There is clearly a lot of fancy optimization going on under the covers of those 100,000 probes, which one day might be interesting,[1] but right now the main conclusion is that you don't need to worry about operation 3. No, the big concern is operation 2. Even though it was only executed once, that single full table scan took 24.81 of the 24.16 seconds of our statement's elapsed time. That full table scan is where we need to focus our attention.

Fixing the Problem

Once you have identified the specific operation in your SQL statement that is taking the most time, the next thing to do is to figure out how to save some of that time. Always remember that at this stage we are just trying to find out what needs to be fixed and not how to deploy the fix in production.

Check the Statistics

Before you go any further you need to know if your object statistics are appropriate. Object statistics are the key input to the CBO, and I will explain why "appropriate" does not necessarily mean "up to date" in chapter 6. The point is to ensure that you don't spend a lot of effort tuning a query when the statement's poor performance is purely down to stale or otherwise inappropriate statistics.

If you are working on a test system that has production-like data and the object statistics on your test system are out-of-date, then the simplest thing may be to just to re-gather them. However, if you have some extended statistics or hand-crafted histograms on your production system it would be best to make sure that the same extended statistics and histograms are present on your test system, and perhaps the best thing would be to copy the statistics from production to your test system.

I'll be talking a lot more about object statistics in the next chapter and I don't want to get too bogged down at this point. The main point I want to make here is that you need to consider the state of your object statistics early on in your tuning process.

Let us gather statistics on the tables in Listing 5-2 and rerun the query. Listing 5-4 shows the updated results from V$SQL_PLAN_STATISTICS_ALL.

Listing 5-4. Performance after gathering statistics

ID	OPERATION	OPTIONS	Actual Time	Object Name	Last Starts	Actual Rows
0	SELECT STATEMENT		13.390		1	400
1	HASH JOIN		13.390		1	400
2	INDEX	FULL SCAN	.000	SYS_IOT_TOP_100393	1	1
3	TABLE ACCESS	FULL	13.307	T2	1	100000

---

[1]Actually, the reasons that the operation was so fast were, first, that a "consistent get" from a unique index does not actually take out a latch and, second, because most of the time no index entry was found.

We can see that the execution plan has changed and the performance has improved. In fact, the improvement is primarily due to the fact that the data is now cached rather than being due to the change in execution plan. That same full table scan is still the source of our problems.

Changing the Code

There are several reasons why rewriting a query in a functionally equivalent way may help the CBO. I'll mention a couple now. I will cover the topic in more depth in Chapter 16.

Adding Information

There are lots of ways that you can give information to the CBO to help it along. Here is just one example.

Unless a column is guaranteed to always be NOT NULL, you can't add a NOT NULL constraint for it. However, the specific rows you are selecting at the specific time you are selecting them may be guaranteed to be NOT NULL, and you can add a predicate such as "WHERE c1 IS NOT NULL." Now the CBO has one more bit of potentially useful information it can include in its preparation of an execution plan. In the case of the simple query in Listing 5-2 there isn't any useful information that we can add.

Transforming the Query

As I showed in Listings 1-1 and 1-2 there are occasions when you can rewrite a query in an entirely different way and cause the CBO to come up with a completely different execution plan. There doesn't seem to be any useful transformation that we can apply to the query in Listing 5-2 so let us move on.

Adding Hints

Although I consider hints a perfectly acceptable way to get a SQL statement to run fast on a production system, now is not the time for a debate on this topic. At this stage we are just trying to identify a well-performing execution plan via a set of experiments. You will find that all well-known Oracle experts would agree that *for experimental purposes only* you should not in any way be inhibited from using hints, documented or undocumented, in your search for the most efficient execution plan.

Like most of you out there I often ask myself questions like "Why on earth has the CBO used a full table scan instead of using the index that I created specifically for queries like this?" Well, before spending days theorizing on the matter, I usually end up adding an INDEX hint to my query and, if possible, running the query again. There are several possible outcomes:

- After adding the INDEX hint the CBO still used a full table scan. This suggests that the use of the index is illegal in some way. I would now have half the answer to my question. The other half would be: "Why is use of the index illegal?"

- The index was used but the query was actually no faster, or possibly was even slower. I now have a new question: "What false assumption did I make that made me believe the index would be faster?"

- The index was used and the elapsed time of the query was reduced. This experimental result leads to a different new question: "What false assumption did the CBO make that made it believe that the index would not be faster?" If there are hundreds of similar SQL statements out there then this new question is extremely important. At this point, though, these concerns don't worry me too much; I can proceed to tune other parts of the query, leaving the hint in place.

In the case of the query in Listing 5-2 there aren't yet any indexes on table T2. The only hint that might have helped, a PARALLEL hint, didn't work on my laptop because the single local hard disk can't do more than one thing at once. Let us move on.

Making Physical Changes to the Database

The most common physical database change people make to improve query performance is to add one or more indexes. However, there are lots of other physical design changes that may help improve query performance, and I will cover these in Chapter 15. Here are just a few examples.

Provided you have the necessary licenses you might implement partitioning or compression. You might create materialized views or perform some other form of denormalization. Of course, in the specific case shown in Listing 5-2 we could simply remove the PCTFREE 99 that I added deliberately to slow down the full table scan! That may not often be an option in real life, but you might occasionally find that a table has a large amount of free space in its blocks and that by moving the table you can significantly reduce its size and improve access times.

Even when you do decide that adding an index will help query performance, there are still several questions to ask. The first thought in your mind, as with any physical design change, should be to assess the impact that adding the index will have on DML statements. Every time you insert a row into a table, every time you delete a row from a table, and every time you update indexed columns in a table you need to adjust the table's indexes. The more of those indexes you have, the longer the DML will take. Not only that, but indexes take up space in the buffer cache and on disk, space that may be better used for other purposes.

I am contradicting myself a little bit here. After all you are still just running experiments, so you don't have to think everything through at this stage. But some physical design changes take a lot of work and impact other testers, so it may be worth giving some thought to the wider impact of your proposed change before you expend a lot of effort on an idea that may be quite impractical in practice.

Let us assume that you are still keen on the idea of adding an index. You then need to ask yourself what columns to index and in what order. Perhaps adding an extra column to your index would help other queries. Another thing to consider is the possibility of using one or more bitmap indexes, which is not a bad option if data is loaded in bulk and there are few, if any, updates later. For narrow tables, changing to an Indexed Organized Table may be an option as well.

The final thing to consider when adding an index is how many columns, if any, to compress. In the case of table T2 in Listing 5-2, we know that our indexed column will be repeated many times, so it seems sensible to compress it. Listing 5-5 adds an index on T2.C2 and shows the amended data from V$SQL_PLAN_STATISTICS_ALL.

Listing 5-5. Adding a compressed index

```
CREATE INDEX t2_i1
   ON t2 (c2)
   COMPRESS 1;
```

ID	OPERATION	OPTIONS	Actual Time	Object Name	Last Starts	Actual Rows
0	SELECT STATEMENT		**.004**		1	400
1	HASH JOIN		.004		1	400
2	NESTED LOOPS		.003		1	400
3	NESTED LOOPS		.001		1	400
4	STATISTICS COL		.000		1	1
5	INDEX	FULL SCAN	.000	SYS_IOT_TOP_100	1	1
6	INDEX	RANGE SCAN	.001	T2_I1	1	400
7	TABLE ACCESS	BY INDEX ROWID	.001	T2	400	400
8	TABLE ACCESS	FULL	.000	T2	0	0

Wow! Our query now runs in a fraction of a second! We can see that the execution plan has changed almost beyond recognition with the addition of the index. The key point is that our full table scan has been replaced by operation 7, which makes just 400 single-block accesses to T2.

Making Changes to the Environment

If your query seems to be perfectly well tuned and the performance is still unacceptable, what then? Hardware upgrades are always an option, of course, but there are often far less drastic measures available. You may be able to increase the size of the buffer cache to reduce the number of disk reads. You may be able to increase the size of the PGA or set WORAKAREA_SIZE_POLICY to MANUAL so that a sort will complete in memory. We will discuss sorts at length in Chapter 17. You might also want to run the query in parallel, and we will discuss parallel execution plans in Chapter 8.

Running the SQL Tuning Advisor

It is an unfortunate fact of life that DBAs are often assigned responsibility for a large number of applications and databases and are nevertheless called in at the last minute, often at antisocial hours, to deal with performance issues about which they have little or no background knowledge. In these cases it will be difficult to build the detailed business and technical context for the performance issue in the way that I have advocated here.

Fortunately, help may be at a hand. The SQL Tuning Advisor performs automated checks on what it can see in the database. It checks if the statistics are stale or misleading. It looks for hidden correlations in columns and does a few other basic checks. I believe that the way it works is to run parts of the SQL statement to see how well the CBO's theoretical ideas work out in practice.

There is good news and bad news about the SQL Tuning Advisor. The bad news is that the SQL Tuning Advisor is incapable of solving all but the most basic of tuning problems:

- It doesn't have any more SQL transformations available than the CBO and runs through the same sort of costing calculations as the CBO, and so it often comes up with the same conclusions as the CBO.

- It can recommend a new index, but its advice should be taken with a pinch of salt, as the CBO doesn't actually create the index and so doesn't know anything about what index statistics like the *clustering factor* would be.

■ **Tip** Never run the SQL Tuning Advisor when the query involves a temporary table. In real life the application will populate the temporary table before invoking the query, but the SQL Tuning Advisor will not. As a consequence the advice generated will usually be completely wrong.

The good news is that although the SQL Tuning Advisor can only help with the most basic of tuning issues, a lot of tuning issues are, in fact, quite basic! Because of this I sometimes use the SQL Tuning Advisor even when working with an application that I am intimately familiar with. Of course, these days I can often see the solution to a simple tuning issue right away and so my use of the SQL Tuning Advisor is now mostly restricted to lunch time! If I am given a tuning problem just as I am about to head out for something to eat, it is quite straightforward to kick off the SQL Tuning Advisor before I do. Sometimes, the answer is waiting for me by the time I get back from lunch!

You can invoke the SQL Tuning Advisor from *Enterprise Manager* (EM) but by the time you have logged into EM you could have kicked off the task from SQL*Plus and be at lunch. Listing 5-6 shows a generic SQL script that you can use.

Listing 5-6. Creating a SQL Tuning Advisor task from SQL*Plus

```
VARIABLE t VARCHAR2(20)

BEGIN
   :t := DBMS_SQLTUNE.create_tuning_task (sql_id => '&SQL_ID');
   DBMS_SQLTUNE.execute_tuning_task (:t);
END;
/

SET LINES 32767 PAGES 0 TRIMSPOOL ON VERIFY OFF LONG 1000000 LONGC 1000000

SELECT DBMS_SQLTUNE.report_tuning_task (task_name => :t, TYPE => 'TEXT')
  FROM DUAL;

EXEC dbms_sqltune.drop_tuning_task(:t);
SET LINES 200
```

The idea is the same as the SQL Performance Monitor scripts that I showed you earlier. You use the SQL*Plus `DEFINE` command to specify the SQL_ID and then call the script that you have saved somewhere convenient. Do you see the highlighted section that says TYPE => 'TEXT'? In this case, the only supported type is 'TEXT', and so rather than generating an HTML report for viewing in a browser this script just sends the report to the terminal.

The `DBMS_SQLTUNE.CREATE_TUNING_TASK` procedure has several options that you might want to look at. For example, the default time allotted for the tuning task is 30 minutes, and that is frequently insufficient. All that happens then when the SQL Tuning Advisor hits its time limit is that it produces a curt report saying that it has run out of time. You might want to increase the timeout, particularly if you are planning a long lunch!

Shall we see what the SQL Tuning Advisor makes of the query in Listing 5-2? Have a look at Listing 5-7.

Listing 5-7. Dropping the index from Listing 5-5 and running the SQL Tuning Advisor

```
DROP INDEX t2_i1;
DEFINE SQL_ID=cwktrs03rd8c7
@@run_tuning_advisor

--- Edited output

2- Using New Indices
--------------------
Plan hash value: 3119652813
```

Id	Operation	Name	Rows	Bytes	Time
0	SELECT STATEMENT		333	652K	00:00:05
1	NESTED LOOPS				
2	NESTED LOOPS		333	652K	00:00:05
3	INDEX FULL SCAN	SYS_IOT_TOP_446365	1	3	00:00:01
* 4	INDEX RANGE SCAN	IDX$$_126C0001	333		00:00:01
5	TABLE ACCESS BY INDEX ROWID	T2	333	652K	00:00:05

The `@run_tuning_advisor` call in Listing 5-7 assumes that the code in Listing 5-6 has been saved in a script called `run_tuning_advisor.sql`. We can see that the SQL Tuning Advisor suggests the use of the index that we just dropped and that we know helps tremendously. Thankfully, you aren't required to use the name IDX$$_126C0001 that the SQL Tuning Advisor has used for the index!

Rethink the Requirement

On occasions the cost and complexity of a solution seem to be out of all proportion to the problem being addressed. Is it really worth all of the time and effort? Will running 200 parallel query slaves flat out for half an hour have too much impact on the rest of the system? There are times when these sorts of questions really need to be asked. Perhaps the daily report you have been asked to tune could be run just once on the weekend when the system is otherwise idle. Maybe the query could be simplified and still provide data that is perfectly serviceable to the business consumers.

Although you shouldn't be afraid to ask these sorts of questions when the time is right, you need to make sure you have your facts straight before you do. You don't want your boss to have your colleague "take another look" and for him or her to find a quick solution. That would be embarrassing! If you are in any doubt, why not review your findings with a colleague first?

Summary

This chapter has provided an overview of a systematic approach to tuning a SQL statement. You need to begin by getting as thorough an understanding of the problem at hand as is practical. The next step is to get a breakdown of where the time is being spent. Finally, an iterative process of change and retest is used until such time as the performance reaches an acceptable level.

At this stage I haven't given you much in the way of examples of query transformations, no information on how to hint properly, and only discussed physical database transformations very briefly. These topics will all be discussed in much more detail later in the book.

Always remember that tuning is an experimental process to determine what has gone wrong and why. It has little to do with deployment in the production system. Let us move onto that topic now in Chapter 6.

CHAPTER 6

■ ■ ■

Object Statistics and Deployment

This chapter introduces the second of the two important themes of the book: how to manage the performance of SQL statements in a production environment. This is undoubtedly the most controversial chapter in this book as some experts may disagree with the views I express here, particularly as they fly in the face of Oracle's stated strategy. Nevertheless, I am very far from alone in reaching the conclusions that I have, and the techniques I describe have been used by a number of people to stabilize the performance of many Oracle databases. Let us begin with some generic observations about performance management.

The Principle of Performance Management

There is an overriding principle that I believe applies to the performance of all types of services. It doesn't have to be a database-related service, and it doesn't even have to be in IT. Let me give you a couple of examples that are not IT related to make the point clear.

The Royal Mail Example

About 20 years ago I was listening to an after-dinner talk by an employee of the Royal Mail. The Royal Mail is the postal service in the United Kingdom, and the speaker started to discuss a survey that his employer had made of its business customers. The Royal Mail wanted to know if their customers would be happy with a 2:00 p.m. delivery time or whether they would pay extra for a 9:00 a.m. delivery. The response from their customer base was that the Royal Mail was asking the wrong question!

At the time, the reliability of the Royal Mail was not particularly great. My own experience of what is known as "First Class Mail" was that correspondence would arrive the following day about 90% of the time. Ten percent of the time the mail wasn't delivered for at least two days. This sort of service is no good at all to a business consumer. Suppose a law firm sends legal documents to their employee John at his office in London. John wants to discuss these documents with Jim, a client of the law firm, also based in London. Do you imagine that John can call Jim and say, "Hey, Jim, why not pop over for a chat about these legal documents? There is a 90% chance that I will have them by then!" That is not how business functions. John needs a *guarantee* of a delivery time. If that guaranteed time is 2:00 p.m. then John might be able to arrange his meeting with Jim for 3:00 p.m. If Jim is only available in the morning then another carrier might be needed, but whichever service provider John uses, that service provider must (paraphrasing a famous advertising slogan from a U.S. parcel service) ensure that the correspondence absolutely, positively, must be there by whatever time was guaranteed.

In real life, of course, there is no such thing as an *absolute* guarantee. There are always factors beyond our control that introduce small levels of risk. But these exceptions need to be very few if consumers are to tolerate them.

The Airport Example

I was driving my adult son Thomas to the airport and told him about the performance management principle that I was trying to explain. I asked if he had any ideas for a second example that most people could relate to. He struggled a bit to come up with a suitable example as we sat over a meal. After we had finished eating, Thomas headed through airport security and I made my way home. About an hour later I got a call from Thomas. He had some good news and some bad news. The bad news was that he had missed his flight, but the good news was that I had a second example for my book!

I used to be a frequent flyer, and I absolutely hate wasting time at an airport. I left Thomas to go through security about 30 minutes before his flight was due to depart. That should have given him enough time, and he wouldn't be stuck in the departures lounge for too long. I thought I was being a good "service provider". Unfortunately, there was an issue with the image of Thomas's electronic boarding pass on his smartphone and he had to go and get a paper copy printed off. By the time Thomas was back at security his flight had closed. He explained to me that optimizing the airport experience to minimize the wait was all very laudable but that next time I would have to ensure that he absolutely, positively did not miss the flight!

Service Level Agreements in IT

Consumers of IT services are no different from consumers of any other type of service. They want *guarantees*. These guarantees are embodied in Service Level Agreements, or SLAs, that are either formal documents or informal understandings. These SLAs aren't written with words like "the batch must finish in one hour 90% of the time" or even "the batch must finish in an average time of less than one hour over the course of a month." These sorts of performance measures are of no use to any service consumer. No, SLAs are always stated to reflect the sentiment that the batch "absolutely, positively must be finished in an hour."

In the vast majority of cases, the consumer will not care whether the one-hour batch finishes in 15 minutes or 59 minutes any more than you would care if your letters arrived at 4:30 in the morning. It would be a rare event for a business consumer of an IT service to call staff at home and say, "Hey, the overnight batch is running ahead of schedule, why not grab an early train and start work early?" Consumers of services make plans based on the guaranteed performance level and often aren't in a position to take advantage of higher levels of performance if they occur.

Of course, the service *provider* of a one-hour batch is very much interested in the difference between a 15 minute and a 59 minute run. In the former case there is plenty of contingency time to deal with unexpected events, while there is none in the latter case. Nevertheless, the consumer's needs come first, and efforts to reduce the elapsed time of a batch can only be made after a predictable performance profile has been established.

Non-database Deployment Strategies

Given the requirements of service consumers, the IT industry has established techniques for ensuring that both the functionality and performance levels of IT services are predictable. There are a number of software development methodologies in existence, but they all share a couple of common attributes:

- New features are tested in some way to provide confidence that the software functions correctly and that performance levels are satisfactory before being delivered for general-purpose consumption.

- Changes, either to software or critical configuration data, involving a production service are controlled in some way to minimize risk. Typically, these controls involve some combination of testing, impact analysis, authorization, and auditing.

All these processes and procedures are there to do one basic thing; they are there so that the consumers absolutely, positively will get the service they have been promised. Of course, we don't always succeed, but that is at least our goal.

The Strategic Direction for the CBO

Up until now I have been talking about the delivery of services to consumers in general. I have done so at length and deliberately avoided any mention of database performance. All this preparation is, as you may have guessed, because in my opinion the strategy that Oracle, and the CBO development team in particular, are following does not reflect the basic requirements for predictable service delivery.

The History of Strategic Features

The CBO was introduced in Oracle 7 as an optional feature. You didn't have to use it, and most of us didn't. The slow take up was for two reasons. Some customers were concerned that, like any major new feature, the CBO might not work well at first. They had a point. The second reason for the slow take up was that the CBO was unpredictable by design. You might get one execution plan one day and then, after gathering object statistics, you might get a completely different execution plan that may or may not work as well.

One of the key things about the old Rule-Based Optimizer (RBO) was that the same statement resulted in the same execution plan every time. The CBO, on the other hand, is designed to be *adaptable*. The CBO tries to get the optimal execution plan each and every time, and if the object statistics suggest that the data has changed then the CBO will quite happily consider a new execution plan.

Despite the concerns about predictability that customers started raising from the outset and continue to raise today, the strategic direction of the CBO continues to be based on adaptability. Features like dynamic sampling and bind variable peeking started to appear. When 11g arrived it became very clear that the CBO team was looking towards ever more adaptable and ever less predictable behaviors. The signals came in the form of *Adaptive Cursor Sharing* in 11gR1 and *Cardinality Feedback* in 11gR2. Both Adaptive Cursor Sharing and Cardinality Feedback can result in the execution plan selected for the first execution of a statement being "upgraded" for the second and subsequent executions, even with no change to object statistics! Usually, these changes are for the better, but there are no *guarantees*.

As if this wasn't bad enough, 12cR1 introduced *Adaptive Execution Plans*. This feature might result in the execution plan of a statement changing in mid-flight! We don't want these features!

- On a test system we don't want these features because they might mask problems that will impact our production service.

- On a production system we don't want these features because the execution plans that we have tested are satisfactory, whatever the CBO thinks; we don't want to risk using an untested plan that might cause performance to degrade.

Implications of the CBO Strategy

Now that we know what the strategy of the CBO development team is, let us look at what it means for us. I'll approach this by looking at comments from two well-known Oracle gurus: Connor McDonald and Dave Ensor.

Connor McDonald's view

If you ask people who the most knowledgeable experts in Oracle database technology are you might soon find yourself in the middle of a disagreement. Sometimes quite a heated disagreement! However, the most entertaining Oracle speaker in the world is surely Connor McDonald. If you come up with another name, you probably haven't heard Connor speak! Oh, and just in case you are wondering, Connor knows a thing or two about Oracle database technology as well!

I have only had the privilege of hearing Connor speak twice, and on the first of those occasions he discussed a topic that is right at the center of the issues we are discussing in this chapter. Connor began his presentation by proposing a very simple change to a software program. A dropdown list had two entries: "MALE" and "Female". The "MALE" is all capital letters but "Female" only has the first letter capitalized. A developer would like to correct this by changing "MALE" to "Male". What needs to be done? Well Connor ran through a long list of tasks that the fictitious developer might have to do: write a business case, have the business case approved, generate a test plan, run through unit testing, subsystem testing, and system testing, document test results, go through a Quality Assurance review. . . the list went on and on and on. All the while Connor's laptop was throwing images of meetings, documents, and various other things that I won't mention in case you see his presentation and I spoil the fun! By the time Connor got to the end of his list I was, along with most of the rest of the audience, chuckling quite loudly. After all, most of us have at some point experienced something similar!

Connor's presentation then took a different tack. Connor proposed a fictitious service impacting incident and the ensuing post-mortem. The incident was caused by a changed execution plan that in turn was caused by a change in object statistics. What! A change that caused an incident! Was this change authorized? Was there a change record? Who is to blame?

Of course the fictitious execution plan changed was caused by an explicitly run job to gather statistics. No authorization, no impact analysis, no testing, nothing. Connor asked the perfectly reasonable question as to why IT organizations routinely precipitate untested execution plan changes on their database systems while at the same time placing most other types of changes under the highest scrutiny. It seemed to Connor that that the world had gone mad. I agree!

The Dave Ensor Paradox

If the award for the most entertaining Oracle speaker in the world goes to Connor McDonald, I would give Dave Ensor the award for most memorable sound bite! I don't know when or where Dave first stated that "the only time that it is safe to gather statistics is when to do so would make no difference." Wherever or whenever he spoke those now famous, or infamous, words, they are now known world-wide as "The Dave Ensor Paradox."

I should point out right away that Dave's assertion is utterly untrue, a fact that I am sure Dave would be the first to acknowledge. However, there are two thought-provoking aspects of his "paradox" that warrant discussion. The first of these is the basis for the original assertion.

When you gather statistics, one of two things might happen to the execution plans of your SQL statements. The first thing that might happen is nothing; the execution plan based on the new statistics is precisely the same as the execution plan that was used the last time the statement ran. Since nothing has changed you obviously haven't done any harm. The second thing that might happen is that the execution plan has changed. We don't know for sure how the new plan will behave in practice, so it isn't safe to gather statistics when that is the outcome. A compelling argument.

The second interesting aspect of Dave Ensor's paradox is the fatal flaw in his argument. We will come to that very soon.

Why We Need to Gather Statistics

If gathering statistics is such a dangerous activity, as both Connor and Dave have suggested, then why on earth do we do it? Listing 6-1 sheds some light on this:

Listing 6-1. How time changes an execution plan, part 1

```
SET LINES 2000 PAGES 0

CREATE TABLE t3
(
   c1
  ,c2
  ,c3
)
```

```
PCTFREE 99
PCTUSED 1
AS
        SELECT ROWNUM, DATE '2012-04-01' + MOD (ROWNUM, 2), RPAD ('X', 2000) c3
          FROM DUAL
    CONNECT BY LEVEL <= 1000;

CREATE INDEX t3_i1
   ON t3 (c2);

EXPLAIN PLAN
   FOR
       SELECT *
         FROM t3
         WHERE t3.c2 = TO_DATE ( :b1, 'DD-MON-YYYY');

SELECT * FROM TABLE (DBMS_XPLAN.display);

VARIABLE b1 VARCHAR2(11)
EXEC :b1 := '01-APR-2012';

BEGIN
   FOR r IN (SELECT *
                FROM t3
                WHERE t3.c2 = TO_DATE ( :b1, 'DD-MON-YYYY'))
   LOOP
      NULL;
   END LOOP;
END;
/

SELECT * FROM TABLE (DBMS_XPLAN.display_cursor (sql_id => 'dgcvn46zatdqr'));
```

Listing 6-1 begins by creating table T3 that includes a column of type DATE. Table T3 is populated with dates from April 2012 and in 12cR1 onwards statistics will be implicitly gathered for both the table and the index. We then use DBMS_XPLAN.DISPLAY to see the results of an EXPLAIN PLAN statement and DBMS_XPLAN.DISPLAY_CURSOR to see the actual execution plan used at runtime. Listing 6-2 shows the results of the experiment.

Listing 6-2. How time changes an execution plan, part 2

```
Plan hash value: 4161002650

-----------------------------------------------------------------------
| Id | Operation          | Name | Rows | Bytes | Cost (%CPU)| Time     |
-----------------------------------------------------------------------
|  0 | SELECT STATEMENT   |      |      |       | 272 (100)|           |
|* 1 |  TABLE ACCESS FULL | T3   |  500 |  982K |  272   (0)| 00:00:01 |
-----------------------------------------------------------------------
```

```
Predicate Information (identified by operation id):
---------------------------------------------------

   1 - filter("T3"."C2"=TO_DATE(:B1,'DD-MON-YYYY'))

SQL_ID  dgcvn46zatdqr, child number 0
-------------------------------------
SELECT * FROM T3 WHERE T3.C2 = TO_DATE ( :B1, 'DD-MON-YYYY')

Plan hash value: 4161002650

---------------------------------------------------------------------------
| Id  | Operation         | Name | Rows  | Bytes | Cost (%CPU)| Time     |
---------------------------------------------------------------------------
|   0 | SELECT STATEMENT  |      |       |       |   272 (100)|          |
|*  1 |   TABLE ACCESS FULL| T3  |   500 |  982K |   272   (0)| 00:00:01 |
---------------------------------------------------------------------------

Predicate Information (identified by operation id):
---------------------------------------------------

   1 - filter("T3"."C2"=TO_DATE(:B1,'DD-MON-YYYY'))
```

The output of the two DBMS_XPLAN calls both show precisely the same execution plan. That is good. Now let us assume some time passes. Listing 6-3 is my attempt to simulate the passage of time from April 2012 until April 2014.

Listing 6-3. How time changes an execution plan, part 3

```
ALTER SYSTEM FLUSH SHARED_POOL;

DELETE FROM t3;

INSERT INTO t3 (c1, c2,c3)
        SELECT ROWNUM, DATE '2014-04-01' + MOD (ROWNUM, 2),rpad('X',2000)
          FROM DUAL
   CONNECT BY LEVEL <= 1000;

EXPLAIN PLAN
   FOR
      SELECT *
        FROM t3
        WHERE t3.c2 = TO_DATE ( :b1, 'DD-MON-YYYY');

SELECT * FROM TABLE (DBMS_XPLAN.display);

VARIABLE b1 VARCHAR2(11)
EXEC :b1 := '01-APR-2014';

BEGIN
   FOR r IN (SELECT *
               FROM t3
               WHERE t3.c2 = TO_DATE ( :b1, 'DD-MON-YYYY'))
```

```
    LOOP
        NULL;
    END LOOP;
END;
/

SELECT * FROM TABLE (DBMS_XPLAN.display_cursor (sql_id => 'dgcvn46zatdqr'));
```

What I have done here is to:

- Flush the shared pool to simulate the aging of the statement from the cursor cache

- Although not required, replace the data in the table with data from April 2014

- Re-execute the EXPLAIN PLAN statement

- Re-execute the DBMS_XPLAN.DISPLAY call

- Re-execute the statement, retrieving data from April 2014

- Re-execute the DBMS_XPLAN.DISPLAY_CURSOR statement

Listing 6-4 shows the results of this second experiment.

Listing 6-4. How time changes an execution plan, part 4

```
Plan hash value: 4161002650
```

Id	Operation	Name	Rows	Bytes	Cost (%CPU)	Time
0	SELECT STATEMENT		500	982K	272 (0)	00:00:01
* 1	TABLE ACCESS FULL	T3	500	982K	272 (0)	00:00:01

```
Predicate Information (identified by operation id):
---------------------------------------------------

   1 - filter("T3"."C2"=TO_DATE(:B1,'DD-MON-YYYY'))

SQL_ID  dgcvn46zatdqr, child number 0
-------------------------------------
SELECT * FROM T3 WHERE T3.C2 = TO_DATE ( :B1, 'DD-MON-YYYY')

Plan hash value: 3225921897
```

Id	Operation	Name	Rows	Bytes	Cost (%CPU)	Time
0	SELECT STATEMENT				2 (100)	
1	TABLE ACCESS BY INDEX ROWID BATCHED	T3	1	2013	2 (0)	00:00:01
* 2	INDEX RANGE SCAN	T3_I1	1		1 (0)	00:00:01

```
Predicate Information (identified by operation id):
---------------------------------------------------

   2 - access("T3"."C2"=TO_DATE(:B1,'DD-MON-YYYY'))
```

We can see that although the output of EXPLAIN PLAN is unchanged, the execution plan used at runtime has changed completely! April fool's! The reason the change in execution plan has occurred is because the object statistics, and in particular the column statistics for column T3.C2, include what I call *time-sensitive data*. The LOW_VALUE and HIGH_VALUE statistics record the minimum and maximum value of a column at the time statistics are gathered. When we execute our statement two years later, the CBO goes through the following metaphorical thought process: "If the maximum value of T3.C2 was April 30th 2012 the last time statistics were gathered, and the value specified for the bind variable B1 is now April 1st 2014, then the number of rows selected from T3 is almost certainly zero". What is the basis for this logic? The CBO assumes that we have specified a date in the future and that the statistics are current rather than the surely more likely case that the date is in the recent past and that the statistics are out of date. Let us see what happens when we re-gather statistics.

Listing 6-5. How time changes an execution plan, part 5

```
BEGIN
   DBMS_STATS.gather_table_stats (SYS_CONTEXT ('USERENV', 'CURRENT_SCHEMA')
                                 ,'T3'
                                 ,no_invalidate   => FALSE);
END;
/

BEGIN
   FOR r IN (SELECT *
               FROM t3
              WHERE t3.c2 = TO_DATE ( :b1, 'DD-MON-YYYY'))
   LOOP
      NULL;
   END LOOP;
END;
/

SELECT * FROM TABLE (DBMS_XPLAN.display_cursor (sql_id => 'dgcvn46zatdqr'));
SQL_ID  dgcvn46zatdqr, child number 0
-------------------------------------
SELECT * FROM T3 WHERE T3.C2 = TO_DATE ( :B1, 'DD-MON-YYYY')

Plan hash value: 3225921897
```

Id	Operation	Name	Rows	Bytes	Cost (%CPU)	Time
0	SELECT STATEMENT				1 (100)	
1	TABLE ACCESS BY INDEX ROWID BATCHED	T3	1	2013	1 (0)	00:00:01
* 2	INDEX RANGE SCAN	T3_I1	1		1 (0)	00:00:01

```
Predicate Information (identified by operation id):
---------------------------------------------------

   2 - access("T3"."C2"=TO_DATE(:B1,'DD-MON-YYYY'))
```

We can see that after we re-gather statistics, thereby updating the LOW_VALUE and HIGH_VALUE column statistics, the execution plan used at runtime for our statement suddenly reverts back to the original.

This experiment leads us to an astonishing conclusion. The following sentence is the single most important in this book.

The reason we gather statistics on a production system is to prevent execution plans from changing, not to ensure that execution plans do change.

Let us pause for a second and consider the enormous implications of this statement. It is now possible to see the flaw in Dave Ensor's paradox. Sometimes the "difference" that gathering statistics makes is to prevent an execution plan change that would otherwise have taken place! So the correct version of Dave Ensor's paradox should be:

The only time that it is safe to gather statistics is when to do so results in no execution plan changes from the last time the SQL statements ran.

It doesn't quite have the same ring to it does it? Our position now seems hopeless. On the one hand, if we don't gather statistics on our production system then sooner or later, as sure as eggs are eggs, execution plans will change and almost certainly for the worse. On the other hand, if we do gather statistics then we are playing a game of Russian Roulette; sooner or later some change in some table, column, or index statistic will result in an undesirable execution plan change that will create a service-impacting incident. What are we to do? We need to sort out one or two more things before addressing that question.

How Often Do We Need to Change Execution Plans?

The implicit assumption made by both Connor McDonald and Dave Ensor is that predictable performance comes from unchanged execution plans. Is that really true? If our database is growing and the sizes of the tables change don't we need, at some point, to change the execution plans of our statements? Wolfgang Breitling can help us answer that question.

Wolfgang Breitling's Tuning by Cardinality Feedback

In 2006 Wolfgang Breitling published a paper entitled "Tuning by Cardinality Feedback (TCF)." You can find his paper here: http://www.centrexcc.com/Tuning%20by%20Cardinality%20Feedback.pdf. This paper may well be the single biggest contribution to the science of Oracle SQL tuning to date.

■ **Note**   I should point out that the 11gR2 cardinality feedback feature that I mentioned earlier has absolutely nothing to do with Wolfgang's paper. However, I think that Wolfgang is quietly pleased that Oracle seems to have named a feature after his invention!

Briefly, Wolfgang's argument is as follows:

- If the CBO is able to correctly determine the cardinality of operations in an execution plan, then the CBO will come up with the optimal execution plan.

- When the CBO comes up with an execution plan that runs substantially slower than the best possible plan, it is because one or more cardinality estimates are out by *multiple orders of magnitude*; cardinality estimates that are out by a factor of two or three may result in the optimal execution plan being missed, but the selected plan will perform almost equivalently to the optimal plan.

- All we need to do to determine the optimal execution plan for a statement is to give the CBO the correct cardinality estimates, and the CBO will do the rest.

Whilst these statements aren't always true, they are true the majority of the time! Now, Wolfgang's paper was about SQL tuning so it may seem odd that I am bringing it up in a chapter that is dedicated to object statistics and deployment. The reason I have done so is because of the TCF corollary.

The TCF Corollary

Let us assume that an operation in an execution plan actually returns 10,000 rows. What TCF says is that if the CBO estimate is 5,000 or 20,000 then there is no need to worry; the plan selected by the CBO will be reasonable. It is only when the CBO estimate is lower than 100 or higher than 1,000,000 that the CBO is likely to come up with a plan that performs really badly.

The corollary to this statement is that if a table doubles or triples in size then no execution plan change is needed. Suppose that statistics are gathered on our 10,000-row table, and the CBO comes up with a plan based on an accurate cardinality estimate of 10,000. Suppose now that the table grows to 20,000 rows. TCF says that when the CBO uses a plan based on the (now) incorrect cardinality estimate of 10,000 it will work fine! That is the theory. Theory doesn't always work in practice, but on this occasion I am happy to report that it does!

Let me be clear about something. Assume we have a SQL statement that joins, say, T1 and T2 and then aggregates the results. On the one hand, if T1 and T2 both double in size then the SQL statement will almost certainly run slower. On the other hand, it is unlikely that that the elapsed time increase can be avoided by changing the execution plan; whatever the original optimal execution plan was is still likely to be optimal, or close to it, after the size increase.

In the overwhelming majority of real-life cases database tables will not often grow (or shrink) by factors of 100 or 1,000; we can live with one set of execution plans for years on end with no execution-plan related performance issues whatsoever! The main exception to this principle is the deployment of an empty table to production that grows rapidly, such as the AUDIT_TRAIL table that I mentioned in chapter 5. We'll deal with this exception a little later in the chapter once we have the main principles worked out.

Concurrent Execution Plans

We have now established that if an execution plan works well one day then it will likely work well the next, but can we always get away with just one execution plan at a time for each SQL statement? Let us look at a couple of cases that seem to suggest that we can't.

Skewed Data and Histograms

There are many database tables that contain skewed data. By that I mean that a limited number of values within a column occur very frequently while others occur much less frequently. Suppose that your company does 60% of its business with a company called AJAX and the other 40% of its business with 100 other customers including ACME.

A query that selects all transactions for AJAX from a table might well be best suited to a full table scan. On the other hand, a query that selects all transactions for ACME might be better off using an index, as only about 0.4% of the transactions will be selected. To enable the CBO to distinguish the AJAX customer from all others, a *histogram* can be used.

The main point to realize here is that bind variables and histograms should be considered mutually exclusive. If you parse a statement using one value for a bind variable, such as AJAX in my example, then that execution plan may be used when other values of the bind variable, such as ACME, are used. To prevent this, you should ensure that you have different SQL_IDs for each execution plan that you need. Listing 6-6 show how this might be done:

Listing 6-6. Using multiple SQL_IDs to allow for multiple execution plans

```
CREATE OR REPLACE PROCEDURE listing_6_6 (p_cust_last_name VARCHAR2)
IS
   cnt    NUMBER;
BEGIN
   IF p_cust_last_name = 'AJAX'
   THEN
      SELECT COUNT (*)
        INTO cnt
        FROM sh.sales s JOIN sh.customers c USING (cust_id)
       WHERE c.cust_last_name = 'AJAX'; -- One plan for AJAX
   ELSE
      SELECT COUNT (*)
        INTO cnt
        FROM sh.sales s JOIN sh.customers c USING (cust_id)
       WHERE c.cust_last_name = p_cust_last_name; -- Another for everybody else
   END IF;
END listing_6_6;
/
```

The above procedure doesn't do anything useful, but rather shows the correct way to code with histograms. The two SQL statements in the PL/SQL procedure will have different SQL_IDs and, therefore, two different execution plans may simultaneously be kept in the cursor cache.

In 11gR1 Oracle introduced Adaptive Cursor Sharing, which allows two or more execution plans to be kept in the cursor cache with the same SQL_ID. This might suggest to you that the complexity shown in Listing 6-6 is no longer needed. The problem with Adaptive Cursor Sharing is that a SQL statement has to perform badly at least once before an alternative execution plan is considered. If you want high-performing SQL each and every time then you still need to use separate SQL statements with separate SQL_IDs.

Workload Variations

There is one other case that I have come across where multiple execution plans were apparently needed for the same SQL statement. Let me explain this extraordinarily rare scenario.

I was working with an ETL process that loaded data from a table R1 in a remote database into a global temporary table TEMP1. An INSERT statement was then used to join TEMP1 with a permanent table T1 and then load the joined data into T2. The ETL process had two operating modes, and this is where things got interesting.

The normal operating mode of the ETL process was referred to as INCREMENTAL. Only the changed data from R1 was loaded into TEMP1. The INCREMENTAL load ran once every 15 minutes and the number of rows loaded into TEMP1 ranged from zero to a few dozen. The second operating mode was FULL. A FULL load was only done under exceptional conditions and involved loading *all* rows from R1 into TEMP1. A FULL load added millions of rows to TEMP1, but the same INSERT statement was used for both INCREMENTAL and FULL loads to insert data into T2.

There were two possible execution plans the CBO might pick depending on the statistics set for TEMP1 or the outcome of dynamic sampling. The first plan involved a NESTED LOOPS join driven by TEMP1 and this worked fine for the INCREMENTAL load. Unfortunately, when the NESTED LOOPS plan was used with a FULL load the ETL process took about two days! The alternative execution plan was to use a HASH JOIN. When a FULL load was done with this plan it finished in a couple of hours, which was more than satisfactory given the infrequent use. Unfortunately, when the HASH JOIN was used for the INCREMENTAL load the process took about one hour, quite unsuitable for a process that was designed to run every 15 minutes!

Now, as you can imagine, a FULL load and an INCREMENTAL load never ran at the same time, but they did occasionally run within a few minutes of each other and so we occasionally observed the same execution plan being used for different modes. We might have used some combination of shared pool flushing, dynamic sampling, and statistics manipulation to solve this problem, but relying on operational staff to follow documentation is a risk that should be avoided when possible. Listing 6-7 gives you an indication of what we did in practice.

Listing 6-7. Using hints to create multiple SQL_IDs

```
CREATE OR REPLACE PROCEDURE listing_6_7 (load_mode VARCHAR2)
IS
BEGIN
   IF load_mode = 'INCREMENTAL'
   THEN
      INSERT INTO t3 (c1, c2)
         SELECT /*+ leading(temp1) use_nl(t3) */
               temp1.c3, t3.c2
           FROM temp1, t3
          WHERE temp1.c1 = t3.c1;
   ELSE -- FULL
      INSERT INTO t3 (c1, c2)
         SELECT /*+ leading(t3) use_hash(temp1) no_swap_join_inputs(temp1) */
               temp1.c3, t3.c2
           FROM temp1, t3
          WHERE temp1.c1 = t3.c1;
   END IF;
END listing_6_7;
/
```

As you can see from the highlighted sections of the code, we used optimizer hints. Don't worry about the specifics of the hints just now. The key point at this stage is that the hints served three purposes:

- Because the SQL_IDs of the two statements are now different, an execution plan in the cursor cache from a FULL load would not be used for an INCREMENTAL load or vice-versa.

- The hints instructed the CBO which execution plan to use. By the time we had worked out the rest of the details of the problem we knew what plans were needed in each case, so we didn't need to risk the possibility that the CBO would get things wrong.

- The hints provided useful documentation so that those that followed had some kind of a clue as to why such obscure logic was used. A few paragraphs of explanatory comments were also added to the code, of course.

I have worked with a significant number of applications based on Oracle technology over the last several years, each of which probably has several tens of thousands of SQL statements. In all that time I have come across exactly one SQL statement that needed this sort of treatment! It is, however, a very nice educational scenario.

Concurrent Execution Plans Wrap Up

There do seem to be some exceptional cases where different execution plans are needed for the same SQL statement to take care of variations in the data being accessed. Fortunately or unfortunately, the only way we can ensure that different execution plans are used in different scenarios is to recode our application so that different SQL statements with different SQL_IDs are used for each scenario. The good news is that once this reality is accepted we have a self-fulfilling prophecy upon which we can base our strategy: We need just one execution plan for each SQL statement!

Oracle's Plan Stability Features

Although the CBO strategy is all about adaptability, Oracle, like any other company, has to do something to address the demands of its largest and most vocal customers. Here are the tactical plan stability measures that Oracle has taken to address customer concerns about predictability.

Stored Outlines

The first response to the customer demand for stable execution plans came in release 8i with the introduction of stored outlines. Loosely speaking, stored outlines involve a repository of execution plans, one for each SQL statement. The repository is held in tables in the OUTLN schema. Stored outlines have a number of drawbacks, but the two key ones are:

- There is no way to determine which stored outlines are no longer required because they refer to SQL statements that have changed or been deleted.

- Even more fatally, there is no way to determine which statements in your application are lacking stored outlines.

SQL Profiles

SQL profiles appeared in 10g and are intimately linked to the SQL Tuning Advisor. Although the example I gave in Listing 5-7 involved the creation of a new index, most SQL Tuning Advisor recommendations relate to cardinality errors and simply involve a different execution plan. To arrange for the new execution plan to be used you are required to "accept" the SQL profile that the SQL Tuning Advisor creates for you. Since the SQL profile overrides the execution plan that the CBO otherwise would have used, most of us initially assumed that SQL profiles were some sort of plan stability offering. They aren't! Even after you have accepted a SQL profile, the next time you gather statistics the original, poorly performing plan may reappear! You might even get a third plan with unknown performance.

SQL profiles are actually an attempt to improve the CBO's guesses. They are not an attempt to remove the guesswork. SQL profiles aren't part of the CBO strategic direction and they don't provide plan stability. SQL profiles fall between two stools, and the CBO team has assured us that SQL profiles won't see a great deal of investment in the future.

SQL Plan Baselines

SQL plan baselines appeared in 11gR1 in a wave of confusion. Very simply put, SQL plan baselines are a direct replacement for stored outlines. One noticeable improvement, at least from a security point of view, is that the repository of execution plans is now held in the data dictionary rather than in a schema with a password that might be compromised.

SQL plan baselines are reasonably easy to use and many customers are using them successfully. However, they suffer the same major drawbacks as stored outlines in that you cannot reconcile the repository of execution plans with the statements in your application. In most other important respects SQL plan baselines have the same advantages and disadvantages as stored outlines.

The confusion arose with respect to licensing. Almost up to the point of release SQL plan baselines were going to be a chargeable feature. In fact many students of the Oracle University who attended an 11g new features course, including me, were told, incorrectly, that SQL plan baselines required the Tuning Pack. In fact, the only part of the SQL plan baselines feature that requires a license is something called *plan evolvement*, a feature that allows execution plans to change! Even then the license is only required when plan evolvement is performed by the SQL Tuning Advisor. So we get the stuff we want for free (the stability part) and have to pay for the stuff we don't want (the adaptability part). It is no wonder that Oracle staff were internally confused about all of this!

Introducing TSTATS

TSTATS is a deployment methodology for managing performance that allows us to take full advantage of the best aspects of the CBO while preventing it from changing execution plans on a whim. No repository of execution plans is involved, so there are no reconciliation issues, and no use of hidden initialization parameters or other unsupported features is involved.

Acknowledgements

The name TSTATS stands for "Tony's Statistics," a name invented by my client to refer to the methodology that I was successfully persuading them to adopt. Although the name appeals to my sense of vanity, it would be wrong of me to suggest that TSTATS is entirely my invention. In the preface I give some details of the history of TSTATS and give credit to both Jonathan Lewis and Wolfgang Breitling. However, the biggest contribution is from Adrian Billington, whose ideas for deleting time-based data from object statistics are at the core of TSTATS. Let us get to that now.

Adjusting Column Statistics

If the CBO's lack of predictability is based on time-sensitive data, in other words statistics that are only valid for a limited period of time, then why don't we just delete those statistics? It turns out that although there are a couple of reasons why deleting time-sensitive data from your object statistics might not be a good idea, and we will discuss these in Chapter 20, most of the time we can do so with impunity. You can't update column statistics to remove the LOW_VALUE and HIGH_VALUE statistics and for reasons that I cannot fathom this created a mental block with me for several years. The solution to this problem, obvious in retrospect, is to delete the column statistics and re-insert them with the time-sensitive bits removed! Listing 6-8 shows how to do this.

Listing 6-8. Updating column statistics with DBMS_STATS

```
DECLARE
    distcnt    NUMBER;
    density    NUMBER;
    nullcnt    NUMBER;
    srec       DBMS_STATS.statrec;
    avgclen    NUMBER;
BEGIN
    DBMS_STATS.get_column_stats (
       ownname    => SYS_CONTEXT ('USERENV', 'CURRENT_SCHEMA')
      ,tabname    => 'T3'
      ,colname    => 'C2'
```

```
      ,distcnt    => distcnt
      ,density    => density
      ,nullcnt    => nullcnt
      ,srec       => srec
      ,avgclen    => avgclen);

   DBMS_STATS.delete_column_stats (
       ownname    => SYS_CONTEXT ('USERENV', 'CURRENT_SCHEMA')
      ,tabname    => 'T3'
      ,colname    => 'C2');

   DBMS_STATS.set_column_stats (
       ownname    => SYS_CONTEXT ('USERENV', 'CURRENT_SCHEMA')
      ,tabname    => 'T3'
      ,colname    => 'C2'
      ,distcnt    => distcnt
      ,density    => density
      ,nullcnt    => nullcnt
      ,srec       => NULL
      ,avgclen    => avgclen);
END;
/
```

Listing 6-8 manipulates T3.C2 and the key point is the highlighted line. The SREC structure holds the data that is destined for the LOW_VALUE and HIGH_VALUE statistics, and this structure is omitted when the statistics are reinserted.

Once these changes have been made and the shared pool flushed, the example statement used in Listings 6-1 through 6-5 will use a full table scan no matter what date you give! In addition, the cost and cardinality calculations will be the same after the deletion of the time-sensitive statistics as they were for contemporary dates before the deletion.

TSTATS in a Nutshell

The removal of time-sensitive data from object statistics is the main idea behind TSTATS. Here is the essence of a process that can be used on the back of that idea:

1. Gather statistics on a selected "master" test system.

2. Fabricate statistics for all global temporary tables.

3. Remove time-sensitive data from object statistics.

4. Perform initial performance testing on the master test system and make adjustments as necessary.

5. Copy the statistics to all other test systems and ultimately to production.

6. Lock the object statistics of your application schemas on all systems.

7. Drop all statistics-gathering jobs for application schemas on all your systems.

8. TSTATS only applies to application schemas, so any jobs that gather dictionary statistics are unaffected.

By following these steps and taking a few other precautions, you can ensure that the execution plans on all your test systems match those of your production systems and that the same SQL statement will have the same execution plan forever, or at least until you decide otherwise!

Does this approach seem familiar? It should; it is the standard approach for deploying software, DML, and configuration changes. Whatever change-control procedures you have in place for software and DML should be applied to object statistics. Typically you would deliver software, DML, and object statistics at the same time as parts of a release.

An Alternative to TSTATS

Stabilizing your application performance by the use of the TSTATS methodology is not straightforward, and some investment of time and effort is required. As you will see in chapter 20 there may be ways to simplify TSTATS to address specific point issues so that you can get a resolution to your key stability issues quickly and easily. Even so, if you are managing an estate of hundreds of databases then adopting any variant of TSTATS as a standard will probably be impractical. That situation will change only in the unlikely event that the CBO team delivers some changes that make a TSTATS-like approach more straightforward.

In 2012 the Real World Performance team from Oracle did a round-the-world tour to try to dispel some myths about Oracle performance and to educate people about performance management. I attended the Edinburgh seminar and found it very stimulating. One of the most interesting suggestions came from Graham Wood. Graham's observation was that many of Oracle's customers gather statistics far too frequently. I want to make it clear that Graham did not say that gathering statistics was only required to prevent execution plan changes, and he most definitely didn't liken gathering statistics to a game of Russian Roulette! However, Graham's recommendation does suggest, quite correctly, that there is some risk to gathering statistics and that by doing it less often you can reduce that risk considerably.

HOW OFTEN DO YOU NEED TO GATHER STATISTICS?

The CBO will reduce its cardinality estimates more slowly the wider the date range of data in your tables, and it is only when the cardinality estimates reduce to very low numbers that execution plans are likely to change. So if you hold a month's worth of data and collect statistics once per week you should be OK. If you hold one year's worth of data then you shouldn't have to gather statistics more than once every three months!

Deployment Options for Tuned SQL

In Chapter 5 I described a systematic process for tuning a SQL statement that involved running a series of experiments. I made it clear that the experimental change and the production deployment change might be different, and it is the process for identifying the latter that I want to talk about now. The considerations involved are the same whether you are using traditional object statistics management techniques or some variant of TSTATS; the primary consideration is whether you want your production change to affect other statements as well.

When Just One SQL Statement Needs to Change

There are several reasons why you might want your production change to be restricted to one specific SQL statement. It may be that your performance problem relates to a construct that is only found in one place and you know that no other SQL statements need to be fixed. You may even suspect that other SQL statements might be suffering from the same issue but these statements are not critical and the time and effort to test the impact of a change cannot be justified. Finally, you might have discovered an issue that affects a number of critical SQL statements but you need to deploy the fix to just one SQL statement now with the fix for other statements being deferred to the next release.

Whatever the reason for deciding to restrict your changes to one SQL statement, that decision is key to determining your deployment strategy.

Transforming SQL Code

This is an easy one. If the successful optimization experiment involved rewriting the SQL statement in some way, then most of the time making that same code change in production is only going to affect that one SQL statement. Since that is the desired effect in this case you can just deploy the experimental code change to production.

To limit the scope of your change you should be reluctant to alter a view definition. It would be better to either create a new view or use a factored subquery instead.

Adding Hints to the SQL Code

If your successful optimization experiment involved adding hints to your SQL statement and you want a deployment option that restricts change to that one SQL statement then you should have no hesitation in deploying hints to production. This recommendation may surprise you, as there is a lot of material in books, conference papers, and blogs that suggests that you should be very reluctant to deploy hints in production code. I disagree strongly with such sentiments and I will return to this topic with a lengthier discussion in Chapter 18.

Just because you used one set of hints to get the desired execution plan does not mean that you should use the same set of hints for production use. For example, you may have taken Wolfgang Breitling's Tuning by Cardinality Feedback message to heart and applied one or more CARDINALITY hints to your code to correct some CBO cardinality errors. If you aren't using TSTATS then these hints will not reliably prevent execution plan changes when statistics are next gathered. It would be best to identify what changes resulted from the CARDINALITY hints and then use other hints to specify the access methods, join orders, and so on directly. In Chapter 8 I will show you how to determine what these hints are, and we will be discussing the meaning of most of them in Part 3.

Physical Database Changes

You should be very careful about making physical database changes just to make one SQL statement run faster. I already explained in the last chapter that adding an index results in extra overhead for all DML. Furthermore, when you add an index or make some other physical database change you can't be sure of the impact on the execution plans of other SQL statements. You should consider making physical database changes to optimize one SQL statement only as a last resort.

When Multiple SQL Statements Need to Change

When you are in the early stages of a major release and still have a lot of test cycles ahead of you might want to make changes that affect a number of SQL statements. The changes you make might even result in sweeping performance improvements across your application.

I was recently tasked with taking a six-hour overnight batch and reducing the elapsed time to two hours. The batch involved hundreds, possibly thousands, of statements and tuning even the top 10% one by one would have been a hopeless task. Even in situations like these I begin by looking at the longest running SQL statement first. But once I understand the issue with that statement I try to find ways of fixing it that might benefit other statements as well. This is often possible when the performance problem is associated with a common construct.

Remember that if you make a change that improves the performance of one hundred statements and causes the performance of two other statements to degrade you can always hint the two that have degraded!

Transforming SQL Code and Adding Hints

I have already said that altering a view definition is a bad idea when you are trying to limit the scope of a change. The corollary is that altering a view definition is a good idea when sweeping changes are needed.

With this exception, changing a single SQL statement, and that includes hinting, is not likely to make a massive difference to the application as a whole unless this particular statement runs very often or very long.

Physical Database Changes

Physical database changes have a huge potential for improving the performance of an application as a whole, and it is the application as a whole that needs to be considered when making such changes. It is not uncommon to discover that an application is performing poorly because of the huge number of indexes that have been added over the years in order to solve point issues with individual queries. Perhaps the way to improve the performance of your application is to drop a number of those indexes! Adding an index is not the only way to address a long-running full table scan, and we shall discuss many of these in Chapter 15.

Altering Statistics

I have made a big fuss about the fact that when object statistics change execution plans might change. In the context of a production system execution plan changes are bad things, but in the context of tuning an entire application on a test system such changes are potentially very good things.

If your successful optimization experiment involved adding hints to your SQL statement and you suspect that a number of other SQL statements are going to be similarly affected, you should try to find a different solution that will fix the issue everywhere. Altering statistics can help.

Extended Statistics

As Wolfgang Breitling's TCF paper explains, one of the most common reasons that the CBO comes up with a poor execution plan is that it has come up with a poor cardinality estimate. And one of the main reasons that the CBO comes up with a poor cardinality estimate is because it is unaware of the correlation between two columns. So if you provide the CBO with the correlation information then you might help the performance of multiple SQL statements.

Imagine that you have a table T1 with 40,000 rows. T1 has two columns C1 and C2. There are 20 different values of C1, 2,000 rows for each value. There are also 20 different values of C2, 2,000 rows for each value. The CBO might need to know how many rows will match a specific value of C1 and also a specific value of C2. The CBO knows that there are 400 possible combinations of C1 and C2, and will normally assume that each of these 400 possible combinations is equally likely. So the CBO will divide 40,000 by 400 to get a cardinality estimate of 100.

Now suppose that the real name of T1 is ORDERS and that the real names of C1 and C2 are ORDER_DATE and a DELIVERY_DATE respectively. The values of ORDER_DATE vary from 1st March to 20th March and the delivery dates vary from 2nd March to 21st March. You run a tight ship and every single DELIVERY_DATE is the day after ORDER_DATE! This means that in reality there are only 20 combinations of ORDER_DATE and DELIVERY_DATE in the table—2,000 rows for each combination. The ORDER_DATE and the DELIVERY_DATE are correlated.

Issues like these are addressed by the use of *extended statistics,* and I will make a detailed walkthrough of extended statistics in chapter 9. By creating extended statistics rather than hinting you might improve the performance of other SQL statements that use the same combination of columns.

Hand-crafted Histograms

Another reason that the CBO comes up with bad cardinality estimates is *data skew*. I introduced the concept of data skew a little earlier in this chapter: it is a situation where a small number of column values occur more frequently than others. Although the normal TSTATS approach to column statistics is to remove all information about specific values, this isn't the correct approach for columns requiring histograms. Histograms are a perfectly reasonable thing to deploy as long as the application doesn't use bind variables for values of the column that has data skew.

In my experience the number of columns in a fully normalized schema that require histograms is very low. Of course in real-life some level of denormalization is common and particular columns requiring a histogram will be replicated across multiple tables. In these cases the replicated columns will usually have the same column name, be easy to identify, and require identical histograms. Whether you are using TSTATS or not, my recommendation would always be to analyze your data and manually set such histograms. We will cover this is detail in Chapter 20. At this point, however, the key message is, as always, that statistic changes can be used to improve the performance of multiple SQL statements at once.

Generating False Object Statistics

The use of extended statistics and histograms are features that Oracle employees frequently discuss and encourage you to use. However, there is far less talk about explicitly setting or overriding other types of statistics with particular values. I would presume that the lack of discussion is because setting statistics to specific values requires a considerably higher level of knowledge and expertise than setting up either extended statistics or histograms.

What I want to emphasize at this point is that setting statistics to particular values is fully supported, and the techniques for doing so are documented with the DBMS_STATS package. There are a few special cases that require setting object statistics to values that do not reflect reality, and we will discuss these in Chapter 20.

■ **Note** The reason object statistics exist is to help the CBO arrive at correct decisions. If accurate statistics result in bad CBO decisions and inaccurate statistics result in good decisions you want to deploy inaccurate statistics.

As with any statistics manipulation you should consider the impact of your change on other SQL statements. Typically knowledge of what types of query prevail in your application and what types rarely if ever occur is critical to determining whether falsifying object statistics will be beneficial or not.

Changing PL/SQL Code and Altering the Environment

I have often seen SQL statements that perform poorly because of repeated function calls that involve recursive SQL. One way to improve matters is to recode the logic that calls the SQL statement so that the function is called once. When calls to a particular function, or set of functions, are known to be called repeatedly by large numbers of SQL statements in an application, it might be cost effective to make those functions DETERMINISTIC or to use the function cache that I described in Chapter 1.

If a sort spills to disk, you might parallelize the query. But if you suspect other sorts may spill to disk as well, you might consider increasing PGA_AGGREGATE_TARGET to help improve those other queries as well. You should consider other environmental changes in the same light.

Summary

This chapter has introduced a deployment methodology known as TSTATS that addresses the requirement for execution plan stability in a production environment without the need for a repository of execution plans. The methodology is complex to set up and will be discussed in detail in chapter 20 of this book, but alternative approaches are needed. You might use a simplified form of TSTATS, but for the bulk of well-behaving applications you should probably just keep the number of times object statistics are gathered to a minimum.

Together with physical database design, object statistics are an important consideration when deploying optimized SQL. In the early stages of a release, adjusting statistics is a great way to improve the performance of multiple parts of an application at once. However, at later stages of the testing lifecycle when the goal is to localize the impact of change, changes to object statistics should be minimized, and a sensible alternative is to add hints to your SQL statements.

PART 2

Advanced Concepts

CHAPTER 7

Advanced SQL Concepts

In this chapter we return to the vagaries of the SQL language to investigate three more of the key concepts that can get you both into a performance jam and out of one.

- The first thing I want to look at is the syntax of query blocks and subqueries. The focus of the discussion is the difference between the way that the CBO treats the two constructs and the way that the SQL Language Reference manual does—a critical issue when we come to analyze execution plans in depth, as we will do in the next chapter.

- The second topic of the chapter is the different types of SQL function. Analytic functions in particular can be really helpful when used correctly and really harmful to performance when used incorrectly.

- The third and final topic in this chapter is the MODEL clause. Many people will go through their whole careers without ever needing to learn what the MODEL clause is or what it does. However, if you, like me, find yourself in desperate need of the MODEL clause you need to recognize when to dive for the Data Warehousing Guide!

Query Blocks and Subqueries

For the Oracle performance specialist the concept of a query block is very important as it is a fundamental processing unit for the CBO and the runtime engine. However, before we can discuss how query blocks work we need to clear up some terminology.

Terminology

The formal definition of a query block in the SQL Language Reference manual is quite complex, but, informally, a query block can be explained quite straightforwardly as "stuff that follows the keyword SELECT.". The same manual defines a subquery, for which there are four possible constructs:

- A query block
- A query block followed by an ORDER BY clause
- A number of query blocks connected by *set operators*
- A number of query blocks connected by set operators followed by an ORDER BY clause

The set operators are UNION, UNION ALL, INTERSECT, and MINUS.

■ **Note**   I have explained the concept of a subquery a little differently than the SQL Language Reference manual did to emphasize that it is illegal for the operands of a set operator to include an ORDER BY clause.

It turns out that the CBO seems to treat all subqueries as query blocks. It does so as follows:

- A subquery involving set operators is considered as a special type of query block that I will refer to as a *set query block.*

- An ORDER BY clause is considered part of the query block that it follows.

From now on when I use of the term "query block" in this book the CBO's interpretation should be assumed; when I use the term "subquery" I will mean it in the normal informal way, namely a query block other than the main query block in a SELECT statement.

How Query Blocks are Processed

Following the SELECT keyword, a query block is written in the following order:

- The optional DISTINCT or UNIQUE operation

- The select list

- Everything else except the ORDER BY clause

- The optional ORDER BY clause

The logical order in which a query block is executed, however, is different:

- Everything else

- The select list

- The optional DISTINCT or UNIQUE operation

- The optional ORDER BY clause

The good news is that with very few exceptions the order in which the various bits and bobs that I have loosely referred to as "everything else" are logically processed in the order in which they appear. In particular, the following clauses, some of which are optional, are written in the same order as they are logically processed:

- The FROM clause

- The WHERE clause

- The GROUP BY clause

- The HAVING clause

- The MODEL clause

Of course, the CBO is free to change the order in which it asks the runtime engine to do things as long as the resulting set of rows is the same as the logical order.

Functions

If your application has been built so that most of your business logic has been implemented outside of the database then you may make very little use of functions in your SQL. However, most commercial and scientific SQL statements are riddled with function calls. The use and abuse of these function calls often results in a huge amount of processing, particularly sorting and aggregation; it is not uncommon for this overhead to dwarf the traditional database overhead of accessing and joining tables. So in this section I want to make sure we all have a clear understanding of how the main function categories work.

The SQL Language Reference manual defines the following function categories:

- Single-row functions

- Aggregate functions

- Analytic functions

- Object reference functions

- Model functions

- OLAP functions

- Data cartridge functions

This section focusses on single-row functions, aggregate functions, and analytic functions. Let us start with aggregate functions.

■ **Note** Throughout this section I will be using built-in functions for my examples, but it is important to understand that you can write your own scalar, aggregate, or analytic functions and the same principles that I am about to discuss will apply.

Aggregate Functions

Some of the readers of this book will feel fairly fluent with aggregate functions, but I think it is important to review the concepts formally so that there is no confusion when we come to looking at analytic functions and the MODEL clause shortly.

The Concept of Aggregation

Simply put, aggregation involves taking a set of items, producing a single value, *and then discarding the input.* Listing 7-1 shows the two different ways that aggregation can be triggered.

Listing 7-1. The use of GROUP BY and analytic functions to trigger aggregation

```
CREATE TABLE t1
AS
        SELECT DATE '2013-12-31' + ROWNUM transaction_date
              ,MOD (ROWNUM, 4) + 1 channel_id
              ,MOD (ROWNUM, 5) + 1 cust_id
              ,DECODE (ROWNUM
                     ,1, 4
                     ,ROWNUM * ROWNUM + DECODE (MOD (ROWNUM, 7), 3, 3000, 0))
                  sales_amount
          FROM DUAL
   CONNECT BY LEVEL <= 100;

-- No Aggregation in next query

SELECT * FROM t1;

--Exactly one row returned in next query

SELECT COUNT (*) cnt FROM t1;

-- 0 or more rows returned in next query

  SELECT channel_id
    FROM t1
GROUP BY channel_id;

-- At most one row returned in next query

SELECT 1 non_empty_flag
  FROM t1
HAVING COUNT (*) > 0;

-- 0 or more rows returned in next query

  SELECT channel_id, COUNT (*) cnt
    FROM t1
GROUP BY channel_id
  HAVING COUNT (*) < 2;
```

Listing 7-1 includes create a table T1 and then issues several queries.

- The first query in Listing 7-1 contains no aggregate function and no GROUP BY clause so no aggregation occurs.

- The second query includes the COUNT (*) aggregate function. Since no GROUP BY clause is specified the whole table is aggregated and exactly one row is returned. To be clear, if T1 were empty the query would still return one row and the value of CNT would be 0.

- The third query includes a GROUP BY clause, and so even though no aggregate function appears in the statement, aggregation still takes place. A GROUP BY operator returns one row for every distinct value of the expressions specified in the GROUP BY clause. So in this case there would be one row for each distinct value of CHANNEL_ID, and when the table is empty no rows are returned.

- The fourth query in Listing 7-1 shows that an aggregate function doesn't need to be placed in the select list to trigger aggregation. The HAVING clause applies a filter *after* aggregation, unlike a WHERE clause that filters before aggregation. So in this case if T1 were empty the value of COUNT (*) would be 0 and the query would return 0 rows. If there are rows in the table the query would return one row.

- Of course, the most common way aggregation is used is with the GROUP BY clause and aggregate functions used together. The GROUP BY clause in the final query in Listing 7-1 ensures that only values of CHANNEL_ID that occur at least once in T1 are returned, so it is not possible for CNT to have a value of 0. The HAVING clause removes any rows where COUNT (*) >= 2, so if this final query returns any rows the value of CNT will be 1 in all cases!

Sorting Aggregating Functions

Many aggregate functions require a sort to operate effectively. Listing 7-2 shows how the MEDIAN aggregate function might be used.

Listing 7-2. Use of a sorting aggregate function

```
SELECT channel_id, MEDIAN (sales_amount) med, COUNT (*) cnt
    FROM t1
GROUP BY channel_id;


----------------------------
| Id  | Operation           |
----------------------------
|   0 | SELECT STATEMENT    |
|   1 |  SORT GROUP BY      |
|   2 |   TABLE ACCESS FULL |
----------------------------
```

■ **Note** The median of an odd number of numbers is the middle one in the sorted list. For an even number of values it is the average (mean) of the two middle numbers. So the median of 2, 4, 6, 8, 100 and 102 is 7 (the average of 6 and 8).

From Listing 7-2 on I will be showing the execution plans for SQL statements in the format produced by DBMS_XPLAN. DISPLAY without using the EXPLAIN PLAN statement and without showing explicit calls to the DBMS_XPLAN.DISPLAY function. Furthermore, I will only be showing the relevant portions of the execution plan. These measures are purely to save space. The downloadable materials are not abbreviated in this way.

Listing 7-2 aggregates the 100 rows in the table T1 we created in Listing 7-1 to return four rows, one for each distinct value of CHANNEL_ID. The value of MED in these rows represents the median of the 25 rows in each group. The basic execution plan for this statement is also shown in Listing 7-2, and operation 1 is the sort used to implement this.

■ **Note**   If the truth be known, there are actually six sorts performed in Listing 7-2! The first sort is by C1 to create the four groups. Then each group is sorted by SALES_AMOUNT as required by the MEDIAN function. If you examine the statistic "*sorts (rows)*" before and after the query in Listing 7-2 you will see that it increases by 200, twice the number in the table; each row is sorted twice. And if multiple aggregate functions with different sort orders are used, then each group may be sorted multiple times.

The code that you can use to examine the statistic is:

```
SELECT VALUE FROM v$mystat NATURAL JOIN v$statname WHERE name = 'sorts (rows)';
```

Non-sorting Aggregating Functions

Not all aggregate functions require a sort. I use the term "*non-sorting aggregate functions*" (NSAFs) to refer to aggregate functions that require no sort. An example of an NSAF is COUNT. COUNT doesn't need to sort: as each row is processed COUNT simply increments a running tally. Other NSAFs, like SUM, AVG, and STDDEV are also implemented by keeping running tallies of one form or another.

When an NSAF and a GROUP BY clause both appear in a query block then the NSAF needs to keep running tallies for each group. Oracle database 10g introduced a feature called *hash aggregation* that allows NSAFs to find the tallies for each group by a lookup in a hash table rather than a lookup from a sorted list. Let us have a look at Listing 7-3, which shows the feature in action.

Listing 7-3. Hash aggregation for NSAFs

```
    SELECT channel_id
          ,AVG (sales_amount)
          ,SUM (sales_amount)
          ,STDDEV (sales_amount)
          ,COUNT (*)
      FROM t1
GROUP BY channel_id;


-------------------------------------
| Id  | Operation          | Name |
-------------------------------------
|   0 | SELECT STATEMENT   |      |
|   1 |  HASH GROUP BY     |      |
|   2 |   TABLE ACCESS FULL| T1   |
-------------------------------------
```

Hash aggregation requires that *all* aggregate functions used in the query block are NSAFs; all of the functions in Listing 7-3 are NSAFs, so the operation HASH GROUP BY is used to avoid any sorting.

■ **Note**   Not all NSAFs can take advantage of hash aggregation. Those that can't include COLLECT, FIRST, LAST, RANK, SYS_XMLAGG, and XMLAGG. These functions use the SORT GROUP BY operation when a GROUP BY clause is used and the non-sorting SORT AGGREGATE operation when no GROUP BY clause is specified. This restriction is presumably due to the variable size of the aggregated values.

Just because the CBO can use hash aggregation doesn't mean that it will. Hash aggregation will not be used when the data being grouped is already sorted or needs to be sorted anyway. Listing 7-4 provides two examples.

Listing 7-4. SORT GROUP BY with NSAFs

```
  SELECT channel_id, AVG (sales_amount) mean
    FROM t1
   WHERE channel_id IS NOT NULL
GROUP BY channel_id
ORDER BY channel_id;

CREATE INDEX t1_i1
   ON t1 (channel_id);

  SELECT channel_id, AVG (sales_amount) mean
    FROM t1
   WHERE channel_id IS NOT NULL
GROUP BY channel_id;

DROP INDEX t1_i1;
```

```
-----------------------------------
| Id  | Operation          | Name |
-----------------------------------
|   0 | SELECT STATEMENT   |      |
|   1 |  SORT GROUP BY     |      |
|*  2 |   TABLE ACCESS FULL| T1   |
-----------------------------------
```

```
------------------------------------------------
| Id  | Operation                   | Name    |
------------------------------------------------
|   0 | SELECT STATEMENT            |         |
|   1 |  SORT GROUP BY NOSORT       |         |
|   2 |   TABLE ACCESS BY INDEX ROWID| T1     |
|*  3 |    INDEX FULL SCAN          | T1_I1   |
------------------------------------------------
```

The first query in Listing 7-4 includes an ORDER BY clause. In this case there is no getting around a sort so hash aggregation gains nothing.

■ **Note**   You might think that it would be more efficient to perform hash aggregation and then sort the aggregated rows. After all, if you have 1,000,000 rows and 10 groups wouldn't it be better to sort the 10 aggregated rows rather than the 1,000,000 un-aggregated ones? In fact, in such a case only 10 rows would be kept in the sort work area; the NSAFs would just keep their running tallies for each group as with hash aggregation.

Before executing the second query in Listing 7-4 we create an index on CHANNEL_ID. The index will return the data in sorted order anyway so we don't need either an explicit sort or a hash table, and the aggregation is processed for each group in turn. Notice that that the name for operation 1 is now self-contradictory: SORT GROUP BY NOSORT. Of course, no sort takes place.

Analytic Functions

Now that we fully understand what aggregate functions are and how they are processed, it is time to move on to the more complex concept of analytic functions. Analytic functions have the potential to make SQL statements easy to read and perform well. They can also make SQL impenetrable and slow when used incorrectly.

The Concept of Analytics

We said that aggregate functions discard the original rows being aggregated. What happens if that is not what we want? Do you remember Listing 3-1? That query listed each row in SCOTT.EMP together with aggregated data about that employee's department. We used a subquery to accomplish that. Listing 7-5 is another example of the same technique using the table T1 from Listing 7-1 and the COUNT function.

Listing 7-5. Use of subqueries to implement analytics

```
SELECT outer.*
      , (SELECT COUNT (*)
            FROM t1 inner
           WHERE inner.channel_id = outer.channel_id)
         med
  FROM t1 outer;
```

```
-----------------------------------
| Id  | Operation          | Name |
-----------------------------------
|   0 | SELECT STATEMENT   |      |
|   1 |  SORT GROUP BY     |      |
|*  2 |   TABLE ACCESS FULL| T1   |
|   3 |  TABLE ACCESS FULL | T1   |
-----------------------------------
```

The query in Listing 7-5 lists the 100 rows in T1 together with an extra column containing the matching count of rows for the corresponding value of CHANNEL_ID. The execution plan for the query seems to suggest that we will perform the subquery for each of the 100 rows in T1. However, as with Listing 3-1, scalar subquery caching will mean that we only perform the subquery four times, one for each distinct value of CHANNEL_ID. Nevertheless, when we add in operation 3 from the main query we will still perform five full table scans of T1 in the course of the query.

Subqueries can also be used to denote ordering. Listing 7-6 shows how we might add a row number and a rank to a sorted list.

Listing 7-6. Numbering output using ROWNUM and subqueries

```
WITH q1
    AS (  SELECT *
             FROM t1
         ORDER BY transaction_date)
  SELECT ROWNUM rn
       , (SELECT COUNT (*)+1
            FROM q1 inner
           WHERE inner.sales_amount < outer.sales_amount)
           rank_sales,outer.*
    FROM q1 outer
ORDER BY sales_amount;

-- First few rows of output
```

RN	RANK_SALES	TRANSACTI	CHANNEL_ID	CUST_ID	SALES_AMOUNT
1	1	01-JAN-14	2	2	4
2	1	02-JAN-14	3	3	4
4	3	04-JAN-14	1	5	16
5	4	05-JAN-14	2	1	25

Id	Operation	Name
0	SELECT STATEMENT	
1	SORT AGGREGATE	
* 2	VIEW	
3	TABLE ACCESS FULL	SYS_TEMP_0FD9D664B_479D89AC
4	TEMP TABLE TRANSFORMATION	
5	LOAD AS SELECT	SYS_TEMP_0FD9D664B_479D89AC
6	SORT ORDER BY	
7	TABLE ACCESS FULL	T1
8	SORT ORDER BY	
9	COUNT	
10	VIEW	
11	TABLE ACCESS FULL	SYS_TEMP_0FD9D664B_479D89AC

The factored subquery Q1 in Listing 7-6 orders the rows in the table, then we use the ROWNUM pseudocolumn to identify the position of each row in the sorted list. The column RANK_SALES differs slightly from RN in that rows with identical sales figures (such as the first two rows) are given equal position. The execution plan for this statement is far from straightforward. There must surely be an easier and more efficient way! Indeed there is; analytic functions offer solutions to many inefficient subqueries.

■ **Note**   All analytic functions have an equivalent formulation involving subqueries. Sometimes the analytic function performs better than the subquery, and sometimes the subquery performs better than the analytic function.

Aggregate Functions Used as Analytics

Most, but not all, aggregate functions can also be used as analytic functions. Listing 7-7 rewrites Listing 7-5, this time using COUNT as an analytic function rather than an aggregate function.

Listing 7-7. An aggregate function used as an analytic function

```
SELECT t1.*, COUNT (sales_amount) OVER (PARTITION BY channel_id) cnt FROM t1;
```

```
------------------------------------
| Id | Operation         | Name |
------------------------------------
|  0 | SELECT STATEMENT  |      |
|  1 |  WINDOW SORT      |      |
|  2 |   TABLE ACCESS FULL| T1  |
------------------------------------
```

The presence of the OVER clause in Listing 7-7 indicates that the MEDIAN function is being used as an analytic function rather than as an aggregate function. The query returns all 100 rows of T1, and the column CNT is added just as in Listing 7-5. Although the rows returned by Listing 7-5 and Listing 7-7 are the same, the way the queries execute are quite different, and the rows will likely be returned in a different order.

The execution plan shown in Listing 7-7 includes the WINDOW SORT operation that is specific to analytic functions. Unlike the SORT GROUP BY operation that may make several sorts, the WINDOW SORT operation performs just one sort of the rows it receives from its child. In the case of Listing 7-7 the rows are sorted by the composite key containing the columns CHANNEL_ID and SALES_AMOUNT, implicitly creating a group for each value of CHANNEL_ID. The COUNT function then processes each group in two phases:

- In the first phase, the group is processed to identify the COUNT for the group as with the aggregate variant of the COUNT function.

- In the second phase, each row from the group is output with the same calculated count being provided as an extra column on each row.

The term PARTITION BY is the analytic equivalent to the GROUP BY clause in aggregation; if the PARTITION BY keywords are omitted then the analytic function processes the entire result set.

Listing 7-8 shows a simple analytic that processes the entire result set.

Listing 7-8. Use of a NSAF in an analytic

```
SELECT t1.*, AVG (sales_amount) OVER () average_sales_amount FROM t1;
```

```
------------------------------------
| Id | Operation         | Name |
------------------------------------
|  0 | SELECT STATEMENT  |      |
|  1 |  WINDOW BUFFER    |      |
|  2 |   TABLE ACCESS FULL| T1  |
------------------------------------
```

The query in Listing 7-8 adds a column, AVERAGE_SALES_AMOUNT, that has the same value for all 100 rows in T1. That value is the average value of SALES_AMOUNT for the entire table. Notice that because AVG is an NSAF and there is no PARTITION BY clause there is no need to sort at all. As a consequence the WINDOW BUFFER operation is used instead of WINDOW SORT.

As with aggregation, when multiple functions are used multiple sorts may be needed. In the case of analytics, however, each sort has its own operation. Look at the difference in the execution plans for the two queries in Listing 7-9.

Listing 7-9. Comparison of multiple sorts with aggregation and analytics

```
SELECT MEDIAN (channel_id) med_channel_id
      ,MEDIAN (sales_amount) med_sales_amount
  FROM t1;
```

```
----------------------------------
| Id  | Operation          | Name |
----------------------------------
|   0 | SELECT STATEMENT   |      |
|   1 |  SORT GROUP BY     |      |
|   2 |   TABLE ACCESS FULL| T1   |
----------------------------------
```

```
SELECT t1.*
      ,MEDIAN (channel_id) OVER () med_channel_id
      ,MEDIAN (sales_amount) OVER () med_sales_amount
  FROM t1;
```

```
-----------------------------
| Id  | Operation           |
-----------------------------
|   0 | SELECT STATEMENT    |
|   1 |  WINDOW SORT        |
|   2 |   WINDOW SORT       |
|   3 |    TABLE ACCESS FULL|
-----------------------------
```

The first query in Listing 7-9 returns one row with the median values of CHANNEL_ID and SALES_AMOUNT. Each aggregate function call requires its own sort: the first a sort by CHANNEL_ID and the second a sort by SALES_AMOUNT. However, that detail is masked by the SORT GROUP BY operation. The second query involves analytic function calls and returns all 100 rows in T1. This second query also requires two sorts. In this case, however, the two sorts each have their own WINDOW SORT operation in the execution plan.

Analytic-only Functions

Although nearly all aggregate functions can operate as analytic functions, there are a lot of analytic functions that have no aggregate counterpart. By way of an example, Listing 7-10 rewrites Listing 7-6 in a way that is both easier to read and more efficient.

Listing 7-10. Introducing the ROW_NUMBER and RANK analytic functions

```
SELECT ROW_NUMBER () OVER (ORDER BY sales_amount) rn
      ,RANK () OVER (ORDER BY sales_amount) rank_sales
      ,t1.*
   FROM t1
ORDER BY sales_amount;
```

```
----------------------------
| Id  | Operation           |
----------------------------
|   0 | SELECT STATEMENT    |
|   1 | WINDOW SORT         |
|   2 |   TABLE ACCESS FULL |
----------------------------
```

The output of the query in Listing 7-10 is identical to that in 7-6. The WINDOW SORT operation sorts the rows by SALES_AMOUNT, and then the ROW_NUMBER analytic function reads the rows from the sorted buffer and adds the additional column indicating the position in the list. The RANK function is similar to ROW_NUMBER except that rows with equal values of SALES_AMOUNT are given the same ranking. Notice that the ORDER BY clause causes no additional overhead as the data is already sorted. But this behavior is not guaranteed, and in case the CBO does something different in future releases it is best to add the ORDER BY clause if the ordering is important.

Analytic Sub-clauses

We have seen that analytic functions include the keyword OVER followed by a pair of parentheses. Inside these parentheses there are up to three optional sub-clauses. These are the *query partition* sub-clause, the *order by* sub-clause, and the *windowing* sub-clause. If more than one of these sub-clauses are present then they must be written in the prescribed order. Let us look at each of these sub-clauses in more detail.

Query Partition Sub-clause

This sub-clause uses the keywords PARTITION BY to separate the rows into groups and then runs the analytic function on each group independently.

■ **Note**   The keywords PARTITION BY when used in analytic functions have nothing to do with the licensed feature that permits indexes and tables to be split into multiple segments. Nor is there any relationship between the term PARTITION BY in analytics and the partitioned outer-join concept that we discussed in Chapter 1.

We have seen an example of the query partition sub-clause in Listing 7-7. Listing 7-11 provides us with another example that is a slight modification of Listing 7-8.

Listing 7-11. NSAF analytic with a PARTITION BY clause

```
SELECT t1.*
     ,AVG (sales_amount) OVER (PARTITION BY channel_id) average_sales_amount
  FROM t1;
```

```
---------------------------
| Id  | Operation          |
---------------------------
|   0 | SELECT STATEMENT   |
|   1 | WINDOW SORT        |
|   2 |   TABLE ACCESS FULL|
---------------------------
```

The only difference between the query in Listing 7-8 and the query in Listing 7-11 is the addition of the query partition clause. So in Listing 7-8 the value of AVERAGE_SALES_AMOUNT for the row where CHANNEL_ID is 1 and SALES_AMOUNT is 16 is 3803.53, as it is for every row. The average value of SALES_AMOUNT of all 100 rows in T1 is 3803.53. On the other hand, the query containing the PARTITION BY clause returns a value of 3896 for AVERAGE_SALES_AMOUNT when CHANNEL_ID is 1 and SALES_AMOUNT is 16. This is the average of the 25 rows where CHANNEL_ID is 1.

You will notice that the execution plan in Listing 7-11 differs from that in Listing 7-8. The query partition clause in Listing 7-11 requires the rows to be sorted by CHANNEL_ID even though the AVG function is an NSAF.

ORDER BY Sub-clause

When the MEDIAN function is used as an analytic function the order in which the rows are sorted is determined by the argument to the MEDIAN function, and in this case the order by sub-clause would be redundant and is illegal. However, we have already seen an example of a legal use of the order by sub-clause in Listing 7-10 that introduced the ROW_NUMBER analytic function. Listing 7-12 shows another use of the order by sub-clause.

Listing 7-12. The NTILE analytic function

```
SELECT t1.*, NTILE (4) OVER (ORDER BY sales_amount) nt FROM t1;
```

The query in Listing 7-12 sorts the 100 rows in T1 by SALES_AMOUNT. The execution plan for this statement appears to be the same as those in Listing 7-10 and 7-11 so I haven't shown it again. The NTILE function identifies percentiles, and its argument indicates how many. In this case the function returns 1 for the 25 rows in the lowest quartile (the rows with the lowest value of SALES_AMOUNT), 2 for the 25 rows in the second quartile, 3 for the 25 rows in the third quartile, and 4 for the 25 rows with the highest values for SALES_AMOUNT.

It is possible to combine the query partition clause and the order by clause in the same function call. Listing 7-13 shows how this is done and introduces a new analytic function at the same time.

Listing 7-13. The LAG analytic functions

```
SELECT t1.*
      ,LAG (sales_amount)
          OVER (PARTITION BY channel_id, cust_id ORDER BY transaction_date)
          prev_sales_amount
   FROM t1
ORDER BY channel_id, sales_amount;
```

The LAG function picks the value of an expression from an earlier row. The function takes three arguments.

- The first, mandatory, argument is the column or expression to pick

- The second, optional, argument is the number of rows back to go and defaults to 1, in other words the preceding row

- The third and final optional argument is the value returned if the offset goes beyond the scope of the window. If you do not specify the third argument then it defaults to NULL.

This call to the LAG function operates by logically grouping the 100 rows into 20 groups of 5 rows based on the distinct values of CHANNEL_ID and CUST_ID. Within each group we take the value of SALES_AMOUNT from the preceding row when ordered by TRANSACTION_DATE. In other words, we see the details of a transaction together with the SALES_AMOUNT from the previous transaction made by the same customer using the same channel. Listing 7-14 shows a few sample rows from the output.

Listing 7-14. Sample output from Listing 7-13

TRANSACTION_DATE	CHANNEL_ID	CUST_ID	SALES_AMOUNT	PREV_SALES_AMOUNT
20/01/2014	**1**	**1**	**400**	
09/02/2014	1	1	1600	400
01/03/2014	1	1	3600	1600
21/03/2014	1	1	9400	3600
10/04/2014	1	1	10000	9400
16/01/2014	**1**	**2**	**256**	

Notice that the highlighted rows are the first in their group. In this case, LAG returns NULL because we didn't specify three arguments to the function. You should know that there is a LEAD function call as well. This takes values from a succeeding, rather than preceding, row.

■ **Note** A call to LEAD with a descending sort order yields the same value as a call to LAG with an ascending sort order and vice versa. Only the order of the rows returned by the WINDOW SORT operation changes.

Windowing Analytic Sub-clause

The windowing sub-clause is the most complex of the three types of sub-clause but also one of the most useful. The rules for its use are quite complex, and I can only provide an introduction here.

- A windowing sub-clause is only allowed for a subset of NSAFs.

- If a windowing sub-clause is specified, an order by sub-clause is also required.

- For those functions that support a windowing sub-clause a default window sub-clause is implied if an order by sub-clause is provided.

Like the query partition clause, the windowing clause restricts the analytic function to a subset of rows, but unlike the query partition clause the range is dynamic. Consider listing 7-15, which shows the windowing clause in action.

Listing 7-15. An implementation of a moving average

```
SELECT t1.*
     ,AVG (
         sales_amount)
     OVER (PARTITION BY cust_id
         ORDER BY transaction_date
         ROWS BETWEEN 2 PRECEDING AND CURRENT ROW)
         mov_avg
  FROM t1;

-- Sample output
```

TRANSACTION_DATE	CHANNEL_ID	CUST_ID	SALES_AMOUNT	MOV_AVG
05-JAN-14	2	1	25	25
10-JAN-14	**3**	**1**	**3100**	**1562.5**
15-JAN-14	**4**	**1**	**225**	**1116.66666666667**
20-JAN-14	**1**	**1**	**400**	**1241.66666666667**

Listing 7-15 implements a traditional moving-average calculation, including the current row and the two that precede it, assuming that they exist. The value returned by the function is the average SALES_AMOUNT of the last three transactions with that customer. The sample output shows some rows where CUST_ID is 1. The first row has a window of one row, the second provides the average of the first two rows, and the third and subsequent rows in the group average three numbers. So the fourth row provides an average of 3100, 225, and 400, which is 1241⅔.

The default windowing specification is ROWS BETWEEN UNBOUNDED PRECEDING AND CURRENT ROW, and one very common use of this is to implement a running total, as shown in Listing 7-16.

Listing 7-16. A running total using SUM with an implied windowing sub-clause

```
SELECT t1.*
     ,SUM (sales_amount)
         OVER (PARTITION BY cust_id ORDER BY transaction_date)
         moving_balance
  FROM t1;

-- Sample output (first few rows)
```

TRANSACTION_DATE	CHANNEL_ID	CUST_ID	SALES_AMOUNT	MOVING_BALANCE
05-JAN-14	2	1	25	25
10-JAN-14	3	1	3100	3125
15-JAN-14	4	1	225	3350
20-JAN-14	1	1	400	3750

At first glance the order by sub-clause used with the SUM function seems ludicrous because the sum of a set of values is the same no matter how they are ordered. However, because SUM supports windowing the implication of the order by sub-clause is that we are summing just the current and preceding rows; the windowing sub-clause is implied. Do you see how the values of SALES_AMOUNT are accumulated in the MOVING_BALANCE column?

Windowing is also supported for logical ranges. Listing 7-17 shows an example of a logical range.

Listing 7-17. Windowing over a specified time period

```
        SELECT t1.*
        ,AVG (
            sales_amount)
        OVER (PARTITION BY cust_id
              ORDER BY transaction_date
              RANGE INTERVAL '10' DAY PRECEDING)
            mov_avg
FROM t1;
```

The query in Listing 7-17 specifies that transactions made in the *eleven* days ending on the transaction date of the current row are included in the window. Notice that I have abbreviated the window specification here; by default the window closes on the current row or value. Because of the way the data was setup in T1, the output of Listing 7-17 is identical to that in Listing 7-15.

■ **Note**   When logical ranges are used the keywords CURRENT ROW, which are implicit in Listing 7-17, really mean current value. So if there were multiple rows with the same value of TRANSACTION_DATE as the current row then the analytic would include the values of SALES_AMOUNT from all such rows in its average.

Why Windowing is Restricted to NSAFs

A while ago a client asked me to implement a moving median, much like the moving average in Listing 7-15. I couldn't use the MEDIAN function with a windowing sub-clause because windowing isn't supported for the MEDIAN function, as it is inefficient.

To understand why calculating a moving median is so difficult, let us take another look at the sample output shown in Listing 7-15. Before calculating the last MOVING_BALANCE the window has to be "slid" to exclude the first row and include the fourth. The rows included in the resultant window are highlighted. To make this "sliding" activity efficient, the WINDOW SORT operation has sorted the rows by CUST_ID and TRANSACTION_DATE.

Once the rows in the window have been identified, it is then time to invoke the analytic function. For NSAFs, such as AVG used in Listing 7-15, this is a simple matter of scanning the values and keeping track of the tally as usual.

■ **Note**   For many functions, including AVG, it is theoretically possible to calculate the new values without scanning all the rows in the window each time. However, for functions like MAX and MIN a scan is required.

Now suppose we wanted to calculate a moving median for SALES_AMOUNT rather than a moving average. The rows in our window are sorted by TRANSACTION_DATE and would have to be re-sorted by SALES_AMOUNT. This re-sort would be required each time the window slides to a new row in T1. The same type of argument can be made for any aggregate function that sorts.

Of course, regardless of the inefficiency of the calculation, my client still had a requirement for a moving median! I'll come back to how I solved this problem shortly when we discuss the MODEL clause.

Analytics as a Double-edged Sword

These analytics seem really cool. Analytic functions allow us to write succinct and efficient code and impress our friends with our SQL prowess at the same time! What could be better? Quite a lot, actually.

Let me create a new table T2 that shows how analytic functions can lead you into the performance mire more often than they can extract you from it. Listing 7-18 shows a test case similar to the one a naïve Tony Hasler developed a few years ago to demonstrate how super-fast analytic functions were. I was in for a shock!

Listing 7-18. The downside of analytic functions

```sql
CREATE TABLE t2
(
   c1              NUMBER
  ,c2              NUMBER
  ,big_column1     CHAR (2000)
  ,big_column2     CHAR (2000)
);

INSERT /*+ APPEND */ INTO t2 (c1
                ,c2
                ,big_column1
                ,big_column2)
      SELECT ROWNUM
            ,MOD (ROWNUM, 5)
            ,RPAD ('X', 2000)
            ,RPAD ('X', 2000)
        FROM DUAL
   CONNECT BY LEVEL <= 50000;

COMMIT;

WITH q1
     AS (  SELECT c2, AVG (c1) avg_c1
             FROM t2
         GROUP BY c2)
SELECT *
  FROM t2 NATURAL JOIN q1;
```

```
---------------------------------------------------------------------------
| Id  | Operation           | Name | Rows  | Bytes | Cost (%CPU)| Time     |
---------------------------------------------------------------------------
|   0 | SELECT STATEMENT    |      | 50000 |  192M | 27106   (1)| 00:00:02 |
|*  1 |  HASH JOIN          |      | 50000 |  192M | 27106   (1)| 00:00:02 |
|   2 |   VIEW              |      |     5 |   130 | 13553   (1)| 00:00:01 |
|   3 |    HASH GROUP BY    |      |     5 |    40 | 13553   (1)| 00:00:01 |
|   4 |     TABLE ACCESS FULL| T2  | 50000 |  390K | 13552   (1)| 00:00:01 |
|   5 |   TABLE ACCESS FULL | T2   | 50000 |  191M | 13552   (1)| 00:00:01 |
---------------------------------------------------------------------------

Predicate Information (identified by operation id):
---------------------------------------------------

   1 - access("T2"."C2"="Q1"."C2")
```

```sql
SELECT t2.*, AVG (c1) OVER (PARTITION BY c2) avg_c1 FROM t2;
```

```
--------------------------------------------------------------------------------
| Id  | Operation          | Name | Rows  | Bytes |TempSpc| Cost (%CPU)| Time     |
--------------------------------------------------------------------------------
|   0 | SELECT STATEMENT   |      | 50000 |  191M |       | 55293   (1)| 00:00:03 |
|   1 |  WINDOW SORT       |      | 50000 |  191M |  195M | 55293   (1)| 00:00:03 |
|   2 |   TABLE ACCESS FULL| T2   | 50000 |  191M |       | 13552   (1)| 00:00:01 |
--------------------------------------------------------------------------------
```

Listing 7-18 creates a test table and then issues two queries that generate precisely the same results. The first query is typical of those from a junior programmer who knows nothing of analytic functions but is keen to show off knowledge of subquery factoring and ANSI syntax. The CBO seems to feel that there will be 5.8 billion rows consuming 21 terabytes of space. All of this horror should surely be avoided.

The second query in Listing 7-18 seems much more efficient. We have eliminated that "offensive" second full table scan of T2. Great—so why is the estimated (and actual) elapsed time for the second higher than for the first?

The clue to the problem lies in the column in the execution plan named "TempSpc" for "Temporary Table Space" that only appears in the execution plan for the second query. The big problem with analytics is that the sort is based on the *entire result set*. The data aggregated in the hypothetical junior programmer's SQL excludes BIG_COLUMN1 and BIG_COLUMN2. We can, therefore, aggregate the data in memory, and because AVG is an NSAF we don't need any sort at all! Unless you have a large enough SGA you are never going to sort the data in the second query in memory, and that disk-based sort will take much longer than an extra full-table scan.

■ **Note** The execution plans shown in Listing 17-18 were prepared on a database with a 512Mb SGA. If you try running these examples on a database with a large SGA you may need to increase the number of rows in T2 from 50,000 to a much larger value to see the effect. Similarly, if you find the second query taking too long you may need to reduce the number of rows to a smaller value.

Combining Aggregate and Analytic Functions

Analytic functions are evaluated after any optional aggregation. The first consequence of this fact is that analytic functions cannot appear in a WHERE clause, a GROUP BY clause, or a HAVING clause; analytic functions can only be used with the MODEL clause, as part of a select list, or as part of an expression in an ORDER BY clause. The second consequence of the late point at which analytics are evaluated is that the results of aggregation can be used as inputs to analytic functions. Listing 7-19 gives an example.

Listing 7-19. Combining aggregate and analytic functions

```
SELECT cust_id
       ,COUNT (*) tran_count
       ,SUM (sales_amount) total_sales
       ,100 * SUM (sales_amount) / SUM (SUM (sales_amount)) OVER ()
           pct_revenue1
       ,100 * ratio_to_report (SUM (sales_amount)) OVER () pct_revenue2
    FROM t1
GROUP BY cust_id;
```

```
-------------------------------------
| Id | Operation         | Name |
-------------------------------------
|  0 | SELECT STATEMENT  |      |
|  1 |  WINDOW BUFFER     |      |
|  2 |   HASH GROUP BY     |      |
|  3 |    TABLE ACCESS FULL| T1   |
-------------------------------------
```

CUST_ID	TRAN_COUNT	TOTAL_SALES	PCT_REVENUE1	PCT_REVENUE2
1	20	80750	21.2302781889455	21.2302781889455
2	20	69673	18.3179835573796	18.3179835573796
4	20	76630	20.1470739024012	20.1470739024012
5	20	78670	20.6834177724377	20.6834177724377
3	20	74630	19.621246578836	19.621246578836

Listing 7-19 aggregates the 100 rows in T1 into five groups, one for each CUST_ID. We use aggregate functions to calculate TRAN_COUNT, the number of transactions with the customer, and TOTAL_SALES, the sum of SALES_AMOUNT for the customer. As you can see from the execution plan, at that point the result of the hash aggregation in operation 2 is passed to the WINDOW BUFFER operation that supports the un-partitioned NSAF analytic function calls.

The last two columns, PCT_REVENUE1 and PCT_REVENUE2, show the percentage of revenue that the customer contributed. Although the values of the two columns are the same, the calculations are performed slightly differently. PCT_REVENUE1 is evaluated by dividing the aggregated sum of SALES_AMOUNT for the customer by the sum of all aggregated sales for all customers. PCT_REVENUE2 makes use of a special analytic function RATIO_TO_REPORT that makes it easier to write such expressions.

I think that some people may find this sort of SQL difficult to read, and I don't suggest that you consider Listing 7-19 good coding practice. A slightly lengthier, but clearer, way to write the SQL in Listing 7-19 is shown in Listing 7-20:

Listing 7-20. Separating aggregation and analytics with subqueries

```
WITH q1
    AS ( SELECT cust_id, COUNT (*) tran_count, SUM (sales_amount) total_sales
            FROM t1
         GROUP BY cust_id)
SELECT q1.*
       ,100 * total_sales / SUM (total_sales) OVER () pct_revenue1
       ,100 * ratio_to_report (total_sales) OVER () pct_revenue2
  FROM q1;
```

The CBO has no trouble transforming the query in Listing 7-20 into that from Listing 7-19, and the two queries have identical execution plans.

Single-row Functions

The term *"single-row function,"* coined by the SQL Language Reference manual, is a bit misleading because the functions referred to can be applied to data aggregated from many rows. Single-row functions are frequently referred to as *scalar functions,* but this is inaccurate because some of the functions in this category, such as SET, operate on non-scalar data. Listing 7-21 shows a few interesting cases of this category of function.

Listing 7-21. Single-row functions in various contexts

```
SELECT GREATEST (
         ratio_to_report (FLOOR (SUM (LEAST (sales_amount, 100)))) OVER ()
         ,0)
         n1
    FROM t1
GROUP BY cust_id;
```

```
-------------------------------------
| Id | Operation            | Name |
-------------------------------------
|  0 | SELECT STATEMENT     |      |
|  1 |  WINDOW BUFFER       |      |
|  2 |   HASH GROUP BY      |      |
|  3 |    TABLE ACCESS FULL | T1   |
-------------------------------------
```

This query doesn't do anything meaningful so I haven't listed the results. The query is constructed purely to show how single-row functions work. The basic evaluation rules are:

- A single-row function is valid in expressions in all clauses in a query block.

- If the arguments of the single-row function include one or more analytic functions then the single-row function is evaluated after the analytic functions, otherwise the single-row function is evaluated before any analytics.

- If the arguments of the single-row function include one or more aggregate functions then the single-row function is evaluated after aggregation, otherwise the single-row function is evaluated before any aggregation (unless the arguments include analytics).

Let us have a look at how these rules affect the various scalar functions used to evaluate N1 in our query.

- The arguments of the single-row function LEAST contain no aggregate or analytic functions and so LEAST is evaluated before any aggregation or analytics.

- The argument to the single-row function FLOOR is an aggregate function, so FLOOR is evaluated after aggregation but before analytics.

- The arguments of the single-row function GREATEST include an analytic function, so the GREATEST function is evaluated after the analytics.

The MODEL Clause

There is a behavior common in the investment banking world, and possibly other sectors as well, that regulators are taking an increasingly dim view of. That behavior is business staff downloading the results of database queries into Excel spreadsheets and then performing complex calculations on them, often using Visual Basic functions. I heard of one case where these calculations were so involved they took over 45 minutes to run! The problem the regulators have with this type of thing is that there is usually very little control of changes to these spreadsheets. The problem we as technicians should have with this behavior is that it is inappropriate to perform such complex calculations on a desktop when there is a massive database server with lots of CPUs that could perform these calculations more quickly.

To address this issue, Oracle introduced the MODEL clause in 10g. In fact, the keyword SPREADSHEET is a synonym for MODEL, a fact that emphasizes the normal use of the clause. In this section I will briefly introduce the concepts. If you have a genuine need to use the MODEL clause you should consult the chapter entitled *SQL for Modeling* in the Data Warehousing Guide.

Spreadsheet Concepts

The one thing that is missing from the Oracle-supplied documentation is a comparison of the terminology and concepts of the MODEL clause with those of an Excel spreadsheet. This is hardly surprising given that Excel is not an Oracle-supplied product! Let me rectify that now. They say that a picture paints a thousand words, so take a look at Figure 7-1.

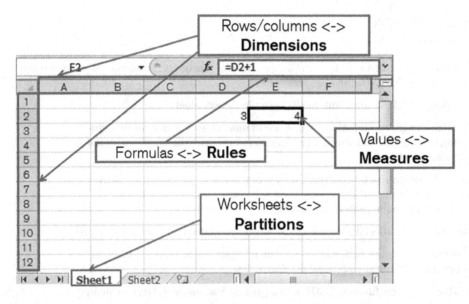

Figure 7-1. *Comparing Excel and MODEL clause concepts*

- An Excel workbook is split into one or more worksheets. The equivalent MODEL clause concept is the PARTITION. Yet another use of this overloaded term!

- A worksheet contains a number of values. The equivalent MODEL clause concept is the MEASURE.

- Values in a worksheet are referenced by the row number and the column letter. In a MODEL partition the measures are referenced by DIMENSION values.

- Some values in an Excel spreadsheet are evaluated by formulas. The formulas in a MODEL clause are referred to as RULES.

There are some important differences between the Excel and MODEL clause concepts that are summarized in Table 7-1.

Table 7-1. *Differences between Excel and MODEL clause concepts*

Model Term	Excel Term	Differences
Partition	Worksheet	It is possible for formulas in one Excel worksheet to reference cells in another. It is not possible for partitions in a model clause to reference each other.
Dimension	Row and column	In Excel there are always exactly two dimensions. In a model clause there are one or more.
Measure	A cell value	In Excel only one value is referenced by the dimensions. The model clause allows one or more measures.
Rules	Formulas	Nested cell references are possible with models.

A Moving Median with the MODEL Clause

Do you remember that we couldn't use the MEDIAN as an analytic function with a windowing clause because it isn't supported? Listing 7-22 shows you how to implement a moving median with the MODEL clause.

Listing 7-22. Implementing a moving median with a MODEL clause

```
ALTER SESSION FORCE PARALLEL QUERY PARALLEL 3;

SELECT transaction_date,channel_id,cust_id,sales_amount,mov_median,mov_med_avg
  FROM t1
MODEL
   PARTITION BY (cust_id)
   DIMENSION BY (ROW_NUMBER () OVER (PARTITION BY cust_id ORDER BY transaction_date) rn)
   MEASURES (transaction_date, channel_id, sales_amount, 0 mov_median, 0 mov_med_avg)
   RULES
      (
      mov_median [ANY] =
              MEDIAN (sales_amount)[rn BETWEEN CV()-2 AND CV ()],
      mov_med_avg [ANY] = ROUND(AVG(mov_median) OVER (ORDER BY rn ROWS 2 PRECEDING))
)
ORDER BY cust_id,transaction_date,mov_median;

ALTER SESSION ENABLE PARALLEL QUERY;

-- Sample output

TRANSACTION_DATE      CHANNEL_ID      CUST_ID   SALES_AMOUNT   MOV_MEDIAN    MOV_MED_AVG
05-JAN-2014           2               1                   25   25            25
10-JAN-2014           3               1                 3100   1562.5        794
15-JAN-2014           4               1                  225   225           604
20-JAN-2014           1               1                  400   400           729
```

```
-------------------------------------------------
| Id | Operation                      | Name     |
-------------------------------------------------
|  0 | SELECT STATEMENT               |          |
|  1 |  PX COORDINATOR                |          |
|  2 |   PX SEND QC (ORDER)           | :TQ10002 |
|  3 |    SORT ORDER BY               |          |
|  4 |     SQL MODEL ORDERED          |          |
|  5 |      PX RECEIVE                |          |
|  6 |       PX SEND RANGE            | :TQ10001 |
|  7 |        WINDOW SORT             |          |
|  8 |         PX RECEIVE             |          |
|  9 |          PX SEND RANGE         | :TQ10000 |
| 10 |           PX BLOCK ITERATOR    |          |
| 11 |            TABLE ACCESS FULL   | T1       |
| 12 |       WINDOW (IN SQL MODEL) SORT|         |
-------------------------------------------------
```

The code in Listing 7-22 begins by forcing parallel query. I only do this so as to demonstrate the parallelization capabilities of the MODEL clause; the dataset is ordinarily too small to warrant parallel query.

The query begins by selecting all rows and columns from T1 and passing the data to the model clause.

- The first sub-clause we see is the optional PARTITION BY clause. This means that the data for each CUST_ID is treated separately—in its own worksheet, if you will.

- The second sub-clause is the DIMENSION BY clause, and the expression here includes an analytic function. The clause defines a new identifier RN that gives the ordering of the rows in our worksheet by transaction date. Normally I would use a factored subquery in a way analogous to Listing 7-20 to make the query easier to read, but here I am just showing what is possible.

- The MEASURES clause identifies what values are addressed by our RN dimension. These include the remaining columns from T1 as well as two new columns. MOV_MEDIAN will be the median for the three most recent transactions and MOV_MED_AVG will be the average (mean) value of MOV_MED from the three most recent transactions. The identifiers are initialized to zero so that the data types of the measures are known.

- The RULES clause then calculates our missing measures.

The first rule uses MEDIAN as an aggregate function, and in the MODEL clause we can explicitly specify the range of measures to be used. The expression in square brackets on the right-hand side is:

```
rn BETWEEN CV()-2 AND CV ()
```

The term CV is an abbreviation for CURRENT_VALUE, a function in the model category that is only legal inside a MODEL clause. The CV function is much like a relative cell reference in Excel. So, for example, when the dimension RN has a value of 7 the expression as a whole would be interpreted as rn BETWEEN 5 and 7. Notice that we are applying the aggregate function in the RULES sub-clause after the analytic function in the DIMENSION BY clause. This is legal because the RULES sub-clause operates independently of the rest of the query block.

The second rule is evaluated after the first and so can use the MOV_MEDIAN measure calculated in the first rule as input, just like the results of one formula in Excel can be input to another. I could have calculated the MOV_MED_AVG in the same way as MOV_MEDIAN, but in this case I have the option to use an analytic function and that is what I have chosen to do.

After the measures have been evaluated by the rules, the results are passed back to the select list and the ORDER BY clause. I have included the MOV_MEDIAN in the ORDER BY clause just to show that it is possible to do so and for no other reason.

The execution plan in Listing 7-22 is somewhat lengthy, but that is more to do with the parallelization than the MODEL clause; individual rules within the model clause are not shown in the execution plan. The first thing about the execution plan I want to mention is the difference between operation 7 and operation 12. Operation 7 is used to evaluate the ROW_NUMBER analytic function outside of the MODEL clause and operation 12 is used to evaluate the AVG analytic function inside the MODEL clause, as you might have guessed from the operation name WINDOW (IN SQL MODEL) SORT. There is no visible operation for the MEDIAN aggregate function. The other thing I want to highlight in the execution plan is operation 6. This examines the value of CUST_ID to determine which parallel query slave to send data to; the parallelization of MODEL clause rule evaluation is always based on the expressions in the PARTITION BY sub-clause to prevent the need for any communication between the parallel query slaves.

Why Not Use PL/SQL?

The MODEL clause seems like heresy! SQL is supposed to be a declarative programming language, and here we are writing a series of rules and specifying not only how the calculations are to be performed but in what order. We have imperative programming languages like PL/SQL with equivalent parallelization capabilities for that, don't we?

The point to realize is that SQL is *declarative* and has the ability to operate on *multiple rows* together. PL/SQL and other imperative languages are *imperative* and *single-row* based. What the MODEL clause provides us with is *imperative* syntax capable of operating on *multiple rows* at a time. Just imagine how difficult it would be to implement a moving median in PL/SQL!

Summary

It is a recurring theme of this book that the more thoroughly you understand things, the easier it is to correctly analyze problems and identify good solutions to those problems. We began this chapter by a look at the syntax of query blocks because without understanding that syntax some aspects of execution plans would be difficult to follow. We then covered functions. A thorough understanding of the main categories of SQL functions is crucial to understanding the increasing number of performance problems that are unrelated to the selection of an index for accessing a table or determining the correct join order. In particular, we saw how the volume of data processed by analytic functions can make them unattractive in some situations. Finally, we introduced the complex topic of the MODEL clause and explained how it can be used to perform analytic calculations on sets of rows when these calculations aren't easily performed by other means.

This chapter marks the end of our analysis of the SQL language itself. It is time to now to return to the topic of performance analysis. In chapter 8 we complete our study of execution plans that we began in Chapter 3.

■ ■ ■

CHAPTER 8

Advanced Execution Plan Concepts

This chapter covers three major topics: the display of execution plans, parallel execution plans, and global hinting.

I have already shown quite a few parts of an execution plan in this book, and in this chapter I will explain most of the remaining parts, most notably the outline hints section. These additional execution plan sections can be displayed with non-default formatting options. The second major topic in the chapter is a discussion of execution plans for statements that run in parallel. There hasn't been a lot written about how parallel execution plans work, and in particular there is a lot of confusion about how to interpret such execution plans. I want to spend some time clearing all that confusion up. The CBO's selection of execution plan can be controlled, or at least influenced, by the use of *optimizer hints,* and there is far more to the topic of hinting than may have been apparent in this book so far. Thus, the third topic in this chapter is *global hints.* Global hints allow a programmer to influence the CBO's treatment of blocks other than the one in which the hint appears. This type of hint is useful for hinting query blocks from data dictionary views without altering the view, among other things.

But let me begin this chapter with the first of the three topics: displaying execution plans.

Displaying Additional Execution Plan Sections

In Chapter 3 I explained the default display of execution plans using the functions in the DBMS_XPLAN package, and in Chapter 4 I explained how additional information from the runtime engine can be displayed in the operation table of DBMS_XPLAN output and in the V$SQL_PLAN_STATISTICS_ALL view. But DBMS_XPLAN can display a lot more information about the CBO's behavior than has been explained so far. If requested to do so by using non-default formatting options, DBMS_XPLAN will display more information in additional sections below the operation table. I will give a brief overview of the formatting options and then explain how to interpret these additional sections.

DBMS_XPLAN Formatting Options

Table 8-1 summarizes the information about the DBMS_XPLAN display options documented in the PL/SQL Packages and Types Reference Manual:

Table 8-1. *Format levels and fine-grained control in calls to DBMS_XPLAN packages*

		Format levels				
Fine-grained Control	**Column/Section**	**Basic**	**Serial**	**Typical**	**All**	**Advanced**
rows	C		X	X	X	X
bytes	C		X	X	X	X
cost	C		X	X	X	X
partition	C		X	X	X	X
predicate	S		X	X	X	X
remote	S		X	X	X	X
note	S		X	X	X	X
parallel	C			X	X	X
projection	S				X	X
alias	S				X	X
peeked_binds	S					X
outline	S					X
adaptive	See discussion of adaptive execution plans below					

When looking at Table 8-1, bear mind the following points:

- Some optional display data appears in additional columns in the operation table and some appears in additional sections following the operation table. The table shows where each data item appears.

- The BASIC level displays only the Id, Operation, and Name columns of the operation table and, with some obscure exceptions[1], no other sections. These basic level columns cannot be suppressed in any display.

- Display levels other than BASIC contain additional columns like Time that cannot be suppressed except by selecting the BASIC level and then adding any desired sections or columns.

- Format keywords are not case sensitive.

- All levels can be customized using fine-grained control together with a minus sign to remove the data or an optional plus sign to add it. So, for example, 'ADVANCED -COST' and 'BASIC +PEEKED_BINDS' are both legal formats.

- Information about adaptive execution plans is not displayed by any level and must be explicitly added with +ADAPTIVE. Explicitly adding ADAPTIVE to the BASIC level doesn't work.

---

[1]'BASIC +ALLSTATS' when STATISTICS_LEVEL=TYPICAL includes a note section. Information about result caching appears even with BASIC formatting.

- Runtime statistics are displayed using format options as described in Chapter 4. So to obtain the fullest possible display from DBMS_XPLAN.DISPLAY_CURSOR you need to specify 'ADVANCED ALLSTATS LAST ADAPTIVE' for the format parameter.

- All levels are documented except ADVANCED and all fine-grained controls are documented except PEEKED_BINDS and OUTLINE.

- The SERIAL level still displays parallel operations for statements executed in parallel. Only the columns in the operation table relating to parallel operations are suppressed.

- Some options don't apply to all procedures in the DBMS_XPLAN package. For example, PEEKED_BINDS is only valid for DBMS_XPLAN.DISPLAY_CURSOR and PREDICATE information is not displayed in the output of DBMS_XPLAN.DISPLAY_AWR.

I have already explained that if you need detailed information about individual row source operations you had best look at the view V$SQL_PLAN_STATISTICS_ALL, so I will focus on the additional sections of the execution plan, presenting them in the order in which they appear.

Running EXPLAIN PLAN for Analysis

The listings in the remaining sections of this chapter use tables created as in Listing 8-1.

Listing 8-1. Creating tables and a loopback database link for execution plan demonstrations

```
CREATE PUBLIC DATABASE LINK "loopback"
USING 'localhost:1521/orcl'; -- Customize for your database name and port

CREATE /*+ NO_GATHER_OPTIMIZER_STATISTICS */ TABLE t1 AS
        SELECT ROWNUM c1 FROM DUAL CONNECT BY LEVEL <= 100;
CREATE /*+ NO_GATHER_OPTIMIZER_STATISTICS */ TABLE t2 AS
        SELECT ROWNUM c2 FROM DUAL CONNECT BY LEVEL <= 100;
CREATE /*+ NO_GATHER_OPTIMIZER_STATISTICS */ TABLE t3 AS
        SELECT ROWNUM c3 FROM DUAL CONNECT BY LEVEL <= 100;
CREATE /*+ NO_GATHER_OPTIMIZER_STATISTICS */ TABLE t4 AS
        SELECT ROWNUM c4 FROM DUAL CONNECT BY LEVEL <= 100;
```

Listing 8-1 creates four tables, each with a single column. To test remote access I have also created a loopback database link. The listing assumes that the database is called ORCL and that the SQLNET port is set to the default of 1521. This is a highly insecure approach, and to test the examples you will probably have to change the database link creation statement to meet your needs.

The listings that follow in the next few sections contain both statements and execution plans. Unless otherwise stated the execution plans should be obtained using EXPLAIN PLAN and a call to DBMS_XPLAN.DISPLAY that specifies the BASIC level with the suitable fine-grained control specified in the section in which the listing appears. BASIC level has been used to keep the operation table as uncluttered as possible so that focus is drawn to the other aspects of the execution plan under discussion.

Query Blocks and Object Alias

If the ALIAS fine-grained control is specified or implied then a section detailing the query blocks and objects used in the explained statement appears immediately after the operation table. Listing 8-2 is a simple query that helps demonstrate the meaning of this section.

Listing 8-2. Simple query with three query blocks

```
WITH q1 AS (SELECT /*+ no_merge */
                   c1 FROM t1)
    ,q2 AS (SELECT /*+ no_merge */
                   c2 FROM t2)
SELECT COUNT (*)
  FROM q1, q2 myalias
 WHERE c1 = c2;
```

Plan hash value: 1978226902

```
-------------------------------------
| Id  | Operation            | Name |
-------------------------------------
|   0 | SELECT STATEMENT     |      |
|   1 |  SORT AGGREGATE      |      |
|   2 |   HASH JOIN          |      |
|   3 |    VIEW              |      |
|   4 |     TABLE ACCESS FULL| T1   |
|   5 |    VIEW              |      |
|   6 |     TABLE ACCESS FULL| T2   |
-------------------------------------
```

Query Block Name / Object Alias (identified by operation id):

```
   1 - SEL$3
   3 - SEL$1 / Q1@SEL$3
   4 - SEL$1 / T1@SEL$1
   5 - SEL$2 / MYALIAS@SEL$3
   6 - SEL$2 / T2@SEL$2
```

The simple statement in Listing 8-2 could, of course, be made even simpler by eliminating the two factored subqueries and instead just joining T1 and T2. In fact, if the NO_MERGE hints were removed the CBO would apply the *simple view merging* transformation to do that for us. As it is, the three query blocks aren't merged and all appear in the final execution plan.

The CBO has provided default names for these three query blocks. These names are SEL$1, SEL$2, and SEL$3 and are allocated in the order in which the SELECT keywords appear in the original statement. The ALIAS section of the execution plan display indicates the query block with which the operations are associated. Where applicable, an *object alias* is also shown. Because operation 2 is associated with the same query block as operation 1 and there is no object alias to display, operation 2 isn't shown in the ALIAS section at all; SEL$3 is implied.

For tables T1 and T2 I didn't specify an alias in the FROM clause so the table name itself is shown for the object alias of operations 4 and 6. You will notice, however, that the table names have been qualified by the name of the query block preceded by an '@' symbol. So for operation 4 T1@SEL$1 means *the row source named T1 that appears in the FROM clause of SEL$1*. This need to qualify row source names arises because the same object (or alias) can be used multiple times in different query blocks within the same SQL statement.

Notice that the alias may be for an object other than a table. Operation 3 references Q1, a factored subquery that was not given an alias in the main clause of Listing 8-2. Operation 5 references MYALIAS, the alias I gave for Q2 in the main query (SEL$3).

Listing 8-3 shows what happens when we remove one of the NO_MERGE hints.

Listing 8-3. Query block merging

```
WITH q1 AS (SELECT c1 FROM t1)
    ,q2 AS (SELECT /*+  no_merge */
                   c2 FROM t2)
SELECT COUNT (*)
  FROM q1, q2 myalias
 WHERE c1 = c2;


Plan hash value: 3055011902


-------------------------------------
| Id  | Operation            | Name |
-------------------------------------
|   0 | SELECT STATEMENT     |      |
|   1 |  SORT AGGREGATE      |      |
|   2 |   HASH JOIN          |      |
|   3 |    TABLE ACCESS FULL | T1   |
|   4 |    VIEW              |      |
|   5 |     TABLE ACCESS FULL| T2   |
-------------------------------------

Query Block Name / Object Alias (identified by operation id):
-----------------------------------------------------------

   1 - SEL$F1D6E378
   3 - SEL$F1D6E378 / T1@SEL$1
   4 - SEL$2         / MYALIAS@SEL$3
   5 - SEL$2         / T2@SEL$2
```

The operation table now has one less row because the removal of the NO_MERGE hint in the first factored subquery has allowed SEL$1 and SEL$3 to be merged. However, the ALIAS section has suddenly become more difficult to parse. What is that gobbledygook alias for operations 1 and 3? This hexadecimal name is actually a name assigned by the CBO by hashing SEL$1 and SEL$3. It turns out that in all releases up to and including 12cR1 (at least) this apparently random name is always precisely the same when SEL$1 is merged into SEL$3 (but not vice versa) irrespective of the statement, the database instance, or the database version! The only factors that determine the name of the merged query block are the names of the blocks being merged.

Operation 3 demonstrates another interesting point. Notice how the referencing query block (SEL$F1D6E378 left of the slash) is the query block related to the *operation,* but the referenced query block (SEL$1 on the right of the slash) is the original query block from where the referenced *object* appears.

When it comes to global hinting we might need to rely on these names, but despite the stability of these names it is actually best practice to explicitly name query blocks when global hints are used. Listing 8-4 shows us how.

Listing 8-4. Naming query blocks using the QB_NAME hint

```
WITH q1 AS (SELECT /*+  qb_name(qb1) */
                   c1 FROM t1)
    ,q2 AS (SELECT /*+  no_merge */
                   c2 FROM t2)
SELECT /*+ qb_name(qb2) */
       COUNT (c1)
  FROM q1, q2 myalias
 WHERE c1 = c2;


Plan hash value: 3055011902


-------------------------------------------
| Id  | Operation            | Name |
-------------------------------------------
|   0 | SELECT STATEMENT     |      |      |
|   1 |  SORT AGGREGATE      |      |      |
|   2 |   HASH JOIN          |      |      |
|   3 |    TABLE ACCESS FULL | T1   |      |
|   4 |    VIEW              |      |      |
|   5 |     TABLE ACCESS FULL| T2   |      |
-------------------------------------------


Query Block Name / Object Alias (identified by operation id):
-----------------------------------------------------------

   1 - SEL$86DECE37
   3 - SEL$86DECE37 / T1@QB1
   4 - SEL$1          / MYALIAS@QB2
   5 - SEL$1          / T2@SEL$1
```

Because we have explicitly renamed SEL$1 to QB1 and SEL$3 to QB2 by means of QB_NAME hints, the fully qualified object aliases have been changed for operations 3 and 4 in Listing 8-4. Furthermore, the query block name for operation 5 has changed from SEL$2 to SEL$1, as operation 5 is now associated with the first unnamed query block in the statement. What is more, the gobbledygook name for the merged query block has changed; whenever a query block named QB1 is merged into QB2 the resulting query block is named SEL$86DECE37. Listing 8-5 shows query block naming in a DML statement.

Listing 8-5. Additional query block with multi-table insert

```
INSERT ALL
  INTO t1 (c1)
  WITH q1 AS (SELECT /*+  qb_name(qb1) */
                     c1 FROM t1)
      ,q2 AS (SELECT /*+  no_merge */
                     c2 FROM t2)
  SELECT /*+ qb_name(qb2) */
         COUNT (c1)
    FROM q1, q2 myalias
   WHERE c1 = c2;


Plan hash value: 3420834736


-------------------------------------------
| Id  | Operation             | Name |
-------------------------------------------
|   0 | INSERT STATEMENT      |      |
|   1 |  MULTI-TABLE INSERT   |      |
|   2 |   VIEW                |      |
|   3 |    SORT AGGREGATE     |      |
|   4 |     HASH JOIN         |      |
|   5 |      TABLE ACCESS FULL | T1  |
|   6 |      VIEW             |      |
|   7 |       TABLE ACCESS FULL| T2  |
|   8 |   INTO               | T1   |
-------------------------------------------


Query Block Name / Object Alias (identified by operation id):
-------------------------------------------------------------

   1 - SEL$1
   2 - SEL$86DECE37 / from$_subquery$_002@SEL$1
   3 - SEL$86DECE37
   5 - SEL$86DECE37 / T1@QB1
   6 - SEL$2          / MYALIAS@QB2
   7 - SEL$2          / T2@SEL$2
```

The presence of the keyword ALL following the INSERT keyword in Listing 8-5 makes it syntactically a multi-table operation even though we are only inserting data into T1. However, the query block associated with the unmerged selection from T2 (operation 7 in Listing 8-5) has changed from SEL$1 to SEL$2. What has happened here is that a hidden query block has been added. The name of our merged query block hasn't changed though, because it is still formed by merging QB1 into QB2. When we look at global hinting later in this chapter the significance of this will become clearer.

In real life, the statements we are asked to tune are usually far more complicated than the simple examples that I have given so far. Listing 8-6 is a little more realistic.

Listing 8-6. Multiple query-block types

```
ALTER SESSION SET star_transformation_enabled=temp_disable;

INSERT /*+ APPEND */ INTO t2 (c2)
   WITH q1
        AS (SELECT *
              FROM book.t1@loopback t1)
   SELECT
          COUNT (*)
     FROM (SELECT *
              FROM q1, t2
             WHERE q1.c1 = t2.c2
             UNION ALL
             SELECT *
               FROM t3, t4
              WHERE t3.c3 = t4.c4
              -- ORDER BY 1 ... see the explanation of column projections below
            )
           ,t3
     WHERE c1 = c3;

COMMIT;

ALTER SESSION SET star_transformation_enabled=false;

Plan hash value: 2044158967
```

```
-------------------------------------------------
| Id  | Operation                      | Name |
-------------------------------------------------
|   0 | INSERT STATEMENT               |      |
|   1 |  LOAD AS SELECT                | T2   |
|   2 |   OPTIMIZER STATISTICS GATHERING |    |
|   3 |    SORT AGGREGATE              |      |
|*  4 |     HASH JOIN                  |      |
|   5 |      TABLE ACCESS FULL         | T3   |
|   6 |      VIEW                      |      |
|   7 |       UNION-ALL                |      |
|*  8 |        HASH JOIN               |      |
|   9 |         REMOTE                 | T1   |
|  10 |         TABLE ACCESS FULL      | T2   |
|* 11 |        HASH JOIN               |      |
|  12 |         TABLE ACCESS FULL      | T3   |
|  13 |         TABLE ACCESS FULL      | T4   |
-------------------------------------------------
```

```
Query Block Name / Object Alias (identified by operation id):
--------------------------------------------------------------

    1 - SEL$2
    5 - SEL$2          / T3@SEL$2
    6 - SET$1          / from$_subquery$_003@SEL$2
    7 - SET$1
    8 - SEL$F1D6E378
    9 - SEL$F1D6E378 / T1@SEL$1
   10 - SEL$F1D6E378 / T2@SEL$3
   11 - SEL$4
   12 - SEL$4         / T3@SEL$4
   13 - SEL$4         / T4@SEL$4
```

■ **Caution**   because of the unpredictable behaviour of dynamic sampling, the operations on lines 9 and 10 may be transposed.

Listing 8-6 shows a single-table INSERT statement that includes four occurrences of the SELECT keyword. As a single-table INSERT statement doesn't introduce an extra query block in the same way that a multi-table INSERT does, these four query blocks have been named SEL$1, SEL$2, SEL$3, and SEL$4. However, SEL$3 and SEL$4 are operands of a UNION ALL operator, and, as I explained at the beginning of Chapter 7, this results in the creation of a new query block that has been named SET$1. SET$1 is an inline view referenced in the main query (SEL$2). Unlike real tables, data dictionary views, and factored subqueries, there is no default object alias for an inline view. And since an alias isn't explicitly specified for the inline view in Listing 8-6, the CBO has made up the name from$_subquery$_003@SEL$2 and shown it for operation 6.

I would like to conclude this explanation of the ALIAS section of an execution plan with two observations:

- Listing 8-6 merges SEL$1 into SEL$3; the resulting query block name, SEL$F1D6E378, is the same as that in Listing 8-3. In both cases the name is formed by hashing SEL$1 and SEL$3.

- There is no entry for operations 2, 3, and 4 in Listing 8-6 because there is no object alias; the associated query block is the same as operation 1, i.e., SEL$2.

Outline Data

Following the ALIAS section of an execution plan display is the OUTLINE section. To explain the purpose and use of this OUTLINE section I will use the same statement as that provided in Listing 8-6. Listing 8-7 just shows the OUTLINE section.

Listing 8-7. Outline data for INSERT in Listing 8-6

```
01    /*+
02        BEGIN_OUTLINE_DATA
03        USE_HASH(@"SEL$F1D6E378" "T1"@"SEL$1")
04        LEADING(@"SEL$F1D6E378" "T1"@"SEL$1" "T2"@"SEL$3")
05        FULL(@"SEL$F1D6E378" "T1"@"SEL$1")
06        FULL(@"SEL$F1D6E378" "T2"@"SEL$3")
07        USE_HASH(@"SEL$4" "T4"@"SEL$4")
08        LEADING(@"SEL$4" "T3"@"SEL$4" "T4"@"SEL$4")
09        FULL(@"SEL$4" "T4"@"SEL$4")
10        FULL(@"SEL$4" "T3"@"SEL$4")
11        USE_HASH(@"SEL$2" "from$_subquery$_003"@"SEL$2")
12        LEADING(@"SEL$2" "T3"@"SEL$2" "from$_subquery$_003"@"SEL$2")
13        NO_ACCESS(@"SEL$2" "from$_subquery$_003"@"SEL$2")
14        FULL(@"SEL$2" "T3"@"SEL$2")
15        FULL(@"INS$1" "T2"@"INS$1")
16        OUTLINE(@"SEL$1")
17        OUTLINE(@"SEL$3")
18        OUTLINE_LEAF(@"INS$1")
19        OUTLINE_LEAF(@"SEL$2")
20        OUTLINE_LEAF(@"SET$1")
21        OUTLINE_LEAF(@"SEL$4")
22        MERGE(@"SEL$1")
23        OUTLINE_LEAF(@"SEL$F1D6E378")
24        ALL_ROWS
25        OPT_PARAM('star_transformation_enabled' 'temp_disable')
26        DB_VERSION('12.1.0.1')
27        OPTIMIZER_FEATURES_ENABLE('12.1.0.1')
28        IGNORE_OPTIM_EMBEDDED_HINTS
29        END_OUTLINE_DATA
30    */
```

This section of an execution plan is just full of that hexadecimal gobbledygook! Hopefully the explanation in the previous section of how query blocks and object aliases are named makes it a little less difficult to parse, but the section is clearly not designed for human readability. Be aware that the line numbers in Listing 8-7 will not appear in real life. I have added line numbers to assist with the explanations that follow.

■ **Note** DML statements make use of additional "query blocks" that don't appear in the alias section. You will see that operation 15 makes reference to a query blocked named INS$1.DELETE, MERGE, and UPDATE statements include a DEL$1, MRG$1, and UPD$1 "query block" respectively. If you explain a CREATE INDEX or ALTER INDEX statement you will also see mention of a CRI$1 "query block."

The purpose of the OUTLINE section of an execution plan is to provide all the hints necessary to fully specify the execution plan for the statement. If you just take the section, which conveniently includes the /*+ */ hint syntax, and paste it into your statement at any point where a hint is legal, the theory is that while the execution plan remains legal it will not change regardless of any changes to object statistics, system statistics, or most initialization parameters; you will have removed all flexibility from the CBO.

These types of hints are actually what are kept in stored outlines and SQL plan baselines, but in fact they do not fully specify the execution plan for Listing 8-6. Let us take a detailed look at the different types of hints so as to understand what is missing.

Outline Interpretation Hints

When customers of Oracle upgraded from 9i to 10g many found that their stored outlines no longer worked as expected. The problem was that the interpretation of hints changed. These days hints like those on lines 24, 25, 26, and 27 of Listing 8-7 control the precise way that the remaining hints are interpreted. Of course, the ALL_ROWS hint might be replaced by one of the FIRST_ROWS variants if you have specified such a hint in your code or have a non-default setting of the OPTMIZER_MODE initialization parameter. The value of the parameter passed to OPTIMIZER_FEATURES_ENABLE may also differ because of the database version or because of a hint or initialization parameter setting.

How these parameters work together with the undocumented DB_VERSION hint need not concern us. All we need to know is that the intention is to avoid changes in behavior when the database version or initialization parameters change. If there are any non-default settings for optimizer initialization parameters, such as the STAR_TRANSFORMATION_ENABLED setting that I changed before explaining the query, one or more OPT_PARAM hints will also be present, such as that found on line 25.

Identifying Outline Data

The hints on lines 2, 28, and 29 in Listing 8-7 work together to ensure that the outline hints are treated differently from other hints in the statement. The IGNORE_OPTIM_EMBEDDED_HINTS hint tells the CBO to ignore *most* hints in the SQL statement except those that are bracketed by BEGIN_OUTLINE_DATA and END_OUTLINE_DATA hints. I have emphasized the word *most* because there are a number of hints that aren't implemented in the OUTLINE section of an execution plan, and thankfully these aren't ignored.

THE TERM "OUTLINE"

The term "outline" is somewhat overloaded, and to avoid confusion I need to explain its different uses:

- There is a section in the output of DBMS_XPLAN functions generated as a result of the OUTLINE fine-grained control that has the heading Outline Data.

- The content of the outline section includes hints that are individually referred to as *outline hints*, and the entire set is referred to simply as an *outline*. These outline hints are bracketed by the two hints BEGIN_OUTLINE_DATA and END_OUTLINE_DATA.

- Outline hints are the basis for the implementation of plan stability features such as stored outlines and SQL plan baselines.

- Outline hints can be pasted into SQL statements where they continue to be referred to as outline hints. Hints other than those bracketed by the BEGIN_OUTLINE_DATA and END_OUTLINE_DATA hints are referred to as *embedded hints*.

- And if that isn't confusing enough, one of these outline hints is named OUTLINE and another is named OUTLINE_LEAF.

Hopefully this helps a bit.

An example of an embedded hint that isn't ignored by IGNORE_OPTIM_EMBEDDED_HINTS is APPEND. APPEND causes a serial direct-path load to occur. Neither the APPEND hint in Listing 8-6, nor any alternative hint that performs the same function, makes an appearance in Listing 8-7, but a serial direct-path load has still occurred. To make this point clearer Listing 8-8 shows how we might move our outline hints into Listing 8-6 to prevent changes to the execution plan.

Listing 8-8. Use of outline hints in source code

```
INSERT /*+ APPEND */
     INTO   t2 (c2)
  WITH q1
       AS (SELECT *
             FROM book.t1@loopback t1)
  SELECT /*+
         BEGIN_OUTLINE_DATA
         <other hints suppressed for brevity>
         IGNORE_OPTIM_EMBEDDED_HINTS
         END_OUTLINE_DATA
       */
         COUNT (*)
  FROM (SELECT *
          FROM q1, t2
          WHERE q1.c1 = t2.c2
         UNION ALL
         SELECT *
          FROM t3, t4
          WHERE t3.c3 = t4.c4)
       ,t3
  WHERE c1 = c3;
```

The highlighted hints in Listing 8-8 originated from Listing 8-7 but have been shortened for brevity. If you look at the execution plan for Listing 8-8 you will see that it is unchanged from that of Listing 8-6 and in particular that operation 1 is still LOAD AS SELECT. If the APPEND hint is removed from Listing 8-8 then operation 1 becomes LOAD TABLE CONVENTIONAL, as no instruction to use direct-path load appears in the outline hints.

■ **Note** Non-default values for optimizer parameters, such as _optimizer_gather_stats_on_load, will also be ignored unless there is an appropriate OPT_PARAM hint included in the outline hints. This is because of the presence of the OPTIMIZER_FEATURES_ENABLE hint that resets optimizer parameters to the default for that release.

For a complete list of hints that are not implemented in an outline you can look at the view V$SQL_HINT. All rows where OUTLINE_VERSION is NULL identify hints that, if included in source code, will not be implemented in an outline and will not be ignored by IGNORE_OPTIM_EMBEDDED_HINTS. Hints that are excluded from outlines include RESULT_CACHE, which we discussed in Chapter 4, as well as MATERIALIZE and INLINE, which control the behavior of factored subqueries. We will look at the materialization of factored subqueries in Chapter 13.

■ **Note** An amusing paradox arises when IGNORE_OPTIM_EMBEDDED_HINTS is supplied as an embedded hint outside of an outline. In fact, such a hint has no effect. This in effect means that it ignored itself!

I am emphasizing the distinction between hints that appear in outlines and those that don't because many people remove all other embedded hints from their SQL statement when they paste outline hints into their code. Don't remove any embedded hints until you are sure that they are truly unnecessary!

Final Query Block Structure

The hints OUTLINE_LEAF and OUTLINE appear in Listing 8-7 on lines 16, 17, 18, 19, 20, 21, and 23. These hints indicate which query blocks exist in the final execution plan (OUTLINE_LEAF) and which were merged or otherwise transformed out of existence (OUTLINE).[2]

It is about time I gave you a warning about the undocumented hints you see in outlines. You shouldn't try changing them or using them outside of outlines unless you know what you are doing. For example, if you want to suppress view merging you could use OUTLINE_LEAF to do so. However, it is much safer to use the documented NO_MERGE hint for this purpose in the way I have done several times in this chapter. Reserve the use of hints like OUTLINE and OUTLINE_LEAF to the occasions when you paste outline hints unaltered into your code.

Query Transformation Hints

The MERGE hint on line 22 in Listing 8-7 shows the use of the simple view-merging query transformation applied to query block SEL$1. We will cover most of the query transformations available to the CBO in Chapter 13, and all discretionary query transformations that are used in a statement will be reflected in an outline by hints such as MERGE.

Comments

The NO_ACCESS hint on line 13 in Listing 8-7 is a bit of a mystery to me. It documents the fact that the CBO did not merge a query block. It doesn't actually have any effect when you place it in your code, and it doesn't seem to matter if you remove it from the outline. It seems to be just a comment.

Final State Optimization Hints

This hints on lines 3 to 12 and on lines 14 and 15 in Listing 8-7 look *almost* like the normal embedded hints that appear in SQL statements. They control join order, join method, and access method. I say *almost* because they include global hint syntax and fully qualified object aliases, which, although legal, are rarely found in the source code of SQL statements. We will look into global hints in more detail later in the chapter.

We have now categorized all of the outline hints in Listing 8-7. Let us move on to other sections of the DBMS_XPLAN output.

Peeked Binds

When a call is made to DBMS_XPLAN.DISPLAY_CURSOR, the PEEKED_BINDS section follows the OUTLINE section. Listing 8-6 cannot be used to demonstrate PEEKED_BINDS for two reasons:

- The statement doesn't have any bind variables.

- The statement uses a database link and because of this, in releases prior to 12cR1, no bind variable peeking is performed.

So for the purposes of the PEEKED_BINDS section I will use the script shown in Listing 8-9.

---

[2]Sometimes both an OUTLINE hint and an OUTLINE_LEAF hint appear for a surviving query block.

Listing 8-9. Local database query demonstrating peeked binds

```
DECLARE
    dummy    NUMBER := 0;
BEGIN
    FOR r IN (WITH q1 AS (SELECT /*+ TAG1 */
                                 * FROM t1)
              SELECT *
                FROM (SELECT *
                        FROM q1, t2
                       WHERE q1.c1 = t2.c2 AND c1 > dummy
                       UNION ALL
                       SELECT *
                         FROM t3, t4
                        WHERE t3.c3 = t4.c4 AND c3 > dummy)
                     ,t3
               WHERE c1 = c3)
    LOOP
        NULL;
    END LOOP;
END;
/

SET LINES 200 PAGES 0

SELECT p.*
  FROM v$sql s
      ,TABLE (
           DBMS_XPLAN.display_cursor (s.sql_id
                                     ,s.child_number
                                     ,'BASIC +PEEKED_BINDS')) p
 WHERE sql_text LIKE 'WITH%SELECT /*+ TAG1 */%';

EXPLAINED SQL STATEMENT:
------------------------
WITH Q1 AS (SELECT /*+ TAG1 */ * FROM T1) SELECT * FROM (SELECT * FROM
Q1, T2 WHERE Q1.C1 = T2.C2 AND C1 > :B1 UNION ALL SELECT * FROM T3, T4
WHERE T3.C3 = T4.C4 AND C3 > :B1 ) ,T3 WHERE C1 = C3

Plan hash value: 2648033210
```

```
-------------------------------------
| Id  | Operation            | Name |
-------------------------------------
|   0 | SELECT STATEMENT     |      |
|   1 |  HASH JOIN           |      |
|   2 |   TABLE ACCESS FULL  | T3   |
|   3 |   VIEW               |      |
|   4 |    UNION-ALL         |      |
|   5 |     HASH JOIN        |      |
|   6 |      TABLE ACCESS FULL| T1  |
|   7 |      TABLE ACCESS FULL| T2  |
|   8 |     HASH JOIN        |      |
|   9 |      TABLE ACCESS FULL| T3  |
|  10 |      TABLE ACCESS FULL| T4  |
-------------------------------------

Peeked Binds (identified by position):
-------------------------------------

   1 - :B1 (NUMBER): 0
   2 - :B1 (NUMBER, Primary=1)
```

Unlike the earlier examples in this chapter that imply a call to EXPLAIN PLAN followed by a call to DBMS_XPLAN.DISPLAY, Listing 8-9 actually runs a statement and then calls DBMS_XPLAN.DISPLAY_CURSOR to produce the output. You will see that I included the string TAG1 in the comment of the statement. This comment appears to the PL/SQL compiler as a hint (it isn't, of course) and so the comment isn't removed. After running the statement and discarding the rows returned, I call DBMS_XPLAN.DISPLAY_CURSOR using a *left lateral join* with V$SQL to identify the SQL_ID. I will cover left lateral joins when we talk about join methods in Chapter 11. The output of the call to DBMS_XPLAN.DISPLAY_CURSOR is also shown in Listing 8-9.

We can see that when the query was parsed the value of the bind variable :B1 was looked at in case its value might influence the choice of execution plan. The bind variable was added by PL/SQL as a result of the use of the PL/SQL variable I have named DUMMY. DUMMY was used twice, but there is no need to peek at its value twice. That is the meaning of the Primary=1 part of the output—it indicates that the value of the second use of the bind variable is taken from the first.

It is worthwhile repeating that bind variables are only peeked at when the statement is parsed. With a few exceptions, such as adaptive cursor sharing, the second and subsequent executions of a statement with different values for the bind variables will not cause any more peeking, and the output from DBMS_XPLAN.DISPLAY_CURSOR will not be updated by such calls.

Predicate Information

The PREDICATE section of the DBMS_XPLAN function calls appears after any PEEKED_BINDS section. We have already covered filter predicates in Chapter 3 because the default output level of the DBMS_XPLAN functions is TYPICAL and the PREDICATE section is included in the TYPICAL level. For completeness, Listing 8-10 shows the filter predicates of the statement in Listing 8-6.

Listing 8-10. Predicate information for query in Listing 8-6

```
Predicate Information (identified by operation id):
---------------------------------------------------

   4 - access("C1"="C3")
   8 - access("T1"."C1"="T2"."C2")
  11 - access("T3"."C3"="T4"."C4")
```

The access predicates in this case relate to the three HASH JOIN operations.

Column Projection

The next section of the DBMS_XPLAN output to be displayed shows the columns that are returned by the various row source operations. These may not be the same as those specified by the programmer because in some cases the CBO can determine that they are not required and then eliminate them. Listing 8-11 shows the column projection data for the statement in Listing 8-6.

Listing 8-11. Column projection information for the query in Listing 8-6

```
Column Projection Information (identified by operation id):
----------------------------------------------------------

   1 - SYSDEF[4], SYSDEF[16336], SYSDEF[1], SYSDEF[112], SYSDEF[16336]
   2 - (#keys=3) COUNT(*)[22]
   3 - (#keys=0) COUNT(*)[22]
   4 - (#keys=1) "C3"[NUMBER,22], "C1"[NUMBER,22]
   5 - (rowset=200) "C3"[NUMBER,22]
   6 - "C1"[NUMBER,22]
   7 - STRDEF[22]
   8 - (#keys=1) "T1"."C1"[NUMBER,22], "T2"."C2"[NUMBER,22]
   9 - "T1"."C1"[NUMBER,22]
  10 - (rowset=200) "T2"."C2"[NUMBER,22]
  11 - (#keys=1) "T3"."C3"[NUMBER,22], "T4"."C4"[NUMBER,22]
  12 - (rowset=200) "T3"."C3"[NUMBER,22]
  13 - (rowset=200) "T4"."C4"[NUMBER,22]
```

This section can be useful when you are assessing memory requirements, as you can see not only the names of the columns but also the data types and the size of the columns. Operations 4, 8, and 11 include the text (#keys=1). This means that there is one column used in the join. The columns used in a join or sort are always listed first so, for instance, operation 11 uses T3.C3 for the hash join.

I find the output associated with operation 3 to be amusing. The text (#keys=0) indicates that no columns were used in the sort. As I explained in Chapter 3, there isn't a sort with SORT AGGREGATE! You will also see that operation 7, the UNION-ALL operator, shows an identifier name as STRDEF. I have no idea what STRDEF stands for, but it is used for internally generated column names.

> ■ **Note** The ORDER BY clause in a set query block must specify positions or aliases rather than explicit expressions. A commented-out line in bold in Listing 8-6 gives an example.

Remote SQL

Because Listing 8-6 uses a database link, a portion of the statement needs to be sent to the far side of the link for processing. Listing 8-12 shows this SQL.

Listing 8-12. Remote SQL information for query in Listing 8-6

```
Remote SQL Information (identified by operation id):
---------------------------------------------------

   9 - SELECT /*+ */ "C1" FROM "BOOK"."T1" "T1" (accessing 'LOOPBACK' )
```

You will see that the text of the query sent to the "remote" database has been altered to quote identifiers, specify the schema (in my case BOOK), and add an object alias. If hints were supplied in the original statement then the appropriate subset would be included in the query sent to the "remote" database. This remote SQL statement will, of course, have its own execution plan, but if you need to examine this you will have to do so separately on the remote database.

Adaptive Plans

Adaptive execution plans are new to 12cR1 and are probably the most well-known of the new adaptive features of that release. With the exception of a note, information about execution plan adaptation is only shown when ADAPTIVE is explicitly added to the format parameter of the DBMS_XPLAN call. Contrary to the documentation, ADAPTIVE is a fine-grained control, not a format level.

The idea is of adaptive plans is as follows: You have two possible plans. You start with one and if that doesn't work out you switch to the other in mid-flight. Although *hybrid parallel query distribution*, which we will discuss in the context of parallel queries later in this chapter, is very similar, as of 12.1.0.1 the only truly adaptive mechanism is the table join.

The adaptive join works like this. You find some matching rows from one of the tables being joined and see how many you get. If you get a small number you can access the second table being joined with a nested loops join. If it seems like you are getting a lot then at some point you will give up on the nested loops and start working on a hash join.

We will discuss the ins and outs of nested loops joins and hash joins in Chapter 11, but right now all we need to focus on is understanding what the execution plans are trying to tell us.

Not all joins are adaptive. In fact most are not, so for my demonstration I have had to rely on the example provided in the SQL Tuning Guide. Listing 8-13 shows my adaptation of the SQL Tuning Guide's example of adaptive joins.

Listing 8-13. Use of adaptive execution plans

```
ALTER SYSTEM FLUSH SHARED_POOL;

SET LINES 200 PAGES 0
VARIABLE b1 NUMBER;
EXEC :b1 := 15;

SELECT product_name
  FROM oe.order_items o, oe.product_information p
 WHERE unit_price = :b1 AND o.quantity > 1 AND p.product_id = o.product_id;

SELECT *
  FROM TABLE (DBMS_XPLAN.display_cursor (format => 'TYPICAL +ADAPTIVE'));

  EXEC :b1 := 1000;

SELECT product_name
  FROM oe.order_items o, oe.product_information p
 WHERE unit_price = :b1 AND o.quantity > 1 AND p.product_id = o.product_id;

SELECT *
  FROM TABLE (DBMS_XPLAN.display_cursor (format => 'TYPICAL'));

  EXEC :b1 := 15;

SELECT product_name
  FROM oe.order_items o, oe.product_information p
 WHERE unit_price = :b1 AND o.quantity > 1 AND p.product_id = o.product_id;

SELECT *
  FROM TABLE (DBMS_XPLAN.display_cursor (format => 'TYPICAL'));
```

Before looking at the output from the code in Listing 8-13, let us look at what it does. Listing 8-13 starts by flushing the shared pool to get rid of any previous runs and then sets up a SQL*Plus variable B1, which is initialized to 15 and used as a bind variable in the query based on the OE example schema. After the query returns, the execution plan is displayed using DBMS_XPLAN.DISPLAY_CURSOR. Listing 8-13 specifies ADAPTIVE in the call to DBMS_XPLAN. DISPLAY_CURSOR to show the bits of the execution plan we are interested in.

The value of the SQL*Plus variable B1 is then changed from 15 to 1000 and the query is run a second time. Finally, B1 is changed back to 15 and the query is rerun for the third and final time. After the second and third runs of our query we don't list the adaptive parts of the execution plan in our call to DBMS_XPLAN.DISPLAY_CURSOR.

Listing 8-14 shows the output from Listing 18-13.

Listing 8-14. Execution plans from an adaptive query run multiple times

```
System altered.
 PL/SQL procedure successfully completed.
Screws <B.28.S>
<cut>
Screws <B.28.S>
```

13 rows selected.
SQL_ID g4hyzd4v4ggm7, **child number 0**

SELECT product_name   FROM oe.order_items o, oe.product_information p
WHERE unit_price = :b1 AND o.quantity > 1 AND p.product_id =
o.product_id

Plan hash value: 1553478007

```
---------------------------------------------------------------------------------
| Id  | Operation                        | Name                   | Rows | Time     |
---------------------------------------------------------------------------------
|   0 | SELECT STATEMENT                 |                        |      |          |
| * 1 |  HASH JOIN                       |                        |    4 | 00:00:01 |
|-  2 |   NESTED LOOPS                   |                        |      |          |
|-  3 |    NESTED LOOPS                  |                        |    4 | 00:00:01 |
|-  4 |     STATISTICS COLLECTOR         |                        |      |          |
| * 5 |      TABLE ACCESS FULL           | ORDER_ITEMS            |    4 | 00:00:01 |
|- * 6|      INDEX UNIQUE SCAN           | PRODUCT_INFORMATION_PK |    1 |          |
|-  7 |     TABLE ACCESS BY INDEX ROWID| PRODUCT_INFORMATION    |    1 | 00:00:01 |
|   8 |    TABLE ACCESS FULL             | PRODUCT_INFORMATION    |    1 | 00:00:01 |
---------------------------------------------------------------------------------
```

Predicate Information (identified by operation id):
----

   1 - access("P"."PRODUCT_ID"="O"."PRODUCT_ID")
   5 - filter(("UNIT_PRICE"=:B1 AND "O"."QUANTITY">1))
   6 - access("P"."PRODUCT_ID"="O"."PRODUCT_ID")

Note

   - this is an adaptive plan (rows marked '-' are inactive)

33 rows selected.
 PL/SQL procedure successfully completed.
no rows selected.
SQL_ID g4hyzd4v4ggm7, **child number 1**

SELECT product_name   FROM oe.order_items o, oe.product_information p
WHERE unit_price = :b1 AND o.quantity > 1 AND p.product_id =
o.product_id

Plan hash value: 1255158658

```
---------------------------------------------------------------------------------
| Id  | Operation                      | Name                   | Rows | Time     |
---------------------------------------------------------------------------------
|   0 | SELECT STATEMENT               |                        |      |          |
|   1 |  NESTED LOOPS                  |                        |      |          |
|   2 |   NESTED LOOPS                 |                        |   13 | 00:00:01 |
| * 3 |    TABLE ACCESS FULL           | ORDER_ITEMS            |    4 | 00:00:01 |
| * 4 |    INDEX UNIQUE SCAN           | PRODUCT_INFORMATION_PK |    1 |          |
|   5 |   TABLE ACCESS BY INDEX ROWID| PRODUCT_INFORMATION    |    4 | 00:00:01 |
---------------------------------------------------------------------------------
```

Predicate Information (identified by operation id):
----

   3 - filter(("UNIT_PRICE"=:B1 AND "O"."QUANTITY">1))
   4 - access("P"."PRODUCT_ID"="O"."PRODUCT_ID")

Note

   - statistics feedback used for this statement
   - this is an adaptive plan

30 rows selected.
 PL/SQL procedure successfully completed.
Screws <B.28.S>
Screws <B.28.S>

13 rows selected.
SQL_ID g4hyzd4v4ggm7, **child number 1**

SELECT product_name   FROM oe.order_items o, oe.product_information p
WHERE unit_price = :b1 AND o.quantity > 1 AND p.product_id =
o.product_id

Plan hash value: 1255158658

| Id | Operation | Name | Rows | Time |

0	SELECT STATEMENT			
1	NESTED LOOPS			
2	NESTED LOOPS		13	00:00:01
* 3	TABLE ACCESS FULL	ORDER_ITEMS	4	00:00:01
* 4	INDEX UNIQUE SCAN	PRODUCT_INFORMATION_PK	1	
5	TABLE ACCESS BY INDEX ROWID	PRODUCT_INFORMATION	4	00:00:01

Predicate Information (identified by operation id):
----

   3 - filter(("UNIT_PRICE"=:B1 AND "O"."QUANTITY">1))
   4 - access("P"."PRODUCT_ID"="O"."PRODUCT_ID")

Note

   - statistics feedback used for this statement
   - this is an adaptive plan

30 rows selected.

The first query returns 13 rows—more than the CBO's estimate of 4—and by taking a careful look at the first child cursor for this statement (child 0) you can see that a hash join has been used. You can see this by mentally removing the lines with a minus sign that show the alternative plan that was discarded. When we rerun the same SQL statement, this time with a bind variable that results in no rows being returned, we see that a new child cursor has been created (child 1) and that we have used a nested loops join. This time I didn't use the ADAPTIVE keyword in the format parameter of DBMS_XPLAN.DISPLAY_CURSOR, and the unused portions of the execution plan have not been shown.

■ **Note**   My thanks to Randolf Geist, who, after several attempts, convinced me that the extra child cursor is actually a manifestation of statistics feedback and not of adaptive plans.

All this is very impressive, but what happens when we run the query for the third time, using the original value of the bind variable? Unfortunately, we continue to use the nested loops join and don't revert back to the hash join!

We have already seen one big feature of Oracle database that adapts once and doesn't adapt again: bind variable peeking. Bind variable peeking didn't work out well, but hopefully this same shortcoming of adaptive execution plans will be fixed sometime soon.

Result Cache Information

In Chapter 4 I showed how the runtime engine can make use of the result cache. If the result cache is used in a statement, then a section is placed in the output of all DBMS_XPLAN functions that shows its use. This section cannot be suppressed, but it only contains meaningful information when used with DBMS_XPLAN.DISPLAY and even then only when the level is TYPICAL, ALL, or ADVANCED. Listing 8-15 shows a simple example.

Listing 8-15. Result cache information from a simple statement

```
SET PAGES 0 LINES 300
EXPLAIN PLAN FOR SELECT /*+ RESULT_CACHE */ * FROM DUAL;

Explain complete.

SELECT * FROM TABLE (DBMS_XPLAN.display (format => 'TYPICAL'));

Plan hash value: 272002086
```

Id	Operation	Name	Rows	Bytes	Cost (%CPU)	Time
0	SELECT STATEMENT		1	2	2 (0)	00:00:01
1	RESULT CACHE	9p1ghjb9czx4w7vqtuxk5zudg6				
2	TABLE ACCESS FULL	DUAL	1	2	2 (0)	00:00:01

```
Result Cache Information (identified by operation id):
-----------------------------------------------------

   1 - column-count=1; attributes=(single-row); name="SELECT /*+ RESULT_CACHE */ * FROM DUAL"

14 rows selected.
```

Notes

The NOTE section of the execution plan provides textual information that may be useful. There are lots of different types of notes that can appear in this section. We have already seen notes relating to adaptive plans. Here are some more of the notes that I have seen:

```
- rule based optimizer used (consider using cbo)

- cbqt star transformation used for this statement

- Warning: basic plan statistics not available. These are only collected when:
    * hint 'gather_plan_statistics' is used for the statement or
    * parameter 'statistics_level' is set to 'ALL', at session or system level
```

The first note will be displayed when the execution plan is produced by the RBO and not the CBO, perhaps because a RULE hint is used. The second hint is displayed when cost-based query transformation (CBQT) results in a star transformation. The third note is displayed when you have selected a format parameter such as ALLSTATS but the statistics from the runtime engine are not available, perhaps for the reasons given in the note or perhaps because you have used DBMS_XPLAN.DISPLAY and the SQL statement hasn't actually been run.

In the case of the statement in Listing 8-6 a fourth type of note appears, and this is shown in Listing 8-16.

Listing 8-16. Note for the query in Listing 8-6

```
Note
-----
    - dynamic sampling used for this statement (level=2)
```

This note is displayed because I used hints to suppress the gathering of statistics on the example tables as they were created. As a consequence, the CBO sampled the data in the tables to generate statistics for its plan evaluation.

That concludes our discussion of execution plan displays. Let us move on to the second major topic of this chapter, parallel execution plans.

Understanding Parallel Execution Plans

When a SQL statement uses parallel execution, two or more *parallel execution servers* (sometimes known as parallel execution slaves or parallel query slaves) are allocated to the original session. Each of the parallel query servers can perform a portion of the total workload, thus allowing the SQL statement as a whole to finish more quickly.

The topic of parallel execution is a lengthy one, and a general book on Oracle database performance could spend a chapter dedicated entirely to the topic. In fact, the chapter entitled "*Using Parallel Execution*" in the *VLDB and Partitioning Guide* does just that. However, at this point I just want to focus on interpreting execution plans that include parallel operations and analyzing the performance of same. But before looking at an example execution plan I need to lay some groundwork. Let us start off with a look at which SQL statements can be run in parallel and which cannot be.

Operations That Can Be Run in Parallel

The following DDL statements can be run in parallel:

- CREATE INDEX

- CREATE TABLE ... AS SELECT

- ALTER INDEX ... REBUILD

- ALTER TABLE ... [MOVE|SPLIT|COALESCE] PARTITION

- ALTER TABLE ... MOVE

- ALTER INDEX ... [REBUILD|SPLIT] PARTITION

■ **Tip**   When you validate a constraint there is a recursive query involved, and that recursive query can also be performed in parallel.

When a DDL statement is parallelized, multiple blocks of the object being created are written simultaneously. All DML operations can be run in parallel as well, and once again multiple blocks can be written or updated in parallel. The terms *parallel DDL* and *parallel DML* are used to refer to these types of parallel operations.

The third, and most common, type of parallel operation is referred to as *parallel query*. The term *parallel query* doesn't just refer to running SELECT statements in parallel. The term is also used to refer to the parallelization of subqueries in a DDL or DML statement. So, for example, if you run the query portion of a CREATE TABLE ... AS SELECT statement in parallel but you write the data to disk serially, you are performing parallel query but not a parallel DDL.

Parallel query is conceptually more complex than parallel DDL or parallel DML. A query, or subquery, usually involves multiple row source operations. It is normal to see an execution plan within which some of the row source operations run in parallel and some run serially. The reasons why there is often a mix of serial and parallel operations within an execution plan will become clear as we go on.

Controlling Parallel Execution

There are subtle differences in the mechanisms for controlling parallel DDL, parallel DML, and parallel query, so I want to look at them separately. Let us start off with parallel DDL.

Controlling Parallel DDL

The two main considerations for running parallel DDL are the session status and the syntax of the DDL statement. By default, parallel DDL is enabled, but it can be altered for the current session using one of the following commands:

- ALTER SESSION DISABLE PARALLEL DDL

- ALTER SESSION ENABLE DDL

- ALTER SESSION FORCE PARALLEL DDL [PARALLEL n]

You can see which, if any, of these statements was issued last by looking at the PDDL_STATUS column in V$SESSION. PDDL_STATUS has valid values of DISABLED, ENABLED, or FORCED. We will see what these commands do in a moment, but first we need to look at Listing 8-17, which shows the syntactic construct for running parallel DDL.

Listing 8-17. Syntax for parallel DDL

```
CREATE INDEX t1_i1
   ON t1 (c1)
   PARALLEL 10;
```

Listing 8-17 uses the PARALLEL clause, which is available in all statements that support parallel DDL, to *suggest* that the contents of the index are written in parallel. The *degree of parallelism* (DOP) is specified as "10" in the statement. This PARALLEL clause could have been abbreviated to just PARALLEL if I didn't want to explicitly specify the DOP. I will explain what the DOP is in a few pages after explaining a few more concepts.

The value of PDDL_STATUS can be interpreted as follows:

- If the value of PDDL_STATUS is DISABLED then the index T1_I1 in Listing 8-17 will not be built in parallel despite the presence of the PARALLEL clause.

- If the value of PDDL_STATUS is ENABLED the index will be built with the specified or default value of parallelism.

- If the value of PDDL_STATUS is FORCED the index will be built in parallel using the degree specified in the ALTER SESSION FORCE PARALLEL DDL statement. In fact, if the value of PDDL_STATUS is FORCED the table will be created in parallel even if no PARALLEL clause is specified in the SQL statement.

■ Tip   In releases prior to 12cR1, specifying the DOP when performing parallel DDL also set the default DOP for subsequent parallel queries. I can't tell you the number of times that I have seen cases where a DBA or developer has forgotten to issue an ALTER INDEX xxx PARALLEL 1 statement after an index is created or rebuilt. Sensibly, if you move a table or rebuild an index in parallel in 12cR1 the data dictionary is not updated. However, if you create a table or an index in parallel the data dictionary retains the DOP you specified as it did in previous releases, so continue to be careful!

Controlling Parallel DML

As with parallel DDL, we need to consider the session status and the syntax of a parallel DML statement, but there are other considerations as well. By default, parallel DML is *disabled,* but it can be altered for the current session using one of the following commands:

- ALTER SESSION DISABLE DML

- ALTER SESSION ENABLE PARALLEL DML

- ALTER SESSION FORCE PARALLEL DML [PARALLEL n]

You can see which, if any, of these statements was issued last by looking at the PDML_STATUS column in V$SESSION.

I will explain why parallel DML is disabled by default shortly. First of all, take a look at Listing 8-18, which shows how to use parallel DML when it is enabled.

Listing 8-18. Syntax for parellel DML

```
ALTER SESSION ENABLE PARALLEL DML;

INSERT INTO t2 (c2)
   SELECT /*+ parallel */
        c1 FROM t1;

INSERT /*+ parallel(t3 10) */
     INTO  t3 (c3)
   SELECT c1 FROM t1;

ALTER TABLE t3 PARALLEL 10;

INSERT INTO t3 (c3)
   SELECT c1 FROM t1;

COMMIT;
```

The first INSERT statement in Listing 8-18 uses a *statement-level hint* to allow parallel DML and parallel queries throughout the statement. Because it is a statement-level hint it can appear in any legal location.

The second query in Listing 8-18 shows an alternative variant of the PARALLEL hint that specifies a particular object, specifically table T3, together with an optional DOP. For the hint to apply to parallel DML it needs to be placed in the query after the INSERT keyword as shown. This is because the hint applies to the INS$1 query block that we discussed earlier.

The third query in Listing 8-18 includes no hint. However, parallel DML will still be possible because the preceding ALTER TABLE command set a default DOP for the object. The value of PDML_STATUS can be interpreted as follows:

- If the value of PDML_STATUS is DISABLED then none of the statements in Listing 8-18 will use parallel DML.

- If the value of PDML_STATUS is ENABLED all of the statements in Listing 8-18 will use parallel DML.

- If the value of PDML_STATUS is FORCED all of the statements in Listing 8-18 will use parallel DML using the degree specified in the ALTER SESSION FORCE PARALLEL DML statement. In fact, if the value of PDML_STATUS is FORCED parallel DML will be used even if no hint is specified in the SQL statement and none of the tables concerned specify a DOP greater than one.

Let me return now to the question of why parallel DML is disabled at the session level by default. It will help if we look at what happens when we try to run the code seen in Listing 8-19.

151

Listing 8-19. Trying to read a table after it has been modified in parallel

```
ALTER SESSION ENABLE PARALLEL DML;

-- The statement below succeeds

INSERT INTO t2 (c2)
   SELECT /*+ parallel */
         c1 FROM t1;

-- The statement below fails

INSERT INTO t2 (c2)
   SELECT c1 FROM t1;

COMMIT;

-- The statement below succeeds

INSERT INTO t2 (c2)
   SELECT c1 FROM t1;

-- The statement below succeeds

INSERT INTO t2 (c2)
   SELECT c1 FROM t1;

COMMIT;
```

If you try running the code in Listing 8-19 you will find that the second INSERT statement fails, even though it doesn't use parallel DML. The error code is

```
ORA-12838: cannot read/modify an object after modifying it in parallel
```

The problem is that parallel DML statements may use what is known as *direct path writes,* which means that the inserted rows are not in the SGA and can only be read from disk after the transaction commits. This change in semantics is the reason that parallel DML is not enabled by default. Notice that as of 12cR1 direct path writes are only used when inserting rows into a table and even then not always. When rows are updated or deleted direct path writes are never used. However, you will get the same error message regardless of which DML statement is performed in parallel.

Controlling Parallel Query

We now come to the most complicated of the three ways that a SQL statement can be parallelized: parallel query. Parallel query is enabled at the session level by default, and at the risk of appearing repetitive, here are the three commands that affect parallel query at the session level:

- `ALTER SESSION DISABLE PARALLEL QUERY`
- `ALTER SESSION ENABLE QUERY`
- `ALTER SESSION FORCE PARALLEL QUERY [PARALLEL n]`

■ **Caution**   Whereas parallel DDL and parallel DML can be forced with `ALTER SESSION FORCE` statements, `ALTER SESSION FORCE PARALLEL QUERY` does not force parallel query! I will explain why shortly after we have laid some more groundwork.

You can see which, if any, of these statements was issued last by looking at the PQ_STATUS column in V$SESSION.

As with parallel DML, parallel query can be managed at the statement level by setting the DOP for an object and/or by using hints. However, there are more hints to look at when discussing parallel query. These are the hints that I will be discussing in the forthcoming sections:

- PARALLEL

- PARALLEL_INDEX

- PQ_DISTRIBUTE

- PQ_REPLICATE

I am not quite ready to provide examples of parallel query. We need to cover a few more concepts first, beginning with *granules of parallelism*.

Granules of Parallelism

There are two types of granule that can be allocated when an object is accessed in parallel. We will discuss *block-range granules* first and then move on to *partition granules*. Always remember that when multiple objects are accessed in the same SQL statement, some may be accessed using block-range granules, some with partition granules, and some may be accessed serially without any use of granules.

Block-range Granules

When an object is accessed using multi-block reads we can parallelize those reads. For example, when a TABLE FULL SCAN operation is needed a number of parallel query servers can be used to each read a portion of the table.

To help with this, the table is split into what are known as block-range granules. These block-range granules are identified at runtime, and there is nothing in the execution plan that tells you how many block-range granules there are or how big they are. The number of block-range granules is usually a lot larger than the DOP.

Block-range granules can be used even when multiple partitions from a partitioned table are accessed. Figure 8-1 shows the basic idea.

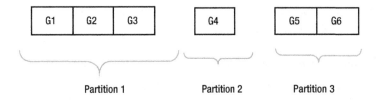

Figure 8-1. *Block-range granules on a partitioned table*

Figure 8-1 shows how a table with three partitions is split into six block-range granules of roughly equal size even when the partition sizes vary significantly. We could, for example, use two parallel query servers, and each server would probably end up reading data from three of the block-range granules.

■ **Tip** When block-range granules are in use the operation PX BLOCK ITERATOR appears in an execution plan. The child of this operation is the object from which the granules are derived.

For large tables there are often dozens or even hundreds of granules, with many granules being allocated to each parallel query server.

Let us move on now to the second type of granule—partition granules.

Partition Granules

When a table or an index is partitioned it is possible to allocate partition granules rather than block-range granules. In this case there is exactly one granule per partition (or subpartition). This doesn't sound like a good idea, as the granules may vary in size significantly, as Figure 8-2 shows:

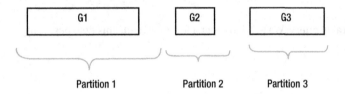

Figure 8-2. Partition granules on a partitioned table

As you can see, there are now only three granules for three partitions, and these granules are all of different sizes. Partition granules can result in some parallel query servers doing most of the work while others lay idle.

■ **Tip** When partition granules are in use one of the many operations that begin PX PARTITION ... appears in an execution plan. The child of this operation is the object from which the granules are derived.

There are three main reasons to use partition granules. These are:

- When performing parallel DDL or parallel DML it is often more efficient to have only one parallel query server writing to a partition rather than many.

- As we will see in Chapter 10, it is possible to perform neither an INDEX RANGE SCAN nor an INDEX FULL SCAN on an unpartitioned index in parallel. However, it is possible for one parallel query server to scan one partition of an index while other parallel query servers scan different partitions.

- *Partition-wise joins* require partition granules. We will cover partition-wise joins in Chapter 11.

Now that we know how data is split up for parallelization, it is time to look at how parallel query servers are organized to enable them access to this granular data.

Data Flow Operators

The Oracle documentation talks about something called a ***Data Flow Operator***, or DFO. Personally, I think that grammatically it should be called a Data Flow Operation, but since I will be using the abbreviation DFO from now on we don't need to be too worried about this nicety.

A DFO is basically one or more row source operations in an execution plan that form a single unit of parallelized work. To explain this I finally need to show an actual execution plan with a parallel query! Listing 8-20 shows an execution plan with just one DFO.

Listing 8-20. An execution plan with one DFO

```
CREATE TABLE t5
PARTITION BY HASH (c1)
   PARTITIONS 16
AS
       SELECT ROWNUM c1, ROWNUM c2
          FROM DUAL
   CONNECT BY LEVEL <= 10000;

CREATE INDEX t5_i1
   ON t5 (c2) local;

SELECT /*+ index(t5) parallel_index(t5) */
       *
  FROM t5
 WHERE c2 IS NOT NULL;
```

Id	Operation	Name	TQ	IN-OUT	PQ Distrib
0	SELECT STATEMENT				
1	PX COORDINATOR				
2	PX SEND QC (RANDOM)	:TQ10000	Q1,00	P->S	QC (RAND)
3	**PX PARTITION HASH ALL**		Q1,00	PCWC	
4	**TABLE ACCESS BY LOCAL INDEX ROWID BATCHED**	T5	Q1,00	PCWP	
5	**INDEX FULL SCAN**	T5_I1	Q1,00	PCWP	

Listing 8-20 begins by creating a partitioned table T5 and an associated local index T5_I1. The table is then queried, specifying hints that cause T5 to be accessed by the index. Since block-range granules can't be used for an INDEX FULL SCAN, you can see the PX PARTITION HASH ALL operation that shows the use of partition granules. Each parallel query server will access one or more partitions and perform operations 4 and 5 on those partitions.

As each parallel query server reads rows from the table, those rows are sent onto the *query coordinator (QC)* as shown by operation 2. The QC is the original session that existed at the beginning. Apart from receiving the output of the parallel query servers, the QC is also responsible for doling out granules, of whatever type, to the parallel query servers.

Notice the contents of the IN-OUT column in the execution plan. Operation 3 shows PCWC, which means *Parallel Combined with Child*. Operation 5 shows PCWP, which means *Parallel Combined with Parent*. Operation 4 is combined with both parent and child. This information can be used to identify the groups of row source operations within each DFO in an execution plan. Incidentally, the IN-OUT column of operation 2 shows P->S, which means *Parallel to Serial*; the parallel query servers are sending data to the QC.

That wasn't too difficult to understand, was it? Let me move on to a more complex example that involves multiple DFOs.

Parallel Query Server Sets and DFO Trees

The execution plan in Listing 8-20 involved just one DFO. An execution plan may involve more than one DFO. The set of DFOs is what is referred to as a *DFO tree*. Listing 8-21 provides an example of a DFO tree with multiple DFOs.

Listing 8-21. Parallel query with multiple DFOs

```
BEGIN
   FOR i IN 1 .. 4
   LOOP
      DBMS_STATS.gather_table_stats (
          ownname   => SYS_CONTEXT ('USERENV', 'CURRENT_SCHEMA')
          ,tabname   => 'T' || i);
   END LOOP;
END;
/

WITH q1
     AS ( SELECT c1, COUNT (*) cnt1
             FROM t1
          GROUP BY c1)
     ,q2
      AS ( SELECT c2, COUNT (*) cnt2
             FROM t2
          GROUP BY c2)
SELECT /*+ monitor optimizer_features_enable('11.2.0.3') parallel */
       c1, c2, cnt1
  FROM q1, q2
 WHERE cnt1 = cnt2;
```

Id	Operation	Name	TQ	IN-OUT	PQ Distrib
0	SELECT STATEMENT				
1	**PX COORDINATOR**				
2	**PX SEND QC (RANDOM)**	:TQ10003	Q1,03	P->S	QC (RAND)
3	HASH JOIN BUFFERED		Q1,03	PCWP	
4	VIEW		Q1,03	PCWP	
5	HASH GROUP BY		Q1,03	PCWP	
6	**PX RECEIVE**		Q1,03	PCWP	
7	**PX SEND HASH**	:TQ10001	Q1,01	P->P	HASH
8	PX BLOCK ITERATOR		Q1,01	PCWC	
9	TABLE ACCESS FULL	T1	Q1,01	PCWP	
10	**PX RECEIVE**		Q1,03	PCWP	
11	**PX SEND BROADCAST**	:TQ10002	Q1,02	P->P	BROADCAST
12	VIEW		Q1,02	PCWP	
13	HASH GROUP BY		Q1,02	PCWP	
14	**PX RECEIVE**		Q1,02	PCWP	
15	**PX SEND HASH**	:TQ10000	Q1,00	P->P	HASH
16	PX BLOCK ITERATOR		Q1,00	PCWC	
17	TABLE ACCESS FULL	T2	Q1,00	PCWP	

After gathering missing object statistics, Listing 8-21 issues a parallel query. I specified the `optimizer_features_enable('11.2.0.3')` hint; the 12.1.0.1 plan would have presented some new features somewhat prematurely.

Using the `IN-OUT` column of Listing 8-21 to identify the DFOs is possible but a little awkward. It is easier to look at the TQ column and see that there are four distinct values reflecting the four DFOs in this plan. We can also look at the operation above each `PX SEND` operation to see where each DFO is sending its data.

For complex parallel execution plans like this one it is often helpful to draw out the DFO tree. Figure 8-3 shows one way to depict the DFO tree associated with Listing 8-21.

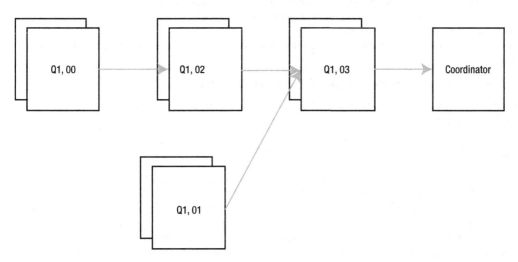

Figure 8-3. *Pictorial representation of the DFO tree for Listing 8-21*

From Figure 8-3 we can see that three of the four DFOs send data to another DFO, whereas the DFO named `Q1,03` (operations 2 through 6 and operation 10 in the execution plan of Listing 8-21) sends data to the QC.

DFO trees are neither height balanced nor binary; the leaves of the tree are varying distances from the root, and a branch node may have one or several children. The leaves of the tree tend to be operations like full table scans, whereas the branches tend to be joins, aggregations, or sorts.

In order to support multiple concurrent DFOs Oracle database has created the concept of a *parallel query server set (PQSS)* with each set operating on one DFO at a time. Now, if we had a PQSS for every DFO we would end up with an awful lot of processes for a complex DFO tree. In fact, we only have at most *two* PQSSs for each DFO tree.

■ **Tip** The number of servers in a PQSS is known as the *Degree Of Parallelism* (DOP), and if there are two PQSSs in a DFO tree the DOP will be the same for both. Furthermore, if you use hints to specify a DOP of 4 for one table and 5 for another, the higher number will normally be used, resulting in the allocation of 10 parallel query servers (although this number may be reduced to conserve resources).

To understand how we can get away with just two PQSSs, it is time to look at how the DFOs communicate with each other and the QC. It is time to introduce *table queues*.

Table Queues and DFO Ordering

The arrows connecting the nodes in Figure 8-3 represent data being sent from one DFO to another or to the QC. Such communication is facilitated by means of a *table queue (TQ)*. Each table queue has a producer and a consumer. The name of the table queue is shown in the NAME column of the execution plan for PX SEND operations and shows a remarkable similarity to the name of the DFO that is the producer for the TQ. This isn't a coincidence!

When a producer sends data to a TQ there absolutely *must* be a consumer actively waiting for that data; don't let the term *queue* mislead you into thinking that large amounts of data can be buffered in a TQ. It can't. I will refer to a TQ as *active* if a producer and consumer are exchanging data using the TQ. It's a little odd talking about a piece of memory being active, but I am sure you get the idea.

So how does the runtime engine process this entire DFO tree with just two PQSSs? Well, the runtime engine has to follow a few rules:

1. At any point in time there can be at most one TQ active for a DFO tree.

2. On receipt, the consumer for a TQ must not forward data to another TQ. This is usually accomplished by buffering the data in a workarea.

3. The runtime engine always starts off with :TQ10000 and processes each TQ in numerical order.

Understanding this third rule is the key to reading a parallel execution plan. To quote Jonathan Lewis: *Follow the TQs*. Let's use these rules to follow through the sequence of events in Listing 8-21.

The two PQSSs are initially allocated to :TQ10000, one PQSS (let us call it PQSS1) producing and one (let us call it PQSS2) consuming. This means that PQSS1 starts by running DFO Q1, 00 and PQSS2 starts by running Q1, 02. There is a HASH GROUP BY aggregation on line 13 that buffers data so that PQSS2 can comply with rule 2 above. Once all the data from table T2 has been grouped, DFO Q1, 00 is complete. Here is a highlight of the set of operations associated with :TQ10000.

Id	Operation	Name	TQ	IN-OUT	PQ Distrib
13	HASH GROUP BY		Q1,02	PCWP	
14	PX RECEIVE		Q1,02	PCWP	
15	PX SEND HASH	:TQ10000	Q1,00	P->P	HASH
16	PX BLOCK ITERATOR		Q1,00	PCWC	
17	TABLE ACCESS FULL	T2	Q1,00	PCWP	

The runtime engine now moves on to :TQ10001. One PQSS starts reading T1 on line 9 (DFO Q1, 01) and sending the data to the other PQSS (DFO Q1, 03). This consuming PQSS groups the data it receives with a HASH GROUP BY operation and then builds a workarea for a hash join. Here is a highlight of the set of operations associated with :TQ10001.

Id	Operation	Name	TQ	IN-OUT	PQ Distrib
3	HASH JOIN BUFFERED		Q1,03	PCWP	
4	VIEW		Q1,03	PCWP	
5	HASH GROUP BY		Q1,03	PCWP	
6	PX RECEIVE		Q1,03	PCWP	
7	PX SEND HASH	:TQ10001	Q1,01	P->P	HASH
8	PX BLOCK ITERATOR		Q1,01	PCWC	
9	TABLE ACCESS FULL	T1	Q1,01	PCWP	

At this stage it may not be immediately obvious which PQSS is the producer for :TQ10001 and which is the consumer, but that will soon become clear.

The runtime engine now moves on to :TQ10002. What happens here is that the data from the workarea on line 13 is extracted and then sent from one PQSS to another. Here is a highlight of the set of operations associated with :TQ10002.

```
---------------------------------------------------------------------
| Id  | Operation               | Name     |   TQ  |IN-OUT| PQ Distrib |
---------------------------------------------------------------------
|  3  |    HASH JOIN BUFFERED   |          | Q1,03 | PCWP |            |
< lines not involved cut>                                  |
| 10  |     PX RECEIVE          |          | Q1,03 | PCWP |            |
| 11  |      PX SEND BROADCAST  | :TQ10002 | Q1,02 | P->P | BROADCAST  |
| 12  |       VIEW              |          | Q1,02 | PCWP |            |
| 13  |        HASH GROUP BY    |          | Q1,02 | PCWP |            |
---------------------------------------------------------------------
```

The final TQ in our DFO tree is :TQ10003, but let us pause briefly before looking at that in detail.

We always use the same PQSS for all operations in a DFO, so the producer for :TQ10002 must be PQSS2 as PQSS2 ran Q1, 02 when Q1, 02 was the consumer for :TQ10000. This, in turn, means that the consumer for :TQ10002 is PQSS1, and as this is DFO Q1, 03, we can work backwards and conclude that the consumer for :TQ10001 must also have been PQSS1 and that the producer for :TQ10001 must have been PQSS2. If your head is spinning a bit from this explanation take another look at Figure 8-3. Any two adjacent nodes in the DFO tree must use different PQSSs, and so after allocating PQSS1 to DFO Q1, 00 there is only one way to allocate PQSSs to the remaining DFOs.

You can now see that PQSS1 runs Q1, 00 and Q1, 03 and that PQSS2 runs Q1, 01 and Q1, 02. You can confirm this analysis if you produce a SQL Monitor report (despite the fact that the query ran almost instantly, this report is available due to the MONITOR hint in Listing 8-21) using one of the scripts shown in Listing 4-6. Figure 8-4 shows a snippet from the report.

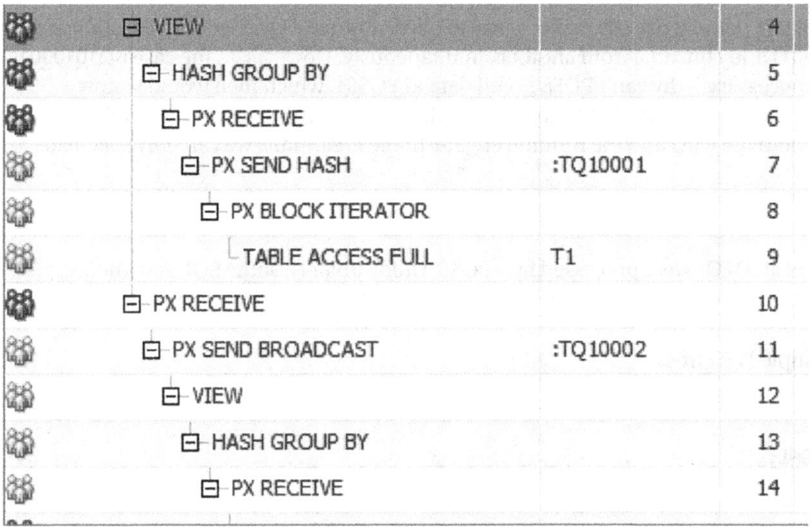

Figure 8-4. *Snippet from SQL Monitor report showing relationship of DFO and Parallel Query Server Sets*

Figure 8-4 shows PQSS1 by three blue people (dark gray in the absence of color) in a huddle and PQSS2 as three pink people (light gray in the absence of color).

This is all very tricky, so let me walk through DFO Q1, 02 and DFO Q1, 03 again. Each member of PQSS2 builds a workarea associated with the HASH GROUP BY on line 13 when acting as the consumer for :TQ10000. DFO Q1,02 is then effectively suspended while :TQ10001 is active. PQSS2 resumes DFO Q1,02, this time acting as a producer, when :TQ10002 becomes active and reads the data from the workarea.

Rule 2 above states that the consumer of a TQ cannot forward the data to another TQ. Yet—on receipt of the data on line 10—it looks like the second part of the hash join on line 3 will start producing rows and sending them to the coordinator on line 2. Isn't this a violation of rule 2? It looks like :TQ10002 and :TQ10003 will both be active at the same time. The clue, as you might have guessed, comes from the word BUFFERED in line 3. In actual fact, the data from line 10 is not joined at this point—it is just buffered. I will provide a more detailed explanation of the HASH JOIN BUFFERED operation in Chapter 11 when I cover joins in more detail.

Once all the data has been sent from PQSS2 to PQSS1 and buffered, PQSS1 moves on to :TQ10003. PQSS1 can now read the data that it just buffered, perform the join on line 3, and send the data to the QC. Here are the steps associated with :TQ10003:

```
-----------------------------------------------------------------------
| Id  | Operation              | Name      | TQ    |IN-OUT| PQ Distrib |
-----------------------------------------------------------------------
|  1  | PX COORDINATOR         |           |       |      |            |
|  2  |   PX SEND QC (RANDOM)   | :TQ10003  | Q1,03 | P->S | QC (RAND)  |
|  3  |    HASH JOIN BUFFERED   |           | Q1,03 | PCWP |            |
-----------------------------------------------------------------------
```

To recap:

- Rows are placed into the workarea of the HASH GROUP BY on line 13 when :TQ10000 is active and those rows are extracted when :TQ10002 is active.

- Rows are placed into the in-memory hash cluster of the HASH JOIN BUFFERED operation on line 3 when :TQ10001 is active, rows for the probe row source are buffered when :TQ10002 is active, and the actual join is performed when :TQ10003 is active.

Now you might have a question at this point. It usually makes sense to have only one TQ active at once, otherwise a PQSS might have to produce on one TQ and consume from another simultaneously. However, in the case of :TQ10002 and :TQ10003 the restriction seems unnecessary. Why can't PQSS2 send data to PQSS1, which then would simply forward the results of the join to the QC? Many of us would like to know. Perhaps one day Oracle will either tell us the reason or remove the restriction from both the CBO and the runtime engine. In the meantime, we can only speculate.

Multiple DFO Trees

Listing 8-21 only had one DFO tree, and all DFOs were processed by a PQSS. Unfortunately, some SQL statements require more than one DFO tree, and sometimes a DFO is processed by the QC. Listing 8-22 demonstrates these points.

Listing 8-22. Parallel query with multiple DFO trees

```
COMMIT;

ALTER SESSION DISABLE PARALLEL DML;

WITH q1
    AS ( SELECT /*+
                    parallel(T1)
                    full(t1)
                    no_parallel(t2)
                    no_pq_replicate(t2)
                    no_gby_pushdown
```

```
                     pq_distribute(t2 none broadcast)
                     */
                  c1 + c2 c12, AVG (c1) avg_c1, COUNT (c2) cnt_c2
              FROM t1, t2
             WHERE c1 = c2 + 1
          GROUP BY c1 + c2
          ORDER BY 1)
    ,q2 AS (SELECT ROWNUM rn, c12 FROM q1)
  SELECT /*+ leading(q1)
             pq_distribute(q2 none broadcast) */
         *
    FROM q1 NATURAL JOIN q2
ORDER BY cnt_c2;
```

```
---------------------------------------------------------------------------------------
| Id  | Operation                | Name            |  TQ   |IN-OUT| PQ Distrib |
---------------------------------------------------------------------------------------
|   0 | SELECT STATEMENT         |                 |       |      |            |
|   1 |  TEMP TABLE TRANSFORMATION|                |       |      |            |
|   2 |   PX COORDINATOR         |                 |       |      |            |
|   3 |    PX SEND QC (RANDOM)    | :TQ10002        | Q1,02 | P->S | QC (RAND)  |
|   4 |     LOAD AS SELECT        | SYS_TEMP_0FD9D6 | Q1,02 | PCWP |            |
|   5 |      SORT GROUP BY        |                 | Q1,02 | PCWP |            |
|   6 |       PX RECEIVE          |                 | Q1,02 | PCWP |            |
|   7 |        PX SEND RANGE      | :TQ10001        | Q1,01 | P->P | RANGE      |
|   8 |         HASH JOIN BUFFERED |                | Q1,01 | PCWP |            |
|   9 |          PX BLOCK ITERATOR|                 | Q1,01 | PCWC |            |
|  10 |           TABLE ACCESS FULL| T1             | Q1,01 | PCWP |            |
|  11 |          PX RECEIVE       |                 | Q1,01 | PCWP |            |
|  12 |           PX SEND BROADCAST| :TQ10000       | Q1,00 | S->P | BROADCAST  |
|  13 |            PX SELECTOR     |                 | Q1,00 | SCWC |            |
|  14 |             TABLE ACCESS FULL| T2           | Q1,00 | SCWP |            |
|  15 |   PX COORDINATOR          |                 |       |      |            |
|  16 |    PX SEND QC (ORDER)     | :TQ20003        | Q2,03 | P->S | QC (ORDER) |
|  17 |     SORT ORDER BY         |                 | Q2,03 | PCWP |            |
|  18 |      PX RECEIVE           |                 | Q2,03 | PCWP |            |
|  19 |       PX SEND RANGE       | :TQ20002        | Q2,02 | P->P | RANGE      |
|  20 |        HASH JOIN BUFFERED |                 | Q2,02 | PCWP |            |
|  21 |         VIEW              |                 | Q2,02 | PCWP |            |
|  22 |          PX BLOCK ITERATOR|                 | Q2,02 | PCWC |            |
|  23 |           TABLE ACCESS FULL| SYS_TEMP_0FD9D6| Q2,02 | PCWP |            |
|  24 |         PX RECEIVE        |                 | Q2,02 | PCWP |            |
|  25 |          PX SEND BROADCAST| :TQ20001        | Q2,01 | S->P | BROADCAST  |
|  26 |           BUFFER SORT     |                 | Q2,01 | SCWP |            |
|  27 |            VIEW           |                 | Q2,01 | SCWC |            |
|  28 |             COUNT         |                 | Q2,01 | SCWP |            |
|  29 |              PX RECEIVE   |                 | Q2,01 | SCWP |            |
|  30 |               PX SEND 1 SLAVE| :TQ20000     | Q2,00 | P->S | 1 SLAVE    |
|  31 |                VIEW       |                 | Q2,00 | PCWP |            |
|  32 |                 PX BLOCK ITERATOR|          | Q2,00 | PCWC |            |
|  33 |                  TABLE ACCESS FULL| SYS_TEMP_0FD9D6| Q2,00 | PCWP |      |
---------------------------------------------------------------------------------------
```

Don't worry about what the query in Listing 8-22 does. Focus on the execution plan instead. The first thing to look at is operation 4. The LOAD AS SELECT has a value of PCWP (Parallel Combined with Child) in the IN-OUT column, clearly showing that we are loading a table in parallel. This may surprise you because Listing 8-22 begins by disabling parallel DML. But the purpose of disabling parallel DML is to prevent the ORA-12838 error, as in Listing 8-19. Since the temporary table we are loading has been created for materializing the factored subquery Q1 and will cease to exist at the end of this statement, such an error is impossible; we can use parallel DML even though it is ostensibly disabled.

Next look at operations 12, 13, and 14. These operations read table T2 serially, as you can see from the IN-OUT column values. The PX SELECTOR operation on line 13 is new to 12cR1 and indicates that the serial operation is done by a parallel query server from PQSS1 and not by the QC as in earlier releases. Line 12 shows that all selected rows from T2 are broadcast to all members of PQSS2. We will look at other ways that parallel query servers can communicate with each other shortly.

Now take a look at the operation on line 30. There are two things to notice about this operation. First, the newly created temporary table is read in parallel by PQSS1 (I have truncated the table name to save space on the page), but all rows are sent to a single member of PQSS2, as suggested by the operation name and confirmed by the IN-OUT column. All rows are processed by one slave in PQSS2 because of the use of the ROWNUM pseudo-column in the query. Once again, the PX SEND 1 SLAVE operation is new to 12cR1, and in prior releases this operation would have been PX SEND QC (RANDOM), as the COUNT operation that implements the ROWNUM pseudo-column would have been performed by the QC.

The second thing to note about operation 30 is that the name of the DFO is Q2,00 and the TQ name is :TQ20000. These names show that a second DFO tree is used in the statement, and all lines from 16 to 33 are performed by this second DFO tree. When multiple DFO trees are involved in a statement each DFO tree usually gets its own parallel query server set or its own pair of parallel query server sets, and indeed the DOP may differ from one DFO tree to the next. The parallel query server sets that support a particular DFO tree are known as a *parallel group*. So in the case of Listing 8-22 there are a total of four parallel query slave server sets—two sets per group.

Finally, I want to turn your attention to operation 26. Do you recall that a consumer from a TQ must buffer its data? On line 3 in Listing 8-21 and on line 20 in Listing 8-22 this buffering is incorporated into the HASH JOIN BUFFERED operation, but on line 26 in Listing 8-22 the buffering is a separate and explicit operation. Don't worry about the word *sort*. This is one of numerous cases where the BUFFER SORT operation doesn't sort.

Parallel Query Distribution Mechanisms

Listings 8-21 and 8-22 use the PX SEND HASH, PX SEND RANGE, PX SEND BROADCAST, PX SEND QC (RANDOM), and PX_SEND QC (ORDER) operations. These myriad ways in which producers send data through table queues reflect the variety of *data distribution* mechanisms with which these operations are associated. It is now time to explain these distribution mechanisms. We will begin with data-loading distribution mechanisms for partitioned tables and then move on to the distribution mechanisms associated with joins and other operations.

Data-loading Distribution Mechanisms for Partitioned Tables

Although there have been a number of data-loading distribution mechanisms available for some time, they were only documented in the context of the hints that control them in 11gR2. In this section I will discuss just two data-loading distribution mechanisms that can be used when loading data into multiple partitions of a partitioned table. For further information you can consult the description of the PQ_DISTRIBUTE hint in the SQL Reference Manual.

Imagine you are loading data into a hash partitioned table with eight partitions. The natural thing to do would be to have one parallel query server per partition of the table being loaded, wouldn't it? Yes, it would! Listing 8-23 demonstrates.

Listing 8-23. Loading data with no skew into a hash partitioned table

```
CREATE TABLE t_part1
PARTITION BY HASH (c1)
    PARTITIONS 8
AS
    SELECT c1, ROWNUM AS c3 FROM t1;

CREATE TABLE t_part2
PARTITION BY HASH (c2)
    PARTITIONS 8
AS
    SELECT c1 AS c2, ROWNUM AS c4 FROM t1;

ALTER SESSION ENABLE PARALLEL DML;

INSERT /*+ parallel(t_part1 8) pq_distribute(t_part1 PARTITION) */
      INTO  t_part1
    SELECT  c1,c1 FROM t1;
```

```
-------------------------------------------------------------------------------
| Id | Operation                      | Name      | TQ    |IN-OUT| PQ Distrib |
-------------------------------------------------------------------------------
|  0 | INSERT STATEMENT               |           |       |      |            |
|  1 |  PX COORDINATOR                |           |       |      |            |
|  2 |   PX SEND QC (RANDOM)          | :TQ10001  | Q1,01 | P->S | QC (RAND)  |
|  3 |    LOAD AS SELECT              | T_PART1   | Q1,01 | PCWP |            |
|  4 |     OPTIMIZER STATISTICS GATHERING |       | Q1,01 | PCWP |            |
|  5 |      PX RECEIVE                |           | Q1,01 | PCWP |            |
|  6 |       PX SEND PARTITION (KEY)  | :TQ10000  | Q1,00 | S->P | PART (KEY) |
|  7 |        PX SELECTOR             |           | Q1,00 | SCWC |            |
|  8 |         TABLE ACCESS FULL      | T1        | Q1,00 | SCWP |            |
-------------------------------------------------------------------------------
```

After creating a couple of partitioned tables and enabling parallel DML, Listing 8-23 copies data from one unpartitioned table into a partitioned table using one loading server per partition. We have used hints to demonstrate how to force this loading technique. In this case, the unpartitioned table T1 is read serially; each row is then sent to whichever parallel query slave is responsible for loading data into the partition for which the row is destined.

That seems all well and good, but what if most of the data you are reading goes into just one or two partitions? Having just one process writing to a partition won't help much. Take a look at Listing 8-24.

Listing 8-24. Loading data with skew into a hash partitioned table

```
INSERT /*+ parallel(t_part1 8) pq_distribute(t_part1 RANDOM)  */
    INTO  t_part1
  SELECT /*+ parallel(t_part2 8) */ * FROM t_part2;
```

Id	Operation	Name	TQ	IN-OUT	PQ Distrib
0	INSERT STATEMENT				
1	PX COORDINATOR				
2	PX SEND QC (RANDOM)	:TQ10001	Q1,01	P->S	QC (RAND)
3	LOAD AS SELECT	T_PART1	Q1,01	PCWP	
4	OPTIMIZER STATISTICS GATHERING		Q1,01	PCWP	
5	PX RECEIVE		Q1,01	PCWP	
6	**PX SEND ROUND-ROBIN**	:TQ10000	Q1,00	S->P	RND-ROBIN
7	PARTITION HASH ALL				
8	TABLE ACCESS FULL	T_PART2			

The data-loading mechanism used in Listing 8-24 will be most effective when most data is targeted for one or two partitions as each server can load data into all partitions. Because of the way direct path writes work, this would be inefficient when rows are evenly distributed among partitions.

Correlated Subquery Distribution Mechanisms

Prior to 12cR1 the evaluation of correlated subqueries that could not be unnested was either done serially or by an entirely separate DFO tree. 12cR1 introduced several ways in which correlated subqueries could be evaluated in parallel. It also introduced the PQ_FILTER hint to give you some control over that mechanism. Listing 8-25 shows two of four options.

Listing 8-25. Parallel execution of correlated subquery evaluation

```
SELECT /*+                          SELECT /*+
parallel(t1) full(t1)               parallel(t1) full(t1)
pq_filter(NONE)                     pq_filter(HASH)
*/                                  */
      *                                   *
  FROM t1                             FROM t1
WHERE EXISTS                        WHERE EXISTS
        (SELECT null                        (SELECT null
            FROM t2                             FROM t2
          WHERE t1.c1 != t2.c2);            WHERE t1.c1 != t2.c2);
```

```
---------------------------------------------    ---------------------------------------------
| Id  | Operation            | Name    |      | Id  | Operation            | Name     |
---------------------------------------------    ---------------------------------------------
|  0  | SELECT STATEMENT     |         |      |  0  | SELECT STATEMENT     |          |
|  1  |  PX COORDINATOR      |         |      |  1  |  PX COORDINATOR      |          |
|  2  |   PX SEND QC (RANDOM)| :TQ10000|      |  2  |   PX SEND QC (RANDOM)| :TQ10001 |
|  3  |    FILTER            |         |      |  3  |    BUFFER SORT       |          |
|  4  |     PX BLOCK ITERATOR|         |      |  4  |     FILTER           |          |
|  5  |      TABLE ACCESS FULL| T1     |      |  5  |      PX RECEIVE      |          |
|  6  |      TABLE ACCESS FULL| T2     |      |  6  |       PX SEND HASH   | :TQ10000 |
---------------------------------------------    |  7  |        PX BLOCK ITERATOR|       |
                                                 |  8  |         TABLE ACCESS FULL| T1   |
                                                 |  9  |         TABLE ACCESS FULL| T2   |
                                                 ---------------------------------------------
```

The query in Listing 8-25 reads T1 in parallel and filters the results using a correlated subquery, which cannot be unnested.

Suppose that T1 is huge, the evaluation of the correlated subquery is cheap, and the filter gets rid of most of the rows from T1. In that case, the PQ_FILTER (NONE) hint on left-hand side would be a good idea, as the resulting execution plan evaluates the subquery with the same parallel query server that reads T1, and there is only one DFO; we don't send all the unfiltered data through a TQ. This is probably the most sensible approach in most cases.

On the other hand, suppose that T1 isn't that big but the calculations performed by the correlated subquery are very expensive. In that case, you can arrange for the filtering to be done by a separate DFO concurrently with the parallelized full table scan of T1. This is accomplished by the use of the PQ_FILTER (HASH) hint on the right-hand side of Listing 8-25.

The execution plan on the right-hand side of Listing 8-25 shows that as PQSS1 reads rows from T1 it sends them to a member of PQSS2 based on a hash of T1.C1. Note that the presence of the second DFO means that data needs to be buffered after filtering before sending data to the QC, and, at the risk of sounding repetitive, I want to remind you again that there is no sort involved in operation 3 despite appearances.

There are two more legal values for the PQ_FILTER hint parameter. PQ_FILTER (SERIAL) causes all correlated subquery evaluations to be performed by the QC as with 11gR2 and earlier. Having the QC perform filtering might be a good idea if the number of distinct values of the correlated column T1.C1 is low, as scalar subquery caching may prevent the subquery from being evaluated repeatedly.

If you specify the PQ_FILTER (RANDOM) hint, rows are sent from PQSS1 to PQSS2 on a round-robin basis rather than based on a hash function on T1.C1, as with the PQ_FILTER (HASH) distribution mechanism. According to the documentation, this distribution mechanism should be used when there is skew in the data, but this makes no sense to me. Suppose all the rows in T1 had exactly the same value for T1.C1. The PX SEND HASH operation shown on line 6 of the execution plan on the right-hand side of Listing 8-25 would send all the rows to the same member of PQSS2, but scalar subquery caching would prevent the multiple evaluations of the subquery that would arise with PQ_FILTER (RANDOM).

Subqueries that can't be unnested are a rarity these days, and the occasions when they need to be evaluated in parallel are even rarer. I must confess that I have no practical experience with this 12cR1 feature; the above analysis is purely theoretical and could be flawed. At least now you know as much as I do!

Other Parallel Distribution Mechanisms

The PQ_DISTRIBUTE hint isn't used only to control different approaches to loading data. In fact, by far the most common use of this hint is to control the different approaches for joining tables in parallel. I will cover these distribution mechanisms in Chapter 11 once I have covered the different methods for joining tables serially.

There are one or two other ways that a producing PQSS can distribute its data through a TQ, but these are for specific situations and there is no choice of distribution mechanism; the PQ_DISTRIBUTE hint is neither legal nor required.

For example, you will see the PX SEND RANGE operation on line 7 in Listing 8-22. This is because the consumer of the TQ performs a sort in parallel. Chapter 17 is dedicated to sorts; we will take a look at the parallelization of sorts there. The same listing shows a PX SEND QC (RANDOM) operation on line 3 and a PX SEND QC (ORDER) operation on line 16. Both distribution mechanisms involve sending data to the QC, but in the former case the order in which members of the PQSS send data to the QC is of no relevance—the PQSS members just notify the QC that they have finished loading data and the QC just wants to know when everything is done. In the latter case the order in which the PQSS members send rows to the QC is important because the final result set needs to be ordered by CNT_C2.

Why Forcing Parallel Query Doesn't Force Parallel Query

The PARALLEL and PARALLEL_INDEX hints are used to *authorize* the CBO to use parallel execution to perform operations in parallel and optionally to specify the DOP to be used. However, if the CBO has the choice to use an operation that cannot be performed in parallel, such as an index range scan, then it may elect to choose that access method and run it serially rather than use an alternative, more expensive, parallel operation.

The statement ALTER SESSION FORCE PARALLEL QUERY essentially adds PARALLEL and PARALLEL_INDEX statement-level hints to each SQL statement in the session; Listing 8-26 demonstrates that parallel execution isn't guaranteed by the statement.

Listing 8-26. Understanding FORCE PARALLEL QUERY

```
ALTER SESSION FORCE PARALLEL QUERY PARALLEL 2;

SELECT *
  FROM sh.customers c
 WHERE cust_id < 100;


-----------------------------------------------------------------------
| Id  | Operation                           | Name         | Cost (%CPU)|
-----------------------------------------------------------------------
|   0 | SELECT STATEMENT                    |              |   54   (0)|
|   1 |  TABLE ACCESS BY INDEX ROWID BATCHED| CUSTOMERS    |   54   (0)|
|*  2 |   INDEX RANGE SCAN                  | CUSTOMERS_PK |    2   (0)|
-----------------------------------------------------------------------

Predicate Information (identified by operation id):
---------------------------------------------------

   2 - access("CUST_ID"<100)

SELECT /*+ full(c) */
       *
  FROM sh.customers c
 WHERE cust_id < 100;


---------------------------------------------------------
| Id  | Operation              | Name      | Cost (%CPU)|
---------------------------------------------------------
|   0 | SELECT STATEMENT       |           |  235   (1)|
|   1 |  PX COORDINATOR        |           |            |
|   2 |   PX SEND QC (RANDOM)  | :TQ10000  |  235   (1)|
|   3 |    PX BLOCK ITERATOR   |           |  235   (1)|
|*  4 |     TABLE ACCESS FULL  | CUSTOMERS |  235   (1)|
---------------------------------------------------------
```

Predicate Information (identified by operation id):
----

   4 - filter("CUST_ID"<100)

ALTER SESSION FORCE PARALLEL QUERY PARALLEL **20**;

```
SELECT *
  FROM sh.customers c
 WHERE cust_id < 100;
```

```
-----------------------------------------------------------
| Id  | Operation             | Name      | Cost (%CPU)|
-----------------------------------------------------------
|   0 | SELECT STATEMENT      |           |    23   (0)|
|   1 |  PX COORDINATOR       |           |            |
|   2 |   PX SEND QC (RANDOM) | :TQ10000  |    23   (0)|
|   3 |    PX BLOCK ITERATOR  |           |    23   (0)|
|*  4 |     TABLE ACCESS FULL | CUSTOMERS |    23   (0)|
-----------------------------------------------------------
```

Predicate Information (identified by operation id):
----

   4 - filter("CUST_ID"<100)

ALTER SESSION ENABLE PARALLEL QUERY;

Listing 8-26 begins by "forcing" a DOP of two before querying the SH.CUSTOMERS table. The resultant execution plan uses an index range scan that is run serially with a cost of 54. When I force a full table scan with a hint, you can see that the CBO elects to run it in parallel, but the cost of 235 is much higher than the alternative serial index range scan. However, the final query in Listing 8-26 runs with a DOP of 20. Now the cost of the parallel full table scan is 23 because each parallel query slave now has fewer blocks to read; the CBO calculates that the parallel query operation will now complete quicker than the equivalent index range scan.

In Chapter 10 we will look at the index range scan in more detail and it will become clear why block-range granules cannot be used to run an index range scan in parallel.

Further Reading

There is a lot more to the topic of parallel execution than I have covered in this chapter. There are several initialization parameters that control such things as the minimum and maximum number of parallel execution slaves that an instance can support. There are features such as *statement queuing* and *DOP downgrade* that determine what happens when the desired number of parallel query servers aren't available. You can also the use the *resource manager* to prioritize parallel execution. For details on all of these features and information about the views that can be used to monitor parallel execution, I repeat my recommendation to take a look at the VLDB and Partitioning Guide.

That concludes our discussion on parallel execution. It is time to move on to the third and final major topic of this chapter: global hints.

Understanding Global Hints

The vast majority of embedded hints in SQL statements are *local* hints, meaning that they apply to the query block in which they are placed. In an outline, all the hints for all query blocks are placed in one place and so some way has to be found to indicate the query block to which each hint applies. This is accomplished by means of an '@' symbol as the leading character of the first argument to the hint, marking it as *global*. Take a look at lines 4, 8, and 12 in Listing 8-7. These are all LEADING hints, but line 4 applies to the query block SEL$F1D6E378, which as I explained earlier is the query block formed by the merge of query blocks SEL$1 into SEL$3, whereas the hints on lines 8 and 12 apply to query blocks SEL$2 and SEL$4, respectively.

Global hints are documented in the SQL Language Reference manual, are fully supported when embedded in SQL statements, and are often invaluable. There are at least three types of occasions that warrant the use of global hints, seen here:

- You want to hint a block originating in a data dictionary view. To use a local hint in this case would require the definition of the view to be altered and would affect other users of the view.

- You want to hint a query block that is the result of a query transformation. In these cases local hints can be confusing to the reader.

- Where hints are so numerous that they impair the readability of the original statement, global hints allow them all to be collected in one place.

I will provide simple examples of the first two scenarios, but providing a simple example of complex hinting is somewhat of an oxymoron. After demonstrating these scenarios I will focus in on the NO_MERGE hint, as the multiple variants of this very common hint are somewhat daunting. If you can grasp the NO_MERGE hint you can consider yourself a master of global hinting!

Hinting Data Dictionary Views

Listing 8-27 creates a data dictionary view and uses that view in a query. To keep things simple, I also drop the index on T1 and disable parallel query.

Listing 8-27. Simple query using a data dictionary view

```
ALTER SESSION DISABLE PARALLEL QUERY;

DROP INDEX t1_i1

CREATE OR REPLACE VIEW v1
AS
    SELECT c1, MEDIAN (c2) med_c2
      FROM t1, t2
     WHERE t1.c1 = t2.c2
  GROUP BY t1.c1;

SELECT *
  FROM v1, t3
 WHERE v1.c1 = t3.c3;

Plan hash value: 808098385
```

```
----------------------------------------
| Id  | Operation             | Name |
----------------------------------------
|  0  | SELECT STATEMENT      |      |
|  1  |  HASH JOIN            |      |
|  2  |   VIEW                | V1   |
|  3  |    HASH GROUP BY      |      |
|  4  |     HASH JOIN         |      |
|  5  |      TABLE ACCESS FULL| T1   |
|  6  |      TABLE ACCESS FULL| T2   |
|  7  |   TABLE ACCESS FULL   | T3   |
----------------------------------------
```

Query Block Name / Object Alias (identified by operation id):

```
   1 - SEL$1
   2 - SEL$2 / V1@SEL$1
   3 - SEL$2
   5 - SEL$2 / T1@SEL$2
   6 - SEL$2 / T2@SEL$2
   7 - SEL$1 / T3@SEL$1
```

Outline Data

```
  /*+
      BEGIN_OUTLINE_DATA
      USE_HASH_AGGREGATION(@"SEL$2")
      USE_HASH(@"SEL$2" "T2"@"SEL$2")
      LEADING(@"SEL$2" "T1"@"SEL$2" "T2"@"SEL$2")
      FULL(@"SEL$2" "T2"@"SEL$2")
      FULL(@"SEL$2" "T1"@"SEL$2")
      USE_HASH(@"SEL$1" "T3"@"SEL$1")
      LEADING(@"SEL$1" "V1"@"SEL$1" "T3"@"SEL$1")
      FULL(@"SEL$1" "T3"@"SEL$1")
      NO_ACCESS(@"SEL$1" "V1"@"SEL$1")
      OUTLINE_LEAF(@"SEL$1")
      OUTLINE_LEAF(@"SEL$2")
      ALL_ROWS
      DB_VERSION('12.1.0.1')
      OPTIMIZER_FEATURES_ENABLE('12.1.0.1')
      IGNORE_OPTIM_EMBEDDED_HINTS
      END_OUTLINE_DATA
  */
```

Now imagine that you wish to change the HASH JOIN of T1 and T2 to a nested loops join driven by T1. Of course, this doesn't make sense from a performance perspective, but I am just trying to explain the principle with a simple example at this point. Listing 8-28 shows how to do this without editing the view definition.

Listing 8-28. Applying a hint to a query block embedded in a data dictionary view

```
SELECT
/*+
    LEADING(@"SEL$2" "T1"@"SEL$2" "T2"@"SEL$2")
    USE_NL(@"SEL$2" "T2"@"SEL$2")
*/
*
  FROM v1, t3
 WHERE v1.c1 = t3.c3;

Plan hash value: 1369664419

----------------------------------------
| Id  | Operation              | Name |
----------------------------------------
|   0 | SELECT STATEMENT       |      |
|   1 |  HASH JOIN             |      |
|   2 |   VIEW                 | V1   |
|   3 |    HASH GROUP BY       |      |
|   4 |     NESTED LOOPS       |      |
|   5 |      TABLE ACCESS FULL | T1   |
|   6 |      TABLE ACCESS FULL | T2   |
|   7 |   TABLE ACCESS FULL    | T3   |
----------------------------------------

Query Block Name / Object Alias (identified by operation id):
------------------------------------------------------------

   1 - SEL$1
   2 - SEL$2 / V1@SEL$1
   3 - SEL$2
   5 - SEL$2 / T1@SEL$2
   6 - SEL$2 / T2@SEL$2
   7 - SEL$1 / T3@SEL$1

Outline Data
------------

  /*+
      BEGIN_OUTLINE_DATA
      USE_HASH_AGGREGATION(@"SEL$2")
      USE_NL(@"SEL$2" "T2"@"SEL$2")
      LEADING(@"SEL$2" "T1"@"SEL$2" "T2"@"SEL$2")
      FULL(@"SEL$2" "T2"@"SEL$2")
      FULL(@"SEL$2" "T1"@"SEL$2")
      USE_HASH(@"SEL$1" "T3"@"SEL$1")
      LEADING(@"SEL$1" "V1"@"SEL$1" "T3"@"SEL$1")
      FULL(@"SEL$1" "T3"@"SEL$1")
      NO_ACCESS(@"SEL$1" "V1"@"SEL$1")
      OUTLINE_LEAF(@"SEL$1")
      OUTLINE_LEAF(@"SEL$2")
```

```
    ALL_ROWS
    DB_VERSION('12.1.0.1')
    OPTIMIZER_FEATURES_ENABLE('12.1.0.1')
    IGNORE_OPTIM_EMBEDDED_HINTS
    END_OUTLINE_DATA
  */
```

What I did here was to look at the highlighted lines from the ALIAS and OUTLINE sections of the execution plan for the original statement in Listing 8-27 to determine the correct query block name and object aliases to use. Since a query block isn't listed for operation 4, I could determine the correct query block by looking at the query block for operation 3. I then used that information to construct suitable global hints to embed in my SQL statement. The execution plan for the statement in Listing 8-28 shows that the hints had the desired result.

▪ **Note**   It is important to realize that, unlike local hints, the place that global hints appear is irrelevant; they can be placed in any legal location in a SQL statement and the effect will be the same.

Applying Hints to Transformed Queries

Generally speaking, local hints are preferable to global hints as they are easier for a reader to understand, but this isn't always the case. In Chapter 13 of this book I will discuss the *star transformation* and *subquery unnesting transformation*. These two transformations, amongst others, can result in an execution plan that seems to bear little resemblance to the original SQL statement, and local hints seem meaningless. Even when there have been few, if any, transformations, there comes a point where large numbers of local hints scattered around a complex statement become impediments to the readability of the original code. In these hopefully rare cases, a single block of global hints can, in my opinion, make understanding the statement and its associated hints easier. Providing a simple example of obfuscation is a bit of a challenge, but Listing 8-29 might just help make my point.

Listing 8-29. Local hints applied to an unnested subquery

```
SELECT *
  FROM t1
 WHERE NOT EXISTS
          (SELECT /*+ unnest use_nl(t2) */
                  1
             FROM t2
            WHERE t2.c2 = t1.c1);
```

I have deliberately withheld the execution plan for Listing 8-29 in order to simulate the experience of the programmer reading through source code. The USE_NL hint controls join mechanism and seems meaningless as it appears in a block that contains only one row source. Nevertheless, this hint is valid because it is applied to a transformed block that contains multiple row sources. Since these hints only make sense when looking at the transformed execution plan, it is surely best to group all such hints in one place so that the business logic remains uncluttered.

The NO_MERGE Hint

I would like to conclude this discussion of global hints with a note about the MERGE and NO_MERGE hints. When used as local hints, the MERGE and NO_MERGE hints have two variants. Both local variants have equivalent global forms, thus making a total of four variants. It is easy to confuse these four variants, so let me clear things up. For simplicity I will stick to the NO_MERGE hint, as it is by far the more common embedded hint.

- When used as a local hint with no arguments, NO_MERGE instructs the CBO not to merge the *query block* in which the hint appears.

- When used as a local hint with one argument (not preceded by an '@' symbol), that argument is assumed to be a data dictionary view, a factored subquery, or an inline view. The NO_MERGE hint instructs the CBO not to merge the *row source* named in the argument.

- When used as a global hint with one argument preceded by an '@' symbol, the NO_MERGE hint instructs the CBO not to merge the *query block* named in the argument.

- When used as a global hint with two arguments (the first preceded by an '@' symbol), the second argument is assumed to be a data dictionary view, a factored subquery, or an inline view appearing in the query block specified by the first argument. The NO_MERGE hint instructs the CBO not to merge the *row source* named in the second argument that appears in the *query block* specified in the first argument.

Confused? Perhaps Listing 8-30 can shed some light.

Listing 8-30. The four variants of the NO_MERGE hint

```
WITH fs AS (SELECT /*+ qb_name(qb1) no_merge */
                   * FROM t1)
SELECT /*+ qb_name(qb2) */
       *
  FROM fs myalias, t2
 WHERE myalias.c1 = t2.c2;

WITH fs AS (SELECT /*+ qb_name(qb1) */
                   * FROM t1)
SELECT /*+ qb_name(qb2) no_merge(myalias) */
       *
  FROM fs myalias, t2
 WHERE myalias.c1 = t2.c2;

WITH fs AS (SELECT /*+ qb_name(qb1) */
                   * FROM t1)
SELECT /*+ qb_name(qb2) no_merge(@qb1) */
       *
  FROM fs myalias, t2
 WHERE myalias.c1 = t2.c2;

WITH fs AS (SELECT /*+ qb_name(qb1) no_merge(@qb2 myalias) */
                   * FROM t1)
SELECT /*+ qb_name(qb2) */
       *
  FROM fs myalias, t2
 WHERE myalias.c1 = t2.c2;

Plan hash value: 2191810965
```

```
-------------------------------------
| Id  | Operation          | Name  |
-------------------------------------
|   0 | SELECT STATEMENT   |       |
|   1 |  HASH JOIN         |       |
|   2 |   VIEW             |       |
|   3 |    TABLE ACCESS FULL| T1   |
|   4 |   TABLE ACCESS FULL | T2   |
-------------------------------------
```

With the exception of hints, the four statements in Listing 8-30 are identical. They all contain two query blocks that would be merged unless a hint prevented it. Each of the four statements contains one NO_MERGE hint that succeeds in preventing the merge, but these four hints are subtly different.

The key to understanding how the hints operate is to understand the three different ways by which the first query block is named.

- **FS** is the name of the factored subquery and allows the main query to reference it just like a table.

- **QB1** is the name of the query block. This has been assigned by the QB_NAME hint and is relevant only for global hints.

- **MYALIAS** is an object alias assigned in the FROM clause of the main query. Its primary purpose is to qualify the names of columns in the main query block, but it also has uses in the NO_MERGE hint. The existence of an object alias renders further reference to the identifier FS illegal.

With this in mind let us look at the four hints in turn.

- In the first query the NO_MERGE hint has no arguments. It is a local hint that instructs the CBO not to merge the block in which the hint appears. Like any local hint, it must be placed in the block to which it applies, in this case the subquery.

- The second query also uses a local NO_MERGE hint, but this time an argument is supplied. The argument specifies the object alias of the row source that must not be merged. Accordingly, the correct argument value is MYALIAS. Like any local hint, it must be placed in the block to which it applies, in this case the main query because the row source appears in the FROM clause of the main query.

- The third variant uses global hint syntax. The supplied query block name QB1 indicates that the hint should operate like a local hint in QB1. There being no other argument apart from the query block name, the hint operates just like the first variant with the exception that the hint can appear anywhere in the statement.

- The fourth variant is also a global hint. The supplied query block name QB2 indicates that the hint should operate like a local hint placed in QB2. The second argument in the fourth variant, MYALIAS, is treated like the first argument in the second variant. Like any global hint, its location in the statement is irrelevant—the hint always operates on the main query block QB2.

Are you scratching your head at this point? Don't worry. Of course you are far too sensible to use the fourth hint variant, but keep this page handy for when you come across somebody else's illegible hints!

Summary

This chapter has covered three important related topics. I have covered most of the previously unexplained parts of an execution plan made available by using a non-default formatting argument to DBMS_XPLAN functions. I have also explained how to interpret execution plans for statements run in parallel, and I have explained my views on global hints.

Global hints give some insight into the operation of the outlines that appear in the output of DBMS_XPLAN functions and form the basis for Oracle's plan-stability features. Global hints also significantly improve our ability to control CBO behavior without making business logic unreadable or impacting other users of data dictionary views.

Whereas the novice SQL programmer will never hint and the average SQL programmer will use local hints only occasionally, the expert tuning specialist is often called in when all others have given up. For that person, a mastery of both parallel execution plans and global hinting is essential to understanding what the CBO is up to as well as to getting it to do the right thing.

But why are all these shenanigans necessary? In Chapter 9 we will look at object statistics, which are the main inputs to the CBO decision-making process. An understanding of what object statistics are and how the CBO uses them puts us onto the road that leads to understanding why the CBO gets things right much of the time and why it sometimes lets us down.

CHAPTER 9

Object Statistics

Although the CBO makes its decisions about how to optimize a statement using data from various sources, the majority of the important information the CBO needs comes from object statistics. Most of this chapter is dedicated to an explanation of object statistics, although we will conclude this chapter with a few short points about other sources of information that the CBO uses.

In principle, and largely in practice, the use of object statistics as the basis for optimization is ideal. For example, we need some way to distinguish a tiny configuration table with ten rows from a transactional table with terabytes of data—object statistics can do that for us. Notice that if the CBO was designed to get its input from the actual size of a table, rather than a separate statistic, we would have no way to control changes to the CBO input data; every time we added a row to a table the execution plan for a statement might change.

We can categorize object statistics in two ways: by object type and by level. We have *table statistics*, *index statistics*, and *column statistics*, and for each table, column, or index, we may hold data at the *global*, *partition*, or *subpartition* level.

Note If you use *domain indexes* you can create your own object statistics types. For details see the *Data Cartridge Developer's Guide*. There are also various statistics associated with user-defined object types and object tables. For information see the *Object-Relational Developer's Guide*. I will not be covering domain indexes or object-relational concepts in this book.

This chapter will explain what each statistic is and how it is used, as well as explain why we have three different levels of statistics. But I would like to begin by making some general points about the application of object statistics and explaining how they are obtained in the first place.

The Purpose of Object Statistics

Let us assume that the CBO is considering accessing a table using a full table scan (FTS). There are three crucial metrics that the CBO needs to estimate:

- **Cost.** In other words, the CBO needs to know how long the FTS is likely to take. If it is quick then the FTS may be a good idea and if it takes ages then maybe not.

- **Cardinality.** When deciding whether to do an FTS or use an index to access a table, the number of rows returned isn't directly relevant; the same number of rows will be returned no matter how we access the table. On the other hand, the number of rows input to the *parent* operation may be of crucial importance. For example, suppose that the result of the FTS is then used as the driving row source of a join with another row source. If the FTS returns only one or two rows then a nested loop may be a good idea. If the FTS returns 10,000 rows then maybe a hash join would be better. The cardinality of an FTS can be determined in two stages. First, we need to know the **number of rows** in the table, and second, we need to know the **selectivity** of the predicates. So, for example, if a table has 1,000 rows and we have a 10% selectivity (otherwise expressed as a selectivity of 0.1) then the number of rows returned by the full table scan will be 10% of 1,000, i.e., 100.

- **Bytes.** Like cardinality, the number of bytes returned by a table access will be the same no matter whether an FTS or an index is used. However, if the CBO wants to perform a hash join on two tables, each with 10,000 rows, then the driving row source will be selected based on the smaller of the two tables as measured in bytes.

Although I have used an FTS as my example, the same three metrics are critical to all row-source operations, and the main purpose of object statistics is to help the CBO estimate them as accurately as possible.

In a small number of cases, most notably when accessing a table through an index, estimates for multiple row-source operations need to be obtained together. We will consider this special case as part of our discussion of the *clustering factor* index statistic shortly.

Creating Object Statistics

The CBO reads object statistics from the data dictionary, but these statistics need to be put into the data dictionary in the first place. There are four different ways to create or update object statistics using the DBMS_STATS package: *gathering, importing, transferring,* and *setting* statistics. Furthermore:

- By default, object statistics are generated for an index when it is created or rebuilt.

- By default, in database release 12cR1 onwards, object statistics for a table and its associated columns are generated when a table is created with the CREATE TABLE ... AS SELECT option or when an empty table is loaded in bulk with an INSERT statement.

Let me go through these options one at a time.

Gathering Object Statistics

Gathering statistics is by far the most common way to create or update statistics, and for application objects one of four different procedures from the DBMS_STATS package needs to be used:

- DBMS_STATS.GATHER_DATABASE_STATS gathers statistics for the entire database.

- DBMS_STATS.GATHER_SCHEMA_STATS gathers statistics for objects within a specified schema.

- DBMS_STATS.GATHER_TABLE_STATS gathers statistics for a specified table, table partition, or table subpartition.

  - When statistics are gathered for a partitioned table it is possible to gather them for all partitions and subpartitions, if applicable, as part of the same call.

  - Whether statistics are gathered for a table, partition, or subpartition the default behavior is to gather statistics for all associated indexes as part of the same call.

  - In addition to table statistics, this procedure gathers statistics for some or all columns in the table at the same time; there is no option to gather column statistics separately.

- DBMS_STATS.GATHER_INDEX_STATS gathers statistics for a specified index, index partition, or index subpartition. As with DBMS_STATS.GATHER_TABLE_STATS it is possible to gather statistics at the global, partition, and subpartition level as part of the same call.

■ **Note**   Objects in the data dictionary also need object statistics. These are obtained using the DBMS_STATS.GATHER_DICTIONARY_STATS and DBMS_STATS.GATHER_FIXED_OBJECT_STATS procedures.

All the statistics-gathering procedures in the DBMS_STATS work in a similar way: the object being analyzed is read using recursive SQL statements. Not all blocks in the object need be read. By default, data is randomly sampled until DBMS_STATS thinks that additional sampling will not materially affect the calculated statistics. The logic to determine when to stop is remarkably effective in release 11gR1 onward in the vast majority of cases.

■ **Note**   In some cases, such as when you have a column that has the same value for 2,000,000 rows and a second value for 2 rows, the random sampling is likely to prematurely determine that all the rows in the table have the same value for the column. In such cases, you should simply set the column statistics to reflect reality!

There are a lot of optional parameters to the DBMS_STATS statistics-gathering procedures. For example, you can indicate that statistics should only be gathered on an object if they are missing or deemed to be *stale*. You can also specify that statistics gathering is done in parallel. For more details see the *PL/SQL Packages and Types Reference* manual.

You should be aware that when Oracle database is first installed a job to gather statistics for the database as a whole is automatically created. I suspect this job is there to cater to the not insubstantial number of customers that never think about object statistics. For most large-scale systems, customization of this process is necessary and you should review this job carefully. The job is scheduled in a variety of different ways depending on release, so for more details see the SQL Tuning Guide (or the Performance Tuning Guide for release 11g or earlier).

In the vast majority of cases, the *initial* set of statistics for an object should be gathered. It is the only practical way. On the other hand, as I explained in Chapter 6, statistics gathering on production systems should be kept to a minimum. I am now going to explain one way in which statistics gathering on a production system can be eliminated altogether.

Exporting and Importing Statistics

If you are a fan of cooking shows you will be familiar with expressions like "here is one that I created earlier." Cooking takes time and things sometimes go wrong. So on TV cooking shows it is normal, in the interest of time, to show the initial stages of preparing a meal and then shortcut to the end using a pre-prepared dish.

In some ways, gathering statistics is like cooking: it takes some time and a small slip-up can ruin things. The good news is that DBAs, like TV chefs, can often save time and avoid risk by importing pre-made statistics into a database. The use of pre-made statistics is one of a few key concepts in the TSTATS deployment approach that I introduced in Chapter 6, but there are many other scenarios where the use of pre-made object statistics is useful. One such example is a lengthy data conversion, migration, or upgrade procedure. Such procedures are often performed in tight maintenance windows and rehearsed several times using data that, if not identical to production, are very similar. Object statistics derived from this test data may very well be suitable for use on the production system. Listing 9-1 demonstrates the technique.

Listing 9-1. Copying statistics from one system to another using DBMS_STATS export and import procedures

```
CREATE TABLE statement
(
    transaction_date_time   TIMESTAMP WITH TIME ZONE
   ,transaction_date        DATE
   ,posting_date            DATE
   ,posting_delay           AS (posting_date - transaction_date)
   ,description             VARCHAR2 (30)
   ,transaction_amount      NUMBER
   ,amount_category         AS (CASE WHEN transaction_amount < 10 THEN 'LOW'
                                     WHEN transaction_amount < 100 THEN 'MEDIUM' ELSE 'HIGH'
                              END)
   ,product_category        NUMBER
   ,customer_category       NUMBER
)
PCTFREE 80
PCTUSED 10;

INSERT INTO statement (transaction_date_time
                      ,transaction_date
                      ,posting_date
                      ,description
                      ,transaction_amount
                      ,product_category
                      ,customer_category)
      SELECT   TIMESTAMP '2013-01-01 12:00:00.00 -05:00'
               + NUMTODSINTERVAL (TRUNC ( (ROWNUM - 1) / 50), 'DAY')
              ,DATE '2013-01-01' + TRUNC ( (ROWNUM - 1) / 50)
              ,DATE '2013-01-01' + TRUNC ( (ROWNUM - 1) / 50) + MOD (ROWNUM, 3)
                   posting_date
              ,DECODE (MOD (ROWNUM, 4)
                      ,0, 'Flight'
                      ,1, 'Meal'
                      ,2, 'Taxi'
                      ,'Deliveries')
              ,DECODE (MOD (ROWNUM, 4)
                      ,0, 200 + (30 * ROWNUM)
                      ,1, 20 + ROWNUM
                      ,2, 5 + MOD (ROWNUM, 30)
                      ,8)
```

```
              ,TRUNC ( (ROWNUM - 1) / 50) + 1
              ,MOD ( (ROWNUM - 1), 50) + 1
         FROM DUAL
   CONNECT BY LEVEL <= 500;

CREATE INDEX statement_i_tran_dt
   ON statement (transaction_date_time);

CREATE INDEX statement_i_pc
   ON statement (product_category);

CREATE INDEX statement_i_cc
   ON statement (customer_category);

BEGIN
   DBMS_STATS.gather_table_stats (
      ownname        => SYS_CONTEXT ('USERENV', 'CURRENT_SCHEMA')
      ,tabname       => 'STATEMENT'
      ,partname      => NULL
      ,granularity   => 'ALL'
      ,method_opt    => 'FOR ALL COLUMNS SIZE 1'
      ,cascade       => FALSE);
END;
/

BEGIN
   DBMS_STATS.create_stat_table (
      ownname    => SYS_CONTEXT ('USERENV', 'CURRENT_SCHEMA')
      ,stattab   => 'CH9_STATS');

   DBMS_STATS.export_table_stats (
      ownname    => SYS_CONTEXT ('USERENV', 'CURRENT_SCHEMA')
      ,tabname   => 'STATEMENT'
      ,statown   => SYS_CONTEXT ('USERENV', 'CURRENT_SCHEMA')
      ,stattab   => 'CH9_STATS');
END;
/

-- Move to target system

BEGIN
   DBMS_STATS.delete_table_stats (
      ownname    => SYS_CONTEXT ('USERENV', 'CURRENT_SCHEMA')
      ,tabname   => 'STATEMENT');

   DBMS_STATS.import_table_stats (
      ownname    => SYS_CONTEXT ('USERENV', 'CURRENT_SCHEMA')
      ,tabname   => 'STATEMENT'
      ,statown   => SYS_CONTEXT ('USERENV', 'CURRENT_SCHEMA')
      ,stattab   => 'CH9_STATS');
END;
/
```

- Listing 9-1 creates a table called STATEMENT that will form the basis of other demonstrations in this chapter. STATEMENT is loaded with data, some indexes are created, and then statistics are gathered. At this stage you have to imagine that this table is on the source system, i.e., the test system in the scenario I described above.

- The first stage in the process of statistics copying is to create a regular heap table to hold the exported statistics. This has to have a specific format and is created using a call to DBMS_STATS.CREATE_STAT_TABLE. I have named the heap table CH9_STATS, but I could have used any name.

- The next step is to export the statistics. I have done so using DBMS_STATS.EXPORT_TABLE_STATS that by default exports statistics for the table, its columns, and associated indexes. As you might imagine, there are variants of this procedure for the database and schema, amongst others.

- The next step in the process is not shown but involves moving the heap table to the target system, i.e., the production system in the scenario I described above. This could be done by use of a database link or with the datapump utility. However, my preferred approach is to generate either a SQL Loader script or just a bunch of INSERT statements. This allows the script to be checked into a source-code control system along with other project scripts for posterity.

- You now have to imagine that the remaining code in Listing 9-1 is running on the target system. It is good practice to delete any existing statistics on your target table or tables using DBMS_STATS.DELETE_TABLE_STATS or DBMS_STATS.DELETE_SCHEMA_STATS first. Otherwise you may end up with a hybrid set of statistics.

- A call to DBMS_STATS.IMPORT_TABLE_STATS is then performed to load object statistics from the CH9_STATS heap table into the data dictionary, where the CBO can then use them for SQL statements involving the STATEMENT table.

In case there is any doubt, the time that these export/import operations take bears no relation to the size of the objects concerned. The time taken to perform export/import operations is purely the result of the number of objects involved, and for most databases importing statistics is a task that can be completed within a couple of minutes at most.

Transferring Statistics

Oracle database 12cR1 introduced an alternative to the export/import approach for copying statistics from one database to another. The DBMS_STATS.TRANSFER_STATS procedure allows object statistics to be copied without having to create a heap table, such as CH9_STATS used by Listing 9-1. Listing 9-2 shows how to transfer statistics for a specific table directly from one database to another.

Listing 9-2. Transferring statistcs between databases using a database link

```
BEGIN
   DBMS_STATS.transfer_stats (
       ownname    => SYS_CONTEXT ('USERENV', 'CURRENT_SCHEMA')
      ,tabname    => 'STATEMENT'
      ,dblink     => 'DBLINK_NAME');
END;
/
```

If you want to try this you will need to replace the DBLINK_NAME parameter value with the name of a valid database link on your target database that refers to the source database. The statistics for the table STATEMENT will be transferred directly from one system to another.

Perhaps I am a little old fashioned, but it seems to me that if your statistics are important enough to warrant copying then they are worth backing up. On that premise, the approach in Listing 9-1 is superior to that in Listing 9-2. But then again, maybe you just can't teach an old dog new tricks.

Setting Object Statistics

Although the vast majority of object statistics should be gathered, there are a few occasions where statistics need to be directly set. Here are a few of them:

- Users of the DBMS_STATS.COPY_TABLE_STATS package may need to set statistics for some columns for the partition that is the target of the copy. We will discuss DBMS_STATS.COPY_TABLE_STATS in Chapter 20.

- The TSTATS deployment model requires the minimum and maximum values of columns to be deleted for some columns. The TSTATS model for stabilizing execution plans will also be discussed in Chapter 20.

- Gathering statistics on temporary tables can be tricky because at the time that statistics are gathered the temporary table is likely to be empty, particularly when ON COMMIT DELETE ROWS is set for the table.

- In my opinion, histograms should be manually set on all columns that require them. I advocate manually setting histograms so that the number of test cases is limited. Listing 9-8 later in this chapter gives an example of how to directly set up histograms and explains the benefits in more detail.

Creating or Rebuilding Indexes and Tables

Gathering object statistics on large indexes can be a time-consuming affair because data needs to be read from the index. However, statistics for an index can be generated as the index is being built or rebuilt with virtually no additional overhead. and this is the default behavior unless statistics for the table being indexed are locked. Notice that this behavior cannot be suppressed even when an index is being created for an empty table that is yet to be loaded.

It is also possible to generate table and column statistics when a CREATE TABLE ... AS SELECT statement is run and when data is bulk loaded into an empty table using SQL Loader, or by using an INSERT ... SELECT statement. Curiously, the ability to generate statistics for a table during creation or loading did not appear until 12cR1. Here are some general tips applicable to 12cR1 and later:

- When statistics are generated by a bulk data load, no column histograms are generated and the statistics for any indexes are not updated.

- Statistics can be generated for bulk loads into non-empty tables by use of the GATHER_OPTIMIZER_STATISTICS hint.

- Statistic generation for CREATE TABLE ... AS SELECT statements and bulk loading of empty tables can be suppressed by the NO_GATHER_OPTIMIZER_STATISTICS hint.

The above rules might lead you to believe that if you load data in bulk and then create indexes then you will not need to gather any more statistics. However, *function-based indexes* add *hidden columns* to a table, and the statistics for these columns can only be obtained after the indexes are created. There are also complications involving partitioning and indexed organized tables. For precise details of how and when objects statistics are gathered during table creation and bulk inserts please refer to the SQL Tuning Guide.

Creating Object Statistics Wrap Up

I have now explained five different ways that object statistics can be loaded into the data dictionary. The primary mechanism is to gather object statistics directly using procedures such as DBMS_STATS.GATHER_TABLE_STATS. We can also load pre-made statistics using DBMS_STATS.IMPORT_TABLE_STATS or DBMS_STATS.TRANSFER_STATS. A fourth option is to set the object statistics to specific values using procedures such as DBMS_STATS.SET_TABLE_STATS. Finally, object statistics may be generated by DDL or DML operations, such as CREATE INDEX.

Now that we have loaded our object statistics into the database it would be nice to be able to look at them. Let us deal with that now.

Examining Object Statistics

Object statistics are held both in the data dictionary and in tables created by DBMS_STATS.CREATE_STAT_TABLE. Let us see how we can find and interpret these statistics, beginning with the data dictionary.

Examining Object Statistics in the Data Dictionary

Statistics in the data dictionary can be obtained by calls to procedures in the DBMS_STATS package, such as DBMS_STATS.GET_COLUMN_STATS. However, it is generally more convenient to use views on the data dictionary. Table 9-1 lists the primary views for examining object statistics.

Table 9-1. *Views for examining object statistics in the data dictionary*

	Global	Partition	Subpartition
Table	ALL_TAB_STATISTICS	ALL_TAB_STATISTICS	ALL_TAB_STATISTICS
Index	ALL_IND_STATISTICS	ALL_IND_STATISTICS	ALL_IND_STATISTICS
Column	ALL_TAB_COL_STATISTICS	ALL_PART_COL_STATISTICS	ALL_SUBPART_COL_STATISTICS
Histograms	ALL_TAB_HISTOGRAMS	ALL_PART_HISTOGRAMS	ALL_SUBPART_HISTOGRAMS

At this point I need to define some terms to avoid confusion.

- Object statistics are associated with a table, index, or column. In this chapter I will use the terms *object table*, *object index*, and *object column* when referring to entities that have object statistics. My use of these terms in this chapter is unrelated to their normal use as defined in the Object-Relational Developer's Guide.

- Object statistics can be displayed using the views in Table 9-1, among others. I will refer to such a view as a *statistic view* and a column in a statistic view as *statistic column*.

- I will use the term *export table* to refer to a table created by DBMS_STATS.CREATE_STAT_TABLE. I will use the term *export column* to refer to a column in an export table.

■ **Tip** Although the normal way to load data into an export table is with DBMS_STATS.EXPORT_TABLE_STATS it is also possible to use procedures such as DBMS_STATS.GATHER_TABLE_STATS to gather statistics directly into export tables without updating the data dictionary.

Consider the following when looking at Table 9-1:

- Histograms are a special type of column statistic. Unlike other types of column statistic, more than one row in the statistic view is required for each object column. Because of this, histograms are shown in a separate set of statistic views than other column statistics.

- The views listed in Table 9-1 all begin with ALL. As with many data dictionary views there are alternative variants prefixed by USER and DBA. USER views just list statistics for objects owned by the current user. Suitably privileged users have access to DBA variants that include objects owned by SYS and other objects that the current user does not have access to. The views in Table 9-1 begin with ALL and display object statistics for all objects that the current user has access to, including objects owned by other users. Objects that the current user has no access to are not displayed.

- Object statistics are included in many other common views, such as ALL_TABLES, but these views may be missing some key columns. For example, the column STATTYPE_LOCKED indicates whether statistics for a table are locked, and this column is not present in ALL_TABLES; it is present in ALL_TAB_STATISTICS.

- The view ALL_TAB_COL_STATISTICS excludes object columns that have no statistics, and the three histogram statistic views do not necessarily list all object columns. The other eight tables in Listing 9-1 include rows for objects that have statistics and for objects that have no statistics.

Examining Exported Object Statistics

When you look at an export table you will see that most export columns have deliberately meaningless names. For example, in an export table created in 11gR2 there are 12 numeric columns with names from N1 to N12. There are two columns of type RAW named R1 and R2, 30-byte character columns named C1 to C5, and columns CH1, CL1, and D1. These last three columns are a 1000-byte character column, a CLOB, and a DATE respectively. Additional columns have been added in 12cR1.

All sorts of statistics can be held in export tables, not just object statistics, and these meaningless column names reflect the multi-purpose nature of an export table. Theoretically, you shouldn't need to interpret the data in such tables. Unfortunately, in practice you may well have to. One common scenario that involves manipulating exported statistics directly involves partitioned tables. Suppose you take a backup of partition-level statistics for a table partitioned by date and want to restore these statistics a year later. Some partitions will have been dropped and others created and so the names of the partitions will likely have changed. The most practical thing to do is just to update the names of the partitions in the export table before importing.

There are some columns in an export table that have meaningful, or semi-meaningful, names:

- **TYPE** indicates the type of statistic. T means `table`, I means index, and C indicates that the row holds column statistics. When an object column has histograms there are multiple rows in the export table for the same object column. All such rows in the export table have a TYPE of C.

- **FLAGS** is a bitmask. For example, if the value of TYPE is C and FLAGS is odd (the low order bit is set), the statistics for the object column were set with a call to DBMS_STATS.SET_COLUMN_STATS. After import, the statistic column USER_STATS in ALL_TAB_COL_STATISTICS will be YES.

- **VERSION** applies to the layout of the export table. If you try to import statistics into an 11g database from an export table created in 10g you will be asked to run the DBMS_STATS.UPGRADE_STAT_TABLE procedure. Among other things, the value of the VERSION column will be increased from 4 to 6 in all rows in the export table.

- **STATID** is an export column that allows multiple sets of statistics to be held for the same object. The value of STATID can be set when calling DBMS_STATS.EXPORT_TABLE_STATS, and the set to be imported can be specified in calls to DBMS_STATS.IMPORT_TABLE_STATS.

Now that we know the statistic views that show us object statistics in the data dictionary and we know at a high level how to interpret rows in an export table, we can move on to describing what the individual statistics are and what they are used for.

Statistic Descriptions

So far in this chapter I have explained how to load statistics into the data dictionary, how to export the statistics, and how to examine statistics using statistic views and export tables. It is now time to look at individual object statistics so that we can understand what they each do. Tables 9-2, 9-3, and 9-4 provide descriptions of the table, index, and column statistics respectively.

It is important to realize that the CBO is a complex and ever-changing beast. Without access to the source code for all releases of Oracle database it is impossible to say with certainty precisely how, if at all, a particular statistic is used. Nevertheless, there is a fair amount of published research that can be used to give us some idea.[1] Let us begin by looking at the table statistics.

Table Statistics

Table 9-2 provides a description of each table statistic and the name by which that statistic is identified in both a statistic view and an export table. Table 9-2 also provides the name of the parameter to use in a call to DBMS_STATS.SET_TABLE_STATS.

---

[1]As mentioned in the preface, my main source of information on statistics usage is the book *Cost Based Oracle* by Jonathan Lewis (2006).

Table 9-2. *Descriptions of table statistics*

Statistic column name	SET_TABLE_STATS parameter	Export column name	Description
OWNER	OWNNAME	C5	The table owner
TABLE_NAME	TABNAME	C1	The table name
PARTITION_NAME	PARTNAME	C2	The partition within the table for partition-level statistics
SUBPARTITION_NAME	PARTNAME	C3	The subpartition within the table for subpartition-level statistics
NUM_ROWS	NUMROWS	N1	The number of rows in the table or (sub) partition
BLOCKS	NUMBLKS	N2	The number of blocks below the high water mark
AVG_ROW_LEN	AVGRLEN	N3	The average size of a row in bytes
CHAIN_CNT	N/A	N9	Not gathered, settable, or used in 12cR1 or below
AVG_CACHED_BLOCKS	CACHEDBLK	N10	Not gathered or used by the CBO in 12cR1 or below
AVG_CACHE_HIT_RATIO	CACHEHIT	N11	Not gathered or used in 12cR1 or below
SAMPLE_SIZE	N/A	N4	Gathered but not settable or used
LAST_ANALYZED	N/A	D1	Date and time that statistics were last changed

Table 9-2 shows that, as far as I can tell, the CBO only makes use of three table **statistics**.

- **NUM_ROWS.** This statistic is used in conjunction with the estimated *selectivity* of a row source operation to estimate the cardinality of the operation; in other words the number of rows that the operation is anticipated to return. So if NUM_ROWS is 1,000 and the selectivity is calculated as 0.1 (10%), then the estimated cardinality of the operation will be 100. The NUM_ROWS statistic is used for determining neither the number of bytes that each returned row will consume nor the cost of the operation.

- **BLOCKS.** This statistic is only used for full table scans and only to estimate the cost of the row source operation, in other words, how long the full table scan will take. This statistic is not used for estimating cardinality or bytes.

- **AVG_ROW_LEN.** This statistic is used only to estimate the number of bytes that each row returned by a row source operation will consume. In fact, only when all columns in a table are selected does the CBO have the option to use this statistic. Most of the time the column statistic AVG_COL_LEN is used for estimating the number of bytes returned by a row source operation.

The one piece of information that we are missing is the selectivity of the operation. We use column statistics to calculate selectivity, and we will come onto column statistics after looking at index statistics.

Index Statistics

Table 9-3 provides a description of each index statistic and the name by which that statistic is identified in both a statistic view and an export table. Table 9-3 also provides the name of the parameter to use in a call to DBMS_STATS.SET_INDEX_STATS.

Table 9-3. Descriptions of table statistics

Statistic column name	SET_INDEX_STATS parameter	Stats table column name	Description
OWNER	OWNNAME	C5	The table owner.
INDEX_NAME	INDNAME	C1	The table name.
PARTITION_NAME	PARTNAME	C2	The partition within the index for partition level statistics.
SUBPARTITION_NAME	PARTNAME	C3	The subpartition within the index for subpartition-level statistics.
NUM_ROWS	NUMROWS	N1	The number of rows in the index or (sub) partition.
LEAF_BLOCKS	NUMLBLKS	N2	The number of leaf blocks in the index.
DISTINCT_KEYS	NUMDIST	N3	The number of distinct key values within the index.
AVG_LEAF_BLOCKS_PER_KEY	AVGLBLK	N4	Average number of leaf index blocks for each key value. Always 1 for a unique index.
AVG_DATA_BLOCKS_PER_KEY	AVGDBLK	N5	The average number of blocks in the table referenced by each index value.
CLUSTERING_FACTOR	CLSTFCT	N6	Together with index selectivity, the clustering factor is used to determine the efficacy of a B-tree index. See discussion below.
BLEVEL	INDLEVEL	N7	The "height" of an index. An index with just one block that is both the root and leaf block has a BLEVEL of 0.
SAMPLE_SIZE	N/A	N8	The number of rows sampled during a gather operation. Not gathered, settable, or used by the CBO in 12cR1 or earlier.
PCT_DIRECT_ACCESS	GUESSQ	N9	Only used for secondary indexes on index-organized tables. The percentage probability that the row hasn't moved since the index entry was created.
AVG_CACHED_BLOCKS	CACHEDBLK	N10	Not gathered or used by CBO in 12cR1 or earlier releases.
AVG_CACHE_HIT_RATIO	CACHEHIT	N11	Not gathered or used by the CBO in 12cR1 or earlier releases.

The first thing I want to say about index statistics is that they are entirely independent of table and column statistics and can be gathered solely by looking at the index without any access to the table. As an example, the statistic AVG_DATA_BLOCKS_PER_KEY, which appears to relate to the table, can be determined by looking at the ROWIDs in the index entries.

Index statistics are used to determine not only the cost, cardinalities, and bytes of an index access, but also the cost of accessing the table when the index access is a child operation of a TABLE ACCESS BY [LOCAL|GLOBAL] ROWID operation. However, before looking at how index statistics are used to cost table access, let us consider the index operation itself.

How Index Statistics are Used for Index Operations

There are a number of row source operations for accessing an index. These include INDEX RANGE SCAN, INDEX FULL SCAN, and several more. We will look at them all in chapter 10. Once the index has been accessed, the ROWIDs returned may or may not be used to access the table itself. For now let us focus on how the CBO uses index statistics for generating estimates for the index access itself.

- **NUM_ROWS.** If a B-tree index is made up entirely of non-null columns then the value of NUM_ROWS for the index will exactly match the value of NUM_ROWS for the table. However, when the indexed column or columns are NULL then no entry is made for a row in a B-tree index and the value of NUM_ROWS for the index may be lower than that for the table. It turns out that sometimes the CBO estimates the cardinality of an index operation by making use of the NUM_ROWS statistic for the index, but most of the time the index statistic is ignored and the NUM_ROWS statistic for the table is used for cardinality calculations.

- **LEAF_BLOCKS.** This statistic is used to help determine the cost of an index operation. If the selectivity is 10% (excluding filter predicates) then the number of leaf blocks accessed is assumed to be 10% of the value of the LEAF_BLOCKS statistic.

- **BLEVEL.** Most index access operations involve accessing the root block of the index and working down to the leaf blocks. The BLEVEL statistic can be used directly for the estimated cost of this traversal and is added to the calculation based on LEAF_BLOCKS to arrive at the overall cost for the index operation. The costing algorithm for an INDEX FAST FULL SCAN is the one algorithm that doesn't make use of the BLEVEL statistic, as the leaf blocks are not read by traversing the index from the root block. I will cover the INDEX FAST FULL SCAN operation in the context of other access methods in Chapter 10.

The number of bytes returned by index access operations is determined by summing the AVG_COL_LEN column statistic for all columns returned by the index operation and adding some overhead. We need to use column statistics to determine the selectivity of an index operation, just as we do for a table operation, and I will look at column statistics after explaining how index statistics are used to cost table access.

How Index Statistics are Used to Cost Table Access

When a table is accessed through an index the estimated cost of that access is determined by index—*not* table—statistics. On the other hand, index statistics are used to determine neither the number of rows nor the number of bytes returned by the table access operation. That makes sense because the number of rows selected from a table is independent of which index, if any, is used to access the table.

Figures 9-1 and 9-2 show how difficult it is to determine the cost of accessing a table through an index.

  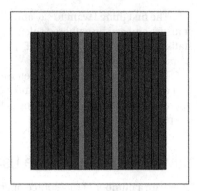

Figure 9-1. *Table blocks from a weakly clustered index*

 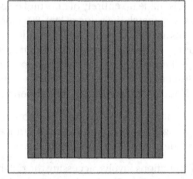 

Figure 9-2. *Table blocks from a strongly clustered index*

Figure 9-1 shows three table blocks from an imaginary table with ten blocks that each contain 20 rows, making a total of 200 rows in the table. Let us assume that 20 rows in the table have a specific value for a specific column and that column is indexed. If these 20 rows are scattered around the table then there would be approximately two matching rows per block. I have represented this situation by the highlighted rows in Figure 9-1.

As you can see, every block in the table would need to be read to obtain these 20 rows, so a full table scan would be more efficient than an indexed access, primarily because multi-block reads could be used to access the table, rather than single block reads. Now take a look at Figure 9-2.

In this case all 20 rows that we select through the index appear in a single block, and now an indexed access would be far more efficient, as only one table block needs to be read. Notice that in both Figure 9-1 and Figure 9-2 selectivity is 10% (20 rows from 200) so knowing the selectivity isn't sufficient for the CBO to estimate the cost of access to a table via an index. Enter the *clustering factor*. To calculate the cost of accessing a table through an index (as opposed to the cost of accessing the index itself) we multiply the clustering factor by the selectivity. Since strongly clustered indexes have a *lower* clustering factor than weakly clustered indexes, the cost of accessing the table from a strongly clustered index is lower than that for accessing the table from a weakly clustered index. Listing 9-3 demonstrates how this works in practice.

Listing 9-3. Influence of clustering factor on the cost of table access

```
SELECT index_name, distinct_keys, clustering_factor
  FROM all_ind_statistics I
  WHERE     i.table_name = 'STATEMENT'
        AND i.owner = SYS_CONTEXT ('USERENV', 'CURRENT_SCHEMA')
        AND i.index_name IN ('STATEMENT_I_PC', 'STATEMENT_I_CC')
ORDER BY index_name DESC;

SELECT *
  FROM statement t
 WHERE product_category = 1;

SELECT *
  FROM statement t
 WHERE customer_category = 1;

SELECT /*+ index(t (customer_category)) */
       *
  FROM statement t
 WHERE customer_category = 1;
--
-- Output of first query showing the clustering factor of the indexes
--


INDEX_NAME                        DISTINCT_KEYS                  CLUSTERING_FACTOR
STATEMENT_I_PC                    10                             17
STATEMENT_I_CC                    50                             500


--
-- Execution plans for the three queries against the STATEMENT table
--


---------------------------------------------------------------------------
| Id | Operation                              | Name            | Cost (%CPU)|
---------------------------------------------------------------------------
|  0 | SELECT STATEMENT                       |                 |    3   (0)|
|  1 |  TABLE ACCESS BY INDEX ROWID BATCHED| STATEMENT         |    3   (0)|
|  2 |   INDEX RANGE SCAN                     | STATEMENT_I_PC  |    1   (0)|
---------------------------------------------------------------------------

-------------------------------------------------------
| Id | Operation         | Name      | Cost (%CPU)|
-------------------------------------------------------
|  0 | SELECT STATEMENT  |           |    7   (0)|
|  1 |  TABLE ACCESS FULL| STATEMENT |    7   (0)|
-------------------------------------------------------

---------------------------------------------------------------------------
| Id | Operation                              | Name            | Cost (%CPU)|
---------------------------------------------------------------------------
|  0 | SELECT STATEMENT                       |                 |   11   (0)|
|  1 |  TABLE ACCESS BY INDEX ROWID BATCHED| STATEMENT         |   11   (0)|
|  2 |   INDEX RANGE SCAN                     | STATEMENT_I_CC  |    1   (0)|
---------------------------------------------------------------------------
```

I have arranged for the first 50 rows inserted into STATEMENT to have one value for PRODUCT_CATEGORY, the next 50 a second value, and so on. There are, therefore, 10 distinct values of the PRODUCT_CATEGORY, and the data is strongly clustered because all of the rows for one PRODUCT_CATEGORY will be in a small number of blocks. On the other hand, the 50 values for CUSTOMER_CATEGORY have been assigned using a MOD function, and so the rows for a specific CUSTOMER_CATEGORY are spread out over the entire table.

When we select the rows for a particular PRODUCT_CATEGORY we multiply the selectivity (1/10) by the clustering factor of the STATEMENT_I_PC index, which Listing 9-3 shows us is 17. This gives us a value of 1.7. The index access itself has a cost of 1, so the total cost of accessing the table via the index is 2.7. This is rounded to 3 for display purposes.

There are 50 different values of CUSTOMER_CATEGORY and so when we select rows for one value of CUSTOMER_CATEGORY we get only 10 rows rather than the 50 that we got when we selected rows for a particular PRODUCT_CATEGORY. Based on selectivity arguments only, you would think that if the CBO used an index to access 50 rows it would use an index to access 10 rows. However, because the selected rows for a particular CUSTOMER_CATEGORY are scattered around the table, the clustering factor is higher, and now the CBO estimates that a full table scan would be cheaper than an indexed access. The reported cost for the full table scan in Listing 9-3 is 7. When we force the use of the index with a hint, the cost of accessing the table through the index is calculated as the selectivity (1/50) multiplied by the clustering factor of the STATEMENT_I_CC index (500). This yields a cost of 10, which is added to the cost of 1 for the index access itself to give the displayed total cost of 11. Since the estimated total cost of table access via an index is 11 and the cost of a full table scan is 5, the unhinted selection of rows for a particular CUSTOMER_CATEGORY uses a full table scan.

NESTED LOOP ACCESS VIA A MULTI-COLUMN INDEX

There is an obscure case where the cost of an index range scan is calculated in an entirely different way from how I have described above. The case involves nested loops on multi-column indexes where there is a strong correlation between the values of the indexed columns and where equality predicates exist for all indexed columns. This obscure case is identified by a low value for DISTINCT_KEYS, and the calculation involves simply adding BLEVEL and AVG_LEAF_BLOCKS_PER_KEY for the index access; the cost of the table access is AVG_DATA_BLOCKS_PER_KEY. I only mention this case to avoid leaving you with the impression that the DISTINCT_KEYS, AVG_LEAF_BLOCKS_PER_KEY, and AVG_DATA_BLOCKS_PER_KEY index statistics are unused. For more information on this obscure case see Chapter 11 of *Cost-Based Oracle* by Jonathan Lewis (2006).

Function-based Indexes and TIMESTAMP WITH TIME ZONE

It is possible to create an index on one or more expressions involving the columns in a table rather than just the columns themselves. Such indexes are referred to as *function-based indexes*. It may come as a surprise to some of you that any attempt to create an index on a column of TIMESTAMP WITH TIME ZONE results in a function-based index! This is because columns of type TIMESTAMP WITH TIME ZONE are converted for the index in the way shown in Listing 9-4.

Listing 9-4. A function-based index involving TIMESTAMP WITH TIME ZONE

```
SELECT transaction_date_time
  FROM statement t
 WHERE transaction_date_time = TIMESTAMP '2013-01-02 12:00:00.00 -05:00';
```

```
------------------------------------------------------------------
| Id  | Operation                        | Name                |
------------------------------------------------------------------
|  0  | SELECT STATEMENT                 |                     |
|  1  |  TABLE ACCESS BY INDEX ROWID BATCHED| STATEMENT        |
|  2  |   INDEX RANGE SCAN               | STATEMENT_I_TRAN_DT |
------------------------------------------------------------------

Predicate Information (identified by operation id):
---------------------------------------------------

   2 - access(SYS_EXTRACT_UTC("TRANSACTION_DATE_TIME")=TIMESTAMP'
            2013-01-02 17:00:00.000000000')
```

If you look at the filter predicate for the execution plan of the query in Listing 9-4 you will see that the predicate has changed to include a function SYS_EXTRACT_UTC that converts the TIMESTAMP WITH TIME ZONE data type to a TIMESTAMP data type indicating *Universal Coordinated Time* (UTC)[2]. The fact that the original time zone in the literal is five hours earlier than UTC is reflected in the TIMESTAMP literal in the predicate, which is shown in the execution plan. The reason that this conversion is done is because two TIMESTAMP WITH TIME ZONE values that involve different time zones but are actually simultaneous are considered equal. Notice that since the function-based index excludes the original time zone the table itself needs to be accessed to retrieve the time zone, even though no other column is present in the select list.

■ **Note**   Since all predicates involving columns of type TIMESTAMP WITH TIME ZONE are converted to use the SYS_EXTRACT_UTC function, column statistics on object columns of type TIMESTAMP WITH TIME ZONE cannot be used to determine cardinality!

Bitmap Indexes

The structure of the root block and branch blocks of a bitmap index are identical to that of a B-tree index, but the entries in the leaf blocks are bitmaps that refer to a number of rows in the table. Because of this the NUM_ROWS statistic for a bitmap index (which should be interpreted as "number of index entries" in this case) will usually be considerably less than the number of rows in the table, and for small tables will equal the number of distinct values for the column. The CLUSTERING_FACTOR is unused in a bitmap index and is set, arbitrarily, to a copy of NUM_ROWS.

Column Statistics

Finally we come to discuss column statistics. Column statistics have nothing to do with the cost of an operation and everything to do with the size of the rows returned by an operation and the cardinality of an operation. As with table and index statistics, Table 9-4 lists the individual column statistics and provides the associated identifiers in statistic views and export tables. Table 9-4 also provides the names of the parameters to DBMS_STATS.SET_COLUMN_STATS.

---

[2]The abbreviation UTC is a compromise between the English Universal Coordinated Time and the French Temps Universel Coordonné.

Table 9-4. *Descriptions of table statistics*

Statistic column name	SET_COLUMN_STATS parameter	Stats table column name	Description
OWNER	OWNNAME	C5	The table owner.
TABLE_NAME	TABNAME	C1	The table name.
PARTITION_NAME*	PARTNAME	C2	The partition within the table for partition level statistics.
SUBPARTITION_NAME	PARTNAME	C3	The subpartition within the table for subpartition-level statistics.
COLUMN_NAME	COLNAME	C4	The name of the column. This may be a fabricated name in the case of hidden columns. See below for details.
NUM_DISTINCT	DISTCNT	N1	The number of distinct non-null values for the column.
DENSITY	DENSITY	N2	If a histogram is not present this is the inverse of N1. See below for its use with histograms.
Not shown	Not settable	N3	A spare unused statistic set to the same as N2 when statistics are gathered.
SAMPLE_SIZE	N/A	N4	The number of rows sampled during a gather operation. Not used by the CBO.
NUM_NULLS	NULLCNT	N5	The number of rows where the column value is NULL.
Not shown	Part of SREC	N6	Numeric representation of minimum value.
Not shown	Part of SREC	N7	Numeric representation of maximum value.
AVG_COL_LEN	AVGCLEN	N8	The average size of a column value in bytes.
ENDPOINT_NUMBER	Part of SREC	N10	For histograms, a cumulative sum of the number of rows for all endpoints with values less than or equal to the value of N11.
ENDPOINT_VALUE	Part of SREC	N11	A numeric representation of the histogram value. For character strings only the first six characters are represented.
ENDPOINT_ACTUAL_VALUE	Part of SREC	CH1	The actual value of a character column. Only populated when two successive endpoints are identical in the first six characters.
LOW_VALUE	Part of SREC	R1	Raw representation of minimum value.
HIGH_VALUE	Part of SREC	R2	Raw representation of maximum value.
HISTOGRAM	Part of SREC	N/A	Indicates the type of a histogram, if any.
NUM_BUCKETS	Part of SREC	N/A	Indicates the number of endpoints in a histogram.

Although column statistics can be set and exported independently of table statistics, column statistics can only be gathered along with a table. The METHOD_OPT parameter to the DBMS_STATS gathering procedures controls which column statistics to gather and whether to generate histograms for these columns.

Let me first describe how column statistics are used without histograms and then explain how histograms alter things.

- **NUM_DISTINCT.** This statistic is *sometimes* used to determine selectivity. If you have an equality predicate on a column with five distinct values, the selectivity will be 1/5 or 20%. See also the DENSITY statistic.

- **DENSITY.** *When histograms aren't in use*, this statistic is the inverse of NUM_DISTINCT and is *sometimes* used to determine selectivity. If you have an equality predicate on a column with five distinct values, the DENSITY column will reflect the selectivity of 1/5 or 0.2.

- **NUM_NULLS.** This column statistic is used to help determine cardinality. The statistic is obviously invaluable when you have a predicate such as <object_column> IS NULL or <object_column> IS NOT NULL. In the latter case the number of rows selected is the value of the NUM_ROWS statistic for the object table minus the value of the NUM_NULLS statistic for the object column. The number of rows with non-null values for an object column is also the basis for cardinality calculations for equality, inequality, and range predicates.

- **LOW_VALUE and HIGH_VALUE.** The primary purpose of these column statistics is to handle range predicates such as TRANSACTION_DATE < DATE '2013-02-11'. Since the maximum value of TRANSACTION_DATE in the STATEMENT table created in Listing 9-1 is known to be 10th January 2013, the selectivity of that predicate is estimated at 100%. I will return to the LOW_VALUE and HIGH_VALUE column statistics for a lengthier explanation in Chapter 20.

- **AVG_COL_LEN.** This statistic is used to determine the number of bytes returned by an operation. If, for example, you select five columns from a table then the estimate for the number of bytes returned by the operation for each row will be the sum of the AVG_COL_LEN statistics for each of those five columns plus a variable-sized overhead per row.

This explanation of column statistics seems to leave a lot out. If you pick a few SQL statements at random from a typical application and try to reproduce the CBO's cardinality calculations based solely on the object statistics and my explanation so far you will probably succeed in very few cases. But first of all, let us look at Listing 9-5 and work through a very simple example.

Listing 9-5. Simple cardinality and bytes calculation based on column statistics

```
SELECT num_rows
      ,column_name
      ,num_nulls
      ,avg_col_len
      ,num_distinct
      ,ROUND (density, 3) density
  FROM all_tab_col_statistics c, all_tab_statistics t
 WHERE     t.owner = SYS_CONTEXT ('USERENV', 'CURRENT_SCHEMA')
       AND t.table_name = 'STATEMENT'
       AND c.owner = SYS_CONTEXT ('USERENV', 'CURRENT_SCHEMA')
       AND c.table_name = 'STATEMENT'
       AND c.column_name IN ('TRANSACTION_DATE'
                            ,'DESCRIPTION'
                            ,'POSTING_DATE'
                            ,'POSTING_DELAY');
```

```
SELECT *
  FROM statement
 WHERE description = 'Flight' AND posting_delay = 0;
```

NUM_ROWS	COLUMN_NAME	NUM_NULLS	AVG_COL_LEN	NUM_DISTINCT	DENSITY
500	TRANSACTION_DATE	0	8	10	0.1
500	POSTING_DATE	0	8	12	0.083
500	POSTING_DELAY	0	3	3	0.333
500	DESCRIPTION	0	7	4	0.25

```
------------------------------------------------------------
| Id | Operation       | Name      | Rows | Bytes | Time     |
------------------------------------------------------------
|  0 | SELECT STATEMENT |          |   42 | 2310  | 00:00:01 |
|  1 |  TABLE ACCESS FULL| STATEMENT |  42 | 2310  | 00:00:01 |
------------------------------------------------------------
```

Listing 9-5 begins by selecting a few pertinent column statistics from our statistics views and looking at the execution plan of a simple, single table select statement on the table created in Listing 9-1.

- The first selection predicate is an equality operation on the DESCRIPTION column, and the NUM_DISTINCT column statistic for the DESCRIPTION object column is 4 (the DENSITY being 1/4).

- The second selection predicate is an equality operation on the POSTING_DELAY column, and the NUM_DISTINCT column statistic for the POSTING_DELAY object column is 3 (the DENSITY being 1/3).

- The NUM_ROWS statistic for the STATEMENT table is 500, and the NUM_NULLS statistic for the DESCRIPTION and POSTING_DELAY columns is 0, so the estimated number of rows from which we are selecting is 500.

- Given selectivities of 1/4 and 1/3 from 500 rows the estimated cardinality for the statement is 500/4/3 = 41.67, and after rounding up that is what DBMS_XPLAN displays.

That is all very well, you may say, but real-life queries have expressions and function calls in select lists and predicates. Listing 9-6 is only a little more complicated, but now the CBO's estimates start to become a lot less scientific and a lot less accurate.

Listing 9-6. CBO calculations in the absence of column statistics

```
SELECT *
  FROM statement
 WHERE SUBSTR (description, 1, 1) = 'F';
```

```
------------------------------------------------------------
| Id | Operation       | Name      | Rows | Bytes | Time     |
------------------------------------------------------------
|  0 | SELECT STATEMENT |          |    5 |  275  | 00:00:01 |
|  1 |  TABLE ACCESS FULL| STATEMENT |   5 |  275  | 00:00:01 |
------------------------------------------------------------
```

This time our predicate involves a function call. We have no column statistic that we can use, so the CBO has to pick an arbitrary selectivity. When faced with an equality predicate and no statistics on which to base a selectivity estimate, the CBO just picks 1%! Hardcoded! So our estimated cardinality is 500/100 = 5. If you run the query you actually get 125 rows, so the estimate is out by a factor of 25.

To be fair I have given an exceptionally simplified explanation of the CBO's cardinality-estimating algorithm, but that does not detract from the validity of the point that the CBO often makes arbitrary estimates in the absence of meaningful input data.

Histograms

The explanation of column statistics given so far means that the CBO has to treat most equality predicates involving a column name and a literal value in the same way, irrespective of the supplied value. Listing 9-7 shows how this can be problematic.

Listing 9-7. An example of a missing histogram

```
SELECT *
  FROM statement
 WHERE transaction_amount = 8;
```

```
-----------------------------------------------------------------------------
| Id  | Operation          | Name      | Rows  | Bytes | Cost (%CPU)| Time     |
-----------------------------------------------------------------------------
|   0 | SELECT STATEMENT   |           |     2 |   106 |     8   (0)| 00:00:01 |
|*  1 |  TABLE ACCESS FULL | STATEMENT |     2 |   106 |     8   (0)| 00:00:01 |
-----------------------------------------------------------------------------
```

There are 262 distinct values of `TRANSACTION_AMOUNT` in `STATEMENT` varying from 5 to 15200. The CBO assumes, correctly in this case, that 8 is one of those 262 values but assumes that only about 500/262 rows will have `TRANSACTION_AMOUNT` = 8. In actuality there are 125 rows with `TRANSACTION_AMOUNT` = 8. The way to improve the accuracy of the CBO's estimate in this case is to define a histogram. Before creating the histogram I want to define what I will call a *histogram specification* that documents the different estimates that we want the CBO to make. I would propose the following histogram specification for `TRANSACTION_AMOUNT`:

> *For every 500 rows in STATEMENT the CBO should assume that 125 have a value of 8 for TRANSACTION_AMOUNT and the CBO should assume 2 rows for any other supplied value.*

Listing 9-8 shows how we might construct a histogram to make the CBO make these assumptions.

Listing 9-8. Creating a histogram on TRANSACTION_AMOUNT

```
DECLARE
   srec    DBMS_STATS.statrec;
BEGIN
   FOR r
      IN (SELECT *
             FROM all_tab_cols
            WHERE    owner = SYS_CONTEXT ('USERENV', 'CURRENT_SCHEMA')
                 AND table_name = 'STATEMENT'
                 AND column_name = 'TRANSACTION_AMOUNT')
```

```
   LOOP
      srec.epc := 3;
      srec.bkvals := DBMS_STATS.numarray (600, 400, 600);
      DBMS_STATS.prepare_column_values (srec
                                       ,DBMS_STATS.numarray (-1e7, 8, 1e7));
      DBMS_STATS.set_column_stats (ownname   => r.owner
                                  ,tabname   => r.table_name
                                  ,colname   => r.column_name
                                  ,distcnt   => 3
                                  ,density   => 1 / 250
                                  ,nullcnt   => 0
                                  ,srec      => srec
                                  ,avgclen   => r.avg_col_len);
   END LOOP;
END;
/

SELECT *
  FROM statement
 WHERE transaction_amount = 8;


------------------------------------------------------------
| Id | Operation         | Name      | Rows | Bytes | Time     |
------------------------------------------------------------
|  0 | SELECT STATEMENT  |           |  125 |  6875 | 00:00:01 |
|  1 |  TABLE ACCESS FULL| STATEMENT |  125 |  6875 | 00:00:01 |
------------------------------------------------------------


SELECT *
  FROM statement
 WHERE transaction_amount = 1640;


------------------------------------------------------------
| Id | Operation         | Name      | Rows | Bytes | Time     |
------------------------------------------------------------
|  0 | SELECT STATEMENT  |           |    2 |   110 | 00:00:01 |
|  1 |  TABLE ACCESS FULL| STATEMENT |    2 |   110 | 00:00:01 |
------------------------------------------------------------
```

This PL/SQL "loop" will actually only call DBMS_STATS.SET_COLUMN_STATS once, as the query on ALL_TAB_COLS[3] returns one row. The key to defining the histogram on TRANSACTION_AMOUNT is the SREC parameter that I have highlighted in bold. This structure is set up as follows:

1. Set SREC.EPC. EPC is short for *End Point Count* and in this case defines the number of distinct values for the object column. I recommend setting EPC to two more than the number of values for the column that the *histogram specification* defines. In our case the only value in our histogram specification is 8 so we set EPC to 3.

---

[3]Incidentally I use ALL_TAB_COLS instead of ALL_TAB_COL_STATISTICS in case there are no pre-existing statistics for the column.

2. Set `SREC.BKVALS`. BKVALS is short for bucket values and in this case the list of three bucket values indicates the supposed number of rows for each endpoint. So in theory 600 rows have one value for `TRANSACTION_AMOUNT`, 400 rows have a second value, and 600 rows have a third value. Those three values together suggest that there are 1600 rows in the table (600+400+600=1600). In fact, the actual interpretation of these values is that *for every 1600* rows in the table 600 rows have the first, as yet unspecified, value for `TRANSACTION_AMOUNT`, 400 rows have the second value, and 600 rows have the third value.

3. Call `DBMS_STATS.PREPARE_COLUMN_VALUES` to define the actual object column values for each endpoint. The first endpoint is deliberately absurdly low, the middle endpoint is the value of 8 from our histogram specification, and the last value is absurdly high. The addition of the absurdly low and absurdly high values at the beginning and end of our ordered set of values is why we set `SREC.EPC` to two more than the number of values in our histogram specification. We will never use the absurd values in our predicates (or they wouldn't be absurd) so the only statistic of note is that 400 rows out of every 1600 have a value of 8. This means that when we select from 500 rows the CBO will give a cardinality estimate of `500 x 400 / 1600 = 125`.

4. Call `DBMS_STATS.SET_COLUMN_STATS`. There are two parameters I want to draw your attention to.

   • **DISTCNT** is set to 3. We have defined three values for our column (`-1e7, 8,` and `1e7`) so we need to be consistent and set `DISTCNT` to the same value as `SREC.EPC`. This arrangement ensures that we get what is called a *frequency histogram*.

   • **DENSITY** is set to 1/250. When a frequency histogram is defined this statistic indicates the selectivity of predicates with values not specified in the histogram. The supplied value of 1/250 in Listing 9-8 indicates that for 500 non-null rows the CBO should assume 500/250 = 2 rows match the equality predicate when a value other than the three provided appears in a predicate.

After the histogram is created we can see that the CBO provides a cardinality estimate of 125 when the `TRANSACTION_AMOUNT = 8` predicate is supplied and a cardinality estimate of 2 when any other literal value is supplied in the predicate.

Creating histograms in this way is often referred to as *faking histograms*. I don't like this term because there is a connotation that gathered histograms (not faked) are somehow superior. They are not. For example, when I allowed histograms to be created automatically for `TRANSACTION_AMOUNT` on my 12cR1 database I got a histogram with 254 endpoints. In theory, that would mean that I might get 255 different execution plans (one for each defined endpoint and one for values not specified in the histogram) for every statement involving equality predicates on `TRANSACTION_AMOUNT`. By manually creating a frequency histogram using a histogram specification defined with testing in mind you can limit the number of test cases. In the case of Listing 9-8 there are just two test cases for each statement: `TRANSACTION_AMOUNT = 8` and `TRANSACTION_AMOUNT = <anything else>`.

Bear in mind the following when manually creating histograms this way:

   • Manually creating a frequency histogram with absurd minimum and maximum values means that you don't have to worry about new column values that are either higher than the previous maximum value or lower than the previous minimum. However, range predicates such as `TRANSACTION_AMOUNT > 15000` may yield cardinality estimates that are far too high. If you use range predicates you may have to pick sensible minimum and maximum values.

   • Don't pick values for the `srec.bkvals` array that are too small or a rounding error may creep in. Don't, for example, replace 600, 400, and 600 in Listing 9-8 with 6, 4, and 6. This will alter the results for predicates such as `TRANSACTION_AMOUNT > 8`.

- The CBO will get confused if the default selectivity from DENSITY is higher than the selectivity for the supplied endpoints.

- The selectivity of unspecified values of a column is only calculated using the DENSITY statistic for manually created histograms. When histograms are gathered (USER_STATS = 'NO' in ALL_TAB_COL_STATISTICS) then the selectivity of unspecified values is half of that for the lowest supplied endpoint.

- There are other types of histograms. These include *height-based histograms*, *top frequency histograms*, and *hybrid histograms*. Top frequency and hybrid histograms appear for the first time in 12cR1. In my experience, which may or may not be typical, the type of manually created frequency histogram that I have described here is the only one I have ever needed.

When you use one of the views listed in Table 9-1 to view histograms you may be momentarily confused. Listing 9-9 shows the histogram on TRANSACTION_AMOUNT that I created in Listing 9-8:

Listing 9-9. Displaying histogram data

```
SELECT table_name
      ,column_name
      ,endpoint_number
      ,endpoint_value
      ,endpoint_actual_value
  FROM all_tab_histograms
 WHERE    owner = SYS_CONTEXT ('USERENV', 'CURRENT_SCHEMA')
      AND table_name = 'STATEMENT'
      AND column_name = 'TRANSACTION_AMOUNT';
```

TABLE_NAME	COLUMN_NAME	ENDPOINT_NUMBER	ENDPOINT_VALUE	ENDPOINT_ACTUAL_VALUE
STATEMENT	TRANSACTION_AMOUNT	600	-10000000	
STATEMENT	TRANSACTION_AMOUNT	1000	8	
STATEMENT	TRANSACTION_AMOUNT	1600	10000000	

The two things to be wary of are:

1. The ENDPOINT_ACTUAL_VALUE is only populated for character columns where the first six characters are shared by consecutive endpoints.

2. The ENDPOINT_NUMBER is cumulative. It represents a running sum of cardinalities up to that point.

Virtual and Hidden Columns

I have already mentioned that a function-based index creates a hidden object column and that the hidden object column can have statistics just like a regular object column. But because the column is hidden it is not returned by queries that begin SELECT * FROM. Such hidden columns are also considered to be *virtual columns* because they have no physical representation in the table.

Oracle database 11gR1 introduced the concept of unhidden virtual columns. These unhidden virtual columns are explicitly declared by CREATE TABLE or ALTER TABLE DDL statements rather than being implicitly declared as part of the creation of a function-based index. From the perspective of the CBO, virtual columns are treated in almost the same way, irrespective of whether they are hidden or not. Listing 9-10 shows how the CBO uses statistics on the virtual columns of the STATEMENT table created in Listing 9-1.

Listing 9-10. CBO use of statistics on virtual columns

```
--
-- Query 1: using an explictly declared
-- virtual column
--
SELECT *
  FROM statement
 WHERE posting_delay = 1;
------------------------------------------------
| Id  | Operation         | Name      | Rows  |
------------------------------------------------
|   0 | SELECT STATEMENT  |           |   167 |
|*  1 |   TABLE ACCESS FULL| STATEMENT |   167 |
------------------------------------------------

Predicate Information (identified by operation id):
---------------------------------------------------

   1 - filter("POSTING_DELAY"=1)
--
-- Query 2: using an expression equivalent to
-- an explictly declared virtual column.
--
SELECT *
  FROM statement
 WHERE (posting_date - transaction_date) = 1;
------------------------------------------------
| Id  | Operation         | Name      | Rows  |
------------------------------------------------
|   0 | SELECT STATEMENT  |           |   167 |
|*  1 |   TABLE ACCESS FULL| STATEMENT |   167 |
------------------------------------------------

Predicate Information (identified by operation id):
---------------------------------------------------

   1 - filter("STATEMENT"."POSTING_DELAY"=1)
--
-- Query 3: using an expression not identical to
-- virtual column.
--
SELECT *
  FROM statement
 WHERE (transaction_date - posting_date) = -1;
------------------------------------------------
| Id  | Operation         | Name      | Rows  |
------------------------------------------------
|   0 | SELECT STATEMENT  |           |     5 |
|*  1 |   TABLE ACCESS FULL| STATEMENT |     5 |
------------------------------------------------
```

```
Predicate Information (identified by operation id):
---------------------------------------------------

   1 - filter("TRANSACTION_DATE"-"POSTING_DATE"=(-1))

--
-- Query 4: using a hidden column
--
SELECT /*+ full(s) */ sys_nc00010$
  FROM statement s
 WHERE sys_nc00010$ = TIMESTAMP '2013-01-02 17:00:00.00';
---------------------------------------------------
| Id  | Operation        | Name      | Rows  |
---------------------------------------------------
|   0 | SELECT STATEMENT |           |   50  |
|*  1 |  TABLE ACCESS FULL| STATEMENT |   50  |
---------------------------------------------------

Predicate Information (identified by operation id):
---------------------------------------------------

   1 - filter(SYS_EXTRACT_UTC("TRANSACTION_DATE_TIME")=TIMESTAMP'
             2013-01-02 17:00:00.000000000')
--
-- Query 5: using an expression equivalent to
-- a hidden column.
--

SELECT SYS_EXTRACT_UTC (transaction_date_time)
  FROM statement s
 WHERE SYS_EXTRACT_UTC (transaction_date_time) =
          TIMESTAMP '2013-01-02 17:00:00.00';
----------------------------------------------------------
| Id  | Operation        | Name             | Rows  |
----------------------------------------------------------
|   0 | SELECT STATEMENT |                  |   50  |
|*  1 |  INDEX RANGE SCAN| STATEMENT_I_TRAN_DT |   50  |
----------------------------------------------------------

Predicate Information (identified by operation id):
---------------------------------------------------

   1 - access(SYS_EXTRACT_UTC("TRANSACTION_DATE_TIME")=TIMESTAMP'
             2013-01-02 17:00:00.000000000')
--
-- Query 6: using the timestamp with time zone column
--

SELECT transaction_date_time
  FROM statement s
 WHERE transaction_date_time = TIMESTAMP '2013-01-02 12:00:00.00 -05:00';
```

```
-------------------------------------------------------------------------
| Id  | Operation                           | Name               | Rows |
-------------------------------------------------------------------------
|   0 | SELECT STATEMENT                    |                    |  50  |
|   1 |  TABLE ACCESS BY INDEX ROWID BATCHED| STATEMENT          |  50  |
|*  2 |   INDEX RANGE SCAN                  | STATEMENT_I_TRAN_DT|  50  |
-------------------------------------------------------------------------
```

Predicate Information (identified by operation id):

```
   2 - access(SYS_EXTRACT_UTC("TRANSACTION_DATE_TIME")=TIMESTAMP'
           2013-01-02 17:00:00.000000000')
```

The first query in Listing 9-10 involves a predicate on an explicitly declared virtual column. The statistics for the virtual column can be used and the CBO divides the number of non-null rows by the number of distinct values for POSTING_DELAY. This is 50/3, which after rounding gives us 167. The second query uses an expression identical to the definition of the virtual column, and once again the virtual column statistics are used to yield a cardinality estimate of 167. Notice that the name of the virtual column appears in the predicate section of the execution plan of the second query. The third query uses an expression that is similar, but not identical, to the definition of the virtual column, and now the statistics on the virtual column cannot be used and the CBO has to fall back on its 1% selectivity guess.

We see similar behavior when we use predicates on the hidden column. The fourth query in Listing 9-10 somewhat unusually, but perfectly legally, references the hidden column explicitly generated for our function-based index. The CBO has been able to use the fact that there are ten distinct values of the expression in the table to estimate the cardinality as 500/10, i.e., 50. I have forced the use of a full table scan to emphasize the fact that, although the hidden column exists purely by virtue of the function-based index, the statistics can be used regardless of the access method. The fifth and sixth queries in Listing 9-10 also make use of the statistics on the hidden column. The fifth query uses the expression for the hidden column and the sixth uses the name of the TIMESTAMP WITH TIME ZONE column. Notice that in the last query the table has to be accessed to retrieve the time zone information that is missing from the index. A final observation on the last three queries is that the predicate section in the execution plan makes no reference to the hidden column name, a sensible variation of the display of filter predicates from explicitly declared virtual columns.

Extended Statistics

Like the columns created implicitly by the creation of function-based indexes, extended statistics are hidden, virtual columns. In Chapter 6 I explained the main purpose of extended statistics, namely to let the CBO understand the correlation between columns. Let me now give you an example using the STATEMENT table I created in Listing 9-1. Listing 9-11 shows two execution plans for a query, one before and one after creating extended statistics for the DESCRIPTION and AMOUNT_CATEGORY columns.

Listing 9-11. The use of multi-column extended statistics

```
--
-- Query and associated execution plan without extended statistics
--
SELECT *
  FROM statement t
 WHERE     transaction_date = DATE '2013-01-02'
       AND posting_date = DATE '2013-01-02';
```

```
----------------------------------------------------------------
| Id  | Operation          | Name      | Rows  | Time     |
----------------------------------------------------------------
|  0  | SELECT STATEMENT   |           |     4 | 00:00:01 |
|* 1  |  TABLE ACCESS FULL | STATEMENT |     4 | 00:00:01 |
----------------------------------------------------------------

--
-- Now we gather extended statistics for the two columns
--
DECLARE
    extension_name   all_tab_col_statistics.column_name%TYPE;
BEGIN
    extension_name :=
      DBMS_STATS.create_extended_stats (
          ownname       => SYS_CONTEXT ('USERENV', 'CURRENT_SCHEMA')
         ,tabname       => 'STATEMENT'
         ,extension     => '(TRANSACTION_DATE,POSTING_DATE)');
      DBMS_STATS.gather_table_stats (
          ownname       => SYS_CONTEXT ('USERENV', 'CURRENT_SCHEMA')
         ,tabname       => 'STATEMENT'
         ,partname      => NULL
         ,GRANULARITY   => 'GLOBAL'
         ,method_opt    => 'FOR ALL COLUMNS SIZE 1'
         ,cascade       => FALSE);
END;
/
--
-- Now let us look at the new execution plan for the query
--
----------------------------------------------------------------
| Id  | Operation          | Name      | Rows  | Time     |
----------------------------------------------------------------
|  0  | SELECT STATEMENT   |           |    17 | 00:00:01 |
|* 1  |  TABLE ACCESS FULL | STATEMENT |    17 | 00:00:01 |
----------------------------------------------------------------
```

The query in Listing 9-11 includes predicates on the TRANSACTION_DATE and POSTING_DATE columns. There are 10 values for TRANSACTION_DATE and 12 values for POSTING_DATE, and so without the extended statistics the CBO assumes that the query will return 500/10/12 rows, which is about 4. In fact, there are only 30 different combinations of TRANSACTION_DATE and POSTING_DATE, and after the extended statistics are gathered the execution plan for our query shows a cardinality of 17, which is the rounded result of 500/30.

■ **Note** I might have created the TRANSACTION_DATE column as a virtual column derived by the expression TRUNC (TRANSACTION_DATE_TIME). However, extended statistics, such as that defined in Listing 9-11, cannot be based on virtual columns.

I have said that with respect to cardinality estimates we shouldn't be overly concerned by errors of factors of 2 or 3, and the difference between 17 and 4 isn't much more than that. However, it is quite common to have several predicates on a number of correlated columns, and the cumulative effect of these sorts of cardinality errors can be disastrous.

■ **Note**   In Chapter 6, I mentioned that when you begin to analyze the performance of a new application or a new major release of an existing application it is a good idea to look for ways to improve the execution plans of large numbers of statements. Extended statistics are a prime example of this sort of change: if you set up extended statistics properly, the CBO may improve execution plans for a large number of statements.

There is a second variety of extended statistics that can be useful. This type of extension is just like the hidden virtual column that you get with a function-based index but without the index itself. Listing 9-12 shows an example.

Listing 9-12. Extended statistics for an expression

```
SELECT *
  FROM statement
 WHERE CASE
         WHEN description <> 'Flight' AND transaction_amount > 100
         THEN
            'HIGH'
       END = 'HIGH';


------------------------------------------------------------
| Id  | Operation         | Name      | Rows  | Time     |
------------------------------------------------------------
|   0 | SELECT STATEMENT  |           |     5 | 00:00:01 |
|*  1 |   TABLE ACCESS FULL| STATEMENT |     5 | 00:00:01 |
------------------------------------------------------------

Predicate Information (identified by operation id):
---------------------------------------------------

   1 - filter(CASE  WHEN ("DESCRIPTION"<>'Flight' AND
             "TRANSACTION_AMOUNT">100) THEN 'HIGH' END ='HIGH')

DECLARE
   extension_name   all_tab_cols.column_name%TYPE;
BEGIN
   extension_name :=
      DBMS_STATS.create_extended_stats (
         ownname     => SYS_CONTEXT ('USERENV', 'CURRENT_SCHEMA')
         ,tabname     => 'STATEMENT'
         ,extension   => q'[(CASE WHEN DESCRIPTION <> 'Flight'
                                    AND TRANSACTION_AMOUNT > 100
                             THEN 'HIGH' END)]');
```

```
    DBMS_STATS.gather_table_stats (
        ownname        => SYS_CONTEXT ('USERENV', 'CURRENT_SCHEMA')
        ,tabname       => 'STATEMENT'
        ,partname      => NULL
        ,method_opt    => 'FOR ALL COLUMNS SIZE 1'
        ,cascade       => FALSE);
END;
/


---------------------------------------------------------------
| Id  | Operation         | Name      | Rows  | Time     |
---------------------------------------------------------------
|   0 | SELECT STATEMENT  |           |   105 | 00:00:01 |
|*  1 |   TABLE ACCESS FULL| STATEMENT |   105 | 00:00:01 |
---------------------------------------------------------------

Predicate Information (identified by operation id):
---------------------------------------------------------------

   1 - filter(CASE  WHEN ("DESCRIPTION"<>'Flight' AND
              "TRANSACTION_AMOUNT">100) THEN 'HIGH' END ='HIGH')
```

The query in Listing 9-12 lists all transactions with AMOUNT > 100 that aren't flights. The query has had to be constructed in a special way so that we can take advantage of extended statistics. Before the creation of the extended statistic the estimated cardinality is 5 based on our good old 1% estimate. After the creation of an extended statistic on our carefully constructed expression, and the subsequent gathering of statistics on the table, we can see that the CBO has been able to accurately estimate the number of rows that would be returned from the query at 105.

Viewing Information on Virtual and Hidden Columns

As we have seen, the statistics for hidden and virtual columns are the same as for regular columns; the CBO uses these statistics in similar ways. However, there are two more things to be said about hidden and virtual columns. I want to explain how extended statistics are exported, but first let us look at how to examine information on hidden and virtual columns in the data dictionary.

Data Dictionary Views for Hidden and Virtual Columns

Hidden columns are not displayed by the view ALL_TAB_COLUMNS and only appear in ALL_TAB_COL_STATISTICS if statistics exist on the hidden columns. There are two views that display information on hidden columns regardless of whether they have statistics or not:

- ALL_TAB_COLS displays similar information as ALL_TAB_COLUMNS but includes hidden columns. The ALL_TAB_COLS statistic view includes two statistic columns—VIRTUAL_COLUMN and HIDDEN_COLUMN—that indicate if the object column is virtual or hidden, respectively.

- ALL_STAT_EXTENSIONS lists information about all virtual columns, including hidden virtual columns, whether they are associated with function-based indexes; unhidden, explicitly declared virtual columns; or hidden columns associated with extended statistics. ALL_STAT_EXTENSIONS includes a column—EXTENSION—with a data type of CLOB that defines the expression upon which the virtual column is based.

Exporting Extended Statistics

With the exception of extended statistics, hidden and virtual columns are exported and imported in precisely the same way as regular columns. However, there is an additional row in an export table for each extended statistic.

You cannot import statistics for a hidden column associated with a function-based index without creating the function-based index first using a CREATE INDEX statement. You cannot import statistics for an explicitly declared virtual column without declaring the column first using a CREATE TABLE or ALTER TABLE statement. The DDL statements that create function-based indexes and explicitly declared virtual columns cause the expressions on which the virtual column is based to be stored in the data dictionary.

On the other hand, you can import extended statistics without first calling DBMS_STATS.CREATE_EXTENDED_STATS; the import operation implicitly creates the hidden virtual column. This implicit creation of virtual columns that occurs when statistics are imported means that the export table needs to contain information about the expression on which the virtual column is based. This information is held in an extra row in the export table that has a TYPE of E, and the expression is stored in the export column CL1 that is of type CLOB. Listing 9-13 shows how extended statistics can be exported and imported.

Listing 9-13. Exporting and importing extended statistcs

```
TRUNCATE TABLE ch9_stats;

BEGIN
   DBMS_STATS.export_table_stats (
      ownname    => SYS_CONTEXT ('USERENV', 'CURRENT_SCHEMA')
      ,tabname    => 'STATEMENT'
      ,statown    => SYS_CONTEXT ('USERENV', 'CURRENT_SCHEMA')
      ,stattab    => 'CH9_STATS');

   DBMS_STATS.drop_extended_stats (
      ownname       => SYS_CONTEXT ('USERENV', 'CURRENT_SCHEMA')
      ,tabname       => 'STATEMENT'
      ,extension    => '(TRANSACTION_DATE,POSTING_DATE)');

   DBMS_STATS.drop_extended_stats (
      ownname       => SYS_CONTEXT ('USERENV', 'CURRENT_SCHEMA')
      ,tabname       => 'STATEMENT'
      ,extension    => q'[(CASE WHEN DESCRIPTION <> 'Flight'
                                     AND TRANSACTION_AMOUNT > 100
                                THEN 'HIGH' END)]');

   DBMS_STATS.delete_table_stats (
      ownname    => SYS_CONTEXT ('USERENV', 'CURRENT_SCHEMA')
      ,tabname    => 'STATEMENT');
END;
/

SELECT c1, SUBSTR (c4, 1,10) c4, DBMS_LOB.SUBSTR (cl1,60,1) cl1
  FROM ch9_stats
 WHERE TYPE = 'E';
```

```
-- Output from select statement
C1                 C4              CL1
STATEMENT          SYS_STU557      SYS_OP_COMBINED_HASH("TRANSACTION_DATE","POSTING_DATE")
STATEMENT          SYS_STUN6S      CASE  WHEN ("DESCRIPTION"<>'Flight' AND "TRANSACTION_AMOUNT"


  SELECT extension_name
    FROM all_stat_extensions
  WHERE     owner = SYS_CONTEXT ('USERENV', 'CURRENT_SCHEMA')
        AND table_name = 'STATEMENT'
ORDER BY extension_name;

-- Output from select statement

EXTENSION_NAME
AMOUNT_CATEGORY
POSTING_DELAY
SYS_NC00010$

BEGIN
  DBMS_STATS.import_table_stats (
      ownname    => SYS_CONTEXT ('USERENV', 'CURRENT_SCHEMA')
     ,tabname    => 'STATEMENT'
     ,statown    => SYS_CONTEXT ('USERENV', 'CURRENT_SCHEMA')
     ,stattab    => 'CH9_STATS');
END;
/

  SELECT extension_name
    FROM all_stat_extensions
  WHERE     owner = SYS_CONTEXT ('USERENV', 'CURRENT_SCHEMA')
        AND table_name = 'STATEMENT'
ORDER BY extension_name;

-- Output from select statement

EXTENSION_NAME
AMOUNT_CATEGORY
POSTING_DELAY
SYS_NC00010$
SYS_STU557IEAHGZ6B4RPUZEQ_SX#6
SYS_STUN6S71CM11RD1VMYVLKR9$GJ
```

Listing 9-14 exports the object statistics for STATEMENT into a freshly truncated export table and then drops both extended statistics with the DBMS_STATS.DROP_EXTENDED_STATISTICS procedure. The remaining statistics are dropped as well just for good measure.

A query against the export table shows that the specification of the extended statistics expressions has been saved. Notice the use of the SYS_OP_COMBINED_HASH function for the multi-column statistic. Once the extended statistics are dropped we can see that they are no longer visible in the output of a query against ALL_STAT_EXTENSIONS.

Once we import the statistics we can see the extended statistics reappear in ALL_STAT_EXTENSIONS.

Statistics Descriptions Wrap-up

I have explained what the statistics associated with tables, indexes, and columns are and how they are used by the CBO for optimization. I have also explained the major different types of hidden and virtual columns that can be created and used by the CBO. What I have yet to do is to explain the various different levels of statistics that can be used on partitioned tables. Let us get into that now.

Statistics and Partitions

The *partitioning option* is a separately licensed feature of Oracle Database Enterprise Edition. With this option you are able to partition your tables and indexes and enjoy a number of performance and administrative benefits. I will briefly look at the performance benefits of partitioning in Chapter 15, but for the moment I want to focus on the statistics associated with partitioned tables.

As I mentioned in the introduction to this chapter, when the partitioning option is used, table, index, and column statistics can all be maintained at the global, partition, and, in the case of composite partitioned tables, subpartition level. The statistics associated with a table or index partition are precisely the same as those at the global level. For example, the AVG_ROW_LEN statistic for a table partition indicates the average size of a row in the table partition. The BLEVEL statistic of an index partition indicates how many blocks have to be visited on the way from the index partition's root block to a leaf block within the index partition. The NUM_NULLS statistic for an object column defined at the partition level indicates the number of rows within the specified table partition where the object column is NULL.

In this section I want to clear up some confusion around how and when the CBO uses partition- and subpartition-level statistics and when global statistics are used. I also want to clearly explain the difference between the use of partition-level statistics by the CBO and *partition elimination* by the runtime engine.

Before getting into these topics, however, I need to explain how partition-level statistics are obtained. Setting, exporting, and importing statistics for a particular partition or subpartition is the same as doing so for the table or index as a whole, barring the specification of the partition or subpartition name; I won't revisit these topics. However, there are a couple of complications regarding gathering statistics at the partition or subpartition level, which I will cover now.

The relationship between table statistics and partition-level statistics can be extended to the relationship between partition-level statistics and subpartition-level statistics. To be concise, I will ignore composite partitioned tables and subpartition-level statistics for most of the rest of this section.

Gathering Statistics on Partitioned Tables

When we call routines such as DBMS_STATS.GATHER_TABLE_STATS providing the name of a partitioned table as a parameter, we have the opportunity to specify a value for the GRANULARITY parameter. For partitioned tables the default value for GRANULARITY is ALL, which means that both global and partition-level statistics are gathered.

You might think that by scanning the data in each partition of a partitioned table it would be possible to construct global and partition-level statistics at the same time. This is not the default behavior.

If you specify ALL for the GRANULARITY parameter of DBMS_STATS.GATHER_TABLE_STATS and NULL for the PARTNAME parameter, what actually happens by default is that all the partitions are scanned twice. One scan is used to obtain the global statistics and another to obtain the partition-level statistics. So if your table has five partitions you will have a total of ten partition scans.

If you specify ALL for the GRANULARITY parameter of DBMS_STATS.GATHER_TABLE_STATS and the name of a specific partition for the PARTNAME parameter, then partition-level statistics are gathered only for the specified partition, but *all* partitions are scanned to gather global statistics. Thus, if your table has five partitions you have a total of six partition scans.

Many users like to gather partition-level statistics when data is loaded into a previously empty partition and the overhead of scanning all partitions to update global statistics is unacceptable. As a consequence, it is normal for calls to DBMS_STATS.GATHER_TABLE_STATS to specify a value of PARTITION for the GRANULARITY parameter when gathering statistics on a single partition. This setting means that only one scan is made on the specified partition and no scans are made on any other partition. Fortunately, the negative impact of this shortcut is far less than you might think. Listing 9-14 shows what happens to global statistics when they aren't explicitly gathered.

Listing 9-14. Gathering statistics with GRANULARITY set to PARTITION

```
CREATE /*+ NO_GATHER_OPTIMIZER_STATISTICS */ TABLE statement_part
PARTITION BY RANGE
    (transaction_date)
    (
        PARTITION p1 VALUES LESS THAN (DATE '2013-01-05')
       ,PARTITION p2 VALUES LESS THAN (maxvalue))
AS
    SELECT * FROM statement;

BEGIN
    DBMS_STATS.gather_table_stats (
        ownname         => SYS_CONTEXT ('USERENV', 'CURRENT_SCHEMA')
       ,tabname         => 'STATEMENT_PART'
       ,partname        => 'P1'
       ,GRANULARITY     => 'PARTITION'
       ,method_opt      => 'FOR ALL COLUMNS SIZE 1');

    DBMS_STATS.gather_table_stats (
        ownname         => SYS_CONTEXT ('USERENV', 'CURRENT_SCHEMA')
       ,tabname         => 'STATEMENT_PART'
       ,partname        => 'P2'
       ,GRANULARITY     => 'PARTITION'
       ,method_opt      => 'FOR ALL COLUMNS SIZE 1');
END;
/

SELECT a.num_rows p1_rows
      ,a.global_stats p1_global_stats
      ,b.num_rows p2_rows
      ,b.global_stats p2_global_stats
      ,c.num_rows tab_rows
      ,c.global_stats tab_global_stats
  FROM all_tab_statistics a
       FULL JOIN all_tab_statistics b USING (owner, table_name)
       FULL JOIN all_tab_statistics c USING (owner, table_name)
  WHERE     owner = SYS_CONTEXT ('USERENV', 'CURRENT_SCHEMA')
        AND table_name = 'STATEMENT_PART'
        AND a.partition_name = 'P1'
        AND b.partition_name = 'P2'
        AND c.partition_name IS NULL;
```

P1_ROWS	P1_GLOBAL_STATS	P2_ROWS	P2_GLOBAL_STATS	TAB_ROWS	TAB_GLOBAL_STATS
200	YES	300	YES	500	NO

Listing 9-14 creates a table STATEMENT_PART that has the same content as STATEMENT, but all virtual columns have become real and the table is partitioned by range using the TRANSACTION_DATE column. Two partitions are created; they are named, somewhat unimaginatively, P1 and P2. I have specified the NO_GATHER_OPTIMIZER_STATISTICS hint so that on 12cR1 and later global statistics are not gathered automatically.

Once STATEMENT_PART is created and populated, statistics are gathered on the two partitions—P1 and P2—individually. Listing 9-14 then proceeds to look at the NUM_ROWS and GLOBAL_STATS statistic columns for the two partitions and for the table as a whole. We can see that there are apparently 200 rows in partition P1 and 300 rows in P2. However, in apparent contradiction to my explanation of the GRANULARITY parameter above, there are global statistics for the table as a whole because NUM_ROWS in ALL_TAB_STATISTICS has been set to 500!

The key to understanding what has happened is to look at the value of the column named GLOBAL_STATS. Now, I was utterly confused by this column for many years. I used to think that GLOBAL_STATS, which is set to YES or NO, had something to do with whether the statistics were global statistics or not. I hope you can sympathize with my mistake. If I had read the Reference manual properly I would have seen the following:

> *GLOBAL_STATS VARCHAR2 (3) Indicates whether statistics were calculated without merging underlying partitions (YES) or not (NO)*

It was only a short while ago that I was put out of my misery by Doug Burns (http://oracledoug.com/index.html), who explained the concept properly in a conference presentation. You see, once statistics are available for all partitions in a table or index, these partition-level statistics can be merged to determine the global statistics. In this case the numbers 200 from P1 and 300 from P2 are just added up to get 500 for STATEMENT_PART as a whole.

This method of merging partition-level statistics might seem to render the need for gathering global statistics unnecessary. However, this isn't quite true. Listing 9-15 shows the one issue that relates to merging partition-level statistics.

Listing 9-15. NUM_DISTINCT calculations when merging partition-level statistics

```
SELECT column_name
      ,a.num_distinct p1_distinct
      ,b.num_distinct p2_distinct
      ,c.num_distinct tab_distinct
  FROM all_part_col_statistics a
       FULL JOIN all_part_col_statistics b
          USING (owner, table_name, column_name)
       FULL JOIN all_tab_col_statistics c
          USING (owner, table_name, column_name)
 WHERE     owner = SYS_CONTEXT ('USERENV', 'CURRENT_SCHEMA')
       AND table_name = 'STATEMENT_PART'
       AND a.partition_name = 'P1'
       AND b.partition_name = 'P2';
```

COLUMN_NAME	P1_DISTINCT	P2_DISTINCT	TAB_DISTINCT
CUSTOMER_CATEGORY	50	50	50
PRODUCT_CATEGORY	4	6	10
AMOUNT_CATEGORY	3	3	3
TRANSACTION_AMOUNT	112	166	166
DESCRIPTION	4	4	4
POSTING_DELAY	3	3	3
POSTING_DATE	**6**	**8**	**8**
TRANSACTION_DATE	4	6	10
TRANSACTION_DATE_TIME	4	6	10

Listing 9-15 queries the NUM_DISTINCT statistic columns for partitions P1 and P2 and for the table as a whole. We can see that there are four distinct values of TRANSACTION_DATE_TIME in P1 and six distinct values in P2. The DBMS_STATS package had correctly determined that there are a total of ten distinct values of TRANSACTION_DATE_TIME in the table as a whole because the maximum value of TRANSACTION_DATE_TIME in P1 is lower than the minimum value in P2. On the other hand, DBMS_STATS sees that there are six distinct values of POSTING_DATE in P1 and eight in P2, but it has no way of knowing whether the number of distinct values of POSTING_DATE in the table as a whole is 8, 14, or something in between. The confusion arises because the maximum value of POSTING_DATE in P1 is greater than the minimum value in P2. The actual number of distinct values of POSTING_DATE in STATEMENT_PART is 12. DBMS_STATS always takes the minimum possible value in these circumstances.

Oracle database 11gR1 introduced a fancy new feature that allows us to get accurate, or almost accurate, global column statistics by merging partition column statistics. Listing 9-16 shows us how we can do this.

Listing 9-16. Incremental gathering of global statistics

```
BEGIN
    DBMS_STATS.set_table_prefs (
        ownname    => SYS_CONTEXT ('USERENV', 'CURRENT_SCHEMA')
        ,tabname    => 'STATEMENT_PART'
        ,pname      => 'INCREMENTAL'
        ,pvalue     => 'TRUE');
END;
/

BEGIN
    DBMS_STATS.gather_table_stats (
        ownname          => SYS_CONTEXT ('USERENV', 'CURRENT_SCHEMA')
        ,tabname          => 'STATEMENT_PART'
        ,partname         => 'P1'
        ,GRANULARITY      => 'APPROX_GLOBAL AND PARTITION'
        ,method_opt       => 'FOR ALL COLUMNS SIZE 1');

    DBMS_STATS.gather_table_stats (
        ownname          => SYS_CONTEXT ('USERENV', 'CURRENT_SCHEMA')
        ,tabname          => 'STATEMENT_PART'
        ,partname         => 'P2'
        ,granularity      => 'APPROX_GLOBAL AND PARTITION'
        ,method_opt       => 'FOR ALL COLUMNS SIZE 1');
END;
/

SELECT column_name
        ,a.num_distinct p1_distinct
        ,b.num_distinct p2_distinct
        ,c.num_distinct tab_distinct
   FROM all_part_col_statistics a
        FULL JOIN all_part_col_statistics b
           USING (owner, table_name, column_name)
        FULL JOIN all_tab_col_statistics c
           USING (owner, table_name, column_name)
  WHERE     owner = SYS_CONTEXT ('USERENV', 'CURRENT_SCHEMA')
        AND table_name = 'STATEMENT_PART'
        AND a.partition_name = 'P1'
        AND b.partition_name = 'P2';
```

COLUMN_NAME	P1_DISTINCT	P2_DISTINCT	TAB_DISTINCT
CUSTOMER_CATEGORY	50	50	50
PRODUCT_CATEGORY	4	6	10
AMOUNT_CATEGORY	3	3	3
TRANSACTION_AMOUNT	112	166	262
DESCRIPTION	4	4	4
POSTING_DELAY	3	3	3
POSTING_DATE	**6**	**8**	**12**
TRANSACTION_DATE	4	6	10
TRANSACTION_DATE_TIME	4	6	10

Listing 9-16 uses the DBMS_STATS.SET_TABLE_PREFS procedure to set up what are called *synopses* for partitions. Statistics for partitions P1 and P2 are then gathered with the GRANULARITY of "APPROX_GLOBAL AND PARTITION," and at that point the calculation for the global NUM_DISTINCT statistics has been corrected. In particular, notice that the number of distinct values of POSTING_DATE for the table as a whole is now 12.

■ **Note**   There are a number of other preferences that you can set with DBMS_STATS.SET_DATABASE_PREFS, DBMS_STATS.SET_SCHEMA_PREFS, and DBMS_STATS.SET_TABLE_PREFS. I will explain shortly why you should leave most of them alone.

For columns with a small number of distinct values, a synopsis is essentially just a list of those distinct values, and statistics merging is 100% accurate, as in Listing 9-16. When there are a large number of distinct values some fancy hashing occurs possibly, resulting in some slight inaccuracies in the merged statistics. In most cases the use of incrementally maintained global statistics will reduce the total amount of time needed to gather statistics, and the global statistics that result will be perfectly usable. On the other hand, synopses take up space and increase the time that it takes to gather partition-level statistics. Many users still like to gather partition-level statistics as quickly as possible (without synopses) during the week and gather global statistics on the weekend when the system is less busy.

Here are a few points to wrap up the topic of gathering partition-level statistics:

- When the INCREMENTAL preference is used and APPROX_GLOBAL AND PARTITION is specified for GRANULARITY, then GLOBAL_STATS=YES for the table/index as a whole despite the fact that the statistics have actually been obtained by merging partition-level statistics.

- When GLOBAL_STATS=NO for a partition it means that statistics for the partition have been merged from subpartition-level statistics. GLOBAL_STATS has no meaning for subpartition-level statistics.

- GLOBAL_STATS and USER_STATS are both set to YES by DBMS_STATS.SET_xxx_STATS procedures.

- Updating global statistics by merging partition statistics doesn't always happen. For example, merging doesn't happen when there are existing statistics for the table/index as a whole and those statistics have GLOBAL_STATS=YES. It doesn't matter how old these unmerged statistics are, they will never be updated by statistics merged from partition-level statistics unless the APPROX_GLOBAL AND PARTITION GRANULARITY parameter value is used when gathering partition-level statistics. There are, apparently, other undocumented scenarios where merging of partition-level statistics into global statistics will not occur.

- If the INCREMENTAL preference has been set to TRUE with a call to DBMS_STATS.SET_TABLE_PREFS, then gathering statistics for the table as a whole, specifying a value of GLOBAL for GRANULARITY, will actually gather partition-level statistics and merge them. So GLOBAL and ALL appear to be equivalent values for GRANULARITY in such a case.

How the CBO Uses Partition-level Statistics

Now that we have covered what partition-level statistics are and how we obtain them, it is time to look at how the CBO uses them. It seems that a lot of people get the use of partition-level statistics by the CBO confused with the concept of partition elimination by the runtime engine. Listings 9-17 through 9-20 should help clear things up.

Listing 9-17. Partition elimination by the runtime engine and partition statistics by the CBO

```
SELECT *
  FROM statement_part
 WHERE      transaction_date = DATE '2013-01-01'
       AND posting_date = DATE '2013-01-01';
```

Id	Operation	Name	Rows	Bytes	Time	Pstart	Pstop
0	SELECT STATEMENT		8	424	00:00:01		
1	PARTITION RANGE SINGLE		8	424	00:00:01	1	1
* 2	TABLE ACCESS FULL	STATEMENT_PART	8	424	00:00:01	1	1

```
SELECT *
  FROM statement_part
 WHERE      transaction_date = DATE '2013-01-06'
       AND posting_date = DATE '2013-01-06';
```

Id	Operation	Name	Rows	Bytes	Time	Pstart	Pstop
0	SELECT STATEMENT		6	324	00:00:01		
1	PARTITION RANGE SINGLE		6	324	00:00:01	2	2
* 2	TABLE ACCESS FULL	STATEMENT_PART	6	324	00:00:01	2	2

Because of the predicate on TRANSACTION_DATE in the queries in Listing 9-17, the CBO knows precisely which partition will be accessed. In the first query, the CBO knows that only the first partition, P1, will be referenced. The CBO tells us this by listing the number 1 in the PSTART (partition start) and PSTOP (partition stop) columns in the operation table. Accordingly, the CBO can use the partition-level statistics for P1 in its calculations. The partition-level statistics for P1 indicate the following:

- There are 300 rows in partition P1.

- There are six different values for TRANSACTION_DATE and six different values for POSTING_DATE in partition P1.

- So that gives us an estimated cardinality of 300/6/6 = 8.33 rows (rounded to 8).

The second query in Listing 9-17 is known by the CBO to use the second partition, so the statistics for P2 are used:

- There are 200 rows in partition P2.

- There are four different values for TRANSACTION_DATE and eight different values for POSTING_DATE in partition P2.

- So that gives us an estimated cardinality of 200/4/8 = 6.25 rows (rounded to 6).

The different cardinality estimates for the two queries is clear evidence that the CBO has used partition-level statistics in its calculations. Listing 9-18 shows us a third query that differs only slightly from those in Listing 9-17, but that difference is crucial.

Listing 9-18. Partition elimination by the runtime engine and use of global statistics by the CBO

```
SELECT *
  FROM statement_part
 WHERE     transaction_date = (SELECT DATE '2013-01-01' FROM DUAL)
       AND posting_date = DATE '2013-01-01';
```

```
-------------------------------------------------------------------------------------------
| Id | Operation              | Name           | Rows | Bytes | Time     | Pstart| Pstop |
-------------------------------------------------------------------------------------------
|  0 | SELECT STATEMENT       |                |    4 |   220 | 00:00:01 |       |       |
|  1 |  PARTITION RANGE SINGLE|                |    4 |   220 | 00:00:01 | KEY   | KEY   |
|* 2 |   TABLE ACCESS FULL    | STATEMENT_PART |    4 |   220 | 00:00:01 | KEY   | KEY   |
|  3 |    FAST DUAL           |                |    1 |       | 00:00:01 |       |       |
-------------------------------------------------------------------------------------------
```

Listing 9-18 doesn't use a literal for the TRANSACTION_DATE value. It uses an expression. That simple change means that the CBO loses track of which partition will be referenced, a fact that is made clear by the use of the word "KEY" in the PSTART and PSTOP columns of the operation table. As a consequence of this lack of certainty the CBO falls back on global statistics, as follows:

- There are 500 rows in STATEMENT_PART, according to the global statistics.

- There are 10 different values for TRANSACTION_DATE in STATEMENT_PART, according to the global statistics.

- There are 12 different values for POSTING_DATE in STATEMENT_PART, according to the global statistics.

- So that gives us an estimated cardinality of 500/10/12 = 4.17 rows (rounded to 4).

I want to be absolutely clear about something: the CBO *does* know that only a single partition will be referenced. That is why it was able to specify the PARTITION RANGE SINGLE operation. The runtime engine will be able to restrict its access to one partition. However, *which* partition the runtime engine will use remains unknown until the little subquery is actually run. So even though only a single partition is accessed at runtime the CBO needs to use global statistics to estimate the cardinality, because the CBO doesn't know which set of partition-level statistics to use.

The last two listings have covered queries that access just a single partition. Listing 9-19 shows a query that references multiple partitions:

Listing 9-19. Use of global statistics when multiple partitions are referenced

```
SELECT *
  FROM statement_part
 WHERE     transaction_date IN (DATE '2013-01-04', DATE '2013-01-05')
       AND posting_date = DATE '2013-01-05';
```

Id	Operation	Name	Rows	Bytes	Time	Pstart	Pstop
0	SELECT STATEMENT		8	440	00:00:01		
1	PARTITION RANGE INLIST		8	440	00:00:01	**KEY(I)**	**KEY(I)**
* 2	TABLE ACCESS FULL	STATEMENT_PART	8	440	00:00:01	**KEY(I)**	**KEY(I)**

Listing 9-19 references two values of TRANSACTION_DATE in different partitions. The CBO knows which partitions are used for each value of the inlist, so theoretically the CBO could use the statistics for partition P1 to estimate the number of rows where TRANSACTION_DATE is 4th January and the statistics for P2 to estimate the number of rows where TRANSACTION_DATE is 5th January. This would have yielded a cardinality estimate of 14 (8+6). However, the CBO is designed to use only one set of statistics at a time and so uses the global statistics for both dates. Hence the cardinality estimate of 8 (4+4). Notice the PSTART and PSTOP columns in the operation table have a value of KEY (I), indicating the presence of an inlist.

There is one final reason why global statistics might be used, and that is because partition-level statistics do not exist! For completeness, Listing 9-20 demonstrates this case.

Listing 9-20. Deleting partition-level statistics

```
BEGIN
   DBMS_STATS.delete_table_stats (
       ownname    => SYS_CONTEXT ('USERENV', 'CURRENT_SCHEMA')
      ,tabname    => 'STATEMENT_PART'
      ,partname   => 'P1');
END;
/

SELECT *
  FROM statement_part
 WHERE     transaction_date = DATE '2013-01-01'
       AND posting_date = DATE '2013-01-01';
```

Id	Operation	Name	Rows	Bytes	Time	Pstart	Pstop
0	SELECT STATEMENT		4	220	00:00:01		
1	PARTITION RANGE SINGLE		4	220	00:00:01	1	1
* 2	TABLE ACCESS FULL	STATEMENT_PART	4	220	00:00:01	1	1

Listing 9-20 shows an execution plan for the same query as that in Listing 9-17 except that the partition-level statistics are deleted. We can see that the CBO still knows the specific partition to be referenced, but the cardinality estimate of 4 shows that we have used global statistics as the basis for estimation in the same way as in Listing 9-18.

Why We Need Partition-level Statistics

Now that I have explained what partition-level statistics are, I can address the question of why partition-level statistics are needed in the first place. To be clear: partition-level statistics aren't always required. The CBO can often work out fairly reasonable plans perfectly well with just global statistics. There are three main reasons why people bother with partition level statistics:

- The amount of data varies substantially from one partition to the next and so different execution plans may be needed when querying different partitions.

- It takes too long to gather global statistics.

- Partition-level statistics appear to result in the CBO picking better performing plans.

Let us look at each of these reasons in turn.

Skew in Partition Size

When the partitioning option is used to facilitate what the *VLDB and Partitioning Guide* calls *Information Lifecycle Management (ILM),* tables are partitioned by a column of type DATE. The idea is that old data can be easily dropped or archived by dropping or exporting entire partitions rather than deleting individual rows. When partitioning is used for ILM in this way there are usually performance benefits as well because queries often specify a predicate on the partitioning column, and partition elimination can occur. ILM is probably the most common of all uses of the partitioning option.

When partitioning is used for ILM the partitions are usually of similar size. However, when tables are partitioned in other ways, such as by PRODUCT or CUSTOMER, significant skew is possible because, for example, your company may owe its survival to one particularly successful product or one big customer. Even when tables are partitioned by date they may be subpartitioned in such a way that some subpartitions are considerably larger than others.

In extreme circumstances you may need to have one execution plan for a small partition and another for a large partition. In these cases having the CBO understand that a full table scan will be very fast for one partition and very slow for another may be useful.

Partition-level statistics were almost certainly invented to address these types of scenarios. Nevertheless, while not unheard of, this type of scenario is quite rare. The usual reasons why partition-level statistics are used are to reduce statistics-gathering time or to improve the quality of execution plans.

Reducing the Time to Gather Statistics

As I explained in Chapter 6, your execution plans will change for the worse unless you either use a TSTATS-like deployment approach or you keep your statistics at least reasonably up-to-date. This is true whether your tables are partitioned or not.

Suppose a table has daily partitions based on a column called BUSINESS_DATE for ILM.

- Each weekday you load a ton of data into that day's partition and then subsequently query the loaded data. The application isn't used at the weekend.

- You keep two weeks' worth of data online. Each weekend you create five new partitions for the weekdays of the upcoming week and you drop five partitions for the week before last. So, for example, on Saturday, March 14, 2015, you would create partitions for Monday, March 16, 2015, through Friday, March 20, 2015, and drop partitions for March 2, 2015, through March 6, 2015, leaving the partitions for Monday, March 9, 2015, to Friday March 13, 2015, online. After you perform partition maintenance you gather statistics for the table as a whole.

After gathering statistics you might cross your fingers and hope that you can survive until the next weekend, because it just takes too long to gather statistics during the week. If so, you will have one of two problems:

- If you do not explicitly set the GRANULARITY parameter when gathering statistics it will default to ALL. When statistics are gathered with GRANULARITY set to ALL, statistics will be gathered for all partitions, including the empty ones. On Monday when you query the data loaded, the CBO will use the partition-level statistics that indicate that Monday's partition is empty and will almost certainly come up with a very bad execution plan.

- If you carefully set the GRANULARITY parameter to GLOBAL then partition-level statistics will not be created for the empty partitions. You might accomplish the same thing by gathering statistics before creating the new, empty partitions. On Monday your execution plans may be reasonable, but by Friday the execution plans will change. This is because the CBO will look at the LOW_VALUE and HIGH_VALUE column statistics for BUSINESS_DATE. On Friday, March 21, 2015, the statistics will say that the lowest value for BUSINESS_DATE is Monday, March 9, 2015, and the maximum value for BUSINESS_DATE is Friday, March 14, 2015. The CBO will assume that there is no chance that there is any data in the table for Friday, March 21, 2015. You will run into the stale statistics issue that I demonstrated in Chapter 6.

Something has to be done to ensure that you don't get unwanted execution plan changes during the week. Many people opt to gather statistics each day after the data is loaded but before it is queried. This statistics-gathering activity may delay the execution of the queries, and in some cases statistics gathering may be the biggest contributor to the elapsed time of an overnight batch run.

To mitigate the impact of the delay that statistics gathering creates it is usual in these cases just to gather statistics for the partition just loaded and specify a GRANULARITY of PARTITION. Provided that queries in the application are written to include equality predicates on BUSINESS_DATE, the gathering of partition-level statistics in this way will prevent the unwanted execution plan changes related to stale statistics.

The tone of my explanation may lead you to conclude that I do not believe that this common use of partition-level statistics purely to reduce statistics-gathering time is appropriate. If so, your conclusion would be correct, and in Chapter 20 we will go into this in depth as it is a key element of the TSTATS methodology. I take an equally dim view of the third and final reason people use partition-level statistics. Let us look at that now.

Superior Execution Plans from Partition-level Statistics

Since partition-level statistics are specific to a particular partition it seems intuitive that the CBO may be able to make more accurate estimates with their use than with the use of global statistics. Indeed, if we look at the execution plan in Listing 9-20, where global statistics are used, the cardinality estimate is 4. This is lower than the cardinality estimate of 8 in Listing 9-17 for the same query where partition-level statistics are used. Since the actual number of rows returned by the query is 18 we can see that the estimate based on the partition-level statistics is, although not perfect, the more accurate one.

Without necessarily understanding all of the computer science involved, many people have experienced real-life issues with the poor quality of execution plans based on global statistics and develop an unjustified love of partition-level statistics. But let us step back from this problem for a minute.

What is the difference between the problem the CBO has with estimating cardinality for a query issued on STATEMENT_PART and the problem the CBO has with estimating cardinality for a query issued on STATEMENT? The answer is none. How did we deal with cardinality errors for queries issued on the STATEMENT table? The answer is that we created extended statistics. We can do the same thing with STATEMENT_PART, as Listing 9-21 demonstrates.

Listing 9-21. Extended global statistics on a partitioned table

```
BEGIN
  DBMS_STATS.delete_table_stats (
     ownname            => SYS_CONTEXT ('USERENV', 'CURRENT_SCHEMA')
```

```
      ,tabname          => 'STATEMENT_PART'
      ,partname         => NULL
      ,cascade_parts    => TRUE);

   DBMS_STATS.set_table_prefs (
      ownname     => SYS_CONTEXT ('USERENV', 'CURRENT_SCHEMA')
      ,tabname    => 'STATEMENT_PART'
      ,pname      => 'INCREMENTAL'
      ,pvalue     => 'FALSE');
END;
/

DECLARE
   extension_name    all_tab_cols.column_name%TYPE;
BEGIN
   extension_name :=
      DBMS_STATS.create_extended_stats (
         ownname       => SYS_CONTEXT ('USERENV', 'CURRENT_SCHEMA')
         ,tabname      => 'STATEMENT_PART'
         ,extension    => '(TRANSACTION_DATE,POSTING_DATE)');

   DBMS_STATS.gather_table_stats (
      ownname          => SYS_CONTEXT ('USERENV', 'CURRENT_SCHEMA')
      ,tabname         => 'STATEMENT_PART'
      ,partname        => NULL
      ,granularity     => 'GLOBAL'
      ,method_opt      => 'FOR ALL COLUMNS SIZE 1'
      ,cascade         => FALSE);
END;
/

SELECT *
  FROM statement_part
 WHERE      transaction_date = DATE '2013-01-01'
        AND posting_date = DATE '2013-01-01';
```

```
----------------------------------------------------------------------------
| Id  | Operation                | Name           | Rows | Time      | Pstart| Pstop |
----------------------------------------------------------------------------
|   0 | SELECT STATEMENT         |                |   17 | 00:00:01  |       |       |
|   1 |  PARTITION RANGE SINGLE  |                |   17 | 00:00:01  |    1  |    1  |
|*  2 |   TABLE ACCESS FULL      | STATEMENT_PART |   17 | 00:00:01  |    1  |    1  |
----------------------------------------------------------------------------
```

To avoid any ambiguity Listing 9-21 begins by deleting all the statistics for STATEMENT_PART and resetting the INCREMENTAL statistic-gathering preference to FALSE. I have explicitly specified PARTNAME as NULL, implying the table as a whole, and CASCADE_PARTS as TRUE to ensure that statistics for all underlying partitions are deleted as well. These two settings are the default, but I wanted to be crystal clear.

Listing 9-21 then creates multi-column extended statistics for STATEMENT_PART in the same way that Listing 9-11 did for STATEMENT and then gathers *global* statistics *only*. When we now look at the execution plan for our query we can see that we have a cardinality estimate of 17, which is almost exactly correct and is a far superior result than that from the non-extended partition-level statistics.

■ **Tip** The use of partition-level statistics can often mask the need for extended statistics on multiple columns that include the partitioning column.

One reason for partition-level statistics being used far more frequently than extended global statistics is that extended statistics were only introduced as part of 11gR1 and old practices die hard. People haven't yet woken up to all the benefits that extended statistics bring.

Statistics and Partitions Wrap-up

In this section I have looked at the different levels of statistics that might exist for a partitioned table. I have explained how to gather partition-level statistics, how the CBO uses them, and why partition-level statistics are so popular. Although partition-level statistics have rare legitimate uses for tables with skewed partition sizes, they are more often than not used for what, in my opinion, are inappropriate purposes and we will return to this discussion in Chapter 20.

Restoring Statistics

In Chapter 6 I expressed the view that gathering statistics is like a game of Russian roulette. Well, what if you get shot? What happens if the moment after you gather statistics execution plans "flip" and performance deteriorates dramatically? The good news is that you can restore the previous set of statistics quite quickly as a short-term measure so that you have time to find out what went wrong and put a permanent solution in place. Listing 9-22 is a somewhat contrived demonstration of restoring statistics.

Listing 9-22. Restoring table statistics with DBMS_STATS.RESTORE_TABLE_STATS

```
SET SERVEROUT ON

DECLARE
    original_stats_time   DATE;
    num_rows              all_tab_statistics.num_rows%TYPE;
    sowner                all_tab_statistics.owner%TYPE;
BEGIN
    SELECT owner, last_analyzed
      INTO sowner, original_stats_time
      FROM all_tab_statistics
     WHERE    owner = SYS_CONTEXT ('USERENV', 'CURRENT_SCHEMA')
          AND table_name = 'STATEMENT_PART'
          AND partition_name IS NULL;

    DELETE FROM statement_part;

    DBMS_STATS.gather_table_stats (ownname      => sowner
                                  ,tabname      => 'STATEMENT_PART'
                                  ,partname     => NULL
                                  ,GRANULARITY  => 'GLOBAL'
                                  ,method_opt   => 'FOR ALL COLUMNS SIZE 1'
                                  ,cascade      => FALSE);
```

```
    SELECT num_rows
      INTO num_rows
      FROM all_tab_statistics
     WHERE      owner = sowner
            AND table_name = 'STATEMENT_PART'
            AND partition_name IS NULL;

    DBMS_OUTPUT.put_line (
       'After deletion and gathering num_rows is: ' || num_rows);

    DBMS_STATS.restore_table_stats (
       ownname             => sowner
      ,tabname             => 'STATEMENT_PART'
      ,as_of_timestamp     => original_stats_time + 1 / 86400
      ,no_invalidate       => FALSE);

    SELECT num_rows
      INTO num_rows
      FROM all_tab_statistics
     WHERE      owner = sowner
            AND table_name = 'STATEMENT_PART'
            AND partition_name IS NULL;

    DBMS_OUTPUT.put_line (
       'After restoring earlier statistics num_rows is: ' || num_rows);

    INSERT INTO statement_part
       SELECT * FROM statement;

    COMMIT;
END;
/

-- Output

After deletion and gathering num_rows is: 0
After restoring earlier statistics num_rows is: 500
```

Listing 9-22 first identifies the time at which the statistics for STATEMENT_PART were last gathered. The rows from the table are then deleted and statistics are gathered. The output shows that the statistics now correctly reflect the fact that there are no rows in the table. We then make a call to DBMS_STATS.RESTORE_TABLE_STATS to restore the previous statistics. The procedure includes an AS_OF_TIMESTAMP parameter. This parameter is used to identify which set of statistics to restore. In an attempt to make the example reproducible, Listing 9-22 specifies a time that is one second after the statistics were originally gathered. Here are some points to bear in mind when restoring statistics:

- There are several procedures for restoring statistics including DBMS_STATS.RESTORE_SCHEMA_STATS.

- User statistics set with DBMS_STATS.SET_xxx_STATS procedures are not restored. So, for example, any hand-crafted histogram would have to be reapplied after statistics are restored.

- Although this is normally the default behavior, it is good practice to explicitly invalidate any bad plans in the shared pool by using the NO_INVALIDATE => FALSE parameter setting, as performed by Listing 9-22.

- The view DBA_OPTSTAT_OPERATIONS provides a history of gather and restore operations.

- By default superseded statistics are retained for 31 days. This can be managed by the function DBMS_STATS.GET_STATS_HISTORY_RETENTION and the procedure DBMS_STATS.ALTER_STATS_HISTORY_RETENTION.

Once you have restored your statistics you probably want to stop some well-meaning soul from re-gathering them two minutes later. Let us see what can be done.

Locking Statistics

There are a lot of reasons why you might want to stop people gathering statistics on one or more tables. Perhaps these tables have lots of hand-crafted changes done with DBMS_STATS.SET_xxx_STATS procedures. Perhaps gathering is a time-consuming activity that you know isn't necessary or will not be necessary for some time. Perhaps, as discussed in the last section, you have restored statistics and you know that re-gathering will cause problems. Perhaps the statistics for a small but growing table have been imported from a test system and reflect future large volumes and you want to make sure that these imported statistics are not overwritten by statistics that reflect the current low row count.

Whatever the reason for wanting to prevent statistics from being gathered, you can do so by calling one of these procedures: DBMS_STATS.LOCK_SCHEMA_STATS, DBMS_STATS.LOCK_TABLE_STATS, and DBMS_STATS.LOCK_PARTITION_STATS. Bear in mind the following when using these routines:

- A determined individual can always gather or set statistics on a locked object by use of the FORCE parameter. No extra privileges are required to override statistic locks.

- If you lock statistics for one or more tables then gathering statistics for a schema will normally avoid the locked tables (unless FORCE is set to TRUE).

- Some people lock statistics on table partitions that have become read-only. This might happen for historic partitions in an ILM environment. Locking read-only partitions can reduce the time it takes to gather statistics when GRANULARITY is set to ALL.

- When you lock the statistics for a table you lock the statistics for all the partitions, columns, and indexes for the table. You can't lock statistics for just one index.

- As previously stated, when statistics are locked for a table, no statistics are generated for an index on that table, as the index is being created or rebuilt, and no statistics are generated for the table, as data is bulk loaded.

In a TSTATS environment you don't want to gather statistics on any application object in a production environment so it is best practice to lock statistics for all tables in your application schema.

Pending Statistics

What if you suspect that a histogram would solve your production problem but you don't have a suitable test system dedicated to your personal use? Is there a way to investigate the impact of a statistics change without impacting other users?

The concept of pending statistics has been developed to help in these situations. Normally, when statistics are gathered, imported, or set they are immediately *published* meaning that all users can see and make use of them. However, it is possible to generate statistics first and to publish them later. Statistics that have been generated and are not yet published are known as *pending* statistics. Listing 9-23 shows how pending statistics work.

Listing 9-23. Testing the effect of a histogram by using pending statistics

```
001 BEGIN
002   2       DBMS_STATS.set_table_prefs (
003   3            ownname    => SYS_CONTEXT ('USERENV', 'CURRENT_SCHEMA')
004   4           ,tabname    => 'STATEMENT_PART'
005   5           ,pname      => 'PUBLISH'
006   6           ,pvalue     => 'TRUE');
007   7   END;
008   8   /
009
010 PL/SQL procedure successfully completed.
011
012
013 BEGIN
014   2       DBMS_STATS.gather_table_stats (
015   3            ownname       => SYS_CONTEXT ('USERENV', 'CURRENT_SCHEMA')
016   4           ,tabname       => 'STATEMENT_PART'
017   5           ,partname      => NULL
018   6           ,GRANULARITY   => 'GLOBAL'
019   7           ,method_opt    => 'FOR ALL COLUMNS SIZE 1'
020   8           ,cascade       => FALSE);
021   9   END;
022  10   /
023
024 PL/SQL procedure successfully completed.
025
026
027 BEGIN
028   2       DBMS_STATS.set_table_prefs (
029   3            ownname    => SYS_CONTEXT ('USERENV', 'CURRENT_SCHEMA')
030   4           ,tabname    => 'STATEMENT_PART'
031   5           ,pname      => 'PUBLISH'
032   6           ,pvalue     => 'FALSE');
033   7   END;
034   8   /
035
036 PL/SQL procedure successfully completed.
037
038
039 DECLARE
040   2       srec    DBMS_STATS.statrec;
041   3   BEGIN
042   4       FOR r
043   5          IN (SELECT *
044   6                  FROM all_tab_cols
045   7                 WHERE    owner = SYS_CONTEXT ('USERENV', 'CURRENT_SCHEMA')
046   8                      AND table_name = 'STATEMENT_PART'
047   9                      AND column_name = 'TRANSACTION_AMOUNT')
048  10       LOOP
049  11          srec.epc := 3;
050  12          srec.bkvals := DBMS_STATS.numarray (600, 400, 600);
```

```
051  13            DBMS_STATS.prepare_column_values (srec
052  14                                   ,DBMS_STATS.numarray (-1e7, 8, 1e7));
053  15            DBMS_STATS.set_column_stats (ownname   => r.owner
054  16                                 ,tabname   => r.table_name
055  17                                 ,colname   => r.column_name
056  18                                 ,distcnt   => 3
057  19                                 ,density   => 1 / 250
058  20                                 ,nullcnt   => 0
059  21                                 ,srec      => srec
060  22                                 ,avgclen   => r.avg_col_len);
061  23      END LOOP;
062  24  END;
063  25  /
064
065  PL/SQL procedure successfully completed.
066
067
068  SET AUTOTRACE OFF
069
070  SELECT endpoint_number, endpoint_value
071   2      FROM all_tab_histograms
072   3     WHERE    owner = SYS_CONTEXT ('USERENV', 'CURRENT_SCHEMA')
073   4           AND table_name = 'STATEMENT_PART'
074   5           AND column_name = 'TRANSACTION_AMOUNT';
075
076  ENDPOINT_NUMBER ENDPOINT_VALUE
077  --------------- --------------
078               0              5
079               1          15200
080
081  2 rows selected.
082
083
084  SELECT endpoint_number, endpoint_value
085   2      FROM all_tab_histgrm_pending_stats
086   3     WHERE    owner = SYS_CONTEXT ('USERENV', 'CURRENT_SCHEMA')
087   4           AND table_name = 'STATEMENT_PART'
088   5           AND column_name = 'TRANSACTION_AMOUNT';
089
090  ENDPOINT_NUMBER ENDPOINT_VALUE
091  --------------- --------------
092             600      -10000000
093            1000              8
094            1600       10000000
095
096  3 rows selected.
097
098
099  SET AUTOTRACE TRACEONLY EXPLAIN
100
```

```
101 SELECT *
102   2    FROM statement_part
103   3   WHERE transaction_amount = 8;
104
105 ------------------------------------------------------------------------------
106 | Id  | Operation           | Name           | Rows | Time     | Pstart| Pstop |
107 ------------------------------------------------------------------------------
108 |  0  | SELECT STATEMENT    |                |    2 | 00:00:01 |       |       |
109 |  1  |  PARTITION RANGE ALL|                |    2 | 00:00:01 |    1  |    2  |
110 |* 2  |   TABLE ACCESS FULL | STATEMENT_PART |    2 | 00:00:01 |    1  |    2  |
111 ------------------------------------------------------------------------------
112
113
114 ALTER SESSION SET optimizer_use_pending_statistics=TRUE;
115
116 Session altered.
117
118
119 SELECT *
120   2    FROM statement_part
121   3   WHERE transaction_amount = 8;
122
123 ------------------------------------------------------------------------------
124 | Id  | Operation           | Name           | Rows | Time     | Pstart| Pstop |
125 ------------------------------------------------------------------------------
126 |  0  | SELECT STATEMENT    |                |  125 | 00:00:01 |       |       |
127 |  1  |  PARTITION RANGE ALL|                |  125 | 00:00:01 |    1  |    2  |
128 |* 2  |   TABLE ACCESS FULL | STATEMENT_PART |  125 | 00:00:01 |    1  |    2  |
129 ------------------------------------------------------------------------------
130
131
132 BEGIN
133   2    DBMS_STATS.publish_pending_stats (
134   3        ownname   => SYS_CONTEXT ('USERENV', 'CURRENT_SCHEMA')
135   4       ,tabname   => 'STATEMENT_PART');
136   5 END;
137   6 /
138
139 PL/SQL procedure successfully completed.
140
141
142 ALTER SESSION SET optimizer_use_pending_statistics=FALSE;
143
144 Session altered.
145
146
147 SELECT *
148   2    FROM statement_part
149   3   WHERE transaction_amount = 8;
150
```

```
151 ---------------------------------------------------------------------
152 | Id  | Operation           | Name           | Rows  | Time     | Pstart| Pstop |
153 ---------------------------------------------------------------------
154 |   0 | SELECT STATEMENT    |                |   125 | 00:00:01 |       |       |
155 |   1 |  PARTITION RANGE ALL|                |   125 | 00:00:01 |     1 |     2 |
156 |*  2 |   TABLE ACCESS FULL | STATEMENT_PART |   125 | 00:00:01 |     1 |     2 |
157 ---------------------------------------------------------------------
158
159
160 SET AUTOTRACE OFF
161
162 SELECT endpoint_number, endpoint_value
163   2    FROM all_tab_histograms
164   3   WHERE     owner = SYS_CONTEXT ('USERENV', 'CURRENT_SCHEMA')
165   4         AND table_name = 'STATEMENT_PART'
166   5         AND column_name = 'TRANSACTION_AMOUNT';
167
168 ENDPOINT_NUMBER ENDPOINT_VALUE
169 --------------- ---------------
170            1000               8
171            1600        10000000
172             600       -10000000
173
174 3 rows selected.
175
176
177 SELECT endpoint_number, endpoint_value
178   2    FROM all_tab_histgrm_pending_stats
179   3   WHERE     owner = SYS_CONTEXT ('USERENV', 'CURRENT_SCHEMA')
180   4         AND table_name = 'STATEMENT_PART'
181   5         AND column_name = 'TRANSACTION_AMOUNT';
182
183 no rows selected
```

This is quite a long script, and the layout is atypical for this book. I have just pasted the output from running the script, showing the commands and the output interspersed.

The first couple of statements in Listing 9-23 are just there to make the script re-runnable; let us start with the statement on line 27. The call to DBMS_STATS.SET_TABLE_PREFS sets the PUBLISH preference for STATEMENT_PART to a non-default value of TRUE. This means that when the histogram is set on the TRANSACTION_AMOUNT column on line 39 it has no effect on execution plans derived in the standard way. We can come to that conclusion because the query of ALL_TAB_HISTOGRAMS on line 70 shows just two endpoints, inconsistent with the 3 endpoints we set up in our histogram. On the other hand, the histogram is displayed when we query the ALL_TAB_HISTGRM_PENDING_STATS view.

The execution plan for the query on line 101 seems not to have used the histogram as the cardinality estimate is only 2. On the other hand, when the initialization parameter OPTIMIZER_USE_PENDING_STATISTICS is set to the non-default value of TRUE we can see from lines 126, 127, and 128 that the cardinality estimate has jumped to 125. This is because we are now using the unpublished pending statistics. The results look good, so on line 132 we call DBMS_STATS.PUBLISH_PENDING_STATS. After that call the statistics are used by the CBO, even after we set OPTIMIZER_USE_PENDING_STATISTICS back to its default value of FALSE. Now when we query ALL_TAB_HISTOGRAMS on line 162 the three endpoints are visible, but now that the statistics have been published the histogram has disappeared from ALL_TAB_HISTGRM_PENDING_STATS.

There are actually twelve views associated with pending statistics. As usual there are variants of the views beginning DBA, ALL, and USER. The four views beginning with ALL are:

- ALL_TAB_PENDING_STATS

- ALL_IND_PENDING_STATS

- ALL_COL_PENDING_STATS

- ALL_TAB_HISTGRM_PENDING_STATS

The idea of pending statistics sounds good and has some value. However, I would dearly love to be able to restore historical statistics to pending status just so I could investigate the effect before publishing the restored statistics. But I gather that there are some implementation difficulties making this awkward.

A Footnote on Other Inputs to the CBO

Although this chapter has focused on object statistics, you should be aware that there are at four more sources of information that the CBO uses. These are:

- Optimizer hints

- Initialization parameters

- System statistics

- Other data dictionary information

We will be discussing optimizer hints throughout this book, and Chapter 18 is dedicated to the topic. Let us look at the other three information sources one by one, starting with initialization parameters.

Initialization Parameters

There are a substantial number of documented initialization parameters that are either specific to the CBO or affect the CBO in some way, shape, or form. There are also a large number of hidden initialization parameters that allow you to influence specific aspects of CBO behavior. Unless you get a recommendation from your third-party software supplier you should almost always endeavor to use default values for almost all of these parameters.

Apart from the fact that you are unlikely to improve the performance of either the CBO or the runtime engine by mucking about with non-default values of optimizer-related initialization parameters, you may run into bugs as the CBO will not necessarily have been tested with your settings.

To make my point, let me pick an example of an initialization parameter that is not directly related to the CBO but impacts CBO behavior. The default value of DB_BLOCK_SIZE is 8192 bytes. In days gone by experts used to recommend using larger values for data warehouses. These days most experts would concur with the following comment from Jonathan Lewis' *Cost-Based Oracle* book:

> *You may be able to find a few special cases where you can get a positive benefit by changing an object from one block size to another; but in general you may find that a few side effects due to the optimizer changing its arithmetic may outweigh the perceived benefits of your chosen block size.*

Quite. Two other initialization parameters that people used to play with are OPTIMIZER_INDEX_COST_ADJ and OPTIMIZER_INDEX_CACHING. These two parameters work at a system wide level (a dubious concept at the best of times) to make index access more or less favorable than full table scans. One problem with these parameters is that they work on reducing the cost of indexed access rather than increasing the cost of full table scans so rounding errors can occur. Just leave them be.

There are a few initialization parameters that you should feel free to change. These are:

- DB_FILE_MULTIBLOCK_READ_COUNT

- PARALLEL_DEGREE_POLICY

- OPTIMIZER_FEATURES_ENABLE

- OPTIMIZER_ADAPTIVE_FEATURES

- OPTIMIZER_ADAPTIVE_REPORTING_ONLY

The default behavior of DB_FILE_MULTIBLOCK_READ_COUNT is a bit confusing, to put it mildly. You should explicitly set this parameter to the maximum I/O size for your platform and block size. For most platforms the maximum I/O size is 1MB, which means that the best value of this parameter is 128, assuming that you have an 8K block size. By explicitly setting the parameter you make the CBO assume that multi-block reads are efficient—which they are.

In Chapter 2 I explained how to set up automatic degree of parallelism by setting PARALLEL_DEGREE_POLICY to AUTO. My experience with this feature has been extremely positive, and I wouldn't be surprised if AUTO became the default setting of PARALLEL_DEGREE_POLICY at some point in the future.

If you upgrade your database to a new version and have no opportunity to thoroughly test (or you do test and run into problems) you can set OPTIMIZER_FEATURES_ENABLE to a non-default value to disable new CBO features and minimize the risk that these new CBO features will disturb your execution plans.

Finally, I just want to mention two new initialization parameters that come with 12cR1. Setting OPTIMIZER_ADAPTIVE_FEATURES to FALSE allows you to turn off all the new adaptive features that were introduced in 12cR1 and that I discussed in Chapter 6. As an alternative to changing OPTIMIZER_ADAPTIVE_FEATURES you can set OPTIMIZER_ADAPTIVE_REPORTING_ONLY to TRUE. With this setting, the information required for an adaptive optimization is gathered, but no action is taken to change the plan. In other words, an adaptive plan will always choose the default (optimizer-chosen) plan, but information is collected on which plan to adapt to in non-reporting mode. I must confess that I do not yet have enough experience to make a firm recommendation on how to set these parameters, but my initial feeling is that production systems at least should generally run with OPTIMIZER_ADAPTIVE_FEATURES set to FALSE until the adaptive features are more mature.

And just in case you are wondering, I do not recommend leaving *all* your initialization parameters at default values! No, your database doesn't have to be named *orcl* and you might want to change the value of SGA_TARGET or MEMORY_TARGET! My comments in this section relate purely to deliberate attempts to influence the CBO.

System Statistics

What takes longer: a 1MB multi-block read or 40 single-block reads issued sequentially? Theoretically the answer to that question depends on your hardware. Indeed, given the potential for caching on enterprise storage your answer might depend on workload as well. Theoretically, the CBO might need to know the answer to this question. But the CBO doesn't just have to choose between multi-block I/Os and single-block I/Os; it may, on occasion, have to choose between, say, a CPU-intensive aggregation in memory and a disk access to read a materialized view. Once again the CBO would like to know something about the relative capabilities of the CPU and the disk subsystems.

Enter system statistics. System statistics were introduced in 10gR1 and received a moderately warm welcome. However, my rather unscientific straw poll of experts suggests that the pendulum of expert opinion has swung very firmly against the use of system statistics. First of all, it is extremely unlikely that an execution plan will change as a result of the presence of system statistics, and even if it does you are unlikely to see much of an improvement in performance as a result.

The same arguments that are made to dissuade people from trying to influence the CBO by adjusting initialization parameters can be made to try and dissuade people from either gathering or setting system statistics: the risk that you will run into some kind of bug or other discrepancy outweighs any benefit that you may get from using system statistics. My recommendation would be to call DBMS_STATS.DELETE_SYSTEM_STATS. This procedure call will restore what are known as *default noworkload statistics* that are used by most Oracle databases on the planet.

If you do choose to use non-default system statistics it is vital that you use DBMS_STATS.EXPORT_SYSTEM_STATS and DBMS_STATS.IMPORT_SYSTEM_STATS to replicate these non-default system statistics from your performance test system on production. Otherwise your production system may pick different execution plans than those that you have so carefully tested.

Other Data Dictionary Information

Obviously, the CBO needs to know what tables and indexes exist and what columns are in said tables and indexes. This type of schema information, the object statistics associated with same, and any system statistics that may have been gathered or set are all held in the data dictionary. However, there are at least two other bits of information that the CBO may extract from the data dictionary.

I mentioned in Chapter 2 that you can decorate a table or an index by specifying the degree of parallelism to be used for queries when PARALLEL_DEGREE_POLICY has the default value of MANUAL. This information is held in the data dictionary and is not considered to be an object statistic. The CBO may also be interested in the number of partitions in a table. We will return to this last point in Chapter 20. I just mention it here for completeness.

Summary

The subject of object statistics is a complex one, and this lengthy chapter has still only provided a high-level view. It is important to realize that we need statistics that get the CBO to do something sensible that we can test, not necessarily object statistics that reflect reality, and so manipulation of statistics is sometimes necessary. On the other hand, if you do change statistics manually you should be very careful that the statistics are *self-consistent*. You shouldn't, for example, set the NUM_ROWS statistic for an index to a value greater than NUM_ROWS for the table. That kind of behavior is likely to send the CBO down code paths that nobody has ever tested.

This chapter concludes the part of the book that deals with advanced concepts, and it is now time to move on to Part 3 and a more detailed look at the job of the CBO. Chapter 10 kicks things off with a look at the access methods from which the CBO must choose.

The Cost-Based Optimizer

■ ■ ■

Access Methods

In this chapter we will look at the primary methods that the runtime engine uses to access data held in the database. In each case we provide basic details of the algorithm used, the execution plan operation names, and the hint that can be used to explicitly specify the access method. I will begin by a discussion of what a *ROWID* is and the various ways it can be used to access a table. This will lead nicely into two sections that discuss the various ways in which B-tree and bitmap indexes can be used to generate ROWIDs. The last three sections in this chapter discuss the much maligned full table scan, the little understood TABLE and XMLTABLE operators, and for completeness cluster access, which most people will never need to use.

Access by ROWID

The most efficient way to access a row in a table is to specify the ROWID. There are many different types of ROWIDs, and I will be explaining what they are and how they are linked to index operations before giving examples of how to use a ROWID.

ROWID Concepts

The ROWID is the fundamental way to address a row in a table. A ROWID has several formats:

- Restricted ROWID (smallfile tablespaces)
- Restricted ROWID (bigfile tablespaces)
- Extended ROWID (smallfile tablespaces)
- Extended ROWID (bigfile tablespaces)
- Universal ROWID (physical)
- Universal ROWID (logical)
- Universal ROWID (foreign tables)

The most commonly used ROWID format is the restricted ROWID for smallfile tablespaces. It has the following parts:

- Relative file number (10 bits)
- Block number (22 bits)
- Row number (16 bits)

This makes a total of 48 bits, or 6 bytes. The first 32 bits are together often called the *relative data block address (RDBA)*, as the RDBA identifies a block in a tablespace.

Restricted ROWIDs are used when the segment that contains the addressed row can be unambiguously determined, for example in row piece pointers, for B-tree indexes on non-partitioned tables, and local indexes on partitioned tables. This ROWID format means that

- A table, partition, or subpartition segment can have at most 4,294,967,296 (2^{32}) blocks

- Each block can hold at most 65,536 (2^{16}) rows

A variation on the restricted ROWID format is used for *bigfile tablespaces*. A bigfile tablespace has only one datafile, so the whole of the first 32 bits of the ROWID can be used for the block number, and that one datafile can have 4,294,967,296 blocks! Notice, however, that the maximum number of blocks in a bigfile and a smallfile tablespace are the same. The main purpose of bigfile tablespaces is actually to deal with huge databases that would otherwise run into the 65,535 datafile limit. However, bigfile tablespaces can also ease administration because you don't have to keep adding datafiles to a growing tablespace. Bigfile tablespaces can also reduce the number of file descriptors a process needs to have open, a potentially serious issue on huge databases.

The extended ROWID formats are used when there is ambiguity in the segment to be referenced. They are found in global indexes of partitioned tables. Extended ROWIDs include an extra four bytes for the data object ID of the table, partition, or subpartition being referenced.

Universal ROWID is an umbrella type that is used to describe three situations not covered so far:

- Logical ROWIDs contain the primary key of a row in an index organized table and a "guess" as to its location.

- Foreign ROWIDs contain gateway-specific information for accessing data in databases from vendors other than Oracle.

- Physical ROWIDs are just extended ROWIDs represented as a universal ROWID.

The physical representation of a universal ROWID begins with a byte that indicates which one of the above three types applies. Bear in mind the following:

- Any column, expression, or variable of type ROWID is an extended ROWID.

- Any column, expression, or variable of type UROWID is a universal ROWID.

- The ROWID pseudo-column is an extended ROWID for heap- or cluster-organized tables and a universal ROWID for index-organized tables.

Now that we know what ROWIDs are we can start to discuss how to use them to access table data.

Access by ROWID

There are five ways that a ROWID can be used to access a table; they are listed in Table 10-1 and then discussed in more detail.

Table 10-1. *The four ROWID methods for table access*

Execution Plan Operation	Hint
TABLE ACCESS BY USER ROWID	ROWID
TABLE ACCESS BY ROWID RANGE	ROWID
TABLE ACCESS BY INDEX ROWID	Not applicable
TABLE ACCESS BY GLOBAL INDEX ROWID	Not applicable
TABLE ACCESS BY LOCAL INDEX ROWID	Not applicable

When a table is accessed using a one or more ROWID or UROWID variables supplied by the caller, or involves the use of the ROWID pseudo-column, either operation TABLE ACCESS BY USER ROWID or operation TABLE ACCESS BY ROWID RANGE appears in the execution plan. However, when the runtime engine identifies the ROWID itself by use of one or more indexes then the following are true:

- TABLE ACCESS BY INDEX ROWID indicates access to a non-partitioned table using a restricted ROWID obtained from one or more indexes.

- TABLE ACCESS BY LOCAL INDEX ROWID indicates access to a partition or subpartition using a restricted ROWID obtained from one or more local indexes.

- TABLE ACCESS BY GLOBAL INDEX ROWID indicates access to a partition or subpartition using an extended ROWID obtained from one or more global indexes.

Because the optimizer is accessing the table after visiting one or more indexes there are no hints for these three operations. You *could* hint the indexed access, but the table access, if required, inevitably follows.

BATCHED ROW ACCESS

A variant to the TABLE ACCESS BY [LOCAL|GLOBAL] INDEX ROWID operations appeared in 12cR1. This variant manifests itself by the appearance of the word BATCHED at the end of the operation name and is presumably an optimization of some kind. However, most commentators have observed that the various optimizations that the runtime engine can apply to indexed access apply whether batching is used or not. The keyword BATCHED only appears under certain circumstances and can be forced or suppressed by use of the BATCH_TABLE_ACCESS_BY_ROWID and NO_BATCH_TABLE_ACCESS_BY_ROWID.

I will provide examples of ROWID access via an index when I cover the index operations themselves, but I will first show the two operations involving direct ROWID access. I will start with Listing 10-1, which involves a single ROWID being passed into a statement.

Listing 10-1. Accessing a table by specifying a single ROWID

```
CREATE TABLE t1
(
   c1    NOT NULL
  ,c2    NOT NULL
  ,c3    NOT NULL
  ,c4    NOT NULL
  ,c5    NOT NULL
  ,c6    NOT NULL
)
AS
       SELECT ROWNUM
              ,ROWNUM
              ,ROWNUM
              ,ROWNUM
              ,ROWNUM
              ,ROWNUM
          FROM DUAL
    CONNECT BY LEVEL < 100;

CREATE BITMAP INDEX t1_bix2
   ON t1 (c4);

BEGIN
   FOR r IN (SELECT t1.*, ORA_ROWSCN oscn, ROWID rid
                FROM t1
                WHERE c1 = 1)
   LOOP
      LOOP
         UPDATE /*+ TAG1 */
                t1
            SET c3 = r.c3 + 1
          WHERE ROWID = r.rid AND ORA_ROWSCN = r.oscn;

         IF SQL%ROWCOUNT > 0 -- Update succeeded
         THEN
            EXIT;
         END IF;
         -- Display some kind of error message
      END LOOP;
   END LOOP;
END;
/

SELECT p.*
  FROM v$sql s
      ,TABLE (
          DBMS_XPLAN.display_cursor (sql_id => s.sql_id, format => 'BASIC')) p
```

```
WHERE sql_text LIKE 'UPDATE%TAG1%';
```

```
-----------------------------------------------
| Id | Operation                  | Name |
-----------------------------------------------
|  0 | UPDATE STATEMENT           |      |
|  1 |  UPDATE                    | T1   |
|  2 |   TABLE ACCESS BY USER ROWID| T1  |
-----------------------------------------------
```

Listing 10-1 creates a table and an associated index before executing a PL/SQL block, which demonstrates the basic techniques involved in what is referred to as *optimistic locking*, used in interactive applications. The idea is that when data is displayed to a user (not shown) the ROWID and the ORA_ROWSCN pseudo-columns are saved. If and when the user decides to update the displayed row, it is updated directly by specifying the previously saved ROWID. Any change to the row by another user between the time the row is displayed, and the time it is updated will be reflected in a change to the ORA_ROWSCN pseudo-column. The predicate ORA_ROWSCN = r.oscn in the update statement is used to ensure that that no such change has occurred.

Notice that I have applied two of my favorite shortcuts: first, the use of a cursor that returns one row so as to avoid declaring PL/SQL variables and second, the extraction of the execution plan for the embedded UPDATE statement by means of a lateral join and a hint-like tag in the PL/SQL code. This is the same approach that I used in Listing 8-9.

Listing 10-1 covered the use of a ROWID to access a single row. It is also possible to use ROWIDs to specify a physical range of rows. The most common use of this mechanism is to parallelize a query or update manually. Listing 10-2 shows how you might update the second set of ten rows in T1.

Listing 10-2. Updating a range of rows in the middle of a table

```
MERGE /*+ rowid(t1) leading(q) use_nl(t1) */
    INTO   t1
    USING (WITH q1
                AS (  SELECT /*+ leading(a) use_nl(b) */  ROWID rid, ROWNUM rn
                        FROM t1
                     ORDER BY ROWID)
          SELECT a.rid min_rid, b.rid max_rid
            FROM q1 a, q1 b
           WHERE a.rn = 11 AND b.rn = 20) q
        ON (t1.ROWID BETWEEN q.min_rid AND q.max_rid)
WHEN MATCHED
THEN
    UPDATE SET c3 = c3 + 1;
```

```
--------------------------------------------------------------------
| Id  | Operation                        | Name                     |
--------------------------------------------------------------------
|  0  | MERGE STATEMENT                  |                          |
|  1  |  MERGE                           | T1                       |
|  2  |   VIEW                           |                          |
|  3  |    NESTED LOOPS                  |                          |
|  4  |     VIEW                         |                          |
|  5  |      TEMP TABLE TRANSFORMATION   |                          |
|  6  |       LOAD AS SELECT             | SYS_TEMP_0FD9D6626_47CA26D6 |
|  7  |        SORT ORDER BY             |                          |
|  8  |         COUNT                    |                          |
|  9  |          BITMAP CONVERSION TO ROWIDS |                      |
| 10  |           BITMAP INDEX FAST FULL SCAN| T1_BIX2               |
| 11  |       NESTED LOOPS               |                          |
| 12  |        VIEW                      |                          |
| 13  |         TABLE ACCESS FULL        | SYS_TEMP_0FD9D6626_47CA26D6 |
| 14  |        VIEW                      |                          |
| 15  |         TABLE ACCESS FULL        | SYS_TEMP_0FD9D6626_47CA26D6 |
| 16  |     TABLE ACCESS BY ROWID RANGE  | T1                       |
--------------------------------------------------------------------
```

   Try to imagine that there are 100,000,000 rows in T1 and not 100. Imagine that there are ten threads each performing some complex manipulation on 1,000,000 rows each rather than a trivial operation on the second set of ten rows from 100, as is shown in Listing 10-2.

   The subquery in the MERGE statement of Listing 10-2 identifies the eleventh and twentieth ROWIDs from the table, which are then used to indicate the physical portion of the table to update. Since table T1 is so small, a number of hints, including the ROWID hint, are required to demonstrate the TABLE ACCESS BY ROWID RANGE operation that would otherwise be quite correctly considered by the CBO to be inefficient.

Of course, Listing 10-2 is highly artificial. One of several issues with the example is that I have written it in such a way so as to suggest that the job of identifying the ROWID ranges is replicated by each of the imagined ten threads. A better approach would be to have the identification of the ROWID ranges for all threads done once by use of information from the data dictionary view DBA_EXTENTS. In fact, there is a package—DBMS_PARALLEL_EXECUTE—that does that for you. For more details, see the PL/SQL Packages and Types Reference manual.

B-tree Index Access

This section discusses the various ways that a B-tree index can be used to access table data, while the next section discusses bitmap indexes. Table 10-2 enumerates the various B-tree access methods.

Table 10-2. *B-tree index access methods*

Execution Plan Operation	Hint	Alternative Hint
INDEX FULL SCAN	INDEX	
INDEX FULL SCAN (MIN/MAX)	INDEX	
INDEX FULL SCAN DESCENDING	INDEX_DESC	
INDEX RANGE SCAN	INDEX	INDEX_RS_ASC
INDEX RANGE SCAN DESCENDING	INDEX_DESC	INDEX_RS_DESC
INDEX RANGE SCAN (MIN/MAX)	INDEX	
INDEX SKIP SCAN	INDEX_SS	INDEX_SS_ASC
INDEX SKIP SCAN DESCENDING	INDEX_SS_DESC	
INDEX UNIQUE SCAN	INDEX	INDEX_RS_ASC
INDEX FAST FULL SCAN	INDEX_FFS	
INDEX SAMPLE FAST FULL SCAN	INDEX_FFS	
HASH JOIN	INDEX_JOIN	
AND-EQUAL	AND_EQUAL	

There seem to be a bewildering number of ways to access a B-tree index, but I think I have them all listed above. Let us start with a detailed analysis of the INDEX FULL SCAN at the top and then work our way quickly down.

INDEX FULL SCAN

Figure 10-1 provides a simplified view of an index that we will be using as our guide.

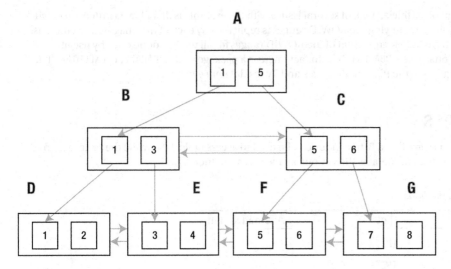

Figure 10-1. *A simplified view of a B-tree index*

Figure 10-1 depicts an index root block A, two branch blocks B and C, and four leaf blocks D, E, F, and G. I have drawn only two index entries per block. In real life there might be hundreds of entries. So if there were 200 entries per block there might be one root block, 200 branch blocks, 40,000 leaf blocks, and 8,000,000 index entries in those leaf blocks.

An INDEX FULL SCAN begins at the root of the index: block A in Figure 10-1. We use pointers in the blocks to descend the left side of the index structure until we have the block containing the smallest value of our leading indexed column, block D. We then follow the forward pointers along the leaf nodes visiting E, F, and G.

The index scan creates an intermediate result set containing rows with all the columns in the index and the ROWID. Of course if there are selection predicates in our WHERE clause (or predicates in the FROM list that can be treated as selection predicates) then we can filter out rows as we go. And equally clearly, we can discard any columns that we don't need and create new columns based on expressions in our select list.

If the only columns we want from this table are in the index, we don't need to do anything more. We are done. However, most of the time we will use the ROWID to access the associated table, table partition, or table subpartition using a TABLE ACCESS BY [LOCAL|GLOBAL] INDEX ROWID operation.

Be aware of the following:

- The layout of the blocks in the diagram is purely a logical sequence. The order on disk may be quite different.

- Because of this we must use single-block reads and follow the pointers. This can slow things down.

- The order of rows returned by an INDEX FULL SCAN is automatically sorted by the indexed columns, so this access method may avoid a sort. This can speed things up.

Listing 10-3 is an example of an INDEX FULL SCAN forced with the use of the INDEX hint:

Listing 10-3. INDEX FULL SCAN operation

```
CREATE INDEX t1_i1
   ON t1 (c1, c2);

SELECT /*+ index(t1 (c1,c2)) */ * FROM t1;
```

```
---------------------------------------------
| Id  | Operation                   | Name  |
---------------------------------------------
|   0 | SELECT STATEMENT            |       |
|   1 |  TABLE ACCESS BY INDEX ROWID| T1    |
|   2 |   INDEX FULL SCAN           | T1_I1 |
---------------------------------------------
```

Listing 10-3 creates a multi-column index on T1. The select statement includes a hint that specifies the use of the index.

■ **Note**   Notice that the name of the index isn't used in the hint. It is legal, and indeed encouraged, to specify the columns in the index you want to use, enclosed in parentheses, rather than the index name itself. This is to ensure that hints don't break if somebody renames an index. All index hints displayed in the OUTLINE section of an execution plan use this approach.

Under certain circumstances the optimizer can make a huge improvement here and do something completely different under the guise of what is supposedly an INDEX FULL SCAN. Listing 10-4 shows an aggregate operation in use on an indexed column:

Listing 10-4. INDEX FULL SCAN with MIN/MAX optimization

```
      SELECT /*+ index(t1 (c1,c2)) */
            MAX (c1) FROM t1;
```

```
---------------------------------------------
| Id  | Operation                   | Name  |
---------------------------------------------
|   0 | SELECT STATEMENT            |       |
|   1 |  SORT AGGREGATE             |       |
|   2 |   INDEX FULL SCAN (MIN/MAX) | T1_I1 |
---------------------------------------------
```

What actually happens in Listing 10-4 is that we move down from the root block in our index using the trailing edge of the tree. In this case that would be A, C, and G. We can identify the maximum value of C1 straightaway without scanning the whole index. Don't worry about the SORT AGGREGATE. As I explained in Chapter 3, the SORT AGGREGATE operation never sorts.

There are many restrictions and special cases that I researched for Oracle Database 10g in my blog in September 2009, seen here:

http://tonyhasler.wordpress.com/2009/09/08/index-full-scan-minmax/

I suspect this is a moving target and that much of what I said back then may not apply in later versions of Oracle Database, so if you are looking for this operation and can't get it to work, you may just have to fiddle around a bit with your predicates.

There is also an INDEX FULL SCAN DESCENDING operation. This just starts off with the maximum value and works its way back through the index using the backward pointers. The difference is that the rows come back in descending order, which can avoid a sort, as Listing 10-5 shows.

Listing 10-5. INDEX FULL SCAN DESCENDING

```
SELECT /*+ index_desc(t1 (c1,c2)) */
       *
     FROM t1
ORDER BY c1 DESC, c2 DESC;
```

```
---------------------------------------------
| Id  | Operation                  | Name  |
---------------------------------------------
|   0 | SELECT STATEMENT           |       |
|   1 |  TABLE ACCESS BY INDEX ROWID| T1   |
|   2 |   INDEX FULL SCAN DESCENDING| T1_I1 |
---------------------------------------------
```

Notice the absence of a sort operation despite the presence of the ORDER BY clause. Now, let us move on to the next access method in our list.

INDEX RANGE SCAN

The INDEX RANGE SCAN is very similar to the INDEX FULL SCAN. So similar, in fact, that the same hint is used to select it. The difference is that when a suitable predicate on one or more leading columns of the index is present in the query block we might be able to start our scan of leaf blocks somewhere in the middle and/or stop somewhere in the middle. In our diagram above, a predicate C1 BETWEEN 3 AND 5 would enable us to go from the root block A down to B, read E and F, and then stop. Listing 10-6 demonstrates:

Listing 10-6. INDEX RANGE SCAN

```
SELECT /*+ index(t1 (c1,c2)) */
       *
     FROM t1
   WHERE c1 BETWEEN 3 AND 5;
```

```
---------------------------------------------
| Id  | Operation                  | Name  |
---------------------------------------------
|   0 | SELECT STATEMENT           |       |
|   1 |  TABLE ACCESS BY INDEX ROWID| T1   |
|   2 |   INDEX RANGE SCAN         | T1_I1 |
---------------------------------------------
```

Performing an INDEX FULL SCAN when an INDEX RANGE SCAN is available never makes sense and the optimizer will never select it. I guess this is the reason that a separate hint for the INDEX RANGE SCAN hasn't been documented.

There are some who would recommend the use of the alternative, undocumented INDEX_RS_ASC hint as it is more specific. Personally, I have no qualms whatsoever about using an undocumented hint, but I don't see the point when a documented one exists!

The same comments I made about INDEX FULL SCANS apply to INDEX RANGE SCANS.

- We must use single-block reads and follow the pointers. This can slow things down.

- The order of rows returned by an INDEX RANGE SCAN is automatically sorted by the indexed columns, so this access method may avoid a sort. This can speed things up.

INDEX RANGE SCAN DESCENDING is the descending variant of INDEX RANGE SCAN and is shown in Listing 10-7.

Listing 10-7. INDEX RANGE SCAN DESCENDING

```
SELECT /*+ index_desc(t1 (c1,c2)) */
       *
  FROM t1
 WHERE c1 BETWEEN 3 AND 5
ORDER BY c1 DESC;
```

```
-----------------------------------------------
| Id  | Operation                   | Name  |
-----------------------------------------------
|   0 | SELECT STATEMENT            |       |
|   1 |  TABLE ACCESS BY INDEX ROWID| T1    |
|   2 |   INDEX RANGE SCAN DESCENDING| T1_I1 |
-----------------------------------------------
```

Listing 10-8 shows that the MIN/MAX optimization can be used with a range scan as with an INDEX FULL SCAN.

Listing 10-8. INDEX RANGE SCAN with MIN/MAX optimization

```
SELECT /*+ index(t1 (c1,c2)) */
       MIN (c2)
  FROM t1
 WHERE c1 = 3
ORDER BY c1 DESC;
```

```
-----------------------------------------------
| Id  | Operation                   | Name  |
-----------------------------------------------
|   0 | SELECT STATEMENT            |       |
|   1 |  SORT AGGREGATE             |       |
|   2 |   FIRST ROW                 |       |
|   3 |    INDEX RANGE SCAN (MIN/MAX)| T1_I1 |
-----------------------------------------------
```

Notice the sudden appearance of an extra operation—FIRST ROW. This sometimes pops up when the MIN/MAX optimization is used. I haven't worked out what it means yet, and I suggest you just ignore it.

The INDEX RANGE SCAN requires there to be a suitable predicate on the leading column of the index. What happens when there are one or more predicates on non-leading columns but no predicate on the leading column? The INDEX SKIP SCAN is an option in this case.

INDEX SKIP SCAN

If the number of distinct values of the leading column is low, then a series of range scans, one for each value of the leading column, may be more efficient than an INDEX FULL SCAN. When the value of the leading column changes, the INDEX SKIP SCAN operation moves back up the B-tree and then descends again looking for the range associated with the new value of the leading column. Listing 10-9 demonstrates the operation.

Listing 10-9. INDEX SKIP SCAN

```
SELECT /*+ index_ss(t1 (c1,c2)) */
       *
  FROM t1
 WHERE c2 = 3
ORDER BY c1, c2;
```

```
--------------------------------------------
| Id | Operation                 | Name  |
--------------------------------------------
|  0 | SELECT STATEMENT          |       |
|  1 |  TABLE ACCESS BY INDEX ROWID| T1   |
|  2 |   INDEX SKIP SCAN         | T1_I1 |
--------------------------------------------
```

Listing 10-10 shows the descending variant.

Listing 10-10. INDEX SKIP SCAN DESCENDING

```
SELECT /*+ index_ss_desc(t1 (c1,c2)) */
       *
  FROM t1
 WHERE c2 = 3
ORDER BY c1 DESC, c2 DESC;
```

```
--------------------------------------------
| Id | Operation                 | Name  |
--------------------------------------------
|  0 | SELECT STATEMENT          |       |
|  1 |  TABLE ACCESS BY INDEX ROWID| T1   |
|  2 |   INDEX SKIP SCAN DESCENDING| T1_I1 |
--------------------------------------------
```

Incidentally, in Oracle Database 10g it was not possible to request that an index be used AND say that an INDEX SKIP SCAN NOT be used. This is no longer true. Just use an INDEX hint and you will get an INDEX FULL SCAN.

INDEX UNIQUE SCAN

The INDEX UNIQUE SCAN is used when accessing at most one row from a unique index. This is a separate operation because it is implemented in a more efficient way than reading a row from a non-unique index that happens to only have one row. Listing 10-11 creates a unique index and then shows the operation.

Listing 10-11. INDEX UNIQUE SCAN

```
CREATE UNIQUE INDEX t1_i2
   ON t1 (c2);

SELECT /*+ index(t1 (c2)) */
          *
       FROM t1
       WHERE c2 = 1;
```

```
---------------------------------------------
| Id  | Operation                  | Name  |
---------------------------------------------
|   0 | SELECT STATEMENT           |       |
|   1 |  TABLE ACCESS BY INDEX ROWID| T1    |
|   2 |   INDEX UNIQUE SCAN        | T1_I2 |
---------------------------------------------
```

Notice that there is no "descending" variant of this plan because we are retrieving only one row.

INDEX FAST FULL SCAN

The next indexed access method is the INDEX FAST FULL SCAN. Well, we like that word *fast*, don't we? The obvious question is: If we have a full scan that is fast, why do we need the slow one? The truth is that the INDEX FAST FULL SCAN has one big restriction and is not always faster than a regular INDEX FULL SCAN.

An INDEX FAST FULL SCAN reads the whole index with multi-block reads. Forget about all those pesky pointers. Just suck the whole index in!

Of course, multi-block reads are always a faster way to read a lot of data than single-block reads. However:

- We are reading all the data in the index—not just the leaf blocks we need.

- The data is provided in physical order, not logical order.

As to the first point, it doesn't matter too much. Nearly all the blocks in an index are leaf blocks anyway, so we are only throwing away a small portion. As to the second point, we may not be interested in the order. Even if we are interested in the order, combining an INDEX FAST FULL SCAN with an explicit sort may be cheaper than alternative access methods.

The really disappointing thing about the INDEX FAST FULL SCAN is that unlike all the other index access methods discussed so far we can't use the ROWIDs to access the table. As to why the developers have imposed this restriction, I have no idea.

If you are reading this because you have just received a call due to a performance problem and suspect that an INDEX FAST FULL SCAN with subsequent table access would help you, skip ahead to Chapter 19, where I document a workaround.

Listing 10-12 shows the operation.

Listing 10-12. INDEX FAST FULL SCAN

```
SELECT /*+ index_ffs(t1 (c1, c2)) */
         c1, c2
      FROM t1
      WHERE c2 = 1;
```

```
-------------------------------------
| Id | Operation          | Name  |
-------------------------------------
|  0 | SELECT STATEMENT    |       |
|  1 |  INDEX FAST FULL SCAN| T1_I1 |
-------------------------------------
```

This example demonstrates that we don't necessarily need all the rows in the index to use an INDEX FAST FULL SCAN; our WHERE clause is free to dispose of some of them. Of course, if you want to use an index but do not want to use a fast full scan, use the INDEX or INDEX_DESC hints.

INDEX SAMPLE FAST FULL SCAN

The final index access method that uses just one B-tree index is probably most used by the DBMS_STATS package when gathering index statistics. It is only used when taking samples in combination with a fast full scan. Listing 10-13 demonstrates.

Listing 10-13. INDEX SAMPLE FAST FULL SCAN

```
SELECT /*+ index_ffs(t1 (c1, c2)) */
         c1, c2
      FROM t1 SAMPLE (5);
```

```
---------------------------------------------
| Id  | Operation             | Name  |
---------------------------------------------
|  0  | SELECT STATEMENT       |       |
|  1  |  INDEX SAMPLE FAST FULL SCAN| T1_I1 |
---------------------------------------------
```

All the access methods discussed so far involve only a single B-tree index. There are two access methods available in all editions of Oracle database that allow B-tree indexes to be combined. Let us look at the first of these now.

INDEX JOIN

Listing 10-14 shows an example of an INDEX JOIN using tables from the HR example schema.

Listing 10-14. Index join example

```
SELECT
      e.first_name
  FROM hr.employees e
 WHERE e.manager_id >=100 AND e.last_name LIKE '%ran%';
```

```
--------------------------------------------------
| Id | Operation             | Name               |
--------------------------------------------------
|  0 | SELECT STATEMENT      |                    |
|* 1 |  VIEW                 | index$_join$_001   |
|* 2 |   HASH JOIN           |                    |
|* 3 |    INDEX RANGE SCAN    | EMP_MANAGER_IX     |
|* 4 |    INDEX FAST FULL SCAN| EMP_NAME_IX        |
--------------------------------------------------
```

Listing 10-14 joins two indexes on the EMPLOYEES tables as if they were themselves tables. The joined column is the ROWID from the table. What has effectively happened is that Listing 10-14 has been transformed into Listing 10-15.

Listing 10-15. Manually transformed index join

```
WITH q1
     AS (SELECT /*+ no_merge */ first_name, ROWID r1
           FROM hr.employees
          WHERE last_name LIKE '%ran%')
     ,q2
     AS (SELECT /*+ no_merge */ ROWID r2
           FROM hr.employees
          WHERE manager_id >=100)
SELECT first_name
  FROM q1, q2
 WHERE r1 = r2;
```

Subquery Q1 in Listing 10-15 can be satisfied by a range scan on the EMP_NAME_IX index with no need to access the table itself, as the only columns we are selecting come from the index. Subquery Q2 can similarly restrict its access to the EMP_MANAGER_IX index. The main query then joins the results of the two subqueries using the ROWIDs from the two indexes.

Be aware that an index join is only possible if the only columns required from the table whose indexes are being joined are those present in the indexes. However, it is possible to combine index joins with regular table joins under certain circumstances, as demonstrated in Listing 10-16.

Listing 10-16. Complex INDEX JOIN example

```
SELECT /*+ leading(e) index_join(e) */
       e.first_name, m.last_name
  FROM hr.employees e, hr.employees m
  WHERE     m.last_name = 'Mourgos'
        AND e.manager_id = m.employee_id
        AND e.last_name = 'Grant'
        AND e.department_id = 50;
```

```
---------------------------------------------------------
| Id  | Operation                   | Name              |
---------------------------------------------------------
|   0 | SELECT STATEMENT            |                   |
|   1 |  NESTED LOOPS               |                   |
|   2 |   NESTED LOOPS              |                   |
|*  3 |    VIEW                     | index$_join$_001  |
|*  4 |     HASH JOIN               |                   |
|*  5 |      HASH JOIN              |                   |
|*  6 |       INDEX RANGE SCAN      | EMP_DEPARTMENT_IX |
|*  7 |       INDEX RANGE SCAN      | EMP_NAME_IX       |
|   8 |      INDEX FAST FULL SCAN   | EMP_MANAGER_IX    |
|*  9 |    INDEX UNIQUE SCAN        | EMP_EMP_ID_PK     |
|* 10 |   TABLE ACCESS BY INDEX ROWID| EMPLOYEES        |
---------------------------------------------------------
```

Since there are only two employees with a surname of Grant and only one of these with Mourgos as a manager, an index join is not suitable on performance grounds for this particular query, but we can use hints for demonstration purposes.

Notice that the reference to M.LAST_NAME doesn't prohibit the index join as it doesn't come from the copy of the EMPLOYEES table with table alias E.

- Index joins require that only columns in the indexes being joined are referenced. You can't even reference the ROWID!

- Index joins are only possible on the first table in a set of joined tables (hence the LEADING hint above).

- Index joins can be forced (when legal) with the INDEX_JOIN hint as in Listing 10-16 above.

If you do see index joins happening a lot you might want to consider creating a multi-column index, as this will be slightly more efficient than the index join, but in my experience index joins aren't usually the source of serious performance issues.

You might think that an index join might sometimes be suitable even when you do want to reference rows in the main table. Well, there is a way to do this.

AND_EQUAL

Listing 10-17 shows the AND_EQUAL access method, but the optimizer will no longer use it unless hinted and that hint is deprecated.

Listing 10-17. Depreccated AND_EQUAL access method

```
SELECT /*+ and_equal(e (manager_id) (job_id)) */
       employee_id
       ,first_name
       ,last_name
       ,email
  FROM hr.employees e
 WHERE e.manager_id = 124 AND e.job_id = 'SH_CLERK';
```

```
-----------------------------------------------------
| Id  | Operation                  | Name           |
-----------------------------------------------------
|   0 | SELECT STATEMENT           |                |
|*  1 |  TABLE ACCESS BY INDEX ROWID| EMPLOYEES     |
|   2 |   AND-EQUAL                |                |
|*  3 |    INDEX RANGE SCAN        | EMP_MANAGER_IX |
|*  4 |    INDEX RANGE SCAN        | EMP_JOB_IX     |
-----------------------------------------------------
```

Listing 10-17 shows the two sets of ROWIDs being merged as before (but perhaps using a different mechanism), but then we use the ROWIDs to access the table and pick up the additional columns.

- This is a deprecated feature.

- There are numerous restrictions, one of which is that the indexes must be single-column, non-unique indexes.

- It requires the AND_EQUAL hint. The optimizer will never generate this plan unless hinted.

- This mechanism will rarely provide a performance improvement, but if it does then a multi-column index is usually warranted.

- There are alternative approaches for both standard edition users and enterprise edition users. We will discuss an option for standard edition users in Chapter 19. The next section on bitmap indexes shows several ways to combine indexes for enterprise edition users.

Bitmap Index Access

The physical structure of a bitmap index is actually very similar to that of a B-tree index, with the root and branch block structures being identical.

The difference comes at the leaf block. Let us suppose that we have a B-tree index on column C1 on T1 and that there are 100 rows in T1 that have a value of 'X' for C1. The B-tree index would contain 100 index entries, each with a ROWID for a particular matching row in the table.

The bitmap index would instead have a bitmap for value 'X' that had one bit for every row in the table or partition; for the 100 rows in the table with value 'X' for C1 the bit would be set, but it would be clear for the remaining rows.

These bitmaps in the leaf blocks are compressed to remove long stretches of clear bits so the more clustered the data in the table is, the smaller the index is. This compression generally means that even if there is an average of only two rows for each value, the bitmap index will be smaller than its B-tree counterpart.

You should always remember that bitmaps are representations of collections of *restricted* ROWIDs. It is, therefore, not possible to

- create a global bitmap index;

- convert ROWIDs from a global index into a bitmap; or

- convert variables or expressions of type ROWID or UROWID to bitmaps.

The operations to access a bitmap index are, unsurprisingly, similar to those for a B-tree index (see Table 10-3).

Table 10-3. Bitmap-indexed access operations

Execution Plan Operation	Hint	Alternative Hint
BITMAP INDEX SINGLE VALUE	INDEX	BITMAP_TREE / INDEX_RS_ASC
BITMAP INDEX RANGE SCAN	INDEX	BITMAP_TREE /INDEX_RS_ASC
BITMAP INDEX FULL SCAN	INDEX	BITMAP_TREE
BITMAP INDEX FAST FULL SCAN	INDEX_FFS	
BITMAP CONSTRUCTION	N/A	
BITMAP COMPACTION	N/A	

Looking at Table 10-3 you will notice the following

- There are no descending or skip scan variants.

- There are no MIN/MAX optimizations available.

- There is no UNIQUE option—hardly surprising as the silly idea of a unique bitmap index isn't even supported.

The BITMAP INDEX SINGLE VALUE operation is used when an equality predicate is supplied for the column or columns in the index and implies the processing of a single bitmap.

The BITMAP CONSTRUCTION and BITMAP COMPACTION are provided for completeness. If you run EXPLAIN PLAN on a CREATE BITMAP INDEX or ALTER INDEX...REBUILD command you will see these operations appear. They are DDL specific.

We can do a whole lot more with bitmaps other than just accessing them in indexes. Table 10-4 shows the full set of operations.

Table 10-4. *Bitmap manipulation operations*

Execution Plan Operation	Hint	Alternative Hint
BITMAP CONVERSION FROM ROWIDS		
BITMAP CONVERSION TO ROWIDS		
BITMAP AND	INDEX_COMBINE	BITMAP_TREE
BITMAP OR	INDEX_COMBINE	BITMAP_TREE
BITMAP MINUS	INDEX_COMBINE	BITMAP_TREE
BITMAP MERGE	INDEX_COMBINE	BITMAP_TREE
BITMAP CONVERSION COUNT		
BITMAP KEY ITERATION	STAR_TRANSFORMATION	

The operation BITMAP CONVERSION FROM ROWIDS is used to convert restricted ROWIDs from a B-tree index into a bitmap, and the operation BITMAP CONVERSION TO ROWIDS is used to convert bitmaps to restricted ROWIDs.

The BITMAP AND, BITMAP OR, and BITMAP MINUS operations perform Boolean algebra operations in the expected way; complex trees of bitmap operations can be formed. The BITMAP MERGE operation is similar to BITMAP OR but is used in some contexts where the ROWID sets are known to be disjointed.

Usually, after all this manipulation of bitmaps, the final result is passed to the BITMAP CONVERSION TO ROWIDS operation. However, sometimes all we want is a count of the number of rows. This can be done by the BITMAP CONVERSION COUNT operation.

The BITMAP KEY ITERATION operation is used in star transformations, which we will discuss in Chapter 13.

It is not unusual to see a lot of bitmap operations in one query, as in Listing 10-18.

Listing 10-18. Bitmap operations

```
CREATE INDEX t1_i3
   ON t1 (c5);

CREATE BITMAP INDEX t1_bix1
   ON t1 (c3);

SELECT /*+ index_combine(t) no_expand */
       *
       FROM t1 t
       WHERE (c1 > 0 AND c5 = 1 AND c3 > 0) OR c4 > 0;
```

```
-------------------------------------------------------
| Id | Operation                          | Name     |
-------------------------------------------------------
|  0 | SELECT STATEMENT                   |          |
|  1 |  TABLE ACCESS BY INDEX ROWID       | T1       |
|  2 |   BITMAP CONVERSION TO ROWIDS      |          |
|  3 |    BITMAP OR                       |          |
|  4 |     BITMAP MERGE                   |          |
|  5 |      BITMAP INDEX RANGE SCAN       | T1_BIX2  |
|  6 |     BITMAP AND                     |          |
|  7 |      BITMAP CONVERSION FROM ROWIDS |          |
|  8 |       INDEX RANGE SCAN             | T1_I3    |
|  9 |      BITMAP MERGE                  |          |
| 10 |       BITMAP INDEX RANGE SCAN      | T1_BIX1  |
| 11 |      BITMAP CONVERSION FROM ROWIDS |          |
| 12 |       SORT ORDER BY                |          |
| 13 |        INDEX RANGE SCAN            | T1_I1    |
-------------------------------------------------------
```

Listing 10-18 begins by creating two more indexes. The execution plan for the query looks a bit scary, but the first thing to understand when reading execution plans like this is that you should not panic. You can follow them easily enough if you take it step by step.

Let us start at operation 5, which is the first operation without a child. This performs a BITMAP INDEX RANGE SCAN on T1_BIX2, which is based on column C4. This range scan will potentially process multiple bitmaps associated with different values of C4, and these are merged by operation 4. This merged bitmap represents the first operand of the BITMAP OR on line 3. We then move on to look at the second operand of the BITMAP OR, which is defined by the operation on line 6 as well as its children.

We now look at operation 8, which is the second operation with no child. This is an INDEX RANGE SCAN on T1_I3, which is a B-tree index based on C5. In this case we have an equality predicate, C5 = 1, and that means all the rows returned have the same index key. A little known fact is that entries from a non-unique index that have the same key value are sorted by ROWID. This means that all the rows returned by the INDEX RANGE SCAN will be in ROWID order and can be directly converted to a bitmap by operation 7. This BITMAP MERGE forms the first operand of the BITMAP AND operation on line 6.

We move on to line 10, an INDEX RANGE SCAN on T1_BIX1, a bitmap index based on C3. Once again, multiple values of C3 are possible and so the various bitmaps need to be merged by line 9, finalizing the second operand of operation 6, the BITMAP AND.

But there is a third operand of operation 6. We begin the evaluation of this third operand by looking at line 13, an INDEX RANGE SCAN on T1_I1, a B-tree index on C1 and C2. Because the range scan may cover multiple key values, the index entries may not be returned in ROWID order; we need to sort the ROWIDs on line 12 before converting them into a bitmap on line 11.

We now have the three operands to the BITMAP AND operation on line 6 and the two operands to the BITMAP OR operation on line 3. After all bitmap manipulation, the final bitmap is converted to a set of ROWIDs on line 2, and these are finally used to access the table on line 1.

Listing 10-19 changes Listing 10-18 slightly to return the count of rows rather than the contents; we can see that the conversion of the bitmap to ROWIDs can be eliminated.

Listing 10-19. BITMAP CONVERSION COUNT example

```
SELECT /*+ index_combine(t) */
          COUNT (*)
       FROM t1 t
       WHERE (c1 > 0 AND c5 = 1 AND c3 > 0) OR c4 > 0;
```

```
--------------------------------------------------------
| Id  | Operation                        | Name    |
--------------------------------------------------------
|  0  | SELECT STATEMENT                 |         |
|  1  |  SORT AGGREGATE                  |         |
|  2  |   BITMAP CONVERSION COUNT        |         |
|  3  |    BITMAP OR                     |         |
|  4  |     BITMAP MERGE                 |         |
|  5  |      BITMAP INDEX RANGE SCAN     | T1_BIX2 |
|  6  |     BITMAP AND                   |         |
|  7  |      BITMAP MERGE                |         |
|  8  |       BITMAP INDEX RANGE SCAN    | T1_BIX1 |
|  9  |      BITMAP CONVERSION FROM ROWIDS|        |
| 10  |       INDEX RANGE SCAN           | T1_I3   |
| 11  |      BITMAP CONVERSION FROM ROWIDS|        |
| 12  |       SORT ORDER BY              |         |
| 13  |        INDEX RANGE SCAN          | T1_I1   |
--------------------------------------------------------
```

The main difference between this plan and the last one is the presence of the BITMAP CONVERSION COUNT operation on line 2 and the absence of any BITMAP CONVERSION TO ROWIDS operation.

One major restriction of bitmap operations, which we will investigate in detail when we discuss the star transformation in Chapter 13, is that this mechanism cannot deal with "in lists" with subqueries such as is unsuccessfully attempted in Listing 10-20.

Listing 10-20. INDEX COMBINE attempt with INLIST

```
SELECT /*+ index_combine(e) */
       /* THIS HINT INNEFFECTIVE IN THIS QUERY */
       employee_id
      ,first_name
      ,last_name
      ,email
  FROM hr.employees e
 WHERE    manager_id IN (SELECT employee_id
                           FROM hr.employees
                          WHERE salary > 14000)
       OR job_id = 'SH_CLERK';
```

```
---------------------------------------------------------
| Id | Operation                   | Name          |
---------------------------------------------------------
|  0 | SELECT STATEMENT            |               |
|  1 |  FILTER                     |               |
|  2 |   TABLE ACCESS BY INDEX ROWID| EMPLOYEES    |
|  3 |    INDEX FULL SCAN          | EMP_EMP_ID_PK |
|  4 |   TABLE ACCESS BY INDEX ROWID| EMPLOYEES    |
|  5 |    INDEX UNIQUE SCAN        | EMP_EMP_ID_PK |
---------------------------------------------------------
```

Full Table Scans

We now come to the pariah of operations in an execution plan: the much maligned full table scan (see Table 10-5).

Table 10-5. Full table scan operations

Operation	Hint
TABLE ACCESS FULL	FULL
TABLE ACCESS SAMPLE	FULL
TABLE ACCESS SAMPLE BY ROWID RANGE	FULL PARALLEL

Although we all refer to the operation as a full table scan, the actual name of the operation in an execution plan display is TABLE ACCESS FULL. Both terms are slightly misleading because in the case of a partitioned table, the "table" being scanned is actually an individual partition or subpartition. Perhaps to avoid an over-specific term it might have been called "segment full scan," but that wouldn't be specific enough; we aren't talking about indexes here, after all. To keep it simple I will assume that we are looking at non-partitioned tables for the remainder of this section; the mechanics don't change. I'll also use the abbreviation FTS for brevity.

The FTS operation sounds simple enough: we read all the blocks in the table from beginning to end.

However, it is actually a lot more complicated than that. We need to

- access the segment header to read the extent map and identify the high water mark (HWM);

- read all the data in all the extents up to the HWM; and

- re-read the segment header to confirm that there are no more rows.

Even if we are talking only about serial, as opposed to parallel, operations, that still isn't the full story. Once all the data has been returned to the client an extra FETCH operation may be required to reconfirm that there is no more data. That will result in a third read of the segment header.

These extra reads of the segment header aren't usually a major factor when we are looking at a large, or even medium-sized, table, but for a tiny table of, say, one block these extra reads might be an issue. If the tiny table is frequently accessed you may need to create an index or just convert the table to an index-organized table.

Some people will tell you that the key to tuning badly performing SQL is to search out FTSs and eliminate them by adding indexes. This is a dangerous half-truth. It is certainly the case that a missing index *can* cause performance problems and that those performance problems might be recognized by the presence of a TABLE FULL SCAN operation in an execution plan. However, FTSs are very often the most efficient way to access a table, as I explained when I introduced the concept of the index clustering factor in Chapter 9. If you have forgotten, take a look back at Figure 9-1.

Listing 10-21 shows the basic FTS operation in action.

Listing 10-21. FULL TABLE SCAN

```
SELECT /*+ full(t1) */
       * FROM t1;


-----------------------------------
| Id  | Operation        | Name |
-----------------------------------
|   0 | SELECT STATEMENT |      |
|   1 |  TABLE ACCESS FULL| T1  |
-----------------------------------
```

Listing 10-22 shows the second operation listed at the top of this section. As with INDEX FAST FULL SCAN, the use of a sample changes the operation.

Listing 10-22. TABLE ACCESS SAMPLE

```
SELECT /*+ full(t1) */
           *
       FROM t1 SAMPLE (5);


-----------------------------------
| Id  | Operation          | Name |
-----------------------------------
|   0 | SELECT STATEMENT   |      |
|   1 |  TABLE ACCESS SAMPLE| T1  |
-----------------------------------
```

Listing 10-22 requests a 5 percent sample from the table. The final FTS variant is demonstrated in Listing 10-23, which shows a query with parallel sampling.

Listing 10-23. TABLE ACCESS SAMPLE in parallel

```
SELECT /*+ full(t1) parallel */
            *
        FROM t1 SAMPLE (5);
```

```
-------------------------------------------------------------
| Id | Operation                         | Name      |
-------------------------------------------------------------
|  0 | SELECT STATEMENT                  |           |
|  1 |  PX COORDINATOR                   |           |
|  2 |   PX SEND QC (RANDOM)             | :TQ10000  |
|  3 |    PX BLOCK ITERATOR              |           |
|  4 |     TABLE ACCESS SAMPLE BY ROWID RANGE| T1    |
-------------------------------------------------------------
```

TABLE and XMLTABLE

The list of functions in the SQL Language Reference manual includes XMLTABLE. For reasons that will shortly become clear, I will inaccurately refer to XMLTABLE as an "operator." A sibling to XMLTABLE is TABLE, but that "operator" is curiously documented in a completely different part of the manual than XMLTABLE.

The XMLTABLE "operator" has an Xquery "operand," and the result of the "operation" is a row source that can appear in a FROM clause just like a regular table or view.

I am not an XML guru, but Listing 10-24 is a quick example of the use of XMLTABLE.

Listing 10-24. XMLTABLE example

```
CREATE TABLE xml_test (c1 XMLTYPE);

SELECT x.*
    FROM xml_test t
        ,XMLTABLE (
                    '//a'
                    PASSING t.c1
                    COLUMNS "a" CHAR (10) PATH '@path1'
                           ,"b" CHAR (50) PATH '@path2'
                    ) x;
```

```
----------------------------------------------
| Id  | Operation          | Name    |
----------------------------------------------
|  0  | SELECT STATEMENT   |         |
|  1  |  NESTED LOOPS      |         |
|  2  |   TABLE ACCESS FULL| XML_TEST |
|  3  |   XPATH EVALUATION |         |
----------------------------------------------
```

The TABLE "operator" has an "operand" that is a *nested table*. The nested table operand has one of three formats:

- A data dictionary or casted PL/SQL nested table object
- A function that returns a nested table object. Such functions are typically pipelined functions
- A CAST...MULTISET expression

The second of these three forms is the most common, and the pipelined functions are often referred to as "table functions." This common use of the term "table function" makes it easier to refer to the keywords TABLE and XMLTABLE as "operators" rather than functions.

Nested tables in the data dictionary aren't a very good idea. The tables themselves aren't stored inline and so you might as well have a child table with a referential integrity constraint linking it to the parent. This way you would at least have the option of accessing the child data without visiting the parent.

■ **Note**   We will see in Chapter 13 that these days the CBO can perform the table elimination transformation so that any unnecessary reference to the parent table is eliminated.

However, if you have inherited some nasty nested tables from your predecessor, Listing 10-25 shows how you query them.

Listing 10-25. Querying a nested table

```
CREATE TYPE order_item AS OBJECT
(
   product_name VARCHAR2 (50)
  ,quantity INTEGER
  ,price NUMBER (8, 2)
);
/

CREATE TYPE order_item_table AS TABLE OF order_item;
/

CREATE TABLE orders
(
   order_id      NUMBER PRIMARY KEY
  ,customer_id   INTEGER
  ,order_items   order_item_table
)
NESTED TABLE order_items
   STORE AS order_items_nt;

SELECT o.order_id
      ,o.customer_id
      ,oi.product_name
      ,oi.quantity
      ,oi.price
  FROM orders o, TABLE (o.order_items) oi;
```

```
-------------------------------------------------------------------
| Id | Operation                    | Name                        |
-------------------------------------------------------------------
|  0 | SELECT STATEMENT             |                             |
|  1 |  NESTED LOOPS                |                             |
|  2 |   NESTED LOOPS               |                             |
|  3 |    TABLE ACCESS FULL         | ORDERS                      |
|  4 |    INDEX RANGE SCAN          | SYS_FK0000127743N00003$     |
|  5 |   TABLE ACCESS BY INDEX ROWID| ORDER_ITEMS_NT              |
-------------------------------------------------------------------
```

As you can see, there is a nested loop from our newly created parent table ORDERS to our nested table ORDER_ITEMS_NT via an automatically created index on a hidden column. Other join orders and methods are possible.

■ **Note** Information about all columns, including column statistics, in nested tables can be seen in the view ALL_NESTED_TABLE_COLS. This view also shows the hidden NESTED_TABLE_ID column on which the index is built.

A pipelined table function is a much better use of the table operator. Listing 10-26 shows a common example.

Listing 10-26. DBMS_XPLAN.display example

```
SELECT * FROM TABLE (DBMS_XPLAN.display);
```

```
------------------------------------------------------
| Id | Operation                        | Name    |
------------------------------------------------------
|  0 | SELECT STATEMENT                 |         |
|  1 | COLLECTION ITERATOR PICKLER FETCH| DISPLAY |
------------------------------------------------------
```

You can see the operation COLLECTION ITERATOR PICKLER FETCH to signify a call to the pipelined function to retrieve rows. In fact, these rows are batched so you don't get a context switch between the calling SQL statement and the pipelined function for every row retrieved.

The third and final way to use the table operator is with a subquery. Listing 10-27 shows what may be somewhat unfamiliar syntax, and it requires the use of user-defined types to get it working.

Listing 10-27. CAST MULTISET example

```
SELECT *
  FROM TABLE (CAST (MULTISET (SELECT 'CAMERA' product, 1 quantity, 1 price
                               FROM DUAL
                             CONNECT BY LEVEL <= 3) AS order_item_table)) oi;
```

```
------------------------------------------------------
| Id | Operation                        | Name |
------------------------------------------------------
|  0 | SELECT STATEMENT                 |      |
|  1 |  COLLECTION ITERATOR SUBQUERY FETCH|    |
|  2 |   COUNT                          |      |
|  3 |    CONNECT BY WITHOUT FILTERING  |      |
|  4 |     FAST DUAL                    |      |
------------------------------------------------------
```

Here I have queried DUAL to generate a collection of three rows and then cast the result into a nested table using the ORDER_ITEM_TYPE that I created in Listing 10-25. The table operator then allows me to treat this nested table as a row source. The query results are the same as that of the original SELECT from DUAL.

The execution plan in Listing 10-27 shows the subquery on lines 2, 3, and 4, while the COLLECTION ITERATOR SUBQUERY FETCH operation on line 1 has been generated by the TABLE operator.

This all seems very complicated and unnecessary. Why go to all the trouble of creating a nested table from a bunch of rows only to expand them back into rows? However, the use of this technique in combination with the left lateral joins that I touched on earlier can be very useful on some occasions, as we will see in Chapter 17.

Cluster Access

I need to mention clusters in this chapter for the sake of completeness (see Table 10-8).

Table 10-6. *Cluster access operations*

Operation	Hint
TABLE ACCESS HASH	HASH
TABLE ACCESS CLUSTER	CLUSTER

Let me go through this example. Listing 10-28 is the final in this chapter.

Listing 10-28. Cluster access methods

```
CREATE CLUSTER cluster_hash
(
  ck                              INTEGER
)
HASHKEYS 3
HASH IS ck;

CREATE TABLE tch1
(
   ck   INTEGER
  ,c1   INTEGER
)
CLUSTER cluster_hash ( ck );

CREATE CLUSTER cluster_btree
(
  ck                              INTEGER,
  c1                              INTEGER
);

CREATE INDEX cluster_btree_ix
   ON CLUSTER cluster_btree;

CREATE TABLE tc2
(
   ck   INTEGER
  ,c1   INTEGER
)
CLUSTER cluster_btree ( ck, c1 );

CREATE TABLE tc3
(
   ck   INTEGER
  ,c1   INTEGER
)
CLUSTER cluster_btree ( ck, c1 );
```

```
SELECT /*+ hash(tch1) index(tc2) cluster(tc3) */
            *
        FROM tch1, tc2, tc3
     WHERE        tch1.ck = 1
            AND tch1.ck = tc2.ck
            AND tch1.c1 = tc2.c1
            AND tc2.ck = tc3.ck
            AND tc2.c1 = tc3.c1;
```

```
--------------------------------------------------------
| Id  | Operation              | Name              |
--------------------------------------------------------
|   0 | SELECT STATEMENT       |                   |
|   1 |  NESTED LOOPS          |                   |
|   2 |   NESTED LOOPS         |                   |
|   3 |    TABLE ACCESS HASH   | TCH1              |
|   4 |    TABLE ACCESS CLUSTER| TC2               |
|   5 |     INDEX UNIQUE SCAN   | CLUSTER_BTREE_IX  |
|   6 |   TABLE ACCESS CLUSTER | TC3               |
--------------------------------------------------------
```

Listing 10-28 begins by creating a hash cluster, a B-tree cluster, and three associated tables. Table TCH1 is created in the single table hash cluster and tables TC2 and TC3 are created in the B-tree cluster.

The execution plan for the query in Listing 10-28 begins by accessing table TCH1. Because we included the predicate TCH1.CK = 1 in our query and CK is our hash cluster key, we are able to go directly to the block or blocks that contain the matching rows from TCH1 without the use of an index. For each of the matching rows in TCH1 we use the value of CK and C1 to access our cluster index on CLUSTER_BTREE. Cluster indexes are special in that they only have one entry per key value, hence why we get an INDEX UNIQUE SCAN operation on line 5 even though there may be many rows in TC2 that match the particular values of CK and C1 extracted from TCH1.

Because columns CK and C1 were both defined in CLUSTER_BTREE and were also specified as join conditions for TC2 and TC3, we know that the rows we want in TC3 are collocated with those of TC2. In fact, the single index entry lookup on line 5 helps us find all the rows we need in both TC2 and TC3 that match our row from TCH1.

All this looks pretty cool. In fact, clusters are used extensively in the data dictionary. However, I personally have never worked on any production Oracle database that has used any kind of cluster outside of the data dictionary.

So why are they so unpopular? Well, in the vast majority of cases the main overhead of accessing data through an index is in accessing the data in the table, not in doing the index lookup. This is because the index structure itself is likely to be cached and the table data may well not be. This tends to limit the benefit of hash clusters. Hash clusters are also a little difficult to manage because you have to know roughly how many rows will match each particular hash key. On the one hand, if you get this value too small then the hash chains become long. On the other hand, if you make the value too large then your cluster is unnecessarily large and you end up with more logical and/or physical I/O than you need. Whether you set the HASHKEYS parameter too large or too small, the performance benefit you thought you might get would rapidly disappear.

But what about regular B-tree clusters? You don't have to worry about setting HASHKEYS, and you still get the main performance benefit of clusters, don't you?

Imagine you have a table called ORDERS with a primary key, ORDER_ID, and an ORDER_ITEMS table with a referential integrity constraint linking it to the parent table. Wouldn't it be nice to be able to make one single-block read and get one row from the ORDERS table and its corresponding rows from the ORDER_ITEMS table? Surely that is better than making two I/Os to retrieve the data from the two tables separately, isn't it?

Well, yes. However, queries that retrieve data for just one order are going to complete quite quickly anyway, and you may not notice the performance improvement. On the other hand, if you are running a report that looks at large numbers of orders and their associated line items you are going to read lots of blocks anyway, so how the data is split between these blocks is of little consequence.

You may have a system with hundreds or thousands of interactive users, so the ORDERS and ORDER_ITEMS tables may be huge and unable to be cached in the SGA, so you really want to halve these I/Os to improve capacity.

Fine. Unfortunately, there is one big problem with this scenario: you can't partition clustered tables. That is a big "gotcha." Partitioning provides significant administrative and performance benefits for large tables, and few people are prepared to give them all up just to enjoy the benefits of clusters.

But if partitioning is out of the picture for you, perhaps because of licensing issues, and you frequently perform joins between tables as I have described, then clustering may seem like a good option.

Even in these rare circumstances, most people end up denormalizing their data or finding some other workaround rather than using something like a cluster that, rightly or wrongly, is viewed as a big unknown. I won't be mentioning clusters again in this book.

Summary

I am afraid that even this lengthy discussion of access methods is incomplete. We haven't discussed access to LOB objects, use of REF data types, or the use of domain indexes. But even so, this chapter has covered all the access methods that you are likely to encounter in the vast majority of SQL statements in commercial applications.

Having covered the various ways to access a single row source within a query it is now time to turn our attention to the topic of joining these row sources together. On to Chapter 11.

CHAPTER 11

Joins

Every SQL query or subquery has a FROM clause that identifies one or more *row sources*. These row sources may be tables, data dictionary views, inline views, factored subqueries, or expressions involving the TABLE or XMLTABLE operators. If there is more than one row source then the rows produced by these row sources need to be *joined*, there being one less join operation than there are row sources. In Chapter 1 I covered the various different syntactic constructs for joins. These constructs included inner joins, left outer joins, right outer joins, full outer joins, and partitioned outer joins. I also explained which types of join could be constructed with traditional syntax and which required ANSI join syntax.

In this chapter I will look at the different methods that the runtime engine has for implementing joins of any type, the rules surrounding the order in which the row sources are joined, and how parallel execution can be used in joins. I will also look at two types of *subquery unnesting*: semi-joins and anti-joins. Subquery unnesting is an *optimizer transformation* for constructing additional row sources and joins that aren't present in the FROM clause of the original query. But first let me review the four types of join method.

Join Methods

There are four methods that the runtime engine has at its disposal for implementing any join. These four methods are *nested loops, hash join, merge join*, and *Cartesian join*. The Cartesian join is just a simplified form of a merge join, so in a sense there are just three and a half join methods.

When an execution plan is displayed by DBMS_XPLAN the two operands of a join operation appear, one on top of the other, at the same level of indentation. In Chapter 1 I introduced the terms *driving row source* to refer to the top row source in the display and *probe row source* to refer to the bottom row source. As we shall shortly see, this terminology is appropriate for nested loops, merge joins, and Cartesian joins. To avoid confusion I will also refer to the top row source of a hash join as the driving row source and the bottom operand as the probe source, even though, as will be soon made clear, the terms aren't entirely appropriate in the case of a hash join.

Chapter 1 also introduced some syntax for describing join orders. The syntax (T1 ➜ T2) ➜ T3 describes what I will refer to as a *join tree* involving two joins. The first join to occur is between T1 and T2, with T1 being the driving row source and T2 being the probe row source. This join creates an *intermediate result set* that becomes the driving row source of a second join operation, with T3 as the probe row source. I will continue to use the same terminology throughout this chapter. Let us now look at the first of the four join methods, nested loops.

Nested loops

The nested loops join method, and only the nested loops join method, can be used to support *correlated row sources* by means of a left lateral join. I will address left lateral joins shortly, but let me first look at what I will refer to as traditional nested loops, which implement joins between uncorrelated row sources.

Traditional nested loops

Listing 11-1 joins the two most famous Oracle database tables from the most famous example database schema.

Listing 11-1. Joining EMP and DEPT using nested loops (10.2.0.5)

```
SELECT  /*+
gather_plan_statistics
optimizer_features_enable('10.2.0.5')
leading(e)
use_nl(d)
index(d)
*/
      e.*, d.loc
  FROM scott.emp e, scott.dept d
 WHERE hiredate > DATE '1980-12-17' AND e.deptno = d.deptno;

SET LINES 200 PAGES 0

SELECT * FROM TABLE (DBMS_XPLAN.display_cursor (format=>
                        'BASIC +IOSTATS LAST -BYTES -ROWS +PREDICATE'));
```

```
-----------------------------------------------------------------
| Id  | Operation                    | Name    | Starts | A-Rows |
-----------------------------------------------------------------
|   0 | SELECT STATEMENT             |         |      1 |     13 |
|   1 |  NESTED LOOPS                |         |      1 |     13 |  -- Extra columns
|*  2 |   TABLE ACCESS FULL          | EMP     |      1 |     13 |  -- removed
|   3 |   TABLE ACCESS BY INDEX ROWID| DEPT    |     13 |     13 |
|*  4 |    INDEX UNIQUE SCAN         | PK_DEPT |     13 |     13 |
-----------------------------------------------------------------

Predicate Information (identified by operation id):
---------------------------------------------------

   2 - filter("HIREDATE">TO_DATE(' 1980-12-17 00:00:00', 'syyyy-mm-dd
           hh24:mi:ss'))
   4 - access("E"."DEPTNO"="D"."DEPTNO")
```

Listing 11-1 joins the EMP and DEPT tables from the example SCOTT schema. I have once again used hints to generate the execution plan I want to discuss, as the CBO would have picked a more efficient plan otherwise. I have used the LEADING hint to specify that the driving row source is the EMP table and an INDEX hint so that DEPT is accessed by an index. So that I can explain different aspects of nested loops in stages, I have also used the OPTIMIZER_FEATURES_ENABLE hint so that the 10.2.0.5 implementation is used. The GATHER_PLAN_STATISTICS hint is used to get runtime data from DBMS_XPLAN.DISPLAY_CURSOR.

The NESTED LOOPS operation on line 1 begins by accessing the driving table EMP. The semantics of an inner join mean that logically all predicates in the WHERE clause are processed after the join operation. However, in reality the predicate hiredate > DATE '1980-12-17' is specific to the EMP table and the CBO eliminates any row that doesn't match this filter condition as soon as possible, as is confirmed by the predicate section of the execution plan in Listing 11-1 that shows the filter being applied by operation 2. As each of the 13 rows in EMP with a suitable hiring date are found, the rows from DEPT matching the join predicate e.deptno = d.deptno are identified and returned.

Although three matching rows in EMP have a DEPTNO of 10, five have a DEPTNO of 20, and five of the thirteen rows have a value of 30 for DEPTNO, it is still possible to use an index on DEPT.DEPTNO. The pseudo-code looks something like this:

```
For each row in EMP subset
LOOP
        For each matching row in DEPT
        LOOP
        <return row>
        END LOOP
END LOOP
```

Hence the term *nested loops*. You can see from the STARTS column of the DBMS_XPLAN.DISPLAY_CURSOR results that the index lookup on PK_DEPT on line 4 and the DEPT table access on line 3 have been performed 13 times, once for each matching row from EMP.

■ **Tip** The STARTS column for the probe row source of a nested loops operation usually matches the A-ROWS columns for the driving row source. This same tip applies to the LAST_STARTS and LAST_OUTPUT_ROWS in V$STATISTICS_PLAN_ALL. *Semi-joins* and *anti-joins* are exceptions to this rule as these take advantage of scalar subquery caching. I will cover semi-joins and anti-joins shortly.

Listing 11-2 lets us see what happens when we change the OPTIMIZER_FEATURES_ENABLE hint to enable some 11gR1 functionality.

Listing 11-2. Joining EMP and DEPT using a nested loop (11.2.0.1)

```
SELECT   /*+
gather_plan_statistics
optimizer_features_enable('11.2.0.1')
leading(e)
use_nl(d)
index(d)
no_nlj_batching(d)
*/
        e.*, d.loc
  FROM scott.emp e, scott.dept d
WHERE hiredate > DATE '1980-12-17' AND e.deptno = d.deptno;

SET LINES 200 PAGES 0

SELECT * FROM TABLE (DBMS_XPLAN.display_cursor (format=>
                          'BASIC +IOSTATS LAST -BYTES -ROWS +PREDICATE'));
```

```
-----------------------------------------------------------------------
| Id  | Operation                   | Name    | Starts | E-Rows | A-Rows |
-----------------------------------------------------------------------
|   0 | SELECT STATEMENT            |         |    0 |        |      0 |
|   1 |  TABLE ACCESS BY INDEX ROWID| DEPT    |    1 |      1 |     13 |
|   2 |   NESTED LOOPS              |         |    1 |     13 |     27 |
|*  3 |    TABLE ACCESS FULL        | EMP     |    1 |     13 |     13 |
|*  4 |    INDEX UNIQUE SCAN        | PK_DEPT |   13 |      1 |     13 |
-----------------------------------------------------------------------
```

Predicate Information (identified by operation id):

```
   3 - filter("HIREDATE">TO_DATE(' 1980-12-17 00:00:00', 'syyyy-mm-dd hh24:mi:ss'))
   4 - access("E"."DEPTNO"="D"."DEPTNO")
```

In addition to the change in the OPTIMIZER_FEATURES_ENABLE parameter, Listing 11-2 also disables one of the new features of 11gR1 by using the NO_NLJ_BATCHING hint. The execution plan in Listing 11-2 differs from that in Listing 11-1 in that the join operation is a child of operation 1—the TABLE ACCESS BY INDEX ROWID. This approach is called nested loop prefetching and was available in 9i for an INDEX RANGE SCAN, but only became available for an INDEX UNIQUE SCAN in 11gR1. Nested loop prefetching allows operation 1 to obtain a number of ROWIDs from its child operation on line 2 before deciding what to do next. In the case where the returned ROWIDs are in consecutive blocks, none of which are in the buffer cache, operation 1 can gain some performance by making a single multi-block read in lieu of multiple single-block reads. Notice that in Listing 11-1 the TABLE ACCESS BY INDEX ROWID operation on line 3 shows a value of 13 in the STARTS column, as opposed to operation 1 in Listing 11-2, which shows a value of 1. In the latter case one invocation of operation 1 is sufficient as all the ROWIDs are obtained from the child on line 2.

Listing 11-3 shows what happens when we remove the two hints in bold from Listing 11-2.

Listing 11-3. Nested loops join batching

```
SELECT   /*+
gather_plan_statistics
leading(e)
use_nl(d)
```

```
index(d)
*/
      e.*, d.loc
  FROM scott.emp e, scott.dept d
WHERE hiredate > DATE '1980-12-17' AND e.deptno = d.deptno;

SET LINES 200 PAGES 0

SELECT *
  FROM TABLE (
          DBMS_XPLAN.display_cursor (
              format   => 'BASIC +IOSTATS LAST -BYTES +PREDICATE'));
```

```
---------------------------------------------------------------------------
| Id  | Operation                   | Name    | Starts | E-Rows | A-Rows |
---------------------------------------------------------------------------
|   0 | SELECT STATEMENT            |         |      1 |        |     13 |
|   1 |  NESTED LOOPS               |         |      1 |        |     13 |
|   2 |   NESTED LOOPS              |         |      1 |     13 |     13 |
|*  3 |    TABLE ACCESS FULL        | EMP     |      1 |     13 |     13 |
|*  4 |    INDEX UNIQUE SCAN        | PK_DEPT |     13 |      1 |     13 |
|   5 |   TABLE ACCESS BY INDEX ROWID| DEPT   |     13 |      1 |     13 |
---------------------------------------------------------------------------
```

Here we have employed an optimization known as *nested loop batching*. We now have two NESTED LOOPS operations for one join. Although nested loop batching is *not* officially an optimizer transformation, the CBO has effectively transformed the original query into that shown in Listing 11-4.

Listing 11-4. Simulating 11g nested loops in 10g

```
SELECT  /*+ leading(e d1)
use_nl(d)
index(d)
rowid(d)
optimizer_features_enable('10.2.0.5') */
      e.*, d.loc
  FROM scott.emp e, scott.dept d1, scott.dept d
 WHERE     e.hiredate > DATE '1980-12-17'
       AND e.deptno = d1.deptno
       AND d.ROWID = d1.ROWID;
```

```
-------------------------------------------------
| Id  | Operation                   | Name    |
-------------------------------------------------
|   0 | SELECT STATEMENT            |         |
|   1 |  NESTED LOOPS               |         |
|   2 |   NESTED LOOPS              |         |
|   3 |    TABLE ACCESS FULL        | EMP     |
|   4 |    INDEX UNIQUE SCAN        | PK_DEPT |
|   5 |   TABLE ACCESS BY USER ROWID| DEPT    |
-------------------------------------------------
```

The execution plan in Listing 11-4 is remarkably similar to that in Listing 11-3 even though the OPTIMIZER_FEATURES_ENABLE hint disables all 11g features. The query in Listing 11-4 includes two copies of DEPT and one copy of EMP, making three row sources in total, and, therefore, two joins are necessary. The one difference between the execution plans in Listings 12-3 and 12-4 is that since we have specified ROWIDs ourselves in Listing 11-4 the access to the table is by means of a TABLE ACCESS BY USER ROWID operation rather than by the TABLE ACCESS BY INDEX ROWID operation in Listing 11-3.

The performance benefits of nested loop batching are not obvious from the DBMS_XPLAN display: the STARTS column for operations 4 and 5 in Listing 11-3 still shows 13 probes for 13 rows, but in some cases physical and logical I/O operations may be reduced nonetheless.

■ **Tip** You will notice in Listing 11-3 see that the E-ROWS column (estimated rows) for operations 4 and 5 of the execution plan shows a value of 1 and the A-ROWS column (actual rows) shows a value of 13. This is *not* a cardinality error by the CBO. In the case of NESTED LOOPS the estimated row count is *per iteration* of the loop whereas the actual row count is for *all iterations* of the loop.

Nested loops have the desirable property that they usually *scale linearly*. By that I mean that if EMP and DEPT double in size the nested loop will take twice as much time (as opposed to much more).

However, nested loops have two undesirable performance properties:

- Unless the probe table is part of a hash cluster (oops! I said I wouldn't mention hash clusters again) or is very small, an index is required on the joined column or columns, in this case DEPT.DEPTNO. If such an index is not present then we might need to visit every row in DEPT for every row in EMP. Not only is this often very costly in itself, it also wrecks the scalability property of the join: if we double the size of EMP and DEPT then the loop takes four times as long because we access DEPT twice as often, because EMP is twice as big, and each scan takes twice as long, because DEPT is twice as big. Note that indexing is usually not possible if the probe row source of the nested loop is a subquery or inline view. For this reason, when joining a table and a subquery or inline view using nested loops, the probe row source will almost always be the table.

- When the probe row source is a table, blocks in the probed table may be visited many times, picking out different rows each time.

Left Lateral Joins

Prior to release 12cR1, a left lateral join was only available in conjunction with the TABLE and XMLTABLE operators that we covered in Chapter 10. I have showed an example of a join involving DBMS_XPLAN.DISPLAY in Listing 8-9. In release 12cR1 this useful feature has become more accessible by means of the LATERAL keyword. Listing 11-5 shows an example of its use.

Listing 11-5. Left lateral join

```
SELECT e1.*, e3.avg_sal
  FROM scott.emp e1
      ,LATERAL (SELECT AVG (e2.sal) avg_sal
                  FROM scott.emp e2
                 WHERE e1.deptno != e2.deptno) e3;
```

```
-------------------------------------------------
| Id  | Operation             | Name            |
-------------------------------------------------
|   0 | SELECT STATEMENT      |                 |
|   1 |  NESTED LOOPS         |                 |
|   2 |   TABLE ACCESS FULL   | EMP             |
|   3 |   VIEW                | VW_LAT_A18161FF |
|   4 |    SORT AGGREGATE     |                 |
|*  5 |     TABLE ACCESS FULL | EMP             |
-------------------------------------------------

Predicate Information (identified by operation id):
---------------------------------------------------

   5 - filter("E1"."DEPTNO"<>"E2"."DEPTNO")
```

Listing 11-5 lists the details of each employee together with the average salaries of all employees in departments other than that in which the employee in question works.

A left lateral join is always implemented by nested loops, and the inline view preceded by LATERAL is always the probe row source. The key advantage of lateral joins is that predicates can be used in the inline view derived from columns in the driving row source. I will use lateral joins to great effect when I look at optimizing sorts in Chapter 17.

It is possible to perform an outer lateral join by placing the characters (+) after the inline view, but as I explained in Chapter 1 I prefer to use ANSI syntax for outer joins. ANSI syntax uses the keywords CROSS APPLY for an inner lateral join and OUTER APPLY for an outer lateral join; I will provide examples of both variants when I cover optimizer transformations in Chapter 13.

Hash joins

There are two variants of the hash join depending on whether join inputs are swapped or not. Let us discuss the standard hash join without join input swapping first and then consider the variation in which join inputs are swapped as part of a wider discussion of join orders a little later in this chapter.

Let us begin by looking at Listing 11-6, which changes the hints in Listing 11-3 to specify a hash join rather than a nested loop.

Listing 11-6. Hash join

```
SELECT /*+ gather_plan_statistics
leading(e)
use_hash(d)
*/
      e.*, d.loc
  FROM scott.emp e, scott.dept d
 WHERE hiredate > DATE '1980-12-17' AND e.deptno = d.deptno;

SELECT *
  FROM TABLE (DBMS_XPLAN.display_cursor (format => 'BASIC +IOSTATS LAST'));
```

```
--------------------------------------------------------------
| Id  | Operation          | Name | Starts | E-Rows | A-Rows |
--------------------------------------------------------------
|   0 | SELECT STATEMENT   |      |      1 |        |     13 |
|*  1 |  HASH JOIN         |      |      1 |     13 |     13 |
|*  2 |   TABLE ACCESS FULL| EMP  |      1 |     13 |     13 |
|   3 |   TABLE ACCESS FULL| DEPT |      1 |      4 |      4 |
--------------------------------------------------------------

Predicate Information (identified by operation id):
---------------------------------------------------

   1 - access("E"."DEPTNO"="D"."DEPTNO")
   2 - filter("HIREDATE">TO_DATE(' 1980-12-17 00:00:00', 'syyyy-mm-dd
             hh24:mi:ss'))
```

The hash join operates by placing the 13 rows from EMP that match the selection predicate into a workarea containing an in-memory hash cluster keyed on EMP.DEPTNO. The hash join then makes a single pass through the probe table DEPT, and for each row we apply the hash to D.DEPTNO and find any matching rows in EMP.

In this regard the hash join is similar to a nested loops join, with DEPT as the driving row source and the copy of the EMP table stored in the in-memory hash cluster as the probe row source. Nevertheless, for consistency I will continue to refer to EMP as the driving row source in our join. Hash joins have the following advantages over nested loops when the probe row source is a table:

- Every block in the probe table is visited at most once and not potentially multiple times as with a nested loop.

- No index is required on the join column in the probe table.

- If a full table scan (or fast full index scan) is used for accessing the probe table then multi-block reads can be used, which are much more efficient than single-block reads through an index.

- Join inputs can be swapped. We will discuss *hash join input swapping* very shortly.

However, hash joins have the following disadvantages:

- If a block in the probe table contains no rows that match any of the rows in the driving row source it may still be visited. So, for example, if the size of the probe table was 1TB, there was no selection predicate, and only two rows matched the join predicates, we would scan the whole 1TB table rather than picking out two rows through an index.

- While both join operands are small, hash joins scale linearly as nested loops do. However, if the driving row source gets too big the hash table will spill onto disk, ruining the linear performance properties.

- Hash joins can only be used with equality join predicates.

When an index is available on the probe row source it may be that a nested loops join will visit some blocks multiple times and some not at all. Deciding between the nested loops join with an index and the hash join that visits all blocks exactly once via a full table scan can be difficult. The optimizer uses the selectivity of the join predicate in conjunction with the clustering factor of the index to help determine the correct course of action, as we discussed in Chapter 9.

Merge joins

A merge join is very similar to a merge sort. Both the driving and probe row sources are sorted to start with and placed into process-private workareas. We then proceed in a way similar to that for a nested loops join: for each row in the driving row source we look for all the rows in the probe row source that match that one row in the driving row source. In the case of an equality join predicate such as T1.C1=T2.C2 we can proceed through the two sorted sets in step. However, merge joins can also take advantage of *range-based join predicates,* such as T1.C1 < T2.C2. In this case, we may need to "backup" the point at which we examine the sorted probe row source as we advance through the driving row source.

Consider Listing 11-7, which includes a range-based join predicate.

Listing 11-7. Query containing a range-based join predicate

```
CREATE TABLE t1
AS
    SELECT ROWNUM c1
      FROM all_objects
     WHERE ROWNUM <= 100;

CREATE TABLE t2
AS
    SELECT c1 + 1 c2 FROM t1;

CREATE TABLE t3
AS
    SELECT c2 + 1 c3 FROM t2;

CREATE TABLE t4
AS
    SELECT c3 + 1 c4 FROM t3;

SELECT /*+ leading (t1) use_merge(t2) */
       *
  FROM t1, t2
 WHERE t1.c1 > 3 AND t2.c2 < t1.c1;
```

```
-------------------------------------
| Id  | Operation          | Name |
-------------------------------------
|   0 | SELECT STATEMENT   |      |
|   1 |  MERGE JOIN        |      |
|   2 |   SORT JOIN        |      |
|   3 |    TABLE ACCESS FULL| T1  |
|   4 |   SORT JOIN        |      |
|   5 |    TABLE ACCESS FULL| T2  |
-------------------------------------
```

Figure 11-1 shows how a merge join driven by T1 would be implemented:

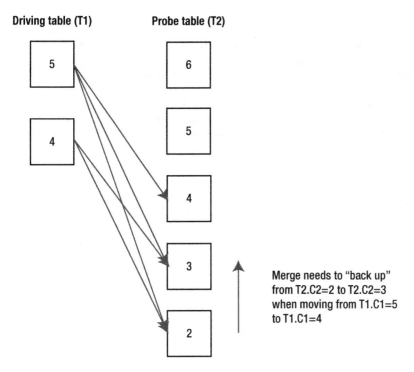

Driving table (T1)   **Probe table (T2)**

Merge needs to "back up"
from T2.C2=2 to T2.C2=3
when moving from T1.C1=5
to T1.C1=4

Figure 11-1. *A merge join*

Notice how:

- Both T1 and T2 have been sorted in descending order because of the "<" predicate. If the predicate were "=", ">", or ">=" both tables would have been sorted in ascending order.

- Because of the selection predicate the workarea for T1 only contains two rows.

Merge joins are a relatively rare choice of join mechanism these days but can be useful under one or more of the following conditions:

- The first row source is already sorted, avoiding the need for the first of the two sorts normally performed by the merge join. Be aware that the second row source is always sorted even if it is sorted to start with!

- The row sources are required to be sorted by the join column (for example, because of an ORDER BY clause). As the results of the join are generated ready-sorted, the extra step is avoided.

- There is no index on the joined columns and/or the selectivity/clustering factor is weak (making nested loops unattractive).

- The join predicate is a range predicate (ruling out hash joins).

- Both row sources being joined are so large that neither can be hashed into memory (making hash joins unattractive). Be aware that merge joins can also spill onto disk, but the impact may not be as bad as for hash joins that spill onto disk.

Cartesian joins

Cartesian joins are very similar to merge joins (they appear as MERGE JOIN CARTESIAN in the execution plan). This is the join method of last resort and is almost only used when there is no join predicate available (unless you use the undocumented and probably useless USE_MERGE_CARTESIAN hint). This join method operates just like a merge join except that as every row in the driving row source matches every row in the probe row source no sorts take place. It may seem like one sort occurs because you will see a BUFFER SORT operation in the execution plan but this is misleading. There is buffering but no sorting. If there are m rows in the driving row source and n rows in the probe row source then there will be m x n rows returned by the join. Cartesian joins should not be a performance concern provided that m x n is small and/or either m or n is zero. Listing 11-8 shows a Cartesian join.

Listing 11-8. Cartesian join

```
SELECT /*+ leading (t1) use_merge_cartesian(t2) */
       *
  FROM t1, t2;
---------------------------------------
| Id | Operation            | Name |
---------------------------------------
|  0 | SELECT STATEMENT     |      |
|  1 |  MERGE JOIN CARTESIAN|      |
|  2 |   TABLE ACCESS FULL  | T1   |
|  3 |   BUFFER SORT        |      |
|  4 |    TABLE ACCESS FULL | T2   |
---------------------------------------
```

Just to repeat, the BUFFER SORT operation buffers but does *not* sort.

Join Orders

Hash join input swapping is a mechanism for generating additional join orders that wouldn't otherwise be available to the CBO. However, before we get into hash join input swapping let us make sure we understand the legal join orders available without hash join input swapping first.

Join orders without hash join input swapping

Prior to the implementation of hash join input swapping the following restrictions on join order applied:

- The first join would have been between two row sources from the FROM clause generating an intermediate result set.

- The second and all subsequent joins would use the intermediate result set from the preceding join as the driving row source and a row source from the FROM clause as the probe row source.

Let me provide an example. If we join the four tables we created in Listing 1-18, T1, T2, T3, and T4, with inner joins, then one possible join tree is ((T1 ➜ T2) ➜ T3) ➜ T4. You can shuffle the tables around. You have four choices for the first table, three for the second, two for the third, and one for the fourth, generating 24 possible legal join orders. This type of join ordering results in what is known as a *left-deep join tree*. The reason for the term is clear if we draw the joins in a diagram as in Figure 11-2.

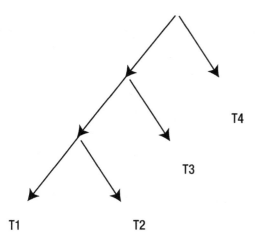

Figure 11-2. *Left-deep join tree*

Figure 11-2 shows arrows pointing downwards because the join operations invoke their children to access the tables. However, you might prefer to draw the arrows pointing upwards; doing so would reflect how the data flows.

The left-deep join tree leads to a simple set of optimizer hints for specifying join order and join method:

- The LEADING hint specifies the first few (or all) row sources in the join. For example, LEADING(T1 T2) forces the CBO to join T1 and T2 to start with. T1 must be the driving row source and T2 the probe row source. Whether T3 or T4 is joined next is up to the CBO.

- The hints USE_NL, USE_HASH, USE_MERGE, and USE_MERGE_CARTESIAN specify join methods. To identify which join the hint refers to, we use the name of the probe row source.

This is all a bit abstract, but hopefully the example in Listing 11-9 will make things clear.

Listing 11-9. Fully specifying join orders and join methods

```
SELECT /*+
leading (t4 t3 t2 t1)
use_nl(t3)
use_nl(t2)
use_nl(t1)
*/
       *
  FROM t1
       ,t2
       ,t3
       ,t4
 WHERE t1.c1 = t2.c2 AND t2.c2 = t3.c3 AND t3.c3 = t4.c4;
```

```
-------------------------------------
| Id | Operation            | Name |
-------------------------------------
|  0 | SELECT STATEMENT     |      |
|  1 |  NESTED LOOPS        |      |
|  2 |   NESTED LOOPS       |      |
|  3 |    NESTED LOOPS      |      |
|  4 |     TABLE ACCESS FULL| T4   |
|  5 |     TABLE ACCESS FULL| T3   |
|  6 |    TABLE ACCESS FULL | T2   |
|  7 |   TABLE ACCESS FULL  | T1   |
-------------------------------------
```

The LEADING hint in Listing 11-9 has specified all the tables, so the join order is fixed as ((T4 ➜ T3) ➜ T2) ➜ T1. When hinting the join mechanisms, the three joins are identified by their respective probe row sources: T3, T2, and T1. In this case a hint specifying T4 would be meaningless as it is not the probe row source in any join.

Join orders with hash join input swapping

In the case of hash joins, and hash joins only, the optimizer can swap the inputs to a join without the need for inline views. So, for example, suppose we started out with a join order ((T1 ➜ T2) ➜ T3) ➜ T4 and we swapped the inputs to the final join with T4. We end up with T4 ➜ ((T1 ➜ T2) ➜ T3). We now have, for the first time, a join with a probe row source that is an intermediate result set. Let us continue the process and swap the join inputs for the second join with T3. This yields T4 ➜ (T3 ➜ (T1 ➜ T2)). We also have the option of swapping the join with T2. The result of swapping the join inputs of the join of T1 and T2 is (T4 ➜ (T3 ➜ (T2 ➜ T1))). Swapping the join inputs of the join of T1 and T2 seems pointless: we could just change the join order instead. But let us not get distracted. I'll soon show you why swapping the join inputs of the first join might be useful. Listing 11-10 shows how we might hint the query in Listing 11-9 in different ways to control join input swapping.

Listing 11-10. A simple example comparing swapped and unswapped join inputs

```
SELECT /*+                        SELECT /*+
leading (t1 t2 t3 t4)             leading (t1 t2 t3 t4)
use_hash(t2)                      use_hash(t2)
use_hash(t3)                      use_hash(t3)
use_hash(t4)                      use_hash(t4)
no_swap_join_inputs(t2)                swap_join_inputs(t2)
```

```
no_swap_join_inputs(t3)                          swap_join_inputs(t3)
no_swap_join_inputs(t4)                          swap_join_inputs(t4)
*/                                          */
        *                                           *
   FROM t1                                       FROM t1
       ,t2                                           ,t2
       ,t3                                           ,t3
       ,t4                                           ,t4
  WHERE t1.c1 = t2.c2                          WHERE t1.c1 = t2.c2
    AND t2.c2 = t3.c3                            AND t2.c2 = t3.c3
    AND t3.c3 = t4.c4;                           AND t3.c3 = t4.c4;
```

Id	Operation	Name		Id	Operation	Name
0	SELECT STATEMENT			0	SELECT STATEMENT	
1	HASH JOIN			1	HASH JOIN	
2	|HASH JOIN			2	|TABLE ACCESS FULL	T4
3	| |HASH JOIN			3	|HASH JOIN	
4	| | |TABLE ACCESS FULL	T1		4	| |TABLE ACCESS FULL	T3
5	| | |TABLE ACCESS FULL	T2		5	| |HASH JOIN	
6	| |TABLE ACCESS FULL	T3		6	| | |TABLE ACCESS FULL	T2
7	|TABLE ACCESS FULL	T4		7	| | |TABLE ACCESS FULL	T1

The left-hand side of Listing 11-10 shows the traditional left-deep join tree with none of the join inputs swapped. This has been enforced with the use of NO_SWAP_JOIN_INPUTS hints. You will notice that the intermediate result set from the join on line 3 is used as the driving row source of the join on line 2 (line 3 is vertically above line 6) and that the intermediate result set of the join on line 2 is the driving row source of the join on line 1 (line 2 is vertically above line 7). I have added some lines to the DBMS_XPLAN output in order to make the alignment clear.

On the other hand, the right-hand side of Listing 11-10 swaps all join inputs by means of SWAP_JOIN_INPUTS hints. Now you can see that the intermediate result set formed by the join on line 5 is the probe row source of the join on line 3 (line 5 is vertically below line 4), and the intermediate result set formed by the join on line 3 is the probe row source of the join on line 1 (line 3 is vertically below line 2). The result of swapping all join inputs is referred to as a right-deep join tree and is depicted pictorially by Figure 12-3.

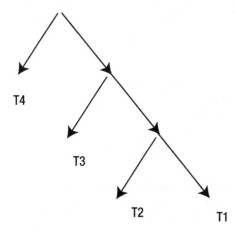

Figure 11-3. *Right-deep join tree*

■ **Note** If some joins in a query have their inputs swapped and others do not then the resulting join tree is referred to as a *zigzag* tree. Join trees such as (T1 ➜ T2) ➜ (T3 ➜ T4) are referred to as *bushy* joins, but bushy joins are never considered by the CBO.

Now that the CBO has created this right-deep join tree, what does the runtime engine do with it? Well, despite the LEADING hint claiming that we start with table T1, the runtime engine actually begins by placing the selected rows from T4 into an in-memory hash cluster in a workarea. It then places the contents of T3 into a second workarea and T2 into a third. What then happens is that T1 is scanned and rows from T1 are matched with T2. The results of any matches of T1 and T2 are matched with rows from T3. Finally, the matching rows from the joins of T1, T2, and T3 are matched against the rows from T4.

The benefits of a right-deep join tree may not be immediately apparent. At first glance a left-deep join tree seems more memory efficient than a right-deep join tree. The runtime engine begins processing the join operation on line 3 in the left-deep join tree in Listing 11-10 by placing T1 into a workarea. As T2 is scanned and matches are found, the joined rows are placed into a second workarea associated with the join on line 2. At the conclusion of the scan of T2 the workarea containing T1 is no longer required and is dropped before the new workarea needed by operation 1 to receive the results of the join with T3 is created. So a left-deep join tree only ever has two workareas. On the other hand, a right-deep join tree with n joins requires n concurrent workareas.

The best way to understand the benefits of right-deep join trees is to look at an example from data warehousing. Listing 11-11 uses tables from the SH example schema.

Listing 11-11. Swapped hash join inputs in a data warehousing environment

```
SELECT *                            SELECT /*+
  FROM sh.sales                              leading (sales customers products)
     JOIN sh.products                        use_hash(customers)
        USING (prod_id)             use_hash(products)
     LEFT JOIN sh.customers         no_swap_join_inputs(customers)
        USING (cust_id);            swap_join_inputs(products)
                                          */ *
                                    FROM sh.sales
                                       JOIN sh.products USING (prod_id)
                                       LEFT JOIN sh.customers USING (cust_id);
```

```
-------------------------------------------    -------------------------------------------
| Id| Operation             | Name        |    | Id| Operation             | Name        |
-------------------------------------------    -------------------------------------------
|  0 | SELECT STATEMENT      |             |    |  0 | SELECT STATEMENT      |             |
|  1 |  HASH JOIN            |             |    |  1 |  HASH JOIN            |             |
|  2 |   TABLE ACCESS FULL   | PRODUCTS    |    |  2 |   TABLE ACCESS FULL   | PRODUCTS    |
|  3 |   HASH JOIN RIGHT OUTER|            |    |  3 |   HASH JOIN OUTER     |             |
|  4 |    TABLE ACCESS FULL  | CUSTOMERS   |    |  4 |    PARTITION RANGE ALL|             |
|  5 |    PARTITION RANGE ALL |            |    |  5 |     TABLE ACCESS FULL | SALES       |
|  6 |     TABLE ACCESS FULL | SALES       |    |  6 |    TABLE ACCESS FULL  | CUSTOMERS   |
-------------------------------------------    -------------------------------------------
```

Listing 11-11 joins the SALES table with the CUSTOMERS and PRODUCTS tables, both with and without hints. The actual SALES data always specifies a customer for each sale, but for demonstration purposes I want to protect against the possibility that the CUST_ID field in the SALES table may be NULL, so I will use an outer join to ensure rows in SALES are not lost.

The biggest table in Listing 2-9 is SALES, with 918,843 rows, and so we would like to read that table last to avoid building a huge hash cluster that may not fit into memory. The PRODUCTS table has 72 rows and the CUSTOMERS table has 55,500 rows, but, unfortunately, there is no predicate on which to join the PRODUCTS and CUSTOMERS tables, and the result of joining them with a Cartesian join would be to yield an intermediate result with 3,996,000 rows (72 x 55,500). Let us see how the CBO addresses the problem.

If you look closely you will see that the join order from the unhinted query is PRODUCTS ➔ (CUSTOMERS ➔ SALES)—a right-deep join tree. Rather than joining PRODUCTS and CUSTOMERS with a Cartesian join, generating one huge workarea, we have created one workarea with 72 rows and another workarea with 55,500 rows. The SALES table is then scanned once, and the query returns rows from SALES that match both the CUSTOMERS and PRODUCTS tables. So that's the answer. Right-deep join trees can be used when joining one big table with multiple small tables by creating multiple small workareas rather than one or more big ones.

There is one more interesting observation to make about the unhinted execution plan in Listing 11-11: the preserved row source in the outer join on line 3 is the probe row source.

The HASH JOIN RIGHT OUTER operation in Listing 11-11 works as follows:

- Rows from CUSTOMERS table are placed into a hash cluster.

- All the partitions of SALES are scanned. Each row from SALES is matched against CUSTOMERS and any matches are passed to the join with PRODUCTS.

- If there are no matches in CUSTOMERS for a row from SALES then the row from SALES is still passed up to the join with PRODUCTS.

The right-hand side of Listing 11-11 uses hints to suppress the swapping of the inputs of the SALES and CUSTOMERS tables but is otherwise identical to the left-hand side. The HASH JOIN OUTER operation works in a completely different way:

- The SALES table is placed into the in-memory hash cluster (not good for performance on this occasion).

- The CUSTOMERS table is scanned and any matches found in SALES are passed up to the join with PRODUCTS.

- When matches are found, the entries in the SALES in-memory hash cluster are marked.

- At the end of the scan of CUSTOMERS any entries from the SALES hash cluster that have not been marked are passed to the join with PRODUCTS.

OUTER JOIN OPERATIONS

There are a number of operations that support different flavors of outer join. These include NESTED LOOPS OUTER, HASH JOIN OUTER, HASH JOIN RIGHT OUTER, HASH JOIN FULL OUTER, MERGE JOIN OUTER, and MERGE JOIN PARTITION OUTER.

- Only the hash join mechanism directly supports full outer joins.

- For some reason the first operand of a HASH JOIN FULL OUTER operation has to be the row source written to the left of the word FULL, but the join inputs can be swapped.

- You cannot get a HASH JOIN RIGHT OUTER operation by changing the join order. You need to swap join inputs.

- With the exception of the HASH JOIN RIGHT OUTER operation, the driving row source is preserved and the probe row source is optional.

- Only nested loops and merge joins support partitioned outer joins.

Although we have now covered the implementation of all explicitly written join operations, the CBO can generate additional joins that aren't written as such. Let us move on to semi-joins, the first of the two types of joins that the CBO can fabricate.

Semi-joins

It turns out that the optimizer can transform some constructs that you don't write as joins into joins. We will begin by looking at semi-joins and then move on to anti-joins. There are two types of semi-join: standard and null-accepting semi-joins. Let us look at standard semi-joins first.

Standard semi-joins

Consider Listing 11-12, which looks for countries that have customers:

Listing 11-12. Semi-join

```
SELECT *                              SELECT *
  FROM sh.countries                     FROM sh.countries
 WHERE country_id IN (SELECT          WHERE country_id IN (SELECT /*+ NO_UNNEST */
country_id FROM sh.customers);                        country_id FROM sh.customers);
```

```
-------------------------------------      -------------------------------------
| Id| Operation          | Name      |     | Id| Operation          | Name      |
-------------------------------------      -------------------------------------
| 0 | SELECT STATEMENT   |           |     | 0 | SELECT STATEMENT   |           |
| 1 |  HASH JOIN SEMI    |           |     | 1 |  FILTER            |           |
| 2 |   TABLE ACCESS FULL| COUNTRIES |     | 2 |   TABLE ACCESS FULL| COUNTRIES |
| 3 |   TABLE ACCESS FULL| CUSTOMERS |     | 3 |   TABLE ACCESS FULL| CUSTOMERS |
-------------------------------------      -------------------------------------
```

When the runtime engine runs the execution plan on the left-hand side of Listing 11-12, it begins by creating an in-memory hash cluster of COUNTRIES as with a normal hash join and then processes the CUSTOMERS looking for a match. However, when the runtime engine finds a match, it removes the entry from the in-memory hash cluster so that the same country isn't returned again.

The process of changing a subquery into a join is called *subquery unnesting* and is an example of an optimizer transformation. We will speak more about optimizer transformations in Chapter 13, but this is a sneak preview. Like all optimizer transformations, subquery unnesting is controlled by two hints. The UNNEST hint wasn't required on the left-hand side, as the CBO chose the transformation itself. The transformation was explicitly suppressed on the right-hand side of Listing 11-12 by means of a NO_UNNEST hint. Without the aid of subquery unnesting the CUSTOMERS table is scanned 23 times, once for each row in COUNTRIES.

Nested loops semi-joins, merge semi-joins, and hash semi-joins are all possible.

- The hash join inputs for a semi-join can be swapped as with an outer join, producing a HASH JOIN RIGHT SEMI operation.

- You can control subquery unnesting with the UNNEST and NO_UNNEST hints.

- Applying local hints to execution plans involving subquery unnesting can be a little awkward, as demonstrated earlier by Listing 8-17.

- You may see semi-joins when you use any of the following constructs:

  - IN (...)

  - EXISTS (...)

  - = ANY (...), > ANY(...), < ANY (...)

  - <= ANY (...), >=ANY (...)

  - = SOME (...), > SOME(...), < SOME (...)

  - <= SOME (...), >=SOME (...)

Null-accepting semi-joins

Release 12cR1 extended semi-join unnesting to incorporate queries like the one in Listing 11-13:

Listing 11-13. Null-accepting semi-join in 12cR1

```
SELECT *
  FROM t1
 WHERE   t1.c1 IS NULL OR
       EXISTS
            (SELECT *
               FROM t2
              WHERE t1.c1 = t2.c2);
```

```
-------------------------------------    -------------------------------------
| Id | Operation          | Name |       | Id | Operation          | Name |
-------------------------------------    -------------------------------------
|  0 | SELECT STATEMENT   |      |       |  0 | SELECT STATEMENT   |      |
|* 1 |  FILTER            |      |       |* 1 |  HASH JOIN SEMI NA |      |
|  2 |   TABLE ACCESS FULL| T1   |       |  2 |   TABLE ACCESS FULL| T1   |
|* 3 |   TABLE ACCESS FULL| T2   |       |  3 |   TABLE ACCESS FULL| T2   |
-------------------------------------    -------------------------------------


Predicate Information                    Predicate Information
---------------------                    ---------------------

  1 - filter("T1"."C1" IS NULL OR        1 - access("T1"."C1"="T2"."C2")
      EXISTS (SELECT 0
   FROM "T2" "T2" WHERE "T2"."C2"=:B1))
  3 - filter("T2"."C2"=:B1)
```

Queries like that shown in Listing 11-13 are quite common. The idea is that we return rows from T1 when either a match with T2.C2 is found *or* T1.C1 is NULL. Prior to 12cR1 such constructs would prohibit subquery unnesting and the left-hand execution plan in Listing 11-13 would have resulted. In 12cR1 the HASH JOIN SEMI NA and HASH JOIN RIGHT SEMI NA operations were introduced, which ensure that rows from T1 where T1.C1 is NULL are returned in addition to those that match T2.C2, and the execution plan shown on the right in Listing 11-13 results.

Anti-joins

Another type of subquery unnesting that you might see is called an *anti-join*. An anti-join looks for mismatches rather than matches, which is what we have been doing so far. As with semi-joins, there are two types of anti-joins: standard and null-aware.

Standard anti-joins

Listing 11-14 looks for invalid countries in the customers table.

Listing 11-14. Standard anti-join

```
SELECT /*+ leading(c) */ *              SELECT *
   FROM sh.customers c                    FROM sh.customers c
WHERE country_id                         WHERE country_id  NOT IN (SELECT country_id
NOT IN (SELECT country_id                                         FROM sh.countries);
       FROM sh.countries);
```

```
-------------------------------------          ------------------------------------------------
| Id| Operation          | Name       |        | Id| Operation          | Name           |
-------------------------------------          ------------------------------------------------
| 0 | SELECT STATEMENT   |            |        | 0 | SELECT STATEMENT   |                |
| 1 | NESTED LOOPS ANTI  |            |        | 1 | HASH JOIN RIGHT ANTI|               |
| 2 |  TABLE ACCESS FULL| CUSTOMERS   |        | 2 |  INDEX FULL SCAN   | COUNTRIES_PK   |
| 3 |  INDEX UNIQUE SCAN| COUNTRIES_PK |       | 3 |  TABLE ACCESS FULL  | CUSTOMERS      |
-------------------------------------          ------------------------------------------------
```

I have hinted the left-hand side of Listing 11-14 once again for demonstration purposes. For each row in CUSTOMERS we look for COUNTRIES that match, but return a row from CUSTOMERS only if a match is *not* found. Nested loops anti-joins, merge anti-joins, and hash anti-joins are all possible.

- As usual the join inputs can be swapped for hash joins. The unhinted execution plan shown on the right side of Listing 11-14 uses a hash join with swapped inputs.

- As with semi-joins, unnesting can be controlled with the UNNEST and NO_UNNEST hints.

Anti-joins may be seen when you use any of the following constructs:

- NOT IN (...)

- NOT EXISTS (...)

- != ALL (...), > ALL(...), < ALL (...), <= ALL (...), >=ALL (...)

Null-aware anti-joins

The execution plans we showed in the previous section were possible because the COUNTRY_ID column in the CUSTOMERS and COUNTRIES table were defined with NOT NULL constraints. Can you see the difference between the two queries in Listing 11-15?

Listing 11-15. NOT EXISTS versus NOT IN

```
SELECT COUNT (*)                         SELECT COUNT (*)
  FROM sh.customers c                       FROM sh.customers c
WHERE NOT EXISTS                          WHERE c.cust_src_id NOT IN (SELECT prod_src_id
        (SELECT 1                                        FROM sh.products p);
          FROM sh.products p
         WHERE prod_src_id = cust_src_id);
```

```
-----------------------------------------      -----------------------------------------------
| Id| Operation            | Name      |       | Id| Operation               | Name      |
-----------------------------------------      -----------------------------------------------
| 0 | SELECT STATEMENT     |           |       | 0 | SELECT STATEMENT        |           |
| 1 |  SORT AGGREGATE      |           |       | 1 |  SORT AGGREGATE         |           |
| 2 |   HASH JOIN RIGHT ANTI|          |       | 2 |   HASH JOIN RIGHT ANTI NA|          |
| 3 |    TABLE ACCESS FULL | PRODUCTS  |       | 3 |    TABLE ACCESS FULL    | PRODUCTS  |
| 4 |    TABLE ACCESS FULL | CUSTOMERS |       | 4 |    TABLE ACCESS FULL    | CUSTOMERS |
-----------------------------------------      -----------------------------------------------
```

No? If you run them you will see that the left-hand query returns 55,500 and the right-hand query returns 0! This is because there are products with an unspecified (NULL) PROD_SRC_ID. If a value is unspecified then we can't assert that any value is unequal to it. Listing 11-16 might be a clearer example.

Listing 11-16. Simple query with NULL in an inlist

```
SELECT *
  FROM DUAL
 WHERE 1 NOT IN (NULL);
```

The query in Listing 11-16 returns no rows, because if we don't know the value of NULL it might be 1.

Prior to 11gR1 the possibility of CUST_SRC_ID being NULL or PROD_SRC_ID being NULL would preclude the possibility of subquery unnesting for the query on the right-hand side of Listing 11-15.

The HASH JOIN RIGHT ANTI NA is the swapped join-input variant of the null-aware anti-join. The so-called single null-aware anti-joins operations, such as HASH JOIN ANTI SNA and HASH JOIN RIGHT ANTI SNA operations, would have been possible had the PROD_SRC_ID been non-null but CUST_SRC_ID been nullable. For more details on null-aware anti-joins, just type "Greg Rahn null-aware anti-join" into your favorite search engine. The discussion of null-aware anti-joins wraps up the list of topics related to joining tables in a serial execution plan. But we have some outstanding business from Chapter 8 on parallel execution plans that we are now in a position to address. Let us do that now.

Distribution Mechanisms for Parallel Joins

Chapter 8 introduced the topic of parallel execution, and in particular some of the different ways in which a parallel query server set (PQSS) can communicate through a table queue (TQ). We had to defer discussion about the distribution mechanisms associated with parallel joins until we covered serial joins, but we are now in a position to revisit the topic.

There are quite a few mechanisms by which PQSSs can communicate when they are cooperating in performing a join of two tables, some of which are applicable solely to partitioned tables and some that are applicable to any table. The extent to which the correct choice of join distribution mechanism can affect performance is not widely appreciated, so I will go through each of the distribution mechanisms in detail. But before we do that, let me discuss the way the PQ_DISTRIBUTE hint is used in relation to parallel joins.

The PQ_DISTRIBUTE hint and parallel joins

When PQ_DISTRIBUTE is used as a local hint to control load distribution, only two arguments are supplied, as I demonstrated in Listings 8-23 and 8-24. When used as a local hint to control join distribution there are three arguments. The first argument identifies the join to which the hint applies, and for that we use the name of the probe source in the same way as we do for hints such as USE_HASH. The second and third hints are used in combination to specify the distribution mechanism. I think it is time for an example. Let us start with the first of our join distribution mechanisms, *full partition-wise joins*.

Full partition-wise joins

A full partition-wise join can only happen when both of the following conditions are met:

- Both tables being joined are partitioned tables and are partitioned identically.[1]

- There is an equijoin predicate on the partitioning (or subpartitioning) columns. In other words, the partitioning column or columns from one table are equated with the corresponding partitioning columns from the other.Listing 11-17 shows two examples of the full partition-wise join in action.

Listing 11-17. Full partition-wise joins

```
CREATE TABLE t_part1
PARTITION BY HASH (c1)
   PARTITIONS 8
AS
   SELECT c1, ROWNUM AS c3 FROM t1;

CREATE TABLE t_part2
PARTITION BY HASH (c2)
   PARTITIONS 8
AS
   SELECT c1 AS c2, ROWNUM AS c4 FROM t1;

SELECT *
  FROM t_part1, t_part2
 WHERE t_part1.c1 = t_part2.c2;


-------------------------------------
| Id  | Operation            | Name    |
-------------------------------------
|   0 | SELECT STATEMENT     |         |
|   1 |  PARTITION HASH ALL  |         |
|*  2 |   HASH JOIN          |         |
|   3 |    TABLE ACCESS FULL | T_PART1 |
|   4 |    TABLE ACCESS FULL | T_PART2 |
-------------------------------------
```

---

[1]Some differences can be tolerated when composite partitioning is involved

Predicate Information (identified by operation id):

```
   2 - access("T_PART1"."C1"="T_PART2"."C2")
```

```
SELECT /*+ parallel(t_part1 8) parallel(t_part2 8) leading(t_part1)
           pq_distribute(t_part2 NONE NONE) */
       *
  FROM t_part1, t_part2
 WHERE t_part1.c1 = t_part2.c2;
```

```
-----------------------------------------------------------------------
| Id  | Operation               | Name      |  TQ  |IN-OUT| PQ Distrib |
-----------------------------------------------------------------------
|   0 | SELECT STATEMENT        |           |      |      |            |
|   1 |  PX COORDINATOR         |           |      |      |            |
|   2 |   PX SEND QC (RANDOM)   | :TQ10000  | Q1,00| P->S | QC (RAND)  |
|   3 |    PX PARTITION HASH ALL|           | Q1,00| PCWC |            |
|*  4 |     HASH JOIN           |           | Q1,00| PCWP |            |
|   5 |      TABLE ACCESS FULL  | T_PART1   | Q1,00| PCWP |            |
|   6 |      TABLE ACCESS FULL  | T_PART2   | Q1,00| PCWP |            |
-----------------------------------------------------------------------
```

Predicate Information (identified by operation id):

```
   4 - access("T_PART1"."C1"="T_PART2"."C2")
```

Listing 11-17 begins by recreating the partitioned tables T_PART1 and T_PART2 from Listing 8-23 and then joins them both serially and in parallel. Because both tables are partitioned in the same way and the join condition equates the two partitioning columns, T_PART1.C1 and T_PART2.C2, a full partition-wise join is possible. As you can see in the parallel variant, there is only one TQ and one DFO. Each parallel query server begins by reading data from one partition of T_PART1 and then joining it with the rows from the corresponding partition of T_PART2. If there are more partitions than parallel query servers it may be that a parallel query server needs to repeat the join for multiple partitions.

Full partition-wise joins support both hash joins and merge joins, but for reasons that aren't particularly clear to me nested loops seem to be illegal as of 12.1.0.1.

Because full partition-wise joins process one pair of partitions at a time, memory use is minimized, and when run in parallel there is only one DFO and no need for any communication between parallel query servers. The potential disadvantage of a parallel full partition-wise join is that partition granules are used, so load balancing may be ineffective if some partitions of one or both tables are larger than others. Before addressing this concern let us consider what happens when only one table is partitioned by the equijoin column.

Partial partition-wise joins

Listing 11-18 shows a join involving both a partitioned table and an unpartitioned table.

Listing 11-18. Partial partition-wise join

```
SELECT                                    SELECT
  /*+ parallel(t_part1 8)                   /*+ parallel(t_part1 8)
      parallel(t1 8) full(t1)                   parallel(t1 8) full(t1)
      leading(t_part1)                          leading(t1)
      no_swap_join_inputs(t1)                   swap_join_inputs(t_part1)
      pq_distribute(t1 NONE PARTITION) */       pq_distribute(t_part1 PARTITION NONE) */
      *                                         *
FROM t_part1 JOIN t1 USING (c1);          FROM t_part1 JOIN t1 USING (c1);
```

```
-----------------------------------------------------------------------------
| Id  | Operation                 | Name      |   TQ  |IN-OUT| PQ Distrib |
-----------------------------------------------------------------------------
|   0 | SELECT STATEMENT          |           |       |      |            |
|   1 |  PX COORDINATOR           |           |       |      |            |
|   2 |   PX SEND QC (RANDOM)      | :TQ10001  | Q1,01 | P->S | QC (RAND)  |
|*  3 |    HASH JOIN BUFFERED      |           | Q1,01 | PCWP |            |
|   4 |     PX PARTITION HASH ALL  |           | Q1,01 | PCWC |            |
|   5 |      TABLE ACCESS FULL     | T_PART1   | Q1,01 | PCWP |            |
|   6 |     PX RECEIVE            |           | Q1,01 | PCWP |            |
|   7 |      PX SEND PARTITION (KEY)| :TQ10000  | Q1,00 | P->P | PART (KEY) |
|   8 |       PX BLOCK ITERATOR    |           | Q1,00 | PCWC |            |
|   9 |        TABLE ACCESS FULL   | T1        | Q1,00 | PCWP |            |
-----------------------------------------------------------------------------
```

Predicate Information (identified by operation id):

```
   3 - access("T_PART1"."C1"="T1"."C1")
```

Unlike full partition-wise joins, partial partition-wise joins like the one shown in Listing 11-18 are only seen in execution plans for statements that run in parallel.

Listing 11-18 joins two tables, but only the driving row source in the hash join is partitioned by the column used in the join predicate. We have used two PQSSs here. Partition granules are used for T_PART1 and block-range granules for T1. Rows read from T1 can only match with corresponding rows from one partition in T_PART1, so each row read by PQSS1 is sent to just one server from PQSS2.

Notice that although we have eliminated the need for the probed row source to be partitioned, and as a result have eliminated the risk of load imbalance from skewed data in that row source, we now have the overhead of two DFOs and a TQ: one DFO obtains rows from the driving row source and performs the join, and the second DFO accesses the probed row source. To be clear, this variant of partial partition-wise joins does nothing to help with variations in partition size in the driving row source.

Listing 11-18 shows two different ways we can use hints to obtain the same execution plan. If we don't swap the join inputs we use the keywords NONE PARTITION to force this distribution mechanism, and if we do swap join inputs we swap the keywords as well and specify PARTITION NONE.

We can also use partial partition-wise joins when only the probed table in our join is appropriately partitioned, which I will demonstrate as part of the discussion on bloom filtering shortly.

Broadcast distribution

Listing 11-19 joins two unpartitioned tables.

Listing 11-19. BROADCAST distribution mechanism

```
CREATE INDEX t1_i1
  ON t1 (c1);

SELECT /*+ index(t1) parallel(t2 8)     SELECT /*+ index(t1) parallel(t2 8)
       leading(t1)                              leading(t2)
       use_hash(t2)                             use_hash(t1)
       no_swap_join_inputs(t2)                  swap_join_inputs(t1)
       pq_distribute(t2 BROADCAST NONE)         pq_distribute(t1 NONE BROADCAST)
       no_pq_replicate(t2)                      no_pq_replicate(t1)
       */                                       */
       *                                        *
  FROM t1 JOIN t2 ON t1.c1 = t2.c2;       FROM t1 JOIN t2 ON t1.c1 = t2.c2;
```

```
---------------------------------------------------------------------------
| Id  | Operation             | Name     |  TQ   |IN-OUT| PQ Distrib |
---------------------------------------------------------------------------
|   0 | SELECT STATEMENT      |          |       |      |            |
|   1 |  PX COORDINATOR       |          |       |      |            |
|   2 |   PX SEND QC (RANDOM) | :TQ10001 | Q1,01 | P->S | QC (RAND)  |
|*  3 |    HASH JOIN          |          | Q1,01 | PCWP |            |
|   4 |     PX RECEIVE        |          | Q1,01 | PCWP |            |
|   5 |      PX SEND BROADCAST| :TQ10000 | Q1,00 | S->P | BROADCAST  |
|   6 |       PX SELECTOR     |          | Q1,00 | SCWC |            |
|   7 |        INDEX FULL SCAN| T1_I1    | Q1,00 | SCWP |            |
|   8 |     PX BLOCK ITERATOR |          | Q1,01 | PCWC |            |
|   9 |      TABLE ACCESS FULL| T2       | Q1,01 | PCWP |            |
---------------------------------------------------------------------------

Predicate Information (identified by operation id):
---------------------------------------------------

   3 - access("T1"."C1"="T2"."C2")
```

Listing 11-19 begins by creating an index on T1.C1 and then runs two queries, shown side by side. When the queries run, one slave from PQSS1 reads the rows from T1 using the index and sends each row read to *every* member of PQSS2, where it is placed into a workarea for the HASH JOIN on line 3. Once the read of the T1.T1_I1 index completes, each member of PQSS2 reads a portion of T2 using block-range granules. The rows are joined on line 3 and sent to the QC.

Now, this might seem inefficient. Why do we want to send the rows from T1 to *every* member of PQSS2? Well, if T1 had a large number of wide rows we wouldn't. But if T1 has a small number of narrow rows the overhead of broadcasting the rows may not be that great. But there is still some overhead, so why do it? The answer lies in the fact that we can avoid sending rows from T2 anywhere until after the join! If T2 is much larger than T1 it might be better to send rows from T1 multiple times through a TQ rather than sending rows from T2 through a TQ once.

The broadcast distribution method supports all join methods, and Listing 11-19 shows two variants for hinting hash joins, as with partial partition-wise joins.

■ **Tip** You can't broadcast the preserved row source of an outer join. This is because the existence check on the optional row source has to be performed on all its rows. A similar restriction applies to semi-joins and anti-joins: you can't broadcast the main query because the existence check needs to be applied to all rows in the subquery.

As with the partial partition-wise joins that I showed in Listing 11-18, the broadcast distribution mechanism in Listing 11-19 uses two DFOs, but this time the join is performed by the DFO that accesses the probed row source rather than the driving row source.

It is technically possible to broadcast the probed row source rather than the driving row source, but I can't think what use this has. One way to do this would be to replace NO_SWAP_JOIN_INPUTS with SWAP_JOIN_INPUTS on the left-hand query of Listing 11-19. On the one hand, broadcasting T2 would suggest that T2 is smaller than T1. On the other hand, the fact that T1 has been chosen as the driving row source of the hash join suggests that T1 is smaller than T2. This contradiction means that the CBO is unlikely to choose such an approach to a parallel join, and you probably shouldn't either.

Row source replication

This is a parallel query distribution mechanism introduced in 12cR1, and I haven't seen an official name for yet so I have coined the term *row source replication* for want of a better term. For some reason, the distribution mechanism is hinted not by means of a new variant of PQ_DISTRIBUTE but rather by means of a new hint, PQ_REPLICATE, that modifies the behavior of broadcast replication.

Those of you with eagle eyes will have noticed that the queries in Listing 11-19 included a NO_PQ_REPLICATE hint. Listing 11-20 changes these hints to PQ_REPLICATE.

Listing 11-20. Row source replciation

```
SELECT /*+ parallel(t2 8)            SELECT /*+ parallel(t2 8)
       leading(t1)                          leading(t2)
       index_ffs(t1) parallel_index(t1)     index_ffs(t1) parallel_index(t1)
       use_hash(t2)                         use_hash(t1)
       no_swap_join_inputs(t2)              swap_join_inputs(t1)
       pq_distribute(t2 BROADCAST NONE)     pq_distribute(t1 NONE BROADCAST)
       pq_replicate(t2)                     pq_replicate(t1)
       */                                   */
       *                                    *
  FROM t1 JOIN t2 ON t1.c1 = t2.c2;      FROM t1 JOIN t2 ON t1.c1 = t2.c2;
```

```
---------------------------------------------
| Id  | Operation               | Name     |
---------------------------------------------
|   0 | SELECT STATEMENT         |          |
|   1 |  PX COORDINATOR          |          |
|   2 |   PX SEND QC (RANDOM)    | :TQ10000 |
|*  3 |    HASH JOIN             |          |
|   4 |     INDEX FAST FULL SCAN | T1_I1    |
|   5 |     PX BLOCK ITERATOR    |          |
|   6 |      TABLE ACCESS FULL   | T2       |
---------------------------------------------
```

```
Predicate Information (identified by operation id):
---------------------------------------------------

   3 - access("T1"."C1"="T2"."C2")
```

Now, what has happened here is pretty cool. Since T1 is so small the CBO reasoned that it would be cheaper to have each parallel query server in the joining DFO read T1 in its entirety than to have a separate DFO and a separate TQ for reading T1 and broadcasting the results. After reading the entirety of T1, each parallel query server reads a portion of T2.

This distribution mechanism only makes sense when T1 is small and T2 is large. So, if you were selecting one row from a terabyte version of table T1 the CBO will use the old broadcast distribution mechanism over replication unless hinted.

You will have noticed that I replaced the INDEX (T1) hint in Listing 11-19 with the two hints INDEX_FFS (T1) and PARALLEL_INDEX (T1) in Listing 11-20. T1 is considered to be read in parallel, even though it is actually read serially but multiple times. Since this is replication not parallel execution there is no reason to prohibit index range or full scans. However, this isn't yet supported as of 12.1.0.1, so I have had to use an index fast full scan as an alternative. A full table scan would also have worked.

There is one more distribution mechanism that we have yet to discuss. This join mechanism solves all load imbalance problems related to partition size, but at a price.

Hash distribution

Imagine that you have to join 3GB from one row source with 3GB from another row source. This join is happening at a critical point in your overnight batch. Nothing else is running and nothing else will run until your join is completed, so time is of the essence. You have 15GB of PGA, 32 processors, and 20 parallel query servers. Serial execution is not on. Not only will you fail to avail yourself of all the CPU and disk bandwidth available to you, but also your join will spill to disk: the maximum size of a workarea is 2GB, and you have 3GB of data.

You need to use parallel execution and choose a DOP of 10, but what join distribution mechanism do you think you should use? Your first thought should be a partition-wise join of some kind. But let us assume that this isn't an option. Maybe your row sources aren't partitioned tables. Maybe they are partitioned but all of your 3GB comes from one partition. Maybe the 3GB comes from several partitions but the join condition is unrelated to the partitioning column. For whatever reason, you need to find an alternative to partition-wise joins.

Neither row source replication nor broadcast distribution seem attractive. When you replicate or broadcast 3GB to ten parallel query slaves you use a total of 30GB of PGA. That is more than the 15GB available. Listing 11-21 shows how we solve such problems.

Listing 11-21. HASH distribution

```
ALTER SESSION SET optimizer_adaptive_features=FALSE;
SELECT /*+ full(t1) parallel(t1)
          parallel(t_part2 8)
        leading(t1)
        use_hash(t_part2)
        no_swap_join_inputs(t_part2)
        pq_distribute(t_part2 HASH HASH) */
        *
  FROM t1 JOIN t_part2 ON t1.c1 = t_part2.c4
 WHERE t_part2.c2 IN (1, 3, 5);
```

```
--------------------------------------------------------------------------------------------
| Id  | Operation                | Name     | Pstart| Pstop |    TQ  |IN-OUT| PQ Distrib |
--------------------------------------------------------------------------------------------
|   0 | SELECT STATEMENT         |          |       |       |        |      |            |
|   1 |  PX COORDINATOR          |          |       |       |        |      |            |
|   2 |   PX SEND QC (RANDOM)    | :TQ10002 |       |       |  Q1,02 | P->S | QC (RAND)  |
|*  3 |    HASH JOIN BUFFERED    |          |       |       |  Q1,02 | PCWP |            |
|   4 |     PX RECEIVE           |          |       |       |  Q1,02 | PCWP |            |
|   5 |      PX SEND HASH        | :TQ10000 |       |       |  Q1,00 | P->P | HASH       |
|   6 |       PX BLOCK ITERATOR  |          |       |       |  Q1,00 | PCWC |            |
|   7 |        TABLE ACCESS FULL | T1       |       |       |  Q1,00 | PCWP |            |
|   8 |     PX RECEIVE           |          |       |       |  Q1,02 | PCWP |            |
|   9 |      PX SEND HASH        | :TQ10001 |       |       |  Q1,01 | P->P | HASH       |
|  10 |       PX BLOCK ITERATOR  |          |KEY(I) |KEY(I) |  Q1,01 | PCWC |            |
|* 11 |        TABLE ACCESS FULL | T_PART2  |KEY(I) |KEY(I) |  Q1,01 | PCWP |            |
--------------------------------------------------------------------------------------------
```

Predicate Information (identified by operation id):

```
   3 - access("T1"."C1"="T_PART2"."C4")
  11 - filter("T_PART2"."C2"=1 OR "T_PART2"."C2"=3 OR "T_PART2"."C2"=5)
```

Up until now, all the examples that I have shown involving block-range granules have specified unpartitioned tables. To show that partitioned tables, although not required, are not prohibited either, Listing 11-21 joins T_PART2, a partitioned table, with T1. As you can see from the PSTART and PSTOP columns, the filter predicates on the partitioning column T_PART2.C2 allow for partition elimination, so not all the blocks in the table are scanned. But the remaining blocks of T_PART2 are distributed among the members of PQSS2 with no regard to the partition from which they originate.

Because the join condition uses T_PART2.C4, and T_PART2 is partitioned using T_PART2.C2, a partial partition-wise join isn't available. As an alternative we have used hash distribution.

I want to make the distinction between hash *distribution* and hash *join* clear as both techniques are used in Listing 11-21. Hash distribution is forced with the PQ_DISTRUBUTE (T_PART2 HASH HASH) hint and implemented by the PX SEND HASH operations on lines 5 and 9 of Listing 11-21. In Listing 11-21 a distribution hash function is used on column T1.C1 to ensure that each row from T1 is sent by PQSS1 to exactly one member of PQSS2. That same distribution hash function is used on T_PART2.C4 when PQSS1 scans T_PART2 so that the rows from T_PART2 are sent to the one member of PQSS2 that holds any matching rows from T1.

Caution   Although hash distribution avoids load imbalance related to variations in partition size, load imbalance may still arise as a result of the hash function. For example, if there is only one value of T1.C1, all rows from T1 will be sent to the same member of PQSS2.

A join hash function is forced using the USE_HASH (T_PART2) hint and is implemented by the HASH JOIN BUFFERED operation on line 3. A join hash function is used by the members of PQSS2 on T1.C1 and T_PART2.C4 to match the rows received, as with serial hash joins or parallel joins using other distribution mechanisms. It is possible to use hash distribution with a merge join, but hash distribution doesn't support nested loops joins.

You will notice that hash distribution involves three DFOs: one DFO for obtaining rows for the driving row source, a second DFO for obtaining rows from the probe row source, and a third for the join itself. In Listing 11-21, PQSS1 reads T1 first and then moves on to reading T_PART2. The join is performed by PQSS2.

This seems wonderful, so what is not to like? Well, I have engineered a very nice scenario where nothing goes wrong. But there is a performance threat—a big one. And the clue is in the name of the join operation on line 3. A hash join always involves one workarea, but the HASH JOIN BUFFERED operation on line 3 involves two workareas! I will explain why this is in just a moment, but first I want to show you a nice little enhancement that was made to hash distributions in 12cR1.

Adaptive parallel joins

You may have noticed that Listing 11-21 began with a statement to disable the 12cR1 adaptive features. Listing 11-22 shows what happens if we re-enable them by issuing an ALTER SESSION SET optimizer_adaptive_features=TRUE statement.

Listing 11-22. Execution plan for Listing 11-21 with adaptive features enabled

```
---------------------------------------------------------------------
| Id  | Operation               | Name      |   TQ  |IN-OUT| PQ Distrib |
---------------------------------------------------------------------
|   0 | SELECT STATEMENT        |           |       |      |            |
|   1 |  PX COORDINATOR         |           |       |      |            |
|   2 |   PX SEND QC (RANDOM)   | :TQ10002  | Q1,02 | P->S | QC (RAND)  |
|*  3 |    HASH JOIN BUFFERED   |           | Q1,02 | PCWP |            |
|   4 |     PX RECEIVE          |           | Q1,02 | PCWP |            |
|   5 |      PX SEND HYBRID HASH| :TQ10000  | Q1,00 | P->P | HYBRID HASH|
|   6 |       STATISTICS COLLECTOR|         | Q1,00 | PCWC |            |
|   7 |        PX BLOCK ITERATOR|           | Q1,00 | PCWC |            |
|   8 |         TABLE ACCESS FULL| T1       | Q1,00 | PCWP |            |
|   9 |     PX RECEIVE          |           | Q1,02 | PCWP |            |
|  10 |      PX SEND HYBRID HASH| :TQ10001  | Q1,01 | P->P | HYBRID HASH|
|  11 |       PX BLOCK ITERATOR |           | Q1,01 | PCWC |            |
|* 12 |        TABLE ACCESS FULL| T_PART2   | Q1,01 | PCWP |            |
---------------------------------------------------------------------

Predicate Information (identified by operation id):
---------------------------------------------------

   3 - access("T1"."C1"="T_PART2"."C4")
  12 - filter("T_PART2"."C2"=1 OR "T_PART2"."C2"=3 OR "T_PART2"."C2"=5)
```

The changes to the execution plan are shown in bold in Listing 11-22. What happens here is that the STATISTICS COLLECTOR buffers a certain number of rows from T1 (twice the DOP presently), and if that number isn't reached the original hash distribution mechanism is changed to a broadcast.

You might think that once the rows from T1 are broadcast, T_PART2 would be accessed by the same DFO that does the join and :TQ10001 wouldn't be used. That was certainly my initial assumption. Unfortunately, in 12cR1 the rows from T_PART2 are still sent through a TQ! As far as I can see, the only advantage of broadcasting the rows from T1 is that a round-robin distribution mechanism is used rather than hash distribution, so load imbalance brought about by the hash function can be avoided. Hopefully this redundant DFO will be removed at some point in the future.

Given my earlier comments about adaptive behavior in Chapter 6, you may be surprised to learn that I quite like this feature. The big difference between this feature and all the other adaptive features to date is that the decision to use hash or broadcast distribution is made each and every time that the query runs. So you can use hash distribution on one execution, broadcast the next, and then return to hash distribution the third time. Would I be more enthusiastic about adaptive join methods and the like if the adaptations were not cast in concrete the first time they were made? I certainly would.

VERIFYING ADAPATIVE JOIN METHODS

If you look at the *using parallel execution* chapter in the VLDB and Partitioning Guide you will find information about a few views that you can use to investigate parallel execution behavior and performance. One of the most important is V$PQ_TQSTAT, and the downloadable scripts use this view in a test case that shows that the choice of broadcast versus hash distribution is made on each execution of a cursor.

It is now time to explain what this HASH JOIN BUFFERED operation is and why it is such a threat to performance.

Data buffering

When T1 is 3GB and T_PART2 is also 3GB a hash join executed serially must spill to disk, but a hash join implemented in parallel with hash distribution may not. On the other hand, suppose that T1 is 500MB and T_PART2 is 30GB—the serial hash join may not spill to disk but, assuming the same 15GB of PGA is available, the parallel execution plan will spill to disk!

To understand why this is the case we have to remind ourselves of a rule that we covered in Chapter 8: a consumer of data from any TQ must buffer the data in a workarea before sending it through another TQ. This is true even when the DFO is receiving data from a PQSS and sending it to the QC, as in Listings 11-19 and 11-20. When a DFO that is performing a hash join obtains data for the driving row source from another DFO there is no issue. The data for the driving row source is always placed into a workarea by a hash join. But when the data for a probe row source is obtained from another DFO we do have a problem, because a normal HASH JOIN operation will immediately match the received rows and start sending data to the parent operation.

If you look at the join operations in Listings 11-17 and 11-19, for instance, you will see that a regular HASH JOIN operation is used. This is okay because the data for the probe row source is obtained by the same DFO that performs the join. But in the case of Listings 11-18 and 11-21 the data from the probe row source is received via a TQ from another DFO. The HASH JOIN BUFFERED operation is required to buffer the probe row source data *in addition to* the driving row source data. In Listing 11-21 the matching of the data from the probe row source (T_PART2) with the driving row source (T1) doesn't begin until *both* full table scans are complete!

■ **Tip** If it can be determined that a probed row doesn't match any row in the driving row source, the probed row is discarded and is not buffered. This is what a HASH JOIN BUFFERED operation does that a combination of a HASH JOIN and a BUFFER SORT doesn't.

All serial HASH JOIN operations have a buffered variant. So, for example, if Listing 11-13 were modified to run in parallel using hash distribution, the HASH JOIN SEMI NA operation would become HASH JOIN SEMI NA BUFFERED.

It is important to understand that the CBO has no solution to the problem I have outlined. When you see a lot of direct path write temp and direct path read temp operations associated with parallel joins using buffered hash operations, it may be that there is no better execution plan available. You may have to recode your application to join subsets of data sequentially and/or redesign your tables so that partition-wise joins are an option.

Bloom filtering

Flowers bloom, and sometimes you need to prune them. But if you think that bloom filtering has something to do with partition pruning then think again! In fact, according to the Wikipedia article on bloom filtering, the technology was invented by Burton Howard Bloom in 1970. The technique isn't specific to Oracle databases or databases in general, for that matter. But Oracle makes nice use of it when optimizing parallel joins.

Here is the scenario we are trying to avoid: We send a row from a probe row source through a TQ to a consuming DFO, which performs a join with a driving row source. Unfortunately, the consuming DFO finds that the row it receives doesn't match any row from the driving row source and throws the row from the probe row source away. What a waste!

Somehow it is possible for most non-matching rows from the probe row source to be discarded by the producing DFO before sending them rough the TQ! As far as I am concerned, this is pure magic, but if you really want to understand how Burton's invention is applied to parallel joins in an Oracle database just Google "Christian Antognini Bloom Filtering" and the article that you hit first will explain all.

Bloom filtering involves generating a small amount of data from the driving row source and sending it backwards through the TQ so that it can be used to filter rows. This filtering sometimes doesn't show up in the operation table or the filter predicates, but sometimes it does. Listing 11-23 returns to the partial partition-wise join of Listing 11-18 to see what happens when we partition the probe row source rather than the driving row source.

Listing 11-23. Partial partition-wise join with partitioned probe row source

```
SELECT /*+ parallel(t_part1 8)
           parallel(t1 8) full(t1)
       leading(t1)
       no_swap_join_inputs(t_part1)
       px_join_filter(t_part1)
       pq_distribute(t_part1 PARTITION NONE) */
       *
FROM t_part1 JOIN t1 USING (c1);
```

```
-----------------------------------------------------------------------------------
| Id  | Operation                     | Name    | Pstart| Pstop |  TQ   |IN-OUT|
-----------------------------------------------------------------------------------
|   0 | SELECT STATEMENT              |         |       |       |       |      |
|   1 |  PX COORDINATOR               |         |       |       |       |      |
|   2 |   PX SEND QC (RANDOM)         | :TQ10001|       |       | Q1,01 | P->S |
|*  3 |    HASH JOIN                  |         |       |       | Q1,01 | PCWP |
|   4 |     JOIN FILTER CREATE        | :BF0001 |       |       | Q1,01 | PCWP |
|   5 |      PART JOIN FILTER CREATE  | :BF0000 |       |       | Q1,01 | PCWP |
|   6 |       PX RECEIVE              |         |       |       | Q1,01 | PCWP |
|   7 |        PX SEND PARTITION (KEY)| :TQ10000|       |       | Q1,00 | P->P |
|   8 |         PX BLOCK ITERATOR     |         |       |       | Q1,00 | PCWC |
|   9 |          TABLE ACCESS FULL    | T1      |       |       | Q1,00 | PCWP |
|  10 |     JOIN FILTER USE           | :BF0001 |       |       | Q1,01 | PCWP |
|  11 |      PX PARTITION HASH JOIN-FILTER| |:BF0000|:BF0000| Q1,01 | PCWC |
|* 12 |       TABLE ACCESS FULL       | T_PART1 |:BF0000|:BF0000| Q1,01 | PCWP |
-----------------------------------------------------------------------------------
```

```
Predicate Information (identified by operation id):
---------------------------------------------------

   3 - access("T_PART1"."C1"="T1"."C1")
  12 - filter(SYS_OP_BLOOM_FILTER(:BF0001,"T_PART1"."C1"))
```

Listing 11-23 shows the creation of two bloom filters and the application of those bloom filters. Bloom filter :BF0000 is created on line 5 and is used on line 11 to perform partition pruning when it is known that no rows from a particular partition of T_PART1 could match any selected row from T1—so there is a connection between partition pruning and bloom filtering after all! The second bloom filter, :BF0001, is created on line 4 and used on line 12 to filter rows as they are read.

You will notice that there is a hint, PX_JOIN_FILTER, in the query. Without the hint the CBO would not have applied :BF0001 on this occasion, although bloom filtering for partition pruning cannot be forced with PX_JOIN_FILTER or suppressed with NO_PX_JOIN_FILTER.

Summary

Although there are only four basic methods for joining row sources in a query or subquery, there are substantially more operations that might appear in an execution plan. These variations come about as a result of hash join input swapping and the need to support different types of join: separate join operations are required for inner joins, outer joins, full outer joins, partitioned outer joins, and multiple types of semi-joins and anti-joins.

When multiple row sources in a query or subquery are joined, a join tree is created as a result of the choice of join order made by the CBO, but there are numerous restrictions that limit the choice of join order. In particular, bushy joins are never selected by the CBO, and the preserved row source in an outer join must precede the optional row source. These restrictions cannot be overridden, even with hints, although hash join input swapping is an alternative in some cases.

When parallel execution is used with joins there are several different distribution methods that can be used, but buffering of data from the probe row source is often a hidden threat to performance when partition-wise joins aren't an option.

Chapter 10 covered the ways of accessing row sources, and this chapter covered the ways those row sources are joined. It is an unfortunate fact that the CBO will often make inappropriate selections for accessing and joining row sources, and an understanding of the computer science behind these concepts is vital for SQL tuning. But it isn't good enough to just understand the mechanics of accessing and joining row sources. We also need to understand other aspects of the process that the CBO follows. Chapter 12 focuses on the optimization process before Chapter 13 looks at query transformation.

Final State Optimization

When I introduced the CBO in Chapter 2 I explained that the CBO followed two processes to come up with an execution plan for the runtime engine: query transformation and final state optimization. In this chapter I will cover final state optimization, and transformations will be the focus of Chapter 13. Put another way, this chapter looks at how the CBO evaluates different candidate execution plans after any query transformations have been performed.

In Chapters 10 and 11 I covered the mechanics of accessing and joining the row sources specified in a query. In this chapter I will provide a high-level overview of the approach used by the CBO to determine the optimal join order, join method, and access method. I will also look at *inlist iteration*. Strictly speaking, parallelization is a part of final state transformation, but in chapters 2 and 8 I covered parallelization as a separate topic, and I don't need to revisit it here.

When reading this chapter please bear in mind that none of the topics covered are independent of each other. You cannot always know the best index to access a table, if any, until you know the join order. But the best join order may depend on the access methods for the joined tables. This effectively means that the CBO has to make some evaluations multiple times. Indeed, the whole final state optimization process covered in this chapter needs to be repeated for each candidate query transformation!

Fortunately, as I said in Chapter 2, we don't need to know the finer details of how the CBO sorts all these dependencies out or any shortcuts it uses to get things done in a reasonable amount of time. We just need enough of an idea of how the CBO operates so that when things go wrong we can work out the reason why and figure out what to do about it.

The goal of final state optimization is to come up with the execution plan with the least cost; in other words, the execution plan that the runtime engine is likely to be able execute in the least amount of time. The main ways to achieve this are:

- Avoid retrieving rows and later throwing them away

- Avoid accessing blocks and then throwing away all the rows in the block

- Avoid reading the same block multiple times

- Read multiple consecutive blocks with multi-block reads rather than single-block reads

This theme of avoiding waste is key to this chapter. Let us begin with a look at how the CBO selects an optimal join order.

Join Order

The vagaries of determining the optimal join order for a SQL query are vast and one could write an entire book about them. In fact, in 2003 Dan Tow did exactly that! His book, *SQL Tuning*, published by O'Reilly, is almost entirely dedicated to a description of a systematic approach to determining the optimal join order for a query. That book was published before Oracle starting supporting either hash join input swapping or the star transformation, which we will come onto in Chapter 13. Today the subject of join order optimization is even more complex than it was in 2003.

Fortunately, these days the problems of join ordering are way down on the list of issues the Oracle SQL performance specialist needs to worry about. This is because the CBO does a pretty good job of determining join order itself *if* (and it is a big if) it can make accurate cardinality estimates for each object access and each join. The reliability of the join order algorithm used by the CBO is the key behind Wolfgang Breitling's famous "Tuning by Cardinality Feedback" paper that I mentioned in a different context in Chapter 6. Wolfgang's tuning approach is to correct the cardinality estimates that the CBO makes and then cross your fingers and hope that the CBO does something sensible. And these days the CBO generally *will* do something sensible!

So what makes one join order better than another? Have a look at Listing 12-1, which provides a very simple example.

Listing 12-1. Simple join order optimization

```
SELECT /*+ gather_plan_statistics */
       COUNT (*)
  FROM oe.order_items i JOIN oe.product_descriptions p USING (product_id)
 WHERE i.order_id = 2367 AND p.language_id = 'US';

SET LINES 200 PAGES 0

SELECT *
  FROM TABLE (DBMS_XPLAN.display_cursor (format => 'BASIC ROWS IOSTATS LAST'));
```

```
-------------------------------------------------------------------------
| Id  | Operation            | Name           | Starts | E-Rows | A-Rows |
-------------------------------------------------------------------------
|   0 | SELECT STATEMENT     |                |    1   |        |    1   |
|   1 |  SORT AGGREGATE      |                |    1   |    1   |    1   |
|   2 |   NESTED LOOPS       |                |    1   |   13   |    8   |
|*  3 |    INDEX RANGE SCAN  | ORDER_ITEMS_UK |    1   |    8   |    8   |
|*  4 |    INDEX UNIQUE SCAN | PRD_DESC_PK    |    8   |    2   |    8   |
-------------------------------------------------------------------------

Predicate Information (identified by operation id):
---------------------------------------------------

3 - access("I"."ORDER_ID"=2367)
4 - access("I"."PRODUCT_ID"="P"."PRODUCT_ID" AND "P"."LANGUAGE_ID"='US')
```

Listing 12-1 joins the ORDER_ITEMS and PRODUCT_DESCRIPTIONS tables from the example OE schema. The query has selection predicates on both tables as well as an equijoin predicate on PRODUCT_ID. The only hint in the query is GATHER_PLAN_STATISTICS, which enables runtime statistics to be gathered.

According to the execution plan from DBMS_XPLAN.DISPLAY_CURSOR, the CBO decided on this join order: ORDER_ITEMS → PRODUCT_DESCRIPTIONS. The CBO estimated that there would be eight rows matching from ORDER_ITEMS, and since the E-ROWS and A-ROWS columns from operation 3 match, we know that that was a perfectly accurate guess. Despite the fact that operation 4 is an INDEX UNIQUE SCAN on an index of the PRODUCT_DESCRIPTIONS table, the CBO assumes that more than one row might be returned; 13 rows are estimated to be input to the SORT AGGREGATE operation on line 1 rather than the eight rows that are returned in practice. This doesn't matter. The CBO has selected the right join order. Listing 12-2 lets us see what happens if we try to override the selected join order.

Listing 12-2. Inappropriate join order

```
SELECT /*+ gather_plan_statistics leading(p) */
       COUNT (*)
  FROM oe.order_items i JOIN oe.product_descriptions p USING (product_id)
 WHERE i.order_id = 2367 AND p.language_id = 'US';

SET LINES 200 PAGES 0

SELECT *
  FROM TABLE (DBMS_XPLAN.display_cursor (format => 'BASIC ROWS IOSTATS LAST'));
```

```
-----------------------------------------------------------------------
| Id | Operation              | Name          | Starts | E-Rows | A-Rows |
-----------------------------------------------------------------------
|  0 | SELECT STATEMENT       |               |    1   |        |    1   |
|  1 |  SORT AGGREGATE        |               |    1   |    1   |    1   |
|  2 |   NESTED LOOPS         |               |    1   |   13   |    8   |
|* 3 |    INDEX FAST FULL SCAN| PRD_DESC_PK   |    1   |  288   |  288   |
|* 4 |    INDEX UNIQUE SCAN   | ORDER_ITEMS_UK|  288   |    1   |    8   |
-----------------------------------------------------------------------
```

Predicate Information (identified by operation id):

```
3 - filter("P"."LANGUAGE_ID"='US')
4 - access("I"."ORDER_ID"=2367 AND "I"."PRODUCT_ID"="P"."PRODUCT_ID")
```

The LEADING hint in Listing 12-2 lets us see how the join order PRODUCT_DESCRIPTIONS → ORDER_ITEMS works out. It turns out that 288 rows match the predicate on LANGUAGE_ID, once again perfectly forecasted by the CBO. However, 280 of these 288 product descriptions end up being discarded by the NESTED LOOPS operation on line 2. *What a waste.* Now we know why PRODUCT_DESCRIPTIONS → ORDER_ITEMS is a bad join order.

■ **Tip** If you expect the CBO to pick plan A and it picks plan B for reasons that you don't immediately understand, try adding hints to force plan B. Then look at the cardinalities and cost estimates for plan B. You will probably see the rationale. You should then be able to see where the "misunderstanding" is. Did you miss something, or did the CBO?

I recently worked on a query that returned about 1,000,000 rows from the first row source and 400,000,000 rows after joining with the second row source; the cardinality dropped back down to 1,000,000 rows after the second join with the third row source. If ever you see this kind of effect (cardinalities rising dramatically and then falling) you should strongly suspect a suboptimal join order.

Despite not being current, there are still things to be learned from Tow's book. Let me tell you the two biggest things I learned from the book.

- Get the first row source correct. In most cases that is enough to get a decent execution plan.

- The best choice for the leading row source is usually the one with the strongest selectivity. This is not necessarily the row source with the lowest number of rows.

Join Method

Chapter 11 explained the benefits and drawbacks of each of the four join mechanisms, so I won't repeat them here. However, in case I have given the impression so far in this book that a human expert can always outsmart the CBO, take a look at Listing 12-3.

Listing 12-3. A non-intuitive join method

```
SELECT /*+ gather_plan_statistics */ *
  FROM hr.employees e JOIN hr.departments d USING (department_id)
 WHERE e.job_id = 'SH_CLERK';

SET LINES 200 PAGES 0

SELECT *
  FROM TABLE (
          DBMS_XPLAN.display_cursor (format => 'BASIC ROWS IOSTATS LAST'));
```

Id	Operation	Name	Starts	E-Rows	A-Rows	Bufs
0	SELECT STATEMENT		1		20	5
1	MERGE JOIN		1	20	20	5
2	TABLE ACCESS BY INDEX ROWID	DEPARTMENTS	1	27	6	2
3	INDEX FULL SCAN	DEPT_ID_PK	1	27	6	1
* 4	SORT JOIN		6	20	20	3
5	TABLE ACCESS BY INDEX ROWID BATCHED	EMPLOYEES	1	20	20	3
* 6	INDEX RANGE SCAN	EMP_JOB_IX	1	20	20	1

```
Predicate Information (identified by operation id):
---------------------------------------------------

4 - access("E"."DEPARTMENT_ID"="D"."DEPARTMENT_ID")
    filter("E"."DEPARTMENT_ID"="D"."DEPARTMENT_ID")
6 - access("E"."JOB_ID"='SH_CLERK'
```

This example identifies all of the employees with a JOB_ID of SH_CLERK and lists them with their associated department information. I must confess I would never have come up with the execution plan that the CBO came up with in a month of Sundays. However, on close inspection it looks pretty good!

Why use a MERGE JOIN? The tables are quite small, and both tables have an index on DEPARTMENT_ID, so surely a NESTED LOOPS join is appropriate? None of the simple rules that I advertised in Chapter 11 seem to suggest that a MERGE JOIN is even remotely appropriate. What is going on? Let us take a deeper look.

Operations 2 and 3 only seem to deepen the confusion. The execution plan performs an INDEX FULL SCAN with *no filter predicate* and then accesses the table. This means that operations 2 and 3 will access every row in the table. Why not use a TABLE FULL SCAN? Try and work it out before reading on.

Operations 4, 5, and 6 access the 20 rows from EMPLOYEES that match the JOB_ID predicate through an index and then sort them as required by the MERGE JOIN. No mystery there. But what happens next? Well, the MERGE JOIN probes those 20 rows from EMPLOYEES for each row from DEPARTMENTS *in order*. That is the key to the access of the DEPARTMENTS table via an INDEX FULL SCAN: the results are in DEPARTMENT_ID order and require no further sort! Not only that, but it turns out that the JOB_ID value SH_CLERK means "Shipping clerk," and all shipping clerks are part of the "Shipping" department with DEPARTMENT_ID 50. So when the runtime engine looks at DEPARTMENT_ID 60 (the sixth department) it finds that there are no more rows in EMPLOYEES to probe and stops further access to DEPARTMENTS. This is why the A-ROWS column displays a value of 6; only departments 10, 20, 30, 40, 50, and 60 were accessed.

In case you are interested, the execution plan I would have guessed would be better involves a NESTED LOOPS join. Using the technique of forcing the execution plan that I thought would be better, I could prove that it wasn't. Take a look at Listing 12-4.

Listing 12-4. My inferior execution plan

```
SELECT /*+ gather_plan_statistics leading(e) use_nl(d) */
       *
  FROM hr.employees e JOIN hr.departments d USING (department_id)
 WHERE e.job_id = 'SH_CLERK';

SET LINES 200 PAGES 0

SELECT *
  FROM TABLE (
          DBMS_XPLAN.display_cursor (format => 'BASIC ROWS IOSTATS LAST'));
```

```
---------------------------------------------------------------------------------------
| Id | Operation                              | Name        | Starts | E-Rows | A-Rows | Buffs |
---------------------------------------------------------------------------------------
|  0 | SELECT STATEMENT                       |             |   1    |        |   20   |  27   |
|  1 |  NESTED LOOPS                          |             |   1    |        |   20   |  27   |
|  2 |   NESTED LOOPS                         |             |   1    |   20   |   20   |   7   |
|  3 |    TABLE ACCESS BY INDEX ROWID BATCHED | EMPLOYEES   |   1    |   20   |   20   |   3   |
|* 4 |     INDEX RANGE SCAN                   | EMP_JOB_IX  |   1    |   20   |   20   |   1   |
|* 5 |    INDEX UNIQUE SCAN                   | DEPT_ID_PK  |  20    |    1   |   20   |   4   |
|  6 |   TABLE ACCESS BY INDEX ROWID          | DEPARTMENTS |  20    |    1   |   20   |  20   |
---------------------------------------------------------------------------------------
```

Predicate Information (identified by operation id):

```
   4 - access("E"."JOB_ID"='SH_CLERK')
   5 - access("E"."DEPARTMENT_ID"="D"."DEPARTMENT_ID")
```

You can see that the NESTED LOOPS join repeats the lookup on DEPT_ID_PK 20 times, resulting in a total of 27 buffer accesses rather than the 5 from Listing 12-3.

This is all pretty cool. Did the CBO work all this out? No. You can see that the CBO had no idea that the runtime engine would stop at DEPARTMENT_ID 60. We know this because there are 27 rows in DEPARTMENTS and the value for E-ROWS for operation 2 is 27. So the CBO was guessing and got lucky. But the CBO's guess was far better than mine for all my years of SQL tuning experience.

■ **Tip**   This book spends a lot of time telling you why the CBO gets things wrong a lot of the time. When the CBO gets things horribly wrong it generally does so because it is basing its decisions on information that is either entirely absent or horribly wrong. Listen to Wolfgang. Correct the CBO's misunderstandings and it will usually do a better job than you and I working together would ever do. The only problem is that it is sometimes quite impractical to correct all the CBO's bad assumptions, as we shall see in Chapter 14.

Access Method

As you read in Chapter 10, there are myriad ways to access a table, but the access method choices that are likely to have the most impact on the performance of a query, one way or another, are those related to index range scans: Which index, if any, should be selected?

Just because the join method is nested loops does not mean that access via an index on the join predicate is inevitable, and just because a hash join is used does not mean that a full table scan on the probe table is inevitable. Take a look at Listing 12-5, which uses a hash join but no full table scan.

Listing 12-5. Hash joins with no full table scans

```
SELECT *
  FROM sh.sales s, sh.customers c
 WHERE     c.cust_marital_status = 'married'
       AND c.cust_gender = 'M'
       AND c.cust_year_of_birth = 1976
       AND c.cust_id = s.cust_id
       AND s.prod_id = 136;
```

```
--------------------------------------------------------------------------------
| Id  | Operation                                 | Name                  | Rows |
--------------------------------------------------------------------------------
|   0 | SELECT STATEMENT                          |                       |   40 |
|*  1 |  HASH JOIN                                |                       |   40 |
|   2 |   TABLE ACCESS BY INDEX ROWID BATCHED     | CUSTOMERS             |   38 |
|   3 |    BITMAP CONVERSION TO ROWIDS            |                       |      |
|   4 |     BITMAP AND                            |                       |      |
|*  5 |      BITMAP INDEX SINGLE VALUE            | CUSTOMERS_YOB_BIX     |      |
|*  6 |      BITMAP INDEX SINGLE VALUE            | CUSTOMERS_MARITAL_BIX |      |
|*  7 |      BITMAP INDEX SINGLE VALUE            | CUSTOMERS_GENDER_BIX  |      |
|   8 |   PARTITION RANGE ALL                     |                       |  710 |
|   9 |    TABLE ACCESS BY LOCAL INDEX ROWID BATCHED| SALES               |  710 |
|  10 |     BITMAP CONVERSION TO ROWIDS           |                       |      |
|* 11 |      BITMAP INDEX SINGLE VALUE            | SALES_PROD_BIX        |      |
--------------------------------------------------------------------------------

Predicate Information (identified by operation id):
---------------------------------------------------

   1 - access("C"."CUST_ID"="S"."CUST_ID")
   5 - access("C"."CUST_YEAR_OF_BIRTH"=1976)
   6 - access("C"."CUST_MARITAL_STATUS"='married')
   7 - access("C"."CUST_GENDER"='M')
  11 - access("S"."PROD_ID"=136)
```

The query in Listing 12-5 performs a join of the CUSTOMERS and SALES tables in the SH example schema. The CBO estimates that there are 23 married male customers born in 1976 and that amongst those 23 customers, 24 sales will have been made for product 136. Working on these assumptions the CBO reckoned that a NESTED LOOPS join would need to make 23 probes on SALES. The choice between nested loops with 23 probes and a hash join with a full table scan might have been a close thing, but on this occasion the hash join appears much faster. The reason for this is that there are selective predicates on CUSTOMERS *independent of the join* and a predicate on the SALES table (s.prod_id = 136) that is *independent of the join* so the SALES table can be accessed via an index even with the hash join. Notice the PARTITION RANGE ALL operation on line 8. Regardless of the join method, all partitions need to be accessed as there is no predicate on the partitioning column TIME_ID.

The CBO's analysis of the appropriate join method and access method can't be faulted, but as it happens there are 284 married male customers born in 1976 and the join inputs should be swapped, but it is not a big deal on this occasion.

Listing 12-6 uses nested loops even though there is no index on the joined column.

Listing 12-6. Nested loops with un-indexed join column

```
SELECT *
  FROM oe.order_items i1, oe.order_items i2
 WHERE     i1.quantity = i2.quantity
       AND i1.order_id = 2392
       AND i1.line_item_id = 4
       AND i2.product_id = 2462;
```

```
-----------------------------------------------------------------------
| Id  | Operation                             | Name            | Rows |
-----------------------------------------------------------------------
|   0 | SELECT STATEMENT                      |                 |    1 |
|   1 |  NESTED LOOPS                         |                 |    1 |
|   2 |   TABLE ACCESS BY INDEX ROWID         | ORDER_ITEMS     |    1 |
|*  3 |    INDEX UNIQUE SCAN                  | ORDER_ITEMS_PK  |    1 |
|*  4 |   TABLE ACCESS BY INDEX ROWID BATCHED | ORDER_ITEMS     |    1 |
|*  5 |    INDEX RANGE SCAN                   | ITEM_PRODUCT_IX |    2 |
-----------------------------------------------------------------------

Predicate Information (identified by operation id):
---------------------------------------------------

   3 - access("I1"."ORDER_ID"=2392 AND "I1"."LINE_ITEM_ID"=4)
   4 - filter("I1"."QUANTITY"="I2"."QUANTITY")
   5 - access("I2"."PRODUCT_ID"=2462)
```

Listing 12-6 performs a self-join on the ORDER_ITEMS table in the OE example schema. The query looks for order items that match the order quantity for a specified line item. The join column is QUANTITY, which is not typically in a WHERE clause and is not indexed. The query is perhaps a little unusual but might be used to investigate a suspected data entry issue.

As with Listing 12-5, both row sources in Listing 12-6 have highly selective predicates independent of the join. On this occasion, one of the row sources, I1, is being accessed by a unique index, so a nested loop is appropriate.

So far in this chapter we have covered join order, join method, and access method. However, there are one or two more factors that the CBO might need to consider as part of final state optimization. Let us begin with a discussion of queries with IN lists.

IN List Iteration

When an IN list is specified in a query on column or columns supported by an index, the CBO has a choice of how many columns to use. Look at the query in Listing 12-7.

Listing 12-7. IN list execution plan options—no iteration

```
SELECT *
    FROM hr.employees e
   WHERE last_name = 'Grant' AND first_name IN ('Kimberely', 'Douglas')
ORDER BY last_name, first_name;
```

```
----------------------------------------------------------------
| Id  | Operation                   | Name        | Cost (%CPU)|
----------------------------------------------------------------
|   0 | SELECT STATEMENT            |             |     2  (0)|
|   1 |  TABLE ACCESS BY INDEX ROWID| EMPLOYEES   |     2  (0)|
|*  2 |   INDEX RANGE SCAN          | EMP_NAME_IX |     1  (0)|
----------------------------------------------------------------

Predicate Information (identified by operation id):
---------------------------------------------------

    2 - access("LAST_NAME"='Grant')
        filter("FIRST_NAME"='Douglas' OR "FIRST_NAME"='Kimberely')
```

The EMP_NAME_IX index on the EMPLOYEES table in the HR example schema includes both LAST_NAME and FIRST_NAME columns. There aren't likely to be too many choices for FIRST_NAME for LAST_NAME = 'Grant', so the CBO has chosen a single INDEX RANGE SCAN on LAST_NAME and filtered out any index entries that don't match either of the supplied values for FIRST_NAME. Suppose there were loads and loads of FIRST_NAMES—then an alternative plan might be suitable. Look at the hinted version of the query in Listing 12-8.

Listing 12-8. IN list execution plan options—with iteration

```
  SELECT /*+ num_index_keys(e emp_name_ix 2) */
         *
    FROM hr.employees e
   WHERE last_name = 'Grant' AND first_name IN ('Kimberely','Douglas')
ORDER BY last_name,first_name ;
```

```
-----------------------------------------------------------------
| Id  | Operation                    | Name         | Cost (%CPU)|
-----------------------------------------------------------------
|   0 | SELECT STATEMENT             |              |    2   (0)|
|   1 |  INLIST ITERATOR             |              |            |
|   2 |   TABLE ACCESS BY INDEX ROWID| EMPLOYEES    |    2   (0)|
|*  3 |    INDEX RANGE SCAN          | EMP_NAME_IX  |    1   (0)|
-----------------------------------------------------------------

Predicate Information (identified by operation id):
---------------------------------------------------
```

```
   3 - access("LAST_NAME"='Grant' AND ("FIRST_NAME"='Douglas' OR
               "FIRST_NAME"='Kimberely'))
```

The hint NUM_INDEX_KEYS can be used to indicate how many columns to use when performing an INDEX RANGE SCAN when an IN list is present. The supplied hint specifies that two columns are used. This means that we need to run two INDEX RANGE SCAN operations, driven by the INLIST ITERATOR operation. The first INDEX RANGE SCAN uses LAST_NAME = 'Grant' and FIRST_NAME = 'Douglas' as access predicates and the second INDEX RANGE SCAN uses LAST_NAME = 'Grant' and FIRST_NAME = 'Kimberely' as access predicates. I don't personally find the description of the access predicates in the DBMS_XPLAN display particularly helpful in this case, so I hope my explanation has helped.

Notice that no sort is present in the execution plan in either Listing 12-7 or Listing 12-8. In the former case the index entries are already appropriately ordered. In the latter case, the members of the IN list have been reordered to avoid the need for a sort. The estimated cost of the alternative plans is virtually identical in this case, but on larger tables there may be a substantial benefit from iteration.

Summary

Final state optimization is the name I have given to the most well-known part of the CBO: the part that deals with join order, join method, and access method. However, final state optimization also deals with inlist iteration.

There is, however, a lot more to the CBO than final state optimization. The CBO also has the ability to transform a query that you write into something that may look completely different from the one you supply. This rather large topic is the focus of Chapter 13.

CHAPTER 13

■ ■ ■

Optimizer Transformations

We have seen throughout this book that there are many ways to transform one SQL query (or DML subquery) into another without in any way changing the query's meaning. For all but the most trivial of queries the CBO will consider a number of such transformations, sometimes estimating costing, to determine the best SQL statement on which to perform the final state optimization that we just covered in Chapter 12. This chapter is dedicated to the topic of optimizer transformations; you will see that there are a bewildering number of such transformations. Although not all optimizer transformations are included in this chapter, the vast majority that you will encounter in your day-to-day life are, as well as some that you will rarely encounter.

You may wonder why all this effort has been put into CBO transformations. After all, you may feel that it is a programmer's responsibility to write SQL in an efficient way, and you would be correct in that feeling. However, you will see as this chapter progresses that there are some ways to rewrite a SQL statement that a mere mortal is unlikely to consider, and that these esoteric rewrites sometimes yield highly efficient execution plans.

However, some CBO transformations, such as *join elimination*, which I will cover later in this chapter, seem only to apply to very poorly written code. There are several reasons that such transformations are important:

- Queries often reference data dictionary views designed for a multitude of purposes. Once these views are expanded into a statement, the result is often obviously inefficient.

- Sometimes SQL code is generated by graphical tools or other language processors. Automatically generated code often seems hopelessly naïve.

- Well, there are actually quite a lot of bad SQL programmers out there!

There is a special class of transformations that I call *no-brainers* that I will discuss very shortly. With the exception of the no-brainers, all optimizer transformations can be disabled in one fell swoop by the NO_QUERY_TRANSFORMATION hint. This hint is sometimes useful for analysis and debugging, but I have never used it in a production SQL statement. However, in some cases, you will need to force or disable specific transformations in particular contexts. With the exception of the no-brainers, all optimizer transformations can be forced, where legal, with a hint that is specific to that transformation and can be disabled with another hint that is usually, but not always, generated by prefixing the characters NO_ to the start of the hint. For example, we have already discussed view merging in Chapter 8: the MERGE hint forces view merging while the NO_MERGE hint disables it. Two exceptions to this rule are:

- The *or-expansion* transformation is forced with the USE_CONCAT hint and disabled with the NO_EXPAND hint.

- *Factored subquery materialization* is forced with the MATERIALIZE hint and disabled with the INLINE hint.

Most of the query transformations explained in the chapter can be expressed in terms of legal SQL; in other words, you might have written the transformed SQL yourself in the first place. However, we have already seen in Chapter 11 that *subquery unnesting* can generate *semi-joins* and *anti-joins* that have no equivalent legal SQL syntax, and here we will discuss *group by pushdown*, another example of a transformation that cannot be expressed by legal SQL. Please bear in mind as you read the listings in this chapter that are designed to demonstrate individual transformations that the transformed query text may not be an exact representation. The listings show the original and, where possible, the transformed query together with the associated execution plans and the hints that force and disable the transformations in question.

The fact that the CBO can perform a number of transformations, one after the other, makes the task of grasping what the CBO is up to somewhat difficult. The good news is that, with the exception of the no-brainers, the hints that are associated with the transformations that the CBO has chosen will appear in the outline section of the plans displayed as a result of the DBMS_XPLAN functions, as I described in Chapter 8. You will, however, never see hints like NO_MERGE or NO_EXPAND in the outline section of a displayed execution plan because the presence of OUTLINE and OUTLINE_LEAF hints means that the absence of hints like MERGE or USE_CONCAT implies that the transformations haven't been applied.

This introduction has had to make special mention of no-brainer optimizer transformations on several occasions. Let us get to those now.

No-brainer Transformations

I am sure you will not be surprised to read that Oracle does not officially refer to any of the CBO transformations as *no-brainers*; this is just a term that I have coined myself to refer to a special set of transformations that have some unusual properties. These transformations are so fundamental that they have no associated hints, so they cannot be forced or disabled. In fact, these transformations aren't even disabled by the NO_QUERY_TRANSFORMATION hint. So invisible are these transformations that there are only two ways to know that they exist:

- You can wade through a 10053 trace file. That is what Christian Antognini did.

- You can read Christian's book, *Troubleshooting Oracle Performance*. That is what I did!

There is some merit to discussing a couple of these no-brainers, but I won't attempt to be exhaustive. Let us start with the count transformation.

Count Transformation

Take a look at the two queries and their associated execution plans, shown in Listing 13-1.

Listing 13-1. Count transformation

```
SELECT COUNT (cust_income_level) FROM sh.customers;
------------------------------------------------
| Id | Operation          | Name      |
------------------------------------------------
|  0 | SELECT STATEMENT   |           |
|  1 |  SORT AGGREGATE    |           |
|  2 |   TABLE ACCESS FULL| CUSTOMERS |
------------------------------------------------

SELECT COUNT (cust_id) FROM sh.customers;
-----------------------------------------------------------------
| Id | Operation                   | Name                |
-----------------------------------------------------------------
|  0 | SELECT STATEMENT            |                     |
|  1 |  SORT AGGREGATE             |                     |
|  2 |   BITMAP CONVERSION COUNT   |                     |
|  3 |    BITMAP INDEX FAST FULL SCAN| CUSTOMERS_GENDER_BIX |
-----------------------------------------------------------------
```

Both the execution plans and the results of the two queries are different. It turns out that the CUST_INCOME_LEVEL column in SH.CUSTOMERS does not have a NOT NULL constraint and as such the column may be, and indeed is, NULL for some rows. Such rows are not counted in the first query of Listing 13-1. Since CUST_INCOME_LEVEL is not indexed, the only way to execute COUNT (CUST_INCOME_LEVEL) is to perform a full table scan. However, CUST_ID is NOT NULL and as such COUNT (CUST_ID) can be transformed to COUNT (*). We could implement COUNT (*) by performing a full table scan, but we can also implement COUNT (*) by means of a bitmap index or a B-tree index on a NOT NULL column. In the case of the second query, the index CUSTOMERS_GENDER_BIX is a bitmap index on a non-null column so it is a doubly suitable, cheap alternative to a full table scan.

Getting bored? The next transformation is more interesting, but not by much.

Predicate Move-around

Consider the query and execution plan in Listing 13-2.

Listing 13-2. Predicate move-around

```
WITH cust_q
     AS (  SELECT cust_id, promo_id, SUM (amount_sold) cas
             FROM sh.sales
          GROUP BY cust_id, promo_id)
    ,prod_q
     AS (  SELECT prod_id, promo_id, SUM (amount_sold) pas
             FROM sh.sales
            WHERE promo_id = 999
          GROUP BY prod_id, promo_id)
SELECT promo_id
     ,prod_id
     ,pas
     ,cust_id
     ,cas
  FROM cust_q NATURAL JOIN prod_q;
```

```
-----------------------------------------
| Id  | Operation            | Name  |
-----------------------------------------
|   0 | SELECT STATEMENT     |       |
|*  1 |  HASH JOIN           |       |
|   2 |   VIEW               |       |
|   3 |    HASH GROUP BY     |       |
|   4 |     PARTITION RANGE ALL|     |
|*  5 |      TABLE ACCESS FULL | SALES |
|   6 |   VIEW               |       |
|   7 |    HASH GROUP BY     |       |
|   8 |     PARTITION RANGE ALL|     |
|*  9 |      TABLE ACCESS FULL | SALES |
-----------------------------------------
```

Predicate Information (identified by operation id):

```
   1 - access("CUST_Q"."PROMO_ID"="PROD_Q"."PROMO_ID")
   5 - filter("PROMO_ID"=999)
   9 - filter("PROMO_ID"=999)
```

The query in Listing 13-2 doesn't do anything meaningful. For each combination of product and customer it lists the total amount of sales for PROMO_ID 999 for the customer and the total amount of sales for PROMO_ID 999 for the product. There are two factored subqueries and only one WHERE clause, but the natural join means that, by using transitive closure, we can apply the predicate in the other subquery as well. However, Listing 13-3 makes the query a little more complicated and thus the predicate move-around transformation ceases to function.

Listing 13-3. Predicate move-around not recognized

```
WITH cust_q
    AS (  SELECT cust_id
                ,promo_id
                ,SUM (amount_sold) cas
                ,MAX (SUM (amount_sold)) OVER (PARTITION BY promo_id) max_cust
            FROM sh.sales
        GROUP BY cust_id, promo_id)
    ,prod_q
    AS (  SELECT prod_id
                ,promo_id
                ,SUM (amount_sold) pas
                ,MAX (SUM (amount_sold)) OVER (PARTITION BY promo_id) max_prod
            FROM sh.sales
           WHERE promo_id = 999
        GROUP BY prod_id, promo_id)
SELECT promo_id
      ,prod_id
      ,pas
      ,cust_id
      ,cas
  FROM cust_q NATURAL JOIN prod_q
 WHERE cust_q.cas = cust_q.max_cust AND prod_q.pas = prod_q.max_prod;
```

```
-------------------------------------------
| Id  | Operation              | Name  |
-------------------------------------------
|   0 | SELECT STATEMENT       |       |
|   1 |  MERGE JOIN            |       |
|*  2 |   VIEW                 |       |
|   3 |    WINDOW BUFFER       |       |
|   4 |     SORT GROUP BY      |       |
|   5 |      PARTITION RANGE ALL |     |
|   6 |       TABLE ACCESS FULL | SALES |
|*  7 |   SORT JOIN           |       |
|*  8 |    VIEW                |       |
|   9 |     WINDOW BUFFER      |       |
|  10 |      SORT GROUP BY     |       |
|  11 |       PARTITION RANGE ALL|     |
|* 12 |        TABLE ACCESS FULL | SALES |
-------------------------------------------
```

```
Predicate Information (identified by operation id):
---------------------------------------------------

   2 - filter("CUST_Q"."CAS"="CUST_Q"."MAX_CUST")
   7 - access("CUST_Q"."PROMO_ID"="PROD_Q"."PROMO_ID")
       filter("CUST_Q"."PROMO_ID"="PROD_Q"."PROMO_ID")
   8 - filter("PROD_Q"."PAS"="PROD_Q"."MAX_PROD")
  12 - filter("PROMO_ID"=999)
```

Listing 13-3 does something a lot more meaningful: it identifies the one product that sold the most for PROMO_ID 999 and the one customer for PROMO_ID 999 that bought the most. But the addition of the analytic functions into the subqueries has caused the CBO to lose confidence in the correctness of predicate move-around. To make the query efficient you will have to add the WHERE clause to the CUST_Q factored subquery yourself.

There are one or two other no-brainer transformations:

- **Filter pushdown** is a simpler variant of predicate move-around.

- **Distinct elimination** removes a redundant DISTINCT operation from a query when the operands involve all columns of the primary key, all columns of a unique key that are NOT NULL, or the ROWID.

- **Select list pruning** removes items from the select list of a subquery that aren't referenced.

The key point involving these transformations is that there is no possible downside to their application. For example, there is no chance that you can make a query slower by removing unreferenced items from the select list in a subquery. All of this is of some interest, but not very much, so let us move on to the second group of transformations: set and join transformations.

Set and Join Transformations

There are several transformations related to set and join operations, most of which have only been implemented recently, which is surprising given how useful many of them are. Let us get going with join elimination.

Join Elimination

Join elimination is one of those transformations that can be demonstrated with inline views and factored subqueries but is really intended for general purpose data dictionary views. I will demonstrate this focus on data dictionary views in Listing 13-4, but I will assume the point is understood in future examples.

Listing 13-4. Join elimination with data dictionary views

```
CREATE OR REPLACE VIEW cust_sales
AS
   WITH sales_q
       AS (   SELECT cust_id
                      ,SUM (amount_sold) amount_sold
                      ,AVG (amount_sold) avg_sold
                      ,COUNT (*) cnt
                  FROM sh.sales s
              GROUP BY cust_id)
   SELECT c.*
         ,s.cust_id AS sales_cust_id
         ,s.amount_sold
         ,s.avg_sold
         ,cnt
      FROM sh.customers c JOIN sales_q s ON c.cust_id = s.cust_id;

SELECT sales_cust_id
      ,amount_sold
      ,avg_sold
      ,cnt
  FROM cust_sales;
```

```
-------------------------------------------------
| Id  | Operation                | Name         |
-------------------------------------------------
|   0 | SELECT STATEMENT         |              |
|   1 |  NESTED LOOPS            |              |
|   2 |   VIEW                   |              |
|   3 |    HASH GROUP BY         |              |
|   4 |     PARTITION RANGE ALL  |              |
|   5 |      TABLE ACCESS FULL   | SALES        |
|*  6 |   INDEX UNIQUE SCAN      | CUSTOMERS_PK |
-------------------------------------------------
```

```
CREATE OR REPLACE VIEW cust_sales
AS
   WITH sales_q
       AS (   SELECT cust_id
                      ,SUM (amount_sold) amount_sold
                      ,AVG (amount_sold) avg_sold
                      ,COUNT (*) cnt
                  FROM sh.sales s
              GROUP BY cust_id)
   SELECT c.*
         ,s.cust_id AS sales_cust_id
         ,s.amount_sold
         ,s.avg_sold
         ,cnt
      FROM sh.customers c RIGHT JOIN sales_q s ON c.cust_id = s.cust_id;
```

```
SELECT /*+   eliminate_join(@SEL$13BD1B6A c@sel$2) */
       /* no_eliminate_join(@SEL$13BD1B6A c@sel$2) */ sales_cust_id
       ,amount_sold
       ,avg_sold
       ,cnt
  FROM cust_sales;
```

-- **Untransformed execution plan (NO_ELIMINATE_JOIN)**

```
-----------------------------------------------
| Id  | Operation               | Name         |
-----------------------------------------------
|   0 | SELECT STATEMENT        |              |
|   1 |  NESTED LOOPS OUTER      |              |
|   2 |   VIEW                   |              |
|   3 |    HASH GROUP BY         |              |
|   4 |     PARTITION RANGE ALL  |              |
|   5 |      TABLE ACCESS FULL   | SALES        |
|*  6 |   INDEX UNIQUE SCAN      | CUSTOMERS_PK |
-----------------------------------------------
```

-- **Transformed query**

```
  SELECT cust_id AS sales_cust_id
         ,SUM (amount_sold) amount_sold
         ,AVG (amount_sold) avg_sold
         ,COUNT (*) cnt
     FROM sh.sales s
GROUP BY cust_id;
```

-- **Transformed execution plan (default)**

```
-------------------------------------------
| Id  | Operation               | Name    |
-------------------------------------------
|   0 | SELECT STATEMENT        |         |
|   1 |  HASH GROUP BY          |         |
|   2 |   PARTITION RANGE ALL   |         |
|   3 |    TABLE ACCESS FULL    | SALES   |
-------------------------------------------
```

Listing 13-4 begins by creating data dictionary view CUST_SALES that adds some columns to the SH.CUSTOMERS example schema table, which are obtained by performing aggregation on the SH.SALES table. The query then uses the CUST_SALES view but is only interested in the columns from the SH.SALES table. Unfortunately, the aggregation operation has caused the CBO to lose track of the significance of the referential integrity constraint that ensures that all rows in SH.SALES have exactly one corresponding row in SH.CUSTOMERS. As a result of this the CBO does not apply the join elimination optimization.

Listing 13-4 continues by redefining the CUST_SALES view to use an outer join. This confirms to the CBO that the join of the aggregated SH.SALES data with SH.CUSTOMERS will not result in the loss of any rows and the fact that the join column CUST_ID is the primary key of SH.CUSTOMERS means that the join will not result in the addition of any rows either. The CBO is now confident that the elimination of the join from SH.SALES to SH.CUSTOMERS will not affect the result and proceeds with the transformation.

The second query in Listing 13-4 includes two comments. The first is a hint to force the default behavior. If you remove the first comment and add a plus sign to the second you can disable the transformation. Unfortunately, because the join happens inside a view you have to look at the outline section of DBMS_XPLAN.DISPLAY to identify the query block and generate a global hint if you really want to disable the transformation. Listing 13-4 also shows the execution plan associated with the untransformed query, the transformed query, and the transformed execution plan.

Have a careful look at Listing 13-4 because I will be using this approach as I go through other transformations.

There is one other interesting application of the join elimination that applies to *nested tables*. Because nested tables offer no performance or administrative benefits they aren't seen much in schemas designed in the 21st century. But just in case you are ever need to work with a 20th-century schema, take a look at Listing 13-5, which references the PM.PRINT_MEDIA example schema.

Listing 13-5. Join elimination on a nested table

```
SELECT /*+   eliminate_join(parent_tab) */
       /* no_eliminate_join(parent_tab) */
       nested_tab.document_typ, COUNT (*) cnt
  FROM pm.print_media parent_tab
       ,TABLE (parent_tab.ad_textdocs_ntab) nested_tab
GROUP BY nested_tab.document_typ;

-- Untransformed execution plan (NO_ELIMINATE_JOIN)


-------------------------------------------------
| Id  | Operation            | Name             |
-------------------------------------------------
|   0 | SELECT STATEMENT     |                  |
|   1 |  HASH GROUP BY       |                  |
|   2 |   NESTED LOOPS       |                  |
|   3 |    TABLE ACCESS FULL | TEXTDOCS_NESTEDTAB |
|*  4 |    INDEX UNIQUE SCAN | SYS_C0011792     |
-------------------------------------------------
```

-- Transformed execution plan (default)

```
---------------------------------------------------------------------
| Id  | Operation                            | Name                       |
---------------------------------------------------------------------
|   0 | SELECT STATEMENT                     |                            |
|   1 |  HASH GROUP BY                       |                            |
|   2 |   TABLE ACCESS BY INDEX ROWID BATCHED| TEXTDOCS_NESTEDTAB         |
|*  3 |    INDEX FULL SCAN                   | SYS_FK0000091775N00007$   |
---------------------------------------------------------------------
```

What is interesting about Listing 13-5 is that prior to the introduction of the join elimination transformation in 10gR2 the possibility of referencing a nested table without its parent didn't exist. There is no valid SQL syntax to express the results of the join elimination transformation!

You might think that join elimination should be a *no-brainer*: there can never be any performance benefit to retaining the join. However, I suspect that the creation of hints to control transformations is now a standard, and, if so, I approve. Seeing hints in the outline section of DBMS_XPLAN functions means that you can work out what is happening more easily and allows you to disable the transformation for educational or investigative purposes.

Outer Join to Inner Join

Sometimes an outer join can't be eliminated, but it can be converted to an inner join. Let us take another look at the second definition of the CUST_SALES view in Listing 13-4. Although the change to the view definition helped queries that only needed aggregated SH.SALES data, it made queries that do require columns from SH.CUSTOMERS less efficient. If we change such queries we can eliminate that overhead. Take a look at Listing 13-6.

Listing 13-6. Outer join to inner join transformation

```
SELECT /*+   outer_join_to_inner(@SEL$13BD1B6A c@sel$2) */
       /* no_outer_join_to_inner(@SEL$13BD1B6A c@sel$2) */
       *
 FROM cust_sales c
WHERE cust_id IS NOT NULL;


-- Untransformed execution plan (NO_OUTER_JOIN_TO_INNER)
-----------------------------------------------
| Id  | Operation                | Name      |
-----------------------------------------------
|   0 | SELECT STATEMENT         |           |
|*  1 |  FILTER                  |           |
|*  2 |   HASH JOIN OUTER        |           |
|   3 |    VIEW                  |           |
|   4 |     HASH GROUP BY        |           |
|   5 |      PARTITION RANGE ALL |           |
|   6 |       TABLE ACCESS FULL  | SALES     |
|   7 |    TABLE ACCESS FULL     | CUSTOMERS |
-----------------------------------------------

Predicate Information (identified by operation id):
---------------------------------------------------

   1 - filter("C"."CUST_ID" IS NOT NULL)
   2 - access("C"."CUST_ID"(+)="S"."CUST_ID")

-- Transformed query

WITH sales_q
      AS (  SELECT cust_id
                  ,SUM (amount_sold) amount_sold
                  ,AVG (amount_sold) avg_sold
                  ,COUNT (*) cnt
              FROM sh.sales s
          GROUP BY cust_id)
   SELECT c.*
         ,s.cust_id AS sales_cust_id
         ,s.amount_sold
         ,s.avg_sold
         ,cnt
     FROM sh.customers c JOIN sales_q s ON c.cust_id = s.cust_id;
```

```
-- Transformed execution plan (default)
```

```
---------------------------------------------
| Id | Operation             | Name      |
---------------------------------------------
|  0 | SELECT STATEMENT      |           |
|* 1 | HASH JOIN             |           |
|  2 |  VIEW                 |           |
|  3 |   HASH GROUP BY       |           |
|  4 |    PARTITION RANGE ALL|           |
|  5 |     TABLE ACCESS FULL | SALES     |
|  6 |  TABLE ACCESS FULL    | CUSTOMERS |
---------------------------------------------

Predicate Information (identified by operation id):
---------------------------------------------------

   1 - access("C"."CUST_ID"="S"."CUST_ID")
```

Leaving aside the referential integrity constraint for a minute, the potential difference between an outer join and an inner join with SH.CUSTOMERS is that extra rows might be added with C.CUST_ID NULL. The presence of the WHERE cust_id IS NOT NULL predicate means that any such additional rows would be eliminated, so the CBO will apply the transformation from an outer join to an inner join unless prohibited from doing so by a hint.

Full Outer Join to Outer Join

A logical extension to the outer-join-to-inner-join transformation is the full-outer-join-to-outer-join transformation. Precisely the same principles apply. If you understood Listing 13-6, Listing 13-7 should be self-explanatory.

Listing 13-7. Full outer join to outer join

```
SELECT /*+    full_outer_join_to_outer(cust) */
       /*  no_full_outer_join_to_outer(cust) */
       *
 FROM sh.countries FULL OUTER JOIN sh.customers cust USING (country_id)
WHERE cust.cust_id IS NOT NULL;

-- Untransformed execution plan (NO_FULL_OUTER_JOIN_TO_OUTER)
---------------------------------------------
| Id  | Operation            | Name      |
---------------------------------------------
|   0 | SELECT STATEMENT     |           |
|*  1 |  VIEW                | VW_FOJ_O  |
|*  2 |   HASH JOIN FULL OUTER|          |
|   3 |    TABLE ACCESS FULL | COUNTRIES |
|   4 |    TABLE ACCESS FULL | CUSTOMERS |
---------------------------------------------

Predicate Information (identified by operation id):
---------------------------------------------------

   1 - filter("CUST"."CUST_ID" IS NOT NULL)
   2 - access("COUNTRIES"."COUNTRY_ID"="CUST"."COUNTRY_ID")

-- Transformed query

SELECT *
  FROM sh.countries RIGHT OUTER JOIN sh.customers cust USING (country_id);
```

-- Transformed execution plan (default)

```
-------------------------------------------
| Id  | Operation            | Name      |
-------------------------------------------
|   0 | SELECT STATEMENT     |           |
|*  1 | HASH JOIN RIGHT OUTER|           |
|   2 |  TABLE ACCESS FULL   | COUNTRIES |
|   3 |  TABLE ACCESS FULL   | CUSTOMERS |
-------------------------------------------

Predicate Information (identified by operation id):
---------------------------------------------------

   1 - access("COUNTRIES"."COUNTRY_ID"(+)="CUST"."COUNTRY_ID")
```

Of course, if we were to add a predicate such as WHERE COUNTRIES.COUNTRY_NAME IS NOT NULL to Listing 13-7 we could apply the outer-join-to-inner-join transformation as well and we would get an inner join.

Semi-Join to Inner Join

Although the semi-join-to-inner-join transformation has been around for some time, the hint to manage the transformation is new to 11.2.0.3. Listing 13-8 demonstrates.

Listing 13-8. Semi-join to inner join

```
SELECT *
  FROM sh.sales s
 WHERE EXISTS
         (SELECT /*+   semi_to_inner(c) */
                 /*  no_semi_to_inner(c) */
               1
           FROM sh.customers c
          WHERE    c.cust_id = s.cust_id
                AND cust_first_name = 'Abner'
                AND cust_last_name = 'Everett');
```

-- Untransformed execution plan (NO_SEMI_TO_INNER)

```
---------------------------------------------
| Id  | Operation            | Name      |
---------------------------------------------
|   0 | SELECT STATEMENT     |           |
|*  1 | HASH JOIN RIGHT SEMI |           |
|*  2 |   TABLE ACCESS FULL  | CUSTOMERS |
|   3 |   PARTITION RANGE ALL|           |
|   4 |    TABLE ACCESS FULL | SALES     |
---------------------------------------------
```

Predicate Information (identified by operation id):

```
   1 - access("C"."CUST_ID"="S"."CUST_ID")
   2 - filter("CUST_FIRST_NAME"='Abner' AND "CUST_LAST_NAME"='Everett')
```

-- Transformed query (approximate)

```
WITH q1
     AS (SELECT DISTINCT cust_id
           FROM sh.customers
          WHERE cust_first_name = 'Abner' AND cust_last_name = 'Everett')
SELECT s.*
  FROM sh.sales s JOIN q1 ON s.cust_id = q1.cust_id;
```

-- Transfomed execution plan (default)

```
-----------------------------------------------------------
| Id | Operation                         | Name           |
-----------------------------------------------------------
|  0 | SELECT STATEMENT                  |                |
|  1 |  NESTED LOOPS                     |                |
|  2 |   NESTED LOOPS                    |                |
|  3 |    SORT UNIQUE                    |                |
|* 4 |     TABLE ACCESS FULL             | CUSTOMERS      |
|  5 |     PARTITION RANGE ALL           |                |
|  6 |      BITMAP CONVERSION TO ROWIDS  |                |
|* 7 |       BITMAP INDEX SINGLE VALUE   | SALES_CUST_BIX |
|  8 |    TABLE ACCESS BY LOCAL INDEX ROWID| SALES        |
-----------------------------------------------------------

Predicate Information (identified by operation id):
---------------------------------------------------

   4 - filter("CUST_FIRST_NAME"='Abner' AND "CUST_LAST_NAME"='Everett')
   7 - access("C"."CUST_ID"="S"."CUST_ID")
```

The transformation shown in Listing 13-8 allows additional join orders for nested loops and merge semi-joins. Prior to the creation of this transformation semi-joins required that the unnested subquery be the probe row source of a nested loops or merge semi-join (join inputs can be swapped for hash joins). Now that we can transform the semi-join to an inner join, we can use the subquery as the driving row source.

Notice that there is a SORT UNIQUE operation in the transformed execution plan. The purpose of this operation is to ensure that any row from SH.SALES appears at most once in the result set. However, if you take the transformed query and run DBMS_XPLAN.DISPLAY on *that* query you will not see this SORT UNIQUE operation. This is because the no-brainer distinct elimination transformation is performed if the transformed query is directly executed or explained. I imagine that the redundant SORT UNIQUE operation introduced by the transformation will disappear in a future release.

Subquery Unnesting

We have already seen the subquery unnesting transformation in the context of semi-joins and anti-joins in Chapter 11. We will also be looking at unnesting of subqueries in the select list in Chapter 14. However, there are one or two other variants of subquery unnesting that I want to address here. Take a look at Listing 13-9.

Listing 13-9. Subquery unnesting with decorrelation

```
SELECT c.cust_first_name, c.cust_last_name, s1.amount_sold
  FROM sh.customers c, sh.sales s1
 WHERE      s1.amount_sold = (SELECT /*      unnest */
                                     /*+ no_unnest */
                                     MAX (amount_sold)
                                FROM sh.sales s2
                               WHERE s1.cust_id = s2.cust_id)
       AND c.cust_id = s1.cust_id;
```

-- **Untransformed execution plan (NO_UNNEST)**

```
---------------------------------------------------------------------
| Id  | Operation                                   | Name          |
---------------------------------------------------------------------
|   0 | SELECT STATEMENT                            |               |
|*  1 |  FILTER                                     |               |
|*  2 |   HASH JOIN                                 |               |
|   3 |    TABLE ACCESS FULL                        | CUSTOMERS     |
|   4 |    PARTITION RANGE ALL                      |               |
|   5 |     TABLE ACCESS FULL                       | SALES         |
|   6 |   SORT AGGREGATE                            |               |
|   7 |    PARTITION RANGE ALL                      |               |
|   8 |     TABLE ACCESS BY LOCAL INDEX ROWID BATCHED| SALES        |
|   9 |      BITMAP CONVERSION TO ROWIDS            |               |
|* 10 |       BITMAP INDEX SINGLE VALUE             | SALES_CUST_BIX |
---------------------------------------------------------------------
```

Predicate Information (identified by operation id):

```
   1 - filter("S1"."AMOUNT_SOLD"= (SELECT /*+ NO_UNNEST */
            MAX("AMOUNT_SOLD") FROM "SH"."SALES" "S2" WHERE "S2"."CUST_ID"=:B1))
   2 - access("C"."CUST_ID"="S1"."CUST_ID")
  10 - access("S2"."CUST_ID"=:B1
```

-- **Transformed query**

```
WITH vw_sq_1
     AS (  SELECT cust_id AS sq_cust_id, MAX (amount_sold) max_amount_sold
             FROM sh.sales s2
         GROUP BY cust_id)
SELECT c.cust_first_name, c.cust_last_name, s1.amount_sold
  FROM sh.sales s1, sh.customers c, vw_sq_1
 WHERE      s1.amount_sold = vw_sq_1.max_amount_sold
       AND s1.cust_id = vw_sq_1.sq_cust_id
       AND s1.cust_id = c.cust_id;
```

-- Transfomed execution plan (default)

```
-------------------------------------------------------
| Id  | Operation                   | Name        |
-------------------------------------------------------
|   0 | SELECT STATEMENT            |             |
|   1 |  NESTED LOOPS               |             |
|   2 |   NESTED LOOPS              |             |
|*  3 |    HASH JOIN                |             |
|   4 |     VIEW                    | VW_SQ_1     |
|   5 |      HASH GROUP BY          |             |
|   6 |       PARTITION RANGE ALL   |             |
|   7 |        TABLE ACCESS FULL    | SALES       |
|   8 |     PARTITION RANGE ALL     |             |
|   9 |      TABLE ACCESS FULL      | SALES       |
|* 10 |    INDEX UNIQUE SCAN        | CUSTOMERS_PK|
|  11 |   TABLE ACCESS BY INDEX ROWID| CUSTOMERS  |
-------------------------------------------------------
```

Predicate Information (identified by operation id):

```
   3 - access("S1"."AMOUNT_SOLD"="MAX(AMOUNT_SOLD)" AND
              "S1"."CUST_ID"="ITEM_1")
  10 - access("C"."CUST_ID"="S1"."CUST_ID")
```

The original subquery in the WHERE clause is a *correlated* subquery, meaning that in the untransformed query that subquery is logically executed for every row returned by the join. However, in the transformed query the aggregation is performed just once, aggregating for every value of CUST_ID.

Subquery unnesting is rather unusual in that it is sometimes applied as a *cost-based transformation* and sometimes as a *heuristic transformation*. If you use a construct such as WHERE C1 = (<subquery>), subquery unnesting is cost based. However, in all the listings in this book, subquery unnesting is applied as a heuristic transformation, meaning that the CBO does not use the cost-based framework to determine whether to apply the transformation. In common with all the other transformations we have discussed so far (except the semi-to-inner transformation), subquery unnesting is *always* performed (unless hinted) regardless of whether or not performance is expected to improve. In the cases of all the optimizer transformations that we have discussed so far, there hasn't been any chance that the transformations would harm performance. It definitely *is* possible for subquery unnesting to harm performance in some cases. We will return to the topic of the potential performance impact of heuristic transformations in Chapters 14 and 18, but for now just make a mental note of it. We need to turn our attention to another case of subquery unnesting, seen in Listing 13-10.

Listing 13-10. Subquery unnesting using window functions

```
SELECT c.cust_first_name, c.cust_last_name, s1.amount_sold
  FROM sh.customers c, sh.sales s1
 WHERE      amount_sold = (SELECT /*      unnest */
                                  /*+ no_unnest */
MAX (amount_sold)
                              FROM sh.sales s2
                             WHERE c.cust_id = s2.cust_id)
       AND c.cust_id = s1.cust_id;
```

-- **Untransformed execution plan (NO_UNNEST)**

```
-----------------------------------------------------------------------
| Id  | Operation                                     | Name            |
-----------------------------------------------------------------------
|   0 | SELECT STATEMENT                              |                 |
|*  1 |  FILTER                                       |                 |
|*  2 |   HASH JOIN                                   |                 |
|   3 |    TABLE ACCESS FULL                          | CUSTOMERS       |
|   4 |    PARTITION RANGE ALL                        |                 |
|   5 |     TABLE ACCESS FULL                         | SALES           |
|   6 |   SORT AGGREGATE                              |                 |
|   7 |    PARTITION RANGE ALL                        |                 |
|   8 |     TABLE ACCESS BY LOCAL INDEX ROWID BATCHED | SALES           |
|   9 |      BITMAP CONVERSION TO ROWIDS              |                 |
|* 10 |       BITMAP INDEX SINGLE VALUE               | SALES_CUST_BIX  |
-----------------------------------------------------------------------
```

```
Predicate Information (identified by operation id):
---------------------------------------------------

   1 - filter("AMOUNT_SOLD"= (SELECT /*+ NO_UNNEST */
             MAX("AMOUNT_SOLD") FROM "SH"."SALES" "S2" WHERE "S2"."CUST_ID"=:B1))
   2 - access("C"."CUST_ID"="S1"."CUST_ID")
  10 - access("S2"."CUST_ID"=:B1)
```

-- **Transformed query**

```
WITH vw_wif_1
    AS (SELECT c.cust_first_name
              ,c.cust_last_name
              ,s.amount_sold
              ,MAX (amount_sold) OVER (PARTITION BY s.cust_id) AS item_4
          FROM sh.customers c, sh.sales s
         WHERE s.cust_id = c.cust_id)
SELECT cust_first_name, cust_last_name, amount_sold
  FROM vw_wif_1
 WHERE CASE WHEN item_4 = amount_sold THEN ROWID END IS NOT NULL;
```

```
-- Transformed execution plan (default)
-------------------------------------------
| Id | Operation               | Name      |
-------------------------------------------
|  0 | SELECT STATEMENT        |           |
|* 1 |  VIEW                   | VW_WIF_1  |
|  2 |   WINDOW SORT           |           |
|* 3 |    HASH JOIN            |           |
|  4 |     TABLE ACCESS FULL   | CUSTOMERS |
|  5 |     PARTITION RANGE ALL|           |
|  6 |      TABLE ACCESS FULL  | SALES     |
-------------------------------------------

Predicate Information (identified by operation id):
--------------------------------------------------

   1 - filter("VW_COL_4" IS NOT NULL)
   3 - access("C"."CUST_ID"="S1"."CUST_ID")
```

The difference in the queries shown in Listing 13-9 and Listing 13-10 is difficult to spot. In fact, the correlating column in Listing 13-9 is S1.CUST_ID and in Listing 13-10 it is C.CUST_ID. Given that there is also a predicate in the queries that equates S1.CUST_ID and C.CUST_ID, it may be a surprise that the resulting execution plan in Listing 13-10 differs so much from that in Listing 13-9. This is an example of a problem with *transitive closure,* and we will return to this topic in Chapter 14. For now, let us just accept that because the correlating column (C.CUST_ID) is from one table and the subquery is equated with a column from another table (S1.AMOUNT_SOLD), Listing 13-10 uses a different variant of subquery unnesting than did Listing 13-9. We can see that in Listing 13-9 we have two full scans of SH.SALES (bad) but no sort (good). In Listing 13-10 we have only one scan of SH.SALES (good) as well as a sort (bad). If you have a query like the ones in the last two listings it might be best to experiment with a code change to see which execution plan performs best.

The transformed query in Listing 13-10 sorts all the rows from the result of the join and then selects just the highest ranking. Why the convoluted predicate involving a case expression? I wouldn't want to speculate.

Partial Joins

Partial joins are a new feature of 12cR1, but in my opinion they haven't been explained well. Let me see if I can provide another angle on things. Take a look at Listing 13-11.

Listing 13-11. Partial join transformation

```
SELECT /*+    partial_join(iv) */
       /*  no_partial_join(iv) */
       product_id, MAX (it.quantity)
  FROM oe.order_items it JOIN oe.inventories iv USING (product_id)
GROUP BY product_id;
```

-- Untransformed execution plan (NO_PARTIAL_JOIN)

```
-----------------------------------------------
| Id | Operation             | Name         |
-----------------------------------------------
|  0 | SELECT STATEMENT      |              |
|  1 |  HASH GROUP BY        |              |
|* 2 |   HASH JOIN           |              |
|  3 |    TABLE ACCESS FULL  | ORDER_ITEMS  |
|  4 |    INDEX FAST FULL SCAN| INVENTORY_IX |
-----------------------------------------------
```

Predicate Information (identified by operation id):

```
   2 - access("IT"."PRODUCT_ID"="IV"."PRODUCT_ID")
```
-- Transformed query

```
  SELECT product_id, MAX (quantity)
    FROM oe.order_items it
   WHERE EXISTS
            (SELECT 1
               FROM oe.inventories iv
              WHERE it.product_id = iv.product_id)
GROUP BY it.product_id;
```

-- Transformed execution plan (default)

```
-----------------------------------------------
| Id | Operation             | Name         |
-----------------------------------------------
|  0 | SELECT STATEMENT      |              |
|  1 |  HASH GROUP BY        |              |
|* 2 |   HASH JOIN SEMI      |              |
|  3 |    TABLE ACCESS FULL  | ORDER_ITEMS  |
|  4 |    INDEX FAST FULL SCAN| INVENTORY_IX |
-----------------------------------------------
```

Predicate Information (identified by operation id):

```
   2 - access("IT"."PRODUCT_ID"="IV"."PRODUCT_ID")
```

As you can see, the partial join converts an inner join to a semi-join. But earlier we had the semi-to-inner-join transformation, didn't we? Are you confused? I was. Let me unravel the mystery.

The benefits of the partial join are best explained with a join of two tables that have a many-to-many relationship, so in Listing 13-11 I have temporarily abandoned the SH example schema and used two tables from the OE example schema that have a many-to-many relationship.

Let us take PRODUCT_ID 1797 as an example and see first how the untransformed query processes it. This product forms part of three orders, and the values of QUANTITY in the three matching rows in OE.ORDER_ITEMS are 7, 9, and 12, respectively. PRODUCT_ID 1797 is also in stock at three warehouses, so there are three rows matching PRODUCT_ID 1797 in OE.INVENTORIES. When we join OE.ORDER_ITEMS and OE.INVENTORIES using the PRODUCT_ID we get nine rows for PRODUCT_ID 1797 with values of QUANTITY 7, 9, 12, 7, 9, 12, 7, 9, and 12 (the three rows from OE.ORDER_ITEMS being replicated three times). When we input these nine rows into our HASH GROUP BY operation we get a value of 12 for MAX (QUANTITY). If we had included MIN (QUANTITY), SUM (DISTINCT QUANTITY), AVG (QUANTITY), and SUM (QUANTITY) in our select list we would have got 7, 28, 9⅓, and 84, respectively.

The transformation to the semi-join prevents the duplication of rows from OE.ORDER_ITEMS as a result of any duplicate values of PRODUCT_ID 1797 in OE.INVENTORIES, so the values input to the HASH GROUP BY operation are just 7, 9, and 12. The value of MAX (PRODUCT_ID) is 12, precisely the same as if we had processed all nine rows. The values of MIN (QUANTITY), SUM (DISTINCT QUANTITY), AVG (QUANTITY), and SUM (QUANTITY) based on these rows would be 7, 28, 9⅓, and 28, respectively. All my example aggregate values are the same for the three rows in the transformed query as for the nine rows in the untransformed query, except SUM (QUANTITY), which yields a different result. As a consequence, if you try adding SUM (QUANTITY) to the select list of the query in Listing 13-11 you will find that the partial join is suddenly illegal. In 12.1.0.1 the AVG (QUANTITY) function will also disable partial joins, and I speculate that this is because COUNT (QUANTITY) and SUM (QUANTITY) are both genuinely illegal. This is the sort of thing that might get fixed in a later release.

The main benefit of the partial join is to reduce the number of rows being input to a GROUP BY or DISTINCT operation. In the case of the HASH JOIN SEMI operation in the transformed execution plan, this is accomplished by removing the entries from the hash cluster as soon as one match is found. From then on, no further rows from OE.INVENTORIES with the same PRODUCT_ID will match.

The partial join also has some interesting side benefits when applied to nested loops joins. Take a look at Listing 13-12, which displays edited runtime statistics along with the execution plan.

Listing 13-12. Partial join transformation with nested loops join

```
BEGIN
    FOR r IN (  SELECT /*+ TAGPJ gather_plan_statistics */
                    cust_id, MAX (s.amount_sold)
                FROM sh.customers c JOIN sh.sales s USING (cust_id)
                WHERE s.amount_sold > 1782 AND s.prod_id = 18
            GROUP BY cust_id)
    LOOP
        NULL;
    END LOOP;
END;

SET LINES 200 PAGES 0

SELECT p.*
  FROM v$sql s
      ,TABLE (
          DBMS_XPLAN.display_cursor (s.sql_id
                                    ,s.child_number
                                    ,'BASIC IOSTATS LAST')) p
  WHERE sql_text LIKE 'SELECT /*+ TAGPJ%';
```

```
--------------------------------------------------------------------------
| Id | Operation                   | Name           | Starts | E-Rows | A-Rows |
--------------------------------------------------------------------------
|  0 | SELECT STATEMENT            |                |    1 |        |     83 |
|  1 | HASH GROUP BY               |                |    1 |      3 |     83 |
|  2 |   NESTED LOOPS SEMI         |                |    1 |      3 |    108 |
|  3 |    PARTITION RANGE ALL      |                |    1 |      3 |    108 |
|* 4 |     TABLE ACCESS BY LOCAL IND| SALES         |   28 |      3 |    108 |
|  5 |      BITMAP CONVERSION TO ROW|               |   16 |        |   9591 |
|* 6 |       BITMAP INDEX SINGLE VAL| SALES_PROD_BIX |   16 |        |     16 |
|* 7 |    INDEX UNIQUE SCAN        | CUSTOMERS_PK   |   83 |  55500 |     83 |
--------------------------------------------------------------------------
```

Predicate Information (identified by operation id):

```
4 - filter("SALES"."AMOUNT_SOLD">1782)
6 - access("SALES"."PROD_ID"=18)
7 - access("CUSTOMERS"."CUST_ID"="SALES"."CUST_ID")
```

At first glance the partial join applied to the nested loops join in Listing 13-12 seems pointless. There is a primary key constraint on the CUST_ID column of SH.CUSTOMERS, so there will only be one row obtained by the INDEX UNIQUE SCAN on line 7, so what benefit comes from converting NESTED LOOPS to NESTED LOOPS SEMI? The answer can be seen by looking at the STARTS column of operation 7. Despite the fact that there are 108 rows from SH.SALES that match the predicates SH.PROD_ID=18 and SH.AMOUNT_SOLD > 1782, the INDEX UNIQUE SCAN was only performed 83 times! This is because there are only 83 distinct values of CUST_ID in those 108 rows and the NESTED LOOPS SEMI and NESTED LOOPS ANTI join operations can take advantage of scalar subquery caching. A regular NESTED LOOPS join cannot!

But perhaps we are getting distracted. The main purpose of the partial join transformation is to eliminate rows as early in the process as possible that would otherwise be pointlessly input to a DISTINCT or GROUP BY operation. This requires the conversion of an inner join to a semi-join. On the other hand, the purpose of the semi-to-inner-join transformation is to allow the subquery to act as the driving row source in a NESTED LOOPS or MERGE join operation. These two goals are mutually exclusive. Fortunately, both the partial join and the semi-to-inner-join transformations are cost based, and the CBO will not perform a partial join transformation when it thinks that doing so would create a disadvantageous join order.

Join Factorization

The purpose of the join factorization transformation is to remove common components from the operands of a UNION ALL operation and then apply them once—after the operation. Listing 13-13 provides an example.

Listing 13-13. Join factorization

```
SELECT /*+   factorize_join(@set$1(s@u1 S@u2)) qb_name(u1) */
       /* no_factorize_join(@set$1) */
       *
  FROM sh.sales s, sh.customers c
 WHERE     c.cust_first_name = 'Abner'
       AND c.cust_last_name = 'Everett'
       AND s.cust_id = c.cust_id
/* AND prod_id = 13
AND time_id = DATE '2001-09-13' */

UNION ALL
SELECT /*+ qb_name(u2) */
       *
  FROM sh.sales s, sh.customers c
 WHERE     c.cust_first_name = 'Abigail'
       AND c.cust_last_name = 'Ruddy'
       AND s.cust_id = c.cust_id
/* AND prod_id = 13
AND time_id = DATE '2001-09-13' */;
```

-- **Untransformed execution plan (NO_FACTORIZE_JOIN)**

```
-------------------------------------------------------------
| Id  | Operation                    | Name            |
-------------------------------------------------------------
|   0 | SELECT STATEMENT             |                 |
|   1 |  UNION-ALL                   |                 |
|   2 |   NESTED LOOPS               |                 |
|   3 |    NESTED LOOPS              |                 |
|*  4 |     TABLE ACCESS FULL        | CUSTOMERS       |
|   5 |     PARTITION RANGE ALL      |                 |
|   6 |      BITMAP CONVERSION TO ROWIDS |             |
|*  7 |       BITMAP INDEX SINGLE VALUE  | SALES_CUST_BIX |
|   8 |     TABLE ACCESS BY LOCAL INDEX ROWID| SALES   |
|   9 |   NESTED LOOPS               |                 |
|  10 |    NESTED LOOPS              |                 |
|* 11 |     TABLE ACCESS FULL        | CUSTOMERS       |
|  12 |     PARTITION RANGE ALL      |                 |
|  13 |      BITMAP CONVERSION TO ROWIDS |             |
|* 14 |       BITMAP INDEX SINGLE VALUE  | SALES_CUST_BIX |
|  15 |     TABLE ACCESS BY LOCAL INDEX ROWID| SALES   |
-------------------------------------------------------------

Predicate Information (identified by operation id):
---------------------------------------------------

   4 - filter("C"."CUST_FIRST_NAME"='Abner' AND
              "C"."CUST_LAST_NAME"='Everett')
   7 - access("S"."CUST_ID"="C"."CUST_ID")
```

```
 11 - filter("C"."CUST_FIRST_NAME"='Abigail' AND
             "C"."CUST_LAST_NAME"='Ruddy')
 14 - access("S"."CUST_ID"="C"."CUST_ID")
```

-- Transformed query

```
WITH vw_jf
     AS (SELECT *
           FROM sh.customers c
          WHERE c.cust_first_name = 'Abner' AND c.cust_last_name = 'Everett'
         UNION ALL
         SELECT *
           FROM sh.customers c
          WHERE c.cust_first_name = 'Abigail' AND c.cust_last_name = 'Ruddy')
SELECT *
  FROM sh.sales s, vw_jf
 WHERE s.cust_id = vw_jf.cust_id;
```

-- Transformed execution plan (default)

```
----------------------------------------------------
| Id  | Operation            | Name                 |
----------------------------------------------------
|   0 | SELECT STATEMENT     |                      |
|*  1 |  HASH JOIN           |                      |
|   2 |   VIEW               | VW_JF_SET$F472D255   |
|   3 |    UNION-ALL         |                      |
|*  4 |     TABLE ACCESS FULL| CUSTOMERS            |
|*  5 |     TABLE ACCESS FULL| CUSTOMERS            |
|   6 |   PARTITION RANGE ALL|                      |
|   7 |    TABLE ACCESS FULL | SALES                |
----------------------------------------------------
```

Predicate Information (identified by operation id):
```
----------------------------------------------------

   6 - access("TIME_ID"=TO_DATE(' 2001-09-13 00:00:00', 'syyyy-mm-dd
               hh24:mi:ss'))
   7 - access("PROD_ID"=13)
  10 - filter("C"."CUST_FIRST_NAME"='Abner' AND
              "C"."CUST_LAST_NAME"='Everett')
  11 - access("C"."CUST_ID"="S"."CUST_ID")
  12 - filter("C"."CUST_FIRST_NAME"='Abigail' AND
              "C"."CUST_LAST_NAME"='Ruddy')
  13 - access("C"."CUST_ID"="S"."CUST_ID")
```

The two branches of the original query in Listing 13-13 both reference the SH.SALES table in identical ways. The transformed query extracts the joins in the two branches and performs just one join after the UNION ALL operation. As you can imagine, this transformation may generate huge savings, but in this case we have replaced two indexed accesses with one full table scan and the benefit is small. In fact, if you add the commented out predicates it would actually be disadvantageous to perform join factorization. Fortunately, join factorization is a cost-based transformation and you will find that when the additional predicates are included the transformation will not be applied unless forced with a hint.

Hinting join factorization is tricky because the hint applies to a set query block. This creates a series of cascading complications.

1. It is not possible to use a local FACTORIZE_JOIN hint, and we need to resort to global hint syntax.

2. The global hint syntax means that we need to refer to the row sources being factorized using the query blocks in which they are contained. Although it wasn't strictly necessary, I have named the query blocks in the UNION ALL branches as U1 and U2 using QB_NAME hints to make the example clearer.

3. QB_NAME hinting is only practical with traditional join syntax so I have had to abandon ANSI join syntax in Listing 13-13.

Set to Join

It is possible to express INTERSECT and MINUS set operations as joins. Listing 13-14 shows how this is done.

Listing 13-14. Set to join transformation

```
SELECT /*+ set_to_join(@set$1) */ /* no_set_to_join(@set$1) */
       prod_id
  FROM sh.sales s1
 WHERE time_id < DATE '2000-01-01' AND cust_id = 13
MINUS
SELECT prod_id
  FROM sh.sales s2
 WHERE time_id >=DATE '2000-01-01';
```

```
-- Untransformed execution plan (default)
```

Id	Operation	Name	Cost (%CPU)
0	SELECT STATEMENT		**2396** (99)
1	MINUS		
2	**SORT UNIQUE**		24 (0)
3	PARTITION RANGE ITERATOR		24 (0)
4	TABLE ACCESS BY LOCAL INDEX ROWID BATCHED	SALES	24 (0)
5	BITMAP CONVERSION TO ROWIDS		
* 6	BITMAP INDEX SINGLE VALUE	SALES_CUST_BIX	
7	**SORT UNIQUE**		2372 (1)
8	PARTITION RANGE ITERATOR		275 (2)
9	TABLE ACCESS FULL	SALES	275 (2)

```
Predicate Information (identified by operation id):
-----------------------------------------------------

   6 - access("CUST_ID"=13)
```

-- Transformed query

```
SELECT DISTINCT s1.prod_id
  FROM sh.sales s1
 WHERE     time_id < DATE '2000-01-01'
       AND cust_id = 13
       AND prod_id NOT IN (SELECT prod_id
                             FROM sh.sales s2
                            WHERE time_id >=DATE '2000-01-01');
```

-- Transfomed execution plan (SET_TO_JOIN)

```
--------------------------------------------------------------------------------
| Id  | Operation                                   | Name            | Cost (%CPU)|
--------------------------------------------------------------------------------
|   0 | SELECT STATEMENT                            |                 |  301   (2)|
|   1 |  HASH UNIQUE                                |                 |  301   (2)|
|*  2 |   HASH JOIN ANTI                            |                 |  301   (2)|
|   3 |    PARTITION RANGE ITERATOR                 |                 |   24   (0)|
|   4 |     TABLE ACCESS BY LOCAL INDEX ROWID BATCHED| SALES          |   24   (0)|
|   5 |      BITMAP CONVERSION TO ROWIDS            |                 |           |
|*  6 |       BITMAP INDEX SINGLE VALUE             | SALES_CUST_BIX  |           |
|   7 |    PARTITION RANGE ITERATOR                 |                 |  275   (2)|
|   8 |     TABLE ACCESS FULL                       | SALES           |  275   (2)|
--------------------------------------------------------------------------------
```

```
Predicate Information (identified by operation id):
-----------------------------------------------------

   2 - access("PROD_ID"="PROD_ID")
   6 - access("CUST_ID"=13)
```

The query in Listing 13-14 identifies the products that CUST_ID 13 bought in the 20th century that were not sold to anyone in the 21st century. The untransformed query performs unique sorts on each of the two branches of the UNION ALL operation before identifying the elements of the result set; this is how MINUS and INTERSECT set operations are always implemented. The application of the transformation means that one of these two sorts can be avoided. But take a look at operation 2 in the execution plan of the transformed query—the workarea for the HASH JOIN ANTI operation includes duplicate values, so we need to ask ourselves whether this transformation is, in fact, worthwhile. In this case CUST_ID 13 only made 19 transactions for 6 products in the 20th century, so eliminating 13 rows from this workarea isn't a big deal. However, the transformation has avoided a unique sort of the 72 products from the 492,064 rows from SH.SALES relating to transactions in the 21st century. The transformation is a good idea on this occasion.

Despite the fact that the cost estimates show that the CBO believes (correctly) that the set-to-join transformation results in a superior execution plan, the transformation will not be applied to the unhinted query and will normally *never* be applied unless hinted!

To understand the reason why we need to use the SET_TO_JOIN hint in Listing 13-14, we need to understand a little more about the difference between cost-based transformations and heuristic transformations. When the CBO considers cost-based transformations, it attempts to determine whether the transformation will reduce the elapsed time of the query; if the transformation will reduce the estimated elapsed time of the query—i.e., the cost is lower—the transformation will be applied, otherwise the transformation will not be applied. A heuristic transformation works by applying a rule of some kind. So far all the heuristic transformations that we have come across in this chapter are applied unconditionally unless disabled by a hint. The working assumption in these cases is that the hint will probably, if not certainly, help.,

In the case of the set-to-join heuristic transformation, the heuristic rule is that the transformation is *never* applied unless hinted, the working assumption being that the cases where the transformation is needed are rare. Given the need for the CBO to come up with a plan in milliseconds, the CBO will not waste its time looking at the set-to-join transformation unless you hint it.

If you like playing around with hidden initialization parameters and don't care about the support implications of doing so, you can change the value of "_convert_set_to_join". If you change the value of this parameter from its default value of FALSE to TRUE at the session level, the heuristic rule will be altered so that the transformation is *always* applied. This is the only circumstance in which you would need to use the NO_SET_TO_JOIN hint to disable the transformation.

The set-to-join transformation provides a fitting end to our discussion of set- and join-related transformations. We can now turn our attention to a new class of transformations relating to aggregate operations.

Aggregation Transformations

Aggregations are a surprisingly complex matter in Oracle databases and figure heavily in the life of a SQL tuning specialist. We need to understand what information needs to be aggregated, when it is to be aggregated, and how it is to be aggregated. In recent releases Oracle has included a number of aggregate-related transformations that not only help query performance but also act as excellent educational guides that you can use to aid your analysis of queries containing aggregations. Let us get started with a look at how distinct aggregations can be optimized.

Distinct Aggregation

I don't know about you, but I have always felt that an aggregate function including the DISTINCT keyword is inherently inefficient and that using it is just a bit lazy. I don't have to worry now because these days the CBO will convert my concise query into something less concise but more efficient. Take a look at Listing 13-15.

Listing 13-15. Distinct aggregation transformation

```
SELECT /*+   transform_distinct_agg */
       /* no_transform_distinct_agg */
    COUNT (DISTINCT cust_id) FROM sh.sales;
```

```
-- Untransformed execution plan (NO_TRANSFORM_DISTINCT_AGG)
```

Id	Operation	Name	Cost (%CPU)
0	SELECT STATEMENT		**407** (0)
1	**SORT GROUP BY**		
2	PARTITION RANGE ALL		407 (0)
3	BITMAP CONVERSION TO ROWIDS		407 (0)
4	BITMAP INDEX FAST FULL SCAN	SALES_CUST_BIX	

-- Transformed query

```
WITH vw_dag
    AS (  SELECT cust_id
            FROM sh.sales
        GROUP BY cust_id)
SELECT COUNT (cust_id)
  FROM vw_dag;
```

-- Transformed execution plan (default)

```
-------------------------------------------------------------------
| Id | Operation                   | Name          | Cost (%CPU)|
-------------------------------------------------------------------
|  0 | SELECT STATEMENT            |               |  428    (5)|
|  1 |  SORT AGGREGATE             |               |            |
|  2 |   VIEW                      | VW_DAG_0      |  428    (5)|
|  3 |    HASH GROUP BY            |               |  428    (5)|
|  4 |     PARTITION RANGE ALL     |               |  407    (0)|
|  5 |      BITMAP CONVERSION TO ROWIDS |          |  407    (0)|
|  6 |       BITMAP INDEX FAST FULL SCAN| SALES_CUST_BIX |        |
-------------------------------------------------------------------
```

The distinct aggregation transformation was introduced in 11gR2 and, as far as I can see, is a heuristic transformation that is unconditionally applied where legal. The estimated cost is higher with the transformation than without, but by separating the job of identifying the distinct values from the job of counting them the query is actually much faster.

Distinct Placement

Distinct placement is a cost-based transformation used from 11gR2 onwards to eliminate duplicate rows as soon as possible. Conceptually, distinct placement and group by placement, which we will discuss in the next section, are very similar. Listing 13-16 shows the basic idea.

Listing 13-16. Distinct placement

```
SELECT /*+ no_partial_join(s1) no_partial_join(s2)     place_distinct(s1) */
      /*  no_partial_join(s1) no_partial_join(s2) no_place_distinct(s1) */
      DISTINCT cust_id, prod_id
 FROM sh.sales s1 JOIN sh.sales s2 USING (cust_id, prod_id)
WHERE s1.time_id < DATE '2000-01-01' AND s2.time_id >=DATE '2000-01-01';
```

-- Untransformed execution plan (NO_PLACE_DISTINCT)

```
-------------------------------------------------------------
| Id  | Operation               | Name   | Cost (%CPU)|
-------------------------------------------------------------
|   0 | SELECT STATEMENT        |        |  5302   (1)|
|   1 |  HASH UNIQUE            |        |  5302   (1)|
|*  2 |   HASH JOIN             |        |  1787   (1)|
|   3 |    PARTITION RANGE ITERATOR|     |   246   (2)|
|   4 |     TABLE ACCESS FULL   | SALES  |   246   (2)|
|   5 |    PARTITION RANGE ITERATOR|     |   275   (2)|
|   6 |     TABLE ACCESS FULL   | SALES  |   275   (2)|
-------------------------------------------------------------
```

Predicate Information (identified by operation id):

```
   2 - access("S1"."PROD_ID"="S2"."PROD_ID" AND
             "S1"."CUST_ID"="S2"."CUST_ID")
```
-- Transformed query

```
WITH vw_dtp
    AS (SELECT /*+ no_partial_join(s1) no_merge */
               DISTINCT s1.cust_id, s1.prod_id
          FROM sh.sales s1
         WHERE s1.time_id < DATE '2000-01-01')
SELECT /*+ no_partial_join(s2) */
      DISTINCT cust_id, prod_id
 FROM vw_dtp NATURAL JOIN sh.sales s2
WHERE s2.time_id >=DATE '2000-01-01';
```

-- **Transformed execution plan (default)**

```
---------------------------------------------------------------
| Id  | Operation                      | Name            | Cost (%CPU)|
---------------------------------------------------------------
|   0 | SELECT STATEMENT               |                 | 5595    (1)|
|   1 |  HASH UNIQUE                   |                 | 5595    (1)|
|*  2 |   HASH JOIN                    |                 | 3326    (1)|
|   3 |    VIEW                        | VW_DTP_6DE9D1A7 | 2138    (1)|
|   4 |     HASH UNIQUE                |                 | 2138    (1)|
|   5 |      PARTITION RANGE ITERATOR|                 |  246    (2)|
|   6 |       TABLE ACCESS FULL        | SALES           |  246    (2)|
|   7 |    PARTITION RANGE ITERATOR    |                 |  275    (2)|
|   8 |     TABLE ACCESS FULL          | SALES           |  275    (2)|
---------------------------------------------------------------
```

Predicate Information (identified by operation id):

```
   2 - access("ITEM_2"="S2"."PROD_ID" AND "ITEM_1"="S2"."CUST_ID")
```

The query in Listing 13-16 finds the combinations of customer and product that occurred in both the 20th and 21st centuries. To keep things simple I have disabled the partial join transformation that would have taken place without the NO_PARTIAL_JOIN hints. The addition of the extra HASH UNIQUE operation means that the workarea used by the HASH JOIN operation on line 2 in the transformed execution plan contains only 72 rows as opposed to the 426,779 rows from SH.SALES associated with 20th century sales, which are placed in the workarea associated with operation 2 of the untransformed query. The cost estimates suggest that the transformation isn't worth the trouble, but somehow the CBO performs the transformation anyway and the query runs measurably faster.

Group by Placement

Group by placement is implemented in the same way and for the same reasons as distinct placement. Listing 13-17 highlights some new points, however.

Listing 13-17. Group by placement

```
  SELECT /*+   place_group_by((s p)) */
         /* no_place_group_by */
          cust_id
         ,c.cust_first_name
         ,c.cust_last_name
         ,c.cust_email
         ,p.prod_category
         ,SUM (s.amount_sold) total_amt_sold
    FROM sh.sales s
         JOIN sh.customers c USING (cust_id)
         JOIN sh.products p USING (prod_id)
GROUP BY cust_id
         ,c.cust_first_name
         ,c.cust_last_name
         ,c.cust_email
         ,p.prod_category;
```

-- Untransformed execution plan (NO_PLACE_GROUP_BY)

```
-------------------------------------------------------------------------
| Id  | Operation                  | Name                  | Cost (%CPU)|
-------------------------------------------------------------------------
|   0 | SELECT STATEMENT           |                       | 19957   (1)|
|   1 |  HASH GROUP BY             |                       | 19957   (1)|
|*  2 |   HASH JOIN                |                       |  2236   (1)|
|   3 |    VIEW                    | index$_join$_004      |     2   (0)|
|*  4 |     HASH JOIN              |                       |            |
|   5 |      INDEX FAST FULL SCAN  | PRODUCTS_PK           |     1   (0)|
|   6 |      INDEX FAST FULL SCAN  | PRODUCTS_PROD_CAT_IX  |     1   (0)|
|*  7 |    HASH JOIN               |                       |  2232   (1)|
|   8 |     TABLE ACCESS FULL      | CUSTOMERS             |   423   (1)|
|   9 |     PARTITION RANGE ALL    |                       |   517   (2)|
|  10 |      TABLE ACCESS FULL     | SALES                 |   517   (2)|
-------------------------------------------------------------------------
```

Predicate Information (identified by operation id):

```
   2 - access("S"."PROD_ID"="P"."PROD_ID")
   4 - access(ROWID=ROWID)
   7 - access("S"."CUST_ID"="C"."CUST_ID")
```

-- Transformed query

```
WITH vw_gbc
     AS (  SELECT /*+ no_place_group_by */
                  s.cust_id
                 ,p.prod_category
                 ,SUM (s.amount_sold) total_amt_sold
             FROM sh.sales s JOIN sh.products p USING (prod_id)
         GROUP BY s.cust_id, p.prod_category, prod_id)
```

```
SELECT /*+ no_place_group_by leading(vw_gbc)
           use_hash(c) no_swap_join_inputs(c) */
        cust_id
       ,c.cust_first_name
       ,c.cust_last_name
       ,c.cust_email
       ,vw_gbc.prod_category
       ,SUM (vw_gbc.total_amt_sold) total_amt_sold
  FROM vw_gbc JOIN sh.customers c USING (cust_id)
GROUP BY cust_id
       ,c.cust_first_name
       ,c.cust_last_name
       ,c.cust_email
       ,vw_gbc.prod_category;
```

-- Transformed execution plan (default)

```
-------------------------------------------------------------------------
| Id | Operation                | Name                  | Cost (%CPU)|
-------------------------------------------------------------------------
|  0 | SELECT STATEMENT         |                       | 4802   (1)|
|  1 |  HASH GROUP BY           |                       | 4802   (1)|
|* 2 |   HASH JOIN              |                       | 4319   (1)|
|  3 |    VIEW                  | VW_GBC_1              | 3682   (1)|
|  4 |     HASH GROUP BY        |                       | 3682   (1)|
|* 5 |      HASH JOIN           |                       |  521   (2)|
|  6 |       VIEW               | index$_join$_004      |    2   (0)|
|* 7 |        HASH JOIN         |                       |           |
|  8 |         INDEX FAST FULL SCAN| PRODUCTS_PK        |    1   (0)|
|  9 |         INDEX FAST FULL SCAN| PRODUCTS_PROD_CAT_IX|  1   (0)|
| 10 |        PARTITION RANGE ALL|                      |  517   (2)|
| 11 |         TABLE ACCESS FULL | SALES                |  517   (2)|
| 12 |    TABLE ACCESS FULL     | CUSTOMERS             |  423   (1)|
-------------------------------------------------------------------------
```

```
Predicate Information (identified by operation id):
-------------------------------------------------

   2 - access("ITEM_1"="C"."CUST_ID")
   5 - access("S"."PROD_ID"="P"."PROD_ID")
   7 - access(ROWID=ROWID)
```

The query in Listing 13-17 identifies the total sales by each customer for each product category. The transformed query performs an aggregation after the join of SH.SALES with SH.PRODUCTS so that the workarea for the HASH JOIN on line 2 is small.

There seem to be some restrictions[1] on the application of the group by placement transformation, not all of which I have been able to work out. However, it does seem that on this occasion we can't group the rows from SH.SALES without joining them at least once.

---

[1] I have reason to believe that there may actually be a bug in 12.1.0.1.

In Listing 13-17 the two operands of the join that produce the final result are:

- The intermediate result set formed by the join of SH.SALES and SH.PRODUCTS

- The table SH.CUSTOMERS

It is possible to perform group by placement on either or both of these operands. You can see the syntax for forcing group placement on the first of these operands in Listing 13-17. The hint PLACE_GROUP_BY ((S P) (C)) would be used to perform group placement on both operands.

Listing 13-18 shows what happens when we remove the hints from the transformed query in Listing 13-17 and then run EXPLAIN PLAN.

Listing 13-18. Group placement in a subquery

```
WITH vw_gbc
    AS ( SELECT /*+  place_group_by((s)) */
                /* no_place_group_by */
                s.cust_id, p.prod_category, SUM (s.amount_sold) total_amt_sold
         FROM sh.sales s JOIN sh.products p USING (prod_id)
       GROUP BY s.cust_id, p.prod_category, prod_id)
  SELECT /*+ place_group_by((vw_gbc)) */
         /* no_place_group_by leading(vw_gbc) use_hash(c) no_swap_join_inputs(c) */
         cust_id
        ,c.cust_first_name
        ,c.cust_last_name
        ,c.cust_email
        ,vw_gbc.prod_category
        ,SUM (vw_gbc.total_amt_sold) total_amt_sold
    FROM vw_gbc JOIN sh.customers c USING (cust_id)
GROUP BY cust_id
        ,c.cust_first_name
        ,c.cust_last_name
        ,c.cust_email
        ,vw_gbc.prod_category;

-- Untransformed execution plan (two NO_PLACE_GROUP_BY)
```

Id	Operation	Name	Cost (%CPU)
0	SELECT STATEMENT		29396 (1)
1	**HASH GROUP BY**		29396 (1)
* 2	HASH JOIN		11675 (1)
3	VIEW		9046 (1)
4	**HASH GROUP BY**		9046 (1)
* 5	HASH JOIN		521 (2)
6	VIEW	index$_join$_002	2 (0)
* 7	HASH JOIN		
8	INDEX FAST FULL SCAN	PRODUCTS_PK	1 (0)
9	INDEX FAST FULL SCAN	PRODUCTS_PROD_CAT_IX	1 (0)
10	PARTITION RANGE ALL		517 (2)
11	TABLE ACCESS FULL	SALES	517 (2)
12	TABLE ACCESS FULL	CUSTOMERS	423 (1)

```
Predicate Information (identified by operation id):
--------------------------------------------------

   2 - access("VW_GBC"."CUST_ID"="C"."CUST_ID")
   5 - access("S"."PROD_ID"="P"."PROD_ID")
   7 - access(ROWID=ROWID)
```

-- Transformed query

```
WITH vw_gbc_1
    AS (  SELECT s.cust_id, s.prod_id, SUM (s.amount_sold) AS total_amt_sold
            FROM sh.sales s
        GROUP BY s.cust_id, s.prod_id)
    ,vw_gbc_2
    AS (  SELECT vw_gbc_1.cust_id, vw_gbc_1.total_amt_sold, p.prod_category
            FROM vw_gbc_1 JOIN sh.products p USING (prod_id)
        GROUP BY vw_gbc_1.cust_id
                ,vw_gbc_1.total_amt_sold
                ,p.prod_category
                ,prod_id)
    ,vw_gbc
    AS (  SELECT vw_gbc_2.cust_id
                ,SUM (vw_gbc_2.total_amt_sold) AS total_amt_sold
                ,vw_gbc_2.prod_category
            FROM vw_gbc_2
        GROUP BY vw_gbc_2.cust_id, vw_gbc_2.prod_category)
  SELECT cust_id
        ,c.cust_first_name
        ,c.cust_last_name
        ,c.cust_email
        ,vw_gbc.prod_category
        ,SUM (vw_gbc.total_amt_sold) total_amt_sold
    FROM vw_gbc JOIN sh.customers c USING (cust_id)
GROUP BY cust_id
        ,c.cust_first_name
        ,c.cust_last_name
        ,c.cust_email
        ,vw_gbc.prod_category;
```

-- Transformed execution plan (default)

```
-------------------------------------------------------------------------
| Id  | Operation                     | Name                 | Cost (%CPU)|
-------------------------------------------------------------------------
|   0 | SELECT STATEMENT              |                      | 7224   (1)|
|   1 |  HASH GROUP BY                |                      | 7224   (1)|
|*  2 |   HASH JOIN                   |                      | 6741   (1)|
|   3 |    VIEW                       | VW_GBC_3             | 6104   (1)|
|   4 |     HASH GROUP BY             |                      | 6104   (1)|
|   5 |      VIEW                     |                      | 6104   (1)|
|   6 |       HASH GROUP BY           |                      | 6104   (1)|
|*  7 |        HASH JOIN              |                      | 3022   (1)|
|   8 |         VIEW                  | index$_join$_002     |    2   (0)|
|*  9 |          HASH JOIN            |                      |           |
|  10 |           INDEX FAST FULL SCAN| PRODUCTS_PK          |    1   (0)|
|  11 |           INDEX FAST FULL SCAN| PRODUCTS_PROD_CAT_IX |    1   (0)|
|  12 |         VIEW                  | VW_GBC_2             | 3019   (1)|
|  13 |          HASH GROUP BY        |                      | 3019   (1)|
|  14 |           PARTITION RANGE ALL |                      |  517   (2)|
|  15 |            TABLE ACCESS FULL  | SALES                |  517   (2)|
|  16 |    TABLE ACCESS FULL          | CUSTOMERS            |  423   (1)|
-------------------------------------------------------------------------

Predicate Information (identified by operation id):
---------------------------------------------------

   2 - access("ITEM_1"="C"."CUST_ID")
   7 - access("ITEM_1"="P"."PROD_ID")
   9 - access(ROWID=ROWID)
```

Listing 13-18 shows that the transformed query from Listing 13-17 will undergo further transformations if we run or explain it directly. Now that we have two separate query blocks, the CBO can aggregate the data from SH.SALES before any join. The data is aggregated again after we join with SH.PRODUCTS and before we join with SH.CUSTOMERS. There is an extra and unnecessary aggregation introduced at this stage: the operations on lines 4 and 6 could be merged.

This analysis leads to an interesting SQL tuning technique: by looking at what transformations the CBO has performed, we may be able to further improve matters by running the transformation process iteratively. It may be that not all of these transformations will work out in practice, but at least you will have some ideas to try out!

Group by Pushdown

Group by pushdown does for parallel aggregations what distinct and group by placements do for join aggregations. The idea is the same: do as much aggregation as possible as early in the process as you can. Listing 13-19 shows the group by pushdown transformation in action.

Listing 13-19. Group by pushdown

```
SELECT /*+ parallel gby_pushdown */ /* parallel no_gby_pushdown */
       prod_id
       ,cust_id
       ,promo_id
       ,COUNT (*) cnt
```

```
    FROM sh.sales
   WHERE amount_sold > 100
GROUP BY prod_id, cust_id, promo_id;
```

-- **Untransformed execution plan (NO_GBY_PUSHDOWN)**

```
------------------------------------------------------
| Id  | Operation               | Name     | Cost (%CPU)|
------------------------------------------------------
|   0 | SELECT STATEMENT        |          |   289   (3)|
|   1 |  PX COORDINATOR         |          |            |
|   2 |   PX SEND QC (RANDOM)   | :TQ10001 |   289   (3)|
|   3 |    HASH GROUP BY        |          |   289   (3)|
|   4 |     PX RECEIVE          |          |   288   (2)|
|   5 |      PX SEND HASH       | :TQ10000 |   288   (2)|
|   6 |       PX BLOCK ITERATOR |          |   288   (2)|
|*  7 |        TABLE ACCESS FULL| SALES    |   288   (2)|
------------------------------------------------------
```

Predicate Information (identified by operation id):
----

   7 - filter("AMOUNT_SOLD">100)

-- **Concept of the transformed query**

```
WITH pq
    AS (   SELECT prod_id
                 ,cust_id
                 ,promo_id
                 ,COUNT (*) cnt
             FROM sh.sales
            WHERE amount_sold > 100 AND time_id < DATE '2000-01-01'
         GROUP BY prod_id, cust_id, promo_id
         UNION ALL
           SELECT prod_id
                 ,cust_id
                 ,promo_id
                 ,COUNT (*) cnt
             FROM sh.sales
            WHERE amount_sold > 100 AND time_id >=DATE '2000-01-01'
         GROUP BY prod_id, cust_id, promo_id)
  SELECT prod_id
        ,cust_id
        ,promo_id
        ,SUM (cnt) AS cnt
    FROM pq
GROUP BY prod_id, cust_id, promo_id;
```

-- Transformed execution plan

```
---------------------------------------------------------------
| Id  | Operation              | Name     | Cost (%CPU)|
---------------------------------------------------------------
|   0 | SELECT STATEMENT       |          |   325   (1)|
|   1 |  PX COORDINATOR        |          |            |
|   2 |   PX SEND QC (RANDOM)  | :TQ10001 |   325   (1)|
|   3 |    HASH GROUP BY       |          |   325   (1)|
|   4 |     PX RECEIVE         |          |   325   (1)|
|   5 |      PX SEND HASH      | :TQ10000 |   325   (1)|
|   6 |       HASH GROUP BY    |          |   325   (1)|
|   7 |        PX BLOCK ITERATOR |        |   144   (2)|
|*  8 |         TABLE ACCESS FULL| SALES  |   144   (2)|
---------------------------------------------------------------
```

Predicate Information (identified by operation id):

```
   8 - filter("AMOUNT_SOLD">100)
```

The query in Listing 13-19 is a straightforward COUNT aggregation performed on SH.SALES in parallel. Without the transformation, each row from SH.SALES where AMOUNT_SOLD > 100 would be sent from one parallel query server to another for aggregation. The concept of this transformation is shown in Listing 13-19 by a UNION ALL factored subquery. Each branch of the UNION ALL is supposed to relate to a parallel query server that reads a portion of the SH.SALES table. The conceptual query uses centuries to partition the data between branches, whereas the parallel query would use block-range granules.

In the conceptual query, each branch of the UNION ALL performs its own COUNT aggregation before the main query performs a SUM aggregation on the result to obtain the final result. In the parallel query, each parallel query slave that reads SH.SALES performs a COUNT aggregation on its subset of data so that the number of rows sent to DFO:TQ10001 for a final SUM aggregation is much reduced.

Once again, we can see that the CBO has performed a transformation that actually increases the estimated cost. The evidence is mounting that the cost-based transformation framework doesn't actually perform final state optimization on each possible transformation, but instead performs some kind of approximate costing calculation.

Group by pushdown is a cost-based transformation that works for DISTINCT operations as well as for GROUP BY operations. Since GROUP BY and DISTINCT operations almost always significantly reduce cardinality, group by pushdown is almost always applied where legal.

The group by pushdown transformation is the last of the aggregation transformations that I wanted to cover. It is time now to look at subqueries.

Subquery Transformations

As I explained in Chapter 7, I have used the term *subquery* throughout this book in an informal way to indicate either a set query block or any part of a SQL statement that begins with the keyword SELECT and that is not the main query block of a query. So, for example, an inline view or data dictionary view is considered to be a subquery for the purposes of discussion here.

We have already discussed subquery unnesting both in Chapter 11 and earlier in this chapter, so I won't be revisiting that topic again. But we still have a lot of other transformations to cover. Let us get started by briefly revisiting simple view merging.

Simple View Merging

We have already seen countless examples of simple view merging in this book, but let us take a brief formal look at the transformation in Listing 13-20.

Listing 13-20. Simple view merging

```
WITH q1
    AS (SELECT /*+    MERGE */
               /* NO_MERGE */
               CASE prod_category
                   WHEN 'Electronics' THEN amount_sold * 0.9
                   ELSE amount_sold
               END
                   AS adjusted_amount_sold
           FROM sh.sales JOIN sh.products USING (prod_id))
  SELECT adjusted_amount_sold, COUNT (*) cnt
    FROM q1
GROUP BY adjusted_amount_sold;
```

-- **Untransformed execution plan (NO_MERGE)**

```
---------------------------------------------------------------------
| Id | Operation                  | Name                 | Cost (%CPU)|
---------------------------------------------------------------------
|  0 | SELECT STATEMENT           |                      |  542  (6)|
|  1 |  HASH GROUP BY             |                      |  542  (6)|
|  2 |   VIEW                     |                      |  521  (2)|
|* 3 |    HASH JOIN               |                      |  521  (2)|
|  4 |     VIEW                   | index$_join$_002     |    2  (0)|
|* 5 |      HASH JOIN             |                      |          |
|  6 |       INDEX FAST FULL SCAN | PRODUCTS_PK          |    1  (0)|
|  7 |       INDEX FAST FULL SCAN | PRODUCTS_PROD_CAT_IX |    1  (0)|
|  8 |     PARTITION RANGE ALL    |                      |  517  (2)|
|  9 |      TABLE ACCESS FULL     | SALES                |  517  (2)|
---------------------------------------------------------------------

Predicate Information (identified by operation id):
---------------------------------------------------

   3 - access("SALES"."PROD_ID"="PRODUCTS"."PROD_ID")
   5 - access(ROWID=ROWID)
```

-- **Transformed query**

```
  SELECT CASE prod_category
           WHEN 'Electronics' THEN amount_sold * 0.9
           ELSE amount_sold
         END
           AS adjusted_amount_sold
    FROM sh.sales JOIN sh.products USING (prod_id)
GROUP BY CASE prod_category
           WHEN 'Electronics' THEN amount_sold * 0.9
           ELSE amount_sold
         END;
```

-- Transformed execution plan (default)

```
---------------------------------------------------------------------
| Id  | Operation               | Name                  | Cost (%CPU)|
---------------------------------------------------------------------
|   0 | SELECT STATEMENT        |                       | 3233   (1)|
|   1 |  HASH GROUP BY          |                       | 3233   (1)|
|*  2 |   HASH JOIN             |                       |  521   (2)|
|   3 |    VIEW                 | index$_join$_002      |    2   (0)|
|*  4 |     HASH JOIN           |                       |           |
|   5 |      INDEX FAST FULL SCAN| PRODUCTS_PK          |    1   (0)|
|   6 |      INDEX FAST FULL SCAN| PRODUCTS_PROD_CAT_IX |    1   (0)|
|   7 |    PARTITION RANGE ALL  |                       |  517   (2)|
|   8 |     TABLE ACCESS FULL   | SALES                 |  517   (2)|
---------------------------------------------------------------------
```

Predicate Information (identified by operation id):

```
   2 - access("SALES"."PROD_ID"="PRODUCTS"."PROD_ID")
   4 - access(ROWID=ROWID)
```

The concepts of subquery unnesting and view merging are easy to confuse:

- View merging applies to inline views, factored subqueries, and data dictionary views that appear as row sources in the FROM clause of an enclosing query block. View merging is controlled by the MERGE and NO_MERGE hints.

- Subquery unnesting relates to subqueries in the SELECT list, WHERE clause, or anywhere else that Oracle may in the future support. Subquery unnesting is controlled by the UNNEST and NO_UNNEST hints.

Listing 13-20 shows how the use of a factored subquery can save typing; we didn't have to replicate the GROUP BY expression to the select list. We just used the column alias ADJUSTED_AMOUNT_SOLD from the subquery. Once again, Oracle transformed our concise query into something conceptually simpler, if less concise.

Simple view merging is a heuristic transformation that is unconditionally applied where legal. The main benefit of simple view merging is that additional join orders are possible (though not in Listing 13-20).

I won't go into the restrictions on simple view merging. If you just remember that simple row sources can be merged and complex ones can't then you will be okay. There is one special case where a complex row source can be merged, but not by simple view merging. Let us look at that now.

Complex View Merging

If a subquery contains a GROUP BY clause and/or a DISTINCT keyword, and that is the *only* reason that simple view merging can't be used, then complex view merging is an alternative. Listing 13-21 gives an example.

Listing 13-21. Complex view merging

```
WITH agg_q
     AS (  SELECT /*+   merge */
                  /* no_merge */
                  s.cust_id, s.prod_id, SUM (s.amount_sold) total_amt_sold
            FROM sh.sales s
        GROUP BY s.cust_id, s.prod_id)
SELECT cust_id
      ,c.cust_first_name
      ,c.cust_last_name
      ,c.cust_email
      ,p.prod_name
      ,agg_q.total_amt_sold
  FROM agg_q
       JOIN sh.customers c USING (cust_id)
       JOIN sh.countries co USING (country_id)
       JOIN sh.products p USING (prod_id)
 WHERE     co.country_name = 'Japan'
       AND prod_category = 'Photo'
       AND total_amt_sold > 20000;
```

```
-- Untransformed execution plan (NO_MERGE)
```

```
--------------------------------------------------------------------
| Id  | Operation                       | Name         | Cost (%CPU)|
--------------------------------------------------------------------
|   0 | SELECT STATEMENT                |              |  541    (6)|
|   1 |  NESTED LOOPS                   |              |            |
|   2 |   NESTED LOOPS                  |              |  541    (6)|
|   3 |    NESTED LOOPS                 |              |  540    (6)|
|   4 |     NESTED LOOPS                |              |  539    (6)|
|   5 |      VIEW                       |              |  538    (6)|
|*  6 |       FILTER                    |              |            |
|   7 |        HASH GROUP BY            |              |  538    (6)|
|   8 |         PARTITION RANGE ALL     |              |  517    (2)|
|   9 |          TABLE ACCESS FULL      | SALES        |  517    (2)|
|  10 |      TABLE ACCESS BY INDEX ROWID| CUSTOMERS    |    1    (0)|
|* 11 |       INDEX UNIQUE SCAN         | CUSTOMERS_PK |    0    (0)|
|* 12 |     TABLE ACCESS BY INDEX ROWID | COUNTRIES    |    1    (0)|
|* 13 |      INDEX UNIQUE SCAN          | COUNTRIES_PK |    0    (0)|
|* 14 |    INDEX UNIQUE SCAN            | PRODUCTS_PK  |    0    (0)|
|* 15 |   TABLE ACCESS BY INDEX ROWID   | PRODUCTS     |    1    (0)|
--------------------------------------------------------------------
```

```
Predicate Information (identified by operation id):
---------------------------------------------------

   6 - filter(SUM("S"."AMOUNT_SOLD")>20000)
  11 - access("AGG_Q"."CUST_ID"="C"."CUST_ID")
  12 - filter("CO"."COUNTRY_NAME"='Japan')
  13 - access("C"."COUNTRY_ID"="CO"."COUNTRY_ID")
```

```
14 - access("AGG_Q"."PROD_ID"="P"."PROD_ID")
15 - filter("P"."PROD_CATEGORY"='Photo')
```

-- Transformed query

```
SELECT cust_id
      ,c.cust_first_name
      ,c.cust_last_name
      ,c.cust_email
      ,p.prod_name
      ,SUM (s.amount_sold) AS total_amt_sold
   FROM sh.sales s
        JOIN sh.customers c USING (cust_id)
        JOIN sh.countries co USING (country_id)
        JOIN sh.products p USING (prod_id)
  WHERE co.country_name = 'Japan' AND prod_category = 'Photo'
GROUP BY cust_id
        ,c.cust_first_name
        ,c.cust_last_name
        ,c.cust_email
        ,p.prod_name
  HAVING SUM (s.amount_sold) > 20000;
```

-- Transformed execution plan (default)

```
---------------------------------------------------------------------------
| Id  | Operation                            | Name               | Cost (%CPU)|
---------------------------------------------------------------------------
|   0 | SELECT STATEMENT                     |                    |  948   (2)|
|*  1 |  FILTER                              |                    |           |
|   2 |   HASH GROUP BY                      |                    |  948   (2)|
|*  3 |    HASH JOIN                         |                    |  948   (2)|
|   4 |     TABLE ACCESS BY INDEX ROWID BATCHED| PRODUCTS         |    3   (0)|
|*  5 |      INDEX RANGE SCAN                | PRODUCTS_PROD_CAT_IX|    1   (0)|
|*  6 |     HASH JOIN                        |                    |  945   (2)|
|*  7 |      HASH JOIN                       |                    |  426   (1)|
|*  8 |       TABLE ACCESS FULL              | COUNTRIES          |    3   (0)|
|   9 |       TABLE ACCESS FULL              | CUSTOMERS          |  423   (1)|
|  10 |      PARTITION RANGE ALL             |                    |  517   (2)|
|  11 |       TABLE ACCESS FULL              | SALES              |  517   (2)|
---------------------------------------------------------------------------
```

```
Predicate Information (identified by operation id):
---------------------------------------------------

   1 - filter(SUM("S"."AMOUNT_SOLD")>20000)
   3 - access("S"."PROD_ID"="P"."PROD_ID")
   5 - access("P"."PROD_CATEGORY"='Photo')
   6 - access("S"."CUST_ID"="C"."CUST_ID")
   7 - access("C"."COUNTRY_ID"="CO"."COUNTRY_ID")
   8 - filter("CO"."COUNTRY_NAME"='Japan')
```

Listing 13-21 provides the total sales of photographic products in Japan to each customer. The benefit of view merging here is that the aggregation is deferred until the rows from other countries and other product categories have been filtered out.

Now, you may be wondering why simple and complex view merging are considered separately. After all, both transformations do the same thing, and both are managed with MERGE and NO_MERGE hints. The crucial difference is that simple view merging is a *heuristic* transformation and complex view merging is a *cost-based* transformation.

If you don't merge a complex view you have the opportunity to aggregate early and reduce the rows that are input to the join. If you *do* merge then your join can reduce the number of rows being aggregated. So whether you do the join or the aggregation first depends on which operation will reduce the intermediate result set the most. In fact, if you remove the WHERE clause from the original query in Listing 13-21, complex view merging will not happen unless you include a MERGE hint.

Does this sound familiar? It should. The discussion we are having here is the exact same discussion as the one we had with the distinct placement and group by placement transformations, but in reverse! The downloadable materials show that if you take the transformed query from Listing 13-16 and add a MERGE hint you can recreate the original query by reversing the original transformation.[2]

Factored Subquery Materialization

In Chapter 1 I explained that one of the key benefits of factored subqueries is that they can be used more than once in a query. In fact, when they are used more than once a temporary table is created that is specific to the statement; this table holds the results of the factored subquery. Listing 13-22 demonstrates.

Listing 13-22. Factored subquery materialization

```
WITH q1
    AS (  SELECT prod_name, prod_category, SUM (amount_sold) total_amt_sold
            FROM sh.sales JOIN sh.products USING (prod_id)
           WHERE prod_category = 'Electronics'
        GROUP BY prod_name, prod_category)
    ,q2
    AS (SELECT 1 AS order_col, prod_name, total_amt_sold FROM q1
        UNION ALL
        SELECT 2, 'Total', SUM (total_amt_sold) FROM q1)
  SELECT prod_name, total_amt_sold
    FROM q2
ORDER BY order_col, prod_name;
```

---

[2]Restrictions on complex view merging preclude reversing the transformation in Listing 13-17.

```
--------------------------------------------------------------------------------
| Id  | Operation                              | Name                      | Cost (%CPU)|
--------------------------------------------------------------------------------
|   0 | SELECT STATEMENT                       |                           |  529   (3)|
|   1 |  TEMP TABLE TRANSFORMATION             |                           |           |
|   2 |   LOAD AS SELECT                       | SYS_TEMP_0FD9D672C_4E5E5D |           |
|   3 |    HASH GROUP BY                       |                           |  525   (3)|
|*  4 |     HASH JOIN                          |                           |  522   (2)|
|   5 |      TABLE ACCESS BY INDEX ROWID BATCHED| PRODUCTS                 |    3   (0)|
|*  6 |       INDEX RANGE SCAN                 | PRODUCTS_PROD_CAT_IX      |    1   (0)|
|   7 |      PARTITION RANGE ALL               |                           |  517   (2)|
|   8 |       TABLE ACCESS FULL                | SALES                     |  517   (2)|
|   9 |   SORT ORDER BY                        |                           |    4   (0)|
|  10 |    VIEW                                |                           |    4   (0)|
|  11 |     UNION-ALL                          |                           |           |
|  12 |      VIEW                              |                           |    2   (0)|
|  13 |       TABLE ACCESS FULL                | SYS_TEMP_0FD9D672C_4E5E5D |    2   (0)|
|  14 |      SORT AGGREGATE                    |                           |           |
|  15 |       VIEW                             |                           |    2   (0)|
|  16 |        TABLE ACCESS FULL               | SYS_TEMP_0FD9D672C_4E5E5D |    2   (0)|
--------------------------------------------------------------------------------
```

Predicate Information (identified by operation id):

```
   4 - access("SALES"."PROD_ID"="PRODUCTS"."PROD_ID")
   6 - access("PRODUCTS"."PROD_CATEGORY"='Electronics')
```

Listing 13-22 is a little different from the other listings in this chapter, as I am using an unhinted query and showing only the transformed execution plan. The query shows the total sales by product, with a grand total given at the end. Listing 13-22 shows the sort of query that might be written by somebody unfamiliar with the use of the ROLLUP keyword in GROUP BY operations.

The TEMP TABLE TRANSFORMATION operation signals the creation of one or more temporary tables that exist purely for the duration of the operation. The children of this operation are always one or more LOAD AS SELECT operations that insert rows into the temporary tables along with one extra child for the main query that utilizes the temporary table or tables created.

Listing 13-22 uses the factored subquery Q1 twice, but the subquery is only evaluated once; the results of the query are stored in a temporary table with a bizarre name (SYS_TEMP_0FD9D672C_4E5E5D in this case), and that temporary table is used in the two branches of the UNION ALL operation.

Factored subquery materialization is not possible when an object type or an LOB is selected, and the transformation is also illegal in distributed transactions.

When legal, factored subquery materialization is a heuristic optimization. If a subquery is referenced once then it will not be materialized, but if it is referenced twice or more it normally will be.[3] You can see in Listing 13-22 that factored subquery Q2 is referenced only once and so it is not materialized. The CBO chooses instead to perform simple view merging of the factored subquery with the main query.

All this sounds very sensible, but don't think for one minute that factored subquery materialization is a no-brainer. We will discuss in Chapter 18 *why* you might need to override the heuristic rules, but for now we need to focus on *how* we override the default behavior.

---

[3]Occasionally an INDEX FAST FULL SCAN will not be materialized unless hinted even when referenced multiple times.

The hinting process is a little strange in several ways:

- To force factored subquery materialization you use the MATERIALIZE hint, but to disable it you use the INLINE hint.

- Neither the MATERIALIZE hint nor the INLINE hint support global hint syntax. The hints have to be placed in the factored subquery itself.

- A consequence of the above restriction is that MATERIALIZE and INLINE hints never appear in outline hints, SQL baselines, SQL profiles, etc. Placing a hint in the code is the only way!

Bearing these points in mind, Listing 13-23 shows how you might prevent the materialization of factored subquery Q1 and materialize Q2 (sort of).

Listing 13-23. Use of MATERIALIZE and INLINE hints

```
WITH q1
    AS ( SELECT /*+ inline */
                prod_name, prod_category, SUM (amount_sold) total_amt_sold
           FROM sh.sales JOIN sh.products USING (prod_id)
          WHERE prod_category = 'Electronics'
       GROUP BY prod_name, prod_category)
    ,q2
    AS (SELECT 1 AS order_col, prod_name, total_amt_sold FROM q1
        UNION ALL
        SELECT 2, 'Total', SUM (total_amt_sold) FROM q1)
    ,q3 AS (SELECT /*+ materialize */
                * FROM q2)
  SELECT prod_name, total_amt_sold
    FROM q3
ORDER BY order_col, prod_name;
```

```
----------------------------------------------------------------------------------------
| Id  | Operation                               | Name                      | Cost (%CPU)|
----------------------------------------------------------------------------------------
|   0 | SELECT STATEMENT                        |                           | 1053    (3)|
|   1 |  TEMP TABLE TRANSFORMATION              |                           |            |
|   2 |   LOAD AS SELECT                        | SYS_TEMP_0FD9D672D_4E5E5D |            |
|   3 |    VIEW                                 |                           | 1051    (3)|
|   4 |     UNION-ALL                           |                           |            |
|   5 |      HASH GROUP BY                      |                           | 525     (3)|
|*  6 |       HASH JOIN                         |                           | 522     (2)|
|   7 |        TABLE ACCESS BY INDEX ROWID BATCHED | PRODUCTS               | 3       (0)|
|*  8 |         INDEX RANGE SCAN                | PRODUCTS_PROD_CAT_IX      | 1       (0)|
|   9 |        PARTITION RANGE ALL              |                           | 517     (2)|
|  10 |         TABLE ACCESS FULL               | SALES                     | 517     (2)|
|  11 |      SORT AGGREGATE                     |                           |            |
|  12 |       VIEW                              |                           | 525     (3)|
|  13 |        HASH GROUP BY                    |                           | 525     (3)|
|* 14 |         HASH JOIN                       |                           | 522     (2)|
|  15 |          TABLE ACCESS BY INDEX ROWID BATCHED| PRODUCTS              | 3       (0)|
```

```
|* 16 |        INDEX RANGE SCAN      | PRODUCTS_PROD_CAT_IX      |   1   (0)|
|  17 |        PARTITION RANGE ALL   |                          | 517   (2)|
|  18 |          TABLE ACCESS FULL   | SALES                    | 517   (2)|
|  19 |    SORT ORDER BY             |                          |   2   (0)|
|  20 |     VIEW                     |                          |   2   (0)|
|  21 |      TABLE ACCESS FULL       | SYS_TEMP_0FD9D672D_4E5E5D |   2   (0)|
---------------------------------------------------------------------------

Predicate Information (identified by operation id):
--------------------------------------------------

   6 - access("SALES"."PROD_ID"="PRODUCTS"."PROD_ID")
   8 - access("PRODUCTS"."PROD_CATEGORY"='Electronics')
  14 - access("SALES"."PROD_ID"="PRODUCTS"."PROD_ID")
  16 - access("PRODUCTS"."PROD_CATEGORY"='Electronics')
```

The use of the MATERIALIZE and INLINE hints in Listing 13-23 has resulted in the join of SH.PRODUCTS and SH.SALES being done twice and has also resulted in the results of the UNION ALL being placed in a temporary table, even though said temporary table is referenced only once.

I had to cheat a bit here. You will notice that I have surreptitiously added a third factored subquery, Q3, to Listing 13-23. This is because the query block from Q2 was the set query block SET$1, which could only be hinted using a global hint (a hint applied after the first SELECT would apply to the first branch of the UNION ALL). Given that MATERIALIZE only supports local hinting, the only thing to do was to create a new query block into which SET$1 could be merged and then materialize that.

I want to emphasize that this discussion has focused on the mechanics of factored subquery materialization. I don't want to leave you with the impression that the hinting that I have applied in Listing 13-23 makes any sense from a performance perspective. We will return to performance issues in Chapter 18.

Subquery Pushdown

When a subquery appears in a WHERE clause, the CBO will usually unnest it if it can. If the subquery cannot be unnested for some reason then the CBO is left with a similar question to the one it has with aggregations: should the subquery be evaluated as early as possible or be deferred until after any joins? Curiously, this decision is made by a query transformation.

Although subquery pushdown is implemented as a query transformation it isn't logically a transformation. Indeed, I assumed for some time that the CBO decided when a subquery should be evaluated as part of the final state transformation logic that we discussed in Chapter 12. It certainly isn't possible to provide any kind of transformed SQL that shows the result of the so-called transformation.

It works like this: the CBO begins by assuming that subqueries in a WHERE clause should be evaluated after all joins have been performed. Only if the cost-based transformation framework decides that this should change (or if there is a hint) will this behavior change. Listing 13-24 might help explain the point a bit better.

Listing 13-24. Subquery pushdown

```
WITH q1
     AS ( SELECT prod_id
              FROM sh.sales
          GROUP BY prod_id
          ORDER BY SUM (amount_sold) DESC)
   SELECT c.cust_first_name
         ,c.cust_last_name
         ,c.cust_email
         ,p.prod_name
     FROM sh.sales s
          JOIN sh.customers c USING (cust_id)
          JOIN sh.products p USING (prod_id)
    WHERE prod_id = (SELECT /*+   push_subq */
                            /* no_push_subq */
                            prod_id
                       FROM q1
                      WHERE ROWNUM = 1)
GROUP BY c.cust_first_name
        ,c.cust_last_name
        ,c.cust_email
        ,p.prod_name
   HAVING SUM (s.amount_sold) > 20000;
```

-- Subquery not pushed (NO_PUSH_SUBQ)

```
--------------------------------------------------------------
| Id  | Operation                 | Name      | Cost (%CPU)|
--------------------------------------------------------------
|   0 | SELECT STATEMENT          |           | 10277   (1)|
|*  1 |  FILTER                   |           |            |
|   2 |   HASH GROUP BY           |           | 10277   (1)|
|*  3 |    FILTER                 |           |            |
|*  4 |     HASH JOIN             |           |  2237   (1)|
|   5 |      TABLE ACCESS FULL    | PRODUCTS  |     3   (0)|
|*  6 |      HASH JOIN            |           |  2232   (1)|
|   7 |       TABLE ACCESS FULL   | CUSTOMERS |   423   (1)|
|   8 |       PARTITION RANGE ALL |           |   517   (2)|
|   9 |        TABLE ACCESS FULL  | SALES     |   517   (2)|
|* 10 |    COUNT STOPKEY          |           |            |
|  11 |     VIEW                  |           |   559   (9)|
|* 12 |      SORT ORDER BY STOPKEY|           |   559   (9)|
|  13 |       SORT GROUP BY       |           |   559   (9)|
|  14 |        PARTITION RANGE ALL|           |   517   (2)|
|  15 |         TABLE ACCESS FULL | SALES     |   517   (2)|
--------------------------------------------------------------
```

Predicate Information (identified by operation id):

```
   1 - filter(SUM("S"."AMOUNT_SOLD")>20000)
   3 - filter("P"."PROD_ID"= (SELECT /*+ NO_PUSH_SUBQ */ "PROD_ID" FROM
               (SELECT "PROD_ID" "PROD_ID" FROM "SH"."SALES" "SALES" GROUP BY
              "PROD_ID" ORDER BY SUM("AMOUNT_SOLD") DESC) "Q1" WHERE ROWNUM=1))
   4 - access("S"."PROD_ID"="P"."PROD_ID")
   6 - access("S"."CUST_ID"="C"."CUST_ID")
  10 - filter(ROWNUM=1)
  12 - filter(ROWNUM=1)
```

-- Subquery pushed (default)

```
---------------------------------------------------------------------------------
| Id  | Operation                                  | Name           | Cost (%CPU)|
---------------------------------------------------------------------------------
|   0 | SELECT STATEMENT                           |                |  865   (1)|
|*  1 |  FILTER                                    |                |           |
|   2 |   HASH GROUP BY                            |                |  865   (1)|
|*  3 |    HASH JOIN                               |                |  864   (1)|
|   4 |     NESTED LOOPS                           |                |  441   (0)|
|   5 |      TABLE ACCESS BY INDEX ROWID           | PRODUCTS       |    1   (0)|
|*  6 |       INDEX UNIQUE SCAN                    | PRODUCTS_PK    |    0   (0)|
|*  7 |        COUNT STOPKEY                       |                |           |
|   8 |         VIEW                               |                |  559   (9)|
|*  9 |          SORT ORDER BY STOPKEY             |                |  559   (9)|
|  10 |           SORT GROUP BY                    |                |  559   (9)|
|  11 |            PARTITION RANGE ALL             |                |  517   (2)|
|  12 |             TABLE ACCESS FULL              | SALES          |  517   (2)|
|  13 |     PARTITION RANGE ALL                    |                |  441   (0)|
|  14 |      TABLE ACCESS BY LOCAL INDEX ROWID BATCHED| SALES       |  441   (0)|
|  15 |       BITMAP CONVERSION TO ROWIDS          |                |           |
|* 16 |        BITMAP INDEX SINGLE VALUE           | SALES_PROD_BIX |           |
|  17 |     TABLE ACCESS FULL                      | CUSTOMERS      |  423   (1)|
---------------------------------------------------------------------------------
```

Predicate Information (identified by operation id):

```
   1 - filter(SUM("S"."AMOUNT_SOLD")>20000)
   3 - access("S"."CUST_ID"="C"."CUST_ID")
   6 - access("P"."PROD_ID"= (SELECT /*+ PUSH_SUBQ */ "PROD_ID" FROM  (SELECT
               "PROD_ID" "PROD_ID" FROM "SH"."SALES" "SALES" GROUP BY "PROD_ID" ORDER BY
              SUM("AMOUNT_SOLD") DESC) "Q1" WHERE ROWNUM=1))
   7 - filter(ROWNUM=1)
   9 - filter(ROWNUM=1)
  16 - access("S"."PROD_ID"="P"."PROD_ID")
```

The presence of the ROWNUM=1 predicate in the subquery of Listing 13-24 precludes any subquery unnesting. If the subquery pushdown transformation is suppressed by the NO_PUSH_SUBQ hint then a FILTER operation appears in the execution plan. Theoretically, if you see a FILTER operation with more than one operand then the second and subsequent operands (the subquery or subqueries) are evaluated for each row returned by the first operand (the main query). In fact, in Listing 13-24 the subquery is not correlated, and scalar subquery caching will ensure that the subquery is evaluated only once.

But in the case of Listing 13-24, suppressing the transformation slows down the query. The point is that without the transformation we will be joining all rows from SH.SALES with the SH.PRODUCTS and SH.CUSTOMERS tables, discarding most of the joined rows at the end. What we want to do is to evaluate the subquery early and apply the filtering to the rows from SH.PRODUCTS so as to get the one row back that we want. We can then use a nested loops join and indexed access to get just the rows matching the one value of PROD_ID from SH.SALES.

When subquery pushdown is applied, the subquery gets applied as a child of an operation that you wouldn't normally expect to have any children. In this case, the INDEX UNIQUE SCAN of operation 6 obtains the value of PROD_ID that it needs by evaluating its child.

■ **Caution**   The documentation in the SQL Language Reference manual for the PUSH_SUBQ hint claims that the hint will have no effect when applied to a table that is joined using a merge join. The actual restriction only applies when the subquery is correlated to a second table, in which case the second correlated table must precede the first in the join order, and the first table must be accessed with a nested loops join.

Listing 13-25 shows an example in which subquery pushdown is illegal because of the join method.

Listing 13-25. Subquery pushdown as illegal and as a bad idea

```
SELECT /* leading(p s1) use_nl(s1) */
       -- Add plus sign for hint to be recognised
     *
 FROM sh.sales s1
      JOIN sh.customers c USING (cust_id)
      JOIN sh.products p ON s1.prod_id = p.prod_id
WHERE      s1.amount_sold > (SELECT /*+ push_subq */
                                    -- Hint inapplicable to hash joins
                                    AVG (s2.amount_sold)
                               FROM sh.sales s2
                              WHERE s2.prod_id = p.prod_id)
      AND p.prod_category = 'Electronics'
      AND c.cust_year_of_birth = 1919;

-- Execution plan with hash join (push_subq hint ignored)
```

Id	Operation	Name	Cost (%CPU)
0	SELECT STATEMENT		942 (2)
* 1	FILTER		
* 2	HASH JOIN		610 (2)
* 3	TABLE ACCESS FULL	CUSTOMERS	271 (1)
* 4	HASH JOIN		339 (3)
5	TABLE ACCESS BY INDEX ROWID BATCHED	PRODUCTS	3 (0)

```
|*  6 |       INDEX RANGE SCAN              | PRODUCTS_PROD_CAT_IX |      1   (0)|
|   7 |      PARTITION RANGE ALL            |                      |    334   (3)|
|   8 |       TABLE ACCESS FULL             | SALES                |    334   (3)|
|   9 |     SORT AGGREGATE                  |                      |             |
|  10 |      PARTITION RANGE ALL            |                      |    332   (2)|
|* 11 |       TABLE ACCESS FULL             | SALES                |    332   (2)|
----------------------------------------------------------------------------
```

Predicate Information (identified by operation id):

```
   1 - filter("S1"."AMOUNT_SOLD"> (SELECT /*+ PUSH_SUBQ */
           AVG("S2"."AMOUNT_SOLD") FROM "SH"."SALES" "S2" WHERE "S2"."PROD_ID"=:B1))
   2 - access("S1"."CUST_ID"="C"."CUST_ID")
   3 - filter("C"."CUST_YEAR_OF_BIRTH"=1919)
   4 - access("S1"."PROD_ID"="P"."PROD_ID")
   6 - access("P"."PROD_CATEGORY"='Electronics')
  11 - filter("S2"."PROD_ID"=:B1)
```

-- Transformed query when nested loops used (push_subq hint honored)

```
----------------------------------------------------------------------------------
| Id  | Operation                                    | Name                 | Cost (%CPU)|
----------------------------------------------------------------------------------
|   0 | SELECT STATEMENT                             |                      | 6166   (1)|
|*  1 |  HASH JOIN                                   |                      | 5726   (1)|
|   2 |   TABLE ACCESS BY INDEX ROWID BATCHED        | CUSTOMERS            |   10   (0)|
|   3 |    BITMAP CONVERSION TO ROWIDS               |                      |            |
|*  4 |     BITMAP INDEX SINGLE VALUE                | CUSTOMERS_YOB_BIX    |            |
|   5 |   NESTED LOOPS                               |                      | 5716   (1)|
|   6 |    TABLE ACCESS BY INDEX ROWID BATCHED       | PRODUCTS             |    3   (0)|
|*  7 |     INDEX RANGE SCAN                         | PRODUCTS_PROD_CAT_IX |    1   (0)|
|   8 |    PARTITION RANGE ALL                       |                      | 5716   (1)|
|*  9 |     TABLE ACCESS BY LOCAL INDEX ROWID BATCHED| SALES                | 5716   (1)|
|  10 |      BITMAP CONVERSION TO ROWIDS             |                      |            |
|* 11 |       BITMAP INDEX SINGLE VALUE              | SALES_PROD_BIX       |            |
|  12 |       SORT AGGREGATE                         |                      |            |
|  13 |        PARTITION RANGE ALL                   |                      |  440   (0)|
|  14 |         TABLE ACCESS BY LOCAL INDEX ROWID BATCHED| SALES            |  440   (0)|
|  15 |          BITMAP CONVERSION TO ROWIDS         |                      |            |
|* 16 |           BITMAP INDEX SINGLE VALUE          | SALES_PROD_BIX       |            |
----------------------------------------------------------------------------------
```

Predicate Information (identified by operation id):

```
   1 - access("S1"."CUST_ID"="C"."CUST_ID")
   4 - access("C"."CUST_YEAR_OF_BIRTH"=1919)
   7 - access("P"."PROD_CATEGORY"='Electronics')
   9 - filter("S1"."AMOUNT_SOLD"> (SELECT /*+ PUSH_SUBQ */ AVG("S2"."AMOUNT_SOLD")
           FROM "SH"."SALES" "S2" WHERE "S2"."PROD_ID"=:B1))
  11 - access("S1"."PROD_ID"="P"."PROD_ID")
  16 - access("S2"."PROD_ID"=:B1)
```

Listing 13-25 can't use the USING clause in the join with SH.PRODUCTS because of the need to qualify the reference in the subquery with a table alias. The execution plan for the query in Listing 13-25 uses a hash join to access the SH.SALES table and so it is not possible to evaluate the subquery early. All the illegal hint did was to prevent subquery unnesting. However, if we apply LEADING and USE_NL hints to force a nested loops join, it is now perfectly legal, if inadvisable, to push the subquery so that it is evaluated before the join with SH.CUSTOMERS. The table access on line 9 now has two children. The first child obtains ROWIDs for each row returned by the bitmap index operation. Theoretically, the second child of operation 9 is evaluated for every ROWID, but subquery caching ensures that the subquery is evaluated just 13 times, once for each of the 13 products in the electronics category. If subquery evaluation had been deferred until after the join with SH.CUSTOMERS, the subquery would have been evaluated just 4 times, since customers born in 1919 only bought 4 of the 13 electronics products.

Join Predicate Pushdown

When view merging is inadvisable or impossible, the join predicate pushdown (JPPD) transformation is a fallback option. Take a look at Listing 13-26.

Listing 13-26. Join predicate pushdown

```
WITH agg_q
     AS ( SELECT /*+  push_pred */
                 /* no_push_pred */
             s.cust_id
            ,prod_id
            ,p.prod_name
            ,SUM (s.amount_sold) total_amt_sold
          FROM sh.sales s JOIN sh.products p USING (prod_id)
       GROUP BY s.cust_id, prod_id)
SELECT cust_id
      ,c.cust_first_name
      ,c.cust_last_name
      ,c.cust_email
      ,agg_q.total_amt_sold
  FROM agg_q RIGHT JOIN sh.customers c USING (cust_id)
 WHERE cust_first_name = 'Abner' AND cust_last_name = 'Everett';

-- Untransformed execution plan (NO_PUSH_PRED)
```

Id	Operation	Name	Cost (%CPU)
0	SELECT STATEMENT		5519 (1)
* 1	HASH JOIN OUTER		5519 (1)
* 2	TABLE ACCESS FULL	CUSTOMERS	423 (1)
3	VIEW		5095 (1)
4	HASH GROUP BY		5095 (1)
* 5	HASH JOIN		3021 (1)
6	INDEX FULL SCAN	PRODUCTS_PK	1 (0)
7	VIEW	VW_GBC_6	3019 (1)
8	HASH GROUP BY		3019 (1)
9	PARTITION RANGE ALL		517 (2)
10	TABLE ACCESS FULL	SALES	517 (2)

Predicate Information (identified by operation id):

```
   1 - access("C"."CUST_ID"="AGG_Q"."CUST_ID"(+))
   2 - filter("C"."CUST_FIRST_NAME"='Abner' AND
              "C"."CUST_LAST_NAME"='Everett')
   5 - access("ITEM_1"="P"."PROD_ID")
```

-- Transformed query

```
SELECT c.cust_id
      ,agg_q.prod_id
      ,agg_q.prod_name
      ,c.cust_first_name
      ,c.cust_last_name
      ,c.cust_email
      ,agg_q.total_amt_sold
  FROM sh.customers c
       OUTER APPLY
       (  SELECT prod_id, p.prod_name, SUM (s.amount_sold) total_amt_sold
            FROM sh.sales s JOIN sh.products p USING (prod_id)
          WHERE s.cust_id = c.cust_id
       GROUP BY prod_id, p.prod_name) agg_q
 WHERE cust_first_name = 'Abner' AND cust_last_name = 'Everett';
```

-- Transformed execution plan (default)

```
---------------------------------------------------------------------------------
| Id  | Operation                                    | Name          | Cost (%CPU)|
---------------------------------------------------------------------------------
|   0 | SELECT STATEMENT                             |               |  480   (0)|
|   1 |  NESTED LOOPS OUTER                          |               |  480   (0)|
|*  2 |   TABLE ACCESS FULL                          | CUSTOMERS     |  423   (1)|
|   3 |   VIEW PUSHED PREDICATE                      |               |   58   (0)|
|   4 |    SORT GROUP BY                             |               |   58   (0)|
|*  5 |     HASH JOIN                                |               |   58   (0)|
|   6 |      VIEW                                    | VW_GBC_6      |   55   (0)|
|   7 |       SORT GROUP BY                          |               |   55   (0)|
|   8 |        PARTITION RANGE ALL                   |               |   55   (0)|
|   9 |         TABLE ACCESS BY LOCAL INDEX ROWID BATCHED| SALES     |   55   (0)|
|  10 |          BITMAP CONVERSION TO ROWIDS         |               |           |
|* 11 |           BITMAP INDEX SINGLE VALUE          | SALES_CUST_BIX|           |
|  12 |      TABLE ACCESS FULL                       | PRODUCTS      |    3   (0)|
---------------------------------------------------------------------------------
```

Predicate Information (identified by operation id):

```
   2 - filter("C"."CUST_FIRST_NAME"='Abner' AND "C"."CUST_LAST_NAME"='Everett')
   5 - access("ITEM_1"="P"."PROD_ID")
  11 - access("S"."CUST_ID"="C"."CUST_ID")
```

The query in Listing 13-26 shows the total sales for each product made to the 14 customers named Abner Everett. The use of an outer join precludes both simple and complex view merging, and so without JPPD the GROUP BY operation would generate 328,395 rows for each combination of customer and product. The JPPD transformation requires a nested loops join from SH.CUSTOMERS into the view so that a predicate on CUST_ID can be applied each time the subquery is evaluated. Notice that both variants of the execution plan in Listing 13-26 show the application of the group by placement transformation; rows from SH.SALES are grouped by CUST_ID before joining with the products table.

According to the optimizer team's blog, https://blogs.oracle.com/optimizer/entry/basics_of_join_predicate_pushdown_in_oracle, JPPD is only supported for the following types of view:

- UNION ALL/UNION view

- Outer-joined view

- Anti-joined view

- Semi-joined view

- DISTINCT view

- GROUP-BY view

Why is JPPD restricted in this way? Well, if none of these conditions apply it is almost certain that the heuristic simple view merging transformation will apply anyway, rendering the JPPD restriction moot. However, I will cover in Chapter 19 an obscure case in which neither JPPD nor simple view merging are supported.

JPPD is a cost-based transformation that can easily be recognized in an execution plan by the presence of either the VIEW PUSHED PREDICATE or UNION ALL PUSHED PREDICATE operations. The benefit of filtering at an early stage comes at the cost of having to execute the subquery multiple times. If evaluating the subquery multiple times is too costly, the CBO may elect not to apply the transformation and then use a hash join so that the subquery is evaluated only once.

Although JPPD has been around for a long time, it is only with 12c SQL syntax that we have the ability to show the results of the transformation. The transformed query in Listing 13-26 uses the ANSI syntax variant for an outer lateral join, which should have precisely the same effect as the join predicate pushdown transformation. In 12.1.0.1, however, there seems to be a bug that prevents the CBO from generating an optimal execution plan for the lateral join, even when hinted.

Subquery Decorrelation

JPPD and subquery decorrelation are inverse transformations of each other in the same way that complex view merging and group by placement are inverse transformations of each other. Subquery decorrelation is shown in Listing 13-27.

Listing 13-27. Subquery decorrelation

```
SELECT o.order_id
      ,o.order_date
      ,o.order_mode
      ,o.customer_id
      ,o.order_status
      ,o.order_total
      ,o.sales_rep_id
      ,o.promotion_id
      ,agg_q.max_quantity
```

```
FROM oe.orders o
     CROSS APPLY (SELECT /*+   decorrelate */
                         /* no_decorrelate */
                  MAX (oi.quantity) max_quantity
              FROM oe.order_items oi
              WHERE oi.order_id = o.order_id) agg_q
WHERE o.order_id IN (2458, 2397);
```

-- Untransformed execution plan (NO_DECORRELATE)

```
---------------------------------------------------------------------
| Id  | Operation                              | Name            | Cost (%CPU)|
---------------------------------------------------------------------
|   0 | SELECT STATEMENT                       |                 |    8   (0)|
|   1 |  NESTED LOOPS                          |                 |    8   (0)|
|   2 |   INLIST ITERATOR                      |                 |           |
|   3 |    TABLE ACCESS BY INDEX ROWID         | ORDERS          |    2   (0)|
|*  4 |     INDEX UNIQUE SCAN                  | ORDER_PK        |    1   (0)|
|   5 |   VIEW                                 | VW_LAT_535DE542 |    3   (0)|
|   6 |    SORT AGGREGATE                      |                 |           |
|   7 |     TABLE ACCESS BY INDEX ROWID BATCHED| ORDER_ITEMS     |    3   (0)|
|*  8 |      INDEX RANGE SCAN                  | ITEM_ORDER_IX   |    1   (0)|
---------------------------------------------------------------------
```

Predicate Information (identified by operation id):

```
   4 - access("O"."ORDER_ID"=2397 OR "O"."ORDER_ID"=2458)
   8 - access("OI"."ORDER_ID"="O"."ORDER_ID")
```

-- Transformed query

```
  SELECT o.order_id order_id
        ,o.order_date order_date
        ,o.order_mode order_mode
        ,o.customer_id customer_id
        ,o.order_status order_status
        ,o.order_total order_total
        ,o.sales_rep_id sales_rep_id
        ,o.promotion_id promotion_id
        ,MAX (oi.quantity) max_quantity
    FROM oe.orders o
        LEFT JOIN oe.order_items oi
            ON     oi.order_id = o.order_id
               AND (oi.order_id = 2397 OR oi.order_id = 2458)
    WHERE (o.order_id = 2397 OR o.order_id = 2458)
```

```
GROUP BY o.order_id
        ,o.ROWID
        ,o.promotion_id
        ,o.sales_rep_id
        ,o.order_total
        ,o.order_status
        ,o.customer_id
        ,o.order_mode
        ,o.order_date
        ,o.order_id;
```

-- Transformed execution plan (default)

```
----------------------------------------------------------------------
| Id  | Operation                     | Name        | Cost (%CPU)|
----------------------------------------------------------------------
|   0 | SELECT STATEMENT              |             |    5   (0)|
|   1 |  HASH GROUP BY                |             |    5   (0)|
|*  2 |   HASH JOIN OUTER             |             |    5   (0)|
|   3 |    INLIST ITERATOR            |             |           |
|   4 |     TABLE ACCESS BY INDEX ROWID| ORDERS     |    2   (0)|
|*  5 |      INDEX UNIQUE SCAN        | ORDER_PK    |    1   (0)|
|*  6 |    TABLE ACCESS FULL          | ORDER_ITEMS |    3   (0)|
----------------------------------------------------------------------
```

Predicate Information (identified by operation id):

```
   2 - access("OI"."ORDER_ID"(+)="O"."ORDER_ID")
   5 - access("O"."ORDER_ID"=2397 OR "O"."ORDER_ID"=2458)
   6 - filter("OI"."ORDER_ID"(+)=2397 OR "OI"."ORDER_ID"(+)=2458)
```

I could have used the transformed query from Listing 13-26 to demonstrate subquery decorrelation, but some considerable fancy hinting would have been needed to prevent JPPD from being applied to the decorrelated result! Instead of doing that, I have used a lateral join using the OE.ORDERS and OE.ORDER_ITEMS tables to demonstrate some additional points.

Listing 13-27 lists the two rows from orders 2397 and 2458 in OE.ORDERS together with the maximum value of QUANTITY for the matching order from OE.ORDER_ITEMS.

The transformed query can now use a hash join and is something a mere mortal is unlikely to dream up. Here are some interesting points to note:

- Even though this was an inner lateral join (CROSS APPLY) and not an outer lateral join (OUTER APPLY), the transformed query still used an outer join. This is because the subquery is guaranteed to return exactly one row, even if there were no line items for the order.

- The GROUP BY clause includes O.ROWID. This isn't necessary in this case because a primary key is in the GROUP BY list, but in general this is needed to ensure that there is no aggregation of rows from the left side of the join; aggregation only applies to the right side, in this case OE.ORDER_ITEMS.

- The transformation has successfully applied transitive closure to allow filtering of the OE.ORDERS and OE.ORDER_ITEMS separately.

Subquery Coalescing

Subquery coalescing is a transformation introduced in 11gR2 and is still in its infancy. Listing 13-28 shows one of the few cases where the transformation can be applied.

Listing 13-28. Subquery coalescing

```
SELECT *
  FROM sh.sales s1
 WHERE    EXISTS
            (SELECT /*+   coalsesce_sq */
                   /* no_coalesce_sq */
                   *
             FROM sh.sales s2
            WHERE    s1.time_id = s2.time_id
                 AND s2.amount_sold > s1.amount_sold + 100)
        OR EXISTS
            (SELECT /*+   coalesce_sq */
                   /* no_coalesce_sq */
                   *
             FROM sh.sales s3
            WHERE    s1.time_id = s3.time_id
                 AND s3.amount_sold < s1.amount_sold - 100);
```

-- Untransformed execution plan (NO_COALESCE_SQ)

```
-----------------------------------------------------------------------------------
| Id  | Operation                                | Name           | Cost (%CPU)|
-----------------------------------------------------------------------------------
|   0 | SELECT STATEMENT                         |                | 1205K  (1)|
|*  1 |  FILTER                                  |                |            |
|   2 |   PARTITION RANGE ALL                    |                |   518  (2)|
|   3 |    TABLE ACCESS FULL                     | SALES          |   518  (2)|
|   4 |   PARTITION RANGE SINGLE                 |                |     1  (0)|
|*  5 |    TABLE ACCESS BY LOCAL INDEX ROWID BATCHED| SALES       |     1  (0)|
|   6 |     BITMAP CONVERSION TO ROWIDS          |                |            |
|*  7 |      BITMAP INDEX SINGLE VALUE           | SALES_TIME_BIX |            |
|   8 |   PARTITION RANGE SINGLE                 |                |     1  (0)|
|*  9 |    TABLE ACCESS BY LOCAL INDEX ROWID BATCHED| SALES       |     1  (0)|
|  10 |     BITMAP CONVERSION TO ROWIDS          |                |            |
|* 11 |      BITMAP INDEX SINGLE VALUE           | SALES_TIME_BIX |            |
-----------------------------------------------------------------------------------
```

Predicate Information (identified by operation id):

```
   1 - filter( EXISTS (SELECT /*+ NO_COALESCE_SQ */ 0 FROM "SH"."SALES"
          "S2" WHERE "S2"."TIME_ID"=:B1 AND "S2"."AMOUNT_SOLD">:B2+100) OR  EXISTS
          (SELECT 0 FROM "SH"."SALES" "S3" WHERE "S3"."TIME_ID"=:B3 AND
          "S3"."AMOUNT_SOLD"<:B4-100))
   5 - filter("S2"."AMOUNT_SOLD">:B1+100)
   7 - access("S2"."TIME_ID"=:B1)
   9 - filter("S3"."AMOUNT_SOLD"<:B1-100)
  11 - access("S3"."TIME_ID"=:B1)
```

-- Transformed query

```
SELECT *
  FROM sh.sales s1
 WHERE EXISTS
          (SELECT *
             FROM sh.sales s2
            WHERE       s2.amount_sold > s1.amount_sold + 100
                    AND s2.time_id = s1.time_id
               OR       s2.amount_sold < s1.amount_sold - 100
                    AND s2.time_id = s1.time_id);
```

-- Transformed execution plan (default)

```
---------------------------------------------------------------------------
| Id  | Operation                                   | Name            | Cost (%CPU)|
---------------------------------------------------------------------------
|   0 | SELECT STATEMENT                            |                 | 358K   (1)|
|*  1 |  FILTER                                     |                 |           |
|   2 |   PARTITION RANGE ALL                       |                 | 517    (2)|
|   3 |    TABLE ACCESS FULL                        | SALES           | 517    (2)|
|   4 |   PARTITION RANGE INLIST                    |                 |   5    (0)|
|*  5 |    TABLE ACCESS BY LOCAL INDEX ROWID BATCHED| SALES           |   5    (0)|
|   6 |     BITMAP CONVERSION TO ROWIDS             |                 |           |
|   7 |      BITMAP OR                              |                 |           |
|*  8 |       BITMAP INDEX SINGLE VALUE             | SALES_TIME_BIX  |           |
|*  9 |       BITMAP INDEX SINGLE VALUE             | SALES_TIME_BIX  |           |
---------------------------------------------------------------------------
```

Predicate Information (identified by operation id):

```
   1 - filter( EXISTS (SELECT 0 FROM "SH"."SALES" "S2" WHERE
               ("S2"."TIME_ID"=:B1 OR "S2"."TIME_ID"=:B2) AND ("S2"."TIME_ID"=:B3 AND
               "S2"."AMOUNT_SOLD">:B4+100 OR "S2"."TIME_ID"=:B5 AND
               "S2"."AMOUNT_SOLD"<:B6-100)))
   5 - filter("S2"."TIME_ID"=:B1 AND "S2"."AMOUNT_SOLD">:B2+100 OR
               "S2"."TIME_ID"=:B3 AND "S2"."AMOUNT_SOLD"<:B4-100)
   8 - access("S2"."TIME_ID"=:B1)
   9 - access("S2"."TIME_ID"=:B1)
```

The fact that the two subqueries in Listing 13-28 are combined using OR means that they cannot be unnested. However, the two subqueries can be coalesced. Notice that the execution plan for the untransformed query contains a FILTER operation with three children, implying the separate application of the two subquery filters. The FILTER operation in the transformed execution plan has just two children, implying one filter.

You will see that in the transformed execution plan we have unnecessarily combined the two identical bitmaps from lines 8 and 9. If you rewrite the query yourself this unnecessary step can be avoided.

Subquery coalescing is the last of the subquery-related transformations that I want to discuss. There are however, a few miscellaneous transformations still to cover.

Miscellaneous Transformations

In this chapter I have tried to place the transformations into logical groups, but there are a few that don't conveniently fit into any category. Let us begin by looking at *or expansion*.

Or Expansion

Sometimes it makes sense to change a predicate concisely written with OR and process the bits separately, as Listing 13-29 demonstrates.

Listing 13-29. Or expansion

```
SELECT /*+ use_concat */
       /* no_expand */
       SUM (amount_sold) cnt
 FROM sh.sales JOIN sh.products USING (prod_id)
WHERE time_id = DATE '1998-03-31' OR prod_name = 'Y Box';

-- Untransformed execution plan (NO_EXPAND)

---------------------------------------------------------
| Id | Operation             | Name     | Cost (%CPU)|
---------------------------------------------------------
|  0 | SELECT STATEMENT      |          |  522   (2)|
|  1 |  SORT AGGREGATE       |          |           |
|* 2 |   HASH JOIN           |          |  522   (2)|
|  3 |    TABLE ACCESS FULL  | PRODUCTS |    3   (0)|
|  4 |    PARTITION RANGE ALL|          |  517   (2)|
|  5 |     TABLE ACCESS FULL | SALES    |  517   (2)|
---------------------------------------------------------

Predicate Information (identified by operation id):
---------------------------------------------------

   2 - access("SALES"."PROD_ID"="PRODUCTS"."PROD_ID")
       filter("SALES"."TIME_ID"=TO_DATE(' 1998-03-31 00:00:00',
              'syyyy-mm-dd hh24:mi:ss') OR "PRODUCTS"."PROD_NAME"='Y Box')

-- Transformed query (approximate)

WITH q1
    AS (SELECT amount_sold
          FROM sh.sales JOIN sh.products USING (prod_id)
         WHERE prod_name = 'Y Box'
        UNION ALL
        SELECT amount_sold
          FROM sh.sales JOIN sh.products USING (prod_id)
         WHERE time_id = DATE '1998-03-31' AND LNNVL (prod_name = 'Y Box'))
SELECT SUM (amount_sold) cnt
  FROM q1;
```

-- Transformed execution plan (default)

```
----------------------------------------------------------------------------
| Id  | Operation                                 | Name           | Cost (%CPU)|
----------------------------------------------------------------------------
|   0 | SELECT STATEMENT                          |                | 472   (0)|
|   1 |  SORT AGGREGATE                           |                |          |
|   2 |   CONCATENATION                           |                |          |
|   3 |    NESTED LOOPS                           |                |          |
|   4 |     NESTED LOOPS                          |                | 445   (0)|
|*  5 |      TABLE ACCESS FULL                    | PRODUCTS       |   3   (0)|
|   6 |      PARTITION RANGE ALL                  |                |          |
|   7 |       BITMAP CONVERSION TO ROWIDS         |                |          |
|*  8 |        BITMAP INDEX SINGLE VALUE          | SALES_PROD_BIX |          |
|   9 |     TABLE ACCESS BY LOCAL INDEX ROWID     | SALES          | 445   (0)|
|* 10 |    HASH JOIN                              |                |  27   (0)|
|* 11 |     TABLE ACCESS FULL                     | PRODUCTS       |   3   (0)|
|  12 |     PARTITION RANGE SINGLE                |                |  24   (0)|
|  13 |      TABLE ACCESS BY LOCAL INDEX ROWID BATCHED| SALES      |  24   (0)|
|  14 |       BITMAP CONVERSION TO ROWIDS         |                |          |
|* 15 |        BITMAP INDEX SINGLE VALUE          | SALES_TIME_BIX |          |
----------------------------------------------------------------------------
```

Predicate Information (identified by operation id):

```
   5 - filter("PRODUCTS"."PROD_NAME"='Y Box')
   8 - access("SALES"."PROD_ID"="PRODUCTS"."PROD_ID")
  10 - access("SALES"."PROD_ID"="PRODUCTS"."PROD_ID")
  11 - filter(LNNVL("PRODUCTS"."PROD_NAME"='Y Box'))
  15 - access("SALES"."TIME_ID"=TO_DATE(' 1998-03-31 00:00:00', 'syyyy-mm-dd
             hh24:mi:ss'))
```

Without the availability of the cost-based or-expansion transformation, the presence of the two independent predicates in Listing 13-29 leaves us with no choice but to use a full table scan on SH.SALES. By adding a UNION ALL set operator we can use two indexes to separately obtain the rows that match the individual predicates.

There is, however, a slight semantic difference between an OR expression and a UNION ALL set operator. It turns out that there was one sale of a Y Box on March 31, 1998. A UNION ALL set operator would normally list this row twice, and the OR condition would list it just once. To avoid such duplicates, rows matching both conditions are excluded from the second branch of the UNION ALL by the means of the LNNVL function. If you are not familiar with the function, LNNVL (PRODUCTS.PROD_NAME='Y Box')) means (PROD_NAME != 'Y Box' OR PROD_NAME IS NULL).

Here are a few key points about the or-expansion transformation:

- As mentioned earlier, the way to suppress or-expansion is with the NO_EXPAND hint. There is no NO_USE_CONCAT hint.

- When the UNION ALL operation is created by the or-expansion transformation it is shown as CONCATENATION. However, the UNION ALL and CONCATENATION operations function identically.

- When you interpret an execution plan that contains a CONCATENATION operation bear in mind that the children are typically listed in reverse order to that in which they appear in the original query.

- The documented variant of USE_CONCAT is an all or nothing approach. On the one hand, you can't decide to expand just one of the OR conditions in a WHERE clause that has several. On the other hand, if you look at the outline section of your displayed execution plan you will see that USE_CONCAT has some undocumented parameters that would allow more control, as would the alternative OR_EXPAND hint. However, I haven't worked out how these work. The CBO will, of its own accord, sometimes expand a subset of the OR conditions.

Materialized View Rewrite

The topic of materialized views is a large one, and it would be possible to write an entire chapter about them. In fact, the Data Warehousing Guide has two! At this point I just want to briefly demonstrate the principle of how a query written against some base tables can be transformed into a query against a materialized view. Listing 13-30 provides a simple example.

Listing 13-30. Materialized view rewrite

```
EXEC dbms_mview.refresh('SH.CAL_MONTH_SALES_MV');

ALTER SESSION SET query_rewrite_integrity=trusted;

  SELECT /*+   rewrite(sh.cal_month_sales_mv) */
         /* no_rewrite */
            t.calendar_month_desc, SUM (s.amount_sold) AS dollars
    FROM sh.sales s, sh.times t
   WHERE s.time_id = t.time_id
GROUP BY t.calendar_month_desc;

-- Untransfomed execution plan (NO_REWRITE)
```

```
-----------------------------------------------------------
| Id  | Operation             | Name      | Cost (%CPU)|
-----------------------------------------------------------
|   0 | SELECT STATEMENT      |           |   367   (8)|
|   1 |  HASH GROUP BY        |           |   367   (8)|
|*  2 |   HASH JOIN           |           |   367   (8)|
|   3 |    VIEW               | VW_GBC_5  |   355   (8)|
|   4 |     HASH GROUP BY     |           |   355   (8)|
|   5 |      PARTITION RANGE ALL|         |   334   (3)|
|   6 |       TABLE ACCESS FULL | SALES   |   334   (3)|
|   7 |    TABLE ACCESS FULL  | TIMES     |    12   (0)|
-----------------------------------------------------------
```

```
Predicate Information (identified by operation id):
---------------------------------------------------

   2 - access("ITEM_1"="T"."TIME_ID")
```

-- Transformed query

```
SELECT *
  FROM sh.cal_month_sales_mv mv;
```

-- Transformed execution plan (default)

```
---------------------------------------------------------------------
| Id  | Operation                    | Name             | Cost (%CPU)|
---------------------------------------------------------------------
|  0  | SELECT STATEMENT             |                  |    3   (0)|
|  1  | MAT_VIEW REWRITE ACCESS FULL | CAL_MONTH_SALES_MV|    3   (0)|
---------------------------------------------------------------------
```

Even though we refresh the SH.CAL_MONTH_SALES_MV materialized view before we start, we still have to set query_rewrite_integrity=trusted before the query can be rewritten. The problem is that the referential integrity constraint between SH.SALES and SH.TIMES isn't validated. Although working out when and where a materialized view rewrite is legal and advisable is tricky, the basic concept is straightforward. In this example, the legwork of aggregating the monthly sales data has been done in advance and doesn't need to be repeated.

There is one more materialized view transformation that I want to discuss. This one is quite obscure.

Grouping Sets to Union Expansion

The grouping-sets-to-union-expansion transformation was introduced in 9iR2, but there has been very little written about it. The transformation only applies to queries that involve grouping sets where the rolled-up data can be obtained from a materialized view. Listing 13-31 demonstrates.

Listing 13-31. Grouping sets to union expansion

```
ALTER SESSION SET query_rewrite_integrity=trusted;

  SELECT /*+   expand_gset_to_union */
         /* no_expand_gset_to_union */
         DECODE (GROUPING (t.time_id), 1, 'Month total', t.time_id) AS time_id
        ,t.calendar_month_desc
        ,SUM (s.amount_sold) AS dollars
    FROM sh.sales s, sh.times t
   WHERE s.time_id = t.time_id
GROUP BY ROLLUP (t.time_id), t.calendar_month_desc
ORDER BY calendar_month_desc, time_id;
```

-- **Untransformed execution plan (NOEXPAND_GSET_TO_UNION)**

```
-----------------------------------------------------------
| Id  | Operation                    | Name    | Cost (%CPU)|
-----------------------------------------------------------
|   0 | SELECT STATEMENT             |         | 6340    (1)|
|   1 |  SORT ORDER BY               |         | 6340    (1)|
|   2 |   SORT GROUP BY ROLLUP       |         | 6340    (1)|
|*  3 |    HASH JOIN                 |         |  537    (2)|
|   4 |     PART JOIN FILTER CREATE  | :BF0000 |            |
|   5 |      TABLE ACCESS FULL       | TIMES   |   18    (0)|
|   6 |     PARTITION RANGE JOIN-FILTER|       |  517    (2)|
|   7 |      TABLE ACCESS FULL       | SALES   |  517    (2)|
-----------------------------------------------------------
```

Predicate Information (identified by operation id):

```
   3 - access("S"."TIME_ID"="T"."TIME_ID")
```

-- **Transformed query**

```
WITH vw_gbc
    AS (  SELECT s.time_id, SUM (s.amount_sold) AS dollars
            FROM sh.sales s
        GROUP BY s.time_id)
   ,gset_union
    AS (  SELECT TO_CHAR (vw_gbc.time_id) AS time_id
               ,t.calendar_month_desc
               ,SUM (vw_gbc.dollars) AS dollars
           FROM vw_gbc, sh.times t
          WHERE vw_gbc.time_id = t.time_id
       GROUP BY vw_gbc.time_id, t.calendar_month_desc
       UNION ALL
       SELECT 'Month Total' AS time_id, mv.calendar_month_desc, mv.dollars
         FROM sh.cal_month_sales_mv mv)
```

```
SELECT *
  FROM gset_union u
ORDER BY u.calendar_month_desc, u.time_id;
```

-- Transformed execution plan (default)

```
---------------------------------------------------------------------
| Id  | Operation                    | Name              | Cost (%CPU)|
---------------------------------------------------------------------
|   0 | SELECT STATEMENT             |                   |  369   (8)|
|   1 |  SORT ORDER BY               |                   |  369   (8)|
|   2 |   VIEW                       |                   |  369   (8)|
|   3 |    UNION-ALL                 |                   |           |
|   4 |     HASH GROUP BY            |                   |  367   (8)|
|*  5 |      HASH JOIN               |                   |  367   (8)|
|   6 |       VIEW                   | VW_GBC_6          |  355   (8)|
|   7 |        HASH GROUP BY         |                   |  355   (8)|
|   8 |         PARTITION RANGE ALL  |                   |  334   (3)|
|   9 |          TABLE ACCESS FULL   | SALES             |  334   (3)|
|  10 |       TABLE ACCESS FULL      | TIMES             |   12   (0)|
|  11 |     MAT_VIEW REWRITE ACCESS FULL| CAL_MONTH_SALES_MV |    2   (0)|
---------------------------------------------------------------------
```

```
Predicate Information (identified by operation id):
---------------------------------------------------

   5 - access("ITEM_1"="T"."TIME_ID")
```

The query in Listing 13-31 provides the total value of sales per day with a rolled-up total by month. The untransformed query includes some variant of bloom-filter pruning despite being a serial query, but let us not get distracted.

The transformed query performs a simple GROUP BY with no ROLLUP and then adds rows for the monthly totals from the materialized view. What is interesting is that apart from replacing the SORT GROUP BY ROLLUP operation with a more straightforward HASH GROUP BY operation, the transformation has made group-by-placement possible! Now that the new group-by-placement transformation has been created, the old expand-grouping-sets-to-union transformation might be revisited so as to operate even in the absence of any materialized view. But for now this transformation seems only to operate when a materialized view is available.

Order by Elimination

It is perfectly legal and quite common for ORDER BY expressions to appear in subqueries, and you are entitled to rely on the ordering of any results from such subqueries. For example, in Listing 13-24 I used a ROWNUM=1 predicate on the results of a subquery that included an ORDER BY clause.

Sometimes, however, you may not rely on the ORDER BY clause of a subquery because the result queries are input to another join, aggregation, or set operation. In such cases the CBO feels entitled to remove your apparently superfluous ORDER BY clause.

The question is this: why would you add an ORDER BY clause and not use it? Almost always, superfluous ORDER BY clauses appear in data dictionary views, and it is these cases that the order-by-elimination transformation is intended to address. On the other hand, it is possible to demonstrate the order-by-elimination transformation with inline views, as Listing 13-32 demonstrates.

Listing 13-32. Order-by-elimination

```
SELECT COUNT (*)
  FROM (  SELECT /*+  eliminate_oby */
                 /* no_eliminate_oby */
                 o1.*
            FROM oe.order_items o1
           WHERE product_id = (SELECT MAX (o2.product_id)
                                  FROM oe.order_items o2
                                 WHERE o2.order_id = o1.order_id)
         ORDER BY order_id) v;
```

-- Untransformed execution plan (NO_ELIMINATE_OBY)

```
---------------------------------------------------------------
| Id  | Operation                 | Name          | Cost (%CPU)|
---------------------------------------------------------------
|   0 | SELECT STATEMENT          |               |    5   (0)|
|   1 |  SORT AGGREGATE           |               |           |
|   2 |   VIEW                    |               |    5   (0)|
|   3 |    SORT ORDER BY          |               |    5   (0)|
|*  4 |     HASH JOIN             |               |    5   (0)|
|   5 |      VIEW                 | VW_SQ_1       |    2   (0)|
|   6 |       HASH GROUP BY       |               |    2   (0)|
|   7 |        INDEX FAST FULL SCAN| ORDER_ITEMS_UK |    2   (0)|
|   8 |      TABLE ACCESS FULL    | ORDER_ITEMS   |    3   (0)|
---------------------------------------------------------------
```

Predicate Information (identified by operation id):

```
   4 - access("PRODUCT_ID"="MAX(O2.PRODUCT_ID)" AND
             "ITEM_1"="O1"."ORDER_ID")
```

-- Transformed query

```
SELECT COUNT (*)
  FROM (SELECT o1.*
          FROM oe.order_items o1
         WHERE product_id = (SELECT MAX (o2.product_id)
                               FROM oe.order_items o2
                              WHERE o2.order_id = o1.order_id)) v;
```

-- Transformed execution plan (default)

```
-----------------------------------------------------------------
| Id  | Operation                | Name          | Cost (%CPU)|
-----------------------------------------------------------------
|   0 | SELECT STATEMENT         |               |    2   (0)|
|   1 |  SORT AGGREGATE          |               |           |
|   2 |   NESTED LOOPS           |               |    2   (0)|
|   3 |    VIEW                  | VW_SQ_1       |    2   (0)|
|   4 |     HASH GROUP BY        |               |    2   (0)|
|   5 |      INDEX FAST FULL SCAN| ORDER_ITEMS_UK|    2   (0)|
|*  6 |    INDEX UNIQUE SCAN     | ORDER_ITEMS_UK|    0   (0)|
-----------------------------------------------------------------

Predicate Information (identified by operation id):
-----------------------------------------------

   6 - access("ITEM_1"="O1"."ORDER_ID" AND
               "PRODUCT_ID"="MAX(O2.PRODUCT_ID)")
```

The query in Listing 13-32 contains an unused ORDER BY clause buried within an inline view. The untransformed query includes a SORT ORDER BY operation, which sorts, and a SORT AGGREGATE operation, which doesn't. The transformed query has removed the redundant ORDER BY clause, and the resulting execution plan includes only the non-sorting SORT AGGREGATE operation that evaluates COUNT (*).

You may wonder why I have suddenly abandoned my beloved factored subqueries in Listing 13-32. The reason is that order-by-elimination does not occur with factored subqueries! I actually think this is a sensible thing. If you put an ORDER BY clause in a factored subquery you did so for a reason. It is really only data dictionary views that need the order-by-elimination transformation.

Table Expansion

Table expansion is a transformation introduced in 11gR2 that is specific to partitioned tables. Prior to the introduction of the table-expansion transformation the unusability of a local index on one partition might preclude the use of other usable indexes on other partitions.

To demonstrate this transformation I have to change the usability of index partitions, and so I will create a new table rather than change the state of example schema data. Listing 13-33 creates a partitioned table with an unusable local index and then rebuilds just one partition.

Listing 13-33. Creation of a table for table expansion demonstration

```
CREATE TABLE t
PARTITION BY RANGE
   (d)
   (
      PARTITION
         t_q1_2013 VALUES LESS THAN (TO_DATE ('2013-04-01', 'yyyy-mm-dd'))
      ,PARTITION
         t_q2_2013 VALUES LESS THAN (TO_DATE ('2013-07-01', 'yyyy-mm-dd'))
      ,PARTITION
         t_q3_2013 VALUES LESS THAN (TO_DATE ('2013-10-01', 'yyyy-mm-dd'))
      ,PARTITION
         t_q4_2013 VALUES LESS THAN (TO_DATE ('2014-01-01', 'yyyy-mm-dd')))
PCTFREE 99
PCTUSED 1
AS
      SELECT DATE '2013-01-01' + ROWNUM - 1 d, ROWNUM n
         FROM DUAL
   CONNECT BY LEVEL <= 365;

CREATE INDEX i
   ON t (n)
   LOCAL
   UNUSABLE;

ALTER INDEX i
   REBUILD PARTITION t_q3_2013;
```

Now that we have our partitioned table available, Listing 13-34 can show how the table expansion transformation works.

Listing 13-34. Table expansion transformation

```
SELECT /*+     expand_table(t) */
       /*  no_expand_table(t) */
      COUNT (*)
 FROM t
WHERE n = 8;
```

```
-- Untransformed execution plan (NO_EXPAND_TABLE)
```

```
-------------------------------------------------
| Id  | Operation           | Name | Cost (%CPU)|
-------------------------------------------------
|   0 | SELECT STATEMENT     |      |   45    (0)|
|   1 |  SORT AGGREGATE      |      |            |
|   2 |   PARTITION RANGE ALL|      |   45    (0)|
|*  3 |    TABLE ACCESS FULL | T    |   45    (0)|
-------------------------------------------------
```

```
Predicate Information (identified by operation id):
---------------------------------------------------

   3 - filter("N"=8)
```

-- Transformed query

```
WITH vw_te
     AS (SELECT *
           FROM t PARTITION (t_q3_2013)
          WHERE n = 8
          UNION ALL
          SELECT *
            FROM t
           WHERE     n = 8
                 AND (   d < TO_DATE ('2013-07-01', 'yyyy-mm-dd')
                      OR d >=TO_DATE ('2013-10-01', 'yyyy-mm-dd')))
SELECT COUNT (*)
  FROM vw_te;
```

-- Transformed execution plan (default)

```
-------------------------------------------------------
| Id  | Operation                | Name   | Cost (%CPU)|
-------------------------------------------------------
|   0 | SELECT STATEMENT         |        |    34   (0)|
|   1 |  SORT AGGREGATE          |        |            |
|   2 |   VIEW                   | VW_TE_1|    34   (0)|
|   3 |    UNION-ALL             |        |            |
|   4 |     PARTITION RANGE SINGLE|       |     1   (0)|
|*  5 |      INDEX RANGE SCAN    | I      |     1   (0)|
|   6 |     PARTITION RANGE OR   |        |    33   (0)|
|*  7 |      TABLE ACCESS FULL   | T      |    33   (0)|
-------------------------------------------------------
```

```
Predicate Information (identified by operation id):
---------------------------------------------------

   5 - access("N"=8)
   7 - filter("N"=8 AND ("T"."D"<TO_DATE(' 2013-07-01 00:00:00',
             'syyyy-mm-dd hh24:mi:ss') OR "T"."D">=TO_DATE(' 2013-10-01 00:00:00',
             'syyyy-mm-dd hh24:mi:ss') AND "T"."D"<TO_DATE(' 2014-01-01 00:00:00',
             'syyyy-mm-dd hh24:mi:ss')))
```

Without the table-expansion transformation the query in Listing 13-34 would be unable to take advantage of the local index because some of its partitions are unusable. The application of the table-expansion transformation splits the query into two branches of a UNION-ALL operation. The first branch is specific to the partition that has a usable local index, and the second branch is specific to the partitions that have no choice but to use a full table scan.

This transformation is likely to be of benefit to many data warehousing applications that regularly rebuild partitions of local bitmap indexes.

The table expansion transformation is the last of our miscellaneous transformations, but I have saved the best for last. The famous star transformation is quite literally in a class of its own. Let us approach the conclusion of this chapter with an explanation of what this most famous of optimizer transformations does and how it can help us.

Star Transformation

The star transformation is the most difficult to grasp of the optimizer transformations, so we will walk through it carefully. We will begin by considering the problem the CBO faces and then move on to looking at how it may be addressed.

The Distributed Join Filter Problem

Let us begin by looking at Listing 13-35 and considering what we would do if we were the CBO.

Listing 13-35. Candidate query for a star transformation

```
SELECT prod_id
      ,cust_id
      ,p.prod_name
      ,c.cust_first_name
      ,s.time_id
      ,s.amount_sold
  FROM sh.sales s
       JOIN sh.customers c USING (cust_id)
       JOIN sh.products p USING (prod_id)
 WHERE c.cust_last_name = 'Everett' AND p.prod_category = 'Electronics';
```

Let us look at some statistics:

- There are 918,843 rows in the SH.SALES table.

- 116,267 of these 918,843 rows match the product filter.

- 740 of the 918,843 rows match the customer filter.

- 115 rows match both customer and product filters.

So, what join order do we pick?

- If we begin by joining the SH.SALES table with either SH.PRODUCTS or SH.CUSTOMERS we end up reading far too many rows from SH.SALES; over 80% of the rows read from SH.SALES will subsequently be discarded.

- If we join SH.PRODUCTS and SH.CUSTOMERS to start with we end up with 5,760 rows, making even a multi-column index expensive.

This is an example of a *distributed filter* where two or more filtering conditions combine in a way that is far more selective than any individual filter is.

There is a strong similarity between this problem and the problem addressed by the INDEX_COMBINE and AND_EQUAL hints that we discussed in Chapter 10; we want to identify the rows matching both our filters and then just read the rows that match both criteria. The difference here is that our filtering conditions are derived from other tables.

So that is our problem statement. Let us now turn our attention to how we might address it.

Solving the Distributed Join Filter Problem

Listing 13-36 is an attempt at rewriting Listing 13-35.

Listing 13-36. First attempt at solving distributed join filters

```
ALTER SESSION SET star_transformation_enabled=temp_disable;

SELECT /* no_table_lookup_by_nl(s) */
       s.time_id, s.amount_sold
  FROM sh.sales s
 WHERE      s.cust_id IN (SELECT c.cust_id
                            FROM sh.customers c
                           WHERE cust_last_name = 'Everett')
       AND s.prod_id IN (SELECT p.prod_id
                            FROM sh.products p
                           WHERE prod_category = 'Electronics');
```

```
-----------------------------------------------------------------------
| Id  | Operation                      | Name                  | Cost (%CPU)|
-----------------------------------------------------------------------
|   0 | SELECT STATEMENT               |                       |  923   (1)|
|   1 |  VIEW                          | VW_ST_8230C7ED        |  923   (1)|
|   2 |   NESTED LOOPS                 |                       |  498   (1)|
|   3 |    PARTITION RANGE ALL         |                       |  440   (1)|
|   4 |     BITMAP CONVERSION TO ROWIDS|                       |  440   (1)|
|   5 |      BITMAP AND                |                       |           |
|   6 |       BITMAP MERGE             |                       |           |
|   7 |        BITMAP KEY ITERATION    |                       |           |
|   8 |         BUFFER SORT            |                       |           |
|*  9 |          TABLE ACCESS FULL     | CUSTOMERS             |  423   (1)|
|* 10 |         BITMAP INDEX RANGE SCAN| SALES_CUST_BIX        |           |
|  11 |       BITMAP MERGE             |                       |           |
|  12 |        BITMAP KEY ITERATION    |                       |           |
|  13 |         BUFFER SORT            |                       |           |
|* 14 |          VIEW                  | index$_join$_051      |    2   (0)|
|* 15 |           HASH JOIN            |                       |           |
|* 16 |            INDEX RANGE SCAN    | PRODUCTS_PROD_CAT_IX  |    1   (0)|
|  17 |            INDEX FAST FULL SCAN| PRODUCTS_PK           |    1   (0)|
|* 18 |         BITMAP INDEX RANGE SCAN| SALES_PROD_BIX        |           |
|  19 |   TABLE ACCESS BY USER ROWID   | SALES                 |  483   (1)|
-----------------------------------------------------------------------

Predicate Information (identified by operation id):
---------------------------------------------------

   9 - filter("CUST_LAST_NAME"='Everett')
  10 - access("S"."CUST_ID"="C"."CUST_ID")
  14 - filter("PROD_CATEGORY"='Electronics')
  15 - access(ROWID=ROWID)
  16 - access("PROD_CATEGORY"='Electronics')
  18 - access("S"."PROD_ID"="P"."PROD_ID")
```

Note that because CUST_ID is unique in SH.CUSTOMERS and PROD_ID is unique in SH.PRODUCTS the number of rows returned by Listing 13-35 and Listing 13-36 should be the same; if there were more than one row in SH.CUSTOMERS for the same CUST_ID then Listing 13-36 would return fewer rows than Listing 13-35 did.

This rewritten query can't use index combining because, as I mentioned in Chapter 10, the technique doesn't support IN lists. The execution plan in Listing 13-36 shows the star transformation, and this alternative approach gives an efficient plan.

The execution plan shows that an index join on the SH.PRODUCTS table has been used to obtain the list of values for PROD_ID and that these values have been used to make several lookups in the SALES_PROD_BIX index of the SH.SALES table in order to obtain multiple bitmaps. These bitmaps are obtained using the BITMAP KEY ITERATION operation on line 12. The use of BITMAP KEY ITERATION is a signature of the star transformation: every time you have a BITMAP KEY ITERATION you have a star transformation and vice versa.[4] As these bitmaps are obtained, they are merged on line 11 to produce a single bitmap that identifies all the rows in SH.SALES from products in the Electronics category.

A similar process applies to the values of CUST_ID using the SALES_CUST_BIX index. The bitmap on line 6 identifies all sales to the 14 Abner Everetts. The bitmaps generated on lines 6 and 11 are fed into the BITMAP AND operation on line 5 to generate a single bitmap that identifies all the rows that match both predicates. Now that we have the final list of ROWIDs we can access the SH.SALES table to obtain just the rows we need.

■ **Note**   The SH.SALES table is accessed by a nested loops join and a TABLE ACCESS BY USER ROWID operation. The approach is actually the result of another transformation introduced in 11gR2 that can be disabled by adding a plus sign to the comment in bold. If the table-lookup-by-nested-loops transformation is disabled, the BITMAP CONVERSION TO ROWIDS operation on line 4 becomes a child of the TABLE ACCESS BY LOCAL INDEX ROWID BATCHED operation and the nested loops join disappears. I have no idea what benefit the table-lookup-by-nested-loops transformation provides.

Be aware that for the star transformation to be applied you must have enterprise edition, and for unhinted queries the initialization parameter STAR_TRANSFORMATION_ENABLED must be set to TRUE or TEMP_DISABLE (I will explain the difference shortly).

But the query in Listing 13-36 is not the same as the query in Listing 13-35: we have lost the ability to select dimension columns. We can address this by adding the dimension tables back into our list of tables, as shown by Listing 13-37.

Listing 13-37. Adding dimension columns with a star transformation

```
ALTER SESSION SET star_transformation_enabled=temp_disable;

SELECT prod_id
      ,cust_id
      ,prod_name
      ,cust_first_name
      ,time_id
      ,amount_sold
  FROM sh.sales s
      JOIN sh.products USING (prod_id)
      JOIN sh.customers USING (cust_id)
```

---

[4]Actually Jonathan Lewis has shown me a counterexample that uses the SEMIJOIN_DRIVER hint but the CBO will never generate such a plan without such nefarious hinting.

```
WHERE       cust_id IN (SELECT c.cust_id
                        FROM sh.customers c
                        WHERE cust_last_name = 'Everett')
       AND prod_id IN (SELECT p.prod_id
                        FROM sh.products p
                        WHERE prod_category = 'Electronics');
```

```
--------------------------------------------------------------------------
| Id  | Operation                             | Name                 | Cost (%CPU)|
--------------------------------------------------------------------------
|   0 | SELECT STATEMENT                      |                      |  1348   (1)|
|*  1 |  HASH JOIN                            |                      |  1348   (1)|
|   2 |   TABLE ACCESS BY INDEX ROWID BATCHED | PRODUCTS             |     3   (0)|
|*  3 |    INDEX RANGE SCAN                   | PRODUCTS_PROD_CAT_IX |     1   (0)|
|*  4 |   HASH JOIN                           |                      |  1345   (1)|
|*  5 |    TABLE ACCESS FULL                  | CUSTOMERS            |   423   (1)|
|   6 |    VIEW                               | VW_ST_C72FA945       |   923   (1)|
|   7 |     NESTED LOOPS                      |                      |   498   (1)|
|   8 |      PARTITION RANGE ALL              |                      |   440   (1)|
|   9 |       BITMAP CONVERSION TO ROWIDS     |                      |   440   (1)|
|  10 |        BITMAP AND                     |                      |            |
|  11 |         BITMAP MERGE                  |                      |            |
|  12 |          BITMAP KEY ITERATION         |                      |            |
|  13 |           BUFFER SORT                 |                      |            |
|* 14 |            TABLE ACCESS FULL          | CUSTOMERS            |   423   (1)|
|* 15 |           BITMAP INDEX RANGE SCAN     | SALES_CUST_BIX       |            |
|  16 |         BITMAP MERGE                  |                      |            |
|  17 |          BITMAP KEY ITERATION         |                      |            |
|  18 |           BUFFER SORT                 |                      |            |
|* 19 |            VIEW                       | index$_join$_055     |     2   (0)|
|* 20 |             HASH JOIN                 |                      |            |
|* 21 |              INDEX RANGE SCAN         | PRODUCTS_PROD_CAT_IX |     1   (0)|
|  22 |              INDEX FAST FULL SCAN     | PRODUCTS_PK          |     1   (0)|
|* 23 |           BITMAP INDEX RANGE SCAN     | SALES_PROD_BIX       |            |
|  24 |      TABLE ACCESS BY USER ROWID       | SALES                |   483   (1)|
--------------------------------------------------------------------------
```

Predicate Information (identified by operation id):

```
   1 - access("ITEM_1"="P"."PROD_ID")
   3 - access("PROD_CATEGORY"='Electronics')
   4 - access("ITEM_2"="C"."CUST_ID")
   5 - filter("CUST_LAST_NAME"='Everett')
  14 - filter("CUST_LAST_NAME"='Everett')
  15 - access("S"."CUST_ID"="C"."CUST_ID")
  19 - filter("PROD_CATEGORY"='Electronics')
  20 - access(ROWID=ROWID)
  21 - access("PROD_CATEGORY"='Electronics')
  23 - access("S"."PROD_ID"="P"."PROD_ID")
```

The execution plan shown in Listing 13-37 results when STAR_TRANSFORMATION_ENABLED is set to TEMP_DISABLE.

You will notice that lines 6 to 24 in Listing 13-37 are identical to lines 1 to 19 in Listing 13-36, but this time we access the SH.PRODUCTS and SH.CUSTOMERS tables a second time each to get the dimension columns. Although we have accessed the dimension tables twice each, we have avoided most of the expensive table fetches from the SH.SALES table.

Although this query is starting to look a little difficult to read, it still doesn't look optimal: why do we have to access the dimension tables twice? Couldn't we cache the columns for our select list when we read the SH.PRODUCTS and SH.CUSTOMERS tables the first time?

Suppose we ran the script shown in Listing 13-38.

Listing 13-38. A star transformation with manual creation of temporary tables

```
CREATE GLOBAL TEMPORARY TABLE cust_cache ON COMMIT PRESERVE ROWS
AS
    SELECT cust_id, cust_first_name
      FROM sh.customers c
     WHERE cust_last_name = 'Everett';

CREATE GLOBAL TEMPORARY TABLE prod_cache ON COMMIT PRESERVE ROWS
AS
    SELECT prod_id, prod_name
      FROM sh.products p
     WHERE prod_category = 'Electronics';

SELECT s.prod_id
      ,s.cust_id
      ,p.prod_name
      ,c.cust_first_name
      ,s.time_id
      ,s.amount_sold
  FROM sh.sales s
       JOIN cust_cache c ON s.cust_id = c.cust_id
       JOIN prod_cache p ON s.prod_id = p.prod_id
 WHERE     s.prod_id IN (SELECT prod_id FROM prod_cache)
       AND s.cust_id IN (SELECT cust_id FROM cust_cache);
```

```
---------------------------------------------------------------------------
| Id  | Operation                     | Name           | Cost (%CPU)|
---------------------------------------------------------------------------
|   0 | SELECT STATEMENT              |                |  358    (0)|
|*  1 |  HASH JOIN                    |                |  358    (0)|
|   2 |   TABLE ACCESS FULL           | CUST_CACHE     |    2    (0)|
|*  3 |   HASH JOIN                   |                |  356    (0)|
|   4 |    TABLE ACCESS FULL          | PROD_CACHE     |    2    (0)|
|   5 |    VIEW                       | VW_ST_456F1C80 |  354    (0)|
|   6 |     NESTED LOOPS              |                |  350    (0)|
|   7 |      PARTITION RANGE ALL      |                |   58    (0)|
|   8 |       BITMAP CONVERSION TO ROWIDS|             |   58    (0)|
|   9 |        BITMAP AND             |                |            |
|  10 |         BITMAP MERGE          |                |            |
|  11 |          BITMAP KEY ITERATION |                |            |
|  12 |           BUFFER SORT         |                |            |
|  13 |            TABLE ACCESS FULL  | PROD_CACHE     |    2    (0)|
|* 14 |            BITMAP INDEX RANGE SCAN| SALES_PROD_BIX |        |
|  15 |         BITMAP MERGE          |                |            |
|  16 |          BITMAP KEY ITERATION |                |            |
|  17 |           BUFFER SORT         |                |            |
|  18 |            TABLE ACCESS FULL  | CUST_CACHE     |    2    (0)|
|* 19 |            BITMAP INDEX RANGE SCAN| SALES_CUST_BIX |        |
|  20 |      TABLE ACCESS BY USER ROWID| SALES         |  296    (0)|
---------------------------------------------------------------------------
```

Predicate Information (identified by operation id):

```
   1 - access("ITEM_1"="C"."CUST_ID")
   3 - access("ITEM_2"="P"."PROD_ID")
  14 - access("S"."PROD_ID"="P"."PROD_ID")
  19 - access("S"."CUST_ID"="C"."CUST_ID")
```

You may wonder why I created real temporary tables rather than use factored subqueries. Well, the logic flow I am using is, in fact, quite different than the logic that the CBO is really using, and as of 12cR1 it doesn't seem the CBO can cope with such factored subqueries; the CBO even gets confused by the USING clause of an ANSI join in this example.

Note the BUFFER SORT operations on lines 12 and 17. It seems that the BITMAP KEY ITERATION operation requires the inputs be sorted. This happens automatically when the input is an index (as has been the case so far); we could have avoided the sort by making the CUST_CACHE and PROD_CACHE tables index organized, but I am drifting off the point.

The good news is that in real life you don't have to create the temporary tables or do anything else fancy. If you set STAR_TRANSFORMATION_ENABLED to TRUE (as opposed to TEMP_DISABLE), the CBO can sort this all out for you. Listing 13-39 shows the execution plan for Listing 13-35 when STAR_TRANSFORMATION_ENABLED is set to TRUE.

Listing 13-39. Final star transformation with star_transformation_enabled=true

```
-------------------------------------------------------------------------------------
| Id  | Operation                           | Name                      | Cost (%CPU)|
-------------------------------------------------------------------------------------
|   0 | SELECT STATEMENT                    |                           | 509    (1)|
|   1 | TEMP TABLE TRANSFORMATION           |                           |           |
|   2 |  LOAD AS SELECT                     | SYS_TEMP_0FD9D6747_4E5E5D |           |
|*  3 |   TABLE ACCESS FULL                 | CUSTOMERS                 | 423    (1)|
|*  4 |  HASH JOIN                          |                           |  87    (2)|
|   5 |   TABLE ACCESS FULL                 | SYS_TEMP_0FD9D6747_4E5E5D |   2    (0)|
|*  6 |   HASH JOIN                         |                           |  85    (2)|
|   7 |    TABLE ACCESS BY INDEX ROWID BATCHED| PRODUCTS                |   3    (0)|
|*  8 |     INDEX RANGE SCAN                | PRODUCTS_PROD_CAT_IX      |   1    (0)|
|   9 |    VIEW                             | VW_ST_B49D23E2            |  82    (2)|
|  10 |     NESTED LOOPS                    |                           |  78    (2)|
|  11 |      PARTITION RANGE ALL            |                           |  19    (0)|
|  12 |       BITMAP CONVERSION TO ROWIDS   |                           |  19    (0)|
|  13 |        BITMAP AND                   |                           |           |
|  14 |         BITMAP MERGE                |                           |           |
|  15 |          BITMAP KEY ITERATION       |                           |           |
|  16 |           BUFFER SORT               |                           |           |
|  17 |            TABLE ACCESS FULL        | SYS_TEMP_0FD9D6747_4E5E5D |   2    (0)|
|* 18 |           BITMAP INDEX RANGE SCAN   | SALES_CUST_BIX            |           |
|  19 |         BITMAP MERGE                |                           |           |
|  20 |          BITMAP KEY ITERATION       |                           |           |
|  21 |           BUFFER SORT               |                           |           |
|* 22 |            VIEW                     | index$_join$_052          |   2    (0)|
|* 23 |             HASH JOIN               |                           |           |
|* 24 |              INDEX RANGE SCAN       | PRODUCTS_PROD_CAT_IX      |   1    (0)|
|  25 |              INDEX FAST FULL SCAN   | PRODUCTS_PK               |   1    (0)|
|* 26 |            BITMAP INDEX RANGE SCAN  | SALES_PROD_BIX            |           |
|  27 |      TABLE ACCESS BY USER ROWID     | SALES                     |  62    (0)|
-------------------------------------------------------------------------------------

Predicate Information (identified by operation id):
---------------------------------------------------

   3 - filter("C"."CUST_LAST_NAME"='Everett')
   4 - access("ITEM_1"="C0")
   6 - access("ITEM_2"="P"."PROD_ID")
   8 - access("P"."PROD_CATEGORY"='Electronics')
  18 - access("S"."CUST_ID"="C0")
  22 - filter("P"."PROD_CATEGORY"='Electronics')
  23 - access(ROWID=ROWID)
  24 - access("P"."PROD_CATEGORY"='Electronics')
  26 - access("S"."PROD_ID"="P"."PROD_ID")
```

Listing 13-39 shows that even though the CBO can't deal with factored subqueries that you write, it can generate them itself and use them just fine!

Let us go through this step by step. At lines 2 and 3 we scan the customers table, find the matching rows, and store the CUST_FIRST_NAME and CUST_ID columns in a temporary table. Lines 9 through 27 are very similar to the other plans we have seen with the exception of the fact that at line 17 we have used the temporary table to retrieve the CUST_ID. Similarly, we have used the same temporary table at line 5 to pick up the CUST_FIRST_NAME for the select list.

Notice that no temporary table was generated for SH.PRODUCTS; the CBO reckoned that it was better to use an index join for the PROD_ID (lines 22 to 25) and then repeat the index lookup to get PROD_NAME (at lines 7 and 8). This was probably a very close call in terms of cost.

There are many weird things about star transformations. Various restrictions are documented in the Data Warehousing Guide, such as the fact that they don't work if bind variables are in use. However, one documented restriction is untrue. It turns out that star transformations can be used when there are no bitmap indexes: Oracle can convert a b-tree index to a bitmap index and use that.

The star transformation is the last of the optimizer transformations that I want to discuss in this chapter, but before wrapping up I want to give you a quick peek at what may be coming very soon.

In the Future

This chapter is by far the longest in the book and has covered over two dozen optimizer transformations. However, you can expect more to come. In 2009 the VLDB endowment published an academic paper authored by the CBO development team entitled "Enhanced Subquery Optimization in Oracle," which showed what might be coming down the road in the future. Take a look at the two queries and associated execution plans in Listing 13-40.

Listing 13-40. The future of subquery coalescing

-- Original query

```
SELECT prod_id
       ,p1.prod_name
       ,p1.prod_desc
       ,p1.prod_category
       ,p1.prod_list_price
  FROM sh.products p1
 WHERE     EXISTS
               (SELECT 1
                  FROM sh.products p2
                 WHERE     p1.prod_category = p2.prod_category
                       AND p1.prod_id <> p2.prod_id)
       AND NOT EXISTS
                 (SELECT 1
                    FROM sh.products p3
                   WHERE     p1.prod_category = p3.prod_category
                         AND p1.prod_id <> p3.prod_id
                         AND p3.prod_list_price > p1.prod_list_price);
```

```
---------------------------------------------------------------
| Id | Operation               | Name                | Cost (%CPU)|
---------------------------------------------------------------
|  0 | SELECT STATEMENT        |                     |   8   (0)|
|* 1 |  HASH JOIN RIGHT SEMI   |                     |   8   (0)|
|  2 |   VIEW                  | index$_join$_002    |   2   (0)|
|* 3 |    HASH JOIN            |                     |         |
|  4 |     INDEX FAST FULL SCAN| PRODUCTS_PK         |   1   (0)|
|  5 |     INDEX FAST FULL SCAN| PRODUCTS_PROD_CAT_IX|   1   (0)|
|* 6 |   HASH JOIN ANTI        |                     |   6   (0)|
|  7 |    TABLE ACCESS FULL    | PRODUCTS            |   3   (0)|
|  8 |    TABLE ACCESS FULL    | PRODUCTS            |   3   (0)|
---------------------------------------------------------------
```

```
Predicate Information (identified by operation id):
---------------------------------------------------

   1 - access("P1"."PROD_CATEGORY"="P2"."PROD_CATEGORY")
       filter("P1"."PROD_ID"<>"P2"."PROD_ID")
   3 - access(ROWID=ROWID)
   6 - access("P1"."PROD_CATEGORY"="P3"."PROD_CATEGORY")
       filter("P3"."PROD_LIST_PRICE">"P1"."PROD_LIST_PRICE" AND
              "P1"."PROD_ID"<>"P3"."PROD_ID")
```

```
-- A transformation of the future

  SELECT p1.prod_id
        ,p1.prod_name
        ,p1.prod_desc
        ,prod_category
        ,p1.prod_list_price
    FROM sh.products p1 JOIN sh.products p2 USING (prod_category)
   WHERE p1.prod_id <> p2.prod_id
GROUP BY p1.prod_id
        ,p1.prod_name
        ,p1.prod_desc
        ,prod_category
        ,p1.prod_list_price
  HAVING SUM (
            CASE
               WHEN p2.prod_list_price > p1.prod_list_price THEN 1
               ELSE 0
            END) = 0;
```

```
--------------------------------------------------------
| Id | Operation              | Name     | Cost (%CPU)|
--------------------------------------------------------
|  0 | SELECT STATEMENT       |          |    6   (0)|
|* 1 |  FILTER                |          |           |
|  2 |   HASH GROUP BY        |          |    6   (0)|
|* 3 |    HASH JOIN           |          |    6   (0)|
|  4 |     TABLE ACCESS FULL| PRODUCTS |    3   (0)|
|  5 |     TABLE ACCESS FULL| PRODUCTS |    3   (0)|
--------------------------------------------------------

Predicate Information (identified by operation id):
--------------------------------------------------

   1 - filter(SUM(CASE  WHEN "P2"."PROD_LIST_PRICE">"P1"."PROD_LIST_PRIC
              E" THEN 1 ELSE 0 END )=0)
   3 - access("P1"."PROD_CATEGORY"="P2"."PROD_CATEGORY")
       filter("P1"."PROD_ID"<>"P2"."PROD_ID"
```

Both versions of the query in Listing 13-40 identify products that have the highest list price in their category but are not in a category of their own. The latter query in Listing 13-40 has both coalesced the two subqueries and also unnested them. I must say that I had to stare at the published queries for several minutes[5] to convince myself that they were semantically equivalent[6] and that real benefits are obtained by such a transformation.

---

[5]The academic paper didn't use the SH example schema but I have produced an equivalent example.
[6]They are equivalent after the correction of what appears to be a typographical error.

Summary

The CBO has a wide range of optimizer transformations at its disposal. This chapter has covered over two dozen of these transformations, but in the unlikely event that the list is comprehensive at the time of writing it probably won't be by the time the book goes to press. Nevertheless, learning how to recognize, and if necessary influence, the choice of optimizer transformations is crucial to tuning complex queries.

An optimizer transformation may be part of the cost-based framework and may be selected on the basis of calculated benefits in cost. However, several of the optimizer transformations are heuristic, meaning that they are applied or not based on some fixed rules. This means that a transformation can be applied that results in an increase in estimated cost. The increased estimated cost may, of course, be irrelevant if the actual elapsed time of the query is reduced.

One thing that should have become clear throughout this chapter is that for a human being to identify the right way to construct an SQL statement so that an optimal execution plan can be derived by final state optimization alone sometimes requires almost superhuman SQL prowess. Just bear in mind that although we should all be very happy that all these optimizer transformations exist, we can't rest on our laurels and pray that the CBO will transform any bad code we write into good code; really bad code will still confuse the CBO.

Nevertheless, now that we understand the power and flexibility of both the final state optimization process that we covered in Chapter 12 and the breadth and sophistication of the transformations available to the CBO, you may be wondering why there are so many SQL tuning specialists out there. The truth is that in the real world things go wrong—all the time. Let us look at that next in Chapter 14.

PART 4

Optimization

CHAPTER 14

■ ■ ■

Why Do Things Go Wrong?

As I mentioned at the beginning of Chapter 1, SQL is a declarative programming language. In theory, you just have to say what you want to have done and then something works out how to do it. In the case of an Oracle database, that "something" is the CBO, and it should devise an appropriate execution plan for you. In theory you shouldn't have to worry about getting incorrect results and you shouldn't have to worry about performance. Since you are reading this book you have almost certainly realized that life isn't as simple as that and that you do, in fact, have to worry quite a bit. With the exception of bugs, the results of a correctly written SQL statement will be correct, but optimal performance, or even acceptable performance, is far from guaranteed, even from a bug-free database.

So why is performance often so poor? We have touched on many of the issues already in this book. Without the correct set of extended statistics cardinality errors will occur and cardinality errors will totally confuse the CBO. But cardinality errors aren't the only things that confuse the CBO. We discussed scalar subquery caching in Chapter 4. The CBO has no way to assess the benefits of scalar subquery caching nor has it any way of knowing which blocks will be in the buffer cache when the query runs.

The subject of caching is just one example of missing information. Sometimes an index can only be used when the indexed column or columns are known to be not null. The CBO might know that an indexed column is not null because there is a NOT NULL constraint on the column or because an IS NOT NULL predicate appears in the WHERE clause. In the absence of such information the CBO will have to assume that the column may, in fact, be NULL and thus avoid the use of an index.

What about contention? Do you think that if an index is being updated by another session while you are querying it that your performance may suffer? I can tell you that it might. I have seen real-life cases where I have had to use an index that appeared to the CBO to be a poor choice, but the query performed well because my chosen index wasn't being updated by other processes at the time of the query. On the other hand, the CBO's chosen index was being updated by other processes, causing poor performance.

The concept of declarative programming languages means that the CBO is supposed to be omniscient, and so we can easily place most of the blame for poor execution plans on the inadequacies of the CBO. However, it is not within the remit of the CBO to design your physical database; if an index is missing the CBO can't create it for you.

You can see that many of the concepts covered in this chapter have already been addressed earlier in the book, but I want to bring them together in one place and expand on them. Let us begin by taking another look at the single biggest problem for the CBO: cardinality errors.

Cardinality Errors

The term *cardinality error* refers to a significant discrepancy between the CBO's estimate of the number of rows returned by a row source operation in a candidate execution plan and the actual number of rows that would be returned were that execution plan to be selected and run. Cardinality estimates are the most important pieces of information that the CBO generates while performing final state optimization. There are several reasons for cardinality errors. Let me begin with the biggest source of cardinality errors: correlated columns.

Correlation of Columns

I introduced the concept of column correlation in Chapter 6, and in Chapter 9 Listing 9-11 showed a correlation between two columns named TRANSACTION_DATE and POSTING_DATE. The correlation between these two date columns is easy to see, but in other cases it may not be. Consider the columns in the SALES table in the SH schema:

- PROD_ID
- CUST_ID
- TIME_ID
- PROMO_ID
- QUANTITY_SOLD
- AMOUNT_SOLD

These columns are reasonably realistic for a data warehouse table, although the example data is quite artificial. I am going to ask you to imagine that this table is for a wine merchant that has the following:

- 100 types of wine
- 10,000 customers
- 10 years of trading history (assume 10 values of TIME_ID)
- A wine promotion every month
- Sold 10,000,000 bottles of wine
- An average of 10 bottles of wine sold per order

This means that there are 1,000,000 rows in the table.

Let us see which columns in the table are correlated with each other. Let us start with PROD_ID and CUST_ID. At first glance these columns seem to have nothing to do with each other. But hang on; let us assume that we want to estimate the number of sales of a specific bottle of wine. We know that there are 100 types of wine so the selectivity will be 1% and the cardinality estimate (the average number of sales transactions for that wine) will be 1% of 1,000,000, or 10,000. Using the same logic we can see that there are 10,000 customers, so each customer will place 0.01% of the orders and thus the average customer places 100 orders over the ten-year period.

So now let us ask the question: How many bottles of a specific wine did a specific customer buy? Well, the CBO will assume that each customer placed one order for each of the 100 types of wine. This is unlikely to be accurate because typically customers will not sample every wine—they will buy lots of bottles of the wine they like. So CUST_ID and PROD_ID are correlated.

■ **Tip** If you realize that you will not find a row for each possible combination of two columns, the two columns are correlated and the CBO will underestimate cardinalities when predicates on both columns are present and there are no extended statistics.

Does each customer buy wine every year? Probably not. Customers come and go, so CUST_ID and TIME_ID are correlated. Will each customer avail themselves of every promotion? Unlikely. Most customers are likely to place orders of the same or similar amounts each time and it is virtually certain that not every combination of CUST_ID and AMOUNT_SOLD will be found in the table. So CUST_ID is correlated to every other column in the table! What about PROD_ID? Will every wine have been sold in every year? No: a 2012 wine wouldn't have been sold in 2011 or earlier, and after it sells out you can't get any more. Do promotions apply to every product? No. If you keep going with these thoughts you can see that almost every column is correlated to every other.

I have worked with some applications where almost every cardinality estimate in every critical execution plan is significantly lower than it should be because of the impact of column correlation.

Statistics Feedback and DBMS_STATS.SEED_COL_USAGE Features

The fact that determining the correct set of extended statistics to create is nigh on impossible for most complex applications is not lost on the optimizer team, who have provided two approaches for addressing this problem.

Let us start with a look at *statistics feedback*, an extended and renamed variant of the cardinality feedback feature that I mentioned in Chapter 6. If you get a significant cardinality error in 12cR1 or later, and you haven't disabled statistics feedback by setting OPTIMIZER_ADAPTIVE_FEATURES to FALSE, then a *SQL Plan Directive* will most likely be created. The existence of a SQL Plan Directive may or may not precipitate one or both of the following consequences:

- Dynamic sampling for that statement or similar statements executed in the future, whether issued by the same session or a different session.

- The automatic creation of extended statistics for certain column groups the next time statistics are gathered.

In my opinion these sort of dynamic adaptive features are undesirable in a production environment. As I explained in Chapter 6, we don't normally want untested execution plans to be run for the first time in a production environment. But despite the brevity of this overview, I feel that SQL Plan Directives are a potentially useful feature for identifying the need for extended statistics on a test system during the early stages of a project lifecycle. The use of dynamic sampling during these early stages is also useful for identifying issues that extended statistics can't currently address, such as correlated columns in multiple tables. You can read more about SQL Plan Directives in the SQL tuning guide.

An entirely separate feature that may be easier to manage was introduced and supported in 11gR2 but only documented for the first time in 12cR1. The DBMS_STATS.SEED_COL_USAGE procedure allows you to collect information on the need for column group statistics while you run a particular workload. Listing 14-1 shows the basic approach.

Listing 14-1. Obtaining extended statistics through DBMS_STATS.SEED_COL_USAGE

```
BEGIN
    DBMS_STATS.reset_col_usage (ownname => 'SH', tabname => NULL); -- Optional

    DBMS_STATS.seed_col_usage (NULL, NULL, 3600);
END;
/


--- Wait a little over an hour

DECLARE
    dummy    CLOB;
BEGIN
    FOR r
      IN (SELECT DISTINCT object_name
            FROM dba_objects, sys.col_group_usage$
           WHERE obj# = object_id AND owner = 'SH' AND object_type = 'TABLE')
    LOOP
      SELECT DBMS_STATS.create_extended_stats ('SH', r.object_name)
        INTO dummy
        FROM DUAL;
    END LOOP;
END;
/
```

Listing 14-1 begins by calling the undocumented DBMS_STATS.RESET_COL_USAGE procedure to remove any unrepresentative data about the SH schema from previous test runs, but this is optional. The next call is to DBMS_STATS.SEED_COL_USAGE, which starts the monitoring of SQL statements for 3,600 seconds. After the hour has elapsed you can create extended statistics based on the column usage statistics obtained. Notice that the call to DBMS_STATS.CREATE_EXTENDED_STATS omits the specification of any extension as these are automatically obtained from the data dictionary.

You can work out the tables that need extended statistics by looking at the data dictionary table SYS.COL_GROUP_USAGE$ as shown in Listing 14-1. As an alternative, if you pass NULL as the table name (as opposed to omitting the table name) you can create the necessary extensions for the SH schema as a whole in one call.

Let me leave correlated columns now and move on to another major source of cardinality errors: functions.

Functions

When you include a function call in a predicate the CBO will normally have no idea what the selectivity of the predicate will be. Consider Listing 14-2:

Listing 14-2. Function call in predicate

```
SELECT *
  FROM some_table t1, another_table t2
 WHERE some_function (t1.some_column) = 1 AND t1.c1 = t2.c2;
```

Suppose that the object statistics for SOME_TABLE say that the table has 1,000,000 rows. How many rows from SOME_TABLE will remain after applying the filter predicate some_function (t1.some_column) = 1? You can't tell, can you? And neither can the CBO. If only one or two rows are selected from SOME_TABLE then perhaps a NESTED LOOPS join with ANOTHER_TABLE is warranted. But perhaps all 1,000,000 rows will be selected, in which case a HASH JOIN will be the only way to avoid disastrous performance. I deliberately chose meaningless table and function names in the above example. Suppose the function call in Listing 14-2 was actually MOD (t1.some_column, 2)? What then? Since MOD is a function supplied by the SQL engine, surely the CBO should realize that the function call is likely to filter out only about half the rows? Well, not really. The SQL language provides dozens of built-in functions, and it would be impractical for the CBO to hold rules for identifying cardinality estimates for each one. The only practical thing for the CBO to do is to treat them in the same way as it treats user-written functions.

When the CBO has no clue as to how to determine cardinality it makes an arbitrary guess using one of a number of fixed built-in values. In the case of a function call a selectivity estimate of 1% is used.

Stale Statistics

I will be brief here. I have already discussed the topic of stale statistics at length in Chapter 6 and will come back to it again in Chapter 20. Just add stale statistics (in a non-TSTATS environment) to the growing list of reasons why cardinality errors occur.

Daft Data Types

Daft data types is the title of a section in Chapter 6 of the book *Cost Based Oracle Fundamentals*. That chapter is dedicated entirely to the topic of cardinality errors, and I have unashamedly copied the section title. Listing 14-3 is also almost directly copied from the same section in Jonathan Lewis' book.

Listing 14-3. Daft data types

```
CREATE TABLE t2
AS
   SELECT d1
         ,TO_NUMBER (TO_CHAR (d1, 'yyyymmdd')) n1
         ,TO_CHAR (d1, 'yyyymmdd') c1
     FROM (SELECT TO_DATE ('31-Dec-1999') + ROWNUM d1
             FROM all_objects
            WHERE ROWNUM <= 1827);

SELECT *
  FROM t2
 WHERE d1 BETWEEN TO_DATE ('30-Dec-2002', 'dd-mon-yyyy')
              AND TO_DATE ('05-Jan-2003', 'dd-mon-yyyy');
```

```
-----------------------------------------
| Id  | Operation        | Name | Rows  |
-----------------------------------------
|   0 | SELECT STATEMENT |      |     8 |
|*  1 |  TABLE ACCESS FULL| T2  |     8 |
-----------------------------------------
```

```
SELECT *
  FROM t2
 WHERE n1 BETWEEN 20021230 AND 20030105;
```

```
-----------------------------------------
| Id  | Operation        | Name | Rows  |
-----------------------------------------
|   0 | SELECT STATEMENT |      |   396 |
|*  1 |  TABLE ACCESS FULL| T2  |   396 |
-----------------------------------------
```

Listing 14-3 generates one row for each date between January 1, 2000 and December 31, 2004. The first query uses a date column to pick the seven rows between December 30, 2002 and January 5, 2003 inclusive, and the cardinality estimate is almost right. The second query uses a predicate on a numeric column that stores dates in YYYYMMDD format. The cardinality estimate is now way off because when viewed as a number the range 20,021,230 to 20,030,105 seems like quite a big chunk of the total range 20,000,101 to 20,041,231.

I could copy and paste much more of Jonathan's chapter but I don't need to. The key thing is not to try and memorize a bunch of reasons why the CBO gets things wrong but rather to develop a mindset that allows you to work out what goes wrong when you need to.

I think I have said all I want to about cardinality errors. But cardinality errors are not the only reasons why the CBO gets things wrong. Let us continue this story of CBO issues by turning our attention to caching effects.

Caching Effects

Many Oracle specialists develop a habit of using the term "cache" as an abbreviation for "buffer cache." I do that myself all the time. However, there are many different sorts of cache in an Oracle database. I covered the OCI, result, and function caches in Chapter 4 and went into quite some detail about the scalar subquery cache in Chapter 13. All of these caches have an effect on the elapsed time and resource consumption of a SQL statement. The CBO has no way of quantifying the benefits of any of these caches and therefore doesn't consider caching effects in its calculations in any way.

I'd like to discuss one particular case where the CBO might one day be able to think things through a little bit more than it currently does. It involves the index clustering factor statistic that I explained in Chapter 9. Listing 14-4 shows an interesting test case.

Listing 14-4. Caching effects of index clustering with a single-column index

```
ALTER SESSION SET statistics_level=all;

SET PAGES 900 LINES 200 SERVEROUTPUT OFF
COMMIT;
ALTER SESSION ENABLE PARALLEL DML;

CREATE TABLE t1
(
   n1        INT
 ,n2        INT
 ,filler    CHAR (10)
)
NOLOGGING;

INSERT /*+ parallel(t1 10) */
     INTO   t1
   WITH generator
       AS (     SELECT ROWNUM rn
                     FROM DUAL
             CONNECT BY LEVEL <= 4500)
     SELECT TRUNC (ROWNUM / 80000)
          ,ROWNUM + 5000 * (MOD (ROWNUM, 2))
          ,RPAD ('X', 10)
     FROM generator, generator;

COMMIT;

CREATE INDEX t1_n1
    ON t1 (n1)
    NOLOGGING
    PARALLEL 10;

COLUMN index_name FORMAT a10

SELECT index_name, clustering_factor
  FROM all_indexes
 WHERE index_name = 'T1_N1';
INDEX_NAME CLUSTERING_FACTOR
---------- -----------------
T1_N1                  74102

ALTER SYSTEM FLUSH BUFFER_CACHE;
```

```
SELECT MAX (filler)
  FROM t1
 WHERE n1 = 2;

SELECT *
  FROM TABLE (
          DBMS_XPLAN.display_cursor (NULL
                                    ,NULL
                                    ,'basic cost iostats -predicate'));
```

```
---------------------------------------------------------------------------------
| Id  | Operation                    | Name   | Cost (%CPU)| A-Rows |A-Time    | Buffers | Reads |
---------------------------------------------------------------------------------
|  0  | SELECT STATEMENT             |        |  458 (100)|      1 |00:00.58 |   440   |  440  |
|  1  |  SORT AGGREGATE              |        |           |      1 |00:00.58 |   440   |  440  |
|  2  |   TABLE ACCESS BY INDEX RO   | T1     |  458  (1)|  80000 |00:00.56 |   440   |  440  |
|  3  |    INDEX RANGE SCAN          | T1_N1  |  165  (0)|  80000 |00:00.21 |   159   |  159  |
---------------------------------------------------------------------------------
```

```
ALTER SYSTEM FLUSH BUFFER_CACHE;

SELECT /*+ full(t1) */
       MAX (filler)
  FROM t1
 WHERE n1 = 2;

SELECT *
  FROM TABLE (
          DBMS_XPLAN.display_cursor (NULL
                                    ,NULL
                                    ,'basic cost iostats -predicate'));
```

```
---------------------------------------------------------------------------------
| Id  | Operation             | Name | Cost (%CPU)| A-Rows |A-Time    | Buffers | Reads  |
---------------------------------------------------------------------------------
|  0  | SELECT STATEMENT      |      | 19507 (100)|      1 |00:08.67 |  71596  | 71592 |
|  1  |  SORT AGGREGATE       |      |            |      1 |00:08.67 |  71596  | 71592 |
|  2  |   TABLE ACCESS FULL   | T1   | 19507  (1)|  80000 |00:08.67 |  71596  | 71592 |
---------------------------------------------------------------------------------
```

Listing 14-4 creates a table T1 with 20,025,000 rows. The rows are added ordered by column N1. A single-column index, T1_N1, is then created on column N1 and statistics are gathered. The clustering factor of the index is quite low at 74,102. To make it a level playing field I flush the buffer cache before each query.

When we query the table looking for rows with a specific value of N1 the CBO elects to use the index T1_N1. When we force a full table scan with a hint we see a much higher cost and a much higher actual elapsed time. The CBO has, correctly, concluded that a full table scan would take much longer. Listing 14-5 shows us what happens when we add a second column to the index.

Listing 14-5. Caching effects of index clustering with a multi-column index

```
DROP INDEX t1_n1;

CREATE  INDEX t1_n1_n2 ON t1(n1,n2);

select index_name,clustering_factor from all_indexes where index_name='T1_N1_N2';

INDEX_NAME CLUSTERING_FACTOR
---------- -----------------
T1_N1_N2            18991249

ALTER SYSTEM FLUSH BUFFER_CACHE;

SELECT MAX (filler)
  FROM t1
 WHERE n1 =2;

SELECT *
  FROM TABLE (DBMS_XPLAN.display_cursor (NULL,
                                         NULL,
                                         'basic cost iostats -predicate'));
```

Id	Operation	Name	Cost (%CPU)	A-Rows	A-Time	Buffers	Reads
0	SELECT STATEMENT		**19507** (100)	1	**00:09.78**	**71596**	**71592**
1	SORT AGGREGATE			1	00:09.78	71596	71592
2	TABLE ACCESS FULL	T1	19507 (1)	80000	00:09.77	71596	71592

```
ALTER SYSTEM FLUSH BUFFER_CACHE;

SELECT /*+ index(t1 t1_n1_n2) */ MAX (filler)
  FROM t1
 WHERE n1 =2;
```

```
SELECT *
  FROM TABLE (DBMS_XPLAN.display_cursor (NULL,
                                         NULL,
                                         'basic cost iostats -predicate'));
```

Id	Operation	Name	Cost (%CPU)	A-Rows	A-Time	Buffers	Reads
0	SELECT STATEMENT		**75014** (100)	1	**00:00.67**	**74497**	**494**
1	SORT AGGREGATE			1	00:00.67	74497	494
2	TABLE ACCESS BY INDEX R	T1	75014 (1)	80000	00:00.65	74497	494
3	INDEX RANGE SCAN	T1_N1_N2	231 (0)	80000	00:00.23	214	214

Listing 14-5 drops index T1_N1 and creates the index T1_N1_N2 on the columns N1 and N2. When we run the query now a full table scan is selected by the CBO. When we force the use of the new index with a hint we see that the CBO has given a much higher cost to the multi-column index operation than it did when considering access with the single-column index T1_N1. Why? T1_N1_N2 is slightly larger than T1_N1, but that doesn't explain the huge increase in cost. Has the CBO got it wrong?

Well, yes and no. If you look at the runtime statistics for the indexed operation you will see that, in fact, the number of consistent gets has increased massively (from 440 in Listing 14-4 to 74,497 in Listing 14-5) with the addition of N2 to the index, just as the CBO suspected. The reason for the huge increase in logical I/Os is that the index entries for T1_N1_N2 are ordered differently than those in T1_N1. I have constructed the data in such a way that consecutive index entries in T1_N1_N2 are almost guaranteed to reference different table blocks, whereas most consecutive index entries in T1_N1 reference the same table block and can be processed as part of the same logical I/O operation. This difference is reflected in the index clustering factor statistic for T1_N1_N2, which at 18,991,249 (almost equal to the number of rows in the table as expected), is much higher than for T1_N1. This explains how the CBO arrived at the correspondingly higher cost estimate for the query using T1_N1_N2.

Although the CBO has correctly realized that index access through T1_N1_N2 involves a large number of logical I/O operations, it hasn't realized that the operations are to the same small set of table blocks. As a consequence there are just 494 physical I/Os for indexed access and the elapsed time is similarly low. The number of physical I/Os for the full table scan is a massive 71,592 because the table isn't held in its entirety in the buffer cache.

Transitive Closure

If you search the Internet for a definition of transitive closure then you are likely to find a lot of confusing mathematical gobbledygook. Let me give you the layman's explanation: if A=B and B=C then A=C. Pretty simple, really, but you might be surprised at how little Oracle understands transitive closure. Listing 14-6 shows three interesting queries and their associated execution plans.

Listing 14-6. Transitive closure examples

```
CREATE TABLE t3 AS SELECT ROWNUM c1 FROM DUAL CONNECT BY LEVEL <=10;
CREATE TABLE t4 AS SELECT MOD(ROWNUM,10)+100 c1 FROM DUAL CONNECT BY LEVEL <= 100;
CREATE TABLE t5 AS SELECT MOD(ROWNUM,10) c1,RPAD('X',30) filler FROM DUAL
                              CONNECT BY LEVEL <= 10000;

CREATE INDEX t5_i1 ON t5(c1);

SELECT COUNT (*)
  FROM t3, t5
 WHERE t3.c1 = t5.c1 AND t3.c1 = 1;
```

```
-------------------------------------------------
| Id  | Operation              | Name  | Rows  |
-------------------------------------------------
|   0 | SELECT STATEMENT       |       |     1 |
|   1 |  SORT AGGREGATE        |       |     1 |
|   2 |   MERGE JOIN CARTESIAN |       |  1000 |
|*  3 |    TABLE ACCESS FULL   | T3    |     1 |
|   4 |    BUFFER SORT         |       |  1000 |
|*  5 |     INDEX RANGE SCAN   | T5_I1 |  1000 |
-------------------------------------------------
```

```
Predicate Information (identified by operation id):
-------------------------------------------------

   3 - filter("T3"."C1"=1)
   5 - access("T5"."C1"=1)
```

```
SELECT *
  FROM t3, t4, t5
 WHERE t3.c1 = t4.c1 AND t4.c1 = t5.c1;
```

```
--------------------------------------------------------------------------------
| Id  | Operation                   | Name  | Rows | Bytes | Cost (%CPU)| Time     |
--------------------------------------------------------------------------------
|   0 | SELECT STATEMENT            |       |    1 |    39 |   8  (13)| 00:00:01 |
|   1 |  NESTED LOOPS               |       |      |       |          |          |
|   2 |   NESTED LOOPS              |       |    1 |    39 |   8  (13)| 00:00:01 |
|*  3 |    HASH JOIN                |       |    1 |     6 |   7  (15)| 00:00:01 |
|   4 |     TABLE ACCESS FULL       | T3    |   10 |    30 |   3   (0)| 00:00:01 |
|   5 |     TABLE ACCESS FULL       | T4    |  100 |   300 |   3   (0)| 00:00:01 |
|*  6 |    INDEX RANGE SCAN         | T5_I1 | 1000 |       |   1   (0)| 00:00:01 |
|   7 |   TABLE ACCESS BY INDEX ROWID| T5   |    1 |    33 |   1   (0)| 00:00:01 |
--------------------------------------------------------------------------------
```

```
Predicate Information (identified by operation id):
---------------------------------------------------


   3 - access("T3"."C1"="T4"."C1")
   6 - access("T4"."C1"="T5"."C1")
```

```sql
SELECT *
  FROM t3, t4, t5
 WHERE t3.c1 = t5.c1 AND t4.c1 = t5.c1;
```

```
---------------------------------------------------------------------------
| Id  | Operation          | Name | Rows  | Bytes | Cost (%CPU)| Time     |
---------------------------------------------------------------------------
|   0 | SELECT STATEMENT   |      |     1 |    39 |    25   (4)| 00:00:01 |
|*  1 |  HASH JOIN         |      |     1 |    39 |    25   (4)| 00:00:01 |
|*  2 |   HASH JOIN        |      |     1 |    36 |    22   (5)| 00:00:01 |
|   3 |    TABLE ACCESS FULL| T4  |   100 |   300 |     3   (0)| 00:00:01 |
|   4 |    TABLE ACCESS FULL| T5  | 10000 |  322K |    18   (0)| 00:00:01 |
|   5 |    TABLE ACCESS FULL | T3 |    10 |    30 |     3   (0)| 00:00:01 |
---------------------------------------------------------------------------
```

```
Predicate Information (identified by operation id):
---------------------------------------------------


   1 - access("T3"."C1"="T5"."C1")
   2 - access("T4"."C1"="T5"."C1")
```

The predicates in our first query are T3.C1=1 and T3.C1=T5.C1. If you look at the filter predicates shown in the execution plan for this first query you will see that the T3.C1=T5.C1 predicate has been replaced by T5.C1=1. Transitive closure is generally recognized in simple situations when a literal value or bind variable is present, but anything more complex will confuse the CBO. The second and third queries are semantically equivalent. The two predicates T3.C1=T4.c1 AND T4.C1=T5.C1 are clearly equivalent to the two predicates T3.C1=T5.c1 AND T4.C1=T5.C1. Both pairs of predicates imply that all three columns are identical. And yet we can see that the selected execution plans for the last two statements are different: the CBO has no "transitive closure" transformation. Unless performance of the two execution plans is identical they can't both be optimal! However, "transitive closure" is just one of many potential transformations that the CBO might one day implement that don't currently exist. Let us consider the implications of this a bit more.

Unsupported Transformations

Consider the two SQL statements in Listing 14-7. Take a look and see which statement you think is better written.

Listing 14-7. Unsupported transformations

```
CREATE TABLE t6
AS
 SELECT ROWNUM c1, MOD (ROWNUM, 2) c2, RPAD ('X', 10) filler
          FROM DUAL
    CONNECT BY LEVEL <= 1000;
CREATE TABLE t7 AS
      SELECT ROWNUM c1,ROWNUM c2 FROM DUAL CONNECT BY LEVEL <= 10;

CREATE INDEX t6_i1 ON t6(c2,c1);

WITH subq AS
      (SELECT   t6.c2, MAX (t6.c1) max_c1
          FROM t6
       GROUP BY t6.c2)
SELECT c2, subq.max_c1
  FROM t7 LEFT JOIN subq USING (c2);
```

```
-------------------------------------------------------------------------------
| Id  | Operation            | Name | Rows  | Bytes | Cost (%CPU)| Time     |
-------------------------------------------------------------------------------
|   0 | SELECT STATEMENT     |      |    10 |   290 |    4  (23)| 00:00:01 |
|*  1 |  HASH JOIN OUTER     |      |    10 |   290 |    4  (23)| 00:00:01 |
|   2 |   TABLE ACCESS FULL  | T7   |    10 |    30 |    2   (0)| 00:00:01 |
|   3 |   VIEW               |      |     2 |    52 |    2  (20)| 00:00:01 |
|   4 |    HASH GROUP BY      |      |     2 |    14 |    2  (20)| 00:00:01 |
|   5 |     TABLE ACCESS FULL| T6   |  1000 |  7000 |    2   (0)| 00:00:01 |
-------------------------------------------------------------------------------

Predicate Information (identified by operation id):
---------------------------------------------------

   1 - access("T7"."C2"="SUBQ"."C2"(+))
```

```
SELECT c2, (SELECT /*+ no_unnest */ MAX (c1)
              FROM t6
             WHERE t6.c2 = t7.c2) max_c1
  FROM t7;
```

```
---------------------------------------------------------------------------------
| Id  | Operation                       | Name  | Rows | Bytes | Cost (%CPU)| Time     |
---------------------------------------------------------------------------------
|   0 | SELECT STATEMENT                |       |   10 |    30 |     3  (0)| 00:00:01 |
|   1 |  SORT AGGREGATE                 |       |    1 |     8 |           |          |
|   2 |   FIRST ROW                     |       |    1 |     8 |     2  (0)| 00:00:01 |
|*  3 |    INDEX RANGE SCAN (MIN/MAX)   | T6_I1 |    1 |     8 |     2  (0)| 00:00:01 |
|   4 |  TABLE ACCESS FULL              | T7    |   10 |    30 |     3  (0)| 00:00:01 |
---------------------------------------------------------------------------------
```

Predicate Information (identified by operation id):

```
   3 - access("T6"."C2"=:B1)
```

If you look closely at the two statements you will see that they are semantically equivalent. Both queries list all the rows from T7 together with the corresponding maximum value (if any) from T6 for the matching value of C2. So which is the superior construct?

The upper query in Listing 14-7 will obtain the maximum value of C1 in T6 for each value of C2. This calculation is guaranteed to be performed exactly once for each value of C2 in T6.

The lower query is constructed in such a way that the maximum value of C1 is only calculated for values of C2 present in T7. However, the maximum value of C1 for a value of C2 that is present in T7 is potentially calculated more than once. Subquery caching may mitigate this. Furthermore, we have the MAX/MIN optimization introduced in Listing 10-8 to consider.

Seem familiar? Should we do everything one time (including stuff that we may never need to do) or should we avoid doing stuff that we never need to do at the expense of risking doing stuff that we do need to do more than once? This is precisely the same sort of argument surrounding indexed access to a table with nested loops versus hash joins and full table scans. Get your mind thinking this way. This is what it is all about.

So it seems that the nature of the data and the availability of a suitable index should dictate which construct is superior. If T7 is a tiny table with just a few rows and T6 has millions of rows with thousands of values of C2, then it seems that the latter construct would be superior. On the other hand, if T7 has millions of rows and T6 has just a few thousand (small but sufficiently large to risk blowing the scalar subquery cache) then it is probably better to use the former construct.

But there is one final complication: Oracle 12cR1 will normally unnest the subquery in the lower query to transform it into the former. To prevent this heuristic transformation from happening you need to include a NO_UNNEST hint.

Missing Information

Another reason why the CBO may not identify a suitable execution plan is because it doesn't understand business rules. If you don't somehow embed business rules in your SQL the CBO may end up doing the wrong thing. Take look at Listing 14-8, which shows two queries against the ORDERS table in the example OE schema.

Listing 14-8. Missing information

```
select sales_rep_id,sum(order_total) from oe.orders where order_status=7 group by sales_rep_id
order by sales_rep_id;
```

```
----------------------------------------------------------------------
| Id  | Operation          | Name   | Rows | Bytes | Cost (%CPU)| Time     |
----------------------------------------------------------------------
|   0 | SELECT STATEMENT   |        |    9 |  144  |  4  (25)| 00:00:01 |
|   1 |  SORT GROUP BY     |        |    9 |  144  |  4  (25)| 00:00:01 |
|*  2 |   TABLE ACCESS FULL| ORDERS |   73 | 1168  |  3   (0)| 00:00:01 |
----------------------------------------------------------------------
```

```
select sales_rep_id,sum(order_total) from oe.orders
where order_status=7 and sales_rep_id is not null group by sales_rep_id order by sales_rep_id;
```

```
-------------------------------------------------------------------------------
| Id  | Operation                   | Name           | Rows | Cost (%CPU)| Time     |
-------------------------------------------------------------------------------
|   0 | SELECT STATEMENT            |                |    9 |  2   (0)| 00:00:01 |
|   1 |  SORT GROUP BY NOSORT       |                |    9 |  2   (0)| 00:00:01 |
|*  2 |   TABLE ACCESS BY INDEX ROWID| ORDERS        |   49 |  2   (0)| 00:00:01 |
|*  3 |    INDEX FULL SCAN          | ORD_SALES_REP_IX |   70 |  1   (0)| 00:00:01 |
-------------------------------------------------------------------------------
```

The first query lists the total order value for each SALES_REP_ID where ORDER_STATUS is 7. The execution plan uses a full table scan and uses a sort to group the data, as the data is required to be sorted on output.

The second query does precisely the same thing except that we have added an extra predicate and SALES_REP_ID is not null. As you can see, that extra predicate has resulted in a completely different execution plan that, amongst other things, requires no sort. The point is that there is no NOT NULL constraint on SALES_REP_ID because some transactions, including all online sales, have no salesman. You may know, however, that ORDER_STATUS=7 implies the use of a salesman.[1] Unless you supply the extra predicate the CBO has no way of knowing that it is safe to use the index and thus produces a potentially inferior execution plan.

Bad Physical Design

I am one of those individuals who likes to blame other people or other things when things go wrong. My wife will tell you that, in my mind, nothing is ever my fault. That is one of the things I love about the CBO. It is a good fall guy when it comes to poor performance! When my SQL performs poorly (and yes, I sometimes write poorly performing SQL) I can usually claim that the CBO should have figured out what I did wrong and should have fixed it. However, the CBO can't be blamed for a missing index! I would have to find somebody else to blame for that!

There is, of course, much more to physical database design than just working out which indexes to create. Top amongst those considerations is working out which indexes to drop. The next chapter, Chapter 15, will go into the topic of physical database design in much more detail, so I will stop now. I just want you to add bad physical design to the ever-increasing list of reasons why things go wrong.

---

[1]It would have made more sense for more to suggest that direct sales have a sales representative and online sales do not. Unfortunately, the sample data doesn't follow that rule!

Contention

When the CBO considers what execution plan to use for a statement it assumes nothing about what other database activity may be going on at the same time. Consideration of concurrent activity might affect the optimal execution plan.

Consider the following scenario. We run ten jobs one after the other. The first job inserts data into a table T1 with JOB_ID=1. The second job inserts data with JOB_ID=2 and so on. Suppose that during the execution of the last of the ten jobs we decide to query some of the data for JOB_ID=1. Our query specifies WHERE JOB_ID=1 AND PRODUCT_CODE=27. The CBO, blissfully unaware of any contention issues, elects to use an index on PRODUCT_CODE because it is more selective and has a low clustering factor. But the last of the ten jobs is bashing away, inserting lots of rows with PRODUCT_CODE=27. This means that our query might have to do a lot of work to roll back these inserts and reconstruct the blocks as they were at the time the query started.

Now suppose we hint our query to use an index on JOB_ID. The use of the less selective index on JOB_ID might be more efficient, as the section of the index with JOB_ID=1 won't be being updated while the query runs. Furthermore, the table blocks being accessed will have filled up long ago and won't be being updated. The fact that neither the index nor the table blocks being accessed through the JOB_ID index are updated during the course of our query may limit or indeed eliminate the rollback activity. I once worked with a query that was running for several hours and by changing the query to use an ostensibly poor index the execution time dropped to a couple of minutes!

Summary

This chapter may have depressed you. All this negative talk about what seems to be a never-ending list of reasons why things can, and more often than not, do prevent the CBO from coming up with the optimal execution plan may seem daunting. And my list only scratches the surface. There are many more reasons why things go wrong that I haven't even covered here. The more complex a SQL statement is, and in particular the more complex the predicates are, the less likely the CBO is to guess right. Don't get too depressed. The main point of this chapter is to remove any rose-tinted spectacles that you may have been wearing. Once you understand that things do go wrong and the main reasons why they go wrong you are in a better position to do something about it! Let us get started in doing something about it right now. On to Chapter 15 and a look at how good physical database design can help SQL performance.

Physical Database Design

For the runtime engine to execute a SQL statement with adequate performance, you must provide it with a properly sized machine that has an adequate SGA and an adequate PGA. However, physical database design is also crucial: even with a reasonably sized machine, a well-written SQL statement, and a CBO that makes all its cardinality estimates perfectly, you are unlikely to get decent performance unless you pay attention to the physical database design.

A WORD ABOUT EXADATA

There are those who suggest that one of the benefits of Exadata is that you don't have to worry about physical database design: full table scans are so cheap and hardware is so plentiful, so who cares?

I feel that this is a bit of an exaggeration. Yes, it might not be cost-effective to spend months designing your physical model, but there will always be a desire to use hardware effectively. Consideration of physical database design is almost always a good idea.

This chapter reviews the more critical aspects of physical database design, one of the few aspects of SQL performance that we can't blame on the CBO.

All too often people equate "physical database design improvement" with "adding indexes." This is very far from the truth, and we will begin this chapter by comparing both the positive and negative aspects of indexes. Once you have come to the conclusion that one or more indexes are necessary, you still have a lot of decisions ahead of you: what columns do you want in the index, whether to use a bitmap index, and so on. We will go through some of these questions.

The partitioning option is a popular and effective tool to improve performance, and I will cover what I believe to be the three most important performance benefits of partitioning: full table scans on portions of a table, the ability to use partition-wise joins, and the additional possibilities for parallelization.

In some circles the word "denormalization" is considered evil, just like "hinting." And just like hinting, denormalization has a legitimate place in SQL performance tuning. I will cover materialized views and other forms of denormalization later in the chapter. I will round out the chapter with a few comments about compression and LOBs.

Before we start, however, I want to reemphasize that physical database design is almost never about tuning individual SQL statements. You are generally looking to find a way to optimize the entire application. This thought should be at the forefront of your mind as we discuss indexes.

Adding and Removing Indexes

Imagine yourself looking at the execution plan of a query. You see that an index is being used to access a table, but that index is not particularly selective: too often a table block is accessed and then the row specified in the index is thrown away because of a predicate on an un-indexed column. "Aha," you say. "Let me create a new index that includes all the columns referenced by predicates in my query and all will be well." You create your new index (or add columns to an existing index) and . . . voilà! Your query runs fast and you pat yourself on the back. This type of behavior is far too common and reflects an inappropriate way to think about indexing and physical database design in general—you shouldn't add indexes in a piecemeal way to optimize individual queries. You need to think about the optimal set of indexes needed for a particular table for supporting *all* your queries without overburdening DML. Let us first look at indexing strategy from the other side of the table: optimizing DML.

Removing Indexes

One of the most overlooked issues in database performance is the impact of having too many indexes on a table. Let us consider this overhead in some detail before discussing how best to reduce it.

Understanding the Overhead of Indexes on DML

If you have a dozen indexes on a table, every time you add a row to that table you need to add a dozen index entries. Together with the change to the table block itself, that makes 13 block changes. All 13 block changes are guaranteed to be made to different blocks because the changes are being made to different database objects. Don't underestimate this overhead. Indexes take up space in the SGA, increase the amount of redo needed, and often generate lots of I/O. Have you ever seen an INSERT statement constantly waiting on "db file sequential read" wait events? You may have assumed that these wait events were associated with the query portion of the INSERT statement. The easiest way to check this is to look at the CURRENT_OBJ# column in V$ACTIVE_SESSION_HISTORY or DBA_HIST_ACTIVE_SESS_HISTORY. This number represents the OBJECT_ID from DBA_OBJECTS associated with the object being accessed. You may well find that most or all of these wait events are associated with index blocks from the table into which you are inserting rows; you need to read the index block into the SGA prior to adding the index entry. If you can reduce the number of indexes on a table you can substantially improve the performance of DML. The following is a quote from the Performance Tuning Guide:

> *Use this simple estimation guide for the cost of index maintenance: each index maintained by an INSERT, DELETE, or UPDATE of the indexed keys requires about three times as much resource as the actual DML operation on the table. Thus, if you INSERT into a table with three indexes, then the insertion is approximately 10 times slower than an INSERT into a table with no indexes. For DML, and particularly for INSERT-heavy applications, the index design should be seriously reviewed, which might require a compromise between the query and INSERT performance.*

Based on the number of tables I have seen with dozens of indexes, many developers are unaware of the above issue. Either that or the information is forgotten in the heat of the moment when solving query performance issues.

Using V$OBJECT_USAGE to Identify Unused Indexes

As a short-term fix to expensive DML you can look for indexes that aren't being used. This can be done by enabling index monitoring on all the indexes in a table or a schema with the ALTER INDEX ....MONITORING USAGE command. This command creates a row in the view V$OBJECT_USAGE. The V$OBJECT_USAGE view contains a column USED that is initialized to the value NO by the ALTER INDEX command and gets updated to YES when the index is used in an execution plan. The idea is that if the value of the column USED continues to have a value of NO forever than the index isn't used and thus can safely be dropped. Of course, forever is a long time, but the longer your system runs without the index being used the higher the confidence level you have that the index will never be used by the current version of your application.

You should bear in mind the following points about V$OBJECT_USAGE:

- You can only view indexes owned by yourself in V$OBJECT_USAGE. Put another way, you have to log in as the schema owner to use the V$OBJECT_USAGE view.

- The gathering of statistics on the monitored index does not cause the value of the USED column in V$OBJECT_USAGE to change.

- Unusually for a dynamic performance view, restarting the database does not cause the value of the USED column in V$OBJECT_USAGE to change for any indexes.

- Adding or removing index entries by DML does not cause the value of the USED column in V$OBJECT_USAGE to change.

- Rebuilding or coalescing an index does not cause the value of the USED column in V$OBJECT_USAGE to change.

- When an index is used to enforce a primary key, unique key, or foreign key constraint, the value of the USED column in V$OBJECT_USAGE does not change.

This last point is worth emphasizing: just because an index isn't used in an execution plan does not mean it is not fulfilling a purpose, so take care when reviewing the indexes you consider dropping.

Removing Indexes on Columns Used in Foreign Key Constraints

During the 1990s a myth regarding a so-called *best practice* got completely out of hand. That myth was that it was *always* necessary to index the referencing columns in a foreign key constraint. The myth took such a hold that many database design tools automatically generated DDL to create indexes on such columns.

Take the ORDER_ID column in the ORDER_ITEMS table in the OE example schema—this column is used by the ORDER_ITEMS_ORDER_ID_FK foreign key constraint that references the ORDER_ID column in the ORDERS table. Now it *is* necessary to index the ORDER_ID column in the ORDERS table because ORDER_ID is the primary key of the ORDERS table, but it is *not* necessary to index the ORDER_ID column in the ORDER_ITEMS table.

How did the myth that you should *always* index columns like ORDER_ITEMS.ORDER_ID take hold? Well, if you DELETE rows from the ORDERS table (or you change the primary key with an UPDATE or MERGE statement) then a table lock will be required on ORDER_ITEMS unless the ORDER_ITEMS.ORDER_ID column is indexed. But if you don't issue such DELETE statements or the performance of the DELETE statements isn't critical then you don't need the index.

Don't get me wrong—regardless of the fact that the ORDER_ID column in ORDER_ITEMS is used in a foreign key constraint, it may be a good idea to index the column anyway. If you join ORDERS with ORDER_ITEMS using the ORDER_ID columns on both tables, and you wish to drive a nested loop from the ORDERS table into ORDER_ITEMS, then an index on ORDER_ITEMS.ORDER_ID may be a good idea. In fact, the OE.ORDER_ITEMS table does have an index named ITEM_ORDER_IX on ORDER_ID.

But all this business of dropping unused indexes is just a quick fix. The best thing to do is to do a thorough job of understanding your indexing requirements and keep those, and only those, indexes.

Identifying Required Indexes

The Performance Tuning Guide states:

> *Index design is ... a largely iterative process, based on the SQL generated by application designers. However, it is possible to make a sensible start by building indexes that enforce primary key constraints and indexes on known access patterns, such as a person's name.*

It is quite true that index design is an iterative process, but I would caution you to be very conservative in your initial selection of indexes. It is easy to assume that an index is required when in fact it isn't. How can you tell what a *known access pattern* is before you have started testing? If you have the time then I would suggest creating indexes to support primary and unique constraints *only* and then run some tests to see how you get on.

Single-column and Multi-column Indexes

Most non-unique B-tree indexes should be multi-column. Let me first explain why this is and then I will go on to discuss column ordering.

Misuse of Single-column Non-unique B-tree Indexes

Listing 15-1 takes another look at the indexes in the ORDER_ITEMS table in the OE example schema, and at ITEM_ORDER_IX in particular.

Listing 15-1. Misuse of a single-column non-unique index

```
SELECT *
  FROM oe.orders JOIN oe.order_items i USING (order_id)
 WHERE order_id = 2400;
```

```
-----------------------------------------------------------------------------
| Id  | Operation                             | Name         | Cost (%CPU)|
-----------------------------------------------------------------------------
|   0 | SELECT STATEMENT                      |              |    4   (0)|
|   1 |  NESTED LOOPS                         |              |    4   (0)|
|   2 |   TABLE ACCESS BY INDEX ROWID         | ORDERS       |    1   (0)|
|*  3 |    INDEX UNIQUE SCAN                  | ORDER_PK     |    0   (0)|
|   4 |   TABLE ACCESS BY INDEX ROWID BATCHED | ORDER_ITEMS  |    3   (0)|
|*  5 |    INDEX RANGE SCAN                   | ITEM_ORDER_IX|    1   (0)|
-----------------------------------------------------------------------------
```

```
SELECT /*+ index(i order_items_pk) */    *
  FROM oe.orders JOIN oe.order_items i USING (order_id)
 WHERE order_id = 2400;
```

```
-----------------------------------------------------------------------------
| Id  | Operation                             | Name          | Cost (%CPU)|
-----------------------------------------------------------------------------
|   0 | SELECT STATEMENT                      |               |    4   (0)|
|   1 |  NESTED LOOPS                         |               |    4   (0)|
|   2 |   TABLE ACCESS BY INDEX ROWID         | ORDERS        |    1   (0)|
|*  3 |    INDEX UNIQUE SCAN                  | ORDER_PK      |    0   (0)|
|   4 |   TABLE ACCESS BY INDEX ROWID BATCHED | ORDER_ITEMS   |    3   (0)|
|*  5 |    INDEX RANGE SCAN                   | ORDER_ITEMS_PK|    1   (0)|
-----------------------------------------------------------------------------
```

The first query in Listing 15-1 shows the sort of query that one presumes the ITEM_ORDER_IX index was designed for: a query on a particular ORDER_ID. However, the second query in Listing 15-1 uses a hint to force the use of the multi-column index supporting the primary key constraint. The index that enforces the primary key is named ORDER_ITEMS_PK. The ORDER_ITEMS_PK index is a multi-column unique index that has ORDER_ID as the leading column, and the reported estimated cost of the use of ORDER_ITEMS_PK is identical to that of ITEM_ORDER_IX: we don't need both indexes.

Of course the ITEM_ORDER_IX index is slightly smaller than the ORDER_ITEMS_PK index, so in fact there might be a slight performance gain from using ITEM_ORDER_IX over ORDER_ITEMS_PK. In practice, however, the DML overhead of maintaining ITEM_ORDER_IX will be far greater than the benefit the index affords queries, and if this were a real-life table then I would drop the single-column ITEM_ORDER_IX index.

■ **Note**　If the ITEM_ORDER_IX column were to be dropped then there would still be no table lock when rows in ORDERS are deleted. This is because the ORDER_ID is the leading column in ORDER_ITEMS_PK and as such ORDER_ITEMS_PK prevents the table lock.

Correct Use of Multi-column Non-unique Indexes

If you find the need to create a non-unique B-tree index on a column then it almost always makes sense to add additional columns to the index to help queries that use predicates involving multiple columns. This is because adding a column or two to an index generally adds relatively little overhead to either DML or queries, but adding additional indexes is very expensive for DML. Listing 15-2 shows the use of a potentially legitimate index on the OE.CUSTOMERS table.

Listing 15-2. Correct use of a multi-column index

```
SELECT *
  FROM oe.customers
 WHERE UPPER (cust_last_name) = 'KANTH';
```

```
--------------------------------------------------------------------------
| Id  | Operation                            | Name              | Rows  | Cost (%CPU)|
--------------------------------------------------------------------------
|   0 | SELECT STATEMENT                     |                   |    2  |    4   (0)|
|   1 |  TABLE ACCESS BY INDEX ROWID BATCHED | CUSTOMERS         |    2  |    4   (0)|
|*  2 |   INDEX RANGE SCAN                   | CUST_UPPER_NAME_IX |    2  |    2   (0)|
--------------------------------------------------------------------------
```

Predicate Information (identified by operation id):

```
   2 - access(UPPER("CUST_LAST_NAME")='KANTH')
```

```
SELECT *
  FROM oe.customers
 WHERE     UPPER (cust_first_name) = 'MALCOLM'
       AND UPPER (cust_last_name) = 'KANTH';
```

```
--------------------------------------------------------------------------
| Id  | Operation                            | Name              | Rows  | Cost (%CPU)|
--------------------------------------------------------------------------
|   0 | SELECT STATEMENT                     |                   |    1  |    2   (0)|
|   1 |  TABLE ACCESS BY INDEX ROWID BATCHED | CUSTOMERS         |    1  |    2   (0)|
|*  2 |   INDEX RANGE SCAN                   | CUST_UPPER_NAME_IX |    1  |    1   (0)|
--------------------------------------------------------------------------
```

Predicate Information (identified by operation id):

```
   2 - access(UPPER("CUST_LAST_NAME")='KANTH' AND
             UPPER("CUST_FIRST_NAME")='MALCOLM')
```

```
SELECT *
  FROM oe.customers
 WHERE UPPER (cust_first_name) = 'MALCOLM';
```

```
------------------------------------------------------------
| Id  | Operation          | Name      | Rows  | Cost (%CPU)|
------------------------------------------------------------
|   0 | SELECT STATEMENT   |           |    2  |    5   (0)|
|*  1 |  TABLE ACCESS FULL | CUSTOMERS |    2  |    5   (0)|
------------------------------------------------------------
```

```
Predicate Information (identified by operation id):
---------------------------------------------------

   1 - filter(UPPER("CUST_FIRST_NAME")='MALCOLM')
```

CUST_UPPER_NAME_IX is a multi-column, function-based index on two expressions: UPPER (CUST_LAST_NAME) and UPPER (CUST_FIRST_NAME). Listing 15-2 shows that an INDEX RANGE SCAN can be used when a predicate on just the first expression is used or when predicates on both expressions are used. But when only the second expression is used in a query only the expensive and unsuitable INDEX SKIP SCAN is available, so the CBO elects to use a full table scan instead.

Let me close this section with a reminder that if you only select columns from an index the table need not be accessed at all. This means that the performance of some queries might improve by adding columns to an index, even if said queries contain no predicates on the column being added to the index.

Order of Columns in a Multi-column Index

As Listing 15-2 shows it is important to ensure that commonly used columns or expressions appear at the leading edge of an index. But if your query has predicates that specify all the columns in an index does it matter what the order of the columns in the index is? Generally speaking the answer is no: your index range scan will scan precisely the same number of index entries no matter the ordering of the columns in the index. However, apart from queries that specify only a portion of the indexed columns, there are three other considerations in determining the optimal column ordering for an index:

- If you wish to compress only a subset of the indexed columns then these columns need to appear on the leading edge of the index. I will cover index compression a little later in this chapter.

- If queries routinely order data using more than one column from an index, then correctly ordering columns in the index might avoid explicit sorts. I will demonstrate how an index can be used to avoid a sort in Chapter 19.

- In theory, if data is loaded in a sorted or semi-sorted manner then the index clustering factor (and hence query performance) might be improved by ordering the columns in the index in the same way as the table data is sorted. I must say that I personally have never come across a situation where clustering factor was a concern in choosing the order of columns in an index.

■ **Note**   The Performance Tuning Guide states that you should "order columns with most selectivity first." This is a famous documentation error that has not been corrected as of 12cR1.

Bitmap Indexes

So far our discussion of indexing strategy has explicitly or implicitly been restricted to B-tree indexes. Bitmap indexes tend to be tiny and are one way to solve one important problem.

Listing 15-2 showed that queries that don't include a predicate on the leading column of an index often can't use a multi-column index efficiently. Imagine you have a table called PROBLEM_TABLE. You have a few dozen commonly used queries on PROBLEM_TABLE that each specify a subset of two or three columns from a set of half a dozen columns, but there is no column that is used in all the queries. What indexes do you create? This is the sort of situation that leads some developers to create dozens of indexes for each column subset. Not a good idea.

If you load your data in bulk then bitmap indexes solve this problem: you just create six single-column bitmap indexes on PROBLEM_TABLE and the INDEX COMBINE operation that we showed in Listing 10-18 can be used to identify the subset of rows needed from the table before it is accessed. It is important to not try to maintain your bitmap index during the DML operations themselves. Listing 15-3 shows the correct way to load data when bitmap indexes are in use.

Listing 15-3. Loading data into a partitioned table that has bitmap indexes

```
CREATE TABLE statement_part_ch15
PARTITION BY RANGE
   (transaction_date)
   (
      PARTITION p1 VALUES LESS THAN (DATE '2013-01-05')
     ,PARTITION p2 VALUES LESS THAN (DATE '2013-01-11')
     ,PARTITION p3 VALUES LESS THAN (DATE '2013-01-12')
     ,PARTITION p4 VALUES LESS THAN (maxvalue))
AS
   SELECT transaction_date_time
         ,transaction_date
         ,posting_date
         ,description
         ,transaction_amount
         ,product_category
         ,customer_category
     FROM statement;

CREATE BITMAP INDEX statement_part_pc_bix
   ON statement_part_ch15 (product_category)
   LOCAL;

CREATE BITMAP INDEX statement_part_cc_bix
   ON statement_part_ch15 (customer_category)
   LOCAL;

ALTER TABLE statement_part_ch15 MODIFY PARTITION FOR (DATE '2013-01-11') UNUSABLE LOCAL INDEXES;

INSERT INTO statement_part_ch15 (transaction_date_time
                                ,transaction_date
                                ,posting_date
                                ,description
                                ,transaction_amount
                                ,product_category
                                ,customer_category)
   SELECT DATE '2013-01-11'
         ,DATE '2013-01-11'
         ,DATE '2013-01-11'
         ,description
         ,transaction_amount
         ,product_category
         ,customer_category
     FROM statement_part_ch15;

ALTER TABLE statement_part_ch15 MODIFY PARTITION FOR (DATE '2013-01-11')
         REBUILD UNUSABLE LOCAL INDEXES;
```

Listing 15-3 creates a partitioned table `STATEMENT_PART_CH15` using data from the `STATEMENT` table we created in Chapter 9. Before loading data into the previously empty partition for `TRANSACTION_DATE` January 11, 2013, the indexes for the partition are marked unusable. Data is then inserted without maintaining the indexes, and, finally, indexes for the partition (in particular, the bitmap indexes) are rebuilt. Once your bitmap indexes are rebuilt they are available for use.

Let me emphasize that bitmap indexes are only of practical use if you load data first, rebuild the indexes second, and query the data third. This is often very practical in data warehousing applications, but DML against *usable* bitmap indexes is very expensive and concurrency is very poor. The implication is that bitmap indexes are usually impractical for most other types of application.

Alternatives to Bitmap Indexes

Let us return to our `PROBLEM_TABLE` with the six columns used by the predicates of the table's various problematic queries. Suppose now that concurrent DML and queries make bitmap indexes impractical. What then? When we consider each query in isolation the best thing to do is to create a multi-column index that includes all the columns or expressions in that query. But as I have already emphasized, this kind of automatic reaction when repeated for each query can result in a plethora of indexes that severely degrade DML performance. So is there an alternative?

You might consider creating six single-column B-tree indexes because, as I showed in Listing 10-18, the `INDEX COMBINE` operation can be used with B-tree indexes as well as with bitmap indexes. However, the associated conversion of the B-tree index entries to bitmaps can be expensive, and so six single-column B-tree indexes is unlikely to be a good idea. You might create just one big index that includes all six columns. That way if the leading columns of the index aren't used in a particular query an `INDEX FULL SCAN` or `INDEX SKIP SCAN` might be used instead.

At the end of the day you probably have to accept that for some queries you will just have to live with a full table scan and a hash join, even if you know that a nested loops join with an index would make the query perform better.

If you are really desperate I will show you how you might rewrite your SQL to work around this issue in Chapter 19.

Index-organized Tables

In my opinion index-organized tables (IOTs) are best used when both of the following conditions apply:

- Your table (or table partition) is very small (less than 50MB) or very narrow (the primary key is at least 10% of the row size)

- You don't need any indexes other than the one index supporting the primary key

If both of these conditions apply you can store all of the table's columns in the index and thus avoid the need for any actual table at all.

It is possible to create additional indexes on an IOT, but as I mentioned briefly in Chapter 3, secondary indexes on IOTs hold a "guess" as to where the referenced row is, so they may need to be rebuilt frequently when the "guesses" become out-of-date. Some experts are more bullish about IOTs than I am. Martin Widlake is a great fan of IOTs. You can read more in his blog starting with this post: `http://mwidlake.wordpress.com/2011/07/18/index-organized-tables-the-basics/`.

Managing Contention

One of the great things about the Oracle database architecture is that writers don't block readers. Alas, writers block other writers! So this section discusses the performance problems that can arise as a result of multiple processes performing DML on the same database object concurrently.

Sequence Contention

You should endeavor to design your application so that gaps in the numbers generated by a sequence are not problematic and that nothing particularly bad happens if numbers are generated out of order from the sequence. This endeavor is particularly relevant in a RAC environment. Once you are confident in the stability of your application you can alter your sequence and specify the CACHE and NOORDER attributes. This will ensure that communication between nodes in a RAC cluster is minimized when allocating numbers from a sequence.

The Hot-block Problem

When multiple processes concurrently insert rows into a table, the rows will usually be inserted into different blocks in the table whether you use Automatic Segment Space Management (ASSM) or Manual Segment Space Management (MSSM). However, it is often the case that multiple processes will attempt to update the same index block at the same time. This is particularly true when the leading column of the index is a timestamp or a number generated from a sequence.

If you try to access a buffer and it is being updated by another session you will have to wait. In Oracle 9i and earlier you would always have seen this wait as a "buffer busy waits" event, but as of release 10.1 and later a second wait event was split out. The wait event "read by other session" means that the buffer you are trying to access is being updated by another session *and* that the block is being read from disk into the buffer cache by that other session. Both the "buffer busy waits" event and the "read by other session" wait event are indications of contention for a block, although you might also see the "read by other session" wait event when there are concurrent readers of the same block.

When multiple processes are concurrently attempting to update the same block, the block is said to be *hot*. Hot blocks don't always occur in indexes, but most of them do. Let us begin our discussion of hot-block contention by a look at a solution that is specific to indexes.

Reverse Key Indexes

On paper, the idea is simple and elegant. Imagine you have an index I1 on column C1 and you populate the values of C1 by obtaining values from a sequence. Three processes might generate values 123,456; 123,457; and 123,458 from the sequence and then insert rows into your table. The index entries in a traditional index would be consecutive, and most likely the processes would be contending with each other to update the same index leaf block. If you create the index with the keyword REVERSE, the bytes in the index entries will be reversed before inserting. You can think of this by imagining index entries 654,321; 754,321; and 854,321. As you can see, these index entries are no longer even remotely consecutive and will be inserted into different blocks. This isn't quite how it works: the bytes in the index entry are reversed, not the digits in the number, but the concept is the same. Almost magically you seem to have instantly solved your contention problem.

The reality is not quite as elegant as it first appears. There are two big problems. The first is that INDEX RANGE SCANs are restricted to specific values of C1. If you have a query with a predicate WHERE C1 BETWEEN 123456 AND 123458 the CBO will not be able to use a range scan to find the three index entries because they are scattered around the index.

The second issue with reverse key indexes is that the hot-block problem now has become a cold-block problem. Before reversing the index there may have been contention between the processes, but at least only one index block would have to be read into the SGA. When you reverse your index, the index entries will be inserted all over the place, and unless all the leaf blocks from the index can be cached in the SGA there is a very real risk that disk reads on the index will increase dramatically.

I am indebted to Oracle's Real World Performance team for educating me about a potentially superior solution to the hot index block problem. That solution is the global partitioned index.

Global Partitioned Indexes

Whether the underlying table is partitioned or not you can partition an index in a way that is totally independent of any partitioning strategy of the underlying table. Such an index is known as a *globally partitioned index*. Listing 15-4 shows how this is done.

Listing 15-4. Creating a globally partitioned index

```
CREATE TABLE global_part_index_test
(
  c1    INTEGER
  ,c2   VARCHAR2 (50)
  ,c3   VARCHAR2 (50)
);

CREATE UNIQUE INDEX gpi_ix
   ON global_part_index_test (c1)
   GLOBAL PARTITION BY HASH (c1)
      PARTITIONS 32;

ALTER TABLE global_part_index_test ADD CONSTRAINT global_part_index_test_pk PRIMARY KEY (c1);

SELECT *
  FROM global_part_index_test
 WHERE c1 BETWEEN 123456 AND 123458;
```

```
-------------------------------------------------------------------------
| Id | Operation                              | Name                    |
-------------------------------------------------------------------------
|  0 | SELECT STATEMENT                       |                         |
|  1 |  PARTITION HASH ALL                    |                         |
|  2 |   TABLE ACCESS BY INDEX ROWID BATCHED| GLOBAL_PART_INDEX_TEST  |
|  3 |    INDEX RANGE SCAN                    | GPI_IX                  |
-------------------------------------------------------------------------
```

Listing 15-4 creates the index used to support a primary key constraint as a global hash-partitioned index. Insertions into the index will be scattered around the 32 partitions, thus substantially reducing the level of contention, just as with a reverse key index. But unlike our reverse key index, we have not lost our ability to perform range scans across multiple values of C1. As you can see from line 1 in the execution plan, the runtime engine needs to look in all 32 partitions, so index range scans are more expensive than for an unpartitioned index, but at least they are possible.

We have solved our cold-block problem as well. Imagine inserting 1,024 rows into a large table with values of C1 from 1 to 1,024. If C1 is indexed with a reverse key index we are likely to insert index entries into 1,024 different blocks. On the other hand, assuming that we can store over 32 index entries in a block, our 1,024 index entries will be stored in just 32 blocks when C1 is indexed as in Listing 15-4. This is because the 32 values (approximately) of C1 for one hash partition will be consecutive within that partition! So our blocks are "lukewarm," as Graham Wood put it, and it is likely that these 32 blocks can be kept in the buffer cache.

Is there a downside to globally partitioned indexes? Yes. They are difficult to maintain—even more difficult to maintain than an unpartitioned global index on a partitioned table.

Imagine that you have a 1TB table. You create five global hash-partitioned indexes, each using 32 hash partitions. You now upgrade your hardware and use datapump export/import to move the 1TB table to your new machine and then attempt to rebuild your indexes. You would need to scan the entire 1TB table to rebuild each index partition, regardless of any partitioning strategy on the table. That is 5 x 32 = 160 full table scans of your 1TB table!

One solution to the rebuild problem is to partition (or subpartition) your table by hash and then use local indexes. (Sub) partitioning your table has the added benefit of reducing the risk of contention on the table itself.

Initial ITL Entries

When a transaction first updates a block it uses an entry in the interested transaction list (ITL) in the block. If all the ITL entries in a block are used by uncommitted transactions then a new ITL entry is added, assuming that there is space in the block for such an entry. An ITL entry consumes 24 bytes, so if you were to pre-allocate 100 entries you would waste about one quarter of the space in an 8K block. By default the initial number of ITL slots is one for a table block and two for an index. If you see a lot of wait events with the name "enq: TX - allocate ITL entry" then the waiting process is unable to allocate a new ITL entry due to lack of space in the block. The direct approach to solving this problem is to increase the number of ITL entries initially allocated to blocks in your index or table. To increase the initial number of ITL entries in index I1 from two to five, the syntax is ALTER INDEX I1 INITRANS 5, but bear in mind the following:

- The change to INITRANS doesn't affect blocks already formatted in the index or table. You may need to rebuild the index or move the table.

- Just because you solve your ITL contention problem doesn't mean you won't still have other contention issues.

If you have ITL entry contention issues it may be better to avoid the issue rather than to solve it: using a reverse key or global hash-partitioned index might eliminate your ITL problem at the same time because the concurrent addition of new index entries will likely be to different blocks and, therefore, different ITLs. Let us look at another way to reduce block contention now.

Spreading Data Out

Just because two sessions are trying to update the same table block doesn't mean they are trying to update the same row in the block. And just because two sessions are trying to update the same index block doesn't mean they are they are trying to update the same index entry. If your database object is small you might try reducing the number of rows per table block or index entries per index block to alleviate contention.

Let us assume that you have 50 sessions that each frequently updates a tiny session-specific row in a table. If nothing special is done all 50 rows will end up in the same block, and you are likely to see a number of buffer busy wait events. Since the table is very small you can probably afford to spread the rows out one per block to avoid contention. There are actually several ways to achieve this. Listing 15-5 shows one such way.

Listing 15-5. Ensuring that there is only one row per block

```
CREATE TABLE process_status
(
    process_id                  INTEGER PRIMARY KEY
   ,status                      INTEGER
   ,last_job_id                 INTEGER
   ,last_job_completion_time    DATE
   ,filler_1                    CHAR (100) DEFAULT RPAD (' ', 100)
)
PCTFREE 99
PCTUSED 1;
```

```
INSERT INTO process_status (process_id)
       SELECT ROWNUM
          FROM DUAL
   CONNECT BY LEVEL <= 50;

BEGIN
   DBMS_STATS.gather_table_stats (
       ownname       => SYS_CONTEXT ('USERENV', 'CURRENT_SCHEMA')
      ,tabname   => 'PROCESS_STATUS');
END;
/

UPDATE process_status
     SET status = 1, last_job_id = 1, last_job_completion_time = SYSDATE
 WHERE process_id = 1;
```

```
--------------------------------------------------
| Id  | Operation            | Name            |
--------------------------------------------------
|   0 | UPDATE STATEMENT     |                 |
|   1 |  UPDATE              | PROCESS_STATUS  |
|   2 |   INDEX UNIQUE SCAN  | SYS_C005053     |
--------------------------------------------------
```

Listing 15-5 creates a table called PROCESS_STATUS that stores 50 rows, one for each application process. Our first attempt to reduce the number of rows in each block of the PROCESS_STATUS table is to set PCTFREE to 99, meaning that rows will no longer be inserted into the table once 1% of the 8K block has been used. But our rows are less than 81 bytes long, so we need to add an extra column that I have called FILLER_1. Now when we insert our 50 rows they will all go into separate blocks. Any UPDATE statement on a single row will find the dedicated block via the index and there will be no contention with other sessions updating other rows in the table.

Partitioning

A favorite topic of light-hearted debate among experts is whether the main advantages of the partitioning option relate to the ease of administration or improved performance. Of course, partitioning offers both administrative-and performance-related advantages. We have already discussed how global hash-partitioned indexes and hash-partitioned tables can help alleviate hot-block contention. Let us look at some of the other performance-related advantages that partitioning brings us.

Full Table Scans on Partitions or Subpartitions

Imagine your table holds 100,000 rows for 10 business days, making 1,000,000 rows in total. Suppose that you can get about 100 rows per block, so your table has about 10,000 blocks in total. Let us take a rosy view of the world and assume that all the rows are perfectly clustered by business date so that all the rows for a particular business date are located in 1,000 of the 10,000 blocks. Now suppose you want to read all of the 10,000 rows for a particular business date. To keep things simple, let us assume that none of the data is in the buffer cache. Do you think indexed access or a full table scan is best?

Well, in truth, neither option is particularly appealing. If you use a full table scan then you will read and throw away 9,000 of the 10,000 blocks that you read. If you read the table blocks using an index then you will only access the 1,000 blocks you need, but they will be read using 1,000 single-block reads.

What we really want is to read the 1,000 blocks for our selected business date with multi-block reads but to not bother with the other 9,000 blocks. As I shall show you in Chapter 19, it is possible to rewrite SQL to accomplish this, but it is very tricky to do so. If you partition your table by business date you will now have 10 table segments each of a size of 1,000 blocks rather than a single 10,000-block segment. After partition elimination your query can perform a single full table scan of a single 1,000-block segment. If these 1,000 blocks are already in the buffer cache then you might not see a huge performance difference between accessing the blocks via an index or via a full table scan. But if the selected 1,000 blocks all need to be read from disk then the fact that the full table scan will use multi-block reads means that the scan will be substantially faster than when an index is used.

So partitioning makes full table scans more attractive, and this in turn may make some indexes redundant that might otherwise be needed. A double win!

Partition-wise Joins

If you join two tables that are partitioned identically and the partitioning column or columns are included in the join predicates, then you can perform what is referred to as a *full partition-wise join*. Listing 15-6 shows a full partition-wise join in action.

Listing 15-6. A full partition-wise join executed serially

```
CREATE TABLE orders_part
(
    order_id            INTEGER NOT NULL
   ,order_date          DATE NOT NULL
   ,customer_name       VARCHAR2 (50)
   ,delivery_address     VARCHAR2 (100)
)
PARTITION BY LIST
    (order_date)
    SUBPARTITION BY HASH (order_id)
        SUBPARTITIONS 16
    (
        PARTITION p1 VALUES (DATE '2014-04-01')
       ,PARTITION p2 VALUES (DATE '2014-04-02'));

CREATE UNIQUE INDEX orders_part_pk
    ON orders_part (order_date, order_id)
    LOCAL;

ALTER TABLE orders_part
    ADD CONSTRAINT orders_part_pk PRIMARY KEY
    (order_date,order_id);
CREATE TABLE order_items_part
(
    order_id             INTEGER NOT NULL
   ,order_item_id        INTEGER NOT NULL
   ,order_date           DATE NOT NULL
   ,product_id           INTEGER
   ,quantity             INTEGER
   ,price                NUMBER
   ,CONSTRAINT order_items_part_fk FOREIGN KEY
```

```
       (order_date, order_id)
        REFERENCES orders_part (order_date, order_id)
)
PARTITION BY REFERENCE (order_items_part_fk);

CREATE UNIQUE INDEX order_items_part_pk
   ON order_items_part (order_date, order_id, order_item_id)
   COMPRESS 1
   LOCAL;

ALTER TABLE order_items_part
   ADD CONSTRAINT order_items_part_pk PRIMARY KEY
   (order_date,order_id,order_item_id);

SELECT /*+ leading(o i) use_hash(i) no_swap_join_inputs(i) */
       *
   FROM orders_part o JOIN order_items_part i USING (order_id);
```

```
-------------------------------------------------------
| Id  | Operation             | Name              |
-------------------------------------------------------
|  0  | SELECT STATEMENT      |                   |
|  1  |  HASH JOIN            |                   |
|  2  |   PARTITION LIST ALL  |                   |
|  3  |    PARTITION HASH ALL |                   |
|  4  |     TABLE ACCESS FULL | ORDERS_PART       |
|  5  |    PARTITION REFERENCE ALL|               |
|  6  |     TABLE ACCESS FULL | ORDER_ITEMS_PART  |
-------------------------------------------------------
```

```
SELECT /*+ leading(o i) use_hash(i) no_swap_join_inputs(i) */
       *
   FROM orders_part o JOIN order_items_part i USING (order_date, order_id);
```

```
------------------------------------------------------
| Id  | Operation            | Name              |
------------------------------------------------------
|  0  | SELECT STATEMENT     |                   |
|  1  |  PARTITION LIST ALL  |                   |
|  2  |   PARTITION HASH ALL |                   |
|  3  |    HASH JOIN         |                   |
|  4  |     TABLE ACCESS FULL| ORDERS_PART       |
|  5  |     TABLE ACCESS FULL| ORDER_ITEMS_PART  |
------------------------------------------------------
```

Listing 15-6 creates two tables, ORDERS_PART and ORDER_ITEMS_PART. ORDERS_PART is partitioned by list using ORDER_DATE and subpartitioned by hash using ORDER_ID. There are partitions for two values of ORDER_DATE and 16 subpartitions for each ORDER_DATE, making 32 subpartitions in all. The primary key should be just the ORDER_ID, but we have compromised a little by adding the ORDER_DATE to the primary key so that the constraint can be enforced using a local index—a common and practical compromise.

The ORDER_ITEMS_PART table is partitioned by reference, which means that when ORDER_ITEMS_PART is created it has 32 partitions, one for each subpartition of ORDER_ITEMS. For each partition added to or dropped from ORDERS_PART, 16 partitions will be added to or dropped from ORDER_ITEMS_PART.

Now then. What happens when we join the two tables? The first query in Listing 15-6 joins the two tables using only the ORDER_ID column. I have used hints to get an execution plan that is both easy to understand and typical of what might be seen once rows are added to the tables. We can see from line 5 in the execution plan that for each subpartition of ORDERS_PART, all 32 subpartitions of ORDER_ITEMS part are scanned. This is because the CBO doesn't know that a particular value of ORDER_ID is only found in one partition of ORDER_ITEMS_PART. When we add the ORDER_DATE to the list of joined columns we see that the PARTITION REFERENCE ALL operation has disappeared, implying that only one partition of ORDER_ITEMS_PART is scanned for each subpartition of ORDERS_PART. Partition elimination on ORDER_ITEMS_PART has been accomplished in the latter query of Listing 15-6 because all columns used to define the partitions and subpartitions in the two tables appear in the join conditions.

■ **Tip**   One of the supposed benefits of partitioning by reference is that you can partition a child table by columns only present in the parent table. However, Listing 15-6 shows that if you eliminate the ORDER_DATE column from ORDER_ITEMS_PART in an attempt to normalize your design you will find that full partition-wise joins can't be used. All the columns used to partition or subpartition a parent table should be present in the child table.

So what have we gained? If we hadn't partitioned our tables at all we would have one big hash join of the entire table, and now we have 32 small hash joins. The point is that there is a likelihood that the small hash joins can be done entirely in memory as opposed to using the large hash join that has an higher probability to spill to disk.

So far we have only been looking at serial partition-wise joins. The beauty of partition-wise joins becomes really apparent when we consider parallelization.

Parallelization and Partitioning

I gave examples of full and partial partition-wise joins in Listings 11-17 and 11-18 respectively, but just to recap, Listing 15-7 takes the latter query in Listing 15-6 and runs it in parallel.

Listing 15-7. Parallel full partition-wise join

```
SELECT /*+ leading(o i) use_hash(i) no_swap_join_inputs(i)
          parallel(16) PQ_DISTRIBUTE(I NONE NONE)*/
      *
  FROM orders_part o JOIN order_items_part i USING (order_date,order_id);
```

Id	Operation	Name
0	SELECT STATEMENT	
1	PX COORDINATOR	
2	PX SEND QC (RANDOM)	**TQ10000:**
3	PX PARTITION HASH ALL	
4	HASH JOIN	
5	TABLE ACCESS FULL	ORDERS_PART
6	TABLE ACCESS FULL	ORDER_ITEMS_PART

Denormalization

I don't profess to be a leading authority on logical database design, but it is my belief that a logical database design should be normalized. However, once you have your initial neat, normalized, logical model you will often need to denormalize the model as part of the physical database design process in order to obtain decent performance. This section describes some of the ways in which you might need to denormalize your database, starting with materialized views.

Materialized Views

There are two reasons why you might create materialized views. One reason is to automate replication of data from one database to another. The second reason is to denormalize your data for performance purposes. Performance is what we are focusing on here, and there are two main categories of performance-related materialized views:

- **Materialized join views** store the results of a join of two or more tables
- **Materialized summary views** store the results of aggregations

Of course you can create a materialized view that both joins tables and then performs aggregations. If the same joins and/or aggregations are done frequently, it might make sense to create a materialized view so that the work is done only once. Here are some of the nice features that materialized views offer:

- **Query rewrite**. This is an example of an optimizer transformation that I showed in Listing 13-30. You don't need to rewrite your query to take advantage of the materialized view.

- **Materialized view logs**. These can be used to keep track of changes to the tables on which the materialized view is based so that changes can be applied to the materialized view incrementally.

- **Refresh on commit**. With this option every time a change is made to a table on which the materialized view is based the materialized view is updated incrementally using the materialized view logs.

This is just a taste of the features of materialized views. For a full tutorial on this complex feature I would recommend the Data Warehousing Guide. The Data Warehousing Guide also describes DIMENSION database objects, which are used to support in-row aggregate values.

Manual Aggregation and Join Tables

In reality, materialized views can be overkill for many applications. You don't necessarily want to deal with query rewrites that happen or don't happen when expected: you can write the queries so that they access the materialized view data directly. You don't necessarily want to worry about the substantial performance impact that materialized view logs and refresh on commit can have on DML performance: you can refresh the materialized view yourself.

If that is your position then you don't need to use the Oracle materialized view feature at all. For example, in a data warehousing application you might generate aggregated data yourself at the end of your daily load process. You can load the aggregated data into a regular table for use by queries during the online day.

You don't necessarily need to maintain both normalized and denormalized copies of your data either. You can, for example, store commonly used columns from a dimension table in a fact table so that joins can be eliminated. Such denormalization might even avoid the need for a star transformation. But if the high cost or complexity of a star transformation is your primary concern, there is a potentially superior solution. I will cover that solution next.

Just remember that denormalization carries the risk of inconsistency in your database, and you should consider whether you need to build some safeguards, such as reconciliation jobs, to mitigate that risk.

Bitmap Join Indexes

Bitmap join indexes are actually a very specialized form of denormalization. They are primarily used to avoid star transformations. I must say that I personally found the concept of a bitmap join index hard to grasp at first. Let me approach the concept slowly and in stages.

A regular single-column B-tree index takes each distinct value of a column and creates an index entry for each row that has that value. The matching rows in the table being indexed are identified by a ROWID. A bitmap index is similar except that the matching rows are identified by a bitmap rather than a list of ROWIDs. A function-based bitmap index is similar to a regular bitmap index except that the bitmaps are associated with an expression rather than a value that is explicitly stored in the table. Like a function-based bitmap index, the indexed values in a bitmap join index don't explicitly appear as a column in the table being indexed, but rather are associated with the indexed value indirectly. It is time for an example, I think. Take a look at Listing 15-8, which shows how we can use bitmap join indexes to improve the query in Listing 13-35.

Listing 15-8. Bitmap join indexes

```
CREATE TABLE sales_2
PARTITION BY RANGE (time_id)
   (PARTITION pdefault VALUES LESS THAN (maxvalue))
AS
   SELECT *
     FROM sh.sales
    WHERE time_id = DATE '2001-10-18';

CREATE TABLE customers_2
AS
   SELECT * FROM sh.customers;

CREATE TABLE products_2
AS
   SELECT * FROM sh.products;

ALTER TABLE products_2
   ADD CONSTRAINT products_2_pk PRIMARY KEY
 (prod_id) ENABLE VALIDATE;

ALTER TABLE customers_2
   ADD CONSTRAINT customers_2_pk PRIMARY KEY
 (cust_id) ENABLE VALIDATE;

BEGIN
   DBMS_STATS.gather_table_stats (
      ownname  => SYS_CONTEXT ('USERENV', 'CURRENT_SCHEMA')
     ,tabname  => 'SALES_2');
   DBMS_STATS.gather_table_stats (
      ownname  => SYS_CONTEXT ('USERENV', 'CURRENT_SCHEMA')
     ,tabname   => 'CUSTOMERS_2');
   DBMS_STATS.gather_table_stats (
      ownname  => SYS_CONTEXT ('USERENV', 'CURRENT_SCHEMA')
     ,tabname   => 'PRODUCTS_2');
END;
/
```

```
CREATE BITMAP INDEX sales_2_cust_ln_bjx
   ON sales_2 (c.cust_last_name)
   FROM customers_2 c, sales_2 s
   WHERE c.cust_id = s.cust_id
   LOCAL;

CREATE BITMAP INDEX sales_prod_category_bjx
   ON sales_2 (p.prod_category)
   FROM products_2 p, sales_2 s
   WHERE s.prod_id = p.prod_id
   LOCAL;

SELECT prod_name
      ,cust_first_name
      ,time_id
      ,amount_sold
  FROM customers_2 c, products_2 p, sales_2 s
 WHERE     s.cust_id = c.cust_id
       AND s.prod_id = p.prod_id
       AND c.cust_last_name = 'Everett'
       AND p.prod_category = 'Electronics';
```

```
--------------------------------------------------------------------------
| Id  | Operation                                  | Name                  |
--------------------------------------------------------------------------
|   0 | SELECT STATEMENT                           |                       |
|   1 |  NESTED LOOPS                              |                       |
|   2 |   NESTED LOOPS                             |                       |
|   3 |    HASH JOIN                               |                       |
|   4 |     TABLE ACCESS FULL                      | PRODUCTS_2            |
|   5 |     PARTITION RANGE SINGLE                 |                       |
|   6 |      TABLE ACCESS BY LOCAL INDEX ROWID BATCHED| SALES_2           |
|   7 |       BITMAP CONVERSION TO ROWIDS          |                       |
|   8 |        BITMAP AND                          |                       |
|   9 |         BITMAP INDEX SINGLE VALUE          | SALES_2_CUST_LN_BJX   |
|  10 |         BITMAP INDEX SINGLE VALUE          | SALES_PROD_CATEGORY_BJX |
|  11 |    INDEX UNIQUE SCAN                       | CUSTOMERS_2_PK        |
|  12 |   TABLE ACCESS BY INDEX ROWID              | CUSTOMERS_2           |
--------------------------------------------------------------------------
```

Listing 15-8 creates copies of the SH.SALES, SH.CUSTOMERS, and SH.PRODUCTS table rather than making DDL changes to the Oracle-supplied example schemas. Before creating any bitmap join indexes we need to create enabled, validated primary key constraints on our CUSTOMERS_2 and PRODUCTS_2 tables. The constraints in the example schemas aren't validated.

The first bitmap index we create is SALES_2_CUST_LN_BJX. This index identifies all the rows in SALES_2 that are associated with each value of CUST_LAST_NAME in the CUSTOMERS_2 table. This bitmap index allows us to identify all the rows in SALES_2 associated with customers that have the last name Everett without going anywhere near the CUSTOMERS_2 table. Similarly, the SALES_PROD_CATEGORY_BJX allows us to identify the rows in SALES_2 that are associated with products in the "Electronics" category without going anywhere near the PRODUCTS_2 table. By combining these indexes we can find the exact set of rows in SALES_2 that match both sets of predicates.

Although bitmap join indexes are similar to function-based indexes, they are also very similar to materialized join views. You could create a materialized join view that holds the value of CUST_LAST_NAME from CUSTOMERS_2 and the associated ROWID from SALES_2, and you would have essentially the same thing as a bitmap join index. However, the bitmap join index is much more compact and more efficient to use than a materialized join view.

The big problem with bitmap join indexes, as with any bitmap index, is that the DML on the tables associated with the index is inefficient. In fact, parallel DML on the dimension table will mark the bitmap join index as unusable. Accordingly, bitmap join indexes are really only useful in data-warehousing environments.

Compression

Compressing data is not a form of denormalization. With the exception of changes in performance, the use or lack of use of compression has no visible impact on users or developers of SQL. Let us look at index and table compression next. I will cover large object (LOB) compression when I mention LOBs a little later.

As a general rule, both index compression and table compression make DML more expensive and queries cheaper. This may sound counterintuitive, as queries need to decompress data. However, the decompression processes for both indexes and tables are very cheap, as we shall see, and even a modest reduction in logical I/O will more than compensate for the cost of decompressing. On the other hand, if you see an excessive amount of CPU used during data loading then you may want to try turning off compression features to see if it makes a difference.

Index Compression

Index compression is one of those Oracle features that should be used extensively but is often forgotten. Index compression is implemented at the block level. Basically, Oracle uses what is called a *prefix table* to store distinct values of the compressed columns in a block. Now, only a pointer to the prefix table entry is stored in the index entry rather than the values of the column or columns themselves. Oracle allows you to specify which columns, if any, to compress, but your choice is restricted: the syntax allows you to specify the number of columns to compress starting with the leading column. You can't, for example, choose to compress the second column but not the first.

Imagine you have 200 rows per block in a non-compressed index. First of all, if the number of distinct values of the compressed columns is normally just one or two per block, your prefix table will contain just one or two entries and you will be able to store a lot more than 200 rows per block in a compressed index. But suppose there are 150 distinct values of your leading column in the 200 uncompressed rows. Now index compression will be a problem because the 150 entries in the prefix table will consume most of the block, and all the extra overhead is likely to mean that you will no longer be able to fit all 200 rows in the block.

■ **Tip** The ANALYZE INDEX . . . VALIDATE STRUCTURE command can be used to determine the recommended number of columns to compress for an index. The recommended value can be found in the column OPT_CMPR_COUNT from the INDEX_STATS table.

Don't assume that just because an index is unique that it can't benefit from compression. Notice that the ORDER_ITEMS_PART_PK index created in Listing 15-6 was created specifying COMPRESS 1, a perfectly suitable thing to do if there are a large number of line items per day, because if you didn't compress it there would be a large number of index entries for each value of ORDER_DATE. It probably isn't worth compressing the ORDER_ID column unless there are a large number of line items in each order.

Notice that index compression isn't really compression at all. It is actually a form of *deduplication*, as Oracle likes to call it. Accordingly, there is no real work needed by queries for decompression. All the query has to do is follow a pointer to get the column value or values in the prefix table.

Table Compression

There are several flavors of table compression:

- **Basic table compression**. This is a compression variant that compresses table data for direct-path inserts and table moves only, which doesn't need additional licenses.

- **OLTP table compression**. In 11gR1 this feature was called *compression for all operations*. Basically it's the same thing as basic compression, but, unlike basic compression, data is also compressed on non-direct path INSERT operations. OLTP table compression requires either the Personal Edition or Enterprise Edition of the Oracle database product. In the case of Enterprise addition, the Oracle Advanced Compression needs to be purchased separately.

- **Hybrid columnar compression**. This is a totally different feature specific to Exadata- and Oracle-supplied storage. This topic is beyond the scope of this book.

Like index compression, basic compression and OLTP table compression are based on the concept of deduplication within a block. In other words, Oracle attempts to store each repeated value just once within a block. The implementation of table compression is somewhat more complicated than index compression. Oracle can reorder columns, deduplicate combinations of columns, and so on. For a detailed description of the internals of table compression, have a look at Jonathan Lewis' articles, starting here: http://allthingsoracle.com/compression-oracle-basic-table-compression/. Here are some important points to note:

- When you create a table with basic compression PCTFREE defaults to 0. When you create a table with OLTP compression the default value of PCTFREE remains 10.

- When you update a row in a table, the updated values aren't recompressed. This is probably why the 11gR1 name for OLTP compression, compression for all operations, was hurriedly changed!

- You should probably be wary of using either basic or OLTP compression on rows that are modified after insertion. This means that OLTP compression is best used for data loaded by non-direct-path INSERT statements, never modified, and then read repeatedly. As a consequence, you should probably override the value of PCTFREE when you create a table with OLTP compression. Listing 15-9 shows the basic syntax.

Listing 15-9. Creating a table with OLTP compression and overriding PCTFREE

```
CREATE TABLE order_items_compress
(
   order_id         INTEGER NOT NULL
  ,order_item_id    INTEGER NOT NULL
  ,order_date       DATE NOT NULL
  ,product_id       INTEGER
  ,quantity         INTEGER
  ,price            NUMBER
  ,CONSTRAINT order_items_compress_fk FOREIGN KEY
      (order_date, order_id)
      REFERENCES orders_part (order_date, order_id)
)
COMPRESS FOR OLTP
PCTFREE 0;
```

■ **Tip** Whether you use table compression or not, you should set PCTFREE to 0 whenever you are certain that no rows in your table ever increase in size as a result of UPDATE or MERGE operations.

LOBs

The term *LOB* stands for large object. It is not just the LOBs that are large—the topic is large too! In fact, Oracle has an entire manual, the *SecureFiles and Large Objects Developer's Guide,* dedicated to the topic. I will just pick out a few key features here.

- Your LOBs should be created as SecureFiles in a tablespace with Automatic Segment Space Management (ASSM). The other flavor of LOB, BasicFiles, will be deprecated in a future release of Oracle database, according to the manual.

- With the Advanced Compression option you can take advantage of both LOB deduplication and LOB compression.

- You can elect to cache LOBs for reads or for both reads and writes. By default, LOBs are not cached in the SGA at all.

- As long as you don't cache LOB data you can elect not to log LOB data. If you take advantage of this option, performance of INSERT operations will improve, but you will lose the LOB data on media recovery. This might be alright if you can just reload the data.

Summary

This chapter has covered a few features of physical database design that are of importance to SQL performance, but it makes no pretense at being a comprehensive guide. However, it is often the case that SQL performance issues are best addressed by physical database design changes, and hopefully this chapter will help you recognize these cases.

If you remember just one thing from this chapter it should be this: don't blindly add an index to solve a performance problem with a single query—at least not without some thought.

CHAPTER 16

Rewriting Queries

At the beginning of Chapter 1 I explained the naiveté of assuming that the CBO will come up with an optimal execution plan regardless of how you write your SQL statement. So far in this book you have already seen numerous cases where an improperly constructed SQL statement can cause the CBO to pick an inappropriate execution plan, there being quite a few examples in the last chapter alone. This chapter and the next explore the topic of rewriting SQL statements in more detail, but I won't pretend to be giving you a full list of problematic scenarios.

In fact, this chapter is a lot shorter than it would have needed to be if it had been written a few years ago; as the number of optimizer transformations increases, the number of SQL constructs that cause performance problems decreases. Nevertheless, there are still many cases where a SQL statement looks perfectly sensible to the casual reader but will need to be rewritten to achieve acceptable performance.

These days one of the most common reasons for rewriting a SQL statement is to address the problem of poorly performing sorts, and the next chapter is dedicated entirely to that topic. However, before we get into that complex topic let us look at a few simple examples of SQL rewrites that we haven't discussed earlier in the book.

Use of Expressions in Predicates

Generally speaking, you should try hard to avoid using expressions on columns used in predicates. We have already seen in Listing 14-1 that the use of a function in a predicate can cause cardinality errors in the CBO, but that isn't the only issue. Listing 16-1 shows how partition elimination can be affected by expressions.

Listing 16-1. Partition elimination and expressions in predicates

```
SELECT COUNT (DISTINCT amount_sold)
  FROM sh.sales
 WHERE EXTRACT (YEAR FROM time_id) = 1998;
```

Id	Operation	Name	Cost (%CPU)	Pstart	Pstop
0	SELECT STATEMENT		**528** (4)		
1	SORT AGGREGATE				
2	VIEW	VW_DAG_0	528 (4)		
3	HASH GROUP BY		528 (4)		
4	**PARTITION RANGE ALL**		528 (4)	**1**	**28**
5	TABLE ACCESS FULL	SALES	528 (4)	**1**	**28**

```
SELECT COUNT (DISTINCT amount_sold)
  FROM sh.sales
 WHERE time_id >=DATE '1998-01-01' AND time_id < DATE '1999-01-01';
```

Id	Operation	Name	Cost (%CPU)	Pstart	Pstop
0	SELECT STATEMENT		**118** (6)		
1	SORT AGGREGATE				
2	VIEW	VW_DAG_0	118 (6)		
3	HASH GROUP BY		118 (6)		
4	**PARTITION RANGE ITERATOR**		113 (2)	**5**	**8**
5	TABLE ACCESS FULL	SALES	113 (2)	**5**	**8**

Both queries in Listing 16-1 produce the same result: the number of distinct values of AMOUNT_SOLD in the SH.SALES table from 1998. The first query uses the EXTRACT function to identify the year of each sale. The second query uses two predicates to generate a range of dates. We can see that in the latter case we have been able to perform partition elimination and thus only accessed the partitions for 1998. In the former case we have had to access all the partitions in the table because the application of a function to the column value precludes partition elimination.

If there is no straightforward way to avoid using a function on a column used in a predicate, you might need to create a virtual column or add a function-based index as was demonstrated in Listing 15-2. Listing 16-2 shows another approach.

Listing 16-2. Using a join when a function is applied to a column

```
SELECT COUNT (DISTINCT amount_sold)
  FROM sh.sales
 WHERE EXTRACT (MONTH FROM time_id) = 10;
```

Id	Operation	Name	Cost (%CPU)	Pstart	Pstop
0	SELECT STATEMENT		**528** (4)		
1	SORT AGGREGATE				
2	VIEW	VW_DAG_0	528 (4)		
3	HASH GROUP BY		528 (4)		
4	PARTITION RANGE ALL		528 (4)	1	28
5	TABLE ACCESS FULL	SALES	528 (4)	1	28

```
SELECT COUNT (DISTINCT amount_sold)
  FROM sh.sales s, sh.times t
 WHERE EXTRACT (MONTH FROM t.time_id) = 10 AND t.time_id = s.time_id;
```

Id	Operation	Name	Cost (%CPU)	Pstart	Pstop
0	SELECT STATEMENT		**102** (1)		
1	SORT AGGREGATE				
2	VIEW	VW_DAG_0	102 (1)		
3	HASH GROUP BY		102 (1)		
4	NESTED LOOPS				
5	NESTED LOOPS		101 (0)		
6	INDEX FULL SCAN	TIMES_PK	0 (0)		
7	PARTITION RANGE ITERATOR			KEY	KEY
8	BITMAP CONVERSION TO ROWIDS				
9	BITMAP INDEX SINGLE VALUE	SALES_TIME_BIX		KEY	KEY
10	TABLE ACCESS BY LOCAL INDEX ROWID	SALES	101 (0)	1	1

Both queries in Listing 16-2 count the number of distinct values for AMOUNT_SOLD in SH.SALES that were made in the month of October (of any year). The execution plan for the first query accesses all the rows in the table because, as with the first query in Listing 16-1, no partition elimination is possible. The second query in Listing 16-2 performs an INDEX FULL SCAN on the TIMES_PK index of the SH.TIMES table. This extra step adds overhead, but the overhead (a single-block access) is recouped with interest because only the matching rows from the SH.SALES table are accessed. The net benefit may not be obvious, but you can see that on my laptop the CBO estimates a cost of 528 for the first query and 102 for the second. The second query actually ran faster as well!

Equality Versus Inequality Predicates

The use of an inequality operator in a predicate is sometimes unavoidable, but its misuse is so frequent that the SQL Tuning Advisor throws up a warning. Listing 16-3 shows a typical example.

Listing 16-3. Inappropriate use of an inequality operator

```
CREATE TABLE mostly_boring
(
    primary_key_id   INTEGER PRIMARY KEY
   ,special_flag     CHAR (1)
   ,boring_field     CHAR (100) DEFAULT RPAD ('BORING', 100)
)
PCTFREE 0;

INSERT INTO mostly_boring (primary_key_id, special_flag)
      SELECT ROWNUM, DECODE (MOD (ROWNUM, 10000), 0, 'Y', 'N')
        FROM DUAL
   CONNECT BY LEVEL <= 100000;

BEGIN
   DBMS_STATS.gather_table_stats (
       ownname       => SYS_CONTEXT ('USERENV', 'CURRENT_SCHEMA')
      ,tabname       => 'MOSTLY_BORING'
      ,method_opt    => 'FOR COLUMNS SPECIAL_FLAG SIZE 2');
END;
/

CREATE INDEX special_index
   ON mostly_boring (special_flag);

SELECT *
  FROM mostly_boring
 WHERE special_flag != 'N';
```

```
-----------------------------------------------------------------
| Id | Operation         | Name          | Rows | Cost (%CPU)|
-----------------------------------------------------------------
|  0 | SELECT STATEMENT  |               |   10 |  384   (1)|
|  1 |  TABLE ACCESS FULL| MOSTLY_BORING |   10 |  384   (1)|
-----------------------------------------------------------------
```

```
SELECT *
  FROM mostly_boring
 WHERE special_flag = 'Y';
```

```
--------------------------------------------------------------------------------
| Id  | Operation                           | Name           | Rows | Cost (%CPU)|
--------------------------------------------------------------------------------
|   0 | SELECT STATEMENT                    |                |   10 |   2    (0)|
|   1 |   TABLE ACCESS BY INDEX ROWID BATCHED| MOSTLY_BORING |   10 |   2    (0)|
|   2 |    INDEX RANGE SCAN                  | SPECIAL_INDEX  |   10 |   1    (0)|
--------------------------------------------------------------------------------
```

```
SELECT *
  FROM mostly_boring
 WHERE special_flag = 'N';
```

```
--------------------------------------------------------------------
| Id  | Operation         | Name          | Rows  | Cost (%CPU)|
--------------------------------------------------------------------
|   0 | SELECT STATEMENT  |               | 99990 |  384    (1)|
|   1 |  TABLE ACCESS FULL| MOSTLY_BORING | 99990 |  384    (1)|
--------------------------------------------------------------------
```

I have created a table called MOSTLY_BORING that contains 100,000 rows that are, you guessed it, mostly boring. There are, however, ten rows that have SPECIAL_FLAG set to Y; the remaining 99,990 rows have a value of N for SPECIAL_FLAG. When gathering statistics I specified a histogram for SPECIAL_FLAG so that the skew in the two values is recorded. When we query the table using the predicate SPECIAL_FLAG != N we use a full table scan. We can't take advantage of the index that we have set up. When we use the predicate SPECIAL_FLAG = 'Y' we can see that the index is used and a dramatic estimated cost saving is the result.

When we request all the boring rows with the predicate SPECIAL_FLAG = 'N' the CBO correctly selects a full table scan. There is no point in going through the index to read almost all the rows in the table. This means that the entries in the index for boring rows (SPECIAL_FLAG = 'N') will never be used. We can avoid storing these rows and make our index smaller. We can do this by a technique that some database theoreticians will brand as heretical: we can use the absence of a value (NULL) to indicate a boring row. Let us reload the table data this way.

Listing 16-4 reloads the data using a "value" of NULL instead of N to represent the 99,990 boring rows. We no longer need a histogram on SPECIAL_FLAG as there is now only one non-null value. The estimated cost of the modified query that selects the boring rows has reduced. This is expected because the fact that the value of N has been removed from the boring rows means that the table is slightly smaller and the cost of the full table scan has been reduced correspondingly. But what do we see with the query that selects the special rows? The estimated cost has increased from 2 to 11! Why? In fact, the increased estimated cost is correct, and the estimated cost of 2 in Listing 16-3 was too low. Why? Well, the original value of the clustering factor for SPECIAL_INDEX suggested that most of the time consecutive index entries would be in the same block. Whereas this was true for the majority of index entries (those with SPECIAL_FLAG = 'N'), it wasn't the case for our ten special rows, no two of which were in the same block! In fact, the BLEVEL of SPECIAL_INDEX has reduced from 1 to 0 as a result of the data change, so we do get a small performance improvement with the change regardless of what the CBO estimates.

Listing 16-4. Use of NULL to indicate a common value

```
TRUNCATE TABLE mostly_boring;

INSERT INTO mostly_boring (primary_key_id, special_flag)
      SELECT ROWNUM, DECODE (MOD (ROWNUM, 10000), 0, 'Y', NULL)
        FROM DUAL
  CONNECT BY LEVEL <= 100000;

BEGIN
  DBMS_STATS.gather_table_stats (
    ownname    => SYS_CONTEXT ('USERENV', 'CURRENT_SCHEMA')
   ,tabname    => 'MOSTLY_BORING');
END;
/

SELECT *
  FROM mostly_boring
 WHERE special_flag = 'Y';
```

```
-------------------------------------------------------------------------
| Id | Operation                            | Name          | Cost (%CPU)|
-------------------------------------------------------------------------
|  0 | SELECT STATEMENT                     |               |   11   (0)|
|  1 |  TABLE ACCESS BY INDEX ROWID BATCHED | MOSTLY_BORING |   11   (0)|
|  2 |   INDEX RANGE SCAN                   | SPECIAL_INDEX |    1   (0)|
-------------------------------------------------------------------------
```

```
SELECT *
  FROM mostly_boring
 WHERE special_flag IS NULL;
```

```
-------------------------------------------------------------------
| Id | Operation          | Name          | Rows  | Cost (%CPU)|
-------------------------------------------------------------------
|  0 | SELECT STATEMENT   |               | 99990 |   379   (1)|
|  1 |  TABLE ACCESS FULL | MOSTLY_BORING | 99990 |   379   (1)|
-------------------------------------------------------------------
```

Implicit Data-Type Conversions

The fact that the Oracle database automatically converts data from one type to another can be very convenient, particularly for business users throwing together an important ad-hoc query where development time is at a premium. However, this silent conversion may mask serious performance issues. Listing 16-5 shows one way that implicit data-type conversions can mask performance problems.

Listing 16-5. Implicit data-type conversion

```
CREATE TABLE date_table
(
  mydate      DATE
 ,filler_1    CHAR (2000)
)
```

```
PCTFREE 0;

INSERT INTO date_table (mydate, filler_1)
       SELECT SYSDATE, RPAD ('x', 2000)
          FROM DUAL
   CONNECT BY LEVEL <= 1000;

BEGIN
   DBMS_STATS.gather_table_stats (
      ownname  => SYS_CONTEXT ('USERENV', 'CURRENT_SCHEMA')
     ,tabname  => 'DATE_TABLE');
END;
/

CREATE INDEX date_index
   ON date_table (mydate);

SELECT mydate
  FROM date_table
 WHERE mydate = SYSTIMESTAMP;
```

```
---------------------------------------------------------------
| Id  | Operation          | Name       | Rows  | Cost (%CPU)|
---------------------------------------------------------------
|   0 | SELECT STATEMENT   |            |    10 |    70   (0)|
|*  1 |   TABLE ACCESS FULL| DATE_TABLE |    10 |    70   (0)|
---------------------------------------------------------------

Predicate Information (identified by operation id):
---------------------------------------------------

   1 - filter(SYS_EXTRACT_UTC(INTERNAL_FUNCTION("MYDATE"))=SYS_EXTRACT_U
             TC(SYSTIMESTAMP(6)))
```

```
SELECT mydate
  FROM date_table
 WHERE mydate = SYSDATE;
```

```
---------------------------------------------------------------
| Id  | Operation          | Name       | Rows  | Cost (%CPU)|
---------------------------------------------------------------
|   0 | SELECT STATEMENT   |            |     1 |     1   (0)|
|*  1 |   INDEX RANGE SCAN | DATE_INDEX |     1 |     1   (0)|
---------------------------------------------------------------

Predicate Information (identified by operation id):
---------------------------------------------------

   1 - access("MYDATE"=SYSDATE@!)
```

Listing 16-5 creates a table DATE_TABLE that includes an indexed column of type DATE. When we try to compare the column with a value of type TIMESTAMP WITH TIMEZONE, the column is implicitly converted to a TIMESTAMP WITH TIMEZONE data type, thus precluding the use of an index. When our predicate specifies a value of type DATE then the index can be used.

This sort of coding problem may seem obscure; who uses SYSTIMESTAMP rather than SYSDATE? However, this sort of problem actually occurs all the time when bind variables are used, particularly when the same PL/SQL variable is used for multiple SQL statements. Also bear in mind that the SQL*Plus VARIABLE command only supports a limited number of types, and DATE is not one of them.

Bind Variables

Although Oracle has introduced adaptive cursor sharing as a damage limitation exercise after having unleashed the wrath of bind variable peeking on us, I still recommend caution when using bind variables in predicates that involve columns with histograms. Let us put our MOSTLY_BORING table back the way it was in Listing 16-3 and see what happens when we use a bind variable for SPECIAL_FLAG.

Listing 16-6. Inappropriate use of bind variables

```
/*  SEE LISTING 16-3 for setup of MOSTLY_BORING table */

SELECT *
  FROM mostly_boring
 WHERE special_flag = :b1;
```

```
-----------------------------------------------------------------
| Id | Operation           | Name          | Rows  | Cost (%CPU)|
-----------------------------------------------------------------
|  0 | SELECT STATEMENT    |               | 50000 |   384   (1)|
|* 1 |   TABLE ACCESS FULL | MOSTLY_BORING | 50000 |   384   (1)|
-----------------------------------------------------------------
```

There are 100,000 rows in the table and two possible values of SPECIAL_FLAG so the CBO assumes that 50,000 rows will be returned by the query in Listing 16-6 when we use EXPLAIN PLAN. In fact, of course, if we run the statement both the cardinality estimate and the execution plan will be dependent on the supplied bind variable value. We will then end up using the same plan for repeated executions of our statement regardless of the value of the supplied bind variable on each occasion. There are several ways to address this problem. You can replicate code as I did in Listing 6-7 or you could use dynamic SQL to generate code with literal values. These approaches both result in the creation of two different SQL statements with independent plans. Since there are just two different execution plans you could write just one statement with a UNION ALL. Hold that thought for a short while and let us focus on UNION ALL.

UNION, UNION ALL, and OR

As a reader of a book entitled *Expert Oracle SQL* I am sure that you know the difference between the semantics of UNION, UNION ALL, and OR. Fortunately or unfortunately, depending on your perspective, a lot of SQL is written by business users with relatively little understanding of SQL performance issues, and the difference between these constructs is unclear to them. Listing 16-7 shows three statements that return identical results but have quite different execution plans.

Listing 16-7. Three equivalent statements with different plans

```
SELECT *
  FROM sh.customers
 WHERE cust_id = 3228
UNION ALL
```

```
SELECT *
  FROM sh.customers
 WHERE cust_id = 6783;
```

```
-------------------------------------------------------------------------
| Id  | Operation                    | Name         | Rows | Cost (%CPU)|
-------------------------------------------------------------------------
|   0 | SELECT STATEMENT             |              |   2  |   4  (50)|
|   1 |  UNION-ALL                   |              |      |          |
|   2 |   TABLE ACCESS BY INDEX ROWID| CUSTOMERS    |   1  |   2   (0)|
|*  3 |    INDEX UNIQUE SCAN         | CUSTOMERS_PK |   1  |   1   (0)|
|   4 |   TABLE ACCESS BY INDEX ROWID| CUSTOMERS    |   1  |   2   (0)|
|*  5 |    INDEX UNIQUE SCAN         | CUSTOMERS_PK |   1  |   1   (0)|
-------------------------------------------------------------------------
```

```
SELECT *
  FROM sh.customers
 WHERE cust_id = 3228
UNION
SELECT *
  FROM sh.customers
 WHERE cust_id = 6783;
```

```
-------------------------------------------------------------------------
| Id  | Operation                    | Name         | Rows | Cost (%CPU)|
-------------------------------------------------------------------------
|   0 | SELECT STATEMENT             |              |   2  |   4  (50)|
|   1 |  SORT UNIQUE                 |              |   2  |   4  (50)|
|   2 |   UNION-ALL                  |              |      |          |
|   3 |    TABLE ACCESS BY INDEX ROWID| CUSTOMERS   |   1  |   2   (0)|
|*  4 |     INDEX UNIQUE SCAN        | CUSTOMERS_PK |   1  |   1   (0)|
|   5 |    TABLE ACCESS BY INDEX ROWID| CUSTOMERS   |   1  |   2   (0)|
|*  6 |     INDEX UNIQUE SCAN        | CUSTOMERS_PK |   1  |   1   (0)|
-------------------------------------------------------------------------
```

```
SELECT *
  FROM sh.customers
 WHERE cust_id = 3228 OR cust_id = 6783;
```

```
-------------------------------------------------------------------------
| Id  | Operation                    | Name         | Rows | Cost (%CPU)|
-------------------------------------------------------------------------
|   0 | SELECT STATEMENT             |              |   2  |   5   (0)|
|   1 |  INLIST ITERATOR             |              |      |          |
|   2 |   TABLE ACCESS BY INDEX ROWID| CUSTOMERS    |   2  |   5   (0)|
|*  3 |    INDEX UNIQUE SCAN         | CUSTOMERS_PK |   2  |   3   (0)|
-------------------------------------------------------------------------
```

The three statements in Listing 16-7 all return two rows—the same two rows in each case. However, these statements all have different execution plans. To understand why this is, take a look at the three queries in Listing 16-8.

Listing 16-8. UNION, UNION ALL, and OR producing different results

```
SELECT cust_first_name, cust_last_name
  FROM sh.customers
 WHERE cust_first_name = 'Abner'
UNION ALL
SELECT cust_first_name, cust_last_name
  FROM sh.customers
 WHERE cust_last_name = 'Everett';  -- Returns 144 rows
```

```
-------------------------------------------------------------
| Id  | Operation           | Name      | Rows  | Cost (%CPU)|
-------------------------------------------------------------
|   0 | SELECT STATEMENT    |           |  173  |  845  (51)|
|   1 |  UNION-ALL          |           |       |           |
|*  2 |   TABLE ACCESS FULL | CUSTOMERS |   43  |  423   (1)|
|*  3 |   TABLE ACCESS FULL | CUSTOMERS |  130  |  423   (1)|
-------------------------------------------------------------
```

Predicate Information (identified by operation id):

```
   2 - filter("CUST_FIRST_NAME"='Abner')
   3 - filter("CUST_LAST_NAME"='Everett')
```

```
SELECT cust_first_name, cust_last_name
  FROM sh.customers
 WHERE cust_first_name = 'Abner'
UNION
SELECT cust_first_name, cust_last_name
  FROM sh.customers
 WHERE cust_last_name = 'Everett'; -- Returns 10 rows
```

```
-------------------------------------------------------------
| Id  | Operation           | Name      | Rows  | Cost (%CPU)|
-------------------------------------------------------------
|   0 | SELECT STATEMENT    |           |  173  |  845  (51)|
|   1 |  SORT UNIQUE        |           |  173  |  845  (51)|
|   2 |   UNION-ALL         |           |       |           |
|*  3 |    TABLE ACCESS FULL | CUSTOMERS |   43  |  423   (1)|
|*  4 |    TABLE ACCESS FULL | CUSTOMERS |  130  |  423   (1)|
-------------------------------------------------------------
```

Predicate Information (identified by operation id):

```
   3 - filter("CUST_FIRST_NAME"='Abner')
   4 - filter("CUST_LAST_NAME"='Everett')
```

```
SELECT cust_first_name, cust_last_name
  FROM sh.customers
 WHERE cust_first_name = 'Abner' OR cust_last_name = 'Everett' -- Returns 128 rows;


-------------------------------------------------------------
| Id  | Operation          | Name      | Rows  | Cost (%CPU)|
-------------------------------------------------------------
|   0 | SELECT STATEMENT   |           |     1 |   423  (1)|
|*  1 |   TABLE ACCESS FULL| CUSTOMERS |     1 |   423  (1)|
-------------------------------------------------------------


Predicate Information (identified by operation id):
---------------------------------------------------

   1 - filter("CUST_FIRST_NAME"='Abner' AND "CUST_LAST_NAME"='Everett')
```

All three queries in Listing 16-8 combine two subsets of rows from SH.CUSTOMERS. The first query in Listing 16-8 returns the 80 rows that match the first name Abner followed by the 64 rows that match the surname Everett. The second query returns only ten rows. The UNION operator removes all duplicate values from the select list, and it turns out that there are only ten distinct combinations of first and last name that match our predicates. The third query returns a different number of rows again. The OR condition does not remove duplicates, but it does ensure that if a particular row matches both predicates it is only returned once. Since there are 16 rows in the SH.CUSTOMERS table that have a first name of Abner and a last name of Everett, these 16 rows are returned by both halves of the UNION ALL query and only once by the OR operator, so there are 16 more rows in the result set of the UNION ALL query than in that of the query that uses the OR operator.

It is never a good idea to use UNION when UNION ALL is known to produce identical results. UNION just performs a UNION ALL and then performs a SORT UNIQUE operation. If the removal of duplicates is not required then the sort performed by UNION is just an unnecessary overhead, sometimes a significant one. As you can see in Listing 16-8, the OR operator used just one full table scan when the other constructs required two, and generally speaking you should use an OR operator instead of UNION or UNION ALL when the results are known to be identical. But let me show you a possible exception. Listing 16-9 returns to our MOSTLY_BORING table.

Listing 16-9. *Avoiding dynamic SQL with UNION ALL*

```
SELECT *
  FROM mostly_boring
 WHERE special_flag = 'Y' AND :b1 = 'Y'
UNION ALL
SELECT *
  FROM mostly_boring
 WHERE special_flag = 'N' AND :b1 = 'N';
```

```
--------------------------------------------------------------------------
| Id | Operation                          | Name          | Cost (%CPU)|
--------------------------------------------------------------------------
|  0 | SELECT STATEMENT                   |               | 386 (100)|
|  1 |  UNION-ALL                         |               |          |
|  2 |   FILTER                           |               |          |
|  3 |    TABLE ACCESS BY INDEX ROWID BATCHED| MOSTLY_BORING |   2   (0)|
|  4 |     INDEX RANGE SCAN               | SPECIAL_INDEX |   1   (0)|
|  5 |   FILTER                           |               |          |
|  6 |    TABLE ACCESS FULL               | MOSTLY_BORING | 384   (1)|
--------------------------------------------------------------------------
```

```
Predicate Information (identified by operation id):
---------------------------------------------------

   2 - filter(:B1='Y')
   4 - access("SPECIAL_FLAG"='Y')
   5 - filter(:B1='N')
   6 - filter("SPECIAL_FLAG"='N')
```

```
SELECT /*+ use_concat */
       *
  FROM mostly_boring
 WHERE    (special_flag = 'Y' AND :b1 = 'Y')
       OR (special_flag = 'N' AND :b1 = 'N');
```

```
--------------------------------------------------------------------------
| Id | Operation                          | Name          | Cost (%CPU)|
--------------------------------------------------------------------------
|  0 | SELECT STATEMENT                   |               | 387   (1)|
|  1 |  CONCATENATION                     |               |          |
|* 2 |   FILTER                           |               |          |
|  3 |    TABLE ACCESS BY INDEX ROWID BATCHED| MOSTLY_BORING |   2   (0)|
|* 4 |     INDEX RANGE SCAN               | SPECIAL_INDEX |   1   (0)|
|* 5 |   FILTER                           |               |          |
|* 6 |    TABLE ACCESS FULL               | MOSTLY_BORING | 385   (1)|
--------------------------------------------------------------------------
```

```
Predicate Information (identified by operation id):
---------------------------------------------------

   2 - filter(:B1='Y')
   4 - access("SPECIAL_FLAG"='Y')
   5 - filter(:B1='N')
```

```
    6 - filter("SPECIAL_FLAG"='N' AND (LNNVL(:B1='Y') OR
              LNNVL("SPECIAL_FLAG"='Y')))
```

Listing 16-9 shows how two different access paths can be combined in a single statement without dynamic SQL. The first query in Listing 16-9 uses a UNION ALL set operator. The first half of the query only selects rows if the value of the bind variable is Y. As such, an indexed access path is selected. The second half of the first query will only return rows if the value of the bind variable is N, and a full table scan is therefore appropriate. The FILTER operations on lines 2 and 5 ensure that only one of the two operations is performed.

The second query in Listing 16-9 accomplishes the same thing with an OR operator, but a USE_CONCAT hint is required; this is because the CBO doesn't realize that only one of the two halves of the statement will be executed and adds the cost of the full table scan and the cost of the indexed access path to arrive at the total statement cost. We know that only one half of the statement will be run and understand why the CBO costing is wrong. We can, therefore, provide the hint with confidence.

Issues with General Purpose Views

Data dictionary views are very useful, and the more complex the definition the more useful the view may be. Apart from the gains in productivity and the improvement in the readability of the queries that use the complex view, there is the potential to avoid changing code in multiple places when requirements change.

Unfortunately, the more complex the view the more likely it is that inefficiencies may creep in. This risk is much reduced in recent releases of Oracle database, as transformations such as join elimination have been introduced, but problems still exist. Listing 16-10 shows a typical example.

Listing 16-10. Inefficiencies with complex views

```
CREATE OR REPLACE VIEW sales_data
AS
   SELECT *
     FROM sh.sales
          JOIN sh.customers USING (cust_id)
          JOIN sh.products USING (prod_id);

  SELECT prod_name, SUM (amount_sold)
    FROM sales_data
GROUP BY prod_name;
```

```
---------------------------------------------------------------
| Id  | Operation               | Name         | Cost (%CPU)|
---------------------------------------------------------------
|   0 | SELECT STATEMENT        |              |   576   (6)|
|   1 |  HASH GROUP BY          |              |   576   (6)|
|*  2 |   HASH JOIN             |              |   576   (6)|
|   3 |    VIEW                 | VW_GBC_9     |   573   (6)|
|   4 |     HASH GROUP BY       |              |   573   (6)|
|*  5 |      HASH JOIN          |              |   552   (2)|
|   6 |       INDEX FAST FULL SCAN| CUSTOMERS_PK |    33   (0)|
|   7 |       PARTITION RANGE ALL |              |   517   (2)|
|   8 |        TABLE ACCESS FULL | SALES        |   517   (2)|
|   9 |    TABLE ACCESS FULL    | PRODUCTS     |     3   (0)|
---------------------------------------------------------------
```

Listing 16-10 begins by defining a view that joins SH.SALES, SH.CUSTOMERS and SH.PRODUCTS. You want to join SH.SALES and SH.PRODUCTS yourself and decide to use the view provided. After all, you know about the fancy join elimination transformation that the CBO has and are confident that your use of the view will not be inefficient. However, we can see that the execution plan still includes the join with the SH.CUSTOMERS table. The reason is that the referential integrity constraint that ensures that every row in SH.SALES has a corresponding row in SH.CUSTOMERS is not validated, so the join elimination isn't legal. To avoid this extra step you would need to join SH.SALES and SH.PRODUCTS yourself.

How to Use Temporary Tables

I showed in Listing 1-15 that you could, and generally should, use factored subqueries to avoid the use of temporary tables that are only required by a single SQL statement. It is theoretically possible for a temporary table to provide better performance than a factored subquery when an index of the temporary table can be used. However, this theoretical possibility is very rare because the cost of building and maintaining the index generally outweighs any benefit the index might bring to a single statement.

However, if multiple independent SQL statements in the same session use similar constructs then a temporary table might be a good idea to avoid repeating work. Listing 16-11 shows a procedure that is crying out for optimization.

Listing 16-11. Repeated construct in multiple SQL statements

```
CREATE TABLE key_electronics_customers
(
   cust_id                  NUMBER PRIMARY KEY
  ,latest_sale_month        DATE
  ,total_electronics_sold   NUMBER (10, 2)
);

CREATE TABLE electronics_promotion_summary
(
   sales_month              DATE
  ,promo_id                 NUMBER
  ,total_electronics_sold   NUMBER (10, 2)
  ,PRIMARY KEY (sales_month, promo_id)
);

CREATE OR REPLACE PROCEDURE get_electronics_stats_v1 (p_sales_month DATE)
IS
   v_sales_month        CONSTANT DATE := TRUNC (p_sales_month, 'MM'); -- Sanity check
   v_next_sales_month   CONSTANT DATE := ADD_MONTHS (v_sales_month, 1);
BEGIN
   --
   -- Identify key electronics customers from this month
   -- that spent more than 1000 on Electronics
   --
   MERGE INTO key_electronics_customers c
       USING (   SELECT cust_id, SUM (amount_sold) amount_sold
                 FROM sh.sales s JOIN sh.products p USING (prod_id)
                 WHERE     time_id >=v_sales_month
```

```
                        AND time_id < v_next_sales_month
                        AND prod_category = 'Electronics'
                GROUP BY cust_id
                    HAVING SUM (amount_sold) > 1000) t
            ON (c.cust_id = t.cust_id)
    WHEN MATCHED
    THEN
        UPDATE SET
            c.latest_sale_month = v_sales_month
            ,c.total_electronics_sold = t.amount_sold
    WHEN NOT MATCHED
    THEN
        INSERT     (cust_id, latest_sale_month, total_electronics_sold)
            VALUES (t.cust_id, v_sales_month, t.amount_sold);

    --
    -- Remove customers with little activity recently
    --
    DELETE FROM key_electronics_customers
        WHERE latest_sale_month < ADD_MONTHS (v_sales_month, -3);


    --
    -- Now generate statistics for promotions for sales in Electronics
    --
    MERGE INTO electronics_promotion_summary p
        USING (  SELECT promo_id, SUM (amount_sold) amount_sold
                    FROM sh.sales s JOIN sh.products p USING (prod_id)
                    WHERE      time_id >=v_sales_month
                        AND time_id < v_next_sales_month
                        AND prod_category = 'Electronics'
                GROUP BY promo_id) t
            ON (p.promo_id = t.promo_id AND p.sales_month = v_sales_month)
    WHEN MATCHED
    THEN
        UPDATE SET p.total_electronics_sold = t.amount_sold
    WHEN NOT MATCHED
    THEN
        INSERT     (sales_month, promo_id, total_electronics_sold)
            VALUES (v_sales_month, t.promo_id, t.amount_sold);
END get_electronics_stats_v1;
/
```

Listing 16-11 creates two tables and a procedure. KEY_ELECTRONICS_CUSTOMERS identifies the customers that have spent more than 1000 units of currency on electronics in one or more of the last three months. ELECTRONICS_PROMOTION_SUMMARY summarizes the total sales for electronics for each promotion in each month. These tables are maintained by a procedure, GET_ELECTRONICS_STATS_V1, that takes data from the SH.SALES and SH.PRODUCTS tables and merges it into the two tables.

We can see that the two MERGE statements access the SH.SALES and SH.PRODUCTS tables in remarkably similar ways: they both join the same way, they both select only rows for electronics for a particular month, and they both perform some kind of aggregation. We can optimize this code by performing the common work once and saving the results in a temporary table. Listing 16-12 shows the way.

Listing 16-12. Avoiding duplication of effort by using a temporary table

```
CREATE GLOBAL TEMPORARY TABLE electronics_analysis_gtt
(
   cust_id        NUMBER NOT NULL
  ,promo_id       NUMBER NOT NULL
  ,time_id        DATE
  ,amount_sold    NUMBER
) ON COMMIT DELETE ROWS;

CREATE OR REPLACE PROCEDURE get_electronics_stats_v2 (p_sales_month DATE)
IS
   v_sales_month        CONSTANT DATE := TRUNC (p_sales_month, 'MM'); -- Sanity check
   v_next_sales_month   CONSTANT DATE := ADD_MONTHS (v_sales_month, 1);
BEGIN
   --
   -- create semi-aggregated data for later use
   --

   DELETE FROM electronics_analysis_gtt; -- just in case

   INSERT INTO electronics_analysis_gtt (cust_id
                                        ,promo_id
                                        ,time_id
                                        ,amount_sold)
      SELECT cust_id
            ,promo_id
            ,MAX (time_id) time_id
            ,SUM (amount_sold) amount_sold
        FROM sh.sales JOIN sh.products p USING (prod_id)
        WHERE     time_id >=v_sales_month
              AND time_id < v_next_sales_month
              AND prod_category = 'Electronics'
     GROUP BY cust_id, promo_id;


   --
   -- Identify key electronics customers from this month
   -- that spent more than 1000 on Electronics
   --
   MERGE INTO key_electronics_customers c
      USING (  SELECT cust_id, SUM (amount_sold) amount_sold
                 FROM electronics_analysis_gtt
               GROUP BY cust_id
                 HAVING SUM (amount_sold) > 1000) t
         ON (c.cust_id = t.cust_id)
   WHEN MATCHED
```

```
THEN
    UPDATE SET
        c.latest_sale_month = v_sales_month
        ,c.total_electronics_sold = t.amount_sold
WHEN NOT MATCHED
THEN
    INSERT    (cust_id, latest_sale_month, total_electronics_sold)
        VALUES (t.cust_id, v_sales_month, t.amount_sold);

--
-- Remove customers with little activity recently
--
DELETE FROM key_electronics_customers
    WHERE latest_sale_month < ADD_MONTHS (v_sales_month, -3);

--
-- Now generate statistics for promotions for sales in Electronics
--
MERGE INTO electronics_promotion_summary p
    USING (  SELECT promo_id, SUM (amount_sold) amount_sold
                FROM electronics_analysis_gtt
             GROUP BY promo_id) t
        ON (p.promo_id = t.promo_id AND p.sales_month = v_sales_month)
WHEN MATCHED
THEN
    UPDATE SET p.total_electronics_sold = t.amount_sold
WHEN NOT MATCHED
THEN
    INSERT    (sales_month, promo_id, total_electronics_sold)
        VALUES (v_sales_month, t.promo_id, t.amount_sold);
END get_electronics_stats_v2;
/
```

Listing 16-12 begins by creating a global temporary table ELECTRONICS_ANALYSIS_GTT that will be used to store semi-aggregated data for use by our upgraded procedure GET_ELECTRONICS_STATS_V2. The upgraded procedure begins by generating data aggregated for each combination of CUST_ID and PROMO_ID for electronics in the specified month. The two MERGE statements then further aggregate the data in the temporary table.

If you run the procedure specifying 1st December 2001, the temporary table contains 1071 rows. Because we only start out with 4132 matching rows in the SH.SALES table the performance benefits of this optimization are not easy to measure, but in real life the amount of data reduction achieved by semi-aggregation can be much larger and the benefits quite substantial.

Avoiding Multiple Similar Subqueries

Just like the multiple similar aggregations in Listing 16-11, many SQL statements contain multiple similar subqueries. Listing 16-13 shows a typical example.

Listing 16-13. Multiple similar subqueries

```
SELECT p.prod_id
      ,p.prod_name
      ,p.prod_category
      , (SELECT SUM (amount_sold)
           FROM sh.sales s
          WHERE s.prod_id = p.prod_id)
           sum_amount_sold
      , (SELECT SUM (quantity_sold)
           FROM sh.sales s
          WHERE s.prod_id = p.prod_id)
           sum_quantity_sold
   FROM sh.products p;
```

```
-----------------------------------------------------------------
| Id  | Operation              | Name       | Cost (%CPU)|
-----------------------------------------------------------------
|   0 | SELECT STATEMENT       |            |  1078   (6)|
|   1 |  HASH JOIN OUTER       |            |  1078   (6)|
|   2 |   HASH JOIN OUTER      |            |   541   (6)|
|   3 |    TABLE ACCESS FULL   | PRODUCTS   |     3   (0)|
|   4 |    VIEW                | VW_SSQ_2   |   538   (6)|
|   5 |     HASH GROUP BY      |            |   538   (6)|
|   6 |      PARTITION RANGE ALL|           |   517   (2)|
|   7 |       TABLE ACCESS FULL| SALES      |   517   (2)|
|   8 |   VIEW                 | VW_SSQ_1   |   537   (6)|
|   9 |    HASH GROUP BY       |            |   537   (6)|
|  10 |     PARTITION RANGE ALL|            |   516   (2)|
|  11 |      TABLE ACCESS FULL | SALES      |   516   (2)|
-----------------------------------------------------------------
```

The query in Listing 16-13 calculates the total amount and total quantity of sales for each product using two similar subqueries in the select list. I have shown the execution plan from a 12cR1 database, and we can see that the CBO has managed to unnest the two subqueries. Unfortunately, as of the time of writing, the CBO is unable to coalesce these subqueries (I wouldn't be surprised if the CBO is able to do this at some point in the future), and so we are left with two full table scans on the SH.SALES table. We can see that the majority of the estimated cost comes from these two repeated full table scans.

There are actually several different ways to address the problem of replicated subqueries, but in this case we have a simple solution. Listing 16-14 shows how we can use a join to avoid duplicating work.

Listing 16-14. Use of a join to avoid repeated subqueries

```
SELECT p.prod_id
      ,p.prod_name
      ,p.prod_category
      ,SUM (amount_sold) sum_amount_sold
      ,SUM (quantity_sold) sum_quantity_sold
   FROM sh.sales s, sh.products p
  WHERE s.prod_id = p.prod_id
GROUP BY p.prod_id, p.prod_name, p.prod_category;
```

Id	Operation	Name	Cost (%CPU)	
0	SELECT STATEMENT		**541**	(6)|
1	HASH GROUP BY		**541**	(6)|
2	HASH JOIN		541	(6)|
3	VIEW	VW_GBC_5	538	(6)|
4	HASH GROUP BY		538	(6)|
5	PARTITION RANGE ALL|		**517**	(2)|
6	TABLE ACCESS FULL	SALES	**517**	(2)|
7	TABLE ACCESS FULL	PRODUCTS	3	(0)|

We can see that by simply joining the two tables and performing a GROUP BY we can get our aggregated values without the need to replicate our full table scan.

Summary

This chapter has provided examples of what many people refer to as *badly written SQL*. However, we need to bear in mind that code that is easy to read but performs badly today may perform perfectly well tomorrow when the CBO implements its next query transformation. Be that as it may, poorly performing SQL almost always either does work that it doesn't need to do, throwing the results away, or does work that it does need to do more than once. In this chapter I have provided only a taster of the more common scenarios in which the CBO is unable to generate an optimal plan until the query is rewritten. If you see an important SQL statement that seems to do redundant or repeated work you should think about rewriting it.

None of the examples in this chapter have looked at sorting data. I have found that a substantial amount of my time in the last few years has been spent trying to avoid the performance problems of pesky sorts. The next installment of our tale focusses entirely on the subject of sorts.

■ ■ ■

CHAPTER 17

Optimizing Sorts

I speculate that in the 1980s and 1990s the biggest source of SQL performance problems was probably poor join order. If you made the wrong choice of table to start your joins you would likely end up in a world of pain. These days we have a reasonably mature CBO and a sophisticated runtime engine that between them support right-deep join trees, star transformations, and a wealth of other fancy features. On the one hand, these improvements mean that join order is much less of a problem for those of us working with an Oracle database than it was. On the other hand, I seem to spend a lot of time these days sorting out sorts. All too often a SQL statement will apparently hang and gobble up all the temporary table space, bringing the entire database to a screeching halt. This chapter is dedicated entirely to the important topic of optimizing sorts and for the most part focuses on writing or rewriting SQL efficiently.

Sort optimization is almost entirely about one thing: stopping the sort from spilling to disk. And if you can't stop the sort from spilling to disk then you need to minimize the amount of disk activity that occurs. There are really only four ways to achieve this goal:

- Don't sort at all. Or sort less often. The most efficient sort is the one you don't do.

- Sort fewer columns. Fewer columns means less demand for memory.

- Sort fewer rows. Fewer rows means less demand on memory and fewer comparisons as well.

- Grab more memory for your sorts.

These concepts are easy enough to grasp, but achieving them is often quite tough. Before we get started on optimization let us review the basic mechanism that Oracle uses for sorting large amounts of data.

The Mechanics of Sorting

When we think of sorting most of us instinctively think about the ORDER BY clause. But sorting occurs in a number of other places as well. Sort merge joins, aggregate functions, analytic functions, set operations, model clauses, hierarchical queries, index builds and rebuilds and anything else that I have forgotten all involve sorts. All these sorting requirements are satisfied using variations of the same basic sort mechanism.

If you can sort all your rows in memory the sort is referred to as *optimal*. But what happens if you try and sort your data and it won't fit into memory without blowing the limit that the runtime engine has set? At some point your sort will spill to disk. In this section I want to talk about what happens when a sort cannot be fully achieved in memory. But first let me talk briefly about how limits on memory allocation are set.

Memory Limits for Sorts

Sorts are initially performed in an in-memory *workarea*. The upper limit on the size of this workarea is mainly controlled, indirectly, by the four initialization parameters: MEMORY_TARGET, PGA_AGGREGATE_TARGET, WORKAREA_SIZE_POLICY, and SORT_AREA_SIZE. The last two of these four parameters can be set at the session level.

If WORKAREA_SIZE_POLICY is set to AUTO then PGA_AGGREGATE_TARGET (or MEMORY_TARGET, if set) indirectly tries to regulate Program Global Area (PGA) memory allocations including workareas: as more memory is allocated by sessions in the instance the less memory will be allocated for new workareas. If you set WORKAREA_SIZE_POLICY to MANUAL (and you can do this at the session level) you have full control over the limits on workarea allocation. Generally it is a good idea to leave WORKAREA_SIZE_POLICY set to AUTO. However, you should set WORKAREA_SIZE_POLICY to MANUAL when you have a critical batch process that you know will be running at a quiet time of the day (or night) and that will need to allocate a substantial proportion of the available memory.

The algorithms for calculating the amount of memory for a workarea change from release to release, but the following statements apply to 11gR2 (at least):

- The maximum amount of memory that can be allocated to a workarea when the value of WORKAREA_SIZE_POLICY is set to the default value of AUTO is 1GB no matter how big PGA_AGGREGATE_TARGET is.

- The maximum amount of memory that can be allocated to a workarea when you set WOKAREA_SIZE_POLICY to MANUAL is just under 2GB.

- You can allocate more memory to a sort by using parallel query, as each parallel query slave gets its own workarea. However, once you have more than six parallel query slaves the amount of memory allocated to each parallel query slave is reduced to prevent the amount of memory allocated to a specific sort from getting any bigger. This implies that no matter what you do you can't allocate more than 12GB to any one sort.

Of course, these high numbers can't always be achieved. For one thing, a SQL statement may have more than one workarea active at once, and there are various undocumented limits that change from release to release that limit the total amount of memory that can be allocated to all workareas in a process at one time. Let me now discuss what happens when you can't get enough memory for your sort.

Disk-based Sorts

As rows are added to the in-memory workarea they are maintained in sorted order. When the in-memory workarea is full some of the sorted rows are written to the designated temporary tablespace. This disk-based area is known as a *sort run*. Once the sort run has been written to disk, memory is freed up for more rows. This process can be repeated many times until all the rows have been processed. Figure 17-1 illustrates how this works:

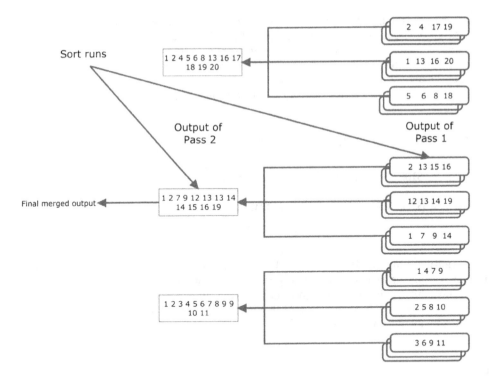

Figure 17-1. *A two-pass sort*

The nine boxes on the right of Figure 17-1 represent nine sort runs. The numbers in the boxes represent sorted rows, although in reality there would normally be many more than four rows in a sort run. Once all the sort runs have been created the first few blocks of each sort run are read back into memory, merged, and output. As the merged rows are output memory is freed up and more data can be read in from disk. This flavor of sort is referred to as a *one-pass sort* as each row is written to disk and read back just once.

However, what happens when there aren't nine sort runs generated by our first pass but 9,000? At that point you may not be able to fit even one block from all 9,000 sort runs into your workarea. In such a case, you read the first portion of only a subset of sort runs into memory and merge those. The merged rows aren't outputted as with a one-pass sort but are written to disk again creating yet another, larger sort run. Figure 17-1 shows nine sort runs produced from the first pass grouped into three subsets of three. Imagine that these three subsets each contain 3,000 sort runs from the first pass rather than just the three shown. Each subset is merged, creating three large sort runs. These three larger sort runs can now be merged to create the final output. This variant of sort is called a *two-pass sort* as each row is written to disk and read back twice. On the first pass each row is written to disk as part of a small sort run and in the second pass the row is written to a larger, merged sort run.

We can continue the thought process to its logical conclusion. What happens when we don't have 9,000 sort runs at the conclusion of our first pass but 9,000,000? Now at the end of our second pass we don't have three large merged sort runs, we have 3,000. At this point we are in serious trouble as we may need to reduce this number of large sort runs even further by creating mega-sized sort runs before we can produce our final sort results. This is a called a *three-pass sort* and by now I am sure you have the idea. As long as we have enough space in our temporary tablespace (and infinite patience) we can sort arbitrarily large sets of data this way.

The easiest way to determine whether an individual sort was optimal, one-pass, or multi-pass is to look at the column LAST_EXECUTION in V$SQL_PLAN_STATISTICS_ALL. Contrary to the documentation, this column will tell you the exact number of passes in a multi-pass sort. Not that you are likely to care too much: if you can't sort your data in one pass you probably will run out of time and patience.

If you run across a multi-pass sort your first thought will probably be to try and allocate more memory to your workarea. The columns ESTIMATED_OPTIMAL_SIZE and ESTIMATED_ONEPASS_SIZE in V$SQL_PLAN_STATISTICS_ALL give a rough idea of how big your workarea would need to be to get your sort to execute as an optimal or one-pass sort, respectively. The reported units are in bytes, and if you see a figure of 1TB (not uncommon) or more you need to figure out how to do less sorting. I'll discuss that in a minute, but just once in a while you may find that a slightly larger workarea will solve your problem. That being the case, you might include the following lines of dynamic SQL from Listing 17-1 in you PL/SQL code:

Listing 17-1. Manually increasing the size of memory for important sorts

```
BEGIN
    EXECUTE IMMEDIATE 'ALTER SESSION SET workarea_size_policy=manual';

    EXECUTE IMMEDIATE 'ALTER SESSION SET sort_area_size=2147483647';
END;
/
```

You should only use the code in Listing 17-1 for sorts that are both important and unavoidably large; you can't magically create more memory by allowing each process to grab as much as it wants. But once you have taken the step to open the floodgates there is no point in going half way: if you don't need the full 2GB it won't be allocated. Once your important sort has concluded your code should issue an ALTER SESSION SET WORKAREA_SIZE_POLICY=AUTO statement to close the floodgates on memory allocation.

Avoiding Sorts

I hope all of this discussion on the inefficiencies of multi-pass sorts has motivated you to avoid unnecessary sorts. I already showed you one way of eliminating a sort in Listing 7-17. In this section I will show you a couple more examples of how you can eliminate sorts.

Non-sorting Aggregate Functions

Imagine that you want to extract the largest value of AMOUNT_SOLD for each PROD_ID from the SH.SALES table and you want to know the CUST_ID with which such sales are associated. Listing 17-2 shows one approach that you may have learned about from other books.

Listing 17-2. Sorting rows with the FIRST_VALUE analytic function

```
WITH q1
    AS (SELECT prod_id
             ,amount_sold
             ,MAX (amount_sold) OVER (PARTITION BY prod_id) largest_sale
             ,FIRST_VALUE (
                 cust_id)
               OVER (PARTITION BY prod_id
                     ORDER BY amount_sold DESC, cust_id ASC)
                largest_sale_customer
         FROM sh.sales)
SELECT DISTINCT prod_id, largest_sale, largest_sale_customer
  FROM q1
 WHERE amount_sold = largest_sale;
```

```
-------------------------------------------------------------
| Id | Operation              | Name  | Rows  | Cost (%CPU)|
-------------------------------------------------------------
|  0 | SELECT STATEMENT       |       |    72 | 5071    (1)|
|  1 |  HASH UNIQUE           |       |    72 | 5071    (1)|
|  2 |   VIEW                 |       | 918K  | 5050    (1)|
|  3 |    WINDOW SORT         |       | 918K  | 5050    (1)|
|  4 |     PARTITION RANGE ALL|       | 918K  |  517    (2)|
|  5 |      TABLE ACCESS FULL | SALES | 918K  |  517    (2)|
-------------------------------------------------------------
```

The FIRST_VALUE analytic function is used in this example to identify the value of CUST_ID that is associated with the largest value of AMOUNT_SOLD per product (the first value when the rows are sorted by AMOUNT_SOLD in descending order). One problem with the FIRST_VALUE function is that when there are multiple values of CUST_ID that all made transactions with the largest value of AMOUNT_SOLD the result is unspecified. To avoid ambiguity we also sort by CUST_ID so that we are guaranteed to get the lowest value from the qualifying set of values of CUST_ID.

As you can see from the execution plan, we sort all 918,843 rows in our factored subquery before throwing all but 72 of those rows away in our main query. This is a very inefficient way to go about things, and I recommend against using the FIRST_VALUE analytic function in most cases. Many professional SQL programmers that I have met use the trick in Listing 17-3 in an attempt to improve matters.

Listing 17-3. Using ROW_NUMBER

```
WITH q1
    AS (SELECT prod_id
               ,amount_sold
               ,cust_id
               ,ROW_NUMBER ()
               OVER (PARTITION BY prod_id
                     ORDER BY amount_sold DESC, cust_id ASC)
                 rn
          FROM sh.sales)
SELECT prod_id, amount_sold largest_sale, cust_id largest_sale_customer
  FROM q1
 WHERE rn = 1;
```

```
-------------------------------------------------------------
| Id | Operation                | Name  | Rows  | Cost (%CPU)|
-------------------------------------------------------------
|  0 | SELECT STATEMENT         |       | 918K  | 5050    (1)|
|  1 |  VIEW                    |       | 918K  | 5050    (1)|
|  2 |   WINDOW SORT PUSHED RANK|       | 918K  | 5050    (1)|
|  3 |    PARTITION RANGE ALL   |       | 918K  |  517    (2)|
|  4 |     TABLE ACCESS FULL    | SALES | 918K  |  517    (2)|
-------------------------------------------------------------
```

The WINDOW SORT PUSHED RANK operation in Listing 17-3 sounds like it might be more efficient than the WINDOW SORT in Listing 17-2, but actually it is less so. If you take a 10032 trace you will see that the ROW_NUMBER analytic function uses what is known as a *version 1 sort*, which is a memory-intensive, insertion-based sort, whereas the FIRST_VALUE function uses a *version 2 sort*, which is apparently a fancy combination of a radix sort and a quick sort[1] that requires much less memory and fewer comparisons.

We can do much better than this. Take a look at Listing 17-4.

Listing 17-4. Optimizing sorts with the FIRST aggregate function

```
SELECT prod_id
      ,MAX (amount_sold) largest_sale
      ,MIN (cust_id) KEEP (DENSE_RANK FIRST ORDER BY amount_sold DESC)
          largest_sale_customer
  FROM sh.sales
GROUP BY prod_id;
```

Id	Operation	Name	Rows	Cost (%CPU)
0	SELECT STATEMENT			72	538 (6)
1	SORT GROUP BY			72	538 (6)
2	PARTITION RANGE ALL			918K	517 (2)
3	TABLE ACCESS FULL	SALES		918K	517 (2)

The FIRST aggregate function has a name that is very similar to FIRST_VALUE, but that is where the similarity ends. FIRST just keeps one row for each of the 72 products and as a result only consumes a tiny amount of memory. The improvement in performance is not quite as significant as the estimated cost suggests but it is still measurable, even with the small volumes from the example schema.

In some cases the FIRST and LAST functions can be even more efficient and avoid a sort altogether! What happens if we just want to know about the largest value of AMOUNT_SOLD in the entire table rather than for each product? Listing 17-5 shows what we get.

Listing 17-5. Avoiding a sort with the FIRST aggregate function

```
SELECT MAX (amount_sold) largest_sale
      ,MIN (cust_id) KEEP (DENSE_RANK FIRST ORDER BY amount_sold DESC)
          largest_sale_customer
  FROM sh.sales;
```

Id	Operation	Name	Rows	Cost (%CPU)
0	SELECT STATEMENT			1	517 (2)
1	SORT AGGREGATE			1	
2	PARTITION RANGE ALL			918K	517 (2)
3	TABLE ACCESS FULL	SALES		918K	517 (2)

---

[1]According to the article on the HelloDBA website http://www.hellodba.com/reader.php?ID=185&lang=en

When we eliminate the GROUP BY clause the SORT GROUP BY operation is replaced by a SORT AGGREGATE operation. I am sure you remember from Chapter 3 that the SORT AGGREGATE operation never sorts.

Index Range Scans and Index Full Scans

An index is basically just a sorted list of values of a column or columns together with the table ROWIDs, and sometimes we can use this pre-sorted list to avoid sorts in our queries. As I explained in Chapter 10, access via an index may be more costly than a full table scan so it isn't always a good idea. But the larger the amount of data being sorted the greater the potential for performance gains when we eliminate a sort. Listing 17-6 shows a fabricated test case.

Listing 17-6. Using an index to avoid a sort

```
SELECT /*+ cardinality(s 1e9) */
       s.*
  FROM sh.sales s
ORDER BY s.time_id;
```

```
---------------------------------------------------------------------------
| Id | Operation                          | Name          | Rows  | Cost (%CPU)|
---------------------------------------------------------------------------
|  0 | SELECT STATEMENT                   |               | 1000M | 3049   (1)|
|  1 |  PARTITION RANGE ALL               |               | 1000M | 3049   (1)|
|  2 |   TABLE ACCESS BY LOCAL INDEX ROWID| SALES         | 1000M | 3049   (1)|
|  3 |    BITMAP CONVERSION TO ROWIDS     |               |       |           |
|  4 |     BITMAP INDEX FULL SCAN         | SALES_TIME_BIX|       |           |
---------------------------------------------------------------------------
```

Listing 17-6 uses a cardinality hint to see what the CBO would do if the SH.SALES table actually held 1,000,000,000 rows and we wanted to sort all the rows by TIME_ID. We can use our index on TIME_ID to avoid any kind of sort because the data is already sorted in the index. Notice how the PARTITION RANGE ALL operation appears *above* the other operations in the execution plan. This is because we are sorting by our partitioning key and the partitions already partially sort our data so that we can go through each partition one after the other.

■ **Tip** It is quite common to partition a table by LIST and for each partition to have just one value. We might, for example, repartition SH.SALES by LIST and have one partition for each TIME_ID. In this type of situation sorts on multiple partitions by the partitioning column can still be achieved by processing partitions one after the other provided that the partitions are in the correct order and that *there is no default partition*!

What if we want to sort our data by a different column? Listing 17-7 shows why things get a little more complicated.

Listing 17-7. A failed attempt to use a local index to sort data

```
SELECT /*+ cardinality(s 1e9) index(s (cust_id)) */
       s.*
  FROM sh.sales s
ORDER BY s.cust_id;
```

```
-------------------------------------------------------------------------------------
| Id | Operation                                   | Name            | Rows  | Cost (%CPU)|
-------------------------------------------------------------------------------------
|  0 | SELECT STATEMENT                            |                 | 1000M | 8723K  (1)|
|  1 |  SORT ORDER BY                              |                 | 1000M | 8723K  (1)|
|  2 |   PARTITION RANGE ALL                       |                 | 1000M | 3472   (1)|
|  3 |    TABLE ACCESS BY LOCAL INDEX ROWID BATCHED| SALES           | 1000M | 3472   (1)|
|  4 |     BITMAP CONVERSION TO ROWIDS             |                 |       |           |
|  5 |      BITMAP INDEX FULL SCAN                  | SALES_CUST_BIX  |       |           |
-------------------------------------------------------------------------------------
```

Listing 17-7 uses a hint to try to force an execution plan similar to that in Listing 17-6, but of course it doesn't work. The local index SALES_CUST_BIX returns rows from each partition in order, but this is not the same thing as sorting data for the table as a whole—we achieved nothing other than adding overhead by adding the hint. Of course a global B-tree index would avoid this issue, but there is an alternative approach shown by Listing 17-8.

Listing 17-8. Use of a dimension table to avoid a global index

```
SELECT /*+ cardinality(s 1e9) */
       s.*
  FROM sh.sales s, sh.customers c
 WHERE s.cust_id = c.cust_id
ORDER BY s.cust_id;
```

```
-------------------------------------------------------------------------------
| Id | Operation                           | Name           | Rows  | Cost (%CPU)|
-------------------------------------------------------------------------------
|  0 | SELECT STATEMENT                    |                | 1000M | 1740K  (1)|
|  1 |  NESTED LOOPS                       |                |       |           |
|  2 |   NESTED LOOPS                      |                | 1000M | 1740K  (1)|
|  3 |    INDEX FULL SCAN                  | CUSTOMERS_PK   | 55500 |  116   (0)|
|  4 |     PARTITION RANGE ALL             |                |       |           |
|  5 |      BITMAP CONVERSION TO ROWIDS    |                |       |           |
|  6 |       BITMAP INDEX SINGLE VALUE     | SALES_CUST_BIX |       |           |
|  7 |    TABLE ACCESS BY LOCAL INDEX ROWID| SALES          | 18018 | 1740K  (1)|
-------------------------------------------------------------------------------
```

To the casual reader the join of SH.SALES with SH.CUSTOMERS serves no purpose, but we now have a full set of customers sorted by CUST_ID. The INDEX FULL SCAN on the dimension table's primary key index returns the customers in the correct order, and for each index entry we can the pick the desired rows from the SH.SALES table. The resulting execution plan is still far from optimal. We have to access all the partitions in the table for each CUST_ID but the performance gain may be just enough to dissuade you from creating a global index on SH.SALES and incurring the attendant maintenance issues.

Avoiding Duplicate Sorts

Sometimes sorts are unavoidable, but let us try not to sort more often than we need to. There's no point in sorting the same data twice, but sometimes that sort of duplication happens. Avoid it whenever you can. Listing 17-9 shows a query resulting in a double-sort. The query looks like a perfectly well-written SQL statement until we look at the execution plan.

Listing 17-9. Redundant sorting

```
  SELECT cust_id
        ,time_id
        ,SUM (amount_sold) daily_amount
        ,SUM (
            SUM (amount_sold))
        OVER (PARTITION BY cust_id
              ORDER BY time_id
              RANGE BETWEEN INTERVAL '6' DAY PRECEDING AND CURRENT ROW)
            weekly_amount
    FROM sh.sales
GROUP BY cust_id, time_id
ORDER BY cust_id, time_id DESC;
```

```
-----------------------------------------------------------
| Id | Operation            | Name  | Rows  | Cost (%CPU)|
-----------------------------------------------------------
|  0 | SELECT STATEMENT     |       |  143K|  5275   (1)|
|  1 |  SORT ORDER BY       |       |  143K|  5275   (1)|
|  2 |   WINDOW SORT        |       |  143K|  5275   (1)|
|  3 |    PARTITION RANGE ALL|      |  143K|  5275   (1)|
|  4 |     SORT GROUP BY    |       |  143K|  5275   (1)|
|  5 |      TABLE ACCESS FULL| SALES |  918K|   517   (2)|
-----------------------------------------------------------
```

Listing 17-9 aggregates the data so that multiple sales by the same customer on the same day are added together. This could have been done using hash aggregation but the CBO decided to use a sort. So be it. We then use a windowing clause in our analytic function to determine the total sales by the current customer in the week up to and including the current day. This requires a second sort. However, we wish the data to be presented by customer in *descending* date order. This seems to require a third sort. With a small change to our code we can avoid one of these sorts. Listing 17-10 shows the way.

Listing 17-10. Avoiding the redundant sort

```
SELECT cust_id
      ,time_id
      ,SUM (amount_sold) daily_amount
      ,SUM (
          SUM (amount_sold))
      OVER (PARTITION BY cust_id
            ORDER BY time_id DESC
            RANGE BETWEEN CURRENT ROW AND INTERVAL '6' DAY FOLLOWING)
          weekly_amount
    FROM sh.sales
GROUP BY cust_id, time_id
ORDER BY cust_id, time_id DESC;
```

```
---------------------------------------------------------------
| Id  | Operation          | Name  | Rows  | Cost (%CPU)|
---------------------------------------------------------------
|   0 | SELECT STATEMENT   |       | 918K| 5745   (1)|
|   1 |  WINDOW SORT       |       | 918K| 5745   (1)|
|   2 |   PARTITION RANGE ALL|     | 918K| 5745   (1)|
|   3 |    SORT GROUP BY   |       | 918K| 5745   (1)|
|   4 |     TABLE ACCESS FULL| SALES | 918K|  517   (2)|
---------------------------------------------------------------
```

Our analytic function now orders the data in the same way as our ORDER BY clause, and this way one sort is eliminated. Notice how the CBO cost estimates make no sense in either the execution plan for Listing 17-9 or for Listing 17-10. Listing 17-10 is, however, more efficient.

Sorting Fewer Columns

Now that we have made sure that we are only sorting when we need to, we can start to focus on optimizing the sorts that remain. One step we can take is to minimize the number of columns we sort. The fewer columns we sort the more likely it is that our sort will fit into our workarea. Let us start out with a sort on an un-indexed column and see what we can do.

Taking Advantage of ROWIDs

Imagine that you worked in a car showroom and wanted to physically sort fifty cars into price order. Would you drive the cars around trying to get the order right? Probably not. You might write the names and prices of the cars on pieces of paper and sort the pieces of paper. Once you had sorted the pieces of paper you could pick the actual cars up one at a time in the correct order.

You can sometimes use an analogous approach to sorting rows in an Oracle database. If the rows are very wide and the sort keys relatively narrow it might be best to replace the columns not required for the sort with a ROWID. After the ROWIDs have been sorted you can use those ROWIDs to retrieve the remaining columns in the table.

It is time for an example. Listing 17-11 shows a fairly costly sort that results from a query written in a fairly natural way.

Listing 17-11. Sorting by an un-indexed column

```
SELECT /*+ cardinality(s 1e9) */
       *
  FROM sh.sales s
       JOIN sh.customers c USING (cust_id)
       JOIN sh.products p USING (prod_id)
ORDER BY cust_id;
```

Id	Operation	Name	Rows	Bytes	TempSpc	Cost
0	SELECT STATEMENT		1000M	364G		59
1	MERGE JOIN		1000M	364G		59
2	**SORT JOIN**		1000M	188G	**412G**	59
* 3	HASH JOIN		1000M	188G		21907
4	TABLE ACCESS FULL	PRODUCTS	72	12456		3
5	PARTITION RANGE ALL		1000M	27G		12955
6	TABLE ACCESS FULL	SALES	1000M	27G		12955
* 7	**SORT JOIN**		55500	10M	**25M**	2709
8	TABLE ACCESS FULL	CUSTOMERS	55500	10M		415

Listing 17-11 makes a natural join between our SH.SALES fact table and two of the dimension tables. The resulting wide rows are then sorted. Once again I have used a cardinality hint to try and simulate a much larger fact table. As you can see, the CBO estimates that we would need 412.025GB of space in our temporary table space to perform two sorts. The CBO has used a MERGE JOIN because the results of this join are automatically sorted and our big join doesn't need the columns from the SH.CUSTOMERS table. Clever, yes, a big win, no.

We can sort a lot less data. One or two optimizer hints are required in Listing 17-12.

Listing 17-12. Sorting fewer columns and using ROWID

```
WITH q1
    AS ( SELECT /*+ cardinality(s1 1e9) */
                    ROWID rid
            FROM sh.sales s1
        ORDER BY cust_id)
SELECT /*+ cardinality(s2 1e9) leading(q1 s2 c p)
        use_nl(s2)
        rowid(s2)
        use_hash(c)
        use_hash(p)
        swap_join_inputs(c)
        swap_join_inputs(p)
        */
        *
  FROM q1
        JOIN sh.sales s2 ON s2.ROWID = q1.rid
        JOIN sh.customers c USING (cust_id)
        JOIN sh.products p USING (prod_id);
```

Id	Operation	Name	Rows	Bytes	TempSpc	Cost
0	SELECT STATEMENT		1088G	411T		4432
* 1	HASH JOIN		1088G	411T		4432
2	TABLE ACCESS FULL	PRODUCTS	72	12456		3
* 3	HASH JOIN		1088G	240T	10M	4423
4	TABLE ACCESS FULL	CUSTOMERS	55500	10M		415
5	NESTED LOOPS		1088G	53T		1006
6	VIEW		1000M	23G		5602
7	**SORT ORDER BY**		1000M	15G	**26G**	5602
8	PARTITION RANGE ALL		1000M	15G		406
9	BITMAP CONVERSION TO ROWIDS		1000M	15G		406
10	BITMAP INDEX FAST FULL SCAN	SALES_CUST_BIX				
11	TABLE ACCESS BY USER ROWID	SALES	1088	31552		1

Take a breath and stay calm. This isn't as complicated as it appears. Let us look at the subquery Q1 in Listing 17-12. We order all the ROWIDs in SH.SALES by CUST_ID. We only need to access the SALES_CUST_BIX index to do this. We don't use an INDEX FULL SCAN as the local index doesn't provide the global ordering that we need, so an INDEX FAST FULL SCAN is more appropriate. Notice that the sort is only estimated to take 26GB as we have just two columns: CUST_ID and ROWID. Once we have the list of ROWIDs in SH.SALES in the right order we can get a hold of the rest of the columns from SH.SALES by using the ROWID. Once we have all the columns from SH.SALES we can access the columns in the dimension tables using nested loops joins. However, a right-deep join tree using hash joins is more efficient as there are fewer logical reads.

Why do we need this complex rewrite and all these hints? Because this is a very complex query transformation, and as I explained in Chapter 14 the CBO can't perform all the query transformations that an expert SQL programmer can. In fact, the CBO doesn't recognize that the rows will be produced in sorted order and will perform a redundant sort if we add an ORDER BY clause.

Another way to use ROWIDs to improve sort performance involves the FIRST and LAST functions. Listing 17-13 shows a concise and efficient alternative to the ROW_NUMBER technique shown in Listing 17-3.

Listing 17-13. Use of the ROWID function with the LAST function

```
WITH q1
     AS (SELECT c.*
              ,SUM (amount_sold) OVER (PARTITION BY cust_state_province)
                  total_province_sales
              ,ROW_NUMBER ()
               OVER (PARTITION BY cust_state_province
                     ORDER BY amount_sold DESC, c.cust_id DESC) rn
          FROM sh.sales s JOIN sh.customers c ON s.cust_id = c.cust_id)
SELECT *
  FROM q1
 WHERE rn = 1;
```

```
-----------------------------------------------------------------
| Id  | Operation                | Name      | Rows  | Cost (%CPU)|
-----------------------------------------------------------------
|   0 | SELECT STATEMENT         |           | 918K| 41847    (1)|
|*  1 |  VIEW                    |           | 918K| 41847    (1)|
|   2 |   WINDOW SORT            |           | 918K| 41847    (1)|
|*  3 |    HASH JOIN             |           | 918K|  2093    (1)|
|   4 |     TABLE ACCESS FULL    | CUSTOMERS | 55500 |   271    (1)|
|   5 |     PARTITION RANGE ALL  |           | 918K|   334    (3)|
|   6 |      TABLE ACCESS FULL   | SALES     | 918K|   334    (3)|
-----------------------------------------------------------------
```

Predicate Information (identified by operation id):

```
   1 - filter("RN"=1)
   3 - access("S"."CUST_ID"="C"."CUST_ID")
```

```
WITH q1
     AS (  SELECT MIN (c.ROWID) KEEP (DENSE_RANK LAST ORDER BY amount_sold, cust_id)
                    cust_rowid
                 ,SUM (amount_sold) total_province_sales
             FROM sh.sales s JOIN sh.customers c USING (cust_id)
         GROUP BY cust_state_province)
SELECT c.*, q1.total_province_sales
  FROM q1 JOIN sh.customers c ON q1.cust_rowid = c.ROWID;
```

```
--------------------------------------------------------------------
| Id  | Operation                    | Name      | Rows  | Cost (%CPU)|
--------------------------------------------------------------------
|   0 | SELECT STATEMENT             |           | 80475 | 1837   (2)|
|   1 |  NESTED LOOPS                |           | 80475 | 1837   (2)|
|   2 |   VIEW                       |           |   145 | 1692   (3)|
|   3 |    SORT GROUP BY             |           |   145 | 1692   (3)|
|*  4 |     HASH JOIN                |           |  918K | 1671   (1)|
|   5 |      TABLE ACCESS FULL       | CUSTOMERS | 55500 |  271   (1)|
|   6 |      PARTITION RANGE ALL     |           |  918K |  334   (3)|
|   7 |       TABLE ACCESS FULL      | SALES     |  918K |  334   (3)|
|   8 |   TABLE ACCESS BY USER ROWID | CUSTOMERS |   555 |    1   (0)|
--------------------------------------------------------------------
```

Predicate Information (identified by operation id):

```
   4 - access("S"."CUST_ID"="C"."CUST_ID")
```

The first query in Listing 17-13 uses the ROW_NUMBER analytic function to identify the customer with the largest single sale for each province and the SUM analytic function to calculate the total AMOUNT_SOLD for that province. The query is inefficient because 918,843 rows are sorted and these rows include all 23 columns from SH.CUSTOMERS. Just like Listing 17-4, the use of the FIRST or LAST functions would improve performance because the workarea for the aggregating sort would only contain one row for each of the 141 provinces (the estimate of 145 is slightly out) rather than the 918,843 rows for the analytic sort.

Despite the potential for performance improvement, the prospect of recoding this query may appear daunting. It looks like you need to write 23 calls to the LAST aggregate function, one for each column in the SH.CUSTOMERS table. However, the second query in Listing 17-13 only requires one call to LAST for the ROWID. Notice that the MIN (C.ROWID) aggregate supplied with LAST could have been MAX (C.ROWID) or even AVG (C.ROWID) with no change in the outcome because the ORDER BY clause has restricted the number of rows being aggregated to one. This use of ROWID saved typing and avoided the lengthy illegible SQL that would arise from 23 separate calls to LAST. Not only is the technique shown in the second query in Listing 17-13 concise, it may further improve performance because now not only has the number of rows being sorted been reduced to 141, but the number of columns in the workarea has been reduced to just 5: CUST_ROWID, CUST_ID, AMOUNT_SOLD, CUST_STATE_PROVINCE, and TOTAL_PROVINCE_SALES.

Solving the Pagination Problem

I would like to think that some of the material in this book has not been written about before. This section is not one of them! There are so many articles on the pagination problem I have no idea who to credit with the original research. In all probability several people have come up with the same ideas independently. So what is the pagination problem? We have all been there. We use a browser to list a long list of sorted items. A Google search on SQL will produce several pages of results. What happens when you select page 2?

Assuming that your browser session ultimately results in a query against an Oracle table and that there are 20 items displayed per browser page, the database query has to pick rows 21 to 40 from a sorted list. Since the query is coming from a stateless web browser interface we can't keep cursors open, as the vast majority of users will never select the second page. Listing 17-14 modifies the query in Listing 17-12 to pick out the second set of 20 rows.

Listing 17-14. A solution to the pagination problem

```
WITH q1
    AS (  SELECT /*+ cardinality(s1 1e9) */
                 ROWID rid
            FROM sh.sales s1
         ORDER BY cust_id)
    ,q2
    AS (SELECT ROWNUM rn, rid
          FROM q1
         WHERE ROWNUM <= 40)
    ,q3
    AS (SELECT rid
          FROM q2
         WHERE rn > 20)
SELECT /*+ cardinality(s2 1e9) leading(q2 s2 c p)
           use_nl(s2)
           rowid(s2)
           use_nl(c) index(c)
           use_nl(p) index(p)
           */
       *
  FROM q3
       JOIN sh.sales s2 ON s2.ROWID = q3.rid
       JOIN sh.customers c USING (cust_id)
       JOIN sh.products p USING (prod_id);
```

```
-----------------------------------------------------------------------------------
| Id  | Operation                      | Name          | Rows  | Bytes |TempSpc|
-----------------------------------------------------------------------------------
|   0 | SELECT STATEMENT               |               | 43533 |   17M |       |
|   1 |  NESTED LOOPS                  |               |       |       |       |
|   2 |   NESTED LOOPS                 |               | 43533 |   17M |       |
|   3 |    NESTED LOOPS                |               | 43533 |   10M |       |
|   4 |     NESTED LOOPS               |               | 43533 | 2295K |       |
|*  5 |      VIEW                      |               |    40 |  1000 |       |
|*  6 |       COUNT STOPKEY            |               |       |       |       |
|   7 |        VIEW                    |               | 1000M |   11G |       |
|*  8 |         SORT ORDER BY STOPKEY  |               | 1000M |   15G |   26G |
|   9 |          PARTITION RANGE ALL   |               | 1000M |   15G |       |
|  10 |           BITMAP CONVERSION TO ROWIDS |        | 1000M |   15G |       |
|  11 |            BITMAP INDEX FAST FULL SCAN| SALES_CUST_BIX |   |       |       |
|  12 |      TABLE ACCESS BY USER ROWID | SALES        |  1088 | 31552 |       |
|  13 |     TABLE ACCESS BY INDEX ROWID | CUSTOMERS    |     1 |   189 |       |
|* 14 |      INDEX UNIQUE SCAN         | CUSTOMERS_PK  |     1 |       |       |
|* 15 |    INDEX UNIQUE SCAN           | PRODUCTS_PK   |     1 |       |       |
|  16 |   TABLE ACCESS BY INDEX ROWID  | PRODUCTS      |     1 |   173 |       |
-----------------------------------------------------------------------------------
```

```
Predicate Information (identified by operation id):
----------------------------------------------------

    5 - filter("RN">20)
    6 - filter(ROWNUM<=40)
    8 - filter(ROWNUM<=40)
   14 - access("S2"."CUST_ID"="C"."CUST_ID")
   15 - access("S2"."PROD_ID"="P"."PROD_ID")
```

Listing 17-14 makes two changes to Listing 17-12. The first change is the addition two factored subqueries, Q2 and Q3, that ensure that we only get the second set of 20 rows from our sorted list. The second change is to use nested loops to access our dimension tables as now we are only getting 20 rows back from SH.SALES. Of course in real life the numbers 21 and 40 would be bind variables.

DO YOU NEED AN ORDER BY CLAUSE?

There is a fair amount of political posturing by Oracle on this topic. Theoretically, Oracle will not guarantee that the database will return rows in the correct order unless you provide an ORDER BY clause. Officially, Oracle will not guarantee that queries in Listing 17-12 and 17-14 will produce results in the correct order in future releases unless you provide an ORDER BY clause.

Oracle has a good reason to take this stance. When 10gR1 was released a lot of queries that relied on the SORT GROUP BY ordering broke when the execution plans of queries that included a GROUP BY clause without an ORDER BY clause were changed to use the newly introduced, and more efficient, HASH GROUP BY operation. Oracle was unfairly criticized by some customers for breaking customer code that way. Oracle does not want to appear to condone any action that may be interpreted as a precedent and does not want to send a message that ORDER BY clauses are not necessary.

However, when you hint a clause as heavily as I did in Listings 17-12 and 17-14 there is little risk that the code will break in a future release, and even if it does there will have to be a workaround. Let me turn the argument around. It turns out that if you avoid ANSI syntax you can add an ORDER BY clause to Listing 17-14 and no extra sort will occur. I wouldn't do that for the sake of political correctness because there is a risk that an extra sort may creep in if you upgrade to a later release!

If you want to argue Oracle politics after work you can always bring up the topic of sorted hash clusters. Sorted hash clusters are an obscure variant of clusters that were introduced in 10gR1 as a way to optimize sorts. But the optimization only works if you do *not* include an explicit ORDER BY clause!

In reality this is all nonsense. The business need is to get critical queries to run fast, so do what needs to be done, document the risks for future generations in your risk register, and get on with your life.

Sorting Fewer Rows

We have discussed at some length the various ways by which you can reduce the amount of data being sorted by reducing the number of columns that are sorted. The other way to reduce the amount of data being sorted is to sort fewer rows, and this approach also has the potential to reduce CPU by avoiding comparisons. Reducing the number of rows in a sort is sometimes easier said than done. Let us start off with a relatively simple case: adding predicates to queries with analytic functions.

Additional Predicates with Analytic Functions

A couple of years ago I was working with a client—I'll call him John—who worked on the risk management team of an investment bank. John needed his Oracle database to do some fancy analytics—at least they seemed fancy to me as a non-mathematician. Not only did John need to see moving averages, but he needed to see moving standard deviations, moving medians, and a lot of other moving stuff. Usually the moving time window was quite small. Let me paraphrase one of John's problems with the SH.SALES table. Take a look at Listing 17-15, which implements a moving average.

Listing 17-15. A first attempt at a moving average

```
WITH q1
    AS (SELECT s.*
             ,AVG (
                amount_sold)
             OVER (
                PARTITION BY cust_id
                ORDER BY time_id
                RANGE BETWEEN INTERVAL '6' DAY PRECEDING AND CURRENT ROW)
                avg_weekly_amount
        FROM sh.sales s)
SELECT *
  FROM q1
 WHERE time_id = DATE '2001-10-18';
```

```
-------------------------------------------------------------------------
| Id | Operation           | Name  | Rows  | Bytes |TempSpc| Cost |
-------------------------------------------------------------------------
|  0 | SELECT STATEMENT    |       | 918K| 87M|      | 7810|
|* 1 |  VIEW               |       | 918K| 87M|      | 7810|
|  2 |   WINDOW SORT       |       | 918K| 25M| 42M| 7810|
|  3 |    PARTITION RANGE ALL|     | 918K| 25M|      |  440|
|  4 |     TABLE ACCESS FULL | SALES | 918K| 25M|      |  440|
-------------------------------------------------------------------------
```

Predicate Information (identified by operation id):

```
   1 - filter("TIME_ID"=TO_DATE(' 2001-10-18 00:00:00', 'syyyy-mm-dd
            hh24:mi:ss'))
```

Listing 17-15 lists all the rows from SH.SALES that happened on October 18, 2001. An additional column, AVG_WEEKLY_AMOUNT, has been added that lists the average value of transactions made by the current customer in the seven days ending on the current day.

■ **Note** As I explained in Chapter 7, the SQL term CURRENT ROW actually means current value when a RANGE is specified, so all sales from the current day are included even if they appear in subsequent rows.

This query is very inefficient. The inefficiency arises because we sort the entire SH.SALES table before selecting the rows we want—you can see that the filter predicate is applied by the operation on line 1. We can't push the predicate into the view because we need a week's worth of data to calculate the analytic function. We can easily improve the performance of this query by adding a second, different, predicate that is applied *before* the analytic function is invoked. Listing 17-16 shows this approach.

Listing 17-16. Adding additional predicates to optimize analytics

```
WITH q1
    AS (SELECT s.*
              ,AVG (
                  amount_sold)
              OVER (
                  PARTITION BY cust_id
                  ORDER BY time_id
                  RANGE BETWEEN INTERVAL '6' DAY PRECEDING AND CURRENT ROW)
              avg_weekly_amount
        FROM sh.sales s
        WHERE time_id >=DATE '2001-10-12' AND time_id <= DATE '2001-10-18')
SELECT *
  FROM q1
 WHERE time_id = DATE '2001-10-18';
```

```
--------------------------------------------------------------------
| Id | Operation              | Name  | Rows | Bytes | Cost |
--------------------------------------------------------------------
|  0 | SELECT STATEMENT       |       | 7918 | 773K  |  38 |
|* 1 |  VIEW                  |       | 7918 | 773K  |  38 |
|  2 |   WINDOW SORT          |       | 7918 | 224K  |  38 |
|  3 |    PARTITION RANGE SINGLE|     | 7918 | 224K  |  37 |
|* 4 |     TABLE ACCESS FULL  | SALES | 7918 | 224K  |  37 |
--------------------------------------------------------------------

Predicate Information (identified by operation id):
---------------------------------------------------

   1 - filter("TIME_ID"=TO_DATE(' 2001-10-18 00:00:00', 'syyyy-mm-dd
             hh24:mi:ss'))
   4 - filter("TIME_ID"<=TO_DATE(' 2001-10-18 00:00:00', 'syyyy-mm-dd
             hh24:mi:ss') AND "TIME_ID">=TO_DATE(' 2001-10-12 00:00:00', 'syyyy-mm-dd
             hh24:mi:ss'))
```

Listing 17-16 adds a second predicate that limits the data being sorted to just the seven days that are needed, resulting in a huge win in performance.

Now that wasn't too difficult, was it? Unfortunately, real life was nowhere near as simple. Let us look at some ways to generalize our solution.

Views with Lateral Joins

It turns out that John was not using SQL*Plus to run his SQL. He was actually using sophisticated visualization software that was used to prepare reports for external customers. It combined data from multiple brands of databases, spreadsheets, and a number of other sources. This visualization software knew nothing about analytic functions, so all this fancy logic had to be buried in views. Listing 17-17 shows a first approach to defining and using a view called SALES_ANALYTICS.

Listing 17-17. An inefficient implementation of SALES_ANALYTICS

```
CREATE OR REPLACE VIEW sales_analytics
AS
   SELECT s.*
        ,AVG (
            amount_sold)
        OVER (PARTITION BY cust_id
            ORDER BY time_id
            RANGE BETWEEN INTERVAL '6' DAY PRECEDING AND CURRENT ROW)
        avg_weekly_amount
     FROM sh.sales s;

SELECT *
  FROM sales_analytics
 WHERE time_id = DATE '2001-10-18';
```

```
-------------------------------------------------------------------------
| Id  | Operation            | Name            | Rows  | Bytes |TempSpc| Cost |
-------------------------------------------------------------------------
|   0 | SELECT STATEMENT     |                 | 918K|   87M|       | 7810|
|*  1 |  VIEW                | SALES_ANALYTICS | 918K|   87M|       | 7810|
|   2 |   WINDOW SORT        |                 | 918K|   25M|  42M| 7810|
|   3 |    PARTITION RANGE ALL|                | 918K|   25M|       |  440|
|   4 |     TABLE ACCESS FULL | SALES          | 918K|   25M|       |  440|
-------------------------------------------------------------------------
```

```
Predicate Information (identified by operation id):
---------------------------------------------------

   1 - filter("TIME_ID"=TO_DATE(' 2001-10-18 00:00:00', 'syyyy-mm-dd hh24:mi:ss'))
```

The definition of SALES_ANALYTICS can't include the second date predicate in the way we did in Listing 17-16 without hard-coding the date range. Listing 17-18 shows one way to solve this problem that uses the lateral join syntax introduced in 12cR1.

Listing 17-18. Using lateral joins with one dimension table in a view

```
CREATE OR REPLACE VIEW sales_analytics
AS
    SELECT s2.prod_id
          ,s2.cust_id
          ,t.time_id
          ,s2.channel_id
          ,s2.promo_id
          ,s2.quantity_sold s2
          ,s2.amount_sold
          ,s2.avg_weekly_amount
      FROM sh.times t
          ,LATERAL (
             SELECT s.*
                   ,AVG (
                       amount_sold)
                    OVER (
                      PARTITION BY cust_id
                      ORDER BY s.time_id
                      RANGE BETWEEN INTERVAL '6' DAY PRECEDING
                            AND      CURRENT ROW)
                     avg_weekly_amount
               FROM sh.sales s
              WHERE s.time_id BETWEEN t.time_id - 6 AND t.time_id) s2
             WHERE s2.time_id = t.time_id;

SELECT *
  FROM sales_analytics
 WHERE time_id = DATE '2001-10-18';
```

```
---------------------------------------------------------------------------------
| Id  | Operation                 | Name            | Rows  | Bytes |TempSpc| Cost |
---------------------------------------------------------------------------------
|  0  | SELECT STATEMENT          |                 | 27588 | 2667K|        |  772|
|  1  |  NESTED LOOPS             |                 | 27588 | 2667K|        |  772|
|* 2  |   INDEX UNIQUE SCAN       | TIMES_PK        |     1 |    8 |        |    0|
|* 3  |   VIEW                    | VW_LAT_4DB60E85 | 27588 | 2451K|        |  772|
|  4  |    WINDOW SORT            |                 | 27588 |  862K| 1416K|  772|
|  5  |     PARTITION RANGE ITERATOR|               | 27588 |  862K|        |  530|
|* 6  |      TABLE ACCESS FULL    | SALES           | 27588 |  862K|        |  530|
---------------------------------------------------------------------------------
```

Predicate Information (identified by operation id):

```
   2 - access("T"."TIME_ID"=TO_DATE(' 2001-10-18 00:00:00', 'syyyy-mm-dd hh24:mi:ss'))
   3 - filter("S2"."TIME_ID"=TO_DATE(' 2001-10-18 00:00:00', 'syyyy-mm-dd hh24:mi:ss'))
   6 - filter("S"."TIME_ID"<="T"."TIME_ID" AND "S"."TIME_ID">=INTERNAL_FUNCTION("T"."TIME_ID")-6)
```

Notice how Listing 17-18 uses the combination of a lateral join and the SH.TIMES dimension table to include an initial filter predicate without hard-coding a date. Now when we issue our query the predicate *can* be pushed into the view as it can be applied to the SH.TIMES dimension table without modification. Well, technically the predicate isn't pushed. The view is merged but the effect is the same: only one row is selected from the SH.TIMES table.

This is all very clever, but what if we want to see a range of dates? We can accomplish this with the addition of a couple of extra columns to our view definition. Listing 17-19 shows us how.

Listing 17-19. Using lateral joins with two dimension tables in a view

```
CREATE OR REPLACE VIEW sales_analytics
AS
    SELECT t1.time_id min_time, t2.time_id max_time, s2.*
      FROM sh.times t1
          ,sh.times t2
          ,LATERAL (
             SELECT s.*
                   ,AVG (
                       amount_sold)
                    OVER (
                       PARTITION BY cust_id
                       ORDER BY s.time_id
                       RANGE BETWEEN INTERVAL '6' DAY PRECEDING
                              AND      CURRENT ROW)
                    avg_weekly_amount
               FROM sh.sales s
              WHERE s.time_id BETWEEN t1.time_id - 6 AND t2.time_id) s2
             WHERE s2.time_id >= t1.time_id;

   SELECT *
     FROM sales_analytics
    WHERE min_time = DATE '2001-10-01' AND max_time = DATE '2002-01-01';
```

```
-----------------------------------------------------------------------------
| Id  | Operation                  | Name            | Rows  | Bytes |TempSpc| Cost |
-----------------------------------------------------------------------------
|   0 | SELECT STATEMENT           |                 | 27588 | 3125K |       |  772 |
|   1 |  NESTED LOOPS              |                 | 27588 | 3125K |       |  772 |
|   2 |   NESTED LOOPS            |                 |     1 |   16  |       |    0 |
|*  3 |    INDEX UNIQUE SCAN      | TIMES_PK        |     1 |    8  |       |    0 |
|*  4 |    INDEX UNIQUE SCAN      | TIMES_PK        |     1 |    8  |       |    0 |
|*  5 |   VIEW                    | VW_LAT_4DB60E85 | 27588 | 2694K |       |  772 |
|   6 |    WINDOW SORT           |                 | 27588 |  862K | 1416K |  772 |
|   7 |     PARTITION RANGE ITERATOR|               | 27588 |  862K |       |  530 |
|*  8 |     TABLE ACCESS FULL    | SALES           | 27588 |  862K |       |  530 |
-----------------------------------------------------------------------------
```

```
Predicate Information (identified by operation id):
-------------------------------------------------
```

```
   3 - access("T2"."TIME_ID"=TO_DATE(' 2002-01-01 00:00:00', 'syyyy-mm-dd hh24:mi:ss'))
   4 - access("T1"."TIME_ID"=TO_DATE(' 2001-10-01 00:00:00', 'syyyy-mm-dd hh24:mi:ss'))
   5 - filter("S2"."TIME_ID">="T1"."TIME_ID" AND
           "S2"."TIME_ID">=TO_DATE(' 2001-10-01 00:00:00', 'syyyy-mm-dd hh24:mi:ss'))
   8 - filter("S"."TIME_ID"<="T2"."TIME_ID" AND
           "S"."TIME_ID">=INTERNAL_FUNCTION("T1"."TIME_ID")-6)
```

Listing 17-19 adds two columns to our view definition, MIN_TIME and MAX_TIME, that can be used in calling queries to specify the range of dates required. We join the dimension table twice so that we have two values that can be used by the embedded predicate.

Wonderful. But what happens if you have to work on a pre-12c database like John's? Well, it turns out that lateral joins have actually been available in Oracle databases for a very long time. To use them in older versions, however, you need to define a couple of data dictionary types, as shown in Listing 17-20.

Listing 17-20. Lateral joins using data dictionary types

```
CREATE OR REPLACE TYPE sales_analytics_ot
    FORCE AS OBJECT
(
   prod_id NUMBER
  ,cust_id NUMBER
  ,time_id DATE
  ,channel_id NUMBER
  ,promo_id NUMBER
  ,quantity_sold NUMBER (10, 2)
  ,amount_sold NUMBER (10, 2)
  ,avg_weekly_amount NUMBER (10, 2)
);

CREATE OR REPLACE TYPE sales_analytics_tt AS TABLE OF sales_analytics_ot;

CREATE OR REPLACE VIEW sales_analytics
AS
    SELECT t1.time_id min_time, t2.time_id max_time, s2.*
      FROM sh.times t1
          ,sh.times t2
          ,TABLE (
              CAST (
                  MULTISET (
                    SELECT s.*
                          ,AVG (
                              amount_sold)
                          OVER (
                              PARTITION BY cust_id
                              ORDER BY time_id
                              RANGE BETWEEN INTERVAL '6' DAY PRECEDING
                                    AND      CURRENT ROW)
                              avg_weekly_amount
                      FROM sh.sales s
                    WHERE s.time_id BETWEEN t1.time_id - 6 AND t2.time_id)
                      AS sales_analytics_tt)) s2
                  WHERE s2.time_id >= t1.time_id;

  SELECT *
    FROM sales_analytics
   WHERE min_time = DATE '2001-10-01' AND max_time = DATE '2002-01-01';
```

```
---------------------------------------------------------------------------------------
| Id  | Operation                                  | Name          | Rows | Bytes | Cost |
---------------------------------------------------------------------------------------
|   0 | SELECT STATEMENT                           |               | 8168 | 143K  |   29 |
|   1 |  NESTED LOOPS                              |               | 8168 | 143K  |   29 |
|   2 |   NESTED LOOPS                             |               |    1 |   16  |    0 |
|*  3 |    INDEX UNIQUE SCAN                       | TIMES_PK      |    1 |    8  |    0 |
|*  4 |    INDEX UNIQUE SCAN                       | TIMES_PK      |    1 |    8  |    0 |
|   5 |   COLLECTION ITERATOR SUBQUERY FETCH       |               | 8168 | 16336 |   29 |
|*  6 |    WINDOW SORT                             |               | 2297 | 73504 |  275 |
|*  7 |     FILTER                                 |               |      |       |      |
|   8 |      PARTITION RANGE ITERATOR              |               | 2297 | 73504 |  275 |
|   9 |       TABLE ACCESS BY LOCAL INDEX ROWID BATCHED| SALES     | 2297 | 73504 |  275 |
|  10 |        BITMAP CONVERSION TO ROWIDS         |               |      |       |      |
|* 11 |         BITMAP INDEX RANGE SCAN            | SALES_TIME_BIX|      |       |      |
---------------------------------------------------------------------------------------
```

Predicate Information (identified by operation id):

```
   3 - access("T2"."TIME_ID"=TO_DATE(' 2002-01-01 00:00:00', 'syyyy-mm-dd hh24:mi:ss'))
   4 - access("T1"."TIME_ID"=TO_DATE(' 2001-10-01 00:00:00', 'syyyy-mm-dd hh24:mi:ss'))
   6 - filter("T1"."TIME_ID"<=SYS_OP_ATG(VALUE(KOKBF$),3,4,2) AND
              SYS_OP_ATG(VALUE(KOKBF$),3,4,2)>=TO_DATE(' 2001-10-01 00:00:00',
              'syyyy-mm-dd hh24:mi:ss'))
   7 - filter(:B1>=:B2-6)
  11 - access("S"."TIME_ID">=:B1-6 AND "S"."TIME_ID"<=:B2)
```

The execution plan in Listing 17-20 looks a little different, and the cardinality estimate is a fairly well-known fixed value for COLLECTION ITERATOR operations (always 8168 for an 8k block size!), but the effect is basically the same as with the new lateral join syntax.

Avoiding Data Densification

One day my client John came to me not with a performance problem but a functional problem. Paraphrasing again, he wanted to sum the sales for a particular customer for a particular day. He then wanted to calculate the moving average daily amounts and the moving standard deviation daily amounts for all such sums for the preceding week. John was a fairly competent SQL programmer. He knew all about analytic functions. Unfortunately, his own code didn't produce the right results. He explained the problem.

Say there were two rows with AMOUNT_SOLD of 75 on Monday with CUST_ID 99 and another two rows of 30 on Friday for CUST_ID 99. That made a total of 150 on Monday and 60 on Friday. The desired daily average that John wanted was 30 (210 divided by 7) reflecting the fact that there were no rows for the other five days of the week. The results from his query were, however, 105 (210 divided by 2). John understood why he got this answer but didn't know how to modify his query to generate the correct results.

I nodded sagely to John. I explained that his problem was well understood and that the solution was known as data densification. My first attempt at solving the problem was to trot out the textbook data densification solution that I showed in Listing 1-26. Listing 17-21 shows what it looked like.

Listing 17-21. Textbook solution to densification for analytics

```
WITH q1
     AS (  SELECT cust_id
                 ,time_id
                 ,SUM (amount_sold) todays_sales
                 ,AVG (
                      NVL (SUM (amount_sold), 0))
                   OVER (
                      PARTITION BY cust_id
                      ORDER BY time_id
                      RANGE BETWEEN INTERVAL '6' DAY PRECEDING AND CURRENT ROW)
                      avg_daily_sales
                 ,STDDEV (
                      NVL (SUM (amount_sold), 0))
                   OVER (
                      PARTITION BY cust_id
                      ORDER BY time_id
                      RANGE BETWEEN INTERVAL '6' DAY PRECEDING AND CURRENT ROW)
                      stddev_daily_sales
             FROM sh.times t
             LEFT JOIN sh.sales s PARTITION BY (cust_id) USING (time_id)
          GROUP BY cust_id, time_id)
SELECT *
  FROM q1
 WHERE todays_sales > 0 AND time_id >=DATE '1998-01-07';
```

The query in Listing 17-21 produced the desired moving average and moving standard deviation. Notice that we can't get meaningful data for the first six days because records do not go back beyond January 1, 1998. Unfortunately, Listing 17-21 took over two minutes on my laptop! The problem is that the data densification turned 917,177 rows into 12,889,734! John's real-life data was much bigger so his real-life query took over 30 minutes. I took a breath and told John I would get back to him. Some thought was needed.

After a few minutes thought I realized I knew how to calculate the desired moving average without data densification. All I needed to do was to take the moving sum and divide by 7! What about the moving standard deviation? I decided to do a few Google searches, and by the next day I had the query in Listing 17-22.

Listing 17-22. *Avoiding data densification for analytics*

```
WITH q1
     AS ( SELECT cust_id
                ,time_id
                ,SUM (amount_sold) todays_sales
                , SUM (
                    NVL (SUM (amount_sold), 0))
                  OVER (
                    PARTITION BY cust_id
                    ORDER BY time_id
                    RANGE BETWEEN INTERVAL '6' DAY PRECEDING AND CURRENT ROW)
                / 7
                    avg_daily_sales
                ,AVG (
                    NVL (SUM (amount_sold), 0))
                  OVER (
                    PARTITION BY cust_id
                    ORDER BY time_id
                    RANGE BETWEEN INTERVAL '6' DAY PRECEDING AND CURRENT ROW)
                    avg_daily_sales_orig
                ,VAR_POP (
                    NVL (SUM (amount_sold), 0))
                  OVER (
                    PARTITION BY cust_id
                    ORDER BY time_id
                    RANGE BETWEEN INTERVAL '6' DAY PRECEDING AND CURRENT ROW)
                    variance_daily_sales_orig
                ,COUNT (
                    time_id)
                  OVER (
                    PARTITION BY cust_id
                    ORDER BY time_id
                    RANGE BETWEEN INTERVAL '6' DAY PRECEDING AND CURRENT ROW)
                    count_distinct
              FROM sh.sales
          GROUP BY cust_id, time_id)
SELECT cust_id
      ,time_id
      ,todays_sales
      ,avg_daily_sales
      ,SQRT (
          ( ( count_distinct
              * ( variance_daily_sales_orig
                + POWER (avg_daily_sales_orig - avg_daily_sales, 2)))
            + ( (7 - count_distinct) * POWER (avg_daily_sales, 2)))
          / 6)
          stddev_daily_sales
  FROM q1
 WHERE time_id >=DATE '1998-01-07';
```

Let us begin the analysis of Listing 17-22 with a look at the select list from the subquery Q1. We take the CUST_ID and TIME_ID columns from SH.SALES and calculate TODAYS_SALES, the total sales for the day. We then calculate the average daily sales for the preceding week, AVG_DAILY_SALES, by dividing the sum of those sales by 7. After that we generate some more columns that help the main query calculate the correct value for the standard deviation without densification.

With the exception of rounding differences after more than 30 decimal places, the query in Listing 17-22 generates identical results to Listing 17-21 but takes just a couple of seconds to do so! It turns out that although the documentation states that data densification is primarily targeted at analytics, most analytic functions (including medians and semi-standard deviations) can be implemented with some development effort far more efficiently without densification.

MATHEMATICAL BASIS FOR STANDARD DEVIATION CALCULATION

For those of you that are interested, I'll describe the basis for the standard deviation calculation in Listing 17-22. Let me begin by showing you how to calculate the population variance. A quick Google search will generate several references to the standard technique for calculating the combined population variance of two sets of observations. If N_1, $\overline{X}_1$, and S_1^2 are the number of observations, the mean, and the population variance of one set of observations, and N_2, $\overline{X}_2$, and S_2^2 are the number of observations, the mean, and the population variance of a second set of observations, then N_c, $\overline{X}_c$, and S_c^2, the number, mean, and population variance of the combined set of observations, can be given by the formulae:

$$N_c = N_1 + N_2$$

$$\overline{X}_c = \frac{N_1 \overline{X}_1 + N_2 \overline{X}_2}{N_1 + N_2}$$

$$S_c^2 = \frac{N_1 \left[S_1^2 (\overline{X}_1 - \overline{X}_c)^2 \right] + N_2 \left[S_2^2 (\overline{X}_2 - \overline{X}_c)^2 \right]}{N_1 + N_2}$$

When we densify data, we have two sets of observations. The first set of observations is the set of rows in the table and the second set is the bunch of zeroes that we notionally add. So N_2, $\overline{X}_2$, and S_2^2 are $7 - N_1$, 0, and 0, respectively. By plugging these values into the general formula we get the following:

$$S_c^2 = \frac{N_1 \left[S_1^2 (\overline{X}_1 - \overline{X}_c)^2 \right] + (7 - N_1) \left[\overline{X}_c^2 \right]}{7}$$

To get the sample variance we just divide by 6 rather than 7, and to get the sample standard deviation we take the square root of the sample variance.

Parallel Sorts

It is possible to improve the performance of sort operations by having them be done in parallel. Not only can you execute the sort in parallel, but you also have the potential to utilize more memory if your system has it available. But don't get too excited. There are a couple of potential pitfalls. Let us get started with Listing 17-23, which shows a parallel sort.

Listing 17-23. A parallel sort

```
BEGIN
   FOR c IN (  SELECT /*+ parallel(s 4) */
                     *
                FROM sh.sales s
            ORDER BY time_id)
   LOOP
      NULL;
   END LOOP;
END;
/
```

```
-----------------------------------------------------------------------------
| Id  | Operation              | Name     | Rows | Bytes |TempSpc| Cost |
-----------------------------------------------------------------------------
|  0  | SELECT STATEMENT       |          | 918K|   28M|       |  149|
|  1  |  PX COORDINATOR        |          |     |      |       |     |
|  2  |   PX SEND QC (ORDER)   | :TQ10001 | 918K|   28M|       |  149|
|  3  |    SORT ORDER BY       |          | 918K|   28M|   45M|  149|
|  4  |     PX RECEIVE         |          | 918K|   28M|       |  143|
|  5  |      PX SEND RANGE     | :TQ10000 | 918K|   28M|       |  143|
|  6  |       PX BLOCK ITERATOR|          | 918K|   28M|       |  143|
|  7  |        TABLE ACCESS FULL| SALES   | 918K|   28M|       |  143|
-----------------------------------------------------------------------------
```

```
SELECT dfo_number dfo
      ,tq_id
      ,server_type
      ,process
      ,num_rows
      ,ROUND (
           ratio_to_report (num_rows)
               OVER (PARTITION BY dfo_number, tq_id, server_type)
          * 100)
          AS "%"
     FROM v$pq_tqstat
ORDER BY dfo_number, tq_id, server_type DESC;
```

```
       DFO     TQ_ID SERVER_TYPE PROCESS   NUM_ROWS        %
---------- ---------- ----------- -------- ---------- ----------
         1         0 Ranger      QC             12        100
         1         0 Producer    P005        260279         28
         1         0 Producer    P007        208354         23
         1         0 Producer    P006        188905         21
         1         0 Producer    P004        261319         28
         1         0 Consumer    P003        357207         39
         1         0 Consumer    P002        203968         22
         1         0 Consumer    P001         35524          4
         1         0 Consumer    P000        322144         35
         1         1 Producer    P003        357207         39
         1         1 Producer    P002        203968         22
         1         1 Producer    P001         35524          4
         1         1 Producer    P000        322144         35
         1         1 Consumer    QC          918843        100
```

Listing 17-23 shows a query embedded in a PL/SQL block so that it can be run without producing the voluminous output. The execution plan is taken from the embedded SQL. Once the query has run we can look at V$PQ_TQSTAT to see how well the sort functioned.

The way the sort works is that the query coordinator looks at a small number of rows per parallel query slave. This was about 93 rows per slave in earlier versions of Oracle database, but in 12cR1 you can see from the V$PQ_TQSTAT output that the query coordinator only sampled 12 rows in total. The sampling is done to determine what range of values is handled by each of the sorting parallel query servers but isn't visible in the execution plan.

The next thing that happens in Listing 17-22 is that one set of parallel query slaves runs through the blocks in SH.SALES in parallel. These are the producers of rows for :TQ10000 and are shown in the execution plan on lines 5, 6, and 7. Each row that is read is sent to one of a second set of parallel query slaves that will perform the sort of the rows that fall within a particular range, as previously determined by the ranger process. This second set of parallel query servers is the consumer of :TQ10000 and the producer for :TQ10001. The operations are shown on lines 2, 3, and 4 in the execution plan.

At this point each member of the second set of slaves (P000, P001, P002, and P003 in V$PQ_TQSTAT) will have a sorted portion of the rows in SH.SALES. Each parallel query server then sends the resultant output to the query coordinator, one after the other, to get the final result set.

So what are the pitfalls? The first problem is that the small range of sampled rows might not be representative and sometimes nearly all the rows can be sent to one parallel query slave. We can see from the highlighted portion of the V$PQ_TQSTAT that P001 only sorted 4% of the rows, but the rest of the rows were distributed to the other three sorting parallel query servers fairly uniformly. The second pitfall is specific to sorting by the partitioning column in a table. Listing 17-6 showed that serial sorts could sort each of the 28 partitions individually. Listing 17-23 shows that the four concurrent sort processes sort all the data from all partitions at once. This means that each parallel query slave will need a *larger* workarea than was required when the query ran serially.

Because of these pitfalls I would suggest that you only resort to parallel processing when all other options for optimizing your sort have been exhausted.

Summary

This chapter has investigated in some depth the various ways in which sorts can be optimized. Sometimes you can eliminate a sort or replace it with a more efficient alternative. Sometimes you can reduce the number of columns or the number of rows in the sort with the primary objective of reducing memory consumption and the secondary objective of saving CPU by reducing the number of comparisons.

The optimization technique of last resort is parallel processing. The potential for skew in the allocation of rows to sorting slaves may generate unstable performance, and on some occasions memory requirements can actually increase. Some of the time, however, parallel sorts can be of great benefit in reducing elapsed time when memory and CPU resources are plentiful at the time your sort is run.

CHAPTER 18

■ ■ ■

Using Hints

In my experience, the vast majority of complex applications that involve a substantial amount of Oracle SQL are littered with hints. This is done despite the omnipresent warnings that suggest that hints are an extreme measure only to be used as a last resort. The following official warning is an example:

> Hints were introduced in Oracle7, when users had little recourse if the optimizer generated suboptimal plans. Now Oracle provides a number of tools, including the SQL Tuning Advisor, SQL plan management, and SQL Performance Analyzer, to help you address performance problems that are not solved by the optimizer. Oracle **strongly recommends that you use those tools rather than hints**. The tools are **far superior to hints**, because when used on an ongoing basis, they provide **fresh solutions** as your data and database environment change.
>
> **Hints should be used sparingly**, and only after you have collected statistics on the relevant tables and evaluated the optimizer plan without hints using the EXPLAIN PLAN statement. Changing database conditions as well as query performance enhancements in subsequent releases can have significant impact on how hints in your code affect performance.

Oracle 12c SQL Language Reference manual

One well-known SQL expert accepts that hinting is a fact of life but has classified hints as "good, bad, and ugly," implying that, depending on the hint, you may be exposing yourself to substantial risks when hints are used in production code.

The sentiments expressed in these sorts of statements shouldn't be dismissed out-of-hand but are, on occasion, misinterpreted. The fact is that there *are* occasions where the use of one or more hints in a SQL statement provides the best, and sometimes the only, way to ensure that performance is adequate and stable. And these occasions are far more numerous than you might think after reading all of these dire warnings.

Many of the chapters in this book include examples of how hinting can be used legitimately, most notably Chapter 14, which explains some of the many reasons why the optimizer might not arrive at an optimal execution plan all on its own. In this chapter I want to go through a few case studies that show legitimate examples of hinting as an optimization technique that don't crop up in other chapters of the book. But before I do that, let me take a step back and try to provide some balance to the views of the foretellers of doom to help you develop your own perspective on how to approach hinting in production code. It all boils down to the one question: Are hints supportable?

Are Hints Supportable?

One of the assumptions that I know some people make is that if they have a problem with a SQL statement that includes hints, Oracle will not provide them with any support until those hints are removed. That line of reasoning suggests that hints are an inherently unsupportable feature of the SQL language. Let me go through a few real-life experiences of my own to try to determine the merit of such sentiments. Let us begin by revisiting the join subquery pushdown optimizer transformation that I covered in Chapter 13.

The PUSH_SUBQ story

If you were working on a database upgrade from 9i to 10g you would have had a nasty surprise if your code included the PUSH_SUBQ or NO_PUSH_SUBQ hints to control subquery pushdown. In 9i the hint was placed in the *outer* query block and applied to *all* subqueries referenced by the enclosing query block. In 10g the behavior of the hint was enhanced to allow each subquery to be treated differently; these days you place the hint in *each subquery individually* and *not* in the enclosing query block.

This 10g change to a hint that was documented in the 9i SQL Reference manual was not backwardly compatible with existing 9i code, thus all statements that included a PUSH_SUBQ hint needed editing at the time of the upgrade. It is experiences like this that lead some people to conclude that Oracle treats optimizer hints in a different way than it does other parts of the SQL language and that, as a result, the use of optimizer hints is a risky affair. But before you decide whether you agree with these conclusions, think about my next story.

The DML error logging story

One of the legal clauses in a PL/SQL FORALL statement is SAVE EXCEPTIONS, which is demonstrated in Listing 12-13 in the Oracle 12c PL/SQL Language Reference manual. The SAVE EXCEPTIONS clause implements what is known as *batch error mode*. In PL/SQL, batch error mode results in the population of the collection SQL%BULK_EXCEPTIONS, which identifies rows that couldn't be inserted or updated because, for example, of an integrity constraint violation. An alternative approach to solving the same problem is to use *DML error logging* described as part of the INSERT, UPDATE and MERGE statements in the SQL Language Reference manual. The use of both batch error mode and DML error logging in the same statement is illogical, but it worked in 10g. Many customers found that when they upgraded from 10g to 11g they suddenly got ORA-38909 messages saying that their previous working code was now illegal. Just do an Internet search for this error code to see the trouble this caused.

Most customers running into an ORA-38909 error code were using PL/SQL and could make code changes to remove the redundant SAVE EXCEPTIONS clause from their code. However, my client was using ODP.NET, which uses batch error mode *unconditionally*. The use of batch error mode in ODP.NET meant that there was no way to invoke DML that included error logging clauses.

I logged a service request on my client's behalf and after three months or so Oracle accepted that this was indeed a bug. Oracle then asked how big an impact the bug was having so that they could prioritize the fix. Since my client had already recoded their application in the intervening three months, and no other clients had reported the issue, there was no business need for a fix anymore. In 12.1.0.1 it is still not possible to invoke DML with error logging clauses from ODP.NET!

But what does this story have to do with optimizer hints? The point is that sometimes Oracle makes changes to documented features of their product that are not backwardly compatible. If the changes affect a substantial number of clients then Oracle will have to produce either a fix or a workaround. The workaround may involve customers changing their code. There isn't anything different about documented optimizer hints or any other documented feature of the Oracle database product: 99.9% of the time an upgrade will be backwardly compatible, but once in a while something unforeseen happens.

But this book has discussed numerous *undocumented* hints. Should our attitude towards these hints be any different than to documented hints? Let us discuss this now.

Documented versus undocumented hints

The SQL Language Reference manual has a chapter entitled "Basic Elements of Oracle SQL" that includes a description of comments, and hints in particular. There are several dozen hints documented, but a complete (or almost complete) list of hints can be found in the view V$SQL_HINT, which has 314 rows!

You might assume that Oracle makes certain implicit guarantees about the use of documented hints but that Oracle might remove or alter the behavior of undocumented hints at any point with moral impunity. In fact, even working out what constitutes a documented hint isn't straightforward. For example, the Data Warehousing Guide makes mention of the EXPAND_GSET_TO_UNION hint that we covered in Chapter 13 as well as other hints such as NO_MULTIMV_REWRITE and NO_BASETABLE_MULTIMV_REWRITE. None of these hints appear in the current SQL Language Reference manual, although EXPAND_GSET_TO_UNION appears in older versions of said manual. Does Oracle support the use of these hints or not?

Perhaps one of the most talked about undocumented hints is the CARDINALITY hint. At the time of writing this book, Tom Kyte is the product manager for the CBO. Although Tom hasn't been in this role for very long his knowledge of the Oracle database product is very well known. He has published multiple excellent books on the product and has maintained the famous *Ask Tom* website for longer than most of us can remember. In 2010, in response to question 2233040800346569775 on the Ask Tom website, Tom said:

> ...correct [the cardinality hint] is not documented. However, it is—in my opinion—one of the few "safe" undocumented things to use because its use will not lead to data corruption, wrong answers, or unpredictable outcomes. If it works—it will influence a query plan, if it doesn't—it won't. That is all—it is rather "safe" in that respect.

Well, the truth is that that the vast majority of hints are optimizer hints, and the statement about the safety of the CARDINALITY hint can surely be extended to every single one of the optimizer hints can it not? Optimizer hints will either alter the execution plan. . .or not! In fact, I personally think that the CARDINALITY hint is one of the most *dangerous* optimizer hints to use on a production system because its effect is, in fact, unpredictable. I will cover the semantics of the CARDINALITY hint in a little while.

In reality, a lot of hints aren't documented simply because Oracle hasn't gotten around to documenting them. I discussed the GATHER_PLAN_STATISTICS hint in Chapter 4, but this hint didn't appear in the Oracle documentation until 12c! To give another example, it is quite clear that Oracle wants us to be able to use hints to control join order and join method, hence the documentation of the LEADING, USE_NL, USE_MERGE, and USE_HASH hints. But any time we use the LEADING and USE_HASH hints together we absolutely *must* use a SWAP_JOIN_INPUTS or NO_SWAP_JOIN_INPUTS hint so as to be unambiguous in our intentions. The only reason that SWAP_JOIN_INPUTS and NO_SWAP_JOIN_INPUTS haven't been documented is because Oracle hasn't gotten around to documenting them. There is absolutely no supportability issue involved at all.

By this stage in the discussion you might be thinking that my view is that you should have no qualms at all about using any hint, documented or undocumented, and that the number of such hints that float around application code has no impact on the supportability of the application. That would be taking things too far. In fact, there *are* support implications of using hints but they aren't the ones we have discussed so far. Let me use an analogy to make my point.

The MODEL clause corollary

If you feel the need to use the HAVING clause in a SQL statement, go right ahead. If you want to use an analytic function, don't feel inhibited. Whether 1% or 90% of SQL statements in an application contain HAVING clauses is of no concern to the supportability of the application, although if 90% of statements had HAVING clauses it would be a strange application! If someone is reading your code and they don't understand the basic features of the SQL language, that is their problem. They should just go home and read the manual.

But what happens if you feel the urge to use the MODEL clause? Should you just go ahead and start using it with as little thought as when you use an analytic function? Absolutely not. The MODEL clause is used in very few applications, and most programmers have absolutely no knowledge of it. Your colleagues can't just go home and read a couple of pages about the MODEL clause before they go to bed and expect to wake up an expert. It is a complex beast!

So if you want to use the MODEL clause, take a breath. Can you use traditional SQL syntax to obtain the results you need with adequate performance? If so, and if the MODEL clause is not already in use in your application, then you should probably refrain from being the first to introduce it. On the other hand, if you have a clearly defined need (such as the moving median example that I discussed in Chapter 7) then you shouldn't be afraid to use the MODEL clause just because it is unfamiliar. Just make sure that you comment your code and explain to your colleagues what you are doing and why.

A similar thought process should go through your head when you feel the urge to slap one of those plus signs at the start of your comment. You should be asking yourself these sorts of questions:

- Do I know the reason why I need to hint this code? Why has the CBO picked a different plan to the one I think is best?

- Do I know that hinting the code will actually make a positive difference, or am I making a potentially incorrect assumption?

- Are there alternative approaches? Are these alternative approaches better or worse than the use of hints?

- Do I understand what the hints that I plan to use do?

- Are the hints an appropriate and complete set?

- Will my colleagues understand what I have done and why?

If you find that you have satisfactory answers to all of the above questions then go ahead. If not, then try to *get* satisfactory answers or find an alternative solution to your problem.

So where do all the analogies and anecdotes leave us? Here is a summary of my personal thoughts on the use of hints.

Supportability conclusion

If you have a functional or performance problem with your Oracle database product then the response that you get from Oracle will depend upon the extent of your business impact and the number of customers affected by similar problems. By its very nature, a problem with the performance of a single SQL statement is almost always much less serious than, for example, a data corruption issue that prevents a database from starting up. As a consequence, there is a limit to the level of support you will get from Oracle for SQL performance issues regardless of whether the issues are caused by optimizer hints or by other features of the database product and regardless of whether the hints are documented or not.

This is not a dig at Oracle. It is how business works. Indeed, you will find that deprecated hints like ORDERED and AND_EQUAL that are widespread in code written by many customers years ago still work perfectly well in 12c, despite having been removed from the SQL Language Reference manual years ago.

The real issues relating to the supportability of hints are focused closer to home and involve you and your colleagues. The sad fact is that even the documented hints aren't usually documented very well, and there are all sorts of hidden restrictions and limitations that mean that we are all working somewhat in the dark.

At Oracle Open World in 2013, Jonathan Lewis said the words *we don't know how to hint* in one of his talks. These words are still ringing in my ears because they are *not* false modesty! Nobody, and I mean nobody, knows all the ins and outs of every optimizer hint. This means that with the exception of the most trivial of SQL statements, nobody can say with absolute certainty that they have the correct set of hints that will provide optimal and stable performance forever.

However, writing this book has made me realize that writing good SQL is very difficult, and so is coming up with a good physical database design. So not only do we not know how to hint, but also *we don't know how to write SQL* and *we don't know how to design our database* either! We simply have to assess each situation on its merits and provide the simplest and most supportable solution that we can find for our business problem *based upon our knowledge*.

I think I have said enough about philosophy; it's now time to return to detailed technical content and look at the different types of hints at our disposal.

Types of Hints

In the preceding paragraphs I have sometimes talked about hints in general and sometimes talked specifically about optimizer hints. There is a difference because there are a few hints that aren't directed at the optimizer at all. Furthermore, there are a couple of different types of optimizer hints. Let me first talk briefly about the hints that aren't directed at the optimizer.

Edition -based redefinition hints

Edition-based redefinition (EBR) was probably the most talked about new feature of 11gR2 and is needed by customers that want to do rolling application upgrades. I use the term "rolling application upgrade" to mean changing application code and DDL specifications without shutting down your application. An integral part of EBR is a set of three hints that change the semantics of a SQL statement. These hints are:

- IGNORE_ROW_ON_DUPKEY_INDEX

- CHANGE_DUPKEY_ERROR_INDEX

- RETRY_ON_ROW_CHANGE

Let me emphasize that these hints *change what the SQL statement does* and are in that respect quite unlike the vast majority of optimizer hints; optimizer hints are generally intended to have an impact on the performance of the statement and nothing else.

The documentation of EBR hints in the SQL Language Reference manual takes care to point out that the normal dire warnings of a potential performance meltdown do not apply to this special type of hint; if you are using EBR you are encouraged to and indeed have no choice but to use these special hints.

A detailed discussion of EBR is beyond the scope of this book, but if you are interested in reading more there is a chapter dedicated to the topic in the Advanced Application Developer's Guide.

It is almost time to turn our attention to optimizer hints, but the discussion of EBR prompts me to take a brief diversion to discuss a somewhat unusual topic.

Hints that cause errors

If you have experience with hinting you will know that, barring bugs, if a hint is used erroneously it will not cause the associated SQL statement to fail; the SQL statement will just ignore the hint. But did you know that if the hint is *valid* it *may* cause the statement to fail or it may prevent it from failing? I have come across three examples of this. Two of these examples relate to EBR and one to materialized view rewrite. Take a look at the examples in Listing 18-1.

Listing 18-1. Hints that cause errors

```
CREATE TABLE t1
AS
   SELECT 1 c1, 1 c2 FROM DUAL;

CREATE UNIQUE INDEX t1_i1
   ON t1 (c1);

CREATE UNIQUE INDEX t1_i2
   ON t1 (c2);

INSERT /*+ change_dupkey_error_index(t1 (c1)) */
     INTO  t1
   SELECT 2, 1 FROM DUAL;

ORA-00001: unique constraint (BOOK.T1_I2) violated

INSERT /*+ change_dupkey_error_index(t1 (c1)) */
     INTO  t1
   SELECT 1, 2 FROM DUAL;
ORA-38911: unique constraint (BOOK.T1_I1) violated

INSERT /*+ ignore_row_on_dupkey_index(t1 (c1)) */
     INTO  t1
      SELECT ROWNUM + 1, 1
         FROM DUAL
   CONNECT BY LEVEL <= 3;
ORA-00001: unique constraint (BOOK.T1_I2) violated

INSERT /*+ ignore_row_on_dupkey_index(t1 (c1)) */
     INTO  t1
      SELECT ROWNUM, ROWNUM + 1
         FROM DUAL
   CONNECT BY LEVEL <= 3;
2 rows created

ALTER SESSION SET query_rewrite_integrity=enforced;

  SELECT /*+ rewrite_or_error */
       t.calendar_month_desc, SUM (s.amount_sold) AS dollars
    FROM sh.sales s, sh.times t
   WHERE s.time_id = t.time_id
GROUP BY t.calendar_month_desc;
ORA-30393: a query block in the statement did not rewrite
```

Listing 18-1 begins by creating a table T1 that has a single row with two columns, C1 and C2. The values of C1 and C2 in this single row are both 1. We now create two indexes, T1_I1 and T1_I2, that ensure that the values of C1 and C2 respectively remain unique.

Now then, what happens when we try to insert rows into T1 that violate these integrity constraints? The first insertion attempts to generate a duplicate value for C2, violating the constraint enforced by T1_C2. As we would expect, we get an ORA-00001 error. But when we try a second insertion that attempts to duplicate values for C1 in violation of the integrity constraint enforced by T1_C1, we get a different error: ORA-38911! This difference is because of the CHANGE_DUPKEY_ERROR_INDEX hint that specifies the C1 column (and implicitly the constraint enforced by the T1_C1 index), thus causing a different error that can be treated in a special way by an EBR-related exception handler.

The third insertion in Listing 18-1 attempts to insert three rows into T1, one of which is a duplicate of C1. This time, the offending row is ignored and we insert the remaining two rows without error. This behavior arises as a result of the IGNORE_ROW_ON_DUPKEY_INDEX hint that once again specifies the integrity constraint should be ignored.

The final SQL statement in Listing 18-1 has nothing to do with EBR and yet also causes a statement failure. The fact that the referential integrity constraint on the TIME_ID column in SH.SALES is not enforced means that the final query in Listing 18-1 cannot be rewritten to use the materialized view CAL_MONTH_SALES_MV when QUERY_REWRITE_INTEGRITY is ENFORCED. Normally, the query would just run against the base tables, but because of the REWRITE_OR_ERROR hint the statement fails. An EXPLAIN PLAN statement specifying the query also fails with the ORA-30393 error.

I hope you found this distraction interesting, but it is time now to return to performance-related matters. We are not yet, however, ready to discuss optimizer hints. We need to look at runtime engine hints first.

Runtime engine hints

There are one or two hints that affect the behavior of a SQL statement at runtime but bear no relationship to the decisions the CBO makes in relation to transformations and final state optimization, including the following:

- We discussed the GATHER_PLAN_STATISTICS hint in Chapter 4 and also in this chapter. This hint causes the runtime engine to gather actual performance statistics at runtime but has no impact on the execution plan.

- We discussed the NO_GATHER_OPTIMIZER_STATISTICS hint in Chapter 9. This hint, and its counterpart GATHER_OPTIMIZER_STATISTICS, controls whether an OPTIMIZER STATISTICS GATHERING operation is added to the execution for direct-path loads.

- The MONITOR hint can be used to force the collection of data that can be referenced using the DBMS_SQLTUNE.REPORT_SQL_MONITOR function. By default, such data isn't collected for statements that run for less than five seconds. The NO_MONITOR hint can be used to suppress the collection of data for statements running for longer than five seconds. Like the GATHER_PLAN_STATISTICS, (NO_)GATHER_OPTIMIZER_STATISTICS, and the (NO_)MONITOR hints have no impact on the execution plan generated by the CBO.

- The DRIVING_SITE hint can be used to change the way a distributed query runs. Although the DRIVING_SITE hint does change the execution plan produced by the CBO, it does so in a way that is independent of the cost-based or heuristic decisions the CBO makes. I will give an example of the legitimate use of the DRIVING_SITE hint in a moment.

- Like the DRIVING_SITE hint, the APPEND and APPEND_VALUES hints alter the appearance of the execution plan generated by the CBO in ways unrelated to the optimization process, but unlike the DRIVING_SITE hint, the APPEND and APPEND_VALUES hints affect the semantics of the statement, as I will demonstrate shortly.

Listing 18-2 makes use of the loopback link that we created in Listing 8-1 to demonstrate the DRIVING_SITE hint.

Listing 18-2. The DRIVING_SITE hint

```
SELECT /*+ driving_site(s) */
       cust_id
       ,c.cust_first_name
       ,c.cust_last_name
       ,SUM (s.amount_sold) sum_sales
    FROM sh.customers c JOIN sh.sales@loopback s USING (cust_id)
GROUP BY cust_id, c.cust_first_name, c.cust_last_name;
```

```
-----------------------------------------------------------------
| Id  | Operation              | Name      | Rows  | Pstart| Pstop |
-----------------------------------------------------------------
|   0 | SELECT STATEMENT REMOTE|           |  918K |       |       |
|   1 |  HASH GROUP BY         |           |  918K |       |       |
|*  2 |   HASH JOIN            |           |  918K |       |       |
|   3 |    REMOTE              | CUSTOMERS | 55500 |       |       |
|   4 |    PARTITION RANGE ALL |           |  918K |     1 |    28 |
|   5 |     TABLE ACCESS FULL  | SALES     |  918K |     1 |    28 |
-----------------------------------------------------------------
```

```
Predicate Information (identified by operation id):
---------------------------------------------------

   2 - access("A2"."CUST_ID"="A1"."CUST_ID")


Note
-----
   - fully remote statement
   - this is an adaptive plan
```

The query in Listing 18-2 joins the local SH.CUSTOMERS table to SH.SALES, which is accessed over a database link. Without the DRIVING_SITE hint, all 918,843 rows from the SH.SALES table would be pulled over the link to join with the local SH.CUSTOMERS table locally. As a consequence of using the DRIVING_SITE hint, the query is actually run at the remote site, and rather than the 918,843 rows from SH.SALES being pulled over the database link, the 55,500 rows from SH.CUSTOMERS are pushed over the link instead. With the hint in place the join and aggregation are performed at the remote site, and the resulting 7,059 rows are returned from the remote side to the local side.

The use of the DRIVING_SITE hint reduces the amount of data sent over the database link and is a perfectly reasonable thing to do, but as of yet this is not an approach that the CBO even considers in an unhinted query. The only time that an unhinted query is run from a remote site is when *all* the row sources are at that site—in other words, when the query isn't really distributed at all.

It is, of course, possible for a query to reference multiple remote locations. It is for this reason that the DRIVING_SITE hint takes a parameter that specifies the row source associated with the remote site that is expected to drive the query.

That's enough about DRIVING_SITE—let us now move on to APPEND and APPEND_VALUES. Parallel DML statements usually result in direct-path writes, but the APPEND and APPEND_VALUES statements are required when trying to cause direct-path loads to occur for serial INSERT statements.

The APPEND hint has been around for many years, but the hint has always been illegal when a VALUES clause was supplied. However, the VALUES clause can be used to insert large numbers of records, and an APPEND_VALUES hint is now available, as demonstrated in Listing 18-3.

Listing 18-3. Use of the APPEND_VALUES hint

```
CREATE /*+ NO_GATHER_OPTIMIZER_STATISTICS */
       TABLE t2
AS
    SELECT *
      FROM all_objects
     WHERE 1 = 0;

DECLARE
    TYPE obj_table_type IS TABLE OF all_objects%ROWTYPE;

    obj_table    obj_table_type;
BEGIN
    SELECT *
      BULK COLLECT INTO obj_table
      FROM all_objects;

    FORALL i IN 1 .. obj_table.COUNT
        INSERT /*+ TAGAV append_values */
               INTO  t2
               VALUES obj_table (i);

    COMMIT;
END;
/

SET LINES 200 PAGES 0

SELECT p.*
  FROM v$sql s
      ,TABLE (DBMS_XPLAN.display_cursor (s.sql_id, s.child_number, 'BASIC')) p
 WHERE s.sql_text LIKE 'INSERT /*+ TAGAV%';

INSERT /*+ TAGAV append_values */ INTO T2 VALUES (:B1 ,:B2 ,:B3 ,:B4
,:B5 ,:B6 ,:B7 ,:B8 ,:B9 ,:B10 ,:B11 ,:B12 ,:B13 ,:B14 ,:B15 ,:B16
,:B17 ,:B18 )

Plan hash value: 3581094869

-----------------------------------
| Id  | Operation       | Name |
-----------------------------------
|   0 | INSERT STATEMENT |      |
|   1 |  LOAD AS SELECT  |      |
|   2 |   BULK BINDS GET |      |
-----------------------------------
```

Unless I am specifically interested in runtime statistics, this book uses the EXPLAIN PLAN statement and the DBMS_XPLAN.DISPLAY function to obtain the execution plan for a statement, and I don't usually show the calls. But in Listing 18-3 the SQL statement under analysis is buried in a PL/SQL block, and it is more convenient to obtain the execution plan by means of the DBMS_XPLAN.DISPLAY_CURSOR in conjunction with a tagged SQL statement and a lateral join, as I have shown.

The LOAD AS SELECT operation in Listing 18-3 signifies the use of direct-path insertion. As with parallel direct-path inserts, serial direct-path inserts will result in what is, in this case, the slightly misleading ORA-12838: cannot read/modify an object after modifying it in parallel error message if an attempt is made to access the object before a COMMIT statement.

What is perhaps a little surprising in Listing 18-3 is that there is no OPTIMIZER STATISTICS GATHERING operation visible in the execution plan and no object statistics are gathered by the INSERT ... VALUES statement as they would have been with an INSERT ... SELECT statement when the APPEND hint is supplied. This behavior cannot be changed by the use of any GATHER_OPTIMIZER_STATISTICS hint.

Incidentally, the GATHER_OPTIMIZER_STATISTICS hint is in some way akin to the NO_SET_TO_JOIN hint that we discussed in Chapter 13. Because both hints specify default behavior, neither hint has any effect under normal circumstances. However, just as the NO_SET_TO_JOIN hint can be used to disable the set-to-join transformation if you set "_convert_set_to_join" to TRUE, so too can GATHER_OPTIMIZER_STATISTICS can be used to force statistics gathering if you set "_optimizer_gather_stats_on_load" to FALSE!

Unlike the three EBR hints, the GATHER_PLAN_STATISTICS, (NO_)MONITOR, (NO_)GATHER_OPTIMIZER_STATISTICS, DRIVING_SITE, APPEND, and APPEND_VALUES hints are not exempt from the health warning in the SQL Language Reference manual. However, you should think of these eight hints in the same way as you do the three EBR hints, namely as extensions of the SQL language that allow you to express what you want to do, not as a way to express how it should be done.

Like most of the optimizer hints that we will discuss in this chapter, the three EBR hints and the eight hints described here are more like directives than hints: there is no discretion allowed in their application. But you shouldn't think of all optimizer hints as directives. Let us look now at some of the optimizer hints that really are hints and not directives.

Optimizer hints that are hints

Most optimizer hints should properly be regarded as directives in that they tell the CBO either that it must do something or that it must not. Of course, the directives are conditional in nature. For example, the USE_HASH (T) hint says: "Assuming that T is not the leading row source in the join tree, and assuming that T has not been eliminated by the join elimination transformation, or undergone any other transformation rendering this directive moot, then join T with a hash join." Similarly, the PARALLEL (T) hint says: "Assuming that you access T with a full table scan, then perform the scan in parallel."

There are, however, one or two optimizer hints that contain no prescriptive component and really are hints. Let us begin our look at these hints now with OPT_PARAM.

OPT_PARAM

We have just discussed two hidden parameters—"_convert_set_to_join" and "_optimizer_gather_stats_on_load"—that allow specific features of the CBO to be enabled, disabled, or forced. In fact, there are scores of such hidden parameters that control optimizer behavior, and officially you need agreement from Oracle support to change any of them. There are also a few documented parameters that are not hidden that affect optimizer behavior, such as OPTIMIZER_INDEX_COST_ADJ. Documented or not, I would repeat my recommendation that, with the exception of the few parameters that I mentioned in Chapter 9, you leave all optimizer-related initialization parameters well alone unless you have a really convincing reason to use non-default values.

If you just want to override default CBO behavior for one statement, then you have the option to use the OPT_PARAM hint as an alternative to changing the initialization parameter for the entire session. The OPT_PARAM hint has been around forever but is documented in 12cR1 for the first time. As you might expect, the documentation for OPT_PARAM only authorizes overrides to documented initialization parameters such as OPTIMIZER_INDEX_COST_ADJ. Listing 18-4 shows the OPT_PARAM hint in action.

Listing 18-4. The OPT_PARAM hint

```
ALTER SESSION SET star_transformation_enabled=temp_disable;

SELECT /*+ opt_param('_optimizer_adaptive_plans','false')
           opt_param('_optimizer_gather_feedback','false')
       */
     * FROM t2;
---------------------------------------------------------------
| Id | Operation         | Name | Rows  | Bytes | Cost (%CPU)| Time     |
---------------------------------------------------------------
|  0 | SELECT STATEMENT  |      | 100K| 35M|  426   (1)| 00:00:01 |
|  1 |  TABLE ACCESS FULL| T2   | 100K| 35M|  426   (1)| 00:00:01 |
---------------------------------------------------------------

Query Block Name / Object Alias (identified by operation id):
-------------------------------------------------------------

   1 - SEL$1 / T2@SEL$1

Outline Data
-------------

  /*+
      BEGIN_OUTLINE_DATA
      FULL(@"SEL$1" "T2"@"SEL$1")
      OUTLINE_LEAF(@"SEL$1")
      ALL_ROWS
      OPT_PARAM('star_transformation_enabled' 'temp_disable')
      OPT_PARAM('_optimizer_gather_feedback' 'false')
      OPT_PARAM('_optimizer_adaptive_plans' 'false')
      DB_VERSION('12.1.0.1')
      OPTIMIZER_FEATURES_ENABLE('12.1.0.1')
      IGNORE_OPTIM_EMBEDDED_HINTS
      END_OUTLINE_DATA
  */
```

Listing 18-4 sets an initialization parameter at the session level before running a query that includes two OPT_PARAM hints that turn off default CBO features. Interestingly, the outline data section in the displayed execution plan includes an OPT_PARAM hint for the non-default session-level parameter. This is necessary because by default the OPTIMIZER_FEATURES_ENABLE ('12.1.0.1') hint, itself a non-prescriptive hint, implicitly resets the value of most optimizer parameters to the default values for the specified release. Because the OPTIMIZER_FEATURES_ENABLE ('12.1.0.1') hint did not appear in the original query, OPT_PARAM hints are added to the outline data for any non-default session-level settings to override the OPTIMIZER_FEATURES_ENABLE ('12.1.0.1') hint.

The OPT_PARAM hint can be used to enable or disable certain optimizer features, and when used this way OPT_PARAM can be regarded as a directive. However, when parameters like OPTIMIZER_INDEX_COST_ADJ are overridden, the CBO isn't being explicitly told to do or not to do anything. It is just being given some additional information to feed into its deliberations.

Incidentally, the initialization parameter OPTIMIZER_DYNAMIC_SAMPLING can be controlled at the statement level either by the OPT_PARAM hint or by the DYNAMIC_SAMPLING hint. Many of us in the Oracle community were highly amused by the fact that in 12cR1 the maximum value of OPTIMIZER_DYNAMIC_SAMPLING was increased from 10 to 11. There is an old movie with the name *This is Spinal Tap,* and if you look at the YouTube clip entitled "spinal tap: these go to eleven," you will see why many of us giggled somewhat childishly when we learned about the new value of OPTIMIZER_DYNAMIC_SAMPLING!

FIRST_ROWS and ALL_ROWS

As of 12cR1 the valid values of the initialization parameter OPTIMIZER_MODE are FIRST_ROWS_1, FIRST_ROWS_10, FIRST_ROWS_100, FIRST_ROWS_1000, or ALL_ROWS. The last of these is, effectively, FIRST_ROWS_INFINITY and is the default value.

When OPTIMIZER_MODE has a non-default value, default CBO behavior can be obtained at the statement level by use of the ALL_ROWS hint. The FIRST_ROWS hint is more flexible than the initialization parameter setting in that you can specify any positive integer as an argument. Listing 18-5 demonstrates.

Listing 18-5. The FIRST_ROWS hint

```
SELECT /*+ first_rows(2000) */
       *
    FROM sh.sales s JOIN sh.customers c USING (cust_id)
ORDER BY cust_id;
```

```
-------------------------------------------------------------
| Id  | Operation                          | Name           |
-------------------------------------------------------------
|   0 | SELECT STATEMENT                   |                |
|   1 |  NESTED LOOPS                      |                |
|   2 |   NESTED LOOPS                     |                |
|   3 |    TABLE ACCESS BY INDEX ROWID     | CUSTOMERS      |
|   4 |     INDEX FULL SCAN                | CUSTOMERS_PK   |
|   5 |    PARTITION RANGE ALL             |                |
|   6 |     BITMAP CONVERSION TO ROWIDS    |                |
|*  7 |      BITMAP INDEX SINGLE VALUE     | SALES_CUST_BIX |
|   8 |   TABLE ACCESS BY LOCAL INDEX ROWID| SALES          |
-------------------------------------------------------------

Predicate Information (identified by operation id):
---------------------------------------------------

   7 - access("S"."CUST_ID"="C"."CUST_ID")
```

```
SELECT /*+ first_rows(3000) */
       *
    FROM sh.sales s JOIN sh.customers c USING (cust_id)
ORDER BY cust_id;
```

```
-----------------------------------------------
| Id  | Operation               | Name      |
-----------------------------------------------
|  0  | SELECT STATEMENT        |           |
|  1  |  MERGE JOIN             |           |
|  2  |   SORT JOIN             |           |
|  3  |    PARTITION RANGE ALL  |           |
|  4  |     TABLE ACCESS FULL   | SALES     |
|* 5  |   SORT JOIN             |           |
|  6  |    TABLE ACCESS FULL    | CUSTOMERS |
-----------------------------------------------
```

Predicate Information (identified by operation id):

```
   5 - access("S"."CUST_ID"="C"."CUST_ID")
       filter("S"."CUST_ID"="C"."CUST_ID")
```

The two different values of the parameter passed to the FIRST_ROWS hint result in completely different execution plans. When we supply a value of 3000 to the hint we are asking the CBO to devise a plan that will deliver the first 3000 rows of output as quickly as possible, even if the total time for the query to return all rows may be extended. The CBO picks a NESTED LOOPS join using an INDEX FULL SCAN on the CUSTOMERS_PK index, meaning that the rows will be delivered in order without the need for a sort. The query will begin producing rows almost immediately.

When we increase the value of the hint parameter to 4000 the execution plan changes to use a MERGE JOIN. This operation requires that the rows from both tables are sorted first, meaning that there will be some delay before any rows are returned. However, once the data from the two tables have been read and sorted the rows are delivered from the query much quicker than from the NESTED LOOPS join; the CBO believes that by the time 4000 rows have been delivered the MERGE JOIN will have overtaken the NESTED LOOPS approach.

CARDINALITY and OPT_ESTIMATE hints

As I explained in Chapter 14, the CBO frequently makes errors in cardinality estimates. The CARDINALITY and OPT_ESTIMATE hints are really useful for understanding what went wrong. The CARDINALITY hint has been around for a very long time and is far better known than the OPT_ESTIMATE hint, which appeared for the first time in 10gR1 for use internally by SQL profiles. Both the CARDINALITY and OPT_ESTIMATE hints allow you to override the cardinality estimates from the CBO. Although the latter hint is far more flexible than the former, let us begin with the CARDINALITY hint, demonstrated in Listing 18-6.

Listing 18-6. Two examples of the CARDINALITY hint

```
SELECT /*+ cardinality(s 918) */
       *
  FROM sh.sales s
 WHERE amount_sold > 100
       AND prod_id IN (SELECT /*+ no_unnest */
                              prod_id
                         FROM sh.products p
                        WHERE prod_category = 'Hardware');
```

```
-------------------------------------------------------------
| Id | Operation                    | Name        | Rows  |
-------------------------------------------------------------
|  0 | SELECT STATEMENT             |             |   13  |
|* 1 |  FILTER                      |             |       |
|  2 |   PARTITION RANGE ALL        |             |  918  |
|* 3 |    TABLE ACCESS FULL         | SALES       |  918  |
|* 4 |    TABLE ACCESS BY INDEX ROWID| PRODUCTS   |    1  |
|* 5 |     INDEX UNIQUE SCAN        | PRODUCTS_PK |    1  |
-------------------------------------------------------------
```

Predicate Information (identified by operation id):

```
   1 - filter( EXISTS (SELECT /*+ NO_UNNEST */ 0 FROM "SH"."PRODUCTS"
           "P" WHERE "PROD_ID"=:B1 AND "PROD_CATEGORY"='Hardware'))
   3 - filter("AMOUNT_SOLD">100)
   4 - filter("PROD_CATEGORY"='Hardware')
   5 - access("PROD_ID"=:B1)
```

```
SELECT /*+ cardinality(s 918) */
       *
  FROM sh.sales s
 WHERE amount_sold > 100
       AND prod_id IN (SELECT /*+ no_unnest push_subq */
                              prod_id
                         FROM sh.products p
                        WHERE prod_category = 'Hardware');
```

```
----------------------------------------------------------------
| Id  | Operation                       | Name        | Rows  |
----------------------------------------------------------------
|  0  | SELECT STATEMENT                |             |   918 |
|  1  |  PARTITION RANGE ALL            |             |   918 |
|* 2  |   TABLE ACCESS FULL             | SALES       |   918 |
|* 3  |    TABLE ACCESS BY INDEX ROWID  | PRODUCTS    |     1 |
|* 4  |     INDEX UNIQUE SCAN           | PRODUCTS_PK |     1 |
----------------------------------------------------------------
```

Predicate Information (identified by operation id):

```
   2 - filter("AMOUNT_SOLD">100 AND  EXISTS (SELECT /*+ PUSH_SUBQ
            NO_UNNEST */ 0 FROM "SH"."PRODUCTS" "P" WHERE "PROD_ID"=:B1 AND
            "PROD_CATEGORY"='Hardware'))
   3 - filter("PROD_CATEGORY"='Hardware')
   4 - access("PROD_ID"=:B1)
```

Both queries in Listing 18-6 include a subquery that isn't unnested. I could have used a complex subquery to make my point, but to avoid unnecessary complexity I have kept the subquery simple and included a NO_UNNEST hint.

The CARDINALITY hint takes the name of a row source as the first argument and the number of rows expected to be returned from the operation that accesses the row source as the second. To be clear, the cardinality estimate indicates the number of rows returned from the row source *after* the application of predicates but *before* the results of any joins, aggregations, or filters. There are 918,843 rows in SH.SALES, but the CARDINALITY hint in Listing 18-6 specifies a value of just 918. Notice that in the first execution plan shown in Listing 18-6, the cardinality estimate of 918 is applied *after* the application of the AMOUNT_SOLD > 100 predicate but *before* the application of the subquery filtering that is performed as a separate step. The second statement in Listing 18-6 differs from the first only by the presence of a PUSH_SUBQ hint that causes the filtering by the subquery to be performed as part of the full table scan itself. The consequence of this is that the cardinality estimate applies after *both* the AMOUNT_SOLD > 100 filter *and* the subquery filter have been applied. You can see that the statement is expected to return 13 rows in the former case and 918 in the latter.

The confusion about the meaning of the CARDINALITY hint is not limited to the application of subquery filters. Take a look at Listing 18-7, which shows CARDINALITY hints used on the probe tables of NESTED LOOPS joins.

Listing 18-7. CARDINALITY hint with NESTED LOOPS joins

```
SELECT /*+ cardinality(c 46000) leading(co) use_nl(c) */
       *
  FROM sh.countries co JOIN sh.customers c USING (country_id);
```

```
-------------------------------------------------
| Id  | Operation           | Name      | Rows  |
-------------------------------------------------
|   0 | SELECT STATEMENT    |           | 46000 |
|   1 |  NESTED LOOPS       |           | 46000 |
|   2 |   TABLE ACCESS FULL | COUNTRIES |    23 |
|*  3 |   TABLE ACCESS FULL | CUSTOMERS |  2000 |
-------------------------------------------------
```

```
Predicate Information (identified by operation id):
---------------------------------------------------
```

```
   3 - filter("CO"."COUNTRY_ID"="C"."COUNTRY_ID")
```

```
SELECT /*+ cardinality(c 46000) leading(co) use_nl(c) */
       *
  FROM sh.countries co JOIN sh.customers c USING (country_id)
 WHERE country_region = 'Asia';
```

```
-------------------------------------------------
| Id  | Operation           | Name      | Rows  |
-------------------------------------------------
|   0 | SELECT STATEMENT    |           |  9281 |
|   1 |  NESTED LOOPS       |           |  9281 |
|*  2 |   TABLE ACCESS FULL | COUNTRIES |     4 |
|*  3 |   TABLE ACCESS FULL | CUSTOMERS |  2421 |
-------------------------------------------------
```

```
Predicate Information (identified by operation id):
---------------------------------------------------
```

```
   2 - filter("CO"."COUNTRY_REGION"='Asia')
   3 - filter("CO"."COUNTRY_ID"="C"."COUNTRY_ID")
```

The two queries in Listing 18-7 both join SH.COUNTRIES with SH.CUSTOMERS, and we use hints to force a NESTED LOOPS join for demonstration purposes.

In the first query in Listing 18-7 there is no filter predicate on either table being joined. We have specified a CARDINALITY hint to tell the CBO to assume that SH.CUSTOMERS has 46,000 rows, and the statistics on the SH.COUNTRIES table tell the CBO to assume that said table has 23 rows, each with a different value of COUNTRY_ID. When we use a NESTED LOOPS join from SH.COUNTRIES to SH.CUSTOMERS, the CBO reports that it expects each of the 23 probes to return an average of 2,000 rows, making 46,000 rows in total.

That example may only be a little confusing, but things get more complicated when we add a filter condition to SH.COUNTRIES as we have done in the second query of Listing 18-7. Since there are six values of COUNTRY_REGION in SH.COUNTRIES, the CBO now expects that only one sixth of the 23 rows in SH.COUNTRIES will match the filter predicate on COUNTRY_REGION and that the result set will be reduced accordingly. But remember that the CARDINALITY hint specifies the number of rows returned from SH.CUSTOMERS *before* any join condition. Why has the cardinality estimate *per country* increased? The reason is that the column statistics on the COUNTRY_ID column of SH.CUSTOMERS suggest that there are actually only 19 countries with customers, so the cardinality estimate per iteration of the loop is determined to be 46,000/19, i.e., 2,421! The estimated cardinality after the join is 9,281 and is calculated from (46,000/19) x (23/6) because the CBO assumes that none of the four countries without customers are in Asia!

■ **Caution** If you re-gather statistics on the SH schema you may find that a histogram is created for the COUNTRY_REGION column of SH.COUNTRIES. If that happens, the CBO will estimate that there are five countries in Asia.

By this stage you are probably realizing that the semantics of the CARDINALITY hint aren't that straightforward. This is one reason why, despite the inestimable value of the CARDINALITY hint for research, I have never personally used a CARDINALITY hint in production code.

Although the CARDINALITY hint is very useful for research, the OPT_ESTIMATE hint is more flexible. Listing 18-8 shows the flexibility of this hint.

Listing 18-8. The OPT_ESTIMATE hint

```
SELECT /*+ opt_estimate(table c rows=46000) leading(co) use_nl(c) */
       *
  FROM sh.countries co JOIN sh.customers c USING (country_id)
 WHERE country_region = 'Asia';
```

```
-------------------------------------------------
| Id  | Operation            | Name      | Rows  |
-------------------------------------------------
|   0 | SELECT STATEMENT     |           | 9281  |
|   1 |   NESTED LOOPS       |           | 9281  |
|*  2 |    TABLE ACCESS FULL | COUNTRIES |    4  |
|*  3 |    TABLE ACCESS FULL | CUSTOMERS | 2421  |
-------------------------------------------------
```

Predicate Information (identified by operation id):

```
   2 - filter("CO"."COUNTRY_REGION"='Asia')
   3 - filter("CO"."COUNTRY_ID"="C"."COUNTRY_ID")
```

```
SELECT /*+ opt_estimate(join (co, c) rows=20000) leading(co) use_nl(c) */
       *
  FROM sh.countries co JOIN sh.customers c USING (country_id)
 WHERE country_region = 'Asia';
```

```
-------------------------------------------------
| Id  | Operation            | Name      | Rows  |
-------------------------------------------------
|   0 | SELECT STATEMENT     |           | 20000 |
|   1 |   NESTED LOOPS       |           | 20000 |
|*  2 |    TABLE ACCESS FULL | COUNTRIES |    4  |
|*  3 |    TABLE ACCESS FULL | CUSTOMERS | 5217  |
-------------------------------------------------
```

Predicate Information (identified by operation id):

```
   2 - filter("CO"."COUNTRY_REGION"='Asia')
   3 - filter("CO"."COUNTRY_ID"="C"."COUNTRY_ID")
```

```
SELECT /*+ index(c (cust_id))
           opt_estimate(index_scan c customers_pk scale_rows=0.1)
       */
       *
  FROM sh.customers c;
```

```
-----------------------------------------------------------------
| Id  | Operation                        | Name         | Rows  |
-----------------------------------------------------------------
|  0  | SELECT STATEMENT                 |              | 55500 |
|  1  |   TABLE ACCESS BY INDEX ROWID BATCHED| CUSTOMERS| 55500 |
|  2  |    INDEX FULL SCAN               | CUSTOMERS_PK |  5550 |
-----------------------------------------------------------------
```

The OPT_ESTIMATE hint was invented to support SQL profiles and not for SQL tuning but is, in fact, quite useful for that purpose. The first query in Listing 18-8 uses the TABLE variant of the OPT_ESTIMATE hint that behaves in exactly the same way as the cardinality hint. The second variant allows us to specify the number of rows that are returned from the JOIN of two tables. The final variant allows us to specify the number of rows returned from an INDEX SCAN. This last option is not particularly useful for us as the number of rows returned from the table itself is not affected by the hint, but I have included it in the interest of being thorough.

The INDEX SCAN example shows another feature of OPT_ESTIMATE—you don't have to specify the exact cardinality. By using SCALE_ROWS you can multiply the cardinality the CBO would have used by a specified factor, in this case 0.1.

Object statistic hints

If you are investigating the effect of object statistics on CBO behavior, you can use object statistic hints to temporarily override the values of object statistics. For example, Listing 18-9 shows how I double-checked my hypothesis that it was the number of distinct values of COUNTRY_ID in SH.SALES that affected the cardinality estimate in the second query of Listing 18-7.

Listing 18-9. Use of COLUMN_STATS hint

```
SELECT /*+ cardinality(c 46000) leading(co) use_nl(c)
           column_stats(sh.customers, country_id, scale, distinct=23)
           index_stats(sh.customers, customers_pk, scale,
                       clustering_factor=1, index_rows=1 blocks=1000)
           table_stats(sh.customers, scale, blocks=100 rows=46000)
           */
       *
  FROM sh.countries co JOIN sh.customers c USING (country_id)
 WHERE country_region = 'Asia';
-------------------------------------------------------
| Id  | Operation             | Name      | Rows  |
-------------------------------------------------------
|  0  | SELECT STATEMENT      |           | 7667  |
|  1  |  NESTED LOOPS         |           | 7667  |
|* 2  |   TABLE ACCESS FULL   | COUNTRIES |    4  |
|* 3  |   TABLE ACCESS FULL   | CUSTOMERS | 2000  |
-------------------------------------------------------

Predicate Information (identified by operation id):
---------------------------------------------------

   2 - filter("CO"."COUNTRY_REGION"='Asia')
   3 - filter("CO"."COUNTRY_ID"="C"."COUNTRY_ID")
```

Listing 18-9 shows that when the CBO believes that there are 23 distinct values of COUNTRY_ID present in the SH.CUSTOMERS table and that there are 46,000 rows in the table as a whole, the number of rows per country is 2,000 as expected. The CBO doesn't estimate that the join will return 8,000 rows, because the estimated number of countries is estimated at 23/6, not as the rounded value of 4 that is displayed.

Listing 18-9 also shows the syntax for the INDEX_STATS and TABLE_STATS hints, but these have no material effect on the execution plan details in this instance.

■ **Caution**   In version 12.1.0.1 specifically, the TABLE_STATS hint appears to force dynamic sampling. As a consequence of this bug the TABLE_STATS hint is unusable for SQL tuning in that version.

Wrapping up hints that are hints

The non-prescriptive hints that simply adjust the data that the CBO uses in its calculations are extremely useful for investigating the cause of poorly performing execution plans and for devising alternative approaches. However, I wouldn't use them in production systems without a very specific reason.

Although some would argue that it is a good idea to leave the CBO alone to come up with "fresh solutions," as the health warning quoted at the start of this chapter put it, I beg to differ. The whole point of the CBO is that you generally don't have to work out an execution plan yourself. By the time you have done sufficient analysis to come to the conclusion that hints are definitely required, you probably have worked out what execution plan you want. If you then decide to hint your code in production, you should use prescriptive hints, i.e., hints that are really directives. Let us focus on those hints now.

Production-hinting case studies

Let us imagine that you have completed your analysis of an errant SQL statement, you understand why the performance was originally so bad, and you have successfully completed performance testing of your fix. However, since you can only achieve the execution plan you need with hints, you may be unsure of whether you have missed something. Here are a few case studies that might help you with the thought process.

The bushy join

I put a brief note at the bottom of Figure 11-3 that stated that the CBO never considers a *bushy join*. I must say I have been fascinated by the concept of a bushy join ever since I read about it in the first edition of Christian Antognini's book *Troubleshooting Oracle Performance*. It is such an easy concept for a human to grasp and demonstrates the need for hinting so well. In real life, however, the need for a bushy join is extremely rare, and it isn't even easy to come up with a plausible SQL statement using the example schemas. Instead, Listing 18-10 revisits Listing 2-3, which used the entirely artificial tables created in Listing 1-21.

Listing 18-10. The bushy join missed

```
SELECT *
  FROM (t1 JOIN t2 ON t1.c1 = t2.c2)
       JOIN (t3 JOIN t4 ON t3.c3 = t4.c4) ON t1.c1 + t2.c2 = t3.c3 + t4.c4;
```

```
----------------------------------------------------------
| Id | Operation              | Name | Rows | Cost (%CPU)|
----------------------------------------------------------
|  0 | SELECT STATEMENT       |      |    1 |   9   (0)|
|* 1 |  HASH JOIN             |      |    1 |   9   (0)|
|  2 |   MERGE JOIN CARTESIAN |      |   25 |   7   (0)|
|* 3 |    HASH JOIN           |      |    5 |   4   (0)|
|  4 |     TABLE ACCESS FULL  | T1   |    5 |   2   (0)|
|  5 |     TABLE ACCESS FULL  | T2   |    5 |   2   (0)|
|  6 |    BUFFER SORT         |      |    5 |   5   (0)|
|  7 |     TABLE ACCESS FULL  | T3   |    5 |   1   (0)|
|  8 |   TABLE ACCESS FULL    | T4   |    5 |   2   (0)|
----------------------------------------------------------
```

```
Predicate Information (identified by operation id):
---------------------------------------------------

   1 - access("T3"."C3"="T4"."C4")
       filter("T1"."C1"+"T2"."C2"="T3"."C3"+"T4"."C4")
   3 - access("T1"."C1"="T2"."C2")
```

The use of ANSI join syntax in Listing 18-10 suggests a specific join tree. Using the syntax from Chapter 11, that join tree is: (T1 ➔ T2) ➔ (T3 ➔ T4). In other words, we join T1 and T2, creating an intermediate result set, we join T3 and T4, generating a second intermediate result set, and finally we join the two intermediate result sets.

Pictorially, we can show a bushy join as follows:

You might like to compare Figure 18-1 with Figure 11-3, which shows a right-deep join tree, and figure 11-2, which shows the left-deep join tree, (T1 ➔ T2) ➔ (T3 ➔ T4), which the CBO has produced for the query in Listing 18-10. To a human being it is quite clear how to proceed, but we need to both rewrite our code *and* hint it to lead the CBO to reach an execution plan that doesn't involve a Cartesian join. Listing 18-11 shows what we must do.

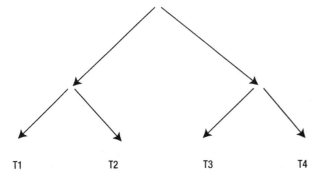

T1   T2   T3   T4

Figure 18-1. *The bushy join*

Listing 18-11. A bushy join with hints

```
WITH t1_t2
     AS (SELECT /*+ no_merge */
              *
          FROM t1 JOIN t2 ON t1.c1 = t2.c2)
    ,t3_t4
     AS (SELECT /*+ no_merge */
              *
          FROM t3 JOIN t4 ON t3.c3 = t4.c4)
SELECT /*+ use_hash(t1_t2) use_hash(t3_t4) */
       *
  FROM t1_t2 JOIN t3_t4 ON t1_t2.c1 + t1_t2.c2 = t3_t4.c3 + t3_t4.c4;
```

```
-------------------------------------------------------------
| Id  | Operation             | Name | Rows | Cost (%CPU)|
-------------------------------------------------------------
|   0 | SELECT STATEMENT      |      |    1 |    8   (0)|
|*  1 |  HASH JOIN            |      |    1 |    8   (0)|
|   2 |   VIEW               |      |    5 |    4   (0)|
|*  3 |    HASH JOIN          |      |    5 |    4   (0)|
|   4 |     TABLE ACCESS FULL| T1   |    5 |    2   (0)|
|   5 |     TABLE ACCESS FULL| T2   |    5 |    2   (0)|
|   6 |   VIEW               |      |    5 |    4   (0)|
|*  7 |    HASH JOIN          |      |    5 |    4   (0)|
|   8 |     TABLE ACCESS FULL| T3   |    5 |    2   (0)|
|   9 |     TABLE ACCESS FULL| T4   |    5 |    2   (0)|
-------------------------------------------------------------
```

```
Predicate Information (identified by operation id):
---------------------------------------------------

   1 - access("T1_T2"."C1"+"T1_T2"."C2"="T3_T4"."C3"+"T3_T4"."C4")
   3 - access("T1"."C1"="T2"."C2")
   7 - access("T3"."C3"="T4"."C4")
```

Without the NO_MERGE hints, the CBO would simply apply the simple view-merging transformation on the rewritten query in Listing 18-11, reproducing the original query in Listing 18-10, and then fail to come up with the optimal plan!

The reason that the hints are necessary in this case is that simple view merging is a *heuristic* transformation. As I explained in Chapter 13, heuristic transformations are applied without any regard to whether they speed up the query or not. In real life, simple view merging is almost always either beneficial or harmless, but in those extremely exceptional cases where a bushy join really is required you will have to use hints to get the right plan.

Although bushy joins are perhaps a once-in-a-lifetime experience, my next example is far more common.

Materialization of factored subqueries

Like simple view merging, factored subquery materialization is a heuristic transformation. The transformation is applied whenever the factored subquery is referenced more than once. Listing 18-12 shows an example of the INLINE hint being used to prevent the CBO from applying the transformation inappropriately.

Listing 18-12. Inappropriate factored subquery materialization

```
WITH q1
    AS ( SELECT /*+ inline */
                time_id
                ,cust_id
                ,MIN (amount_sold) min_as
                ,MAX (amount_sold) max_as
                ,SUM (amount_sold) sum_as
                , 100
                  * ratio_to_report (SUM (amount_sold))
                      OVER (PARTITION BY time_id)
                    pct_total
            FROM sh.sales
        GROUP BY time_id, cust_id)
SELECT *
  FROM q1
 WHERE time_id = DATE '1999-12-31' AND min_as < 100
UNION ALL
SELECT *
  FROM q1
 WHERE time_id = DATE '2000-01-01' AND max_as > 100;
```

-- Execution plan without hint

```
-----------------------------------------------------------------------------------------
| Id  | Operation                   | Name                      | Rows  |TempSpc| Cost (%CPU)|
-----------------------------------------------------------------------------------------
|   0 | SELECT STATEMENT            |                           | 1837K |       | 1233  (51)|
|   1 |  TEMP TABLE TRANSFORMATION  |                           |       |       |           |
|   2 |   LOAD AS SELECT            | SYS_TEMP_0FD9D664A_64B671 |       |       |           |
|   3 |    PARTITION RANGE ALL      |                           |  918K |       | 5745   (1)|
|   4 |     WINDOW BUFFER           |                           |  918K |       | 5745   (1)|
|   5 |      SORT GROUP BY          |                           |  918K |  24M  | 5745   (1)|
|   6 |       TABLE ACCESS FULL     | SALES                     |  918K |       |  517   (2)|
|   7 |   UNION-ALL                 |                           |       |       |           |
|*  8 |    VIEW                     |                           |  918K |       |  616   (1)|
|   9 |     TABLE ACCESS FULL       | SYS_TEMP_0FD9D664A_64B671 |  918K |       |  616   (1)|
|* 10 |    VIEW                     |                           |  918K |       |  616   (1)|
|  11 |     TABLE ACCESS FULL       | SYS_TEMP_0FD9D664A_64B671 |  918K |       |  616   (1)|
-----------------------------------------------------------------------------------------
```

Predicate Information (identified by operation id):

```
    8 - filter("TIME_ID"=TO_DATE(' 1999-12-31 00:00:00', 'syyyy-mm-dd
            hh24:mi:ss') AND "MIN_AS"<100)
   10 - filter("TIME_ID"=TO_DATE(' 2000-01-01 00:00:00', 'syyyy-mm-dd
            hh24:mi:ss') AND "MAX_AS">100)
```

-- Execution plan with hint

Id	Operation	Name	Rows	Cost (%CPU)
0	SELECT STATEMENT		312	**43** (45)
1	UNION-ALL			
* 2	VIEW		207	24 (0)
3	WINDOW BUFFER		207	24 (0)
4	SORT GROUP BY		207	24 (0)
5	**PARTITION RANGE SINGLE**		310	24 (0)
6	**TABLE ACCESS BY LOCAL INDEX ROWID BATCHED**	SALES	310	24 (0)
7	BITMAP CONVERSION TO ROWIDS			
* 8	BITMAP INDEX SINGLE VALUE	SALES_TIME_BIX		
* 9	VIEW		105	19 (0)
10	WINDOW BUFFER		105	19 (0)
11	SORT GROUP BY		105	19 (0)
12	**PARTITION RANGE SINGLE**		153	19 (0)
13	**TABLE ACCESS BY LOCAL INDEX ROWID BATCHED**	SALES	153	19 (0)
14	BITMAP CONVERSION TO ROWIDS			
* 15	BITMAP INDEX SINGLE VALUE	SALES_TIME_BIX		

Predicate Information (identified by operation id):

```
   2 - filter("MIN_AS"<100)
   8 - access("TIME_ID"=TO_DATE(' 1999-12-31 00:00:00', 'syyyy-mm-dd hh24:mi:ss'))
   9 - filter("MAX_AS">100)
  15 - access("TIME_ID"=TO_DATE(' 2000-01-01 00:00:00', 'syyyy-mm-dd hh24:mi:ss'))
```

The factored subquery in Listing 18-12 performs several calculations on data from the SH.SALES table aggregated by TIME_ID and CUST_ID. The specifics of the calculations aren't particularly relevant; just realize that you wouldn't want to type them in twice.

The main query lists a subset of these analytics for the last day of the 20th century and the first day of the 21st century.

Without the INLINE hint the factored subquery will be materialized, and since there is no common predicate to be pushed into the view, data for *all* values of TIME_ID in *all* partitions of SH.SALES is aggregated. When we add the INLINE hint, not only does the estimated cost of the query reduce from 1,233 to 43, but also actual elapsed time reduces as well. The reason for this is that when the factored subquery is merged individually into the two branches of the UNION-ALL operation, not only can partition elimination occur but indexed access to the single partition becomes possible too.

It is possible to devise alternative ways to suppress factored subquery materialization that avoid the use of an undocumented hint. You could, for example, cut and paste the code from the factored subquery to create a duplicate factored subquery, or you could resort to inline views. Rewriting code in such a way just to avoid the use of a hint is bad practice. Not only does it make the code less readable but it also introduces the risk of having an issue with an upgrade: a future version of the CBO might recognize code duplication and "optimize" the duplicate away, recreating the original code! The most maintainable solution, perhaps counteri ntuitively, is to use the undocumented hint; Oracle couldn't possibly stop the INLINE hint from working in a future release given its widespread legitimate use in the existing customer code base.

Suppressing order by elimination and subquery unnesting

This next example will require a little bit of imagination on your part, as it is far from ideal. Let us assume that we want to list all the rows from SH.SALES for the first month of the 21st century together with a column, COUNTRY_SALES_TOTAL, that holds the sum of AMOUNT_SOLD for the associated country for *all* dates. We want to order the results by COUNTRY_SALES_TOTAL. Imagine that the SH.SALES table has many more columns and many more rows than it actually has and that there are many more countries in the world than there actually are.

That being the case, you might find that after trying all the tricks in the last chapter you still can't find a way to sum AMOUNT_SOLD for all countries at once without running into serious problems with temporary tablespace and elapsed time. You make the following plan:

- You realize that there were not sales to all countries in January 2000 and you decide to only aggregate data for those countries that are actually needed. Even so, you still have issues with temporary tablespace.

- You decide to aggregate the data for the identified subset of countries one country at a time, thus avoiding the need for any sort at this point. This might take longer in theory, but you won't need nearly as much temporary tablespace.

- You decide to use the idea from Listing 17-12 and sort just the ROWID from SH.SALES with the associated COUNTRY_ID column from SH.CUSTOMERS.

With these thoughts in mind you devise the SQL in Listing 18-13:

Listing 18-13. Aggregating data piecemeal

```
SELECT /*+ leading(v2) use_nl(s3) */
       s3.*, v2.country_sales_total
  FROM ( SELECT /*+ no_merge */
                v1.sales_rowid
              , (SELECT /*+ no_unnest */
                        SUM (amount_sold)
                   FROM sh.customers c1 JOIN sh.sales s1 USING (cust_id)
                  WHERE c1.country_id = v1.country_id)
                 country_sales_total
           FROM ( SELECT /*+ no_merge no_eliminate_oby */
                         c2.country_id, s2.ROWID sales_rowid
                    FROM sh.customers c2 JOIN sh.sales s2 USING (cust_id)
                   WHERE s2.time_id BETWEEN DATE '2000-01-01'
                                        AND DATE '2000-12-31'
                 ORDER BY c2.country_id, s2.ROWID) v1
         ORDER BY country_sales_total) v2
        ,sh.sales s3
 WHERE s3.ROWID = v2.sales_rowid;
```

Before looking at the execution plans for the query in Listing 18-13, let us look at what the query intends to do without worrying about the embedded hints.

Let us first look at the inline view, tagged V1. This subquery obtains the ROWID from SH.SALES, the COUNTRY_ID from SH.CUSTOMERS, and then sorts them so that all the rows from SH.SALES for the same country are together. The outer subquery, V2, then takes this sorted data and uses a correlated subquery in the SELECT list to obtain the value of COUNTRY_SALES_TOTAL for the country in question. Because the data from V1 is sorted by COUNTRY_ID we can have complete confidence that scalar subquery caching will prevent the aggregation for a particular country being performed more than once.

Now that we have replaced COUNTRY_ID with COUNTRY_SALES_TOTAL in the SELECT list we can use COUNTRY_SALES_TOTAL as a key for a second sort that still has just two columns. Finally, the main query fattens out the rows in the result set with the extra columns from SH.SALES, picking them up via the ROWID.

Listing 18-14 shows two execution plans for the query in Listing 18-13. The first execution plan is obtained without hints, and the second with hints.

Listing 18-14. Execution plans for Listing 18-13

-- Execution plan without hints

```
-----------------------------------------------------------------------
| Id  | Operation                 | Name        | Bytes |TempSpc| Cost (%CPU)|
-----------------------------------------------------------------------
|   0 | SELECT STATEMENT          |             |   42M |       | 12922  (1)|
|   1 |  SORT ORDER BY            |             |   42M |  51M  | 12922  (1)|
|*  2 |   HASH JOIN RIGHT OUTER    |             |   42M |       |  2024  (2)|
|   3 |    VIEW                   | VW_SSQ_1    |  342  |       |   961  (4)|
|   4 |     HASH GROUP BY         |             |  532  |       |   961  (4)|
|*  5 |      HASH JOIN            |             |  193K |       |   961  (4)|
|   6 |       VIEW                | VW_GBC_7    |  124K |       |   538  (6)|
|   7 |        HASH GROUP BY      |             | 70590 |       |   538  (6)|
|   8 |         PARTITION RANGE ALL |           | 8973K |       |   517  (2)|
|   9 |          TABLE ACCESS FULL | SALES       | 8973K |       |   517  (2)|
|  10 |       TABLE ACCESS FULL   | CUSTOMERS   |  541K |       |   423  (1)|
|* 11 |    HASH JOIN              |             | 8796K | 1200K |  1061  (1)|
|  12 |     TABLE ACCESS FULL     | CUSTOMERS   |  541K |       |   423  (1)|
|  13 |     PARTITION RANGE ITERATOR|          | 6541K |       |   131  (2)|
|* 14 |      TABLE ACCESS FULL    | SALES       | 6541K |       |   131  (2)|
-----------------------------------------------------------------------
```

```
Predicate Information (identified by operation id):
---------------------------------------------------

   2 - access("ITEM_1"(+)="C2"."COUNTRY_ID")
   5 - access("C1"."CUST_ID"="ITEM_1")
  11 - access("C2"."CUST_ID"="S2"."CUST_ID")
  14 - filter("S2"."TIME_ID"<=TO_DATE(' 2000-12-31 00:00:00',
          'syyyy-mm-dd hh24:mi:ss'))
```

-- Execution plan with hints

```
-----------------------------------------------------------------------
| Id  | Operation                 | Name        | Bytes |TempSpc| Cost (%CPU)|
-----------------------------------------------------------------------
|   0 | SELECT STATEMENT          |             |   11M |       |  253K  (1)|
|   1 |  SORT AGGREGATE          |             |   20  |       |          |
|*  2 |   HASH JOIN              |             | 7426K |       |   942  (2)|
|*  3 |    TABLE ACCESS FULL     | CUSTOMERS   | 29210 |       |   423  (1)|
|   4 |    PARTITION RANGE ALL    |             | 8973K |       |   517  (2)|
|   5 |     TABLE ACCESS FULL    | SALES       | 8973K |       |   517  (2)|
|   6 |  NESTED LOOPS            |             |   11M |       |  253K  (1)|
|   7 |   VIEW                   |             | 5638K |       | 22723  (1)|
|   8 |    SORT ORDER BY         |             | 5638K | 8184K | 22723  (1)|
|   9 |     VIEW                 |             | 5638K |       |  3162  (1)|
|  10 |      SORT ORDER BY       |             | 7894K |  10M  |  3162  (1)|
```

```
|* 11 |          HASH JOIN               |           | 7894K| 1200K| 1018   (1)|
|  12 |            TABLE ACCESS FULL     | CUSTOMERS |  541K|      |  423   (1)|
|  13 |            PARTITION RANGE ITERATOR|         | 5638K|      |  131   (2)|
|* 14 |              TABLE ACCESS FULL   | SALES     | 5638K|      |  131   (2)|
|  15 | TABLE ACCESS BY USER ROWID       | SALES     |   29 |      |    1   (0)|
--------------------------------------------------------------------------------
```

Predicate Information (identified by operation id):

```
   2 - access("C1"."CUST_ID"="S1"."CUST_ID")
   3 - filter("C1"."COUNTRY_ID"=:B1)
  11 - access("C2"."CUST_ID"="S2"."CUST_ID")
  14 - filter("S2"."TIME_ID"<=TO_DATE(' 2000-12-31 00:00:00',
              'syyyy-mm-dd hh24:mi:ss'))
```

Without hints all the hard work we have put in to get the SQL statement to run just the way we want it to has been undone. We can see evidence of subquery unnesting, group by placement, and order by elimination, among other transformations. The CBO estimate for maximum temporary tablespace consumption is 51M for the sort of the fat rows right at the end.

The execution plan obtained with hints looks more like what we want, although I had to check the column projection data to verify just when the correlated subquery was evaluated. To the casual eye it looks like the subquery is evaluated at the very end, but COUNTRY_SALES_TOTAL is the key for the SORT ORDER BY on line 8, and that is where the correlated subquery is actually evaluated.

With the addition of the hints we can see that the maximum tablespace consumption has been reduced five-fold to 10M. This 10M is needed at the point in the execution plan where we had two active workareas: one for the HASH JOIN on line 11 and one for the SORT ORDER BY on line 2.

But why did we need so many hints? Were they all really necessary? The answer is yes, they were all necessary.[1] In fact, there is a strong case for adding at least one more hint. Here is the analysis:

- The two NO_MERGE hints for V1 and V2 were needed because simple view merging is a heuristic transformation that is unconditionally applied.

- The UNNEST hint for the correlated subquery is also needed because of the unconditional nature of the heuristic subquery unnesting transformation.

- The NO_ELIMINATE_OBY hint in V1 is needed because order by elimination is a heuristic transformation that is always applied when a subsequent sort is required. In fact, I would add a NO_ELIMINATE_OBY to V2 even though the subsequent join doesn't currently trigger order by elimination; the order by elimination transformation might be extended to cover joins in a future release. Of course, in real life I would use factored subqueries, and I have even been known to add NO_ELIMINATE_OBY hints to those on my more paranoid of days!

- The LEADING and USE_NL hints in the main query are needed because we can't include an ORDER BY clause in the main query for reasons that we discussed in the previous chapter.

Even if all the transformations in this last example were cost-based, the CBO probably still wouldn't have gotten it right. For one thing, the CBO is entirely focused on reducing elapsed time and is unconcerned about temporary tablespace utilization; the CBO assumes space in a temporary tablespace never runs out. For another, the CBO currently has no way to measure the benefits of scalar subquery caching and would see no point in retaining the first sort.

---

[1]The NO_QUERY_TRANSFORMATION hint is an alternative that may reduce the number of hints in this case.

Of course, this example is seriously flawed in several ways. For example, even if we wanted to perform our aggregations piecemeal we probably would want to find a way to aggregate data for more than one country at a time. The challenge here, as it is so often in this book, is to find simple examples to generate techniques used in complex situations. In this particular case, the example may be a little oversimplified. However, the principle demonstrated by the example is perfectly valid: sometimes you want to construct SQL in such a way as to force a specific way of evaluating a query, utterly abandoning the concept of the declarative programming language introduced at the start of Chapter 1. In such circumstances you need to apply hints to ensure that your carefully constructed code isn't deconstructed by the CBO.

The v$database_block_corruption view

As you will have gathered from Chapter 9, if you didn't already know, asking the CBO to come up with a decent execution plan when object statistics are stale or otherwise inappropriate is like asking it to fight with both hands tied behind its back. However, a couple of years ago I was unfortunate enough to encounter a situation where the CBO would *always* be fighting with both hands behind its back!

If you select rows from the data dictionary view V$DATABASE_BLOCK_CORRUPTION I sincerely hope, for your sake, that you get no rows back! In a healthy database this view returns no rows, but if RMAN detects corrupt blocks when performing a backup it populates underlying data structures with information about the corrupt blocks, which you can see by looking at this view.

One of the first questions that will run through your mind when you discover corrupt blocks in your database is: *Which segments are corrupt?* There is a well-known article, 472231.1, on the Oracle support website that includes a query that joins V$DATABASE_BLOCK_CORRUPTION, DBA_SEGMENTS, and DBA_EXTENTS to identify the corrupt blocks.

When you run the query provided in that note, the CBO will look at the statistics for the database object X$KCCBLKCOR that V$DATABASE_BLOCK_CORRUPTION references and see that it apparently has no rows, because X$KCCBLKCOR would have contained no rows the last time data dictionary statistics had been gathered. Of course there is no point in running the query in note 472231.1 unless there *are* corrupt blocks, so you *always* need to hint the query to get it to run quickly!

Incidentally, the query in note 472231.1 contains a second weakness in that it reports corruption in segments above their high-water mark, which should not be a cause for a concern. I do have an amended script (submitted to Oracle at the time) that removes the false-positive reports and includes hints to give a reasonable execution plan. The script is too long to print here but is available as corruption.sql in the downloadable materials. Do bear in mind, however, that I have not had the opportunity to verify corruption.sql on a real corrupt database, so I cannot guarantee its correctness or suitability for purpose.

Summary

There are a few hints that are used by edition-based redefinition and a few more that are mainly aimed at the runtime engine, such as the APPEND hint. The vast majority of hints, however, are optimizer hints, which fall into two categories.

On one hand, some optimizer hints really are just hints and are very useful for investigating the cause of poorly performing execution plans and for identifying possible alternatives in a SQL tuning exercise. However, the use of non-prescriptive hints on production systems is generally inadvisable because of their unpredictable behavior.

On the other hand, prescriptive hints, hints that are really directives, can legitimately be used on production systems to solve some classes of performance problems. The use of hints on production systems should only be done after due consideration, not because the hints are likely to cease to function in a future release or because the level of support from Oracle will be negatively impacted but because the supporting documentation is usually very poor or non-existent. That lack of documentation has a tendency to lead to misunderstanding and misuse.

This chapter and the preceding three have covered most of the techniques that are at your disposal in your quest to optimize SQL performance. There are, however, one or two more advanced techniques that may be of use in special situations. On to Chapter 19.

CHAPTER 19

Advanced Tuning Techniques

When I first planned out this book I imagined that this chapter would be a lot longer than it is. In truth, most of the advanced techniques that I use in SQL tuning have already been addressed in earlier chapters. I just have a couple of educational, if obscure, cases to run through. Let us begin with some unusual ways to use the ROWID pseudocolumn.

The availability of the ROWID pseudocolumn is a distinguishing feature of the Oracle database product. This pseudocolumn can be used to get around quite a few of the characteristics of the product. I use the word *characteristics* rather than a more disparaging noun because no criticism is intended. In truth, the CBO has to make a decision on an execution plan in as short a time as possible and it makes little sense to consider options that only make sense once in a blue moon.

Leveraging an INDEX FAST FULL SCAN

In Chapter 10 I explained that the INDEX FAST FULL SCAN access method could only be used when all the columns selected from the table were in the index. However, sometimes this can be a nuisance, and Listing 19-1 shows how to work around the problem in extreme cases.

Listing 19-1. Self-join to use an INDEX FAST FULL SCAN

```
SELECT /*+ no_eliminate_join(t1) no_eliminate_join(t2) leading(t1) use_nl(t2) rowid(t2) */
       t2.*
  FROM sh.sales t1, sh.sales t2
 WHERE MOD (t1.cust_id, 10000) = 1 AND t2.ROWID = t1.ROWID;
```

```
-------------------------------------------------------------------------
| Id  | Operation                     | Name            | Rows  | Cost (%CPU)|
-------------------------------------------------------------------------
|   0 | SELECT STATEMENT              |                 |  9188 |  9597   (1)|
|   1 |  NESTED LOOPS                 |                 |  9188 |    97   (1)|
|   2 |   PARTITION RANGE ALL         |                 |  9188 |   407   (0)|
|   3 |    BITMAP CONVERSION TO ROWIDS|                 |  9188 |   407   (0)|
|   4 |     BITMAP INDEX FAST FULL SCAN| SALES_CUST_BIX |       |            |
|   5 |   TABLE ACCESS BY USER ROWID  | SALES           |     1 |     1   (0)|
-------------------------------------------------------------------------
```

Listing 19-1 selects all the columns from SH.SALES yet somehow has managed to use an INDEX FAST FULL SCAN. The point here is that we have used a self-join, and the only columns referenced from the copy of SH.SALES with alias T1 are CUST_ID and ROWID. Since there is no need to reference the table data from T1, an INDEX FAST FULL SCAN can be used. We then use the ROWID obtained from the T1 copy of SH.SALES to access the T2 copy and from there pick up the rest of the columns.

It is extremely unusual to need to use this sort of approach, which is almost certainly why the CBO doesn't consider it unless a self-join is explicitly coded. In the case of Listing 19-1 we only read three rows (not the arbitrary 1% selectivity that the CBO assumes), but the index entries for these three rows are scattered about the index. An INDEX RANGE SCAN is not an option, and so in this exceptional case we have no good alternative to the INDEX FAST FULL SCAN.

There are two reasons why we need to use all these hints[1] to get the execution plan that we want: first, the estimate for the number of rows that match the MOD function call is too high, and second, join elimination is a heuristic optimizer transformation, as I explained in Chapter 13. Remember that heuristic transformations are applied even if they result in an execution plan with a higher estimated cost.

Because of the small size of the SALES_CUST_BIX index you may find that the use of a traditional INDEX FULL SCAN without a self-join will perform equivalently to Listing 19-1. But when the index is large and isn't cached you should see a significant improvement in performance when using an INDEX FAST FULL SCAN and a self-join.

An INDEX FAST FULL SCAN isn't the only access method with restrictions that we can work around by means of a self-join. Let me now make true on a promise I made in Chapter 13 and show you how users of Oracle database standard edition can simulate a star transformation in extreme circumstances.

Simulating a Star Transformation

Users of Oracle database standard edition have no access to either bitmap indexes or partitioned tables. Listing 19-2 begins by copying the SH.SALES table to an unpartitioned table in the current schema before issuing a rewrite of the query in Listing 13-35.

Listing 19-2. Star transformations for standard edition users

```
CREATE TABLE t1
AS
     SELECT *
       FROM sh.sales s
   ORDER BY time_id, cust_id, prod_id;

CREATE INDEX t1_cust_ix
   ON t1 (cust_id)
   COMPRESS 1;

CREATE INDEX t1_prod_ix
   ON t1 (prod_id)
   COMPRESS 1;

WITH q1
    AS (SELECT /*+ no_merge */
               c.cust_first_name, s.ROWID rid
          FROM sh.customers c JOIN t1 s USING (cust_id)
         WHERE c.cust_last_name = 'Everett')
    ,q2
    AS (SELECT /*+ no_merge */
               p.prod_name, s.ROWID rid
          FROM sh.products p JOIN t1 s USING (prod_id)
         WHERE p.prod_category = 'Electronics')
```

---

[1]Although the hints I have used make my intentions explicit, a single NO_QUERY_TRANSFORMATION hint is a potentially more future-proof alternative to the three NO_ELIMINATE_JOIN hints.

```
SELECT /*+ no_eliminate_join(s) leading(q1 q2 s) use_nl(s) */
      q2.prod_name
      ,q1.cust_first_name
      ,s.time_id
      ,s.amount_sold
  FROM q1 NATURAL JOIN q2 JOIN t1 s ON rid = s.ROWID;
```

```
---------------------------------------------------------------------------------
| Id  | Operation                             | Name                | Rows  | Cost (%CPU)|
---------------------------------------------------------------------------------
|   0 | SELECT STATEMENT                      |                     | 1591  | 2420   (1)|
|   1 |  NESTED LOOPS                         |                     | 1591  | 2420   (1)|
|   2 |   HASH JOIN                           |                     | 1591  |  829   (1)|
|   3 |    VIEW                               |                     | 7956  |  545   (1)|
|   4 |     NESTED LOOPS                      |                     | 7956  |  545   (1)|
|   5 |      TABLE ACCESS FULL                | CUSTOMERS           |   61  |  423   (1)|
|   6 |      INDEX RANGE SCAN                 | T1_CUST_IX          |  130  |    2   (0)|
|   7 |    VIEW                               |                     | 183K  |  284   (1)|
|   8 |     NESTED LOOPS                      |                     | 183K  |  284   (1)|
|   9 |      TABLE ACCESS BY INDEX ROWID BATCHED| PRODUCTS          |   14  |    3   (0)|
|  10 |       INDEX RANGE SCAN                | PRODUCTS_PROD_CAT_IX|   14  |    1   (0)|
|  11 |      INDEX RANGE SCAN                 | T1_PROD_IX          | 12762 |   20   (0)|
|  12 |   TABLE ACCESS BY USER ROWID          | T1                  |    1  |    1   (0)|
---------------------------------------------------------------------------------
```

The query in Listing 19-2 uses two factored subqueries, Q1 and Q2. Q1 joins the dimension table SH.CUSTOMERS to the T1 fact table in order to identify the ROWIDs from T1 that match the specified customers. Only the index on T1.CUST_ID is required; no access to T1 itself is required. Factored subquery Q2 does the same sort of thing with the SH.PRODUCTS dimension table. The main query joins Q1 and Q2 using the ROWIDs from T1 to identify just the rows from T1 that match both sets of conditions before reading those rows from T1.

As usual, we have to litter our code with hints to force this execution plan, which on this sample data is quite inefficient. The main point to note is that the plan contains no use of enterprise edition features such as partitioning or bitmap conversions.

I must admit that I haven't worked with a client that uses standard edition for many years, so the fact that I have never used this technique in a real-life production environment doesn't mean anything. However, from a theoretical point of view I suspect legitimate uses of this type of query are as rare as hens' teeth. To explain why, I will provide a simpler example of this sort of technique in the next section.

Simulating an INDEX JOIN

As I mentioned in Chapter 10, the index join access method only works when all the columns referenced by the query are in the indexes being joined. But as we saw in Listing 19-2, we can code our own hash join on ROWID. Given the availability of the INDEX_COMBINE hint for enterprise edition users, the technique used in Listing 19-3 is probably of most interest to users of standard edition.

Listing 19-3. Simulating an index join

```
WITH q1
    AS (SELECT /*+ no_merge */
                ROWID rid
          FROM t1
         WHERE cust_id = 462)
    ,q2
    AS (SELECT /*+ no_merge */
                ROWID rid
          FROM t1
         WHERE prod_id = 19)
SELECT /*+ leading(q1 q2) use_nl(t1) */
       t1.*
  FROM q1, q2, t1
 WHERE q1.rid = q2.rid AND q2.rid = t1.ROWID;
```

```
-------------------------------------------------------------------
| Id | Operation                  | Name      | Rows  | Cost (%CPU)|
-------------------------------------------------------------------
|  0 | SELECT STATEMENT           |           |   130 |   155  (0)|
|  1 |  NESTED LOOPS              |           |   130 |   155  (0)|
|  2 |   HASH JOIN               |           |   130 |    25  (0)|
|  3 |    VIEW                   |           |   130 |     3  (0)|
|  4 |     INDEX RANGE SCAN      | T1_CUST_IX |   130 |     3  (0)|
|  5 |    VIEW                   |           | 12762 |    22  (0)|
|  6 |     INDEX RANGE SCAN      | T1_PROD_IX | 12762 |    22  (0)|
|  7 |   TABLE ACCESS BY USER ROWID| T1       |     1 |     1  (0)|
-------------------------------------------------------------------
```

Listing 19-3 uses essentially the same technique as Listing 19-2, except that we have eliminated any reference to dimension tables. For the execution plans shown in Listing 19-2 and Listing 19-3 to be optimal, all of the following conditions must be met:

1. The option to use the INDEX_COMBINE hint is unavailable.

2. Neither index can be very selective, otherwise we wouldn't need to join the second index.

3. The combined selectivity of the two indexes must be strong, otherwise we would use a full table scan.

4. The cost savings in accessing fewer rows from the table must be more than the overhead of the additional indexed access and the hash join.

Theoretically it is possible to find a situation in which all these conditions are met. It is the fourth and final condition in the list above that is the most difficult to meet, as the hash join is far more expensive than the BITMAP AND operation used in conjunction with bitmap indexes; an index with poor selectivity is going to generate a large hash table, and the hash join may even spill to disk.

So why am I spending time talking about techniques that I have never used and that you probably will not either? There are two reasons. First, there is a lot of old code out there that uses the AND_EQUAL hint (which is pretty much the same sort of thing), and you should realize that these hints are likely to be counterproductive. The second reason is that there is another scenario where self-joins on ROWID can actually be useful. Let us look at that now.

Joining Multi-Column Indexes

As of release 12.1.0.1 neither the INDEX_JOIN nor the INDEX_COMBINE hints work when the indexes referenced are multi-column indexes with a common prefix. Listing 19-4 replaces the two indexes on T1 that we created in Listing 19-2 with two multi-column indexes that are both prefixed with the TIME_ID column.

Listing 19-4. Attempting to combine multi-column indexes

```
DROP INDEX t1_cust_ix;
DROP INDEX t1_prod_ix;

CREATE INDEX t1_cust_ix2
   ON t1 (time_id, cust_id);

CREATE INDEX t1_prod_ix2
   ON t1 (time_id, prod_id);

SELECT /*+ index_join(t1) index_combine(t1) */
       COUNT (*)
  FROM t1
 WHERE time_id = DATE '2001-12-28' AND cust_id = 1673 AND prod_id = 44;
```

```
---------------------------------------------------------------------
| Id  | Operation                            | Name        | Rows | Cost (%CPU)|
---------------------------------------------------------------------
|   0 | SELECT STATEMENT                     |             |    1 |    4   (0)|
|   1 |  SORT AGGREGATE                      |             |    1 |           |
|   2 |   TABLE ACCESS BY INDEX ROWID BATCHED| T1          |    1 |    4   (0)|
|   3 |    INDEX RANGE SCAN                  | T1_CUST_IX2 |    6 |    3   (0)|
---------------------------------------------------------------------
```

As you can see from Listing 19-4, we end up accessing the T1 table itself despite the presence of INDEX_JOIN and INDEX_COMBINE hints. Neither hint is considered legal. When I came across this situation recently I was glad that I understood how to combine indexes by hand. Listing 19-5 shows a legitimate implementation of a self-join to simulate an index join.

Listing 19-5. Simulating an index join to avoid table access

```
WITH q1
    AS (SELECT /*+ no_merge */
                ROWID rid
          FROM t1
          WHERE time_id = DATE '2001-12-28' AND cust_id = 1673)
    ,q2
    AS (SELECT /*+ no_merge */
                ROWID rid
          FROM t1
          WHERE time_id = DATE '2001-12-28' AND prod_id = 44)
SELECT /*+ leading(q1 q2) use_nl(t1) */
        COUNT (*)
  FROM q1 NATURAL JOIN q2;
```

```
---------------------------------------------------------------
| Id  | Operation          | Name        | Rows  | Cost (%CPU)|
---------------------------------------------------------------
|   0 | SELECT STATEMENT   |             |     1 |     6   (0)|
|   1 |  SORT AGGREGATE    |             |     1 |            |
|   2 |   HASH JOIN        |             |     6 |     6   (0)|
|   3 |    VIEW            |             |     6 |     3   (0)|
|   4 |     INDEX RANGE SCAN| T1_CUST_IX2 |     6 |     3   (0)|
|   5 |    VIEW            |             |    25 |     3   (0)|
|   6 |     INDEX RANGE SCAN| T1_PROD_IX2 |    25 |     3   (0)|
---------------------------------------------------------------
```

Due to the combination of the strong selectivity and the strong clustering factor of the T1_CUST_IX2 index, there is no big difference in the performance of the queries in Listing 19-4 and Listing 19-5, but in real life the gains can be substantial, particularly when the indexes are cached and the table itself is not.

I have one last usage case for the ROWID pseudocolumn, and that is to support application-coded parallel execution. Let us look at that case now.

Using ROWID Ranges for Application-Coded Parallel Execution

Understanding the problem is one of the key themes of this book, and when faced with a query like that in Listing 19-4 it is worthwhile trying to find out why the query is needed in the first place. One possible reason an application might want to know the number of rows satisfying a particular set of conditions is to identify the number of application threads needed to perform some processing in parallel.

This sort of application-driven parallel processing is quite common and is the raison d'être for the DBMS_PARALLEL_EXECUTE package. This package allows you to identify ranges of ROWIDs, referred to as chunks. The idea is that each chunk will be processed by a different application thread. The potential problems with the aforementioned package are that all rows in the table are considered and that the number of rows processed by each chunk may vary wildly.

When I created table T1 in Listing 19-2 I sorted the rows by TIME_ID, CUST_ID, and PROD_ID, reflecting a clustering of data that might well arise in real life. Now suppose the query in Listing 19-5 returned 3,000,000 rows rather than the 3 rows that are actually returned, and that we wanted to split these into three batches of 1,000,000 rows each for some kind of further processing. Listing 19-6 should give you some idea of how to do this.

Listing 19-6. Application-driven parallel execution for clustered data

```
DECLARE
    CURSOR c1
    IS
        WITH q1
            AS (SELECT /*+ no_merge */
                        ROWID rid
                    FROM t1
                   WHERE time_id = DATE '2001-12-28' AND cust_id > 1)
            ,q2
             AS (SELECT /*+ no_merge */
                        ROWID rid
                    FROM t1
                   WHERE time_id = DATE '2001-12-28' AND prod_id > 1)
            ,q3
             AS (SELECT /*+ leading(q1 q2) use_nl(t1) */
                        rid, ROW_NUMBER () OVER (ORDER BY rid) rn
                    FROM q1 NATURAL JOIN q2)
        SELECT TRUNC ( (rn - 1) / 100) + 1 chunk
              ,MIN (rid) min_rowid
              ,MAX (rid) max_rowid
              ,COUNT (*) chunk_size
          FROM q3
        GROUP BY TRUNC ( (rn - 1) / 100);

    CURSOR c2 (
       min_rowid     ROWID
      ,max_rowid     ROWID)
    IS
        SELECT /*+ rowid(t1) */
               *
          FROM t1
         WHERE     ROWID BETWEEN min_rowid AND max_rowid
               AND time_id = DATE '2001-12-28'
               AND prod_id > 1
               AND cust_id > 1;
BEGIN
    FOR r1 IN c1
    LOOP
        FOR r2 IN c2 (r1.min_rowid, r1.max_rowid)
        LOOP
            NULL;
        END LOOP;
    END LOOP;
END;
/
-- Execution plan for cursor C1 below
```

```
---------------------------------------------------------------
| Id | Operation                | Name        | Rows | Cost (%CPU)|
---------------------------------------------------------------
|  0 | SELECT STATEMENT         |             |  628 |    9   (0)|
|  1 |  HASH GROUP BY           |             |  628 |    9   (0)|
|  2 |   VIEW                   |             |  628 |    9   (0)|
|  3 |    WINDOW SORT           |             |  628 |    9   (0)|
|  4 |     HASH JOIN            |             |  628 |    9   (0)|
|  5 |      VIEW                |             |  629 |    5   (0)|
|  6 |       INDEX RANGE SCAN   | T1_CUST_IX2 |  629 |    5   (0)|
|  7 |      VIEW                |             |  629 |    4   (0)|
|  8 |       INDEX RANGE SCAN   | T1_PROD_IX2 |  629 |    4   (0)|
---------------------------------------------------------------
```

Predicate Information (identified by operation id):

```
   4 - access("Q1"."RID"="Q2"."RID")
   6 - access("TIME_ID"=TO_DATE(' 2001-12-28 00:00:00', 'syyyy-mm-dd
           hh24:mi:ss') AND "CUST_ID">1)
   8 - access("TIME_ID"=TO_DATE(' 2001-12-28 00:00:00', 'syyyy-mm-dd
           hh24:mi:ss') AND "PROD_ID">1)
```

-- Execution plan for cursor C2 below

```
------------------------------------------------------------
| Id | Operation                   | Name | Rows | Cost (%CPU)|
------------------------------------------------------------
|  0 | SELECT STATEMENT            |      |    2 | 1206   (1)|
|  1 |  FILTER                     |      |      |           |
|  2 |   TABLE ACCESS BY ROWID RANGE| T1   |    2 | 1206   (1)|
------------------------------------------------------------
```

Predicate Information (identified by operation id):

```
   1 - filter(CHARTOROWID(:B2)>=CHARTOROWID(:B1))
   2 - access(ROWID>=CHARTOROWID(:B1) AND ROWID<=CHARTOROWID(:B2))
       filter("TIME_ID"=TO_DATE(' 2001-12-28 00:00:00', 'syyyy-mm-dd
           hh24:mi:ss') AND "PROD_ID">1 AND "CUST_ID">1)
```

Listing 19-6 shows a PL/SQL block that contains two cursors. The query in cursor C1 identifies the rows in T1 that match our selection predicates (I modified them slightly so that 1,196 rows are returned rather than 3) and then groups them into chunks with a maximum of 100 rows each. Eleven of the 12 chunks in the results of the query relate to 100 rows from T1, and the last chunk relates to 96 rows. The minimum and maximum ROWIDs for each chunk are identified.

The PL/SQL block executes the cursor C2 12 times in sequence, once for each of the 12 chunks identified by cursor C1. In real life these executions would be performed in parallel by separate application threads. Only the small portion of the table containing our clustered data is scanned, and for larger numbers of rows the threads would not compete for blocks in T1 and multi-block reads could be used to read the clustered rows efficiently.

Notice that cursor C2 has to include the original predicates. Not all rows in the ROWID range are guaranteed to be from our set.

That pretty much wraps up what I wanted to say about the ROWID pseudocolumn. I want to switch tack now and talk about a different SQL tuning experience that seems too bizarre to be true.

Converting an Inner Join to an Outer Join

You may think that there is a typographical error in the title of this section. There isn't! This is the story of a real-life experience that involved John, my client working in risk management whom I introduced in the previous chapter.

John (whom you may have guessed is a composite character) came to me with yet another poorly performing query. This query involved a view defined in the data dictionary. Listing 19-7 shows the basic idea.

Listing 19-7. Suboptimal plan involving a data dictionary view

```
CREATE OR REPLACE VIEW sales_simple
AS
    SELECT cust_id
         ,time_id
         ,promo_id
         ,amount_sold
         ,p.prod_id
         ,prod_name
      FROM sh.sales s, sh.products p
     WHERE s.prod_id = p.prod_id;

SELECT *
  FROM sales_simple v JOIN sh.customers c ON c.cust_id = v.cust_id
 WHERE     v.time_id = DATE '1998-03-31'
       AND c.cust_first_name = 'Madison'
       AND cust_last_name = 'Roy'
       AND cust_gender = 'M';
```

Id	Operation	Name	Rows	Cost (%CPU)
0	SELECT STATEMENT		1	448 (1)
1	NESTED LOOPS			
2	NESTED LOOPS		1	448 (1)
3	HASH JOIN		1	447 (1)
4	TABLE ACCESS FULL	CUSTOMERS	1	423 (1)
5	PARTITION RANGE SINGLE		1188	24 (0)
6	TABLE ACCESS BY LOCAL INDEX ROWID BATCHED	SALES	1188	24 (0)
7	BITMAP CONVERSION TO ROWIDS			
8	BITMAP INDEX SINGLE VALUE	SALES_TIME_BIX		
9	INDEX UNIQUE SCAN	PRODUCTS_PK	1	0 (0)
10	TABLE ACCESS BY INDEX ROWID	PRODUCTS	1	1 (0)

The query in Listing 19-6 is suboptimal because there is only one row in the SH.CUSTOMERS table that matches the supplied predicate. The CBO should have picked a join order that allowed it to access the SH.SALES table via the SALES_CUST_BIX index but didn't for reasons that aren't immediately obvious. Not to worry—a couple of hints should do the trick, as shown in Listing 19-8.

Listing 19-8. Data dictionary query with hints in the calling code

```
CREATE OR REPLACE VIEW sales_simple
AS
   SELECT /*+ qb_name(q1)  */
         cust_id
         ,time_id
         ,promo_id
         ,amount_sold
         ,p.prod_id
         ,prod_name
     FROM sh.sales s, sh.products p
    WHERE s.prod_id = p.prod_id;

SELECT /*+ merge(q1) leading(c s@q1 p@q1) use_nl(s@q1) use_nl(p@q1) index(s@q1 (cust_id))*/
       *
  FROM sales_simple v JOIN sh.customers c ON c.cust_id = v.cust_id
 WHERE     v.time_id = DATE '1998-03-31'
       AND c.cust_first_name = 'Madison'
       AND cust_last_name = 'Roy'
       AND cust_gender = 'M';
```

```
-------------------------------------------------------------------------------------
| Id | Operation                                   | Name            | Rows | Cost (%CPU)|
-------------------------------------------------------------------------------------
|  0 | SELECT STATEMENT                            |                 |    1 |   854   (1)|
|  1 |  NESTED LOOPS                               |                 |      |            |
|  2 |   NESTED LOOPS                              |                 |    1 |   854   (1)|
|  3 |    NESTED LOOPS                             |                 |    1 |   853   (1)|
|  4 |     TABLE ACCESS FULL                       | CUSTOMERS       |    1 |   423   (1)|
|  5 |     PARTITION RANGE SINGLE                  |                 |    1 |   853   (1)|
|  6 |      TABLE ACCESS BY LOCAL INDEX ROWID BATCHED| SALES         |    1 |   853   (1)|
|  7 |       BITMAP CONVERSION TO ROWIDS           |                 |      |            |
|  8 |        BITMAP INDEX SINGLE VALUE            | SALES_CUST_BIX  |      |            |
|  9 |    INDEX UNIQUE SCAN                        | PRODUCTS_PK     |    1 |     0   (0)|
| 10 |   TABLE ACCESS BY INDEX ROWID               | PRODUCTS        |    1 |     1   (0)|
-------------------------------------------------------------------------------------
```

The hints in Listing 19-8 are a bit difficult to read but they do the trick: we access the SH.SALES table through the SALES_CUST_BIX index. At this stage John reminded me that he was using his data visualization tool and that all hints would have to go into the view. I could have used global hints or I could have defined a "wrapper" view that encompassed the join with SH.CUSTOMERS. But since John wanted some flexibility to change his queries, neither of these options was particularly appealing. Is there another way?

It occurred to me that if I prevented view merging I might be able to do what I wanted. Listing 19-9 was my first attempt.

Listing 19-9. Attempting to push a predicate into a simple view

```
CREATE OR REPLACE VIEW sales_simple
AS
   SELECT /*+ no_merge leading(s p) push_pred index(s (cust_id)) */
         cust_id
         ,time_id
         ,promo_id
         ,amount_sold
         ,p.prod_id
         ,prod_name
      FROM sh.sales s, sh.products p
   WHERE s.prod_id = p.prod_id;

SELECT *
  FROM sales_simple v JOIN sh.customers c ON c.cust_id = v.cust_id
 WHERE    v.time_id = DATE '1998-03-31'
       AND c.cust_first_name = 'Madison'
       AND cust_last_name = 'Roy'
       AND cust_gender = 'M';
```

```
-----------------------------------------------------------------------------------------
| Id  | Operation                                  | Name            | Rows  | Cost (%CPU)|
-----------------------------------------------------------------------------------------
|   0 | SELECT STATEMENT                           |                 |     1 |   450   (1)|
|*  1 |  HASH JOIN                                 |                 |     1 |   450   (1)|
|*  2 |   TABLE ACCESS FULL                        | CUSTOMERS       |     1 |   423   (1)|
|   3 |   VIEW                                     | SALES_SIMPLE    |  1188 |    27   (0)|
|*  4 |    HASH JOIN                               |                 |  1188 |    27   (0)|
|   5 |     PARTITION RANGE SINGLE                 |                 |  1188 |    24   (0)|
|   6 |      TABLE ACCESS BY LOCAL INDEX ROWID BATCHED| SALES        |  1188 |    24   (0)|
|   7 |       BITMAP CONVERSION TO ROWIDS          |                 |       |            |
|*  8 |        BITMAP INDEX SINGLE VALUE           | SALES_TIME_BIX  |       |            |
|   9 |     TABLE ACCESS FULL                      | PRODUCTS        |    72 |     3   (0)|
-----------------------------------------------------------------------------------------

Predicate Information (identified by operation id):
---------------------------------------------------

   1 - access("C"."CUST_ID"="V"."CUST_ID")
   2 - filter("C"."CUST_FIRST_NAME"='Madison' AND "C"."CUST_LAST_NAME"='Roy' AND
              "C"."CUST_GENDER"='M')
   4 - access("S"."PROD_ID"="P"."PROD_ID")
   8 - access("TIME_ID"=TO_DATE(' 1998-03-31 00:00:00', 'syyyy-mm-dd hh24:mi:ss'))
```

The idea behind the failed optimization attempt of Listing 19-9 was as follows: if we prevent view merging we can force the query to use the SALES_CUST_BIX index using the predicate explicitly pushed into the view with a PUSH_PRED hint. Well, most of what I hinted came to pass: the view was not merged and the desired join order was selected. But the predicate on SH.CUSTOMERS was not pushed into the view! Why on earth not?

After half an hour or so of Googling I found the following blog from the optimizer team:

https://blogs.oracle.com/optimizer/entry/basics_of_join_predicate_pushdown_in_oracle

This blog post explains the circumstances under which the join predicate pushdown (JPPD) transformation will operate and the list of conditions I listed in Chapter 13 were shown. To help you recall, this is the list:

- UNION ALL/UNION view

- Outer-joined view

- Anti-joined view

- Semi-joined view

- DISTINCT view

- GROUP-BY view

As I explained in Chapter 13, this list of conditions is *almost* identical to the list of conditions that prevent simple view merging. The idea seems to be that either a view is merged or JPPD will be legal. But notably absent from the list I have just presented is the presence of a NO_MERGE hint! Now we have what I gather is an unforeseen possibility that simple view merging is suppressed but JPPD is illegal.

With this understanding in mind, I redefined the view and then asked John to click a couple of radio buttons in his data visualization tool to change the query to an outer join. John was somewhat incredulous, pointing out that in his case the results of the query would be unchanged and suggesting that an outer join couldn't possibly outperform an inner join. But nothing ventured, nothing gained. The modified view definition and the modified query generated by the data visualization tool are shown in Listing 19-10.

Listing 19-10. Pushing predicates into an outer join

```
CREATE OR REPLACE VIEW sales_simple
AS
    SELECT /*+ no_merge no_index(s (time_id)) */
           cust_id
           ,time_id
           ,promo_id
           ,amount_sold
           ,p.prod_id
           ,prod_name
      FROM sh.sales s, sh.products p
     WHERE s.prod_id = p.prod_id;

SELECT *
  FROM sales_simple v
       RIGHT JOIN sh.customers c
          ON c.cust_id = v.cust_id AND v.time_id = DATE '1998-03-31'
 WHERE     c.cust_first_name = 'Madison'
       AND cust_last_name = 'Roy'
       AND cust_gender = 'M';
```

```
-------------------------------------------------------------------------------------
| Id  | Operation                                   | Name            | Rows | Cost (%CPU)|
-------------------------------------------------------------------------------------
|   0 | SELECT STATEMENT                            |                 |   1  | 427   (0)|
|   1 |  NESTED LOOPS OUTER                         |                 |   1  | 427   (0)|
|*  2 |   TABLE ACCESS FULL                         | CUSTOMERS       |   1  | 423   (1)|
|   3 |   VIEW PUSHED PREDICATE                     | SALES_SIMPLE    |   1  |   5   (0)|
|   4 |    NESTED LOOPS                             |                 |      |          |
|   5 |     NESTED LOOPS                            |                 |   1  |   5   (0)|
|   6 |      PARTITION RANGE SINGLE                 |                 |   1  |   4   (0)|
|*  7 |       TABLE ACCESS BY LOCAL INDEX ROWID BATCHED| SALES        |   1  |   4   (0)|
|   8 |        BITMAP CONVERSION TO ROWIDS          |                 |      |          |
|*  9 |         BITMAP INDEX SINGLE VALUE           | SALES_CUST_BIX  |      |          |
|* 10 |      INDEX UNIQUE SCAN                      | PRODUCTS_PK     |   1  |   0   (0)|
|  11 |     TABLE ACCESS BY INDEX ROWID             | PRODUCTS        |   1  |   1   (0)|
-------------------------------------------------------------------------------------
```

```
Predicate Information (identified by operation id):
---------------------------------------------------

   2 - filter("C"."CUST_FIRST_NAME"='Madison' AND "C"."CUST_LAST_NAME"='Roy' AND
              "C"."CUST_GENDER"='M')
   7 - filter("TIME_ID"=TO_DATE(' 1998-03-31 00:00:00', 'syyyy-mm-dd hh24:mi:ss'))
   9 - access("CUST_ID"="C"."CUST_ID")
  10 - access("S"."PROD_ID"="P"."PROD_ID")
```

The query in Listing 19-10 has been modified to use an outer join. Notice that I have had to include the predicate on TIME_ID in the outer join conditions to prevent the heuristic outer-join-to-inner transformation.

Now that we have an outer join in place, the conditions for JPPD have been met and I only need two hints defined in the view: the NO_MERGE hint to prevent view merging and the NO_INDEX hint to prevent the SALES_TIME_BIX index being unnecessarily combined with the SALES_CUST_BIX!

I must say that converting an inner join to an outer join to improve performance is one of the weirdest experiences in my SQL tuning career, and I think it a fitting way to end this chapter on advanced techniques.

Summary

This chapter has explained some of the lesser-used techniques in SQL tuning that haven't been covered in previous chapters. As always, you should look at the techniques more as examples of how to think about tuning problems more than as principles that need to be learned by rote. If you do find the need to draw on the lessons learned in this chapter you will probably be solving a problem that is subtly different from the examples found here, so your problem will likely require a solution that differs, subtly or not, from the solutions provided in this chapter.

We have now concluded our discussion of SQL optimization, and it is now time to turn our attention to the problem of stabilizing our finely tuned application in the production environment. I introduced the concept of TSTATS in Chapter 6, and in Chapter 20 we will discuss the details.

Managing Statistics with TSTATS

■ ■ ■

Managing Statistics with TSTATS

This chapter explains a radical approach one can take to the management of object statistics on production systems. This approach has been named TSTATS, for "Tony's Statistics," by one of my clients, and I must say that I like the name. It appeals to my sense of vanity! However, as I have already stated, I am not the only one to have considered the issues addressed in this chapter, and others have developed similar solutions on their own, Adrian Billington being one such person.

I explained the problem that TSTATS addresses in Chapter 6: gathering statistics is a risky activity on production systems and said statistics may result in poor-performing execution plans. But when using traditional approaches in the management of object statistics, as recommended by Oracle, you cannot avoid that risk. TSTATS allows you to eliminate the risky activity of gathering statistics on your production system and allows you to sleep soundly in the knowledge that your execution plans will not change for the worse during your slumbers.

There is good news and bad news when it comes to TSTATS. The bad news is that TSTATS is not a quick "plug and play" solution. You will need to spend weeks, possibly months, preparing for the deployment of TSTATS for a complex application. You will need the services of an Oracle performance expert to get TSTATS going. Notice I said *expert*, not *experienced*. If such an expert isn't available full-time you will need to arrange for one to review plans and make sure that they are okay. Furthermore, you may well run into opposition from your colleagues and management; there are those who will claim, quite incorrectly, that TSTATS will render your database unsupportable by Oracle.

TSTATS AND ORACLE SUPPORT

The procedures in the DBMS_STATS package for manually creating or changing statistics are fully documented and supported. The use of these supplied procedures is quite different from, say, manually updating tables in the data dictionary: use of the supplied procedures is supported, but directly updating rows in the data dictionary is not.

It is true that if you make changes to object statistics that result in worse execution plans than the unaltered statistics would have produced, Oracle support is unlikely to be particularly sympathetic. However, if you run into any other type of issue (such as an ORA-0600 error during execution), you should have the same rights to support from Oracle whether you are using TSTATS or not.

The good news about TSTATS is that when it is developed correctly, it works! After the initial setup, you may never need to gather statistics on any development, test, or production system again, except, of course, to generate statistics for new tables or indexes as they are added to your application.

■ **Caution**   The biggest single mistake I made with TSTATS was to re-gather statistics at the time of a 10g to 11g upgrade. This was totally unnecessary and just created a lot of unnecessary work. Be very cautious about re-gathering statistics on tables after a successful TSTATS deployment.

The two keys to the success of a successful TSTATS deployment are buy-in from management and a commitment to do the job properly—a poorly thought-out implementation will just lead the naysayers to cheer "I told you so," and you will never get a second chance.

With these thoughts in mind, you need to consider your answers to the following questions before proceeding:

- Is your problem with performance stability bad enough to warrant the investment in TSTATS?

- Is there a simpler solution, such as gathering statistics less frequently? How about gathering statistics as part of a quarterly release?

- Is there a way that you can *safely* simplify the TSTATS approach or do you really need all the bells and whistles described in this chapter?

- Is your problem application-wide or can you limit the scope of TSTATS in some way?

- Does this chapter explain all that is needed to solve your problems or is there something special about your application that needs extra consideration? For example, do data volumes vary by multiple orders of magnitude under certain special circumstances?

When you answer these questions bear in mind that there are no right or wrong answers. If, for example, you decide to reduce the scope of TSTATS to a few key tables, decide not to consider histograms, and hint all queries that use range-based predicates you may have underestimated what needs to be done. Like all the issues that are raised in this book and elsewhere in life, decisions are best made with as much information as possible, so speak to your colleagues and take your time.

Now that I have built up the tension, I need to tell you what this wonderful TSTATS technology consists of. There are several elements, as follows:

- The customization of column statistics. This is the most important part of TSTATS, and is a concept I introduced in Chapter 6.

- The management of statistics on partitioned tables. Obviously, if you don't have partitioned tables you don't need to worry about this part of TSTATS.

- The management of statistics for temporary tables.

- Deploying TSTATS.

Let us get started and revisit the topic of column statistics, which I introduced in Chapter 6.

Managing Column Statistics

When you stop gathering statistics on your production system, the most important step towards stabilizing execution plans is to eliminate the high and low values for column statistics in the way shown in Listing 6-8. However, there are several other issues to consider, such as:

- Columns with only one value

- Columns with skewed data values

- Correlated columns and expressions

- Columns used in range predicates

It is important to realize that most columns in most tables will not require any special consideration: the statistics associated with columns not used in WHERE or HAVING clause predicates won't be used by the CBO, and even if a column is used in a predicate, it may not be time based, may not have any skewed data, may not be used in predicates in conjunction with any correlated columns, and may not be used with range predicates. It is important not to underestimate the task at hand, but it is also important not to overestimate the task.

Time-based columns

As we discussed in Chapter 6, time-based columns, such as dates or sequence numbers, can cause unwanted changes to execution plans when statistics are not gathered periodically. You can prevent these unwanted execution plan changes by removing the HIGH_VALUE and LOW_VALUE statistic columns. However, with a few exceptions, which we will discuss shortly, it generally does no harm to remove the HIGH_VALUE and LOW_VALUE statistic columns, even if the column isn't time based.

■ **Caution**   While finalizing this book I discovered that a bug was introduced in release 12.1.0.1 that causes join cardinalities to be calculated incorrectly when HIGH_VALUE and LOW_VALUE are missing from the joined columns of both tables. A workaround to this problem is to set the HIGH_VALUE very high and the LOW_VALUE very low. This workaround is included in the downloadable materials, but to avoid unnecessary complexity the book assumes that there is no issue setting HIGH_VALUE and LOW_VALUE to NULL.

My general recommendation is to begin the setup of TSTATS by eliminating the HIGH_VALUE and LOW_VALUE statistic columns for *all* object columns in your schema unless you know *a priori* that an exception, several of which I will cover shortly, applies. If there are exceptions that you are unaware of, don't worry. You will discover them during your testing.

Listing 20-1 shows a procedure, ADJUST_COLUMN_STATS_V1, within a package called TSTATS, to remove the HIGH_VALUE and LOW_VALUE statistic columns from for a specified table.

Listing 20-1. Removing HIGH_VALUE and LOW_VALUE statistic columns

```
CREATE OR REPLACE PACKAGE tstats
AS
-- Other procedures not shown

    PROCEDURE adjust_column_stats_v1 (
       p_owner all_tab_col_statistics.owner%TYPE DEFAULT SYS_CONTEXT (
                                                          'USERENV'
                                                         ,'CURRENT_SCHEMA')

      ,p_table_name all_tab_col_statistics.table_name%TYPE);

-- Other procedures not shown
END tstats;

CREATE OR REPLACE PACKAGE BODY tstats
AS
-- Other procedures not shown

     PROCEDURE adjust_column_stats_v1 (
     p_owner all_tab_col_statistics.owner%TYPE DEFAULT SYS_CONTEXT (
                                                          'USERENV'
                                                         ,'CURRENT_SCHEMA')
     ,p_table_name all_tab_col_statistics.table_name%TYPE)
   AS
      CURSOR c1
      IS
        SELECT *
          FROM all_tab_col_statistics
         WHERE     owner = p_owner
               AND table_name = p_table_name
               AND last_analyzed IS NOT NULL;
   BEGIN
      FOR r IN c1
      LOOP
         DBMS_STATS.delete_column_stats (ownname      => r.owner
                                        ,tabname      => r.table_name
                                        ,colname      => r.column_name
                                        ,cascade_parts => TRUE
                                        ,no_invalidate => TRUE
                                        ,force        => TRUE);
```

```
        DBMS_STATS.set_column_stats (ownname        => r.owner
                                    ,tabname        => r.table_name
                                    ,colname        => r.column_name
                                    ,distcnt        => r.num_distinct
                                    ,density        => r.density
                                    ,nullcnt        => r.num_nulls
                                    ,srec           => NULL -- No HIGH_VALUE/LOW_VALUE
                                    ,avgclen        => r.avg_col_len
                                    ,no_invalidate  => FALSE
                                    ,force          => TRUE);
      END LOOP;
   END adjust_column_stats_v1;
-- Other procedures not shown
END tstats;
```

The procedure shown in Listing 20-1 loops through all columns in the specified table that have column statistics and then deletes and re-adds the column statistics without the HIGH_VALUE and LOW_VALUE bits.

Columns with NUM_DISTINCT=1

I have discovered a rather peculiar CBO behavior relating to columns that, according to the object statistics, have the same value for every row, where the column value is not NULL. Let me give you an example. Listing 16-4 showed how to minimize index size by using NULL to represent the most common value of a column. The example used a column called SPECIAL_FLAG. If the row was special then SPECIAL_FLAG was set to Y and if not SPECIAL_FLAG was NULL. In this case, the number of distinct values of SPECIAL_FLAG was 1, as NULL doesn't count as a value in the eyes of the CBO (or database theoreticians for that matter).

Immediately after gathering statistics, the HIGH_VALUE and LOW_VALUE of SPECIAL_VALUE would both be Y and the NUM_DISTINCT and DENSITY statistic columns would both be 1. Not unreasonably, the CBO gets somewhat confused when NUM_DISTINCT is 1 and HIGH_VALUE and LOW_VALUE are different! Under these circumstances, the CBO assumes that no rows match any equality predicate that you may supply. Prior to 12cR1, the same behavior is seen when the HIGH_VALUE and LOW_VALUE statistics are removed, as Listing 20-2 demonstrates.

Listing 20-2. Special treatment by the CBO when NUM_DISTINCT=1

```
CREATE TABLE payments
(
   payment_id          INTEGER
  ,employee_id         INTEGER
  ,special_flag        CHAR (1)
  ,paygrade            INTEGER
  ,payment_date        DATE
  ,job_description     VARCHAR2 (50)
)
PCTFREE 0;

INSERT INTO payments (payment_id
                     ,employee_id
                     ,special_flag
                     ,paygrade
                     ,payment_date
                     ,job_description)
   WITH standard_payment_dates
        AS (    SELECT ADD_MONTHS (DATE '2014-01-20', ROWNUM - 1)
                          standard_paydate
                       ,LAST_DAY (ADD_MONTHS (DATE '2014-01-20', ROWNUM - 1))
                          last_day_month
                  FROM DUAL
            CONNECT BY LEVEL <= 12)
       ,employees
        AS (    SELECT ROWNUM employee_id, TRUNC (LOG (2.6, ROWNUM)) + 1 paygrade
                  FROM DUAL
            CONNECT BY LEVEL <= 10000)
       ,q1
        AS (SELECT ROWNUM payment_id
                  ,employee_id
                  ,DECODE (MOD (ROWNUM, 100), 0, 'Y', NULL) special_flag
                  ,paygrade
                  --
                  -- The calculation in the next few lines to determine what day of the week
                  -- the 20th of the month falls on does not use the TO_CHAR function
                  -- as the results of this function depend on NLS settings!
                  --
                  ,CASE
                     WHEN MOD (ROWNUM, 100) = 0
                     THEN
                        standard_paydate + MOD (ROWNUM, 7)
                     WHEN     paygrade = 1
                          AND MOD (last_day_month - DATE '1001-01-06', 7) =
                                5
                     THEN
                        last_day_month - 1
```

```
                    WHEN      paygrade = 1
                        AND MOD (last_day_month - DATE '1001-01-06', 7) =
                                6
                    THEN
                       last_day_month - 2
                    WHEN paygrade = 1
                    THEN
                       last_day_month
                    WHEN MOD (standard_paydate - DATE '1001-01-06', 7) = 5
                    THEN
                       standard_paydate - 1
                    WHEN MOD (standard_paydate - DATE '1001-01-06', 7) = 6
                    THEN
                       standard_paydate - 2
                    ELSE
                       standard_paydate
               END
                  paydate
               ,DECODE (
                  paygrade
                  ,1, 'SENIOR EXECUTIVE'
                  ,2, 'JUNIOR EXECUTIVE'
                  ,3, 'SENIOR DEPARTMENT HEAD'
                  ,4, 'JUNIOR DEPARTMENT HEAD'
                  ,5, 'SENIOR MANAGER'
                  ,6, DECODE (MOD (ROWNUM, 3)
                             ,0, 'JUNIOR MANAGER'
                             ,1, 'SENIOR TECHNICIAN'
                             ,'SENIOR SUPERVISOR')
                  ,7, DECODE (MOD (ROWNUM, 2)
                             ,0, 'SENIOR TECHNICIAN'
                             ,'SENIOR SUPERVISOR')
                  ,8, DECODE (MOD (ROWNUM, 2)
                             ,0, 'JUNIOR TECHNICIAN'
                             ,'JUNIOR SUPERVISOR')
                  ,9, 'ANCILLORY STAFF'
                  ,10, DECODE (MOD (ROWNUM, 2)
                              ,0, 'INTERN'
                              ,'CASUAL WORKER'))
                  job_description
          FROM standard_payment_dates, employees)
   SELECT *
     FROM q1
 ORDER BY paydate;
```

```
BEGIN
   DBMS_STATS.gather_table_stats (
      ownname       => SYS_CONTEXT ('USERENV', 'CURRENT_SCHEMA')
      ,tabname       => 'PAYMENTS'
      ,method_opt   => 'FOR ALL COLUMNS SIZE 1');
END;
/

CREATE UNIQUE INDEX payments_pk
   ON payments (payment_id);

ALTER TABLE payments
   ADD  CONSTRAINT payments_pk PRIMARY KEY (payment_id);

CREATE INDEX payments_ix1
   ON payments (paygrade, job_description);

SELECT *
  FROM payments
 WHERE special_flag = 'Y';
```

```
-------------------------------------------------
| Id  | Operation         | Name      | Rows  |
-------------------------------------------------
|   0 | SELECT STATEMENT  |           |  1200 |
|   1 |  TABLE ACCESS FULL| PAYMENTS  |  1200 |
-------------------------------------------------
```

EXEC tstats.adjust_column_stats_v1(p_table_name=>'PAYMENTS');

```
SELECT *
  FROM payments
 WHERE special_flag = 'Y';
```

```
-------------------------------------------------
| Id  | Operation         | Name      | Rows  |
-------------------------------------------------
|   0 | SELECT STATEMENT  |           |    1 |  -- Releases prior to 12cR1
|   1 |  TABLE ACCESS FULL| PAYMENTS  |    1 |
-------------------------------------------------
```

Listing 20-2 creates a table called PAYMENTS that I will use to make several points in this chapter. The PAYMENTS table includes a SPECIAL_FLAG column that is either Y or NULL. Immediately after gathering statistics we can see that the estimated cardinality of a query that includes an equality predicate on SPECIAL_FLAG is absolutely accurate. However, once the procedure TSTATS.ADJUST_COLUMN_STATS_V1 is called to remove the HIGH_VALUE and LOW_VALUE statistic columns, we see that the CBO gets confused and reduces the cardinality to 0 (rounded up in the display to 1, as usual). This may be a bug, as the behavior cannot be observed in 12.1.0.1.

One way to address this issue would be for the statistic adjustment procedure to avoid processing columns where NUM_DISTINCT is 1. That would certainly work in the example shown in Listing 20-2. However, it is possible for a column with one distinct value to be a time-based column and, if so, leaving HIGH_VALUE and LOW_VALUE in place will create problems, as I will show when we come to look at DBMS_STATS.COPY_TABLE_STATS in a short while.

An alternative approach to dealing with NUM_DISTINCT being 1 is to change the value of NUM_DISTINCT! Listing 20-3 shows the procedure TSTATS.ADJUST_COLUMN_STATS_V2, which solves the problem.

Listing 20-3. Adjusting NUM_DISTINCT and DENSITY to fix cardinality issues

```
CREATE OR REPLACE PACKAGE tstats
AS
-- Other procedures not shown
   PROCEDURE adjust_column_stats_v2 (
      p_owner all_tab_col_statistics.owner%TYPE DEFAULT SYS_CONTEXT (
                                                        'USERENV'
                                                      ,'CURRENT_SCHEMA')

      ,p_table_name all_tab_col_statistics.table_name%TYPE);
-- Other procedures not shown
/END tstats;

CREATE OR REPLACE PACKAGE BODY tstats
AS
-- Other procedures not shown
  PROCEDURE adjust_column_stats_v2 (
      p_owner all_tab_col_statistics.owner%TYPE DEFAULT SYS_CONTEXT (
                                                        'USERENV'
                                                      ,'CURRENT_SCHEMA')

      ,p_table_name all_tab_col_statistics.table_name%TYPE)
   AS
      CURSOR c1
      IS
         SELECT *
           FROM all_tab_col_statistics
          WHERE     owner = p_owner
                AND table_name = p_table_name
                AND last_analyzed IS NOT NULL;

      v_num_distinct all_tab_col_statistics.num_distinct%TYPE;
   BEGIN
      FOR r IN c1
      LOOP
         DBMS_STATS.delete_column_stats (ownname       => r.owner
                                        ,tabname       => r.table_name
                                        ,colname       => r.column_name
                                        ,cascade_parts => TRUE
                                        ,no_invalidate => TRUE
                                        ,force         => TRUE);

         IF r.num_distinct = 1
         THEN
            v_num_distinct := 1 + 1e-14;
         ELSE
            v_num_distinct := r.num_distinct;
         END IF;
```

```
          DBMS_STATS.set_column_stats (ownname         => r.owner
                                      ,tabname         => r.table_name
                                      ,colname         => r.column_name
                                      ,distcnt         => v_num_distinct
                                      ,density         => 1 / v_num_distinct
                                      ,nullcnt         => r.num_nulls
                                      ,srec            => NULL -- No HIGH_VALUE/LOW_VALUE
                                      ,avgclen         => r.avg_col_len
                                      ,no_invalidate   => FALSE
                                      ,force           => TRUE);
      END LOOP;
   END adjust_column_stats_v2;
-- Other procedures not shown
END tstats;
/

EXEC tstats.adjust_column_stats_v2(p_table_name=>'PAYMENTS');
SELECT *
  FROM payments
 WHERE special_flag = 'Y';


-------------------------------------------------
| Id | Operation         | Name     | Rows    |
-------------------------------------------------
|  0 | SELECT STATEMENT  |          | 1200    |
|  1 |  TABLE ACCESS FULL| PAYMENTS | 1200    |
-------------------------------------------------
```

You can see that TSTATS.ADJUST_COLUMN_STATS_V2 now sets NUM_DISTINCT for SPECIAL_FLAG to a non-integer value slightly greater than 1 and the DENSITY to 1/NUM_DISTINCT. Now, it is not logical for the number of distinct values for a column to be anything other than an integer value, but the CBO seems to be unconcerned by this and plugs the non-integer value into its calculations. As we can see by the cardinality estimate of our query, we have avoided the undesirable special code path through the CBO code, and our cardinality estimate has returned to a sensible (and in this case absolutely correct) value.

Let me move on to two more complications with time-based column statistics: skewed column values and range predicates.

Skewed column values and range predicates

Listing 9-8 showed how to set up histograms for a table in order to deal with skewed data that requires different execution plans for the different values specified in equality predicates. I also mentioned in Chapter 9 that you may have to specify realistic values for the high and low endpoints when range predicates are involved (rather than the absurd ones in Listing 9-8). But what if you have time-based skewed data and/or time-based range predicates?

Consider a payroll system that holds 12 months of payroll payments. The vast majority of transactions occur on the 20th day of the month (unless the 20th is a weekend) because that is your company's payday. However, a tiny number of transactions occur on other days to deal with executive pay, errors, adjustments, or other exceptional events.

In this payroll application the popular values will change over time: each month a new standard payday is added and an old one is removed. Personally, I have not worked on an application with time-based histograms like this, but working out how to address such a requirement seems to be a useful exercise. I would propose manually updating the histogram as new payment dates are added and old ones are removed.

Notice that manually updating a histogram with new values is quite different from gathering statistics; in the former case the changes are tightly controlled and there is no risk that undesirable changes to execution plans will creep in, but in the latter case we are back to our game of Russian Roulette. The maintenance procedures for our mythical payroll application would need to call a custom procedure in the TSTATS package at least once per month to keep the histogram current.

This type of application-specific customization of TSTATS is typical of the type of thing you might need to consider and demonstrates why TSTATS isn't usually a plug-and-play solution. Let us now look at the final complication of time-based column statistics: correlation.

Correlated columns and expressions

Listings 9-11 and 9-12 showed how to set up extended statistics in order to handle correlated columns and expressions in predicates. It is worth noting that you can also create histograms on extended statistics and that extended statistics may be time based. Manually setting histograms on column-group statistics is far from straightforward. Theoretically, one should be able to use the SYS_OP_COMBINED_HASH function to set up values for the histogram, but I have been unable to get this to work. Furthermore, the CBO doesn't use extended statistics at all when values are missing from the histogram.

It is easy to imagine more complex scenarios where extended statistics would be even less practical. I recently worked on an application that had so many correlated columns that hundreds of extended statistics would have been needed. However, careful analysis of the poorly performing queries led me to an alternative solution. That solution was to falsify the statistics for some columns.

To illustrate the point, you can see that the PAYMENTS table created by Listing 20-2 includes a column called JOB_DESCRIPTION and that each job description is highly correlated to PAYGRADE. We might know that all the queries in our application that include a predicate on JOB_DESCRIPTION also include a predicate on PAYGRADE. That being the case, it might be practical to falsify the value of NUM_DISTINCT for JOB_DESCRIPTION. By setting NUM_DISTINCT to a very low value we can minimize the extent to which predicates involving JOB_DESCRIPTION cause the CBO to incorrectly reduce cardinality estimates.

But let us take a breath. Rather than using vast amounts of code to manipulate column statistics to solve complex issues we can carefully construct sample data. Let me demonstrate.

Use of sample data for complex statistical issues

The problem with real-life data is that it is unpredictable. One month you may have 2% of exceptions in your payroll and the next month you may have 1% and the month after that 3%. But if you manually create sample data and collect statistics on that sample data you can eliminate this sort of variation. At some point it becomes easier to gather statistics on fabricated data than to try and fabricate the statistics directly. Once gathered, the column statistics from the sample data can be copied to the real-life table.

Whether we are fabricating statistics or fabricating sample data we must begin by analyzing our requirements. So let me propose the following results from an analysis of SQL statements that use the PAYMENTS table created in Listing 20-2.

PAYGRADE column analysis

We discover that the code for processing the payments to the two employees on PAYGRADE 1 is different from the code for processing payments to the 9,998 employees with PAYGRADE 2 to PAYGRADE 10. We need a histogram that shows a small number of payments to those on PAYGRADE 1, but we don't want the histogram to reflect the real-life differences between the remaining pay grades because the same SQL is used to process all pay grades other than 1. We decide that our histogram should show PAYGRADE 1 as having 100 times fewer rows than other pay grades. This means:

- A selectivity of 1/901 for PAYGRADE 1

- A selectivity of 100/901 each for pay grades 2 to 10

Remember, we want a histogram that results in effective and stable execution plans. It doesn't matter that the histogram doesn't accurately reflect the data distribution in the PAYMENTS table.

PAYMENT_DATE column analysis

The vast majority of payroll payments are made on the 20th day of each month (or the preceding Friday if the 20th falls on a weekend). There are a few exceptions for errors, adjustments, and executive pay that might fall later in the month, but these are minimal. If we had no histogram on PAYMENT_DATE then the selectivity for normal pay days would be too low. Since the PAYMENTS table holds one year's data, our histogram should show that almost 1/12th of all payments are made on each of the 12 standard paydays in our PAYMENTS table and it should also show a very small selectivity for other dates in the year.

PAYGRADE and PAYMENT_DATE correlation

It turns out that the two most senior employees of our mythical company (those on PAYGRADE 1) get paid on the last weekday of the month even though everybody else gets paid on or around the 20th of the month. If the special code for processing those two executives on PAYGRADE 1 includes SQL statements that include a predicate on PAYGRADE and PAYMENT_DATE the CBO is unlikely to pick a suitable execution plan if it assumes that most payments are made on the standard pay day.

We can set up column-group statistics for the PAYGRADE and PAYMENT_DATE columns that show two payments are made to the PAYGRADE 1 employees on each of their special paydays. We might also set up non-zero selectivities for days when exceptions might be made so that the column-group statistics are still used.

JOB_DESCRIPTION column analysis

There are 13 job descriptions and 10 pay grades, but there are not 130 combinations of both. We might think of setting up column-group statistics on PAYGRADE and JOB_DESCRIPTION, but as long as the application never uses a predicate on JOB_DESCRIPTION independently of PAYGRADE there is a potentially simpler approach: we can just tell the CBO that there are just two values of JOB_DESCRIPTION. This type of white lie is useful when you have a large number of correlated columns and just want to stop the CBO reducing cardinality estimates too much. You will see how this works once we have fabricated our sample data.

Fabricating sample data

Now that we have identified our problematic columns and decided how we want the CBO to treat them we are ready to fabricate some data that fits our model. Listing 20-4 creates a table, SAMPLE_PAYMENTS, that includes the subset of columns from PAYMENTS that we are interested in, namely PAYGRADE, PAYMENT_DATE, and JOB_DESCRIPTION. Listing 20-4 also shows a procedure TSTATS.AMEND_TIME_BASED_STATISTICS that populates SAMPLE_PAYMENTS. Once SAMPLE_PAYMENTS is populated with data we gather statistics and then copy the column statistics from SAMPLE_PAYMENTS to the real-life PAYMENTS table.

Listing 20-4. Creating and populating the SAMPLE_PAYMENTS table

```
CREATE TABLE sample_payments
(
   paygrade            INTEGER
  ,payment_date        DATE
  ,job_description      CHAR (20)
);

CREATE OR REPLACE PACKAGE tstats
AS
-- Other procedures cut
    PROCEDURE amend_time_based_statistics (
     effective_date    DATE DEFAULT SYSDATE);
-- Other procedures cut
END tstats;
/

CREATE OR REPLACE PACKAGE BODY tstats AS
  PROCEDURE amend_time_based_statistics (
     effective_date    DATE DEFAULT SYSDATE)
   IS
     distcnt    NUMBER;
     density    NUMBER;
     nullcnt    NUMBER;
     srec       DBMS_STATS.statrec;

     avgclen    NUMBER;
   BEGIN
     --
     -- Step 1: Remove data from previous run
     --
     DELETE FROM sample_payments;


     --
     -- Step 2:  Add data for standard pay for standard employees
     --
     INSERT INTO sample_payments (paygrade, payment_date, job_description)
       WITH payment_dates
           AS (   SELECT ADD_MONTHS (TRUNC (effective_date, 'MM') + 19
                                  ,1 - ROWNUM)
                            standard_paydate
                    FROM DUAL
              CONNECT BY LEVEL <= 12)
         ,paygrades
          AS (   SELECT ROWNUM + 1 paygrade
                    FROM DUAL
              CONNECT BY LEVEL <= 9)
         ,multiplier
          AS (   SELECT ROWNUM rid
                    FROM DUAL
              CONNECT BY LEVEL <= 100)
```

```
    SELECT paygrade
         ,CASE MOD (standard_paydate - DATE '1001-01-06', 7)
             WHEN 5 THEN standard_paydate - 1
             WHEN 6 THEN standard_paydate - 2
             ELSE standard_paydate
          END
             payment_date
         ,'AAA' job_description
      FROM paygrades, payment_dates, multiplier;


--
-- Step 3:  Add data for paygrade 1
--
INSERT INTO sample_payments (paygrade, payment_date, job_description)
   WITH payment_dates
        AS (    SELECT ADD_MONTHS (LAST_DAY (TRUNC (effective_date))
                                  ,1 - ROWNUM)
                          standard_paydate
                  FROM DUAL
             CONNECT BY LEVEL <= 12)
   SELECT 1 paygrade
         ,CASE MOD (standard_paydate - DATE '1001-01-06', 7)
             WHEN 5 THEN standard_paydate - 1
             WHEN 6 THEN standard_paydate - 2
             ELSE standard_paydate
          END
             payment_dates
         ,'zzz' job_description
      FROM payment_dates;


--
-- Step 4:  Add rows for exceptions.
--
INSERT INTO sample_payments (paygrade, payment_date, job_description)
   WITH payment_dates
        AS (    SELECT ADD_MONTHS (TRUNC (effective_date, 'MM') + 19
                                  ,1 - ROWNUM)
                          standard_paydate
                  FROM DUAL
             CONNECT BY LEVEL <= 12)
       ,paygrades
        AS (    SELECT ROWNUM + 1 paygrade
                  FROM DUAL
             CONNECT BY LEVEL <= 7)
   SELECT paygrade
         ,CASE MOD (standard_paydate - DATE '1001-01-06', 7)
             WHEN 5 THEN standard_paydate - 2 + paygrade
             WHEN 6 THEN standard_paydate - 3 + paygrade
             ELSE standard_paydate - 1 + paygrade
          END
```

```
                    payment_date
              ,'AAA' job_description
          FROM paygrades, payment_dates;


    --
    -- Step 5:  Gather statistics for SAMPLE_PAYMENTS
    --
    DBMS_STATS.gather_table_stats (
        ownname      => SYS_CONTEXT ('USERENV', 'CURRENT_SCHEMA')
       ,tabname      => 'SAMPLE_PAYMENTS'
       ,method_opt   =>    'FOR COLUMNS SIZE 1 JOB_DESCRIPTION '
                     || 'FOR COLUMNS SIZE 254 PAYGRADE,PAYMENT_DATE, '
                     || '(PAYGRADE,PAYMENT_DATE)');


    --
    -- Step 6:  Copy column statistics from SAMPLE_PAYMENTS to PAYMENTS
    --
    FOR r IN (SELECT column_name, histogram
                FROM all_tab_cols
                WHERE table_name = 'SAMPLE_PAYMENTS')
    LOOP
        DBMS_STATS.get_column_stats (
            ownname   => SYS_CONTEXT ('USERENV', 'CURRENT_SCHEMA')
           ,tabname   => 'SAMPLE_PAYMENTS'
           ,colname   => r.column_name
           ,distcnt   => distcnt
           ,density   => density
           ,nullcnt   => nullcnt
           ,srec      => srec
           ,avgclen   => avgclen);

        DBMS_STATS.set_column_stats (
            ownname   => SYS_CONTEXT ('USERENV', 'CURRENT_SCHEMA')
           ,tabname   => 'PAYMENTS'
           ,colname   => r.column_name
           ,distcnt   => distcnt
           ,density   => density
           ,nullcnt   => nullcnt
           ,srec      => srec
           ,avgclen   => avgclen);
    END LOOP;
  END amend_time_based_statistics;
-- Other procedures cut
END tstats;
/
```

There are several things to note about the code in Listing 20-4:

- We don't need as many rows in SAMPLE_PAYMENTS as there are in PAYMENTS. We just need enough rows to demonstrate the data distribution we want. In fact, SAMPLE_PAYMENTS holds 10,896 rows whereas PAYMENTS currently holds 120,000.

- The table SAMPLE_PAYMENTS doesn't include all columns in PAYMENTS, just the columns that require special treatment.

- After deleting historic data from SAMPLE_PAYMENTS we add 100 rows for each combination of pay grades from 2 to 9 and the 12 standard pay dates. We specify a low value for JOB_DESCRIPTION.

- We then add rows for executive pay—just one row per executive payday. We specify a second, high, value for JOB_DESCRIPTION.

- The last set of rows to be added is for the exceptional entries—one for each day in the week after the standard payday. We specify an arbitrary value of PAYGRADE (not 1) .

- When we gather statistics it is important that we do *not* gather histograms for JOB_DESCRIPTION, as the values we have specified for the columns aren't real. We gather histograms on the remaining columns. Notice an interesting feature of the METHOD_OPT syntax: we can implicitly create extended statistics this way!

- We then copy the column statistics gathered for SAMPLE_PAYMENTS into PAYMENTS.

You may be wondering what we have achieved here. The point of all this is that each month we can regenerate the data in SAMPLE_PAYMENTS and can be 100% certain that the *only* differences in data are the values of PAYMENT_DATE. Everything else will be the same. This means that once we copy the statistics to PAYMENTS, the execution plans will remain the same. Listing 20-5 shows how this works in practice.

Listing 20-5. Demonstrating statistics from fabricated data in action

```
DECLARE
    extension_name      all_stat_extensions.extension_name%TYPE;
    extension_exists    EXCEPTION;
    PRAGMA EXCEPTION_INIT (extension_exists, -20007);
BEGIN
    extension_name :=
        DBMS_STATS.create_extended_stats (
            ownname     => SYS_CONTEXT ('USERENV', 'CURRENT_SCHEMA')
           ,tabname     => 'PAYMENTS'
           ,extension   => '(PAYGRADE,PAYMENT_DATE)');
EXCEPTION
    WHEN extension_exists
    THEN
        NULL;
END;
/

EXEC tstats.amend_time_based_statistics(date '2014-05-01');

ALTER SESSION SET statistics_level='ALL';

SELECT COUNT (*)
  FROM payments
 WHERE paygrade = 1 AND payment_date = DATE '2014-04-30';

SELECT *
  FROM TABLE (DBMS_XPLAN.display_cursor (format => 'BASIC IOSTATS LAST'));
```

```
-----------------------------------------------------------------------------------------
| Id  | Operation                             | Name         | Starts | E-Rows | A-Rows |
-----------------------------------------------------------------------------------------
|   0 | SELECT STATEMENT                      |              |     1  |        |     1  |
|   1 |  SORT AGGREGATE                       |              |     1  |     1  |     1  |
|*  2 |   TABLE ACCESS BY INDEX ROWID BATCHED | PAYMENTS     |     1  |    11  |     2  |
|*  3 |    INDEX RANGE SCAN                   | PAYMENTS_IX1 |     1  |   132  |    24  |
-----------------------------------------------------------------------------------------
```

```
SELECT COUNT (*)
  FROM payments
 WHERE paygrade = 10 AND payment_date = DATE '2014-04-18';

SELECT *
  FROM TABLE (DBMS_XPLAN.display_cursor (format => 'BASIC IOSTATS LAST'));
```

```
-----------------------------------------------------------------
| Id  | Operation            | Name      | Starts | E-Rows | A-Rows |
-----------------------------------------------------------------
|   0 | SELECT STATEMENT     |           |      1 |        |      1 |
|   1 |  SORT AGGREGATE      |           |      1 |      1 |      1 |
|*  2 |   TABLE ACCESS FULL| PAYMENTS    |      1 |   1101 |   4525 |
-----------------------------------------------------------------
```

```
SELECT COUNT (*)
  FROM payments
 WHERE paygrade = 4 AND payment_date = DATE '2014-04-18';
```

```
SELECT *
  FROM TABLE (DBMS_XPLAN.display_cursor (format => 'BASIC IOSTATS LAST'));
```

```
-----------------------------------------------------------------
| Id  | Operation            | Name      | Starts | E-Rows | A-Rows |
-----------------------------------------------------------------
|   0 | SELECT STATEMENT     |           |      1 |        |      1 |
|   1 |  SORT AGGREGATE      |           |      1 |      1 |      1 |
|*  2 |   TABLE ACCESS FULL| PAYMENTS    |      1 |   1101 |     28 |
-----------------------------------------------------------------
```

```
SELECT COUNT (*)
  FROM payments
 WHERE paygrade = 8 AND job_description = 'JUNIOR TECHNICIAN';
```

```
SELECT *
  FROM TABLE (DBMS_XPLAN.display_cursor (format => 'BASIC IOSTATS LAST'));
```

```
-----------------------------------------------------------------
| Id  | Operation            | Name         | Starts | E-Rows | A-Rows |
-----------------------------------------------------------------
|   0 | SELECT STATEMENT     |              |      1 |        |      1 |
|   1 |  SORT AGGREGATE      |              |      1 |      1 |      1 |
|*  2 |   INDEX RANGE SCAN| PAYMENTS_IX1     |      1 |   6674 |   7716 |
-----------------------------------------------------------------
```

```
SELECT COUNT (*)
  FROM payments
 WHERE employee_id = 101;
```

```
SELECT *
  FROM TABLE (DBMS_XPLAN.display_cursor (format => 'BASIC IOSTATS LAST'));
```

```
-------------------------------------------------------------
| Id  | Operation           | Name      | Starts | E-Rows | A-Rows |
-------------------------------------------------------------
|   0 | SELECT STATEMENT    |           |      1 |        |      1 |
|   1 |  SORT AGGREGATE     |           |      1 |      1 |      1 |
|*  2 |   TABLE ACCESS FULL | PAYMENTS  |      1 |     12 |     12 |
-------------------------------------------------------------
```

```
---------------------------------------------------------------------
EXEC tstats.amend_time_based_statistics(date '2015-05-01');
```

```
SELECT COUNT (*)
  FROM payments
 WHERE paygrade = 1 AND payment_date = DATE '2015-04-30';
```

```
SELECT * FROM TABLE (DBMS_XPLAN.display_cursor (format => 'BASIC +ROWS'));
```

```
------------------------------------------------------------------------
| Id  | Operation                            | Name         | Rows  |
------------------------------------------------------------------------
|   0 | SELECT STATEMENT                     |              |       |
|   1 |  SORT AGGREGATE                      |              |     1 |
|   2 |   TABLE ACCESS BY INDEX ROWID BATCHED| PAYMENTS     |    11 |
|   3 |    INDEX RANGE SCAN                  | PAYMENTS_IX1 |   132 |
------------------------------------------------------------------------
```

```
SELECT COUNT (*)
  FROM payments
 WHERE paygrade = 10 AND payment_date = DATE '2015-04-20';
```

```
SELECT * FROM TABLE (DBMS_XPLAN.display_cursor (format => 'BASIC +ROWS'));
```

```
-------------------------------------------------
| Id  | Operation          | Name     | Rows  |
-------------------------------------------------
|   0 | SELECT STATEMENT   |          |       |
|   1 |  SORT AGGREGATE    |          |     1 |
|   2 |   TABLE ACCESS FULL| PAYMENTS |  1101 |
-------------------------------------------------
```

```
SELECT COUNT (*)
  FROM payments
 WHERE paygrade = 4 AND payment_date = DATE '2015-04-20';
```

```
SELECT * FROM TABLE (DBMS_XPLAN.display_cursor (format => 'BASIC +ROWS'));
```

544

```
-----------------------------------------------
| Id | Operation           | Name     | Rows  |
-----------------------------------------------
|  0 | SELECT STATEMENT    |          |       |
|  1 |  SORT AGGREGATE     |          |     1 |
|  2 |   TABLE ACCESS FULL | PAYMENTS | 1101  |
-----------------------------------------------
```

```
SELECT COUNT (*)
  FROM payments
 WHERE paygrade = 8 AND job_description = 'JUNIOR TECHNICIAN';
```

```
SELECT * FROM TABLE (DBMS_XPLAN.display_cursor (format => 'BASIC +ROWS'));
```

```
---------------------------------------------------
| Id | Operation           | Name        | Rows  |
---------------------------------------------------
|  0 | SELECT STATEMENT    |             |       |
|  1 |  SORT AGGREGATE     |             |     1 |
|  2 |   INDEX RANGE SCAN  | PAYMENTS_IX1| 6674  |
---------------------------------------------------
```

```
SELECT COUNT (*)
  FROM payments
 WHERE employee_id = 101;
```

```
SELECT * FROM TABLE (DBMS_XPLAN.display_cursor (format => 'BASIC +ROWS'));
```

```
-----------------------------------------------
| Id | Operation           | Name     | Rows  |
-----------------------------------------------
|  0 | SELECT STATEMENT    |          |       |
|  1 |  SORT AGGREGATE     |          |     1 |
|  2 |   TABLE ACCESS FULL | PAYMENTS |    12 |
-----------------------------------------------
```

Listing 2-5 begins by showing the creation of column-group extended statistics on PAYMENTS for the two columns PAYGRADE and PAYMENT_DATE. This is a one-off task and, unlike the call to TSTATS.AMEND_TIME_BASED_STATISTICS, would not be performed every month.

Normally TSTATS.AMEND_TIME_BASED_STATISTICS would use the current date to generate sample data, but for demonstration purposes Listing 20-5 begins by specifying May 1, 2014. The first query in Listing 20-5 involves PAYGRADE 1. There are 24 rows input to the COUNT function, but the estimated cardinality is too high at 132. Nevertheless, the correct index access method is selected. If there are other issues with the high selectivity some further adjustment to the sample data might be warranted.

The second and third queries in Listing 20-5 involve standard pay grades and the standard pay day of April 18 (April 20, 2014, is a Sunday). The CBO provides the same estimate of 1,101 rows for the two queries. A full table scan is used, which seems reasonable. In the case of PAYGRADE 10 the cardinality estimate is too low, but for PAYGRADE 4 it is too high. However, we have the consistent estimate and the consistent execution plan that we wanted.

The fourth query in Listing 20-5 involves PAYGRADE and JOB_DESCRIPTION. The estimate of 6,674 rows is reasonably close to the actual 7,716 matching rows in the PAYMENTS table despite the fact that we have not created column-group statistics showing that there are only two values of JOB_DESCRIPTION for employees on PAYGRADE 8. This is because the statistics copied from SAMPLE_PAYMENTS lead the CBO to believe that there are only two values of JOB_DESCRIPTION in the entire table! If there are a number of columns that are all correlated to each other, changing column statistics in this way to reflect a significantly reduced number of distinct values can often avoid the CBO underestimating cardinalities.

The next query in Listing 20-5 involves a predicate on EMPLOYEE_ID. Our sample data doesn't include this column, so the statistics for the EMPLOYEE_ID column in the PAYMENTS were not replaced. The CBO based its cardinality estimate on statistics gathered from the PAYMENTS table.

Suppose time passes. Listing 20-5 makes a second call to TSTATS.AMEND_TIME_BASED_STATISTICS for May 1, 2015, simulating the passage of time. We can see that the cardinality estimates for the new dates in 2015 are identical to those in 2014; I haven't shown actual row counts, as the PAYMENTS table hasn't been updated as it would be in real life.

Managing column statistics wrap up

There are numerous reasons why we might wish to change gathered column statistics to help the CBO produce more accurate cardinality estimates and/or to stabilize those cardinality estimates over time. We might start off with the gathered column statistics and just remove the HIGH_VALUE and LOW_VALUE bits. This is the most common approach. To deal with more complex issues, we can fabricate statistics or even gather statistics on fabricated data. The point is that whatever issues we come across, we can find a way to avoid repeatedly gathering statistics on tables used by our application.

Statistics and Partitions

In Chapter 9, I explained some of the reasons why partition-level statistics are used and stated that, in my opinion, partition-level statistics are often more trouble than they are worth. I realize that many of you will still need some convincing on this point. I am also sure that some of you will be concerned, quite rightly, that a change from using partition-level statistics to global statistics is a large change that might involve an unnecessary level of risk for some established applications. Let us take a look at the much overrated procedure, DBMS_STATS.COPY_TABLE_STATS, with the intent of making these issues clearer.

The DBMS_STATS.COPY_TABLE_STATS myth

DBMS_STATS.COPY_TABLE_STATS was first documented in 11gR1 but was actually supported earlier, in 10.2.0.4 and later releases of 10gR2. The procedure is somewhat inappropriately named because the procedure is not used to copy table statistics as such, at least not global table statistics. The procedure is in fact used to copy partition statistics from one partition in a table to another partition in the same table, or to copy subpartition statistics from one subpartition in a table to another subpartition in the same table. Let me begin my coverage of this procedure with an explanation of how things are supposed to work before going on to discuss the drawbacks.

How DBMS_STATS.COPY_TABLE_STATS is supposed to work

There are three key advantages to using DBMS_STATS.COPY_TABLE_STATS over gathering partition-level statistics. The first advantage is that it is far faster to copy statistics than to gather them. The second advantage is that statistics for a partition can only be gathered once the partition has been populated with data, and you might need to query the partition before all the data has been loaded. The third advantage, and the one that most appealed to me initially, is the fact that replicating statistics from one partition to the next minimizes the risk of changes to execution plans. Listing 20-6 shows the basic principle behind DBMS_STATS.COPY_TABLE_STATS.

Listing 20-6. Initial attempt at using DBMS_STATS.COPY_TABLE_STATS

```
CREATE TABLE statement_part
(
    transaction_date_time
   ,transaction_date
   ,posting_date
   ,description
   ,transaction_amount
   ,product_category
   ,customer_category
)
PARTITION BY RANGE
   (transaction_date)
   (
      PARTITION p1 VALUES LESS THAN (DATE '2013-01-05')
     ,PARTITION p2 VALUES LESS THAN (DATE '2013-01-11')
     ,PARTITION p3 VALUES LESS THAN (maxvalue))
PCTFREE 99
PCTUSED 1
AS
      SELECT    TIMESTAMP '2013-01-01 12:00:00.00 -05:00'
              + NUMTODSINTERVAL (TRUNC ( (ROWNUM - 1) / 50), 'DAY')
             ,DATE '2013-01-01' + TRUNC ( (ROWNUM - 1) / 50)
             ,DATE '2013-01-01' + TRUNC ( (ROWNUM - 1) / 50) + MOD (ROWNUM, 3)
             ,DECODE (MOD (ROWNUM, 4)
                     ,0, 'Flight'
                     ,1, 'Meal'
                     ,2, 'Taxi'
                     ,'Deliveries')
             ,DECODE (MOD (ROWNUM, 4)
                     ,0, 200 + (30 * ROWNUM)
                     ,1, 20 + ROWNUM
                     ,2, 5 + MOD (ROWNUM, 30)
                     ,8)
             ,TRUNC ( (ROWNUM - 1) / 50) + 1
             ,MOD ( (ROWNUM - 1), 50) + 1
         FROM DUAL
   CONNECT BY LEVEL <= 500;

CREATE INDEX statement_part_ix1
   ON statement_part (transaction_date)
   LOCAL
   PCTFREE 99;
```

```
BEGIN
    DBMS_STATS.delete_table_stats (
        ownname             => SYS_CONTEXT ('USERENV', 'CURRENT_SCHEMA')
        ,tabname            => 'STATEMENT_PART'
        ,cascade_parts      => TRUE
        ,cascade_indexes    => TRUE
        ,cascade_columns    => TRUE);

    DBMS_STATS.gather_table_stats (
        ownname             => SYS_CONTEXT ('USERENV', 'CURRENT_SCHEMA')
        ,tabname            => 'STATEMENT_PART'
        ,partname           => 'P1'
        ,granularity        => 'PARTITION'
        ,method_opt         => 'FOR ALL COLUMNS SIZE 1');

    DBMS_STATS.copy_table_stats (
        ownname             => SYS_CONTEXT ('USERENV', 'CURRENT_SCHEMA')
        ,tabname            => 'STATEMENT_PART'
        ,srcpartname        => 'P1'
        ,dstpartname        => 'P2');

    DBMS_STATS.copy_table_stats (
        ownname             => SYS_CONTEXT ('USERENV', 'CURRENT_SCHEMA')
        ,tabname            => 'STATEMENT_PART'
        ,srcpartname        => 'P1'
        ,dstpartname        => 'P3');
END;
/

--
-- We can see that the NUM_ROWS statistic has been copied
-- from P1 to other partitions and aggregated to global stats.
--

SELECT partition_name, num_rows
  FROM all_tab_statistics
 WHERE owner = SYS_CONTEXT ('USERENV', 'CURRENT_SCHEMA')
       AND table_name = 'STATEMENT_PART';
```

PARTITION_NAME	NUM_ROWS
	600
P1	200
P2	200
P3	200

```
--
```

```
-- The column statistics have also been copied.
--
SELECT partition_name, num_distinct
  FROM all_part_col_statistics
 WHERE owner = SYS_CONTEXT ('USERENV', 'CURRENT_SCHEMA')
       AND table_name = 'STATEMENT_PART'
       AND column_name = 'DESCRIPTION'
UNION ALL
SELECT 'TABLE' partition_name, num_distinct
  FROM all_tab_col_statistics
 WHERE owner = SYS_CONTEXT ('USERENV', 'CURRENT_SCHEMA')
       AND table_name = 'STATEMENT_PART'
       AND column_name = 'DESCRIPTION';
```

PARTITION_NAME	NUM_DISTINCT
P1	4
P2	4
P3	4
TABLE	4

```
--
-- We can now get reasonable cardinality estimates from
-- queries against partition P2.
--

SELECT COUNT (*)
  FROM statement_part PARTITION (p2)
 WHERE description = 'Flight';
```

```
---------------------------------------------------------------
| Id | Operation             | Name           | Rows | Pstart| Pstop |
---------------------------------------------------------------
|  0 | SELECT STATEMENT      |                |    1 |       |       |
|  1 |  SORT AGGREGATE       |                |    1 |       |       |
|  2 |   PARTITION RANGE SINGLE|              |   50 |    2  |    2  |
|* 3 |    TABLE ACCESS FULL  | STATEMENT_PART |   50 |    2  |    2  |
---------------------------------------------------------------
```

Listing 20-6 recreates the table STATEMENT_PART that we created in Chapter 9, this time with three partitions. I begin by deleting any existing statistics and gathered statistics on partition P1. I then use DBMS_STATS.COPY_TABLE_STATS to copy the statistics from partition P1 to partitions P2 and P3 and show that we now not only have a usable set of statistics for P2 but that global statistics for STATEMENT_PART have also been generated. This all seems pretty cool. However, all is not quite as simple and straightforward as it at first seems.

Drawbacks of DBMS_STATS.COPY_TABLE_STATS

Listing 20-7 highlights the main complications that can arise with DBMS_STATS.COPY_TABLE_STATS.

Listing 20-7. Issues with DBMS_STATS.COPY_TABLE_STATS

```
DELETE FROM statement_part
      WHERE transaction_date NOT IN (DATE '2013-01-01', DATE '2013-01-06');

BEGIN
   DBMS_STATS.delete_table_stats (
      ownname              => SYS_CONTEXT ('USERENV', 'CURRENT_SCHEMA')
      ,tabname             => 'STATEMENT_PART'
      ,cascade_parts       => TRUE
      ,cascade_indexes     => TRUE
      ,cascade_columns     => TRUE);

   DBMS_STATS.gather_table_stats (
      ownname           => SYS_CONTEXT ('USERENV', 'CURRENT_SCHEMA')
      ,tabname          => 'STATEMENT_PART'
      ,partname         => 'P1'
      ,granularity      => 'PARTITION'
      ,method_opt       => 'FOR ALL COLUMNS SIZE 1');

   DBMS_STATS.copy_table_stats (
      ownname           => SYS_CONTEXT ('USERENV', 'CURRENT_SCHEMA')
      ,tabname          => 'STATEMENT_PART'
      ,srcpartname      => 'P1'
      ,dstpartname      => 'P2');

   DBMS_STATS.copy_table_stats (
      ownname           => SYS_CONTEXT ('USERENV', 'CURRENT_SCHEMA')
      ,tabname          => 'STATEMENT_PART'
      ,srcpartname      => 'P1'
      ,dstpartname      => 'P3');
END;
/


CREATE OR REPLACE FUNCTION convert_date_stat (raw_value RAW)
   RETURN DATE
IS
   date_value    DATE;
BEGIN
   DBMS_STATS.convert_raw_value (rawval => raw_value, resval => date_value);
   RETURN date_value;
END convert_date_stat;
/
```

```
    SELECT column_name
          ,partition_name
          ,convert_date_stat (low_value) low_value
          ,convert_date_stat (high_value) high_value
          ,num_distinct
      FROM all_part_col_statistics
     WHERE owner = SYS_CONTEXT ('USERENV', 'CURRENT_SCHEMA')
           AND table_name = 'STATEMENT_PART'
           AND column_name IN ('TRANSACTION_DATE', 'POSTING_DATE')
    ORDER BY column_name DESC, partition_name;

    COLUMN_NAME          PARTITION_NAME      LOW_VALUE HIGH_VALU NUM_DISTINCT
    -------------------- ------------------- --------- --------- ------------
    TRANSACTION_DATE     P1                  01-JAN-13 01-JAN-13            1
    TRANSACTION_DATE     P2                  05-JAN-13 05-JAN-13            1
    TRANSACTION_DATE     P3                  11-JAN-13 11-JAN-13            1
    POSTING_DATE         P1                  01-JAN-13 03-JAN-13            3
    POSTING_DATE         P2                  01-JAN-13 03-JAN-13            3
    POSTING_DATE         P3                  01-JAN-13 03-JAN-13            3

    SELECT COUNT (*)
      FROM statement_part
     WHERE transaction_date = DATE '2013-01-06';


    ----------------------------------------------------------------
    | Id | Operation               | Name               | Rows  |
    ----------------------------------------------------------------
    |  0 | SELECT STATEMENT        |                    |    1  |
    |  1 |  SORT AGGREGATE         |                    |    1  |
    |  2 |   PARTITION RANGE SINGLE|                    |    1  |
    |  3 |    INDEX RANGE SCAN     | STATEMENT_PART_IX1 |    1  |
    ----------------------------------------------------------------
```

Listing 20-7 begins by deleting rows from the table STATEMENT_PART so that each partition has only one TRANSACTION_DATE. Although arguably it makes more sense to partition a table by list when it is guaranteed that there is just one value of the partitioning column per partition, it is not at all uncommon to use range-based partitions in such cases. It is also not uncommon for such ranges to cover more than 24 hours, particularly for businesses that have no data for weekends.

Once statistics for partition P1 have been re-gathered and copied to P2 and P3, we see the first issue: the DBMS_STATS.COPY_TABLE_STATS procedure hasn't just blindly copied the statistics from P2 to P3. It has made what it believes to be a sensible adjustment: the HIGH_VALUE and LOW_VALUE column statistics for column TRANSACTION_DATE in partition P2 have both been set to January 5. In release 11.2.0.2 and 11.2.0.3, the HIGH_VALUE would have been set to January 11, reflecting the range of the partition, but this caused a problem (bug 14607573), as the NUM_DISTINCT column statistic for TRANSACTION_DATE in partition P2 has a value of 1 and yet HIGH_VALUE and LOW_VALUE are different. In any event, since the value of TRANSACTION_DATE for rows in partition P2 is actually January 6, HIGH_VALUE and LOW_VALUE are still misleading, even in 12cR1.

Although DBMS_STATS.COPY_TABLE_STATS attempts to adjust the column statistics for the partitioning column, it makes no attempt to adjust the statistics for other columns, which leads to a second problem. The POSTING_DATE column is correlated to TRANSACTION_DATE, and any time you adjust the statistics for one you should logically adjust the other; if you don't use TSTATS then I would recommend manually adjusting the HIGH_VALUE and LOW_VALUE of all time-based columns when you use DBMS_STATS.COPY_TABLE_STATS on tables partitioned by date.

The logical contradiction with DBMS_STATS.COPY_TABLE_STATS

My first implementation of TSTATS was in 2009. That first application, which I shall call AJAX, included tables partitioned on a column that I shall call BUSINESS_DATE. The programmers for AJAX adhered to a particular coding standard: all SQL statements *must* include an equality predicate on BUSINESS_DATE for every partitioned table level accessed. The intent of this standard was to avoid any dependency on global statistics. Partition-level statistics were used exclusively, and as new partitions were created, statistics for these new partitions were generated using the DBMS_STATS.COPY_TABLE_STATS procedure. Column statistics for BUSINESS_DATE were adjusted manually.

The TSTATS implementation was successful and paved the way for other applications to be converted to TSTATS. I was happy as a clam and thanked my lucky stars for the wonderful DBMS_STATS.COPY_TABLE_STATS procedure.

A couple of years later, for no reason I can think of, I awoke in my bed with a surprising thought: the only legitimate reason to use partition-level statistics would be because partitions are significantly different. But DBMS_STATS.COPY_TABLE_STATS only works when all partitions are similar. So DBMS_STATS.COPY_TABLE_STATS is only usable when there is no need for it!

I often have these sorts of thoughts when I wake up: the whole world seems to have missed something obvious and gone mad. Usually, after I have wiped the sleep from my eyes, had a cup of tea, and eaten my breakfast cereal, the fatal flaw in my sleepy thoughts becomes clear. However, on this occasion no such flaw came to mind. I still believe that despite its widespread use there are few valid use cases for DBMS_STATS.COPY_TABLE_STATS.

Whether you adopt a TSTATS approach or not, the problems you face with global statistics on partitioned tables aren't very different from those you face with statistics on unpartitioned tables: time-based columns cause changes to execution plans, correlated columns and expressions cause cardinality estimate errors, and skewed values for a column may require multiple execution plans for the same statement. Partition-level statistics don't properly address all these issues, as I showed in Listings 9-17 to 9-21 in Chapter 9.

Unfortunately, we can't always treat partitioned tables just like unpartitioned tables. We can't always just delete the partition and subpartition statistics and get on with our lives. Let me stop talking about DBMS_STATS.COPY_TABLE_STATS now and take a more detailed look at global statistics on partitioned tables so that we understand what problems global statistics do and do not pose.

Cardinality estimates with global statistics

Let us try another approach to managing object statistics on STATEMENT_PART. Listing 20-8 gets rid of the partition-level statistics altogether and sets up global statistics alone.

Listing 20-8. Global statistics on STATEMENT_PART

```
BEGIN
   DBMS_STATS.delete_table_stats (
      ownname          => SYS_CONTEXT ('USERENV', 'CURRENT_SCHEMA')
      ,tabname         => 'STATEMENT_PART'
      ,cascade_parts   => TRUE
      ,cascade_indexes => TRUE
      ,cascade_columns => TRUE);

   DBMS_STATS.gather_table_stats (
      ownname          => SYS_CONTEXT ('USERENV', 'CURRENT_SCHEMA')
      ,tabname         => 'STATEMENT_PART'
      ,granularity     => 'GLOBAL'
      ,method_opt      => 'FOR ALL COLUMNS SIZE 1');

   tstats.adjust_column_stats_v2 (
      p_owner          => SYS_CONTEXT ('USERENV', 'CURRENT_SCHEMA')
      ,p_table_name    => 'STATEMENT_PART');
END;
/

SELECT COUNT (*)
  FROM statement_part t
 WHERE transaction_date = DATE '2013-01-06';
```

```
---------------------------------------------------------------------------------
| Id | Operation               | Name                | Rows | Cost (%CPU)| Pstart| Pstop |
---------------------------------------------------------------------------------
|  0 | SELECT STATEMENT        |                     |    1 |   29   (0)|       |       |
|  1 |  SORT AGGREGATE         |                     |    1 |           |       |       |
|  2 |   PARTITION RANGE SINGLE|                     |   50 |   29   (0)|    2  |    2  |
|* 3 |    INDEX FAST FULL SCAN | STATEMENT_PART_IX1  |   50 |   29   (0)|    2  |    2  |
---------------------------------------------------------------------------------
```

```
SELECT /*+ full(t) */
       COUNT (*)
  FROM statement_part t
 WHERE transaction_date = DATE '2013-01-06';
```

```
---------------------------------------------------------------------------------
| Id | Operation               | Name                | Rows | Cost (%CPU)| Pstart| Pstop |
---------------------------------------------------------------------------------
|  0 | SELECT STATEMENT        |                     |    1 |   47   (0)|       |       |
|  1 |  SORT AGGREGATE         |                     |    1 |           |       |       |
|  2 |   PARTITION RANGE SINGLE|                     |   50 |   47   (0)|    2  |    2  |
|* 3 |    TABLE ACCESS FULL    | STATEMENT_PART      |   50 |   47   (0)|    2  |    2  |
---------------------------------------------------------------------------------
```

The global statistics for STATEMENT_PART have been adjusted using the TSTATS.ADJUST_COLUMN_STATS_V2 procedure introduced in Listing 20-3. The cardinality estimates produced by queries against STATEMENT_PART are perfectly reasonable, just as they would be for an unpartitioned table. Notice that our query uses the index we created and that the cost of the plan based on a hinted full table scan is higher. But what happens if we add a few more partitions? Listing 20-9 shows us just that.

Listing 20-9. Adding partitions to STATEMENT_PART

```
ALTER TABLE statement_part
    SPLIT PARTITION p3
        AT (DATE '2013-01-12')
        INTO (PARTITION p3, PARTITION p4);

ALTER TABLE statement_part
    SPLIT PARTITION p4
        AT (DATE '2013-01-13')
        INTO (PARTITION p4, PARTITION p5);

ALTER TABLE statement_part
    SPLIT PARTITION p5
        AT (DATE '2013-01-14')
        INTO (PARTITION p5, PARTITION p6);

SELECT COUNT (*)
  FROM statement_part t
 WHERE transaction_date = DATE '2013-01-06';
```

```
-------------------------------------------------------------------------------
| Id  | Operation              | Name           | Rows | Cost (%CPU)| Pstart| Pstop |
-------------------------------------------------------------------------------
|   0 | SELECT STATEMENT       |                |    1 |   25   (0)|       |       |
|   1 |  SORT AGGREGATE        |                |    1 |           |       |       |
|   2 |   PARTITION RANGE SINGLE|               |   50 |   25   (0)|    2  |    2  |
|*  3 |    TABLE ACCESS FULL   | STATEMENT_PART |   50 |   25   (0)|    2  |    2  |
-------------------------------------------------------------------------------
```

```
SELECT COUNT (*)
  FROM statement_part t
 WHERE transaction_date = DATE '2013-01-13';
```

```
-------------------------------------------------------------------------------
| Id  | Operation              | Name           | Rows | Cost (%CPU)| Pstart| Pstop |
-------------------------------------------------------------------------------
|   0 | SELECT STATEMENT       |                |    1 |   25   (0)|       |       |
|   1 |  SORT AGGREGATE        |                |    1 |           |       |       |
|   2 |   PARTITION RANGE SINGLE|               |   50 |   25   (0)|    5  |    5  |
|*  3 |    TABLE ACCESS FULL   | STATEMENT_PART |   50 |   25   (0)|    5  |    5  |
-------------------------------------------------------------------------------
```

After we add partitions to STATEMENT_PART we can see that our sample query has the same cardinality estimate of 50 both before and after partition maintenance and that a similar query against a newly created partition also has a cardinality estimate of 50. Notice that the value of NUM_DISTINCT for TRANSACTION_DATE is only 2, even though there are partitions for many more values of TRANSACTION_DATE. The reason that I highlight this is because many people have spoken to me who were concerned about such discrepancies. As long as the value of NUM_DISTINCT for the column TRANSACTION_DATE and the value of NUM_ROWS for the table are consistent, the number of rows per TRANSACTION_DATE will be reasonable.

If partition maintenance hasn't changed the cardinality estimates, why are the execution plans in Listings 20-8 and 20-9 different? The answer has nothing to do with cardinality and everything to do with cost.

Costing full table scans of table partitions

There is one significant complication that arises when the total number of partitions in a partitioned table changes while the object statistics for the table aren't changed. Take another look at the execution plans in Listings 20-8 and 20-9. The unhinted query in Listing 20-8 uses an index. The cost associated with the variant that uses a FULL hint is higher—no problem so far.

However, once we add a few more partitions we suddenly find that the unhinted query uses a full table scan! We can see that the cost of the full table scan has been reduced as a result of the partition-maintenance operation. Now the cost of the full table scan is less than that of the index scan, and the execution plan for the unhinted query has changed. If the newly added partitions were dropped, the index access would once again become more attractive.

What has happened here is very unusual. The CBO has estimated the cost of the full table scan of the partition by dividing the value of the NUM_BLOCKS *statistic* by the *current* value of the number of partitions obtained from the data dictionary. Normally, the inputs to the CBO's estimating process are the object statistics, system statistics, and initialization parameters. One exception to this rule is the degree of parallelism specified in the data dictionary for a table or index. The only other case that I know of where the CBO uses data dictionary information, other than statistics, is when it costs full table scans for partitions.

PARTITION-ELIMINATION ANOMALIES

The CBO realizes that performing a full table scan on one partition will take less time than scanning all partitions in a table. However, the same logic is not applied to index scans of any type: the cost of an index scan on one partition of a local index is identical to that of scanning all partitions; this is true in all database releases up to and including 12.1.0.1.

Furthermore, if you use composite partitioning you will find that elimination of subpartitions within a partition will not reduce the cost of a full table scan either. These anomalies may, of course, be corrected at some point in the future.

It seems to me that the CBO development team has missed a trick here. In my opinion, it would be better if there were an object statistic, perhaps called NUM_PARTITIONS, that reflected the number of partitions that existed at the time the object statistics for that table were gathered. But that is just wishful thinking. We need to deal with reality. We can do so simply by increasing the value of the NUM_BLOCKS statistic for the table by the same factor as the increase in the number of partitions. The easiest way to do this is to capture the average number of blocks per partition at the same time as statistics are gathered and then to add a TSTATS hook to the partition-maintenance operations. Listing 20-10 shows one way to do this.

Listing 20-10. Managing NUM_BLOCKS with partition-maintenance operations

```
CREATE OR REPLACE PACKAGE tstats
AS
    -- Other procedures cut

    PROCEDURE adjust_global_stats (
        p_owner all_tab_col_statistics.owner%TYPE DEFAULT SYS_CONTEXT (
                                                            'USERENV'
                                                           ,'CURRENT_SCHEMA')

       ,p_table_name all_tab_col_statistics.table_name%TYPE
       ,p_mode VARCHAR2 DEFAULT 'PMOP');

    PROCEDURE gather_table_stats (
        p_owner all_tab_col_statistics.owner%TYPE DEFAULT SYS_CONTEXT (
                                                            'USERENV'
                                                           ,'CURRENT_SCHEMA')

       ,p_table_name all_tab_col_statistics.table_name%TYPE);

    -- Other procedures cut
END tstats;
/

CREATE OR REPLACE PACKAGE BODY tstats
AS
-- Other procedures cut

PROCEDURE adjust_global_stats (
        p_owner all_tab_col_statistics.owner%TYPE DEFAULT SYS_CONTEXT (
                                                            'USERENV'
                                                           ,'CURRENT_SCHEMA')

       ,p_table_name all_tab_col_statistics.table_name%TYPE
       ,p_mode VARCHAR2 DEFAULT 'PMOP')
    IS
        -- This helper function updates the statistic for the number of blocks in the
        -- table so that the average size of a partition is unaltered. We sneak
        -- this value away in the unused CACHEDBLK statistic.
        --
        numblks     NUMBER;
        numrows     NUMBER;
        avgrlen     NUMBER;
        cachedblk   NUMBER;
        cachehit    NUMBER;
```

```
BEGIN
   DBMS_STATS.get_table_stats (ownname      => p_owner
                              ,tabname      => p_table_name
                              ,numrows      => numrows
                              ,avgrlen      => avgrlen
                              ,numblks      => numblks
                              ,cachedblk    => cachedblk
                              ,cachehit     => cachehit);

   IF p_mode = 'PMOP'
   THEN
      --
      -- Resetting NUMBLKS based on CACHEDBLK
      -- average segment size and current number
      -- of partitions.
      --
      IF cachedblk IS NULL
      THEN
         RETURN; -- No saved value
      END IF;


      --
      -- Recalculate the number of blocks based on
      -- the current number of partitions and the
      -- saved average segment size.
      -- Avoid reference to DBA_SEGMENTS in case
      -- there is no privilege.
      --
      SELECT cachedblk * COUNT (*)
        INTO numblks
        FROM all_objects
       WHERE owner = p_owner
             AND object_name = p_table_name
             AND object_type = 'TABLE PARTITION';
   ELSIF p_mode = 'GATHER'
   THEN
      --
      -- Save average segment size in CACHEDBLK based on NUMBLKS
      -- and current number of partitions.
      --
      SELECT numblks / COUNT (*), TRUNC (numblks / COUNT (*)) * COUNT (*)
        INTO cachedblk, numblks
        FROM all_objects
       WHERE owner = p_owner
             AND object_name = p_table_name
             AND object_type = 'TABLE PARTITION';
   ELSE
      RAISE PROGRAM_ERROR;
   -- Only gets here if p_mode not set to PMOP or GATHER
   END IF;
```

```
        DBMS_STATS.set_table_stats (ownname      => p_owner
                                   ,tabname      => p_table_name
                                   ,numblks      => numblks
                                   ,cachedblk    => cachedblk
                                   ,force        => TRUE);
    END adjust_global_stats;

    PROCEDURE gather_table_stats (
        p_owner all_tab_col_statistics.owner%TYPE DEFAULT SYS_CONTEXT (
                                                          'USERENV'
                                                         ,'CURRENT_SCHEMA')

       ,p_table_name ll_tab_col_statistics.table_name%TYPE)
    IS
    BEGIN
        DBMS_STATS.unlock_table_stats (ownname    => p_owner
                                      ,tabname    => p_table_name);

        FOR r IN (SELECT *
                    FROM all_tables
                   WHERE owner = p_owner AND table_name = p_table_name)
        LOOP
          DBMS_STATS.gather_table_stats (
              ownname        => p_owner
             ,tabname        => p_table_name
             ,granularity    => CASE r.partitioned
                                  WHEN 'YES' THEN 'GLOBAL'
                                  ELSE 'ALL'
                                END
             ,method_opt     => 'FOR ALL COLUMNS SIZE 1');

          adjust_column_stats_v2 (p_owner        => p_owner
                                 ,p_table_name   => p_table_name);

          IF r.partitioned = 'YES'
          THEN
             adjust_global_stats (p_owner        => p_owner
                                 ,p_table_name   => p_table_name
                                 ,p_mode         => 'GATHER');
          END IF;
        END LOOP;

        DBMS_STATS.lock_table_stats (ownname => p_owner, tabname => p_table_name);
    END gather_table_stats;

-- Other procedures cut
END tstats;
/
```

Listing 20-10 shows more procedures from the TSTATS package. TSTATS.GATHER_TABLE_STATS is a wrapper routine that gathers statistics for a table and adjusts the column statistics. In the case of partitioned tables, only global statistics are gathered, and the average number of blocks per partition is saved in the unused CACHEDBLK statistic using procedure TSTATS.ADJUST_TABLE_STATS.

■ **Note**   Using a table statistic reserved by Oracle for future use is very, very naughty. Some of you may be shocked to see such practice shown in a book. Strictly speaking, I should have saved my private data in a legitimate place, such as a regular table, outside of the data dictionary. However, in real life I found the temptation to use the unused statistic irresistible. The fact that the statistic is preserved during calls to DBMS_STATS.EXPORT_TABLE_STATS and DBMS_STATS. IMPORT_TABLE_STATS seems to make the risk of the procedure breaking at some future point in time worth taking. The statistic column is unused in all releases up to and including 12.1.0.1.

The routine TSTATS.ADJUST_TABLE_STATS operates in two modes. When called as part of a statistics-gathering process, the average number of blocks per partition is calculated and saved. When partition-maintenance operations are performed the TSTATS.ADJUST_TABLE_STATS procedure is called with the default mode of "PMOP," which causes the NUM_BLOCKS statistic to be recalculated based on the current number of partitions and the saved value of the number of blocks per partition.

Listing 20-11 shows how we can incorporate TSTATS.ADJUST_TABLE_STATS into our partition-maintenance procedure to avoid having said partition-maintenance operations destabilize our execution plans.

Listing 20-11. Adjusting NUM_BLOCKS as part of partition maintenance

```
--
-- First drop the empty partitions
--
ALTER TABLE statement_part DROP PARTITION p3;
ALTER TABLE statement_part DROP PARTITION p4;
ALTER TABLE statement_part DROP PARTITION p5;
ALTER TABLE statement_part DROP PARTITION p6;
--
-- Now gather statistics on full partitions
--

BEGIN
   tstats.gather_table_stats (
      p_owner        => SYS_CONTEXT ('USERENV', 'CURRENT_SCHEMA')
      ,p_table_name  => 'STATEMENT_PART');
END;
/


--
-- Check plans and cost before partition maintenance
--
SELECT COUNT (*)
  FROM statement_part t
 WHERE transaction_date = DATE '2013-01-06';
```

```
-----------------------------------------------------------------------------------
| Id  | Operation               | Name               | Rows | Cost (%CPU)| Pstart| Pstop |
-----------------------------------------------------------------------------------
|   0 | SELECT STATEMENT        |                    |    1 |   29   (0)|       |       |
|   1 |  SORT AGGREGATE         |                    |    1 |           |       |       |
|   2 |   PARTITION RANGE SINGLE|                    |   50 |   29   (0)|     2 |     2 |
|*  3 |    INDEX FAST FULL SCAN | STATEMENT_PART_IX1 |   50 |   29   (0)|     2 |     2 |
-----------------------------------------------------------------------------------
```

```
SELECT /*+ full(t) */
       COUNT (*)
  FROM statement_part t
 WHERE transaction_date = DATE '2013-01-06';
```

```
-----------------------------------------------------------------------------------
| Id  | Operation               | Name            | Rows | Cost (%CPU)| Pstart| Pstop |
-----------------------------------------------------------------------------------
|   0 | SELECT STATEMENT        |                 |    1 |   69   (0)|       |       |
|   1 |  SORT AGGREGATE         |                 |    1 |           |       |       |
|   2 |   PARTITION RANGE SINGLE|                 |   50 |   69   (0)|     2 |     2 |
|*  3 |    TABLE ACCESS FULL    | STATEMENT_PART  |   50 |   69   (0)|     2 |     2 |
-----------------------------------------------------------------------------------
```

```
--
-- Now recreate the empty partitions

ALTER TABLE statement_part
    ADD PARTITION p3 VALUES LESS THAN (DATE '2013-01-12');

ALTER TABLE statement_part
    ADD PARTITION p4 VALUES LESS THAN (DATE '2013-01-13');

ALTER TABLE statement_part
    ADD PARTITION p5 VALUES LESS THAN (DATE '2013-01-14');

ALTER TABLE statement_part
    ADD PARTITION p6 VALUES LESS THAN (maxvalue);

--
-- Finally call TSTATS hook to adjust NUM_BLOCKS statistic
--

BEGIN
    tstats.adjust_global_stats (
       p_owner          => SYS_CONTEXT ('USERENV', 'CURRENT_SCHEMA')
      ,p_table_name     => 'STATEMENT_PART');
END;
/


--
-- Now re-check plans and costs
--

SELECT COUNT (*)
  FROM statement_part t
 WHERE transaction_date = DATE '2013-01-06';
```

```
---------------------------------------------------------------------------------
| Id  | Operation            | Name              | Rows | Cost (%CPU)| Pstart| Pstop |
---------------------------------------------------------------------------------
|   0 | SELECT STATEMENT     |                   |    1 |   29   (0)|       |       |
|   1 |  SORT AGGREGATE      |                   |    1 |           |       |       |
|   2 |   PARTITION RANGE SINGLE|                |   50 |   29   (0)|    2  |    2  |
|*  3 |    INDEX FAST FULL SCAN | STATEMENT_PART_IX1 |   50 |   29   (0)|    2  |    2  |
---------------------------------------------------------------------------------
```

```
SELECT COUNT (*)
  FROM statement_part t
 WHERE transaction_date = DATE '2013-01-13';
```

```
---------------------------------------------------------------------------
| Id  | Operation                | Name              | Rows  | Cost (%CPU)| Pstart| Pstop |
---------------------------------------------------------------------------
|   0 | SELECT STATEMENT         |                   |    1 |   29   (0)|       |       |
|   1 |  SORT AGGREGATE          |                   |    1 |           |       |       |
|   2 |   PARTITION RANGE SINGLE |                   |   50 |   29   (0)|    5 |    5 |
|*  3 |    INDEX FAST FULL SCAN  | STATEMENT_PART_IX1 |   50 |   29   (0)|    5 |    5 |
---------------------------------------------------------------------------
```

```
SELECT /*+ full(t) */ COUNT (*)
  FROM statement_part t
 WHERE transaction_date = DATE '2013-01-06';
```

```
---------------------------------------------------------------------------
| Id  | Operation                | Name            | Rows  | Cost (%CPU)| Pstart| Pstop |
---------------------------------------------------------------------------
|   0 | SELECT STATEMENT         |                 |    1 |   69   (0)|       |       |
|   1 |  SORT AGGREGATE          |                 |    1 |           |       |       |
|   2 |   PARTITION RANGE SINGLE |                 |   50 |   69   (0)|    2 |    2 |
|*  3 |    TABLE ACCESS FULL     | STATEMENT_PART  |   50 |   69   (0)|    2 |    2 |
---------------------------------------------------------------------------
```

The original cost of the full table scan after gathering and adjusting statistics has changed somewhat as a result of rounding issues, but we can see that by incorporating TSTATS.ADJUST_TABLE_STATS into our partition-maintenance procedure the cost of a full table scan remains unchanged and the unhinted query continues to use the index.

Temporary Tables

I will be honest: temporary tables are a challenging problem for the TSTATS method for two reasons. They are as follows:

- You can't easily gather statistics for a temporary table by an independent job because the temporary table will be empty at the time.

- Whereas it is uncommon for permanent tables to vary in size by orders of magnitude, it is quite common for temporary tables to hold 1,000,000 rows on one occasion and 3 rows shortly after.

When temporary tables are used as staging tables in extract transformation and load (ETL) processes, these difficulties are often apparent. Indeed, permanent tables are sometimes used as staging tables in ETL processes, and the issues discussed in this section apply equally to such tables.

The pros and cons of dynamic sampling

Although it is completely contrary to the philosophy of TSTATS, one pragmatic approach to dealing with wildly varying cardinalities is to rely on dynamic sampling. Unless you explicitly disable it, dynamic sampling will occur automatically on any table that has no object statistics, and that includes temporary tables.

The good thing about dynamic sampling is that it is quite smart and understands all about column correlation and so on, so you don't have to worry about extended statistics or even know what they are! In fact, you are quite likely to get a fairly decent execution plan when your statement is parsed. And if you reparse your statement the next week with wildly different contents in your temporary table then you are likely to get a wildly different plan that is quite appropriate for your modified workload.

■ **Tip**   If you are running 12cR1 or later and you have multiple queries against the same temporary table with the same contents, you can avoid repeated dynamic sampling by gathering statistics on the temporary table that are session specific. For details see the specification of DBMS_STATS.SET_TABLE_PREFS procedure in the PL/SQL Packages and Types Reference manual and look for the GLOBAL_TEMP_TABLE_STATS preference. However, if you use session-specific statistics as an alternative to dynamic sampling you may have to set up extended statistics!

All this is very good, but I am sure you can see the potential downside of dynamic sampling. We still have the same risks of poor performance that inspired TSTATS in the first place, as follows:

- An execution plan resulting from dynamic sampling cannot be predicted with certainty and neither can the resulting performance.

- The execution plan created by one session may be used by the same or a different session when the temporary table contents are quite different than those at the time the statement was parsed.

I must confess that when I first implemented TSTATS for the AJAX application I turned a blind eye to these concerns and hoped that stabilizing the execution plans for all statements not involving temporary tables and relying on dynamic sampling for the remaining statements would be good enough for AJAX to provide a stable service. Unfortunately, I was wrong and had to come up with a way to stabilize plans for queries involving temporary tables. I ended up abandoning dynamic sampling and fabricating statistics for temporary tables.

Fabricating statistics for temporary tables

The idea is simple: use DBMS_STATS.SET_TABLE_STATS, DBMS_STATS.SET_COLUMN_STATS, and, if appropriate, DBMS_STATS.SET_INDEX_STATS to set statistics for global temporary tables and their associated columns and indexes. That way you can ensure that the execution plans that involve your global temporary tables are fixed and testable like all your other queries. The problem is, of course, working out which statistics to fabricate.

To set the stage, let us have a look at Listing 20-12, which performs a merge of a temporary table with a permanent table.

Listing 20-12. Merging a temporary table into a permanent table

```
CREATE GLOBAL TEMPORARY TABLE payments_temp
AS
    SELECT *
      FROM payments
     WHERE 1 = 0;

MERGE /*+ cardinality(t 3) */
    INTO   payments p
    USING payments_temp t
        ON (p.payment_id = t.payment_id)
WHEN MATCHED
THEN
    UPDATE SET p.employee_id = t.employee_id
              ,p.special_flag = t.special_flag
              ,p.paygrade = t.paygrade
              ,p.payment_date = t.payment_date
              ,p.job_description = t.job_description
WHEN NOT MATCHED
THEN
    INSERT     (payment_id
               ,special_flag
               ,paygrade
               ,payment_date
               ,job_description)
        VALUES (t.payment_id
               ,t.special_flag
               ,t.paygrade
               ,t.payment_date
               ,t.job_description);
```

```
-------------------------------------------------------------------------
| Id  | Operation                       | Name         | Rows  | Cost (%CPU)|
-------------------------------------------------------------------------
|   0 | MERGE STATEMENT                 |              |    3  |    5   (0)|
|   1 |  MERGE                          | PAYMENTS     |       |           |
|   2 |   VIEW                          |              |       |           |
|   3 |    NESTED LOOPS OUTER           |              |    3  |    5   (0)|
|   4 |     TABLE ACCESS FULL           | PAYMENTS_TEMP|    3  |    2   (0)|
|   5 |     TABLE ACCESS BY INDEX ROWID | PAYMENTS     |    1  |    1   (0)|
|   6 |      INDEX UNIQUE SCAN          | PAYMENTS_PK  |    1  |    0   (0)|
-------------------------------------------------------------------------
```

```
MERGE /*+ cardinality(t 10000) */
    INTO   payments p
    USING payments_temp t
        ON (p.payment_id = t.payment_id)
WHEN MATCHED
```

```
THEN
   UPDATE SET p.employee_id = t.employee_id
             ,p.special_flag = t.special_flag
             ,p.paygrade = t.paygrade
             ,p.payment_date = t.payment_date
             ,p.job_description = t.job_description
WHEN NOT MATCHED
THEN
   INSERT       (payment_id
                ,special_flag
                ,paygrade
                ,payment_date
                ,job_description)
       VALUES (t.payment_id
              ,t.special_flag
              ,t.paygrade
              ,t.payment_date
              ,t.job_description);
```

```
----------------------------------------------------------------------
| Id | Operation            | Name          | Rows  | Cost (%CPU)|
----------------------------------------------------------------------
|  0 | MERGE STATEMENT      |               | 10000 |   176   (1)|
|  1 |  MERGE               | PAYMENTS      |       |            |
|  2 |   VIEW               |               |       |            |
|  3 |    HASH JOIN OUTER   |               | 10000 |   176   (1)|
|  4 |     TABLE ACCESS FULL| PAYMENTS_TEMP | 10000 |     2   (0)|
|  5 |     TABLE ACCESS FULL| PAYMENTS      |  120K |   174   (1)|
----------------------------------------------------------------------
```

Listing 20-12 shows two MERGE statements and their associated execution plans. The only difference between the two statements is that the argument to the CARDINALITY hint is 3 in one case and 10,000 in the other. We can see that in both cases the CBO elects to use the temporary table as the driving table in the join. In the case where the cardinality is 3 the CBO would like to use a nested loops join, but in the case where the cardinality estimate is 10,000 a hash join is preferred.

We would like to fabricate our statistics so that a reasonable execution plan is selected by the CBO without the need to hint our code. But the optimal execution plan seems to vary depending on the number of rows in our temporary table, so what are we to do?

The key to answering this question lies in the answer to two other questions:

- How bad would it be if we used a nested loops join when there are 10,000 rows in the temporary table?

- How bad would it be if we used a hash join when there are only 3 rows in the table?

Listing 20-13 shows how we might begin our thought process.

Listing 20-13. Assessing the impact of incorrect cardinalities

```
MERGE /*+ cardinality(t 3) leading(t) use_hash(p) no_swap_join_inputs(p) */
     INTO   payments p
     USING payments_temp t
        ON (p.payment_id = t.payment_id)
WHEN MATCHED
THEN
   UPDATE SET p.employee_id = t.employee_id
            ,p.special_flag = t.special_flag
            ,p.paygrade = t.paygrade
            ,p.payment_date = t.payment_date
            ,p.job_description = t.job_description
WHEN NOT MATCHED
THEN
   INSERT     (payment_id
             ,special_flag
             ,paygrade
             ,payment_date
             ,job_description)
      VALUES (t.payment_id
             ,t.special_flag
             ,t.paygrade
             ,t.payment_date
             ,t.job_description);
```

```
------------------------------------------------------------------------
| Id | Operation             | Name          | Rows  | Cost (%CPU)|
------------------------------------------------------------------------
|  0 | MERGE STATEMENT       |               |    3  |  176    (1)|
|  1 |  MERGE                | PAYMENTS      |       |            |
|  2 |   VIEW                |               |       |            |
|  3 |    HASH JOIN OUTER    |               |    3  |  176    (1)|
|  4 |     TABLE ACCESS FULL | PAYMENTS_TEMP |    3  |    2    (0)|
|  5 |     TABLE ACCESS FULL | PAYMENTS      | 120K  |  174    (1)|
------------------------------------------------------------------------
```

```
MERGE /*+ cardinality(t 10000) leading(t) use_nl(p) */
     INTO   payments p
     USING payments_temp t
        ON (p.payment_id = t.payment_id)
WHEN MATCHED
THEN
   UPDATE SET p.employee_id = t.employee_id
            ,p.special_flag = t.special_flag
            ,p.paygrade = t.paygrade
            ,p.payment_date = t.payment_date
            ,p.job_description = t.job_description
WHEN NOT MATCHED
```

```
THEN
    INSERT      (payment_id
                ,special_flag
                ,paygrade
                ,payment_date
                ,job_description)
        VALUES (t.payment_id
                ,t.special_flag
                ,t.paygrade
                ,t.payment_date
                ,t.job_description);
```

```
----------------------------------------------------------------------------
| Id  | Operation                       | Name           | Rows  | Cost (%CPU)|
----------------------------------------------------------------------------
|  0  | MERGE STATEMENT                 |                | 10000 | 10004  (1)|
|  1  |  MERGE                          | PAYMENTS       |       |           |
|  2  |   VIEW                          |                |       |           |
|  3  |    NESTED LOOPS OUTER           |                | 10000 | 10004  (1)|
|  4  |     TABLE ACCESS FULL           | PAYMENTS_TEMP  | 10000 |     2  (0)|
|  5  |     TABLE ACCESS BY INDEX ROWID | PAYMENTS       |     1 |     1  (0)|
|  6  |      INDEX UNIQUE SCAN          | PAYMENTS_PK    |     1 |     0  (0)|
----------------------------------------------------------------------------
```

Listing 12-13 shows the CBO cost estimate for when we force the optimal plan for a 10,000-row temporary table on a 3-row temporary table as well as the cost estimate for when we force the optimal plan for a 3-row temporary table on a 10,000-row temporary table. What we can see in this specific example is that a nested loops join, when applied to a 10,000-row table, would seem disastrous: the cost has jumped from 176 to 10,000. However, the use of a hash join is not particularly disastrous when there are only 3 rows selected from our temporary table, jumping from 5 to 176; this is a big factor but probably only leads to an increase of one or two elapsed seconds. So we can fabricate our temporary table statistics to indicate 10,000 rows in our table and all should be well—at least in this example.

If you select specific rows from your table you might want to prevent the presence of predicates on these columns from reducing the CBO's cardinality estimates to such an extent that a nested loops join method is used. Listing 20-14 shows that by setting the value of NUM_DISTINCT to 2 for each column and bumping up NUM_ROWS for the table to, say, 20,000 we can arrange that a hash join is always, or almost always, selected.

Listing 20-14. Setting statistics to increase the chances of a hash join

```
CREATE OR REPLACE PACKAGE tstats
AS
-- Other procedures omitted
PROCEDURE set_temp_table_stats (
      p_owner all_tab_col_statistics.owner%TYPE DEFAULT SYS_CONTEXT (
                                                          'USERENV'
                                                          ,'CURRENT_SCHEMA')

     ,p_table_name    all_tab_col_statistics.table_name%TYPE
     ,p_numrows       INTEGER DEFAULT 20000
     ,p_numblks       INTEGER DEFAULT 1000
     ,p_avgrlen       INTEGER DEFAULT 400);
-- Other procedures omitted
END tstats;
/

CREATE OR REPLACE PACKAGE BODY tstats
AS
-- Other procedures omitted
PROCEDURE set_temp_table_stats (
      p_owner           all_tab_col_statistics.owner%TYPE DEFAULT SYS_CONTEXT (
                                                          'USERENV'
                                                          ,'CURRENT_SCHEMA')

     ,p_table_name    all_tab_col_statistics.table_name%TYPE
     ,p_numrows       INTEGER DEFAULT 20000
     ,p_numblks       INTEGER DEFAULT 1000
     ,p_avgrlen       INTEGER DEFAULT 400)
   IS
     distcnt    NUMBER;
   BEGIN
     DBMS_STATS.unlock_table_stats (ownname   => p_owner
                                   ,tabname   => p_table_name);
     $IF dbms_db_version.version >=12
     $then
        DBMS_STATS.set_table_prefs (ownname   => p_owner
                                   ,tabname   => p_table_name
                                   ,pname     => 'GLOBAL_TEMP_TABLE_STATS'
                                   ,pvalue    => 'SHARED');
     $END
     DBMS_STATS.delete_table_stats (ownname   => p_owner
                                   ,tabname   => p_table_name);
     DBMS_STATS.set_table_stats (ownname        => p_owner
                                ,tabname        => p_table_name
                                ,numrows        => p_numrows
                                ,numblks        => p_numblks
                                ,avgrlen        => p_avgrlen
                                ,no_invalidate  => FALSE);
     /*
```

We must now set column statistics to limit the effect of predicates on cardinality calculations; by default cardinality is reduced by a factor of 100 for each predicate.

We use a value of 2 for the number of distinct columns to reduce this factor to 2. We do no not use 1 because predicates of the type "column_1 <> 'VALUE_1'" would reduce the cardinality to 1.

```
*/
distcnt := 2;

FOR r IN (SELECT *
              FROM all_tab_columns
             WHERE owner = p_owner AND table_name = p_table_name)
LOOP
   DBMS_STATS.set_column_stats (ownname        => p_owner
                               ,tabname        => r.table_name
                               ,colname        => r.column_name
                               ,distcnt        => distcnt
                               ,density        => 1 / distcnt
                               ,srec           => NULL
                               ,no_invalidate  => FALSE);
   END LOOP;

   DBMS_STATS.lock_table_stats (ownname => p_owner, tabname => p_table_name);
 END set_temp_table_stats;
-- Other procedures omitted
END tstats;
```

EXEC tstats.set_temp_table_stats(p_table_name=>'PAYMENTS_TEMP');

```
SELECT *
  FROM payments_temp JOIN payments USING (payment_id);
```

```
-----------------------------------------------------------------
| Id  | Operation            | Name          | Rows  | Cost (%CPU)|
-----------------------------------------------------------------
|   0 | SELECT STATEMENT     |               | 20000 |   845   (1)|
|   1 |  HASH JOIN           |               | 20000 |   845   (1)|
|   2 |   TABLE ACCESS FULL| PAYMENTS_TEMP | 20000 |   272   (0)|
|   3 |   TABLE ACCESS FULL| PAYMENTS      |  120K |   174   (1)|
-----------------------------------------------------------------
```

```
SELECT *
  FROM payments_temp t JOIN payments p USING (payment_id)
 WHERE t.paygrade = 10 AND t.job_description='INTERN';
```

```
-----------------------------------------------------------------
| Id  | Operation            | Name          | Rows  | Cost (%CPU)|
-----------------------------------------------------------------
|  0  | SELECT STATEMENT     |               | 5000  |  447   (1)|
|  1  |  HASH JOIN           |               | 5000  |  447   (1)|
|  2  |   TABLE ACCESS FULL| PAYMENTS_TEMP  | 5000  |  272   (0)|
|  3  |   TABLE ACCESS FULL| PAYMENTS       |  120K |  174   (1)|
-----------------------------------------------------------------
```

```
SELECT *
 FROM payments_temp t JOIN payments p USING (payment_id)
 WHERE t.paygrade != 10 AND t.payment_date > SYSDATE - 31;
```

```
-----------------------------------------------------------------
| Id  | Operation            | Name          | Rows  | Cost (%CPU)|
-----------------------------------------------------------------
|  0  | SELECT STATEMENT     |               | 6697  |  447   (1)|
|  1  |  HASH JOIN           |               | 6697  |  447   (1)|
|  2  |   TABLE ACCESS FULL| PAYMENTS_TEMP  | 6697  |  272   (0)|
|  3  |   TABLE ACCESS FULL| PAYMENTS       |  120K |  174   (1)|
-----------------------------------------------------------------
```

Listing 20-14 shows another procedure in the TSTATS package. This procedure fabricates statistics on temporary tables. The procedure includes a conditional call to set table preferences that is 12c-specific. After fabricating statistics for PAYMENTS_TEMP, Listing 20-14 shows the execution plans for various two-table joins that use a variety of predicates on our temporary table in combination. Because the cardinality estimates remain quite high, a hash join is used in all cases and the cost estimate remains reasonable. Of course, in real life you wouldn't rely on the CBO's estimates—you would run some real workloads and measure actual elapsed times.

THE RIGHT VALUES FOR COLUMN STATISTICS

In the examples shown in Listing 20-14 the cardinality estimate is kept high by having a low value for NUM_DISTINCT for all columns used in predicates. However, a low value for NUM_DISTINCT will cause a low cardinality when such a column is used in a GROUP BY clause. Some experimentation may be required, and you may well need to resort to hinting in some cases.

The listings have only looked at one SQL statement, and this statement may or may not be typical of the SQL statements in your application. Nevertheless, hash joins often represent the best compromise when the number of rows in a table varies a great deal.

You shouldn't take this discussion of temporary table statistics as a prescriptive solution. Rather, you should consider it as a template for the type of analysis you need to do. If you do your analysis and find that you really must have different execution plans for different sizes of temporary tables, the types of solutions shown in Listings 6-6 and 6-7 are always available as last resorts.

Once you have gathered or set all of the statistics for all of your tables, including the temporary tables, you should have stable execution plans for all the statements in your application on your test system. It is now time to look at how to replicate that stability to other test systems as well as to production.

How to Deploy TSTATS

As I explained in Chapter 6, the TSTATS philosophy is to treat object statistics like application code. And just like application code, object statistics should be placed under version control and be deployed to production and formal test systems using automated deployment scripts according to change control rules. How is this best done?

The process begins on the test system where your object statistics are gathered. The first step is to export the object statistics for the tables in your application to an export table created with the DBMS_STATS.CREATE_STAT_TABLE procedure. For the purposes of discussion, let us assume that your application is called AJAX and that your export table is called TSTATS_AJAX. You now need to use TSTATS_AJAX as the basis for a deployment script that is placed under version control. You can do this by converting the rows in TSTATS_AJAX to insert statements or by creating a SQL*Loader file. Tools such as SQL Developer from Oracle and TOAD from Dell include features for generating such scripts. Your deployment script can create TSTATS_AJAX on your target system and then load the data directly into it using SQL*Plus or SQL*Loader as appropriate.

■ **Note**   You may think that the size of your deployment script will be huge if it includes an insert statement for every table, index, and table column in your application schema. However, bear in mind that you will not have statistics for table partitions, so things probably won't be as bad as you might think.

The final part of your deployment script should import the data from TSTATS_AJAX into the data dictionary on production or on your target test system. Listing 20-15 shows a procedure in the TSTATS package that performs this import.

Listing 20-15. Importing object statistics into the data dictionary

```
CREATE OR REPLACE PACKAGE tstats
AS
-- Other procedures cut
   PROCEDURE import_table_stats (
      p_owner all_tab_col_statistics.owner%TYPE DEFAULT SYS_CONTEXT (
                                                         'USERENV'
                                                        ,'CURRENT_SCHEMA')
     ,p_table_name all_tab_col_statistics.table_name%TYPE
     ,p_statown all_tab_col_statistics.owner%TYPE DEFAULT SYS_CONTEXT (
                                                         'USERENV'
                                                        ,'CURRENT_SCHEMA')
     ,p_stat_table all_tab_col_statistics.table_name%TYPE);
-- Other procedures cut
END tstats;
/

CREATE OR REPLACE PACKAGE BODY tstats
AS
-- Other procedures cut
PROCEDURE import_table_stats (
      p_owner all_tab_col_statistics.owner%TYPE DEFAULT SYS_CONTEXT (
                                                         'USERENV'
                                                        ,'CURRENT_SCHEMA')
     ,p_table_name all_tab_col_statistics.table_name%TYPE
     ,p_statown all_tab_col_statistics.owner%TYPE DEFAULT SYS_CONTEXT (
                                                         'USERENV'
                                                        ,'CURRENT_SCHEMA')
     ,p_stat_table all_tab_col_statistics.table_name%TYPE)
   IS
   BEGIN
     DECLARE
        already_up_to_date    EXCEPTION;
        PRAGMA EXCEPTION_INIT (already_up_to_date, -20000);
     BEGIN
        DBMS_STATS.upgrade_stat_table (ownname   => 'DLS'
                                      ,stattab   => 'DLS_TSTATS');
     EXCEPTION
        WHEN already_up_to_date
        THEN
           NULL;
     END;

     DBMS_STATS.unlock_table_stats (ownname    => p_owner
                                   ,tabname    => p_table_name);
     DBMS_STATS.delete_table_stats (ownname       => p_owner
                                   ,tabname       => p_table_name
                                   ,no_invalidate  => FALSE);
```

```
        DBMS_STATS.import_table_stats (ownname        => p_owner
                                      ,tabname        => p_table_name
                                      ,statown        => p_statown
                                      ,stattab        => p_stat_table
                                      ,no_invalidate  => FALSE);

        -- For partitioned tables it may be that the number of (sub)partitions on
        -- the target systems do not match those on the source system.
        FOR r
           IN (SELECT *
                  FROM all_tables
                WHERE     owner = p_owner
                      AND table_name = p_table_name
                      AND partitioned = 'YES')
        LOOP
           adjust_global_stats (p_owner, p_table_name,'PMOP');
        END LOOP;

        DBMS_STATS.lock_table_stats (ownname => p_owner, tabname => p_table_name);
     END import_table_stats;
-- Other procedures cut
END tstats;
/
```

In case the target system is running a later version of the Oracle database software than the source system, a call is made to DBMS_STATS.UPGRADE_STAT_TABLE to bring TSTATS_AJAX up to date, ignoring any error generated when TSTATS_AJAX is already up to date. The following actions are then performed for each table referenced by TSTATS_AJAX:

- Remove any existing statistics. This is necessary to prevent a mixture of statistics appearing.

- Import the object statistics into the data dictionary using a call to DBMS_STATS.IMPORT_TABLE_STATS.

- Adjust the global statistics for partitioned tables, as the number of partitions on the target system may not match those on the source system.

- Lock the imported statistics.

If in a later release of your application software you wish to add new tables or indexes you can simply create a new version of your deployment script that includes the additional objects, or you can create a new script specific to those objects. You might also include the TSTATS.IMPORT_OBJECT_STATS call in the DML script that creates the new table or index. It is entirely a question of the procedures your organization uses to deploy new objects.

Summary

TSTATS is an approach for managing object statistics that is radically different from the standard approach suggested by Oracle. Nevertheless, TSTATS uses no unsupported features of the Oracle database and effectively allows changes to execution plans to be placed under change control processes without the need for repositories of SQL statements that are difficult, if not impossible, to reconcile with application code.

This chapter has provided some ideas for how you might set up TSTATS. Nevertheless, TSTATS is not a "plug-and-play" tool, and a considerable amount of analysis and customization will usually be required before TSTATS can be successfully deployed for a complex commercial application. Hopefully this chapter has shown the way.

I hope you have found reading this book an educational and enjoyable experience. Good luck!

Index

■ P

Get the eBook for only $10!

> Now you can take the weightless companion with you anywhere, anytime. Your purchase of this book entitles you to 3 electronic versions for only $10.

This Apress title will prove so indispensible that you'll want to carry it with you everywhere, which is why we are offering the eBook in 3 formats for only $10 if you have already purchased the print book.

Convenient and fully searchable, the PDF version enables you to easily find and copy code—or perform examples by quickly toggling between instructions and applications. The MOBI format is ideal for your Kindle, while the ePUB can be utilized on a variety of mobile devices.

Go to www.apress.com/promo/tendollars to purchase your companion eBook.

Apress®
THE EXPERT'S VOICE™

For the Complete Technology & Database Professional

IOUG represents the **voice of Oracle technology and database professionals** - empowering you to be **more productive in your business** and career by **delivering education,** sharing **best practices** and providing technology direction and **networking opportunities.**

Context, Not Just Content

IOUG is dedicated to helping our members become an #IOUGenius by staying on the cutting-edge of Oracle technologies and industry issues through practical content, user-focused education, and invaluable networking and leadership opportunities:

- *SELECT Journal* is our quarterly publication that provides in-depth, peer-reviewed articles on industry news and best practices in Oracle technology

- Our #IOUGenius blog highlights a featured weekly topic and provides **content driven by Oracle professionals and the IOUG community**

- Special Interest Groups provide you the chance to collaborate with peers on the specific issues that matter to you and even take on leadership roles outside of your organization

- COLLABORATE is our once-a-year opportunity to connect with the members of not one, but three, Oracle users groups (IOUG, OAUG and Quest) as well as with the top names and faces in the Oracle community.

Who we are...

... **more than 20,000** database professionals, developers, application and infrastructure architects, business intelligence specialists and IT managers

... **a community of users** that share experiences and knowledge on issues and technologies that matter to you and your organization

Interested? Join IOUG's community of Oracle technology and database professionals at **www.ioug.org/Join.**

Independent Oracle Users Group | phone: (312) 245-1579 | email: membership@ioug.org
330 N. Wabash Ave., Suite 2000, Chicago, IL 60611